D1558890

Cambridge Studies in Early Modern British History

THE CAVALIER PARLIAMENT AND THE RECONSTRUCTION OF THE OLD REGIME, 1661–1667

Cambridge Studies in Early Modern British History

Series editors

ANTHONY FLETCHER
Professor of Modern History, University of Durham

JOHN GUY
Reader in British History, University of Bristol

and JOHN MORRILL
*Lecturer in History, University of Cambridge, and
Fellow and Tutor of Selwyn College*

This is a series of monographs and studies covering many aspects of the history of the British Isles between the late fifteenth century and the early eighteenth century. It includes the work of established scholars and pioneering work by a new generation of scholars. It includes both reviews and revisions of major topics and books which open up new historical terrain or which reveal startling new perspectives on familiar subjects. All the volumes set detailed research into broader perspectives and the books are intended for the use of students as well as of their teachers.

Titles in the series
The Common Peace: Participation and the Criminal Law in Seventeenth-Century England
CYNTHIA B. HERRUP
Politics, Society and Civil War in Warwickshire, 1620–1660
ANN HUGHES
London Crowds in the Reign of Charles II: Propaganda and Politics from the Restoration to the Exclusion Crisis
TIM HARRIS
Criticism and Compliment: The Politics of Literature in the England of Charles I
KEVIN SHARPE
Central Government and the Localities: Hampshire, 1649–1689
ANDREW COLEBY
John Skelton and the Politics of the 1520s
GREG WALKER
Algernon Sidney and the English Republic, 1623–1677
JONATHAN SCOTT
Thomas Starkey and the Commonweal: Humanist Politics and Religion in the Reign of Henry VIII
THOMAS F. MAYER
The Blind Devotion of the People: Popular Religion and the English Reformation
ROBERT WHITING
The Cavalier Parliament and the Reconstruction of the Old Regime, 1661–1667
PAUL SEAWARD

THE CAVALIER PARLIAMENT AND THE RECONSTRUCTION OF THE OLD REGIME, 1661–1667

PAUL SEAWARD

Research Fellow, Christ's College, Cambridge

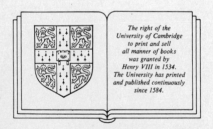

The right of the
University of Cambridge
to print and sell
all manner of books
was granted by
Henry VIII in 1534.
The University has printed
and published continuously
since 1584.

CAMBRIDGE UNIVERSITY PRESS

Cambridge

New York   New Rochelle   Melbourne   Sydney

Published by the Press Syndicate of the University of Cambridge
The Pitt Building, Trumpington Street, Cambridge CB2 1RP
32 East 57th Street, New York, NY 10022, USA
10 Stamford Road, Oakleigh, Melbourne 3166, Australia

First published 1989

Printed in Great Britain at the University Press, Cambridge

British Library cataloguing in publication data
Seaward, Paul
The Cavalier Parliament and the
reconstruction of the Old Regime, 1661–1667.
– (Cambridge studies in early modern British history.)
1. Great Britain. Political events 1661–1667
I. Title
941.06′6

Library of Congress cataloguing in publication data
Seaward, Paul.
The Cavalier Parliament and the reconstruction of the Old Regime,
1661–1667 / Paul Seaward.
p.   cm. – (Cambridge studies in early modern British history)
Bibliography.
Includes index.
ISBN 0 521 34030 6
1. Great Britain – Politics and government – 1660–1688. 2. Great
Britain. Parliamentary – History. 3. Royalists – Great Britain –
History – 17th century. I. Title. II. Series.
DA445.S42 1989
941.06′6–dc 19   88–15603   CIP

ISBN 0 521 34030 6

For Hilary

CONTENTS

ACKNOWLEDGEMENTS

This book is based on a doctoral thesis submitted at the University of Oxford in December 1985, the research for which was supported by a grant from the Department of Education and Science. The thesis was completed, and the book written, during my tenure of a research fellowship at Christ's College, Cambridge. The former institution made my research possible: the latter made it pleasurable. Both Christ's College and the Twenty-Seven Foundation have generously assisted my work. I am grateful to the marquess of Bath, the duke of Beaufort, and Lord Hampton for permission to read and cite manuscripts in their possession. Ruth Spalding kindly allowed me to see her transcription of the Diary of Bulstrode Whitelocke before its publication. I am much indebted to the archivists to the marquess of Bath, the duke of Beaufort, the staff of many libraries and record offices – above all Duke of Humphrey's library in the Bodleian – for their immense patience and assistance.

Ronald Hutton's *The Restoration* appeared in the year my thesis was submitted. Without it, this book would have been scarcely possible, and I am much in his debt for his generous encouragement. Needless to say, my account differs from his on many minor and some major points. I have not chosen to draw attention to all of these, as specialist readers will in any case want to read the two side by side. Mine is intended not to controvert, but to complement his.

Many friends and colleagues have helped me immeasurably with information and advice. I have derived much benefit from the knowledge of David Yale, Mark Goldie, Jeremy Ive, and John Spurr, from discussion with them, with Andrew Coleby and Andrew Swatland on Restoration politics, and from the seventeenth-century seminar run by Anne Whiteman and Blair Worden in Oxford from 1981 to 1985. The examiners of my thesis, Toby Barnard and John Kenyon, were most helpful, as has been John Morrill, one of the editors of this series. Sir Geoffrey Elton generously agreed to read through the typescript. I am most grateful to him for his advice. I am also deeply indebted to Sir John Plumb for his many kindnesses.

My profoundest intellectual debts are to Blair Worden and to my research supervisor, Robert Beddard, both of whose pertinent criticism and unfailing patience and friendship have guided this work through all its stages, and are all-too-meanly rewarded in its results.

One of my greatest creditors has a page to herself.

NOTE

In all quotations in English, spelling and the use of capital letters have been modernised. Alterations to punctuation have been kept to a minimum: where it has been necessary to change it, the change is indicated in a footnote. All dates are old style, with the year regarded as beginning on 1 January; although in the case of documents which have crossed to or from the continent, both old and new dates are given.

ABBREVIATIONS

B.L.	British Library
Bodl.	Bodleian Library, Oxford
Burnet, *History*	*Burnet's history of my own time. Part I: the reign of Charles II*, edited by O. Airy, 2 vols. (Oxford, 1897–1900)
Cal. Cl. S.P.	*Calendar of the Clarendon state papers preserved in the Bodleian Library*, edited by O. Ogle, W. H. Bliss, W. D. Macray, and F. J. Routledge, 5 vols. (Oxford, 1869–1970)
Cal. S.P. Dom	*Calendar of state papers, domestic series, of the reign of Charles II*, edited by M. A. E. Green, F. H. Blackburne Daniel, and F. Bickley, 28 vols. (London, 1860–1939)
Cal. S.P. Ven.	*Calendar of state papers and manuscripts relating to English affairs, existing in the archives and collections of Venice*, edited by R. Brown (London, 1864–)
Carte MSS	Carte Manuscripts, Bodleian Library, Oxford
C.J.	*Journals of the house of commons* (London, 1742–). All references are to vol. VIII, unless otherwise indicated
Chandaman	C. D. Chandaman, *The English public revenue 1660–1668* (Oxford, 1975)
Clarendon, *History*	Edward Hyde, earl of Clarendon, *The history of the Rebellion and Civil Wars in England*, edited by W. D. Macray, 6 vols. (Oxford, 1888)
Clarendon, *Life*	Edward Hyde, earl of Clarendon, *The life of Edward, earl of Clarendon*, 2 vols. (Oxford, 1857)
Clarendon MSS	Clarendon Manuscripts, Bodleian Library, Oxford

Coventry MSS	Coventry papers in the collection of the Marquess of Bath, Longleat House, Wiltshire
D.N.B.	*The dictionary of national biography*, edited by L. Stephen and S. Lee, 63 vols. (London, 1885–1900)
G.E.C.	*The complete peerage*, new edition, edited by G. E. C[okayne] and V. Gibbs, 13 vols. (London, 1910–40)
H.L.R.O.	House of Lords Record Office, House of Lords
H.P.	*The history of parliament: the house of commons, 1660–1690*, edited by B. D. Henning, 3 vols. (London, 1983)
Hutton	Ronald Hutton, *The Restoration: a political and religious history of England and Wales* (Oxford, 1985)
L.J.	*Journals of the house of lords* (London, 1767–). All references are to vol. IX, unless otherwise indicated
Margoliouth	*The poems and letters of Andrew Marvell*, edited by H. M. Margoliouth, 2 vols. (Oxford, 1927)
Milward, *Diary*	*The diary of John Milward Esq.*, edited by Caroline Robbins (Cambridge, 1938)
Parliamentary history	*The parliamentary history of England, from the earliest period to 1803*, edited by W. Cobbett and J. Wright, 36 vols. (London, 1806–20)
Pepys, *Diary*	*The diary of Samuel Pepys*, edited by R. Latham and W. Matthews, 11 vols. (London, 1970–83)
P.R.O.	Public Record Office, London
S.R.	*Statutes of the realm*, 11 vols. (London, 1810–28). All references are to vol. V, unless otherwise indicated
Steele	*Bibliography of royal proclamations of the Tudor and Stuart sovereigns*, 2 vols. (Oxford, 1910)

1

Introduction

By 1660, it had been twenty years since England had known political stability, eighteen since the nation had been torn apart by Civil War, and eleven since the monarchy had been abolished, and most of the old institutions of Church and State swept away with it. But that year saw a transformation in the political scene which astonished contemporaries: in May Charles II was called back from exile by a great revulsion against recent anarchy and instability; no conditions were set upon his return; and the ecstatic enthusiasm with which he was greeted suggested that despite its long absence, the monarchy remained firmly embedded in the hearts of the nation. Yet Charles's laconic comment on his arrival at Whitehall, 'that he doubted it had been his own fault that he had been absent so long, for he saw nobody that did not protest he had ever wished for his return', pointed to the obvious question: how artificial, or at least how profound, was all this sentiment?[1] Did the reaction represent a genuine abandonment of parliamentary interest in controlling and limiting the king? Was it possible that so many years of parliamentary power could be so easily forgotten?

Indeed, within seven years, these questions seemed more apposite still. For as republicans were said to have predicted, by 1667 Crown and parliament were again at one another's throats, England once again plunged into a deep political crisis, her king and people once more divided by a profound mistrust. For those nineteenth- and twentieth-century historians who celebrated England's slow but certain progress towards parliamentary government, the failure of the restored constitution had been in any case inevitable. Whether that constitution was effectively a recreation of the system that had existed before the Civil War, or was one evolutionary stage beyond it – 'the transitional state between the ancient and modern schemes of the English constitution' – it seemed evident, as Henry Hallam wrote in 1854, that 'nothing can more demonstrate the incompatibility of this tory system, which would place the virtual and effective, as well as nominal, administration of the executive

---

[1] Clarendon, *History*, VI, 234.

1

government in the sole hands of the Crown, with the existence of a representative assembly, than the history of this long parliament of Charles II'.[2] Several generations of historians agreed. Committed to a belief that the taste for liberty, once acquired, was never forgotten, they could see the Restoration only as a temporary – if dispiriting – reversal of the freedom that, they conceived, had been fought for in the constitutional struggles of the early seventeenth century. The Revolution, wrote David Ogg in 1954, initiated Englishmen into a political education that was 'almost continuous' until 1688, an education which ultimately fitted them for the responsibility of mature parliamentary rule.[3] The Restoration, Betty Kemp argued, rather more negatively, was 'little more than an experiment to see whether a later generation could get on better in circumstances which their fathers had found impossible' – an experiment which, needless to say, was doomed to failure.[4]

Since R. H. Tawney's famous article of 1941 on the rise of the gentry and its attendant controversy, many historians have identified a social dimension to this political impasse. For if the gentry had been advancing in economic power and political influence in the first half of the seventeenth century, the Restoration seemed to confirm their standing and set a seal on their power. It was they, not the monarchy, who seemed to be the real victors of the Civil War, and from 1660 they were busily exploiting their 'triumph', expanding their roles in local government and their dominance in county society. If the Restoration had settled anything, it was their power: and it was idle of the Crown to suppose it might secure its own constitutional authority for very long in defiance of it.[5]

Such 'whiggish' arguments are no longer much in fashion: and many of these judgements on Restoration politics have, over the past twenty years or so, been called into question. Clayton Roberts, while concurring with Betty Kemp's analysis of the Restoration Settlement as a balance between Crown and parliament resting on the notion of a separation between executive and legislative powers, and accepting that by 1667 that system had effectively broken down, denied that the breakdown was either inevitable, or a natural result of the imperfections of the system. The system failed, he argued, because Charles II and parliamentary leaders grew tired of the restraints it placed on them.[6] Dennis Witcombe, in his study of the middle years of the

[2] Henry Hallam, *The constitutional history of England from the accession of Henry VII to the death of George II*, 3 vols. (London, 1854), II, 353–5.
[3] D. Ogg, *England in the reign of Charles II*, 2nd edn (2 vols., Oxford, 1954), II, 459.
[4] B. Kemp, *King and commons 1660–1832* (London, 1965), p. 10.
[5] See, e.g., Christopher Hill, quoted in Joan Thirsk, *The Restoration* (London, 1976), pp. 27–9.
[6] C. Roberts, *The growth of responsible government in Stuart England* (Cambridge, 1966), pp. 151–4, cf. pp. 195–6, 434.

Cavalier Parliament, went a little further. Only one thing, he wrote, prevented the harmonious recreation of a satisfactory working relationship between king and parliament: Charles II's determination to introduce religious freedom, and parliament's determination to suppress it.[7] Some historians have pointed to the massive power that was still wielded by the government and its agents, and have suggested that there was nothing inevitable about England's progress towards parliamentary government: her evolution might well have proceeded in a different direction, towards a continental-style autocracy.[8]

Recent studies of early Stuart politics have stimulated a more radical criticism of old orthodoxies. Historians of the reigns of James I and Charles I have described the extent to which members of parliament before the Civil War had modest aims: not the seizure of political power and constitutional responsibilities but the winning of benefits, for themselves and their local communities; their actions were guided not by institutional ambitions, but by conventions of consensus. When conflict occurred, its causes were normally to be found in the obscure battles of court factions; and where matters of principle were involved, the principles concerned were usually religious ones. That the first of Charles II's proper parliaments, the 'Cavalier Parliament', was remarkably determined to support the Crown and cherished a striking affection for the restored Church of England has always – even by the most 'whiggish' of writers – been accepted. But the latest studies of Restoration politics take this much further, and stress the similarity between the parliaments of Charles II and the new perceptions of those of his father and his grandfather: M.P.s still abhorred the thought of forcing the king to concessions by withholding supply, conflict was often the result of faction, not of principle, and the principles which did incite men – reluctantly – to oppose the government, were both deeply conservative and steeped in religion. So close is the interpretation to that of pre-Civil War politics that there are signs that Restoration history will shortly end up being contested between the same two camps that have battled over the early Stuart ground.[9]

Part of the problem of reconsidering the meanings of Restoration politics lies in fathoming the purposes – if purposes there were – of government policy. Whigs from Andrew Marvell to John Locke and beyond justified their

---

[7] D. T. Witcombe, *Charles II and the cavalier house of commons, 1663–1674* (Manchester, 1966), p. 177. See also D. R. Lacey, *Dissent and parliamentary politics in England 1661–1689* (New Brunswick, 1969), and R. W. Davis, 'The "presbyterian" opposition and the emergence of party in the house of lords in the reign of Charles II', in *Party and party management in parliament, 1660–1974*, ed. Clyve Jones (Leicester, 1984), pp. 1–35.

[8] J. R. Western, *Monarchy and revolution: the English state in the 1680s* (London, 1972).

[9] J. Miller, 'Charles II and his parliaments', *Trans. Roy. Hist. Soc.*, 5th series, XXXII (1982), 1–23; see also D. Hirst, 'The conciliatoriness of the cavalier commons reconsidered', *Parliamentary History*, VI.ii (1987).

opposition to the court in the 1670s and 1680s by claiming that Charles II and his ministers headed an arbitrary and tyrannical regime, dedicated to smashing the law and the liberties of the people, devouring their property, dismissing parliament, ruling by an army, demolishing the Church and setting up popery in its stead. Few, these days, are so certain that Charles had any such purposes – or if he had, that he very seriously felt able to pursue them. But if it was not a desire to create an 'absolutist' state, such as France was supposed to be, what was it that guided the government's actions? Many have seen the Restoration 'settlement' as a compromise designed by the most powerful minister of the 1660s, Edward Hyde, earl of Clarendon, an attempt to balance the executive power of the Crown with the legislative power of parliament in a way that foreshadowed the eighteenth-century doctrine of the separation of powers. More thorough-going whigs either dismissed the project as unworkable, or answered that Clarendon had no more in his head than to return lock, stock and barrel to the constitution as it existed before the Civil War.[10] But most recent historians have denied that the government owned any very identifiable policy at all. Charles's administration, paralysed by fear of insurrection, by the king's own political lethargy and his ministers' intellectual bankruptcy, had little to do but to survive each crisis as it broke upon them – an activity in which Charles, with practice, came to possess a formidable skill. Charles and his ministers, it is said, had neither the time nor the energy to indulge in anything as luxurious as a constructive policy.[11]

Except, that is, in religion. For the importance of religion in the politics of the 1660s – and indeed, in the Restoration period as a whole – and the government's often counter-productive preoccupation with the issue suggests that on this subject at least, it must have had some more definite objectives. The only difficulty lies in deciding what they were, and who had them. The settlement of the ecclesiastical confusion which had resulted from the demolition of the episcopal Church of England in the 1640s, its partial replacement by presbyterianism, and the wide liberty of conscience permitted in the 1650s, was bound to be one of the restored monarchy's trickiest problems. From the various possible solutions emerged one that had been on the face of it the least likely: the full reconstruction of the anglican Church and the re-imposition of uniformity. Whether the government supported or opposed such a settlement has been much discussed: its occasional gestures

---

[10] See, e.g., E. I. Carlyle, 'Clarendon and the privy council, 1660–1667', *Eng. Hist. Rev.*, XXVII (1912), 251–73. For other instances of this idea, see also Ogg, *England in the reign of Charles II*, I, 189, and C. H. Firth, *Edward Hyde, earl of Clarendon* (Oxford, 1909).

[11] J. Miller, 'The potential for "absolutism" in later Stuart England', *History*, LXIX (1984), 187–207, and 'The later Stuart monarchy', in *The restored monarchy*, ed. J. R. Jones (London, 1979), pp. 30–47; J. R. Jones, *Charles II royal politician* (London, 1986), pp. 187–90.

towards a complete toleration of all nonconformists or a comprehension within the Church of the presbyterians have been judged to have been a genuine effort to introduce liberty of religious conscience, as a demonstration of the deep divisions which existed on the issue within the court, a cover for the real intention – the toleration of catholics – or as merely indicating an occasional concern about the possibility of the dissenters' violent resistance.

Indeed, despite the fact that the religious settlement, because of its importance in the history of English nonconformity, has been more thoroughly studied than any other aspect of Restoration history, its causes are still only partially understood. The legislation of which it was comprised was insisted on by a house of commons whose predecessors, twenty years before, had shown little of their concern for the episcopal Church of England. Various explanations have been advanced for this apparently radical revolution of opinion: the renaissance of anglicanism during its years in the wilderness; the connections so many of its priests formed with the gentry when they were ejected from their benefices and forced to find shelter during the Interregnum; or, more cynically, the gentry's recognition of the Church's role in suppressing sedition and upholding their own dominance. To some, indeed, the triumph of anglicanism has seemed little more than the spiritual equivalent of the triumph of the gentry.[12]

With this exception, although there have been many general accounts of the significance of the 'settlement', there have been few more detailed studies of it – of the pressures and politics which helped to create it – nor of the parliamentary politics of the 1660s as a whole. In contrast to the volumes that have been written on early Stuart parliaments, only one account of any detail exists to cover the early Restoration parliament: Witcombe's *Charles II and the cavalier house of commons*, a book which did much to focus thinking on post-Restoration politics. Since he wrote, several works have appeared which have laid firmer foundations for a new account: the History of Parliament Trust's collection of biographies of M.P.s for 1660–90; an accurately transcribed edition of Pepys's *Diary* with a scholarly commentary; Professor Chandaman's important analysis of *The English public revenue, 1660–1688*; and Ronald Hutton's detailed history of the years 1658–1667. Hutton's book established a basic narrative for the early 1660s, of the type that pre-1660 historians have for a long time taken for granted in the work of S. R. Gardiner and C. H. Firth, and he filled it out with a striking breadth of new

---

[12] R. S. Bosher, *The making of the Restoration settlement: the influence of the Laudians, 1649–1662* (Westminster, 1951); G. R. Abernathy, 'The English presbyterians and the Stuart Restoration, 1648–1663', *Transactions of the American Philosophical Society*, new series, LV, part 2 (1955), and 'Clarendon and the Declaration of Indulgence', *Journal of Ecclesiastical History*, XI (1960); I. M. Green, *The re-establishment of the Church of England, 1660–1663* (Oxford, 1978).

material. This book is intended to build on the work that he and others have done by examining more closely the structure and the course of early Restoration politics. In particular, I have tried to examine the way in which politicians – ministers, officials, Churchmen, and parliamentarians – sought to rebuild the world that had been smashed in the events of the 1640s, and to consider the attitudes they brought to the task. How (if at all) did the government, and others, conceive the structure of the restored monarchy? And what do its intentions, and parliamentary responses to them, reveal about the extent to which the Civil War had changed those attitudes and perceptions about government, religion, and politics? What made the Restoration settlement? And what, in 1667, almost destroyed it?

One major difficulty besets any historian of early Restoration politics. The first years of the Cavalier Parliament are among the most badly reported in all seventeenth-century parliaments.[13] Colonel Reymes's diary of the commons covers a small part of the first session, but only very sketchily;[14] there is some rather meagre and summary coverage of a few debates in the lords from 1664;[15] John Milward's more comprehensive diary begins in 1666, but it was not until the session that began in October 1667 that he was reporting debates with any confidence;[16] and Grey's massive record of debates does not start until 1667.[17] A few scattered private letters provide a little detail on the debates, and pamphlets published in order to influence parliament are sometimes valuable as a guide to opinions and concerns on issues currently being discussed. But letters which include any useful information on parliamentary proceedings are few, and there was an enormous decline soon after the Restoration in the volume of publication. The government's own newspapers preferred rather to suppress information than to disseminate it. The inadequacy of such informal sources force one back on the formal evidence – the Journals of the commons and the lords, and the debris which survives in the House of Lords Record Office and elsewhere left by detailed work on legislation. Not only do such sources illuminate the complex and tedious business of drafting and creating legislation. They can also be used to create a fuller picture of politics: they can hint at government policy, shed light on

[13] See the remarks in *H.P.*, I, xxiii–xxiv.
[14] B.L., Egerton MSS 2043.
[15] Bodl., Rawlinson MSS A. 130. For an identification of the author of this diary as Henchman, see R. W. Davis, 'Committee and other procedures in the house of lords, 1660–1685', *Huntington Library Quarterly*, XLV (1982–3), 29.
[16] *The Diary of John Milward Esq.*, ed. C. Robbins (Cambridge, 1938).
[17] A. Grey, *Debates of the house of commons from the year 1667 to the year 1694* (11 vols., London, 1763), vol. I.

the machinations of court factions, and show how ministers tried to manage parliament.

But the problem of sources is not limited to parliamentary affairs: the government was as reticent about its discussions as was parliament about its debates. Where evidence exists, it is usually to be found in the least trustworthy sources: the fading memories and anecdotes of retired politicians, or the gossip of men only on the fringes of the court. Burnet spent most of the early 1660s in Scotland or abroad: his *History of my own time* relies for this period on second-hand information, and, written in the 1680s, the rather simplistic views of early Restoration politics which it contains are heavily influenced and distorted by later events. James II, then duke of York, was by contrast at the very heart of politics: but his own memoirs, put together mainly after his exile in 1689, are even more misleading, distorted by retrospective musings on the causes of his defeat. Their coverage of the 1660s is sparse, and the fact that only brief notes taken from them in the eighteenth century now exist make their use even more difficult.[18] More contemporary, and more useful, gossip is provided by Pepys: where his source was close to the court – William Coventry, Sir George Carteret or the earl of Sandwich – the information he provides is invaluable. For the period after 1665, when his expertise in naval affairs brought him to the centre of English politics, his diary is one of the least dispensable sources. Foreign ambassadors, too, picked up all the rumour they could. The best reports came from the French, who were closest to the principal politicians at court, until the outbreak of war with them in 1666. But even Louis XIV's experienced diplomats did not possess a truly idiomatic understanding of English politics; and even they were not above writing what their master wished to hear, or failing to distinguish between genuine information and the carefully calculated ministerial indiscretion.

But the most important source for early Restoration history is the remarkable 'Continuation' of the *Life* of Edward Hyde, earl of Clarendon, which he completed in 1672 during his exile in France. Clarendon was Charles II's first lord chancellor, a post he held until his dismissal in 1667, and for much of his time in office he was the king's most trusted minister. His memoir provides the most detailed and most lucid contemporary exposition of the events and policies of the 1660s. Its account is far from perfect: written to defend himself from the charges heaped upon him in 1667, its tone is bitter and self-vindicatory; it was composed without recourse to many documents or to the help of others involved in the events he describes; and it relies almost

---

[18] J. S. Clarke, *The life of James the second, king of England, etc., collected out of memoirs writ of his own hand* (London, 1816). For a discussion of this memoir, see J. Miller, *James II: a study in kingship* (Hove, 1978), appendix.

exclusively on his own memory. Memories can be selective, politicians' memories notoriously so, and there have been many criticisms of the accuracy of the *Life*. But no study of the 1660s can ignore it; even Clarendon's hedgings, his distortions and his silences, can be as informative as a more ingenuous account.

The ministerial correspondence of the period is disappointing. The large collection of political papers amassed by Clarendon, and now deposited largely in the Bodleian library, contain much on foreign affairs, Scotland, and Ireland. On English politics and policy they are strangely reticent. The duke of Ormonde's voluminous correspondence, now preserved in the Carte Manuscripts (also in the Bodleian), are predictably mainly concerned with Irish matters. Nevertheless, from 1662, when he left London for permanent residence in Dublin as lord lieutenant of Ireland, there are many letters to him from English ministers and courtiers, although their references to English politics are frequently oblique and allusive. The state papers of the successive senior secretaries of state, Nicholas and Bennet, which remain in the Public Record Office, are principally administrative and contain little that relates directly to the making of policy. But although such sources give little indication of policy discussions, or provide no satisfactory political reportage, they can sometimes provide useful insights into the mechanics of politics; alliances, patronage, advice and (less commonly) the drafting of legislation.

What follows is cast into three sections: the first considers the attitudes that informed both government policies and parliament's reactions to them, as well as the structures that governed parliamentary politics. The second examines the creation of the legislation of 1661 to 1665 that completed the Restoration 'Settlement' begun by the Convention in 1660. The third part is a narrative of Westminster politics in the period, which concentrates on (and tries to explain) those sessions in which the harmony which normally prevailed between government and parliament broke down, in 1663 and in 1666–7, the latter the crisis which destroyed Clarendon's ministry. That crisis – with which this book concludes – briefly put in doubt the survival of the monarchy. To some it seemed even to confirm the fundamental instability of the regime. To Clarendon it endorsed his own jaundiced conservative's view of the decline of loyalty and virtue in the savage, Hobbesian, post-revolutionary world – a view that was only reinforced as he watched from exile the subsequent course of English affairs. Whatever it meant to individuals, that crisis thoroughly altered the shape of Restoration politics, freeing Charles II of a powerful restraining influence and confirming his distrust and dislike of parliaments. The disastrous politics on which he subsequently, and in part consequently, embarked, led in the 1670s to constant conflict and almost permanent deadlock.

Part One

RECONSTRUCTED POLITICS

2

The making of government policy

In early 1661 the Restoration government was faced with making a set of particularly delicate, and peculiarly important decisions. The Convention Parliament, dissolved in December 1660, had resolved many of the most pressing problems raised by eighteen years of conflict, and had laid the foundations of stability: with the Act of Indemnity it had forestalled any inquisition into the past; it had voted money to pay off the commonwealth army and much of the navy; and it had agreed on a fixed annual revenue for the Crown which was theoretically sufficient to free it from reliance on the generosity of future parliaments. The question of title to land, sequestrated or confiscated by the revolutionary governments from royalists, the Church and the Crown, had been settled without major legislation and with only muted discontent. The government itself had created – in the Worcester House Declaration of October 1660 – a code of ecclesiastical practice which, to their surprise, presbyterians found acceptable. Yet much remained to be done. In some points, the Convention's legislation proved inadequate: the sources it had allotted for the Crown's permanent annual revenue failed to raise the specified sum; the delays in disbanding the republican forces made the whole task much more costly; new laws were required to deal with such problems as recovering Interregnum tax arrears.

But more fundamentally, the whole shape of the restored monarchy remained uncertain. The reforming legislation of 1641–2, which had with the king's assent abolished the instruments of the prerogative government of the 1630s and had established parliament as a regular feature of the constitution, was still in place; and the government faced what it felt to be powerful enemies – radical conspirators, and the members of the old army – protected by little more than the popular enthusiasm which the Restoration had generated. The word of 1660 on the Church was also far from final: the government had prevented the Worcester House Declaration from being enacted as a statute. In February 1661, as the king announced that a new parliament would be summoned to meet on 8 May to confirm the acts of the irregularly assembled Convention and to complete its work, all these things were still

11

matters for political debate.[1] The need for their resolution was every day
emphasised: in January the rebellion of a handful of fifth monarchists
provoked fears of a wider conspiracy;[2] it was unclear to many how far the
Worcester House Declaration superseded the Elizabethan Act of Uniformity;[3] and the legal basis on which the government tried to establish a militia
was questionable.[4]

Four years later, the 'Cavalier Parliament' had completed what is now
known as the 'Restoration Settlement': but to many contemporaries it
seemed curiously incomplete. The Crown's finances were still shaky, and
little of the legislation of 1641–2 had been repealed; the government's
military security seemed scarcely more certain, and plans for a compromise
ecclesiastical settlement had been buried under the rigid imposition of
uniformity. At the time, some blamed Clarendon, the king's *éminence grise*,
for the failure: the chancellor, it was rumoured, had never wanted to restore
royal power to its height; as an M.P. in the early years of the Long Parliament,
they pointed out, he had joined the in resistance to Charles I's prerogative
government. Even now, they said, he retained the same principles, and had no
wish to create a powerful, independent monarchy.[5] Some historians have
concurred at least in regarding the reason why no greater progress towards
'absolutism' was made in the rather favourable climate of the 1660s as the
lack of application from the court: John Miller has argued that while parliament was willing enough to accept a more authoritarian, more centralised
government which could guarantee stability, neither Charles II nor his
ministers were capable of grasping the opportunities this presented. The king
himself lacked the persistence, nerve, or fixity of purpose to develop a
systematically autocratic policy; his ministers were too concerned with the
law, too frightened of parliament, or insufficiently established in power to
guide him in such paths.[6]

Did the court, then, have a policy for the reconstruction of royal power?
Certainly, the government of the 1660s has left behind little that might clarify
its position – no account of its policies, no blueprint of its preferred solution:
indeed, so complex and uncertain a political situation might have precluded
much sophisticated planning. Yet to some extent at least, the attitudes and
assumptions which Charles and his chief advisers brought to the problem of
a political settlement may be recovered; and they suggest that although
immense caution, a sense of the politically possible, and ministers' 'consti-

---

[1] For the king's announcement, see P.R.O., PC 2/55, fol. 69.
[2] Hutton, pp. 150–1.
[3] *Ibid.*, pp. 172–3; Bosher, *The making of the Restoration settlement*, pp. 202–4.
[4] See below, p. 141.
[5] Burnet, *History*, I, 276; Clarke, *James the Second*, I, 391–3.
[6] See especially the works of John Miller, mentioned above, pp. 3–4, nn. 9 and 11.

tutionalist' convictions did play a large part in the government's response to these questions of royal power and authority, it remained far from shy of more autocratic solutions than the 'settlement' which finally emerged. For ministers in the early 1660s had to be deeply wary of alienating that popular support on which the survival of the regime still – in the absence of a really trustworthy army, or even a reliable militia – so precariously depended. The royalist reaction was everywhere obvious; but its depth was less apparent, and in time revealed some awkward ambiguities. For the moment, at least, a desire to increase royal power had, above all, to be tempered by political reality.

Charles's companions and advisers in exile had been a miscellany of royalist officers and wartime counsellors, those too closely identified with the royal cause, too loyal, or too poor, to seek rehabilitation in England. At the Restoration he remarkably widened both their number and their background, appointing a privy council which included many former parliamentarians and Cromwellians.[7] But the council itself, for all Clarendon's pious observations on its importance, quickly became – partly, perhaps, because of their presence – more of a dignified than efficient part of the constitution.[8] Real decisions were taken in a much smaller group: even before the Restoration, according to Clarendon, the king had relied principally on a few trusted advisers. In May 1660 these were, he wrote, himself; the marquis of Ormonde; Lord Colepepper; and the secretary of state, Sir Edward Nicholas.[9] All had been prominent royalists from the early days of the war: Clarendon and Colepepper, in 1640 and early 1641 among the court's principal critics, had in 1641 been recruited to the king's cause, repelled by parliament's mounting radicalism. Both had served as councillors and administrators in exile. Nicholas had been a royal servant for almost his entire career, as secretary to the admiralty, clerk to the privy council, and from 1643 secretary of state. Ormonde was head of one of the great Anglo-Irish families, the Butlers; a member of Strafford's Irish council from 1635, he was for the next fifty years not only the most dominant figure in Irish politics but also deeply respected and enormously influential in England. Others joined them after Charles landed in England: the hero of the Restoration, George Monck, duke of Albemarle; the earl of Southampton, a respected royalist peer, now lord treasurer; and Sir William Morrice, appointed the junior secretary of state. Southampton, like Clarendon and Colepepper, had been brought onto the council in the early 1640s after earlier opposition to

---

[7] See the analysis in Hutton, p. 127.
[8] Clarendon's comments on the council are enumerated in Carlyle, 'Clarendon and the privy council'.
[9] Clarendon, *Life*, I, 270–3.

the policies of Charles I; thereafter, he was widely known as one of the most loyal and weighty of royalist peers. Morrice owed his office to his relationship with Albemarle, although doubtless his great learning and deep sense of religion (the latter something which united Clarendon, Nicholas, Ormonde, and Southampton) also recommended him to the chancellor and the others. Colepepper, however, died shortly after the Restoration, and two years later Ormonde was removed when he left to take up permanent office in Ireland as its lord lieutenant. Nicholas in late 1662 was replaced as secretary by Sir Henry Bennet, the youngest of them all, who during the war had been the duke of York's secretary and then royal ambassador in Madrid.

'Under the notion of foreign affairs', Clarendon wrote, this group was constituted as a committee of the privy council and 'appointed by the king to consult all his affairs before they came to a public debate'.[10] Their meetings have left little trace: only a few very rough notes of them taken by Sir Edward Nicholas in 1660 survive.[11] Nevertheless, it is clear that most important decisions and many minor ones were taken in consultation with a group similar to that which Clarendon had described. The council had little more to do than to comment on and ratify them. In August 1663 Irish business was discussed by the king, his brother James duke of York, Clarendon, Southampton, Albemarle, Sir Henry Bennet, and the earl of Anglesey.[12] In March 1663 Bennet described a meeting attended by the king, York, Clarendon, Southampton, Albemarle, and himself, as well as Manchester and Ashley.[13] At another, in August, the king, York, Clarendon, Southampton, Albemarle, and Bennet were present.[14] When involved in the negotiations in 1662 for the sale of Dunkirk, the French ambassador, the comte D'Estrades, considered the attitudes of the king, York, Clarendon, Southampton, Albemarle, and Sandwich to be the most important.[15] In March 1662 the decision to recommend to the house of lords a proviso to be inserted into the Uniformity Bill was taken by the king with the advice of Clarendon, York, Southampton, and Ormonde.[16] In September 1663 Sir Robert Moray, acting as secretary and agent to the Scottish secretary of state, the earl of Lauderdale,

[10] *Ibid.*, I, 315.
[11] P.R.O., SP 29/23/94, 95.
[12] *Hist. MSS. Comm.* MSS of the marquess of Ormonde, new series (8 vols., 1902–20), III, 67–8, Anglesey to Ormonde, 4 Aug. 1663. This clearly refers to a meeting preparatory to the meeting of the committee of the privy council for Irish affairs at which the ensuing formal decision is taken.
[13] *Hist. MSS. Comm.* MSS of J. M. Heathcote Esq. (1899), pp. 65–6, Bennet to Sir R. Fanshawe, 6 March 1663.
[14] Carte MSS 221, fol. 77v, Bennet to Ormonde, 22 Aug. 1663.
[15] *Collection des lettres et mémoires trouvés dans les porte feuilles du Maréchal de Turenne*, ed. P. H. Le Grimoard (2 vols., Paris, 1782), I, 348–9, D'Estrades to Turenne, 21/31 Aug. 1662.
[16] B.L., Add. MSS 22919, fol. 203, Morrice to Downing, 21 March 1662.

told him of his meeting with the king, the duke of York, Clarendon, and Bennet, after the king had been 'more than an hour close' with them; a few days later he described how Clarendon had arrived at Whitehall an hour before he went off to the council with the king, York, and Bennet.[17] When Pepys was called into a meeting of what he called the 'cabinet council' in November 1664, he found the king, Clarendon, both the secretaries, Gilbert Sheldon, archbishop of Canterbury, and the treasurer of the navy Sir George Carteret. In October 1666, at another meeting of the 'cabinet', it was a much expanded body, including York, Prince Rupert, Clarendon, Southampton, Albemarle, Carteret and Morrice, and a recent addition to the council, York's secretary, William Coventry.[18] Membership of the group evidently varied according to the matter being discussed, but it seems clear that until 1665, at least, its most constant members apart from the king were the duke of York, Albemarle, Clarendon, Southampton, and, after his replacement of Nicholas as chief secretary of state, Sir Henry Bennet.[19] 'Cabinet', or 'cabinet council', were the terms by which this semi-formal body was often known, although there were other names for it:[20] one of its meeting places was the 'green chamber' or 'green-room' at Whitehall, and for some this became a name for the body itself.[21]

Among all the inner councillors, Clarendon was pre-eminent.[22] Yet how responsible he was for the shape and direction of government policy is difficult to judge. He pointed out himself to Ormonde that the king treated the suggestion that anyone 'governed' him with touchy anger, and incidents such as the quarrel over the appointment of his mistress to the queen's bedchamber show his authority to have been a point on which Charles was extremely sensitive.[23] But although there were individual policies of the government against which Clarendon vigorously objected and from which he dissociated himself,[24] it is clear that for the first few years after the Restoration he was invariably consulted and that Charles relied heavily on his advice, particularly in the direction of parliamentary business. As lord chancellor,

[17] B.L., Add. MSS 23120, fol. 29v, 31v, Moray to Lauderdale, 25 and 28 Sept. 1663.
[18] Pepys, *Diary*, V, 316; VII, 312, cf. 260.
[19] Nicholas was probably far less involved in decision making before his removal in any case: he knew nothing, for example, about the Dunkirk negotiations in 1662; see Carte MSS 47, fol. 365, Nicholas to Ormonde, 13 Sept. 1662.
[20] Cf. the reference to 'our Juncto and Counsell' in Carte MSS 32, fols. 597–8v, O'Neill to Ormonde, 20 Jan. 1663, and to 'our meetings', in Carte MSS 47, fol. 56, Clarendon to Ormonde, 19 June 1663.
[21] Pepys, *Diary*, VII, 260, 312; National Library of Scotland, MSS 3136, fol. 23, Lauderdale to Tweedale, 14 Sept. 1667. This usage probably pre-dates the theatrical expression, 'Green room', which is perhaps derived from it. See O.E.D., s.v. 'Green room'.
[22] Clarendon, *Life*, I, 309; cf. 270.
[23] *Ibid.*, I, 358–9; see below, pp. 219–20, 321–2.
[24] E.g. the sale of Dunkirk and the 1662 Declaration of Indulgence. *Ibid.*, II, 10–17, 93–100.

Clarendon was of course Speaker of the house of lords. But his influence in the government's handling of parliamentary affairs went further than this. As the French agent Bartet explained to his master, Mazarin, in early 1661, although Charles recognised that Clarendon lacked interest or ability in foreign affairs, he realised that in parliament his influence, knowledge, and skill made him indispensable.

Le talent du chancelier, qui est la science de la loy d'Angleterre, qui scait le manège du parlement, comment il s'y faut prendre pour faire passer un acte, qui dispose, ou prend le temps pour y portes les esprits, le faict si souvent venir dans le mouvement et dans les affaires qu'il paroist toujours le premier, et le plus grand acteur.[25]

While he controlled parliamentary affairs, Clarendon could direct the government's legislative programme: his opinions and his assumptions would have a great influence on the choice of which measures should be introduced, and how they should be presented and pursued in parliament.

Clarendon's role, indeed, has always been seen as decisive in the politics and policies of the 1660s, although his attitudes have been more often caricatured than investigated.[26] Those who were not inclined to believe the charges of arbitrary rule levelled against him in 1667 took an entirely opposite view. The chancellor, James II had written while smarting in exile from his ignominious flight from the country in 1689, had been 'faulty, in not getting all the destructive laws, in the long rebel parliament of Charles I, repealed; which, most were of opinion, might have been done, and such a revenue settled on the crown, as would have supported the monarchy, and not exposed it to the dangers it has since run'.[27] Gilbert Burnet concurred; Clarendon, he wrote, 'had no mind to put the king out of the necessity of having recourse to parliament'.[28] But the publication in 1759 of Clarendon's *Life*, with its 'Continuation' covering the years of his administration, seemed to show to later writers a less creative, less attractive politician than the young Edward Hyde of the *History of the rebellion*. Ignoring the dramatic changes of the last twenty years, regardless of the fact that new methods were needed for new situations, and romantically, unrealistically, and unimaginatively wedded to the idea of an ancient constitution, Clarendon, it appeared, had at every point sought to return to the methods and institutions of the past. Rather than move forward into a new, balanced constitution, or recognise that the monarchy could only now be supported by a strengthened crown, he retreated incomprehendingly onto the old, unworkable Elizabethan polity.

---

[25] P.R.O., PRO 31/3/109, 31 Jan./10 Feb. 1661.
[26] With the exception of J. R. Jones's 'Introduction' to his *The restored monarchy 1660–88* (London, 1979), pp. 12–15, and cf. his *Charles II royal politician* (London, 1987), p. 56.
[27] James Macpherson, *Original papers containing the secret history of Great Britain from the Restoration to the accession of the house of Hanover* (2 vols., London, 1775), I, 17; cf. 40.
[28] Burnet, *History*, I, 278; cf. 451.

He opposed new institutions, new methods, new faces; the parties some thought essential for running parliament; cabals which bypassed the slow and inefficient privy council; the office of prime minister; all he deprecated. He was, as he quoted the king complaining, one of those 'formal men who liked nothing that was out of the old common road'. With Clarendon in charge, it seemed, government and administration were paralysed by a chronic institutional sclerosis.

Clarendon's visceral, irritating, and often obstructive conservatism can scarcely be denied: yet to concentrate on its many negative aspects is to misrepresent both its real nature and its political significance. Clarendon's conservatism was founded on a theory of politics less logically compelling and less systematic than that, say, of Hobbes, but one rather more sensitive to political reality. Hyde had come to political prominence in 1640 and 1641 not as a visionary, but as a reformer, not as one who wished to change the system, but as one who hoped to preserve the system by changing those who operated it. In the long parliament, he made his reputation in the attack on the abuses committed by the king's servants in the administration of the law:[29] and when he came, after the royal defeat and during the first two years or so of his long exile, to analyse the causes of the war and the means to recover stability, the administration of the law was central to his thinking.

Clarendon's account in the *History of the rebellion* of the origins of the war reflects the conventional royalist theory of a conspiracy of puritans and radicals.[30] But more than most royalist historians, he pointed out the failures, inadequacies, and abuses of Charles I's government: its unnecessary fear of parliaments, the hasty dissolutions, its failure to replenish the exchequer. He criticised most severely, however, those things which had borne the brunt of his own attack in 1640 and 1641: the abuses and corruptions of the law and the lawyers, the creation of 'supplemental acts of state' to supply deficient acts of parliament, the revival of obsolete laws and their vigorous execution, the injustice and unlegal procedures in the privy council and star chamber in enforcing those laws, and the compromising of the independence and integrity of the courts and the judges, who replaced rule of law with reason of state. All these things brought into question not just the government's commitment to law, but the very existence of the law itself; and by so blatantly undermining the very foundations of the law, the government was not just striking at the liberties of the subject, but engineering the collapse of the entire state.[31] For Clarendon's whole thinking about politics was

---

[29] See T. H. Lister, *The life and administration of Edward, first earl of Clarendon* (3 vols., London, 1837–8), I, 73–91.
[30] R. Macgillivray, *Restoration historians and the English Civil War* (The Hague, 1974), pp. 210–13.
[31] Clarendon, *History*, I, 84–92.

centred around the view that the only means to ensure a strict obedience to government was to guarantee that the government would strictly observe the rule of the subject's security, the law. In the past, he argued, the Crown had recognised the importance of preserving the judges as 'the objects of reference and veneration with the people, and that though it might sometimes make sallies upon them by the prerogative, yet the law would keep the people from any invasion of it, and that the king could never suffer whilst the law and the judges were looked upon by the subject as the asyla for their liberties and security'.[32] In the 1630s the Crown had forgotten that principle. At no other time, he wrote, were those 'foundations of right, by which men valued their security . . . more in danger to be destroyed'. If the judges, he argued, 'had preserved the simplicity of their ancestors in severely and strictly defending the laws, other men had observed the modesty of theirs in humbly and dutifully obeying them'.[33]

In practice, Clarendon's commitment to law was tempered both by an appreciation of skill in politics and by a wish to maintain some executive freedom. Like Machiavelli, Clarendon had a fine sense of *virtù*; of Cromwell's 'great parts of courage and industry and judgement', his 'wonderful understanding in the natures and humours of men, and as great a dexterity in the applying them'.[34] He recognised that the principles of statecraft were not always reconcilable with the maxims of law; but as a propagandist, he insisted that it was essential to preserve the form of law while sacrificing the reality. Justice should be done, certainly, but far more important, it should be seen to be done.[35]

In 1660, as Clarendon returned to England, he was acutely aware that the Restoration was an extraordinary event, not to be explained in simply secular terms, and certainly not to be taken as an indication that England might easily settle back into peaceful acquiescence with monarchical rule. The country had not been properly won: it remained to be wooed. Convinced that the best way to do so was by assuring the subject that his closest concerns – the lawful possession of his life, his liberty, and his lands – were guaranteed by the government's firm commitment to the laws of the country and to the settled ways of the constitution, and that wherever so scrupulous an adherence seemed impossible to maintain, at least to follow the form, if not the substance, of order and legality, Clarendon made great efforts to publicise that commitment. In the government's declarations and public statements of the 1660s, many of which he drafted, it was repeatedly emphasised. The Declaration of Breda of April 1660 claimed that the king desired no more 'to enjoy what is ours, than that all our subjects may enjoy what by law is theirs,

[32] *Ibid.*, I, 89.   [33] *Ibid.*, I, 88.   [34] *Ibid.*, VI, 91.   [35] *Ibid.*, I, 90.

by a full and entire administration of justice throughout the land'.[36] The speeches he gave when swearing in new judges and law officers provided the chancellor with another opportunity to trumpet the Crown's determination to uphold the laws. In all these speeches, he later wrote, he had exhorted the judges to be 'strict and precise in their administration of justice according to law, with all equality and without respect of persons'.[37] Swearing in Sergeant Twisden in 1660, he told him that he was fortunate in having a master, Charles II, who had a great respect for the law, and who looked on it as 'the foundation of, and security to, all that reverence and obedience which he expects from his subjects'. It was vital that the lawyers, by their 'civil, upright and generous proceedings', and the judges, by their 'grave deportment . . . and strict administration of justice to all men', should increase public confidence in the law, disposing men to 'such reverence of the laws, and such an estimation of the persons who justly execute those laws, that they may look upon those who could pervert the laws at home, as enemies of the same magnitude, as those who would invade the country from abroad'.[38] In his own and the king's speeches to parliament, Clarendon again extolled the government's commitment to the law, and to the harmonious relationship between Crown and people represented by parliament. Requesting the repeal of the Triennial Act, in 1664, Clarendon was careful to add to Charles's speech that 'never king was so much beholden to parliaments as I have been, nor do I think the crown can ever be happy without frequent parliaments'.[39] In 1661 he contrasted the government's observance of rule and custom, of due process and the formalities of law with the illegality and exorbitance of the Interregnum regimes; the lightness of the monarchy's burden with their weight; the correctness of procedure and the gravity of debate in privy council with their conspiratorial caballing.[40] The Clarendonian regime spared no effort to make known its eagerness to stand by the law and the constitution.

Right at the end of his life, once more in exile after his impeachment and flight in 1667, Clarendon gathered together the threads of his writing, thinking, and his policy of the last three decades in an attack on the philosophy on

---

[36] J. P. Kenyon, *The Stuart constitution 1603–88* (Cambridge, 1966), pp. 357–8.
[37] Clarendon, *Life*, II, 527–8.
[38] Clarendon MSS 73, fol. 93. Cf. his other speeches on similar occasions, at the swearing in of Justice Foster, Sergeant Beave, and Lord Chief Justice Bridgman: Glasgow University Library, MSS T.3.11, fols. 138–40v.
[39] *Parliamentary history*, IV, 291. This speech survives only in a copy in the king's hand (P.R.O., SP 29/95/5), but this contains much evidence that it is copied from another draft, and the prose is unmistakably Clarendon's. (See n. 40 below.)
[40] *Parliamentary history*, IV, 224; for Clarendon's draft see Clarendon MSS 75, fol. 308. The copy that Charles made in his own hand is at H.L.R.O., Main papers, H.L., 20 Nov. 1661. For Clarendon and Charles I employing a similar practice in drafting public statements, see Clarendon, *Life*, I, 101–2.

which, he believed, the most potent threat to the English way of life rested.
Clarendon's *Brief view and survey of the dangerous and pernicious errors to
church and state in Mr. Hobbes's book, entitled Leviathan* was completed in
1670.[41] In it he examined in detail every aspect of Hobbes's influential but
widely condemned book: but inevitably, his work was principally an assault
on its prescription of the absolute sovereignty of the sovereign power as the
just and only effective means of civil peace. Like Hobbes, Clarendon had as
his object peace, security, and prosperity, although he gave considerably
greater emphasis to the enjoyment of property as a motive for political
association – even becoming lyrical in his account of the benefits to be derived
from it, and the miserableness of life in the nomadic existence that its absence
implied.[42] But unlike Hobbes, Clarendon remained sternly convinced that
political obligation derived not from consent, but from the power of God
communicated to a sovereign ruler. Such a gift justified the plenitude of
original sovereign power, and the resumption of that plenitude when it
appeared essential. But two closely linked considerations limited, crucially,
the sovereign's authority in practice. First, Clarendon's assumption that the
benefits to be expected from political society were the benefits that flowed
from the possession of property, meant that political security existed to
guarantee the peaceful possession of property: and this could only be done by
the agreement of laws between the subject and the sovereign, by which the
sovereign accepted bounds to his power for the common benefit. Secondly,
once instituted, these agreements – or laws – are the foundations of the
subject's security in his property, and the main reason why it is in his interest
to continue to accept the sovereign's rule. If they are infringed, the whole
basis of property – and hence society – collapses. While it is within the
sovereign's power to infringe them, both the purpose for which he is instituted by God – the general good – and the prudential motive that, although
the subjects are obliged in any case to obey, they are less likely to if they feel
no earthly benefit to themselves from doing so, should persuade him not to.
While Hobbes had argued that political obligation derived from consent, but
government rested on the sovereign's absolute power, Clarendon countered
that obligation derived from the power of God, but government rested on
consent.[43] Consent was based on trust; and trust was based on an ability to
predict the actions of government; and that predictability was the law. 'All
governments', he urged, 'subsist and are established by firmness and
constancy, by every man's knowing what is his right to enjoy, and what is his

[41] Oxford, 1676.
[42] Edward Hyde, first earl of Clarendon, *A brief view and survey of the dangerous and
    pernicious errors to church and state in Mr. Hobbes's book, entitled Leviathian* (Oxford,
    1676), p. 111.
[43] *Ibid.*, p. 45.

duty to do.'[44] The power and honour of a sovereign, besides, could arise only from the riches, strength, and reputation of his subjects; and it was only the subjects' belief in their secure enjoyment of their lives and goods that gave them the confidence to accumulate them.[45] Law was the key to political stability and economic prosperity: Hobbes's sovereign, for all his pretensions, would achieve neither.

In practice, Clarendon's commitment to the law and to the forms of the constitution set strong limits to the government's ambitions. Yet it did not render it in any way impotent. Clarendon honoured the institution of parliament: he criticised lord treasurer Weston for believing that the 'union, peace and plenty of the kingdom could be preserved without parliaments'.[46] Yet he was a lawyer before he was a parliamentarian; his policy to preserve the law, rather than to perpetuate parliaments. Parliaments themselves might threaten the stability of the law and the constitution: before 1640 their power had grown disproportionately, as governments failed to teach them the true bounds to their freedom; after 1640, as under radical leadership parliament freed itself first of the rules and orders of the institution, then of the laws and liberties of the constitution, that threat became even more apparent.[47] After 1660, it remained as true as ever that without real will by the government, parliament would easily and freely expand its competence and its power.[48] Clarendon also possessed a rather wide sense of the royal prerogative: in the *History* he regretted the failure to raise money by its means in 1640 – something which he was to propose again in 1666 – and in his *Brief view and survey* he defended the right of the Crown to tax without consent in emergencies: 'the laws themselves permit, and allow many things to be done, when the mischief and necessity are in view, which may not warrantably be done upon the pretence of preventing it'.[49] Nor was he much concerned – according to Burnet's story – with the expansion of the royal army, until made aware of its possible implications by Southampton.[50] When he wrote to defend himself from the 1667 impeachment charges, Clarendon carefully skirted around the accusation that he had supported the raising of a standing army. He pointed out, as was true, that he had always insisted that the army should be subject to the Common Law, and that the military were generally his enemies. But the charge itself he failed to deny.[51]

[44] *Ibid.*, p. 124. [45] *Ibid.*, pp. 55–6; cf. 70–1, 82–3. [46] Clarendon, *History*, I, 7–8.
[47] *Ibid.*, I, 9–10, 239–41, 270–2, 311, 343, 355–6, 363, 367, 476–7, 531, 534, 543.
[48] Clarendon, *Life*, II, 450.
[49] Clarendon, *History*, I, 210–20; Clarendon, *Brief view and survey*, pp. 176–80; see below, p. 309.
[50] Burnet, *History*, I, 279–80; see also L. von Ranke, *A history of England, principally in the seventeenth century* (6 vols., Oxford, 1875), III, 339, for Marsin's account of support for an army in 1660.
[51] Clarendon, *Life*, II, 528–9.

For Clarendon, no political scientist but an intensely curious observer of human nature, security lay not in any particular kind of institution or system (although it is clear that he did have an exaggerated reverence and respect for the English constitution's antiquity), but rather in the way it was administered: only the mutual trust of government and people could guarantee peace and prosperity; in recreating that trust it was the behaviour of government, as much as its shape, that was important. Despite the schism in society produced by the war and religion, despite the many changes that had taken place in politics, he believed it was still possible to restore a political system based on co-operation and understanding between Crown and people: but to do so it was essential, by preserving the forms of the constitution and by standing by the law, by ensuring that government behaved in predictable and regular ways, to convince the subject that he had nothing to fear by his obedience.

How well Southampton concurred with his view is uncertain: the treasurer wrote little on such matters. Burnet, indeed, liked to paint him in his favourite whiggish colours: anti-prelatical, an advocate of a more comprehensive church settlement, an opponent of standing armies, a prophet of Charles II's tyrannous ways.[52] But Burnet's gaudy paint-box was inappropriate for the subtler hues of the 1660s. Although Southampton undoubtedly supported an ecclesiastical compromise, and was sternly censorious of the king and his court, his other whiggish qualities are less obvious. He was as anxious as anyone to place the Crown in an unassailable position. If he had originally opposed the establishment of a standing army in late 1660 or early 1661, it was probably because the treasury could not pay for one: he supported later attempts to secure a standing army funded by parliament;[53] and he was, by several accounts, eager to make the Crown so financially secure that it would be freed from dependence on the unreliable goodwill of parliaments – a dependence which he felt was a threat to the prerogatives of monarchy, and which might again provoke a slide into civil war.[54]

Clarendon and Southampton were not, of course, the only men with power or influence: Charles II never took his advice solely from them, nor solely from his private committee. Clarendon felt his desire that the government should abide by constitutional form and legal propriety constantly under threat from those who surrounded the king – if not from the king himself. Bennet knew 'no more of the constitution and laws of England than he did of China, but believed France was the best pattern in the world'.[55] Sir William

[52] Burnet, *History*, I, 162, 170–1, 279–80, 287–8, 316.
[53] See below, pp. 141, 147–8.
[54] Clarendon, *Life*, II, 407; Pepys, *Diary*, IX, 490; B.L., Harleian MSS 1223, fols. 205v–6.
[55] Clarendon, *Life*, I, 615.

Coventry, whose political ability and administrative talents brought him eventually to challenge Clarendon as the most authoritative voice in the government, was a 'declared enemy to all lawyers, and to the law itself', and had 'no principle in religion or state'.[56] Coventry was James's secretary: and James himself, in his complaint of thirty or forty years later that royal power had been insufficiently strengthened at the Restoration, indicated some sort of dissatisfaction with constitutional politics. It was a feeling shared and expressed by several of the military men who surrounded him in the 1660s. In a long treatise on government written shortly before his death in 1678, James's friend and former governor, Lord Berkeley, bitterly reproved the lawyers, who, he claimed, had hoped that the king would lose the Civil War; because had he won by the sword, they feared, he would have been able to 'resume the ancient prerogatives of the crown'. The lawyers had 'batter'd down the star chamber, the council board, the high commission, the court of wards and liveries, with six or seven courts more in my time, all which were so many props and supports of the prerogative royal'.[57] But it was as early as 1663 that another of James's servants, the earl of Peterborough, wrote that 'those old notions of mix'd governments, privileges, and conditions, have by several accidents of state, been put out of the essence of things, they are not to be practis'd any longer, and the consequence of all undertakings can no more be, but monarchy, or a commonwealth'.[58] Peterborough's sentiments were perhaps unusually uncompromising, but the military background and predilections of James and his circle probably made them all less equivocal than other men in calling for large extensions of monarchical power.[59]

Then, of course, there was the king himself: Clarendon complained darkly of 'the ill principles he had received in France', and criticised his enthusiasm for constitutional novelty, his preference for the informal against the formal, his greater appreciation for arguments of immediate expediency, rather than of long-term prudence or justice.[60] If Charles did have ambitions to emulate Louis XIV's 'absolutism', he could not lack encouragement, in particular from the French themselves. Since Charles was eager to form an alliance with the rising power of France, the country's ambassadors could occupy a

---

[56] *Ibid.*, II, 191.
[57] B.L., Sloane MSS 3828, fols. 81–91, particularly fols. 86, 88. The reference to Berkeley's Irish office on fol. 88v shows this to be Lord Berkeley of Stratton, not Berkeley of Berkeley. For his association with James, see Miller, *James II*, pp. 16–22.
[58] P.R.O., SP 28/81/94, Peterborough to Williamson, endorsed as received 14 Oct. 1663 (comma removed between 'undertakings' and 'can'). For Peterborough's connections with James, see *G.E.C.*, X, 497–9, and Miller, *James II*, pp. 72–3.
[59] For James's military circle, see S. S. Webb, ' "Brave men and servants to his Royal Highness": the household of James Stuart in the evolution of English imperialism', *Perspectives in American History*, VIII (1974), 55–80.
[60] Clarendon, *Life*, II, 297. See also I, 428–9, 456–7, II, 21, 80–1, 90, 217, 222, 225–7, 235.

position of unique influence in England. Bartet, Mazarin's agent in London, was not shy in offering advice to Charles concerning his affairs. In early 1661 he spoke frequently and forcefully to him, putting what he believed would be Mazarin's advice.[61] He urged Charles to make himself more secure with a larger standing army, complained that the government had neither force nor boldness enough to make itself the master 'en manière aussi absolue et aussi autorisée et aussi reconnue qu'elle est en France', and lamented the strength of the law in England.[62] Charles was reticent in his answers, although when he invited Bartet to the parade of Monck's regiment at which it was announced that they would be retained in the king's service, he whispered in the agent's ear, as was later reported to Mazarin, 'qu'il falloit vous l'escrire affin que votre excellence vit combien il estimoit vos conseils, et que je n'oubliasse pas de vous mander qu'il venoit de faire là une chose que le feu roy, son père, n'eut jamais osé entreprendre, sans se mettre en danger de perdre sa couronne'.[63] On another occasion, after Charles complained at length to him about the expense of the new troops, the envoy harangued him with his opinions of what was wrong with England, and told him not to abandon the army because of a lack of money. Bartet faithfully reported Charles's avid interest (perhaps caused by a belief that there was the hint of a loan from France in what he was saying).[64] Charles probably did harbour hopes of greater security and a larger army – in September 1660 he told the Spanish general, Marsin, that he was intending to dissolve the Convention and raise an army from his own resources.[65] But Bartet's little chats seem not to have been kept up by his successor, D'Estrades, and they say more about Bartet – a busy-body if ever there was one – than the king.[66] The choice, in fact, was never so stark a one between Clarendonian constitutionalism and French 'absolutism': Charles seemed sufficiently aware of political realities not to take his promptings too seriously unless it sounded as if they were backed by Mazarin's willingness to give money. If Charles did possess wider ambitions, to emulate the power and splendour of Louis XIV, they were perhaps directed as much externally – to cutting an international figure and effacing the humiliating impression of his exile, of an impoverished prince with dwindling supporters and dwindling prospects – as internally, the creation of an 'absolutist' state. The new French ambassador, the Comte D'Estrades, observing Charles's handling of the troublesome Spanish in July 1661, told

[61] P.R.O., PRO 31/3/109, Bartet to Mazarin, 10/20 Jan. 1661.
[62] *Ibid.*, 14/24 Jan. 1661.
[63] *Ibid.*, second letter of 14/24 Jan. 1661.
[64] *Ibid.*, 20/30 Jan. 1661. Cf. 28 Jan./7 Feb. 1661.
[65] Ranke, *A history of England*, III, 337. For Marsin's earlier associations with Charles, see
  F. J. Routledge, *England and the Treaty of the Pyrenees* (Liverpool, 1953), pp. 30, 53, 55, 71.
[66] P.R.O., PRO 31/3/109, 110, *passim*

Mazarin that he seemed to have 'une grande ambition et un desir extreme de faire la guerre'; in the diplomacy of the early 1660s he and his ministers belligerently defended English rights, more, perhaps, than became a small country recovering from a long Civil War.[67]

Clarendon feared rather a cavalier attitude to the law and the constitution which might endanger the Crown's recovery and its reputation, than a determined assault on them; although he, like others, saw the traps of anarchy and arbitrary rule which lay on either side.[68] It was perhaps only during his second exile, as the results of the crisis of 1667 became apparent in the government's new policies, that he began to be more seriously concerned. His *Brief view and survey* of Hobbes was completed in 1670, but only in 1673, in the wake of Charles's withdrawl of his second Declaration of Indulgence, did Clarendon decide to send it off for publication, dedicated to the king, 'that all the world may know, how much you abhor all those extravagant and absurd privileges, which no Christian prince ever enjoyed or affected'.[69] Under Clarendon's care the government was anxious to demonstrate it: it wished to win the 'hearts and affections' of the people of England by showing that it had no intention of making their property and liberty uncertain, and no intention of pushing back the limits of the law. The regime's needs, the dictates of prudence, and Clarendon's own convictions all combine to suggest that while the government's policy would be directed towards strengthening the Crown, it would attempt to do so only within certain limits, and with great caution. To the impatient, caution seemed to indicate reluctance: to the sceptical, hesitancy might demonstrate infirmity of purpose. It was easy to conclude that ministers disfavoured the extension of royal power, or that they lacked the will to carry it through.

If the government's attempts to strengthen the power and authority of the Crown seemed at times feeble or equivocal, its ecclesiastical policy was at best ambiguous and often simply confused. Since 1651 Charles II had been committed at least to the restoration of episcopacy, but did not rule out concessions to presbyterians in the Church's liturgy, ceremonies, and organisation. Some prominent royalists felt that the part played by presbyterians in restoring the king showed their numbers and their influence, and rendered concessions essential. But others saw any compromise as unnecessary, unwelcome, and dangerous: unnecessary because the presbyterian interest was, despite appearances, small and impotent; unwelcome because it would ruin

---

[67] PRO 31/3/109, D'Estrades to Louis XIV, 15/25 July 1661.
[68] Cf. J. W. Daly, 'The implications of royalist politics, 1642–6', *Historical Journal*, XXVII (1984), 745–55.
[69] Epistle dedicatory, dated 10 May 1673. For the events of spring 1673, see D. T. Witcombe, *Charles II and the cavalier house of commons 1663–74* (Manchester, 1966), pp. 125–40.

the integrity of the Church for which Charles I, Archbishop Laud, and count-less royalists had laid down their lives; and dangerous because presbyterians had by no means thrown over their old anti-monarchical principles, and would continue to work for the downfall of Church and State. To add to their disgust, the government even seemed willing to extend its ecclesiastical for-bearance to the many unorthodox religious sects which had sprung up in the 1640s and 1650s; its Declaration of Breda in April 1660 promised a 'liberty to tender consciences, and that no man shall be disquieted or called in ques-tion for differences of opinion in matter of religion which do not disturb the peace of the kingdom; and that we shall be ready to consent to such an act of parliament as upon mature deliberation shall be offered to us for the full granting that indulgence'.[70] If this meant a toleration, many groups had reason to feel uneasy: for anglicans and presbyterians, it threatened the essen-tial religious unity of a national Church, and much else besides; even independents might feel that it could mean liberty not just for the godly, but also for some of the dubious heresies of the 1650s; and all had more than an inkling that 'liberty for tender consciences' would mean the lifting of the penalties against the catholics, almost universally abominated except in the higher echelons of royalism.

Already, in 1660, the government had become aware of the difficulties attendant on any ecclesiastical settlement and the ambivalence in its attitude became more and more obvious. As presbyterians pressed urgently for a moderate episcopalian settlement – something in line, perhaps, with Arch-bishop Ussher's famous scheme of 1641 – the court spoke them fair, offered them preferment, and eventually, in the Worcester House Declaration of October, granted much of what the moderates, at least, had desired. Yet there was enough evidence to suggest that the concession had been wrung from the government rather than freely granted: it was avowedly an interim settle-ment, and when the presbyterians attempted to have the arrangement confirmed in statute, the government's parliamentary agents resisted and defeated them. As time passed, the presbyterians' need for a settlement became more and more pressing: in the early autumn bishops were appointed to most dioceses; by the late summer most cathedral chapters had been fully re-established; everywhere the old liturgy and ceremonies were being restored. The further all these things proceeded the more powerful the anglican establishment, and the more difficult any compromise, would become. To many, it seemed as if the government, recognising this, was merely playing for time, waiting until the presbyterians, now evidently impotent, could be quietly abandoned.

Some historians have accepted, others have rejected such a view of the

---

[70] Kenyon, *The Stuart constitution*, p. 358.

government's policies. Robert Bosher, in the first comprehensive account of the re-establishment of the Church, argued that the influence over both Clarendon and the king of 'Laudian' divines during the Interregnum exile had moulded the government's plans, and although the churchmen, the king and his ministers were willing once they were firmly in power to try to win over moderate dissenters with some concessions, the waverings that there were from a rigidly anglican line had their origins in passing fears of driving the presbyterians to rebellion, rather than in a genuine desire for a fuller comprehension, or even toleration.[71] Other accounts have attributed the settlement's harshness solely to the uncompromising anglicanism of the house of commons. Professor Abernathy argued that the chancellor and the king genuinely sought to obtain a settlement which would include comprehension for moderate presbyterians and toleration for others, but found their efforts constantly frustrated in parliament.[72] Witcombe took a similar view, although he believed that when Clarendon realised in 1663 that parliamentary intolerance rendered any indulgence to dissent impossible he became a strong proponent of persecution.[73] Most recently Ian Green has advanced another explanation: that Clarendon and Charles were at variance in their attitudes towards dissent, and although for a time the chancellor acted the dutiful civil servant and was the public mouthpiece for what was in fact the king's own policy, he had more sympathy with the persecuting anglicanism of the commons. When in 1663 yet another effort to secure an indulgence from parliament was made through the agency of his enemies, his opposition emerged more clearly.[74]

The issue was one on which, indeed, the government was deeply divided: the composition of the privy council guaranteed disagreement, with former presbyterians or at least very deeply protestant episcopalians such as Manchester, Robartes, and Anglesey, rubbing shoulders with much more committed anglicans, such as Ormonde or Nicholas; even at the highest level, amongst the most prominent policy-makers, despite a common and deeply-held anglicanism there were still profound differences over the emphases to be placed on compromise or conformity. Few could have possessed a more vehement hatred of presbyterianism than Sir Edward Nicholas, who attributed to its adherents conspiracies and alliances with even the most radical of sects: he pressed for the removal of presbyterians from office and

---

[71] Bosher, *The making of the Restoration settlement, passim.*
[72] G. R. Abernathy, 'Clarendon and the Declaration of Indulgence', *Journal of Ecclesiastical History*, XI (1960), 55–73, and 'The English presbyterians and the Stuart Restoration, 1648–1663', *Transactions of the American Philosophical Society*, new series, LV, part 2 (1965), 50–94.
[73] Witcombe, *Charles II and the cavalier house of commons*, appendix II, p. 211.
[74] Green, *The re-establishment of the Church of England*, ch. 10.

obstructed measures to lighten the requirements of conformity against them.[75] Yet Southampton, a pattern of anglican pietism, received the praises of Gilbert Burnet for his earnest efforts to achieve the comprehension of at least moderate presbyterians within the Church.[76] The duke of York's position was more complicated. In his memoirs, he criticised Clarendon for having obstructed the 1663 Bill for toleration, which he claimed to have himself supported; he was unusually tolerant in granting offices under his command to those of radical religious belief; and he was well-known to favour catholics and plans for the removal of the penal laws.[77] Yet he seemed to have had little time for presbyterians: in 1663, along with several of his companions, he protested against a decision of the house of lords to weaken the meaning of the declaration of 'assent and consent' to the Act of Uniformity.[78] Perhaps, like some others, he was content that dissenters should be tolerated outside the Church of England, but not that the rules of conformity should be relaxed to comprehend any of them within it.[79]

But it was Clarendon whose attitude to religious policy was widely recognised to be the most crucial in the government's decision: and Clarendon's position was among the least certain. At the time he was criticised from either side; by presbyterians for being uncompromising, by anglicans for being not uncompromising enough.[80] Historians have probed the ambiguity, seeking to square the Hyde of the 1630s, the Hyde of the Great Tew circle, and of ecumenical friends like Chillingworth, Hales and Falkland, with the Hyde of the later years, an apparently determined defender of the Church of England.[81] Because of this, the controversy over the government's ecclesiastical policy has become as much a debate over Clarendon's attitude to the problems of the Church: did he support both toleration and comprehension?[82] Or was he rather an uncompromising anglican who unhappily carried out

---

[75] Clarendon MSS 75, fol. 191, Nicholas to Clarendon, 13 Sept. 1661; Carte MSS 32, fol. 566, Nicholas to Ormonde, 10 June 1663; Carte MSS 47, fols. 351, 361, 363, 365, 367, 385 (letters of Nicholas to Ormonde in late 1662 and early 1663); *Hist. MSS. Comm.*, MSS of R. R. Hastings (4 vols., 1928–47), IV, 104–5, 107, Bishop Parker to Archbishop Bramhall, 20 July, 3 Sept. 1661, and MSS of A. G. Finch Esq. (4 vols., 1913–65), I, 116, 119, 172 (letters of Nicholas to Winchilsea, 1661–2); P. W. Thomas, *Sir John Berkenhead 1617–1679* (Oxford, 1969), pp. 217–20.

[76] Clarendon, *Life*, II. 408–9; Burnet, *History*, I, 170–1, 316; see below, pp. 189, 192–3.

[77] Clarke, *James the Second*, I, 428, 432–3; Pepys, *Diary*, II, 38, IV, 135, V, 350.

[78] See below, pp. 188–9.

[79] See Edward Seymour's speech in the 1668 debates on toleration and comprehension: Milward, *Diary*, p. 221.

[80] For presbyterian criticism, see *Reliquianae Baxterianae; or Mr Richard Baxter's narrative of the most memorable passages of his life and times*, ed. M. Sylvester (London, 1696), part III, pp. 20–1; for anglican, see Carte MSS 45, fol. 232, Sheldon to Ormonde, 29 Oct. 1667.

[81] See H. R. Trevor-Roper, *Edward Hyde, earl of Clarendon* (Oxford, 1975), pp. 22–3.

[82] Abernathy, 'Clarendon and the Declaration of Indulgence', *passim*.

Charles's religious policy?[83] Or was it merely that, while he favoured a full
restoration of the Church of England, he was occasionally willing to offer
presbyterians small concessions whenever he feared that they were likely to
be provoked into rebellion?[84]

Clarendon's position undoubtedly held some deep ambiguities. His own
polemical works against the Roman Catholic Church, and the writings of his
friends of the 1630s, had all been concerned to cut through the involved arguments asserting the accuracy and legitimacy of any particular denomination's
account of Christian truth: scripture contained the essentials of truth, but its
many controverted and difficult matters concerned nothing which was
necessary for salvation. All that was necessary was simple, and easily discovered by plain reason; only the vested interest of individual Churches and
their clerics sought to uphold their own unique infallibility against the claims
of all others.[85] After the Restoration, Clarendon continued to enjoy the
company and conversation of many more than rigid – or even moderate –
anglicans. He often saw his old friend Bulstrode Whitelocke, and discussed
liberty of conscience with him.[86] It was Whitelocke who introduced him to
John Owen, the independent theologian and churchman close to Cromwell,
whom he patronised and admired.[87] He seems also to have found the
company of Katharine, Viscountess Ranelagh, congenial, and was perhaps
sympathetic with her puritan, but essentially pietistic religious views.[88] She,
like Whitelocke, may have been one of Clarendon's lines of communication
with independent ministers.[89]

But religion was not just a question of piety, as the controversies he
deplored sufficiently showed: it was equally a matter of politics. The prince,
Clarendon accepted, could have no authority to meddle with the funda-

[83] Green, *The re-establishment of the Church of England*, ch. 10.
[84] Bosher, *The making of the Restoration settlement*, pp. 267–70.
[85] B. H. G. Wormald, *Clarendon: politics, history and religion 1640–1660* (Cambridge, 1951),
      pp. 243–76.
[86] See Whitelocke's Diary, vol. II (1659–75) in the marquis of Bute's collection. I am most
      grateful to Ruth Spalding, who is currently editing the Diary, for allowing me to see her
      transcription of it. See R. Spalding, *The improbable puritan: a life of Bulstrode Whitelocke,
      1605–75* (London, 1975), pp. 230–1, 233, 234–6, 238, 262. For Whitelocke's religious
      principles, see B. Worden, *The Rump Parliament* (Cambridge, 1974), pp. 131–5.
[87] *A complete collection of the sermons of the reverend and learned John Owen D.D.* (London,
      1721), xxiii–xxiv; Whitelocke, Diary (April, 1664).
[88] B.L., Althorp MSS B6 (Lady Ranelagh's letters to Burlington), and B4 (letters of Clarendon,
      and of Lord Clifford to Burlington); cf. the Countess of Warwick's diary for her, and her
      sister's connections with Clarendon's daughter, the duchess of York: B.L., Add. MSS 27531,
      fol. 110; for Lady Ranelagh and her circle, see C. Webster, *The great instauration: science,
      medicine and reform 1621–60* (London, 1975), pp. 57–67, 501.
[89] Clarendon MSS 78, fol. 231, Lady Ranelagh to Clarendon, May 1663; cf. fol. 247;
      Clarendon MSS 79, fols. 73 (same to same, 17 Feb. 1663), and 270 (same to same, 4 June
      1663).

mentals, the essentials of Christian belief: but to secure good order, peace and unity, he was entitled to organise its inessential matters as he saw fit. The Church of England, in religious terms, was but one way of organising the inessential matters of Christianity: but its government and doctrines were deeply embedded in the history, the law, and the very nature of the English people. Emotionally attached to the English Church, he viewed it not as any more vital to salvation than any other Church, but parochially and unambitiously as 'a part of the government of England'.[90] Change was permissible, of course; all might be re-examined; even a precise uniformity was not strictly necessary. Yet the fundamentals of the English Church could never be given up without irrevocable damage to the English constitution.[91]

There were other objections to an accommodation, as well. It seemed clear that some compromise would have to be reached with the presbyterians, if only because of their reputed strength and numbers, and because the moderates among them were sufficiently close to anglicanism to make such a compromise conceivable. Yet Clarendon, although on excellent terms with some individual presbyterians, detested and distrusted the sect as a whole. Their clericalism was profoundly objectionable to one so antipathetic to the political authority of the clergy as he;[92] and none could forget their role in the origins of the war, their divisive theology, what were seen as their deceptive tactics, above all their anti-monarchical, even popish, doctrines.[93] 'There is no doubt', he wrote to his son Cornbury towards the end of his life, 'every good man would depart from many little things, if the doing so would firmly unite the presbyterians to the Church – which, I confess, I think impossible; for the truth is, they are a pack of knaves; and they who appear less violent will immediately lose the party, who will make no other use of the concessions which shall be granted them, than to ask new and more unreasonable things'.[94] Even before he had decided on its impossibility, he made his distaste for presbyterianism perfectly plain. Visiting Oxford as the university's new chancellor in 1661 he snubbed Dr Henry Wilkinson, principal of Magdalen Hall (his own college) since 1648, an enthusiastic adherent of parliament and presbyterianism, and upbraided him for the college's failure to use the Book of Common Prayer, and for its 'factious and debauched' scholars.[95] He condemned the Covenant, and sought to prevent the election to parliament of men 'inclinable to presbyterian principles'.[96] He criticised churchmen who

---

[90] Quoted in Wormald, *Clarendon*, p. 282.
[91] *Ibid.*, pp. 282–314.   [92] *Ibid.*, pp. 276–80, 289, 306.
[93] See, e.g., Clarendon, *History*, II, 319–22.
[94] Lister, *Life of Clarendon*, III, 483 (10 June 1671).
[95] *The life and times of Anthony Wood, antiquary, of Oxford, 1632–95, described by himself*, ed. Andrew Clark (6 vols., Oxford Historical Society, 1891–1900), I, 413–15.
[96] Clarendon MSS 74, fol. 297, Clarendon to Orrery, 31 March 1661; B.L., M636/18, Lady Rochester to Sir Ralph Verney, 27 Jan. 1662.

were merely 'touched with presbytery'.[97] Clarendon was anxious to crush the unacceptable political doctrines of presbyterianism, and firmly to disavow all those who could not accept the lawful constitution of the Church of England; yet his anti-presbyterianism did not – for the moment at least – impugn his eirenic intentions. By moderating conformity, by coaxing presbyterians back to the Church with concessions and preferments, he hoped eventually to eradicate presbyterianism, and end the schism in the English Church.

Presbyterianism, however, was only part of the problem; for even assuming that it could be eliminated from England by comprehending enough of its adherents within the anglican fold, there remained all those others – the independents and the sects – whose doctrines and whose rejection of a national Church made any accommodation unimaginable. For many anglicans, and others, the only sensible course was to force them into compliance and conformity, to preserve the unity, if not the sanity, of the nation. Yet there were others, some of them at court, who held a different view. Arthur Annesley, earl of Anglesey from 1661, longed for a united reformed Church of England which could reflect his own deep private devotion, and concern about the spread of atheism. But his acquaintance among a wider spectrum of independents as well as presbyterians, and his patronage in the late 1660s of works by Sir Charles Wolseley which urged an end to religious persecution and argued for toleration in a spirit of rational and practical belief, suggests a willingness to go further than a simple comprehension.[98] The duke of Buckingham, a member of the council from April 1662, and one of the king's favourite – if most exasperating – companions, was also known to have a wide acquaintance among dissenters after his marriage to the daughter of Lord Fairfax, although it was only towards the end of the 1660s that he became well known as a supporter of toleration.[99] Anthony Ashley Cooper, Lord Ashley, was one of several Cromwellian *politiques* who had successfully managed the transition to Restoration office, in his case as chancellor of the exchequer. Ashley's loathing of popery and clericalism alike placed him among the most determined opponents of religious compulsion.[100]

Ironically, however, it was only through association with catholicism that

---

[97] Carte MSS 47, fol. 5, Clarendon to Ormonde, 9 Sept. 1662.

[98] For Anglesey, see B. Worden, 'Toleration and the Cromwellian protectorate', pp. 229–30, and M. Goldie, 'Sir Peter Pett, sceptical toryism and the science of toleration in the 1680s', pp. 249–50, both in *Persecution and toleration* (Studies in Church History, XXI, 1984); D. R. Lacey, *Dissent and parliamentary politics in England 1661–1689* (New Brunswick, New Jersey, 1969), pp. 459–62.

[99] See below, pp. 300–1; see Villiers, George, duke of Buckingham, *The works of his grace George Villiers, duke of Buckingham* (2 vols., London, 1775), II, 191–209.

[100] K. H. D. Haley, *The first earl of Shaftesbury* (Oxford, 1968), pp. 28–9, 48–9, 66–7, and cf. R. Ashcraft, *Revolutionary politics and Locke's 'Two treatises of government'* (Princeton, New Jersey, 1986), pp. 80–1.

the movement for toleration could arouse sufficient enthusiasm at court to become realisable. A catholic party, headed in the Civil War by Queen Henrietta Maria, had always seen advantages to itself from the destruction or the enfeeblement of the Church of England; Clarendon deplored her and its policy of seeking an alliance with the prebysterians.[101] By 1661, however, their wider hopes of somehow preventing the Church's re-establishment had clearly been dashed: they hoped, more realistically, only to obtain the removal of the laws against the exercise of their religion. Petitioning like the sects for liberty of conscience outside the established Church, it seemed at times as if their best hope of success lay in joining with them, and seeking a more general toleration. Some catholics at court became, therefore, among the strongest advocates of a wide liberty of conscience. Principal among them was the earl of Bristol, who had served both Charles I and Charles II as secretary of state; his tenure of the post had been ended by his conversion to catholicism. Deprived of office, and even of a place on the privy council, he remained a confidant, friend, and unofficial adviser to the king.[102] Bristol's former secretary, Sir Henry Bennet, whose succession to Nicholas in the secretaryship in 1661 was perhaps due to a promise of the king's to Bristol when the earl was himself forced to surrender it, was also brought to support his position – though whether out of conviction or out of a sense of obligation to and dependence on Bristol's interest is uncertain: at the end of his life, however, Bennet was received into the Roman Church.[103] The queen mother herself continued to agitate for the position of the catholics whenever she was in England, in 1660 and from mid-1662 until her return to France at the beginning of the second Dutch war.[104] Between them, she, Bristol and Bennet, with their various associates, formed for a time a powerful lobby for the relief of the catholics.

ˈ All those factions which sought to extend and to guarantee liberty of conscience for religious minorities sought, and to some degree found, a strong ally in the king himself. But while the king was far from passive in the discussions which surrounded the religious settlement, both his precise role, and his own opinions, remain hard to assess. Charles's personal attitude to religion became quickly famous: he apparently had, as Burnet complained,

---

[101] Clarendon, *History*, I, 566–7, IV, 162–4, 341; see also Green, *The re-establishment of the Church of England*, pp. 26–9.

[102] See, e.g., his employment in the mission to the Treaty of the Pyrenees in 1659, Routledge, *England and the Treaty of the Pyrenees*, pp. 54, 60, 82–3; for Bristol's involvement with Walter Montagu, the queen mother's confessor, and catholic plans in the 1660s, see B.L., Add. MSS 61483, fols. 229 and 231, Bristol to Montagu, 8 Oct. 1660, and Montagu to Bristol, 8 Dec. 1662.

[103] See below, pp. 218–19, and 220–5, for Bennet's relationship with Bristol in 1662–3; V. Barbour, *Henry Bennet, earl of Arlington* (Washington, 1914).

[104] J. Miller, *Popery and politics in England 1660–1688* (Cambridge, 1973), pp. 96–7, 101.

'no sense of religion: both at prayers and sacrament he, as it were, took care to satisfy people that he was in no sort concerned in that about which he was concerned'. He told Burnet that he was 'no atheist, but he could not think God would make a man miserable only for taking a little pleasure out of the way'.[105] With little interest in the formal part of religion, Charles cared little for religious differences: in 1660, when quakerism seemed to many returning exiles and others to be an appalling heresy, he told them (according to the quakers' own account) that they should not be disturbed so long as they lived and worshipped peaceably.[106] But despite his studied indifference, there were a few contemporary rumours and much retrospective speculation concerning his catholicism. Burnet and others appear to have believed that he had been converted towards the end of the exile, possibly in 1659.[107] Charles was plainly emotionally attracted towards a particular, rather unintellectual, kind of catholicism: he was, as Halifax hinted, profoundly superstitious, and the mysteries of catholicism appealed to him.[108] He was close to many catholics; he had discussed, enough times, seeking help from Rome to regain his kingdoms; he recognised the services done him during the Interregnum by many loyal catholics, and was anxious, he told Clarendon, that the laws which prevented them from peacefully worshipping as they pleased should be lifted.[109] Unlike Clarendon, Charles had no very strong sense of the constitutional position of the Church.

But much as all these things inclined Charles to accept as wide a liberty of conscience as was conceivable (and even, to some, inconceivable), his liberalism on the subject was limited. In part, it was limited by a dislike of puritan protestantism: he expressed, among the discussions on his marriage, his contempt for northern protestants and their ugly princesses;[110] he loathed presbyterianism, because of his unhappy experiences in Scotland in 1650–1, because of its strictness and its sermonising, because of the strength it gave to clerical rather than monarchical power. Presbytery, he told the earl of Lauderdale, 'was not a religion for gentlemen'. He enjoyed anti-presbyterian satire, Butler's *Hudibras*, and Jonson's *Bartholomew Fair*.[111]

[105] Burnet, *History*, I, 166–7, cf. 324; see also C. H. Hartmann, *Charles II and Madame* (London, 1934), p. 95, Charles to the duchess of Orleans, 29 Feb. 1664.
[106] *Something that lately passed in discourse between the king and R. Hubberthorne* (London, 1660). Wood's copy (Bodl., Wood 608) dates its publication to 21 July 1660.
[107] Burnet, *History*, I, 133–4, and Airy's notes on these pages
[108] *The complete works of George Savile first marquess of Halifax*, ed. W. Raleigh (Oxford, 1912), pp. 189–91; see also Burnet, *History*, I, 245, and J. P. Kenyon, *The popish plot* (Harmondsworth, 1974), p. 189.
[109] Clarendon, *Life*, I, 533–6.
[110] P.R.O., PRO 31/3/109, Bartet to Mazarin, 10/20 Jan., 28 Jan./7 Feb., 9/19 Feb. 1661.
[111] Burnet, *History*, I, 195; Carte MSS 33, fol. 229, Sir A. Brodrick to Ormonde, 28 Nov. 1663; Bosher, *The making of the Restoration settlement*, pp. 238–9.

And while he was happy to agree to a liberty in matters which did not interest him, he cared deeply that it should not be extended more widely: Burnet wrote that Charles, however much he dissembled on the subject of religion, 'could not help letting himself out against the liberty that under the Reformation all men took of inquiring into matters: for from their inquiring into matters of religion, they carried the humour further, to inquire into matters of state'.[112] Charles's willingness to countenance toleration was at the least conditional on – even intended to produce – the docility of the tolerated, the destruction of militant protestantism which might interfere with the State's wider aims.

In both religion and politics, if the government could have been said to have had a policy in the early 1660s, it was Clarendon's: by standing by the law, to show that monarchical government presented no danger to liberty and property; and by standing by the Church, to reunite the country in the religion to which its constitution and its nature were best suited. But in both cases, these were not the only policies available, nor were they necessarily those most attractive to the king. Clarendon's policies were always threatened, he felt, if not by Charles's absolutist ambitions, at least by a tendency among his other advisers to sacrifice legal and constitutional niceties to expediency, and Charles's own preference for the informal over the formal, for a personal, rather than a bureaucratic power. From parliament, however, government policy faced a different set of threats; from those who feared, rather than exalted, royal power, and from those who felt that policy represented too much compromise, rather than too little. If royal autocracy was limited by Clarendonian policy, it might be limited still further by the temper of the 'Cavalier Parliament'.

[112] Burnet, *History*, I, 166–7

3

Royalism and conservatism in the Cavalier Parliament

In the heyday of 'whiggish' history writing, nothing seemed more natural than to assume that the incomplete reconstruction of royal powers was no more than the logical result of the onward march of parliamentary predominance. During the Civil Wars and Interregnum, parliament had come of age; at the Restoration its maturity was confirmed in a balance of power with the Crown. Some argued that it continued, aggressively, to expand its privileges and authority: others simply that Charles realistically accepted the limitations on its prerogatives that all this implied.[1] Its undoubted anglicanism – like an earlier generation's puritanism – was the mark of parliamentary independence of royal control, the strength and assertiveness of backbench country gentlemen.[2] It was undeniable, however, that no parliament could have had a stronger reputation for royalism, even for docility, than that which opened on 8 May 1661 and continued in existence, with sessions almost every year, for the next eighteen years. Its actions in support of monarchical authority, the legislation it passed to crush the political and ecclesiastical power of presbyterianism and to exalt that of the re-established Church of England, and its reverence for the king and his martyred father, fully earnt it the epithet the 'Cavalier' Parliament. But within seven years of its opening, so loyal a body became so virulent a critic of royal powers and policies that its reluctance to grant supply brought the government to within only a little distance of dissolution. If the Cavalier Parliament was so royalist and so anglican, how could it have provided such determined opposition to the government's wishes?

Exactly how predominant royalists were in the new parliament is difficult to assess. For the house of commons the task has been made simpler by the compilation of information in the *History of parliament*; even so, definition

---

[1] Kemp, *King and commons*, pp. 7–10; Roberts, *The growth of responsible government*, pp. 149–54; Carlyle, 'Clarendon and the privy council'; Sir Keith Feiling, *A history of the Tory party, 1640–1714* (Oxford, 1924).
[2] See, e.g., Witcombe, *Charles II and the cavalier house of commons*, p. 173.

is often a problem. How, for example, can one classify Sir Henry Herbert, whose attempt to avoid commitment in the Civil War was foiled when he was plundered by both sides, carried off to Oxford by royalists, and eventually fined £1,332 by the committee for compounding?[3] Sir Thomas Leigh became technically a delinquent because he happened by accident to be in the cavalier garrison at Lichfield when it surrendered, and was fined accordingly.[4] *Ex parte* statements about individual allegiance made in the aftermath of war should also be treated with caution: after the Restoration John Vaughan claimed that he had been forced to compound, although there is no other evidence of this, and men such as Thomas King magnified their dubious efforts to aid the royal armies.[5] Although in the figures that follow, such cases are usually considered as possible royalists, the figures can only be treated as an approximate account of the political composition of the Cavalier Parliament. For some men, there is not enough information to judge of their Civil War involvement: many may in any case have masked their strong opinions with inactivity.

In the elections of March to May 1661, 501 M.P.s were returned who actually took their seats in the house of commons for the 507 available places. This includes those allowed to sit on double returns who were subsequently ejected; the six places not accounted for were occupied by members who had also been elected elsewhere.[6] A further 119 were chosen in by-elections up to 29 July 1667, including three who had already sat by virtue of elections in 1661, but had been subsequently unseated because of election disputes.[7] So between the opening of the parliament and the end of the brief meeting of July 1667 a total of 617 men were entitled to sit in the house of commons.

Of these, 168 had themselves fought as royalists during the first Civil War, had acted as commissioners of array, or had attended the king at Oxford. A further twenty-three may have been royalists, and ninety-seven, who were not themselves involved in the first Civil War, were sons of royalists. Forty-two who fall within none of the preceding categories, were involved either in the second Civil War, or had taken some part in Interregnum royalist conspiracy. Altogether, some 330 M.P.s had in some way shown their sympathy for the royal cause. At least 141 of these had suffered for it through

---

³ *H.P.*, I, 531–2.   ⁴ *H.P.*, II, 730.   ⁵ *H.P.*, III, 628, II, 684.
⁶ It also includes Lord Holles, created a peer before he was able to take his seat in the commons. Holles is excluded from all the subsequent figures, including the numbers of those entitled to sit between 1661 and 1665. *H.P.* gives the figure for those elected in 1661 as 522 (I, 1). This is because the editors have included in this figure those elected at by-elections resulting from double returns or elections being declared wholly or partly void by the commons (see *H.P.* I, xi–xii). I have regarded all elections after the opening of the Parliament on 8 May 1661 as by-elections, and have not included them in the general election figures.
⁷ Sir James Langham, Sir Henry Lingen, and Edward Nosworthy.

composition fines, sequestration and confiscation: some were still feeling the consequences of their fathers' royalism. Others had been imprisoned, or had suffered the plunder of their lands. Some had spent much of the period in exile. On the other side, fifty-six had fought for parliament, or had clearly demonstrated their sympathy with the cause by continuing to attend the Westminster parliament throughout the Civil War or by serving on county committees. Some forty of these were among the 164 who held office (including minor local office) during the Interregnum.[8]

Parallel figures for the house of lords, which has not received the same prosopographical attention as the commons, are less easily established; information on the activities of some of the more obscure peers is not so readily available. Between 1661 and 1667, 175 temporal peers were entitled to sit in the lords.[9] Seventy-three had fought for the king in the Civil War, had attended him at Oxford, or had shown themselves sympathetic to his cause. A further thirty-six were the sons of royalists, and fourteen more joined the court in exile, fought in the second Civil War, or became involved with royalist conspiracy. Indeed, many received their peerages as rewards for loyalty during the War or Interregnum.[10] Thirty peers had been unequivocal parliamentarians in the Civil War, and others, such as Carlisle and Fauconberg, had become involved with the Interregnum regimes later on. Some, including Ashley, Hunsdon, and Albemarle, became parliamentarians or Cromwellians, having originally supported the royal cause. Others, like Bedford and Willoughby, had moved in the other direction. Lord Paget changed his allegiance several times. Only a few of the forty-eight bishops who sat in the lords during the period had not been ejected and sequestered during the Interregnum. Some had also suffered imprisonment.[11]

Rather over half of the members of the house of commons, 70 per cent of the temporal lords and all of the spiritual lords possessed royalist backgrounds. The government had reason to be pleased: the elections of 1661 had, for the moment, broken much of the political power of presbyterianism

---

[8] Those who changed sides during the war itself have been excluded from the figures.

[9] This figure is based on the list published in 1661, which is reproduced in *Parliamentary history*, IV, 192–3. 'George, Lord Bruce' in this list seems to be a mistake. Heirs of peers who died during the period have been added, as well as the few new elevations to the English peerage (Monmouth, Falmouth, Arundell of Trerice, Butler, Freschville, and Arlington) to arrive at the total number of peer qualified to sit. The main sources used for the lords are *G.E.C.* and *D.N.B.* The figures include peers who were under age when they succeeded, and some who seem not to have been summoned, though qualified, or to have taken their seats.

[10] Some are counted as royalists who really fell foul of the Interregnum authorities only by reason of their Roman Catholicism. Those who changed sides during the Civil War are again excluded from the figures.

[11] A. G. Matthews, *Walker revised* (Oxford, 1948); *Fasti ecclesiae Anglicanae*, ed. J. Le Neve and T. D. Hardy (3 vols., Oxford, 1854).

and independency. Yet the wider meaning of royalist predominance was
more difficult to assess. Some of those who had become royalist conspirators
in the 1650s or who had fought against the army in the second Civil War, had
earlier fought for parliament. Other royalists had taken up arms only reluctantly under immense pressure from relatives, neighbours, friends, or
consciences: finding merit in both sides or none, their commitment had been
grudging, conditional, or agonised. And the other elements, particularly in
the commons, could not be ignored: those who had accepted the commonwealth and the protectorate, or who had lived peacefully under all regimes,
avoiding political or official involvement – even those who had been in arms
for parliament – formed a still substantial minority. The government could be
confident that republicanism – even political presbyterianism – was, if not
extinct, at least dormant. But precisely how far the reaction would allow it to
go in re-imposing royal power was not so obvious: ministers needed to be
wary of taking its royalist supporters for granted, lest they drift away and add
to the strength of those of less certain allegiance. And more important than
the numbers of royalists or parliamentarians, of commonwealth officials or
Interregnum conspirators, were the wider concerns which united many of all
backgrounds. The political instincts and attitudes of the gentry as a whole,
even more than those of royalists in particular, shaped parliament's actions.

From the execution of Strafford in 1641 to the exhumation of Oliver
Cromwell twenty years later, England had experienced rapid, unpredictable
and violent political change. For the gentry, accustomed to political and
social stability and enjoying the material benefits which they helped to bring,
the experience was profoundly disturbing. Old certainties had disintegrated;
with them, it seemed, had gone many of the norms and ethical values of
English life. Clarendon looked sadly back on the 'dilapidations and ruins of
the ancient candour and discipline': 'in a word', he wrote, 'the nation was
corrupted from that integrity, good nature, and generosity, that had been
peculiar to it, and for which it had been signal and celebrated throughout the
world; in the room whereof the vilest craft and dissembling had succeeded'.[12]
Some responded to the turbulence of public life by retreating into the private,
into an introspective religious devotion which emphasised the maintenance
of personal integrity:[13] others chose rather to fight back at the moral
relativism and fashionable cynicism which threatened to swamp tradition
and sociability.[14]

[12] Clarendon, *Life*, I, 307; cf. 305–8.
[13] See J. Spurr, 'Anglican apologetic and the Restoration Church', unpublished D.Phil.
thesis, Oxford University, 1985, pp. 29–35; see also *John Locke: two tracts on government*,
ed. P. Abrams (Cambridge, 1967), pp. 51–3, 57–8.
[14] See S. I. Mintz, *The hunting of Leviathan* (Cambridge, 1962), ch. 7.

But it was a sense of political uncertainty that was more immediately apparent. For a nation which prided itself on the antiquity of its political system and on that system's effectiveness in resolving conflicts, the execution of the king, the abolition of the house of lords, the imposition of military rule, tinkering with the constitution, and the sight of political radicalism at the seat of power were all deeply unsettlint. It was natural to reflect how permanent, how secure, could be the re-establishment of that old system. Despite the seeming success of the Restoration, the danger of imminent political change and violence continued to be felt throughout the 1660s: on one side, there were constant fears of the rebellions and plots of the radicals; on the other, suspicions of plans to make the king absolute, abolishing parliament and law, and replacing the Church of England with popery. The country remained highly sensitive to signs of political crisis: in 1662 Sir Francis Topp, the duke of Newcastle's steward, attributed sluggish land prices and a general decline in economic activity to fears of an uprising and the collapse of government;[15] and in 1663, at the height of the factional struggle for power between Clarendon and the earl of Bristol, Lord Howard of Charlton complained of his inability to repay his debts, because 'all private business in the meantime stands at gaze, nor indeed will any of these dealers part with one penny out of their hands until they be absolutely determined one way or other'.[16] The government was offered advice from all quarters on the best means to preserve political stability.[17] The most terrifying experience of all in the last twenty years had been the reminder of the political power of the people, a multitude 'always craving, never satisfied', over whom 'there can be nothing set . . . which they will not always be reaching at and endeavouring to pull down'.[18] It seemed essential to restore political authority, order and hierarchy; but there remained a nagging doubt: would it be possible to achieve stability under the restored monarchy and the ancient constitution? Thomas Hobbes, notoriously, had blamed the English political system as one of the major causes of the rebellion: James Harrington had argued in his *Oceana* of 1656 that that system was no longer feasible. If the king was restored, he was said to have told the 'Rota' coffee-house meeting in late 1659 or early 1660,

[15] B.L., Loan MSS 29/236, fol. 282, Topp to Newcastle, 6 Aug. 1662; see also Nottingham University Library, Portland Collection, Cavendish MSS PW1/255, Topp to Lord Mansfield, 19 Oct. 1661.
[16] *Hist. MSS. Comm.*, MSS of the marquess of Salisbury at Hatfield House, vol. XXII, 1612–68 (1971), 447, Howard of Charlton to Salisbury, 18 July 1663.
[17] E.g., Edward Chamberlain, *The late war parallel'd, or a brief relation of the five years civil wars of Henry the third* (London, 1660); Roger L'Estrange, *A memento: directed to all those that truly reverence the memory of King Charles the martyr* (London, 1662); see also Newcastle's book of advice to Charles II, Clarendon MSS 109.
[18] Quoted in *John Locke: two tracts*, ed. Abrams, p. 65; cf. Dryden's 'Astraea Redux', ll. 43–8 in *The poems and fables of John Dryden*, ed. J. Kinsley (Oxford, 1970), p. 17.

he would be unable to preserve himself in power for more than three years, for a commonwealth would inevitably return.[19]

Behind this doubt lay a social uncertainty: for Harrington had argued, classically in the 'Second part of the preliminaries' of *Oceana*, that the decline and collapse of monarchical power was best explained by a fundamental shift in the balance of land ownership away from the nobility, and towards a new gentry of independent freeholders. No longer could the monarchy be supported by the might of its natural allies: only a standing army could now sustain it in its unnatural rule. Harrington's use of this analysis was influential, although not unique: many thought that the revolution could somehow be linked with the decay of feudalism, the declining wealth and power of the old nobility, and the rise of a new landed gentry.[20] But a stronger, less academic view of Restoration political sociology saw not just the nobility, but also the higher gentry as under threat, as power and money shifted towards newly rich yeomen and minor gentry, and towards the rapidly expanding wealth of financiers and merchants. The earl of Southampton lamented, in one of his fiscal reports to the king, the Crown's financial difficulties 'when even the genius of the nation tends too much to democracy and that the balance of wealth and election of burgesses (the persons that can only in parliament give the Crown a support) belongs most to merchants, traders and yeomanry'.[21] For royalists, the sense of decline was particularly acute. Since the beginning of the war, the wealthy City oligarchies had been identified as parliamentarian and presbyterian. The war, it seemed, had provided them with an enormous and welcome opportunity of profiting from the embarrassed estates of distressed cavaliers. Parvenu entrepreneurs had managed to establish themselves as landed gentry, complained the heraldic scholar Edward Waterhouse, by using the profits they had derived from 'being in offices of law, plunder, custom, trust or sale of Crown and bishops' lands' to buy up the lands of impoverished royalists, and managed, '(knowing that acts of oblivion, and confirmation of judicial proceedings would come, as of course in all restitutions they do)' so to 'transfer their acquisitions of ill

---

[19] This version of Harrington's prophecy is given by Sir Thomas Dolman (for whom, see *H.P.* II, 219–20) in a letter, possibly to Henry or William Coventry, of Dec. 1663 (Coventry MSS, vol. 4, fol. 5, cf. fols. 1–4). See also John Aubrey's version (*'Brief lives', chiefly of contemporaries, set down by John Aubrey between the years 1669 and 1696*, ed. A. Clarke (2 vols., Oxford, 1898), I, 291) which seems coloured by later events, fitting the prophecy into what actually happened. For Hobbes's contemporary influence, see Mintz, *The hunting of Leviathan*, and Q. Skinner, 'The context of Hobbes's theory of political obligation', in *Hobbes and Rousseau: a collection of critical essays*, ed. M. Cranston and R. S. Peters (New York, 1972), pp. 110–19.

[20] *The political works of James Harrington*, ed. J. G. A. Pocock (Cambridge, 1977), pp. 188–207, cf. p. 117; N. Jose, *Ideas of the Restoration in English literature* (London, 1984), p. 7.

[21] B.L., Harleian MSS 1223, fol. 205v.

title into solid estate'.[22] The comedies of the 1660s bitterly ridiculed the rich, corrupt, hypocritical, presbyterian, who manipulated the unfortunates of the Civil War to make yet greater gains for himself.[23] Religious fanaticism may have been more frightening to the royalist, but presbyterianism was more odious, its adherent the 'state convert' of Samuel Butler's satire, who 'always appeared very faithful and constant to his principles to the very last: for as he first engaged against the crown for no other reason but his own advantage; so he afterwards faced about, and declared for it for the very same consideration'.[24] Royalists watched resentfully as what Sir Robert Howard, in his successful comedy of 1663, *The committee*, referred to as a 'new gentry' of parliamentarians and Interregnum office holders now acquired baronetcies and social respectability to match their new wealth.[25]

For some amongst the nobility and higher gentry, all this raised the spectre of the decay of their power and influence both at the centre of politics and in the country at large. But there was worse to come. Gentry incomes had been bolstered in the early seventeenth century as agricultural production struggled to cope with a growing population, and the consequent scarcities drove up the prices of agricultural commodities and the value of land. But from the 1620s, that growth in population was slackening: ultimately, agriculture was to be faced with the opposite problem, of overproduction and underconsumption. For a time, this was disguised by the bad harvests and dearths of 1640 to 1663, which supported prices, and sometimes pushed them to spectacular levels: but thereafter, as the summers improved, many prices declined heavily. From 1663 to the end of the century grain prices were lower than average; other prices were depressed from 1664.[26] By the mid-to-late 1660s, the resulting drop in rents and land values was beginning seriously to alarm a large proportion of the largely *rentier* gentry. On some estates, the difficulties of tenants meant that landlords were unable to let land by 1665.[27] Not all farmers were equally affected by these problems: but after

---

[22] Edward Waterhouse, *The gentleman's monitor* (London, 1665), pp. 169–70.

[23] See Ben Ross Schneider, *The ethos of Restoration comedy* (Illinois, Urbana, 1971), pp. 41–5.

[24] *The genuine remains in verse and prose of Mr Samuel Butler, author of Hudibras*, ed. R. Thyer (2 vols., London, 1759), II, 62; cf. 63–4 and 393–5.

[25] Sir Robert Howard, *Five new plays* (London, 1700), p. 57; P. Roebuck, *Yorkshire baronets 1640–1760, families, estates and fortunes* (Oxford, 1980), p. 21; see also *The life and times of Anthony Wood*, ed. Clark, I, 299, 301; Roger L'Estrange, *A caveat to the cavaliers: or an antidote against mistaken cordials*; Peniston Whalley, *The civil rights, and conveniences of episcopacy, with the inconvenience of presbytery asserted* (London, 1661), p. 9.

[26] J. Thirsk (ed.), *The agricultural history of England and Wales*, V, i, *Regional farming systems* (Cambridge, 1984), xxiii–xxiv; V, ii, *Agrarian change* (Cambridge, 1985), 1–6, 46–7, 51–2, 55–62, 76–8, appendix III, tables i–vi, xii.

[27] *Ibid.*, pp. 170–8; M. G. Davies, 'Country gentry and falling rents in the 1660s and 1670s', *Midland History*, IV (1977–8), 86–96; see also C. G. A. Clay, 'The price of freehold land in the later seventeenth and eighteenth centuries', *Econ. Hist. Rev.*, 2nd series, XXVII (1974), 174–6.

years of buoyant prices, this sudden and sustained decline, particularly in wheat prices, came as a shock to an agricultural economy unable to adjust quickly, and uncertain of the prospects for the future. By 1669 the notion of a permanent devaluation in rents and land prices had become one of the standard and most persistent themes of English economic debate.[28]

From a society still in great tension, a conservative and authoritarian reaction, loyalist demands for retribution, and the belligerent resurgence of the power of the old gentry were only to be expected: the government had no doubt assumed as much, and had called new elections in 1661 in the hope of reaping the benefit. Yet all the elements of the reaction were complex and ambiguous: the government could not be quite confident that it was a simple reaction which it might easily manipulate in its own interests. For although the solution to all these uncomfortable uncertainties seemed obviously to be the recreation of a powerful authority, able to impose order on the moral, religious, political and social confusion, the form that authority might take could be viewed in several different ways.

'Absolutism', if not exactly in fashion after the Restoration, was at least embraced by some – often clerical – royalist theorists: and some of the Bodinian enthusiasm for an untempered sovereign power spilled over into more practical political discussion.[29] The earl of Peterborough remarked in 1663 that 'those old notions, of mix'd governments, privileges, and conditions, have by severall accidents of state, been put out of the essence of things, they are not to be practised any longer, and the consequences of all undertakings, can no more be, but monarchy, or a commonwealth'.[30] The author of a manuscript tract sent to the duke of Buckingham in 1662 asserted that 'to be really king, the sovereignty is to be really and simply there, it must have no rival, no sharer, it is its own nature individual, indivisible': one way, he suggested, to restore royal power was to recreate feudalism in order to bring the people into a closer, more dependent relationship with their king.[31] Indeed, the recreation of feudalism was more commonly seen as the means to

---

[28] J. Thirsk and J. P. Cooper (eds.), *Seventeenth-century economic documents* (Oxford, 1972), pp. 32–88.

[29] See M. A. Goldie, 'John Locke and Restoration anglicanism', *Political studies*, XXXI (1983), 61–85; see also J. W. Daly, 'The origins and shaping of English royalist thought', *The Canadian Historical Association Historical Papers*, 1974, pp. 15–35, 'John Bramhall and the theoretical problems of royalist moderation', *Journal of British Studies*, XI (1971), 26–44, and *Sir Robert Filmer and English political thought* (Toronto, 1979), for a different view on the extent to which Filmerian-style thinking percolated into royalist political theory.

[30] P.R.O., SP 29/81/94, Peterborough to Williamson, endorsed as received 14 Oct.; cf. the earl of Conway's remark in 1667, Carte MSS 35, fol. 240: see below, p. 289.

[31] B.L., Lansdowne MSS 805, fol. 75v, 76v–77.

re-establish monarchical authority than the imposition of any continental absolutism: another paper of advice, whose author was clearly worried by the Harringtonian argument, proposed the return of the feudal army, and a firm alliance between the monarchy and the nobility – extending even to saving noble and gentry estates from decay. The nobility and gentry, its author claimed, were the fences which preserved the distance between the Crown and the populace.[32] Fabian Phillips, too, based his arguments for as complete a return as possible to the institutions and laws of feudal England on a desire that every proprietor of land should have the direct personal relationship with the king that only tenures *in capite* could provide.[33] John and Robert Heath, in their vigorous defence of the court of wards, likewise insisted that there should be a personal dependence of the subject on the sovereign.[34] Both the Heaths and Phillips argued as they did partly because, as officials of the abolished court of wards, they wanted their jobs back: but even less anti-quarian conservatives, such as Roger L'Estrange, admitted the usefulness of a feudal system.[35] Some merely advocated the resumption of the royal prerogatives that had been abandoned in the 1640s.[36] John Bowring, how-ever, suggested that the government should go rather further, and copy the policies of Charles I in the 1630s, of exploiting all the ancient rights and dues of the crown in order to amass a 'body of private treasure' which the king could use to make himself extremely powerful, 'as absolute as the Grand Signior'. Bowring, who was constantly importuning the government, seems not to have been taken very seriously, and is perhaps representative of the crankiness which some of those who favoured a return to feudalism affected.[37]

Some, mainly military men, reasoned more simply that the security of the regime required, above all else, greater military force.[38] A few of the gentry were occasionally enthusiastic about regular soldiers when they felt particu-larly threatened by the activities of the radicals and fanatics; some of the clergy in the front line of the struggle against sectaries especially favoured a

[32] P.R.O., SP 29/1/81.
[33] D. C. Douglas, *English scholars* (London, 1939), pp. 160–4; J. G. A. Pocock, *The ancient constitution and the feudal law* (reissue, Cambridge, 1987), pp. 215–17.
[34] B.L., Egerton MSS 2979, fols. 26–36, 41–58.
[35] L'Estrange, *A memento*, pp. 77–9; see also [William Constantine], *The reader's speech of the Middle Temple at the entrance into his reading, Febr. 29 1663/4* (London, 1664), pp. 9–10. (For the reader's identity, see A. R. Ingpen, *The Middle Temple bench book* (London, 1912).)
[36] See, e.g., Lord Berkeley in B.L., Sloane MSS 3828, fols. 81–91, esp. fols. 86 and 88. See also below, p. 140.
[37] SP 29/187/47. Cf. SP 29/26/101, and 109/85.
[38] B.L., Sloane MSS 3828, fol. 89v (Lord Berkeley); P.R.O., SP 29/81/94 (Lord Peterborough); SP 29/82/26 (Lord Belasyse); Clarendon MSS 109, pp. 1–6 (the marquess of Newcastle).

stronger permanent army.[39] But other conservatives, even so dedicated a royal polemicist as L'Estrange, found the whole concept of a permanent force distasteful.[40] The reason they did so was characteristic of their thought as a whole. The laws, L'Estrange argued, if properly executed, constituted the 'best public security against sedition'; an army could secure the country only when the nation was rich enough to pay it regularly and adequately and when there were no wealthy and powerful factors contending for power. In those circumstances, there would be scarcely any need for an army: but if one existed while the state was unable to pay it, and while some strong faction might seize control of it, it could only jeopardise stability further. The experience of the 1640s and 1650s had shown, all too clearly, how easily an army could become the creature of an interest: to accept a standing army would be 'to deliver up the strength of the nation, into the hands of a faction'.[41]

For most conservatives, repelled by the behaviour of armies during the war and Interregnum, the most desirable kind of authority was not that imposed by a powerful military force – an army seemed more likely to accelerate change, than to suppress it. The best security lay neither in this, nor in the evanescent constructs of political fashion, but in a return to the most durable standards, of law and custom. 'Though a certain and determinate law may have some mischiefs in relation to particulars, which cannot all by any human prudence at first be foreseen and provided for, yet . . . it is preferable before that arbitrary and uncertain rule which men miscall the law of reason', wrote Sir Matthew Hale, a judge during the Interregnum, yet appointed by Clarendon as chief baron of the exchequer at the Restoration.[42] It was a view shared by many Common Lawyers, 'accidents and artifices of men, are so *various* and *uncertain*, that no government is, was, or ever can be so exact, (no, not that Utopian device, which Mr Wren so well asserted) as can secure against all casual emergents and mischiefs'.[43] Such a view, almost axiomatic among Common Lawyers in the first half of the century, had been confirmed and strengthened by the attacks on the law and on their profession during the war and Interregnum. Yet in England's legal culture, it was one that was not,

---

[39] SP 29/81/16, Sir Thomas Bridges to Bennet, 5 Oct. 1663; Bodl., Tanner MSS 47, fol. 50, Bishop Hall to Bennet, 3 Oct. 1663; B.L., Add. MSS 21922, fol. 251v, Sir John Norton and Sir Humphrey Bennet to Southampton, 18 Aug. 1662.

[40] L'Estrange, *A memento*, pp. 79–84; cf. the mention of a standing army in Milward, *Diary*, pp. 83, 84, 99, 113–14, 120, 218, 219, and below, pp. 141–51, 309–10, 315–17.

[41] L'Estrange, *A memento*, p. 79.

[42] Frederick Pollock and W. S. Holdsworth, 'Sir Matthew Hale on Hobbes: an unpublished MS', *Law Quarterly Review* XXXVII (1921), 290.

[43] [Constantine], *The reader's speech of the Middle Temple*, p. 12; the reference is to Matthew Wren's replies to Harrington, for which, see Pocock, *The political works of James Harrington*, pp. 82–90.

by far, limited to lawyers alone: for many of the gentry, a strict adherence to the laws also seemed to be the best guarantee of security and stability. 'The preservation of our laws ought to be dearest to us, for by them the Crown is kept from tottering on the head of our sovereign, and we protected from oppression', George Sitwell, a Derbyshire gentleman, advised the newly-elected knight of the shire. 'The laws are our birthright, by them every man's property is maintained in what he hath: justice is the sinews of all common-wealths, the strongest tye that can be amongst men, for whilst that is supported there can be no great dissensions among us, nothing is left to an arbitrary power.'[44] L'Estrange, too, extolled the merit of the laws in preserv-ing the bounds of the prince and the people: 'let a prince therefore stick to his ancient laws, and he may be sure his people will stick to him'.[45]

The reaction towards authority was not so much towards the personal power of the Crown as towards the impersonal authority of the law, towards all that the Crown stood for against the confusion of the last twenty years: legalism and legitimacy, the ancient ways of the English constitution.[46] Law represented continuity with the past, and the predictability of the future: for fundamentally, the English gentry wanted to be protected from change. 'There is nothing more dangerous in church or state, than innovations', wrote Roger Coke in a passage echoed by many others. 'It is therefore the most secure way of governing (when men's manners and vices do not require new laws) by the ancient and received laws of a nation.'[47] Even those not particu-larly well-disposed towards Common Lawyers or the Common Law were happy to agree that 'all innovation, we know, is dangerous in any state, whether civil or ecclesiastical'.[48] Innovations provoked, and were provoked by fiery and turbulent spirits: 'alterations are dangerous, although they are specious, and have some reason to justify them; and oftentimes those are the most dangerous, which are most specious', Sir Robert Pointz argued in

---

[44] Sir George Sitwell (ed.), *Letters of the Sitwells and Sacheverells* (2 vols., Scarborough, 1900–1), I, 37–8.

[45] L'Estrange, *A memento*, ch. 10.

[46] See Jose, *Ideas of the Restoration*, p. 50, for Waller's *To the king*, and *Hist. MSS. Comm.*, MSS of the earl of Verulam (1906), pp. 196–8, for Sir Harbottle Grimston's 1665 sessions charge; see also Pocock, *The ancient constitution and the feudal law*, p. 156; and R. Ashton, 'From cavalier to roundhead tyranny, 1642–9', in *Reactions to the English Civil War, 1642–9*, ed. J. S. Morrill (London, 1982), pp. 185–207.

[47] Roger Coke, *Justice vindicated*, 'Elements of power and subjection', p. 69.

[48] T[homas] B[ellamy], *Philanax Anglicus: or a Christian caveat for all kings, princes and prelates, how they entrust a sort of pretended Protestants of integrity, or suffer them to commix with their respective Governments* (London, 1662), preface to the reader. (The preface is a post-war addition to this work, for which, see R. A. Beddard, 'Of the duty of subjects: a proposed fortieth article of religion', *Bodleian Library Record*, X (1978–82), 232, nn. 2 and 3.)

1661.[49] 'By the good constitution, establishment and observation of good laws,' observed the author of a charge at a sessions soon after the Restoration, 'all nations and commonweals which are grown to height and preeminency, have had their prosperous rising, abundant increase and fortunate continuance; but by the want, breach or change of good laws, of which we of this nation have been too sensible, nothing hath ensued but desolation, downfall and inevitable ruin.'[50] By adherence to the laws, the risks of change might be kept at bay. A week before the opening of the new parliament, an old member of the Long Parliament, Robert Hunt, hoped fervently for 'no new laws, but that we may enjoy our good old laws, our protestant religion and a happy peace'.[51]

So strong an emphasis on law and on conservatism carried a fairly evident (and often explicit) warning: that the monarchy was restored as a guarantee of the rights and liberties of Englishment, not at all in contradiction of them. '*Justitia firmat solium*', quoted the Middle Temple reader for the lent term 1664, 'which King James well understood, when he published, that for a king of England to discountenance the common law, was to desert the crown ... the prince is ill advised who ruins the *law*, which is his chief *support*; if for no other cause, yet for this, we have no cause to *fear*'.[52] William Prynne, reader at Lincoln's Inn in the lent term 1661, chose to lecture on the Petition of Right, 'a rehearsal and ratification of the highest nature of all these ancient fundamental laws contrived by the wisdom of all former parliaments and so earnestly contested for in all ages when infringed, that secure the lives limbs liberties franchises inheritances properties estates of all English freemen and subjects'.[53] Prynne's delight in the English laws as the guarantees of liberty was perhaps natural given his actions and affiliations in the 1630s and 1640s: yet the most royalist of lawyers could agree.[54]

Old presbyterians and old royalists were united on the benefits of rule by law. But royalist legalism had its limits: the theories of active resistance, common in the 1640s, again disappeared from the mainstream of English political life. Reluctantly, but inescapably facing the question of how they should behave if the king proved no respecter of the laws and constitution of the kingdom, most writers saw the results of resistance as worse than the tyranny

---

[49]   Sir Robert Pointz, *A vindication of monarchy and the government long established in the Church and kingdom of England* (London, 1661), p. 4.
[50]   Gloucestershire Record Office, D 340.a.23. (Punctuation slightly amended.)
[51]   Bristol University Library, Bull of Shapwick MSS, DM 155/94, Robert Hunt to William Bull, 27 April 1661; for Hunt, see *H.P.*, II, 619–20.
[52]   [Constantine], *The reader's speech of the Middle Temple*, p. 13.
[53]   B.L., Stowe MSS 302, fols. 48v–49; cf. Sir Roger Twysden, *Certain considerations upon the government of England*, ed. J. M. Kemble, Camden Society, old series, XLV (1849), 181.
[54]   See, e.g., Lord Chief Baron Sir Orlando Bridgman, quoted in J. W. Gough, *Fundamental law in English constitutional history* (Oxford, 1955), p. 140.

itself: 'he that trusts to the strength of a steel cap', wrote Twysden, 'may have his head as soon broken as he that wards the blow'.[55] 'The very truth is', summarised L'Estrange,

all government may be tyranny. A king has not the means of governing, if he has not the power of tyrannizing. Here's the short of the matter. We are certainly destroyed without a government, and we may be destroyed with one. So that in prudence, we are rather to choose the hazard of a tyranny, than the certainty of being worried by one another. Without more words, the vulgar end of government is, to keep the multitude from cutting one another's throats.[56]

Indeed, royalist legal conservatism, though in some respects hindering the government's freedom of action, could provide it with a means of re-asserting royal power. For while the disavowal of innovation made it difficult to erect new defences for the Crown's security, it at least made it easier to re-erect the old. It was easy to represent those acts by which the Long Parliament had, with Charles I's assent, limited the Crown's powers, as the innovations which by first breaking into the old standards of the English constitution, had opened the doors to a confused tumult of undesirable novelties. The 1641 Act for Triennial Parliaments, the solicitor general argued in 1664, had over-thrown the fundamental laws by which England was governed: ' 'tis not in the power of a parliament to pass such a law, nor to root out the foundations of that authority under which they sit'.[57] Even if the bishops had consented to their exclusion from the house of lords in 1642 (which they had not), claimed the earl of Dorset in 1661, they could never legally have done so, for they would then be demolishing the constitution itself.[58] In effect, it was alleged, the constitution was based on fundamental laws which parliament, even the power of statute, could not change. The need for order, for the rule of law, might be used to limit the arbitrary powers of parliament as well as the arbitrary power of the crown.

Yet this insistence on the pre-eminence of fundamental law over statute was only one side of an old argument: and even after the Restoration there were those who still maintained the effective sovereignty of parliament and statute.[59] Twysden quoted a remark of Burghley's, 'that he knew not what an act of parliament could not do in England'; and if the power of statute was so transcendent, there could be no fundamental laws or prerogatives, no rights of the king or the people, that it could not alter.[60] The great lawyer John

---

[55] Twysden, *Certain considerations*, p. 105.
[56] L'Estrange, *A memento*, ch. 10.
[57] Leicestershire Record Office, Finch MSS, Box 4965, P.P. 14.
[58] Kent Archives Office, Sackville MSS U269/036; cf. the Act repealing the exclusion, 13 Car. II, c. 2, *S.R.*, 306; the Act had made 'several alterations prejudicial to the constitution and ancient rights of parliament and contrary to the laws of this land'.
[59] See J. P. Somerville, *Politics and ideology in England, 1603–40* (London, 1986), pp. 95–100.
[60] Twysden, *Certain considerations*, p. 173.

Selden had been one of the most cogent proponents of this view in the 1620s and 1640s, and it was his pupil, friend and executor, John Vaughan, who shared with him a slightly iconoclastic view of the common law as nothing more nor less than the law embodied in ancient statutes, who was the master- mind of the resistance to the government's efforts to roll back parliament's legislative advance of 1641–2.[61] But such views were not confined to an intellectual elite. Opposing the restoration of the bishops to the house of lords, Sir John Holland argued that the statutes passed in 1641 with the king's assent were as good in law 'as much as any law to the nation and to say what they have enacted is against the fundamental law of the land is as if it should be said the law of the land is against the law, for one is as much the law as the other'.[62] Holland lost his argument, and the bishops were restored; neither was Vaughan particularly successful in holding back the Crown's *revanche*. After the passage of the repeal of the Triennial Act, Vaughan retired to the country, appalled by his countrymen's carelessness of their rights and privileges, and vowing never to return. Their retreat from their defence he saw as an abdication of constitutional responsibility.[63] Yet the government's failure to incorporate claims that the legislation of 1641–2 was against fundamental law in most of the acts which repealed it indicated that members of parliament remained wary of any strong claims about the constitution one way or another, just as the inability of any form of radical authoritarianism really to take root showed their conservative attachment to the law. Those who sat in parliament in the early 1660s wished above all to resist change, to preserve the constitution, rather than to be inveigled into new debates concerning its nature.[64]

But a retreat onto the law was not the only possible reaction to political turbulence: and indeed, many of the nobility and the landed gentry who sat in the commons found in the law and lawyers objects of irritation and frus- tration rather than guarantees of the *status quo*.[65] Their reaction to the collapse of order and to their perceived decline in power, wealth, and influ-

61 See R. Tuck, ' "The ancient law of freedom": John Selden and the Civil War', in *Reactions to the English Civil War, 1642–9*, ed. J. S. Morrill (London, 1982), pp. 139–45, and R. Tuck, *Natural rights theories: their origin and development* (Cambridge, 1979), pp. 83–4, 97–100, 132–5; for Vaughan, see Clarendon, *Life*, I, 30–1, and below, pp. 94–5.
62 C. Robbins, 'Five speeches, 1661–3, by Sir John Holland, M.P.', *Bull. Inst. Hist. Rev.*, XXVIII (1955), 195.
63 See his speech on the Act, P.R.O., SP 29/53/7; for his retirement, see Carte MSS 215, fol. 359, Brodrick to Ormonde, 30 July 1667.
64 The Act concerning ecclesiastical jurisdiction contains such a declaration (13 Car. II, c. 2, *S.R.*, 306), and the Triennial Act repeal contains a denunciation of the Act as against the prerogative, and makes it 'null and void' (16 Car. II, c. 1, *S.R.*, 513). For the arguments over these statements, see below, pp. 131–3, 165.
65 See, for example, Clarendon MSS 109, p. 25. *H.P.*, I, 48 gives the proportion of lawyers in the house: cf. 4–5.

ence, was as likely to take the form of a vigorous re-imposition of control over their local communities, and a firm suppression of the political aspirations of their new rivals. The determination of the Restoration gentry to suppress political dissidence and to restore the proper social hierarchy was clear enough in the activity of the commissions of the peace, of the Corporation Act commissioners, and in the enthusiastic security measures taken by individuals, sometimes at their own expense.[66] It was obvious that the government might profit from the gentry's concern for their own pre-eminence within their localities, as the gentry saw their own safety bound up with that of the government: but it was equally evident that such an alliance held dangers for the Crown. The gentry, it is frequently argued, constituted the most influential interest group of seventeenth-century England: their efforts for the protection of the monarchy in the 1660s were merely peripheral to their principal concern – the consolidation and expansion of their own power, to establish themselves not simply in their old role, as the mediators between the government and the localities, but in a stronger sense as the almost autonomous governors of their shires and districts. In several pieces of legislation in the 1660s they extended their authority: in the administration of the poor law, of the militia, and over adjacent corporations; while by failing to restore the prerogative courts, they eroded the government's ability to control and discipline them.[67] The gentry, in short, were busy establishing the hegemony they enjoyed in the eighteenth century, confirming Harrington's claim that their wealth and the monarchy's power could not live long together.[68]

So strong a view may be overdrawn. The legislation of the Cavalier Parliament naturally reflected, in some sense, the values and interests of the nobility and gentry who dominated it,[69] as did the way that that legislation was interpreted and enforced reflect those of the innumerable gentry who filled the commissions of the peace. There were certainly aspects of their relationship with the Crown that they were eager to alter. Some were perhaps pleased with the widened administrative role that Restoration legislation gave them. Others were probably dismayed. Yet there is little evidence that they possessed the desire or the confidence to push back the role of the state in local affairs: it was their relationship with their social inferiors, not their

---

[66] A. Fletcher, *Reform in the provinces: the government of Stuart England* (London, 1986), pp. 153, 171, 172, 176–7, 211, 319; S. K. Roberts, *Recovery and Restoration in an English county: Devon local administration 1646–70* (Exeter, 1985), pp. 175–90, 195; C. Holmes, *Seventeenth-century Lincolnshire* (Lincoln, 1980), p. 223.

[67] See, e.g., Fletcher, *Reform in the provinces*, p. 358; Hutton, p. 289; Roberts, *Recovery and Restoration in an English county*, pp. 218–19.

[68] See J. H. Plumb, *The growth of political stability in England, 1675–1725* (Penguin edn, Harmondsworth, 1973), pp. 15–27, 31–5.

[69] See the tables in *H.P.*, I, 10–11.

relationship with the Crown, with which they were most concerned; and while welcoming anything which might bolster their authority amongst their local communities, they saw in this nothing which might contradict the power of the Crown. It was never simple, either, to identify what, exactly, the interest of the gentry might be. Although the gentry of each county both yearned for unity amongst themselves and made some effort to restore it,[70] and although they felt they had interests and aims in common, they were deeply and sadly aware that these were jeopardised by the sharp factional and political divisions which remained between them. Local administrators complained bitterly of the unwillingness of their colleagues to invite unpopularity by undertaking their proper tasks, or of their activities in stirring up local opposition to their own efforts.[71] Civil War allegiance still provoked rows and split county society.[72]

Those who complained most loudly to the government about their neighbours' reluctance to join them in the vigorous execution of the laws tended, naturally, to be those who identified most strongly with the regime: anglican royalists, who believed themselves surrounded by popular dissent and sedition, with most of their colleagues too frightened to come to their aid. Yet it was not only they who saw their interests as close to those of the regime: Sir John Holland, a member of the Long Parliament until Pride's Purge, wrote in one of his parliamentary speeches that if the government was shaken, 'we must unavoidably fall into the hands of unreasonable men, into the hands of an insolent, violent, merciless, frantic, fanatic generation of people, who in hatred to monarchy, magistracy and ministry, would soon destroy all the nobility, gentry, persons of interest and quality throughout the nation'.[73] But the Crown and the gentry were bound together by more than just these ties of mutual protection in a hostile environment: they depended on each other far more fundamentally, and recognised it. From the Crown the gentry received

[70] See, e.g., A. Fletcher, *Sussex 1600–60: a county community in peace and war* (London, 1975), pp. 321–2; M. A. Kishlansky, *Parliamentary selection: social and political choice in early modern England* (Cambridge, 1986), p. 129; Bristol University Library, Bull of Shapwick MSS DM 155/125 and 128, Robert Hunt to William Bull, 24 Nov. and 12 Dec. 1660; Hereford and Worcester Record Office, Microfilm of Pakington MSS in the possession of Lord Hampton, vol. 2, no. 3, Lady Pakington to Bishop Morley, 26 March 1661.

[71] P.R.O., SP 29/62/84, Sir Jordan Crosland to Bennet, 10 Nov. 1662, 91/42, Humphrey Cornwall to Thomas Price, 26 Jan. 1664, 93/64, Peterborough to Williamson, 27 Feb. 1664, 63/141, Evan Lloyd to Sir Henry Bennet, 20 Nov. 1662; see Lambeth Palace Library, MSS 1394 (Twysden's letter book), pp. 55, 60, for the reaction to Sir Roger Twysden's objections to the levying of militia money in 1668.

[72] See Bruce, Thomas, earl of Ailesbury, *Memoirs written by himself* (2 vols., Roxburghe Club, 1890), II, 442; *Hist. MSS. Comm.*, MSS of the earl of Verulam (1906), pp. 59–72; Clarendon MSS 78, fol. 65, Sir Robert Broke to Clarendon, 1 Nov. 1662.

[73] Bodl., Tanner MSS 239, fol. 53.

all those social and administrative distinctions which gave them local standing: rank, office, the perquisites of power. On the gentry the Crown relied for
their service and loyalty in administering the country. Without the Crown,
most of the gentry's influence would disappear (as it had, at times, during the
Interregnum): without the gentry, the Crown, with only a minute army and
no resources for a large professional administration, would be unable to
rule.[74] It was the natural way of things: 'what can be of greater consequence',
the assessors for one country's subsidies were asked in 1661, 'than that his
Majesty be enabled to protect his subjects, and to overcome the difficulties of
government, what greater honour can any subject desire, than in things of
such necessity, of so great and universal concernment, to be called to serve his
king?'[75] The Restoration gentry, like those earlier in the century, felt it right
that they should be heard, their opinions respected by the government, and
themselves treated with consideration, with offices, gratuities, and honours;
in return, they acknowledged their duty to help the government in its business
of governing.

Yet this community of interest could easily be obscured: as Halifax wrote
at the end of the century, 'the interest of the governors and the governed is in
reality the same, but by mistakes on both sides it is generally very differing.
He who is a courtier by trade, and the country gentleman who will be
popular, right or wrong, help to keep up this unreasonable distinction'.[76] The
corruption of ministers and courtiers could easily block the channels of communication and favour, stopping the normal and natural flow of intercourse
of country with court, of gentry and nobility with the king. If it did so, the
government would soon feel the effects in the loss of political goodwill.[77] The
dangers of corruption remained as common a feature of Restoration, as of
early seventeenth century, political advice; and the ministers and courtiers of
the 1660s soon made it appear of uncommon relevance.[78] Clarendon pointed
out in his autobiography, how necessary it had been for the king's advisers to
'endeavour to compose the public disorders, and to provide for the peace and
settlement of the kingdom, before they applied themselves to make or
improve their own particular fortunes': but as early as 1661 he was himself
being likened to Cardinal Wolsey; monstrously corrupt and monstrously

[74] See C. S. Russell, *Parliaments and English politics, 1621–29* (Oxford, 1979), pp. 17–21;
D. Hirst, 'Court, country and politics before 1629', in *Faction and parliament: essays in early
Stuart history*, ed. K. Sharpe (Oxford, 1978), pp. 105–37.
[75] Bodl., Tanner MSS 47, fol. 45v.
[76] Raleigh (ed.), *The complete works of . . . Halifax*, pp. 219–20.
[77] Cf. the opposition to the first duke of Buckingham: K. Sharpe, 'The earl of Arundel, his
circle, and the opposition to the first duke of Buckingham, 1618–28', in *Faction and parliament*, ed. K. Sharpe, pp. 242–4.
[78] Cf. Chamberlain, *The late war parallel'd*, p. 21.

powerful, a corpulent blockage in the arteries of favour.[79] In 1667 he was
dismissed, and in a play produced the following year, Sir Robert Howard, one
of the foremost parliamentary assailants of government corruption,
examined the problem of the too-powerful favourite through a story of
Philip III of Spain's *privado*, the Duke of Lerma, a figure whom many
identified with Clarendon himself. As Lerma's daughter, Maria, is made to
tell the king,

> he that does engross your beams
> Robs others of your light, and is a cloud
> That hangs upon your brightness; breeding
> Ill weather to all the World besides; while he seems
> To make you practice power unlimited;
> Just when you have the least, obeying his.[80]

Like the gentry's attitudes to the constitution, their attitude to government
was essentially conservative: interpreting politics in the same ways as they
had in the first half of the century, they asked for little more than a reconstruction of the norms which had then obtained, of harmony and mutually
beneficial exchange between the government and the localities. If the Crown
wanted to retain their goodwill, it would need to respect that conservatism.

The claim of the gentry as a whole to a special relationship with the Crown
was, though, far outshone by that of the royalists. Their title to the king's
affection and favour was unique, bound to him as they were by ties of the
greatest loyalty, of shared experience and shared suffering. Royalists saw
themselves as a breed apart, distinguished by their courageous defence of a
virtuous, though unfortunate cause, and by their resolute renunciation of
private advantage for honour and public service: some drew up memoirs or
catalogues to celebrate their loyalty, 'because', wrote one of them, 'loyalty,
shall not be hurried with silence to the grave of oblivion, with ignobleness,
and disloyalty';[81] many marked their strong personal devotion to the memory

---

[79] Clarendon, *Life*, I, 274; Clarendon MSS 74, fol. 77, 'examination concerning Lord
Salisbury'.
[80] Sir Robert Howard, *The great favourite, or, the duke of Lerma* (London, 1668), p. 34, cf.
pp. 22, 31.
[81] B.L., Harleian MSS 2043, fol. 38v, cf. fols. 137ff. See also J. Heath, *A new book of loyal
English martyrs and confessors* (London, 1663); W. Winstanley, *The loyal martyrology, or,
brief catalogues and characters of the most eminent persons who suffered for their
conscience during the late times of rebellion* (London, 1665); David Lloyd, *Memoirs of the
lives, actions, sufferings and deaths of those noble, reverend, and excellent personages that
suffered* (London, 1668); R. M. Kidson (ed.), 'The gentry of Staffordshire', and 'Active
parliamentarians during the Civil War', *Collections for a history of Staffordshire*, Staffordshire Record Society, 4th series, II (1958); S. C. Newton (ed.), 'The gentry of Derbyshire in
the seventeenth century', *Derbyshire Archaeological Journal*, LXXVI (1966), 1–30; *Hist.
MSS. Comm.*, 10th report, appendix, part IV (1885), MSS of Stanley Leighton Esq., M.P.,
p. 377; Northamptonshire Record Office, Finch Hatton MSS 576 and 4284.

of their martyred king at the services to commemorate his execution, or in the dedication of new churches.[82]

Such loyalty, it might seem, could blossom into a close political alliance with the government: with the help of the royalists, they sometimes argued, the king could make himself truly secure. As the 'loyal society' of prominent cavalier officers told Clarendon, while seeking relief for impoverished royalist soldiers, 'as it ever was our fixed resolution to prostrate all our concerns, lives, and fortunes for the maintenance of his Majesty's royal person and dignity; so shall it ever be (to our lives end) our practice in all things to submit unto his Majesty's pleasure'.[83] Royalists urged the king to rely only on themselves: it was logical to give trust to those who had shown already some signs of deserving it, madness to give it to those who, having once rebelled, might well do so again.[84] Yet royalism, although its adherents were unlikely to attempt (as some presbyterians had done in 1660) to construct new limits to royal powers, was unlikely either to provide a secure basis for their extension. Royalists, after all, had been many and various, their motives for espousing the king's cause complex. For some, the laws and liberties of the country had seemed, ultimately, to depend on supporting the Crown: they saw devotion to the royal cause also as devotion to the law, the execution of Charles I not just as an outrageous impiety, but also as an act of breathtaking illegality. The rhetoric of royalism stressed law almost as much as it did loyalty.[85]

If this consideration made royalism only a little more of an asset for the government than the desire of the gentry as a whole to stand firmly by the laws and liberties of the country, there were others which made it almost an embarrassment. Viewing themselves as in a peculiarly special relationship with the government, their reaction when they judged that relationship to have been ignored was peculiarly resentful. For while they thought themselves especially qualified as defenders of the royal cause, they thought the crown had an equal obligation towards themselves. They were the natural recipients of royal favour: when they failed to receive it, they instantly smelt corruption. The government, however, handicapped by its estimate of the necessity of reconciling leading presbyterians, was forced to withhold from them many of the highest positions in the administration. The presbyterians,

---

[82] Frances Arnold Foster, *Studies in church dedications* (3 vols., London, 1899), II, 346–7; see also R. A. Beddard, 'Wren's mausoleum for Charles I and the cult of the royal martyr', *Architectural History*, XXVII (1984), 36–49.

[83] Clarendon MSS 75, fol. 337.

[84] See Clarendon MSS 109, pp. 60–1; L'Estrange, *A memento*, ch. 12; Carte MSS 232, fol. 19, William Legge to Ormonde, 1 Feb. 1664.

[85] See, e.g., *The plea, case, and humble proposals of the truly-loyal and suffering officers* (1663), p. 6; and Sir Richard Ford's speech to his regiment of London militia, *The diurnal of Thomas Rugg, 1659–61*, ed. W, L. Sachse, Camden Society, 3rd series, XCI (1961), 160.

Sir John Bramston complained, had duped the king and his advisers into believing that they had been responsible for the Restoration; securing the credit, they scooped the spoils.[86] Royalist discontent appeared as soon as appointments began to be made, within a few weeks of the Restoration. Two weeks after the king had ridden into London in triumph, Lord Falkland exploded on hearing that he was unlikely to be appointed lord lieutenant of Oxfordshire. 'I cannot be so impudent and so importunate as some men are, to get places', he told George Morley, but 'I can and shall be as sensible as any man, if I be very much disobliged'. Many royalists, Morley told Clarendon, had similar complaints.[87] Throughout the 1660s, their failure to gain many of the richest prizes in the gift of the Crown rankled with cavaliers. L'Estrange angrily dismissed James Howell's pious exhortations to patience and articulated the suspicion among royalists that those of his old enemies whom the king had placed in office were bent on the ruin of his greatest friends.[88] The insult to their honour was as hard to bear as the blow to their hopes. 'Are not these sufficient causes to move passion in civil men to break out beyond reason sometimes?' asked Charles Hammond in a plea for the proper administration of the charity for distressed royalists; 'when our poverty for our fidelity shall make us ridiculous, our inferiors predominating over us, our superiors more countenancing our enemies than hearkening to us, and our own party not able to help one another, our complaints being kept from his majesty's ear, as our persons, by our poverty, are kept from his presence.[89]

The royalists' reaction was considerably shriller than the situation warranted: even if they failed to monopolise the highest offices, their entrenchment in the middle-ranking offices of state was difficult to miss. Yet the presence of ex-parliamentarians and Cromwellians in prominent posts and in the privy council was striking. In senior offices, and on the council, were the duke of Albemarle, captain general, once Cromwell and the Rump's commander in Scotland; the earl of Manchester, lord chamberlain, who had been a leading opponent of Charles I; the earl of Anglesey, vice-treasurer of Ireland, was well known for his presbyterianism, and had been president of

[86] *The autobiography of Sir John Bramston*, ed. Lord Braybrooke, Camden Society, old series, XXXII (1845), p. 117; see also *A lively pourtraict of our new-cavaliers, commonly called presbyterians clearly shewing that His Majesty came in not upon their account. In a compendious narrative of our late Revolutions* (London, 1661).

[87] Clarendon MSS 73, fol. 64, Morley to Clarendon, 15 June 1660; *Hist. MSS. Comm.*, 5th report (1876), part 1, appendix, MSS of the duke of Sutherland, pp. 174, 184, 194, 196.

[88] L'Estrange, *A caveat to the cavaliers: or an antidote against mistaken cordials* (London, 1661), pp. 8–9. For this exchange, see my 'A Restoration publicist: James Howell and the earl of Clarendon, 1661–6', *Historical Research*, LXI (1988), 123–31.

[89] 'Truth's discovery; or the cavaliers' case clearly stated by conscience and plain dealing', in *A collection of scarce and valuable tracts . . . selected from public as well as private libraries, particularly that of the late Lord Somers*, ed. W. Scott (13 vols., London, 1809–15), VIII, 563.

the council of state in the early months of 1660. Lauderdale, secretary of state for Scotland, had been a covenanter early in the war. The earl of Sandwich, now vice-admiral of the kingdom, had been a close associate of Cromwell; Lord Robartes, now lord privy seal, and briefly lord deputy of Ireland, had been a presbyterian and a parliamentarian. Lord Ashley, chancellor of the exchequer, had been another of Cromwell's allies. Denzil Holles, one of Charles I's presbyterian opponents, and constant in his efforts to limit the constitutional power of the monarchy, was created a baron and was ambassador to Paris from 1663 to 1666. Charles Howard, who had fought against the king, and sat in the Cromwellian parliaments, became earl of Carlisle and a privy councillor, and was sent on several diplomatic missions. Sir William Morrice, one of the secretaries of state, was a relation of Albemarle's and known to be of presbyterian views. This parliamentarian, Cromwellian, and presbyterian presence in the offices of state was strengthened by others who simply sat on the privy council; principal Civil War politicians such as Viscount Say and Sele, and the earl of Northumberland. Roger Boyle, Lord Broghill, an intimate of Cromwell, was created earl of Orrery and remained President of Munster. Others, such as John Crew, the earls of Lincoln, Pembroke, and Suffolk, received various marks of favour. Rewards to the king's old enemies were conspicuous, too, in the law: Harbottle Grimston, a prominent presbyterian member of the Long Parliament, was now master of the rolls, Matthew Hale lord chief baron of the exchequer. Clarendon was also responsible for the promotion of Sir John Maynard and Sir John Glynne as king's sergeants, particularly galling for royalists because these two, together with Sir John Trevor (whose son became a secretary of state in 1668) were all heavily involved in the most notorious case of the sale of sequestered royalist estates, the 1652 purchase of the Stanley lands.[90] Like the gentry as a whole, royalists who saw the flow of patronage and favour diverted from what they considered to be its natural channel felt disappointed and aggrieved. The royalism of the 1650s had been a philosophy of virtue in adversity, of distance from the corruption and stained principles of political life. Instead of converting royalism into a set of values and ideas which would firmly uphold the government after the Restoration, the court's actions helped to confirm its preference for the 'country', and its contempt for the court, its longing for the clarity of rural fresh air against the smog of city politics. Royalism soon became more of a vehicle for conservatism than for autocracy.

[90] Lists of the council and of officers of state are included in James Heath, *The glories and magnificent triumphs of the blessed restitution of his sacred majesty K. Charles II* (London, 1662); for the Stanley case, and for royalist cynicism about Interregnum turncoats, see below, ch. 8.

For parliament's strongest instincts were highly conservative ones: faced with changes of alarming speed and profundity for the last two decades, its members wished above all else to arrest it, to restore the stable and friendly world they once knew – and which doubtless grew more stable and friendly in their imaginations. Naturally, they recognised that an entire reconstruction of that old world was unlikely to be possible or desirable, and they were reluctant to revive those things which had contributed, in the first place, to its demise: but they had little sympathy for any more fundamental changes. 'Fear God, and honour the king', quoted Evelyn, watching the dismemberment of the exhumed bodies of Cromwell, Bradshaw, and Ireton on 30 January 1661, and he appended another sentence of scripture; 'but meddle not with them who are given to change'.[91]

The 'principal care' of the parliament elected in 1661, wrote the anglican polemicist Samuel Parker, was 'to take care of the Church, and to reinstate it in its ancient dignity'.[92] And indeed, the measures it passed for the benefit of the Church were notorious, closing all the hopes of an indulgence to tender consciences raised by the Declaration of Breda, or of a moderate episcopal church settlement raised by the Worcester House Declaration of October 1660. It restored the bishops to the house of lords; it revived the ecclesiastical courts; and it enacted a new Act of Uniformity which would expel from the Church's ministry even moderate presbyterians, and men who professed to be moderate episcopalians. The Conventicle Act of 1664, and the Five Mile Act of 1665, drew the bonds of nonconformists even tighter.

That the members of the Cavalier Parliament should have been anglicans was scarcely surprising. Even if widespread anglican sentiment had not, self-interest would have made many of the electors of 1661 recognise the sense in choosing as their representative a man identified with the already obviously powerful and influential restored Church of England. Presbyterians almost everywhere either gave up the attempt to get elected, or retreated to safe family boroughs. When parliament met, both houses took steps which would strengthen their anglican majorities. On 13 May the commons voted that every M.P. should take communion according to the use of the Book of Common Prayer at St Margaret's a fortnight later: Sir Anthony Cope, Sir John Bramston, Sir Philip Warwick, Sir Allen Brodrick, and Sir George Ryve, all great churchmen, were appointed to ensure that all did so.[93] The anglican character of the house of lords was immensely strengthened by the

[91] *The diary of John Evelyn*, ed. E. S. de Beer (5 vols., Oxford, 1955), III, 269.
[92] *Bishop Parker's history of his own time*, tr. Thomas Newlin (London, 1727), p. 26.
[93] C.J., 247, 289; there must be, however, some doubt about how successfully, or determinedly, it was enforced: see B.L., Egerton MSS 2043, fol. 10.

restoration to it, in November 1661, of the spiritual lords: the twenty-four bishops and two archbishops now added weight to the Church's cause in the upper house. In both houses, the number of those who openly failed to conform to the Church of England was extremely small. Even those whose dissent from the established church was more limited – perhaps amounting merely to keeping a presbyterian as private chaplain – were few. D. R. Lacey has attempted to calculate the numbers of dissenters in either house from 1661 to 1689: his catalogue includes forty M.P.s and eight peers who sat between 1661 and 1667.[94] Even this may over-estimate their numbers, as the dissent of some dates from after 1667, even the 1680s, and the evidence of their opinions is often small.

On the other hand, these figures can give a false impression of the real extent of sympathy for dissent, or at least of the extent of support for a much more moderate settlement than that finally achieved. The many M.P.s who had been members of the Long Parliament up to, and after Pride's Purge, as well as many of those conformable enough to the Interregnum regimes to have been appointed to office in the 1650s, cannot have been enthusiastic about the imposition of a rigid anglican uniformity. During all the debates on ecclesiastical matters measures against the sects received willing support from almost every quarter of either house. But measures against presbyterians were pushed through the commons against powerful opposition in extremely close votes. How was it, then, that the legislation of the Cavalier Parliament demonstrated a resolute determination not only to enforce the Church of England's hold over the religious life and worship of the nation, but also to create a Church which would exclude both from its ministry and its congregations many who genuinely desired to participate in them?

One reason was perhaps the gentry's feeling that support for the Church was inseparable from their own interests. I. M. Green has described their mutual dependence: 'through its prayers and its sermons, its patronage, tithes, and leases of Church land, the episcopal church furnished theoretical and practical support for the social supremacy of crown and gentry. The gentry in their turn attacked those forces which challenged the ecclesiastical hierarchy and the existing order of society.'[95] Undoubtedly most of the gentry believed that unity and uniformity in religion were essential for the maintenance of stability and order. Some royalist gentry viewed the meetings of dissenters in conventicles as a direct personal threat. Sir Roger Langley, the sheriff of Yorkshire, told Sir Henry Bennet in the summer of 1664 that he would give half of what he had 'to be out of danger of having his throat cut'

---

[94] Lacey, *Dissent and parliamentary politics*, appendices 1 and 2.
[95] Green, *The re-establishment of the Church of England*, p. 180.

by them.[96] Somerset gentry complained in April 1663 of the freedom with which presbyterian conventicles were held: Bennet was assured that 'they are very confident they shall be destroyed if some speedy course be not taken'.[97] Such hysterical reactions were perhaps natural – even justified – among Anglican royalist gentry actively persecuting dissent in areas where it was unusually strong. Others, appreciating that uniformity would help to ensure civil harmony and suppress the subversive effects of allowing each to follow his own religious conscience, rejected a toleration which could only 'bring in all manner of confusion and ruin'.[98] But this dictated no more than uniformity, not the form it should take: it amounted to far less than the ready enthusiasm for the anglican Church, and the unwillingness to compromise on its traditions, ceremonies, or organisation, which informed parliament's approach to ecclesiastical questions.

Nor do the links between the gentry and the clergy within their communities, their shared responsibilities in local religious and secular life, really explain parliament's vehement churchmanship. The links were indeed close: the clergy were drawn principally from the gentry's ranks; they co-operated with the gentry in local commissions of the peace, and sought their help in the upkeep of church fabric. The gentry, in turn, controlled large portions of ecclesiastical patronage, benefited from impropriated tithes, and held tenancies of church lands.[99] But the intimacy of the relationship did not imply an identity of interest. One of the first of a series of Restoration reviews of the condition of the Church, *Ichabod*, published in 1663, hinted that the gentry saw their patronage as a source of material rather than spiritual profit, a complaint that John Eachard's sharper attack of 1670, *The grounds and occasions of the contempt of the clergy and religion enquired into*, took much further.[100] The Church's leases – which Green stresses as an important aspect of the community of interest between Church and gentry – were in fact a particular source of friction. At the Restoration, the Crown instructed Churchmen to offer favourable terms – preferential leases and reduced fines – to the Interregnum purchasers of its lands and to its ancient tenants. But the complex problem of sorting out competing claims to leases, as well as the

[96] P.R.O., SP 29/100/85. For Langley, see A. Browning, *Thomas Osborne earl of Danby* (3 vols., Glasgow, 1951), I, 29, 38–9, 45.
[97] SP 29/72/12, Sir John Warre to Bennet; cf. SP 29/126/109, Warre and Sir William Portman to Arlington, 15 July 1665. For Warre, see *H.P.*, III, 672.
[98] Milward, *Diary*, p. 326 (Speech of Sir John Holland on religion, 1668).
[99] Green, *The re-establishment of the Church of England*, pp. 196–200; J. H. Pruett, *The parish clergy under the later Stuarts: the Leicestershire experience* (Urbana, Illinois, 1978), pp. 37–8, 57–65.
[100] *Ichabod: or five groans of the Church: prudently foreseeing, and passionately bewailing, her second fall* (London, 1663), pp. 80–1. Later editions attributed the work to Thomas Ken, the bishop and nonjuror.

eagerness of some clerical landlords to restore ecclesiastical revenues as fully and as rapidly as possible, soon provoked bitterness even among dedicated anglican royalists.[101] Clarendon admitted the justice of the charge, though he excused the offence: the bishops and clergy

had been very barbarously used themselves; and that had too much quenched all tenderness towards others. They did not enough distinguish between persons: nor did the suffering any man had undergone for fidelity to the king, or his affection to the church eminently expressed, often prevail for the mitigation of his fine; or if it did sometimes, three or four stories of the contrary, and in which there had been some unreasonable hardness used, made a greater noise and spread further than their examples of charity and moderation.[102]

John Cosin's harsh treatment of the tenants of the church of Peterborough while he was dean was one such story: the bishop of Ely's dealings with Thomas Culpepper was another.[103] Such cases invited a good deal of resentment at the Church's wealth, a resentment which gave Sheldon cause for some concern.[104] 'My lord', one of his chaplains told him in December 1662, 'it hath ever been the fate of the Church's revenue to be the subject of envy. And even those, who seemed to long very much for the Church's restoration, cannot now with any complacency look upon it returned with its honours and endowments.'[105]

The Church might have expected more goodwill from the gentry in its struggle against dissent: here at least their interests seemed identical. Yet here, too, they were deceived. Certainly, the gentry were easily united in action against those religious sects which seemed particularly pernicious. The apocalyptic language and threatening and anarchistic behaviour of the religious radicals, especially the quakers, in the upheavals since the death of Oliver Cromwell had done much to encourage many, otherwise unattracted by an anglican settlement, to accept the re-imposition of uniformity. In the early months of 1660, as hopes increased of a restoration of order and government, the gentry led a violent assault against the liberty that quakers and other sectaries had assumed. Widespread antipathy towards them con-

---

[101] Green, *The re-establishment of the Church of England*, pp. 196–7; J. Thirsk, 'The Restoration land settlement', *Journal of Modern History*, XXVI (1954), 319–20, 326–7.
[102] Clarendon, *Life*, I, 453; cf. Burnet, *History*, I, 329–30.
[103] For Cosin, see H. J. Habakkuk, 'The land settlement and the Restoration of Charles II', *Trans. Roy. Hist. Soc.*, 5th series, XXVIII (1978), 206, 211–12; see also Beddard, 'The Restoration Church' in *The restored monarchy*, ed. Jones, p. 163; for Culpepper, see H.L.R.O., Main Papers, H.L., 1 July 1661; *L.J.*, 295; Bodl., MS Eng. Hist. e. 87, fol. 16. Cf. Pepys, *Diary*, VIII, 198–9.
[104] See, e.g., Lord Berkeley's memoir, B.L., Sloane MSS 3828, fols. 88–9; and cf. Clarendon MSS 109, pp. 17, 18, 21.
[105] Bodl., Tanner MSS 48, fol. 71, Jos. Goulston to Sheldon, 8 Dec. 1662; cf. *The correspondence of John Cosin: with other papers*, vol. II, Surtees Society, LV (1872), 101, Sheldon to Cosin, 26 Dec. 1662.

tinued to provoke spontaneous attacks well into the 1660s, although it was
gradually worn down by government leniency and the daunting problems of
arresting, imprisoning, and punishing so many.[106] With anglicans, presbyterians and independents united in their horror of the theological and social
doctrines of the quakers and sects like them, the only limits to their persecution were apparently those of administrative indigestion. But persecution
of the presbyterians and some of the independents themselves was far less
general and spontaneous. The conventicle acts – designed to catch all who
frequented nonconformist religious assemblies, including presbyterians –
were used largely against quakers, and their execution tended to depend on
the determined action of individual J.P.s rather than on the persecuting
venom of the gentry as a class.[107] The gentry were equally unreliable when it
came to ridding the Church of its less than orthodox ministers: as Green has
accepted, 1660 saw no great explosion of persecutions of Interregnum clergy
who refused to use the Book of Common Prayer, only a few isolated
instances. The Five Mile Act of 1665, intended to limit the opportunities that
ejected presbyterian ministers had to establish conventicles, was often left
unenforced.[108] Conflicting with the intellectual and emotional arguments for
a strict conformity and the enforcement of the law were the realities of the
local situation: ties of friendship, the assumption of consensus in the community, administrative inertia, even a gradual recognition of the increasing
quietism of dissent. The wide and divided sympathies of the gentry as a whole
were reflected in the commissions of the peace issued in the spirit of national
unity and reconciliation of 1660, and little altered during the decade thereafter.[109] In some areas powerful factions of ex-presbyterian gentry could
protect and even encourage local dissent;[110] and for other dissenting ministers
and congregations, safety might be ensured by the attitudes of prominent
ex-presbyterian politicians.[111] The adept use of the law by many noncon-

[106] B. Reay, 'The quakers, 1659, and the Restoration of the monarchy', *History*, LXIII (1978),
       192–213, and 'The authorities and early Restoration quakerism', *Journal of Ecclesiastical
       History*, XXXIV (1983), 69–84.
[107] A. Fletcher, 'The enforcement of the Conventicle Acts, 1663–1679', in *Persecution and
       toleration*, Studies in Church History, XXI (1984), 235–6; see also J. J. Hurwich, 'A
       "fanatick town": the political influence of dissenters in Coventry, 1660–1720', *Midland
       History*, IV (1977), 15–48; Holmes, *Seventeenth-century Lincolnshire*, p. 229; A. M.
       Coleby, *Central government and the localities: Hampshire 1649–1689* (Cambridge, 1987),
       pp. 134–41.
[108] Holmes, *Seventeenth-century Lincolnshire*, pp. 229–30.
[109] See Fletcher, *Reform in the provinces*, pp. 19–20.
[110] See, e.g., P. Jenkins, *The making of a ruling class: the Glamorgan gentry 1640–1790*
       (Cambridge, 1983), pp. 117–24.
[111] See, for example, the earl of Northumberland's reluctance to take action against dissent in
       his Sussex lieutenancy: West Sussex Record Office, Chichester, Wiston MSS 5426/2 and 3,
       Northumberland to the deputy lieutenants of Sussex and to Henry Goring, 3 and 5 Nov.
       1661.

formists perplexed their assailants.[112] All these things contributed to a lack of enthusiasm for the attack on dissent; however much the gentry might have been theoretically attracted by the notions of unity and uniformity, many were less certain about the form that such uniformity should take, and considerably less enthusiastic when it came to enforcing it.

Leaders of the Church and prominent anglican royalist politicians looked on all this with irritation and alarm. Sheldon commiserated with bishops in his province on the feeble support they received from local J.P.s, and the signs of official countenance of, or at least indifference to dissent.[113] He himself complained loudly about the obstructions to his campaign for conformity. 'I need not tell you what you cannot but observe from all parts of England', he wrote in 1665 to one sympathetic layman,

how hard those that wish not well to the ecclesiastical jurisdiction, nay the common lawyers too, who should help to defend us in the just execution of the laws, do press upon our heels if we transgress or fall short in the least punctilio of the law ... when you gentlemen and justices of the country with the lawyers shall join hands to assist us, we may hope for remedy, till then, I fear we shall have all cause to complain without help in many things.[114]

Sheldon, at least, believed that the Church derived little profit from its close association with the gentry.

If that association can explain no more than a general revulsion and reaction against the more frightening types of sectary, it seems necessary to look for the harshness with which the Cavalier Parliament approached the ecclesiastical settlement in its members' genuine attachment to the episcopal Church of England, for its ceremonies, its liturgy, even for the ancient structure of its government, and to face the paradox that this could so quickly revive despite the parlous condition of anglicanism during the Interregnum. Indeed, a widespread affection for the services of the Book of Common Prayer was manifest in their celebration all over the country throughout the Civil War and Interregnum, notwithstanding official and unofficial attempts to suppress them.[115] It was more than a few determined ejected ministers here and there who kept the traditions alive: despite parliamentary campaigns against 'scandalous' and 'malignant' parish clergy there remained many incumbents willing to use the Common Prayer beside, or instead of, the

---

[112] See, e.g., Holmes, *Seventeenth-century Lincolnshire*, pp. 223–6.
[113] Bodl., MSS Add. C. 308, fol. 73v, Sheldon to the bishop of Bristol, 11 Oct. 1666; cf. MSS Add. C. 305, fols. 142 and 144, Bishop Ward of Exeter to Sheldon, 9 Dec. 1663 and n.d.; and MSS Add. C. 302, fol. 55 ? to Williamson, 10 May 1666.
[114] Bodl., MSS Add. C. 308, fol. 29, Sheldon to ?, 22 June 1665.
[115] Bosher, *The making of the Restoration settlement*, pp. 11–13; J. S. Morrill, 'The Church in England, 1642–9', in *Reactions to the English Civil War*, ed. Morrill, pp. 89–114.

presbyterian Directory; and plenty of their parishioners were willing to hear them.[116]

But this common level of respect for the anglican rite was still insufficient to bring down the crushing legislative attack on its alternatives between 1661 and 1665. Many who shared that respect would still be reluctant to expel the presbyterians, or at least moderate presbyterians, from their churches. As Green has argued, the Church of England had always been a broad one, and could still readily embrace moderate puritan mentalities.[117] Those who pleaded for a wider ecclesiastical settlement pointed to that tradition: the Church of England in the time of James I, Sir Thomas Littleton asserted in the debate on religion in March 1668, had been calvinist; it was Archbishop Laud who had sought to change it, not the puritans.[118] Even those who strongly supported the church were not necessarily enthusiastic for a full prelatical anglicanism: Samuel Pepys, a regular attender at illegal anglican services during the Interregnum, and a professed devotee of the Church of England, found the ceremonies introduced at Whitehall chapel after the Restoration distasteful ('they do so overdo them'), objected to prelacy, and sympathised with the plight of the nonconformists.[119] The earl of Southampton, than whom there could be few better examples of virtuous anglican royalism, was nevertheless 'not generally believed by the bishops to have an affection keen enough for the government of the church, because he was willing and desirous, that somewhat more might have been done to gratify the presbyterians than they thought just'.[120] Sir John Talbot, a firm royalist and churchman, did much in parliament to try to moderate the laws against nonconformity.

What was more important than a common affection for the rite and tradition of the Church of England was the disproportionate influence wielded within parliament by men with more rigid and specific views about the Church and its organisation, and an uncompromising attitude to those who did not share them. High-flying, prelatical anglicanism was not, it seems, characteristic of the country, the gentry, or even the clergy as a whole: yet parliament was deeply imbued with it, not because such men dominated it in numbers, but because they dominated it in political weight and the effectiveness of their rhetoric.

In part, the creation of a party of ultras among the anglican royalist gentry

---

[116] I. M. Green, 'The persecution of "scandalous" and "malignant" parish clergy during the English Civil War', *Eng. Hist. Rev.*, XCIV (1979), 507–31, esp. 522–6.
[117] Green, *The re-establishment of the Church of England*, pp. 155–77.
[118] Milward, *Diary*, p. 218.
[119] Pepys, *Diary*, I, cxix–cxx, 76, 210, X, 350–4; see also the index entries s.v. 'Religion' and 'Church'.
[120] Clarendon, *Life*, II, 408–9.

was the achievement of those clergy who held to their Church of England principles strongly enough to be ejected from their livings during the Interregnum. Barred from the public ministry they found refuge in the homes of gentry and nobility sympathetic either to their cause or to their plight. Some nailed their colours more firmly to the mast of the royalist flagship by going overseas to minister to the forlorn peripatetic groups of exiled royalists.[121] In most cases the refuges they found were already anglican royalist ones. There were a few exceptions. Sir Christopher Yelverton, a member of the Long Parliament until secluded in 1648, took in the aged (and firmly calvinist) Bishop Morton of Durham. Morton's influence on Yelverton's son, Sir Henry, M.P. for Northampton from 1664, made him into a learned and devout defender of episcopacy and the Church of England, and helped to give his opinion some weight among the Northamptonshire clergy – which he exercised in favour of a prelatical settlement.[122] The member for Bedfordshire, Lord Bruce's conversion from both his father's puritanism and a youthful hedonism may be attributed to the influence of his father's chaplain, Thomas Frampton; although his father, the earl of Elgin, was hardly an enthusiastic adherent of the parliamentary cause, and his aunt, Christiana, dowager countess of Devonshire, was closely linked to devout anglican and royalist circles.[123] The achievement of the ejected clergy, however, was not really in the conversions they effected among the puritan or moderate gentry: nor was it (as Bosher has argued) their success in obtaining the support of the highest of policy-makers – men like Clarendon and Sir Edward Nicholas – whose undoubted adherence to a strong anglican royalism would always have to be tempered by political considerations. It was rather to confirm and strengthen their alliance with the royalist gentry, and to help bring out of it a clique of men and women deeply committed to a prelatical anglicanism. They did not, by any means, include all the royalist gentry: Southampton, as has been argued, was at least one notable exception. Yet they were a powerful and prominent group within it, made even more powerful and prominent by the central role many of them had taken in royalist conspiracy, which made them among the most trusted, and certainly the most obvious agents of

[121] Bosher, *The making of the Restoration settlement*, pp. 39–40, 146–7, 170; Beddard, 'The Restoration Church', pp. 156–9.

[122] H.P., III, 786; A. Wood, *Athenae Oxonienses*, ed. P. Bliss (5 vols., London, 1813–20), III, 906; Bodl., MS Eng. Lett. c. 210, *passim*, Yelverton's letters to Archdeacon Palmer.

[123] H.P., I, 738; for his father, see Sir Philip Warwick, *Memoirs of the reign of King Charles I* (2nd edn, London, 1702), pp. 169–71; Richard Pearson, *Enoch's translation, in a sermon preached at the funeral of the right honourable Thomas, earl of Elgin, baron of Whorlton & c.* (1664), pp. 26–8; for the countess of Devonshire, see *D.N.B.*, and Forster, *Studies in church dedications*, II, 347. Bruce's assimilation into anglican royalist society was perhaps marked by the marriage of his daughter in 1666 to the son of the doyen of Interregnum lay anglicanism, Sir Robert Shirley: E. P. Shirley, *Stemmata Shirleiana* (London, 1873), p. 161.

the restored monarchy, and gave them large claims to favour and reward. Despite their complaints about the numbers of ex-presbyterian and ex-parliamentarian ministers in government, it was the royalist political elite which really held power after the Restoration, which dominated parliament and filled the middle ranks of administration. Within that elite, this committed anglican clique possessed the greatest power, particularly in parliament, where they provided some of the government's most important spokesmen. It was a position of great strength, and one which the Church employed to its full advantage.

Their ultra-anglicanism was not necessarily derived from the zealous anti-puritanism of the Laudian regime; but many of them were strongly identified with it. Sir John Berkenhead, M.P. for Walton, editor of the government newsbooks and licenser of the press, had been an Oxford protégé of the archbishop.[124] Sir John Robinson, M.P. for Rye, lieutenant of the Tower of London, and in 1662–3 lord mayor of London, was his half-nephew, and devoted to his memory.[125] John, Lord Lucas, a notable and much admired sufferer in the royal cause, was perhaps close to Laud, as he acted in 1634 as one of the commissioners for raising funds for the repair of St Paul's, a project dear to the archbishop's heart.[126] Viscount Scudamore was famous for his friendship with Laud and his dedication to the Church: both his son, James Scudamore, and his ward, Sir Henry Lingen, sat in the cavalier house of commons.[127] Richard Aldworth, member for Reading, had been successively secretary to Laud, Juxon and Sheldon.[128] Some were connected to the Laudian regime, if not to Laud himself: Dr Thomas Burwell, M.P. for Ripon, was one of the arminian set which had formed around John Cosin at Durham before the Civil War;[129] Sir Edmund Peirce, M.P. for Maidstone and a master in chancery, had been notorious for his harsh action against puritans as commissary of the archdeacon of Suffolk in the late 1630s.[130]

Yet more important, and certainly more renowned, were the lay connections built up during the Interregnum by the group of anglican apologists and activists who strenuously sought to defend the Church of England against the assaults of Rome and of presbytery, and the temptations of hopelessness. Their refusal to compromise with the Interregnum regimes was an inspiration for the anglican royalist cliques which sheltered and surrounded them. Henry Hammond, the most popular of them, famously found refuge at Westwood,

[124] Thomas, *Sir John Berkenhead*, pp. 15–18, 21–4.
[125] *H.P.*, III, 340.
[126] W. D. Grant, *Margaret the first: a biography of Margaret Cavendish duchess of Newcastle* (London, 1957), p. 48.
[127] H. R. Trevor-Roper, *Archbishop Laud 1573–1645* (London, 1940), pp. 62–3, and appendix; *H.P.*, II, 745, III, 407.
[128] *H.P.*, I, 524–5.   [129] *H.P.*, I, 752–3.   [130] *H.P.*, III, 216–17.

the Worcestershire home of Sir John and Lady Dorothy Pakington.[131] Pakington became M.P. for Worcestershire in 1661, and was active in the suppression of dissent and sedition.[132] But it was his wife, the daughter of Lord Coventry, who maintained the family's wide connection among divines (many of them, such as George Morley and John Barwick, deeply involved in royalist conspiracy), and devout lay anglicans.[133] Her brothers were Henry and William Coventry, both prominent royalists and government spokesmen in the Cavalier Parliament: although the latter's religious interests were no more than conventional, Henry Coventry, a fellow of All Souls in the 1640s during Sheldon's wardenship and while his colleagues included Berkenhead and Jeremy Taylor, was close and sympathetic to the Restoration ecclesiastical hierarchy.[134] Lady Pakington's sister in 1655 married Thomas Chicheley, an M.P., a commissioner of the ordnance, a friend of Sheldon's, and, according to Pepys, a 'great defender of the Church of England'.[135] Another sister, Mary, married Sir Henry Frederick Thynne: their son, Thomas, later Viscount Thynne, was in the 1660s groom of the bedchamber to the duke of York, and an envoy to Sweden; in the 1650s he had been a regular correspondent of Hammond's and one of the prize pupils of the alternative anglican private university established in Oxford by the ejected dons.[136] By his marriage in 1673 to Frances Finch, Thynne became linked to another great anglican political dynasty of the Restoration: she was a cousin of Sir Heneage Finch, whose activity on behalf of the monarchy in the parliament of 1660 brought him the post of solicitor-general, and whose family was firm in its anglican principles and piety.[137] Another, though less well documented circle formed around Gilbert Sheldon and his host, Sir Robert Shirley, in Stafford-

---

[131] Bosher, *The making of the Restoration settlement*, chs. 1–3; J. W. Packer, *The transformation of Anglicanism, 1643–1660, with special reference to Henry Hammond* (London, 1969), pp. 29–35, 37–8.

[132] R. L. Greaves, *Deliver us from evil: the radical underground in Britain, 1660–3* (New York, 1986), pp. 72–7, 131; H.P., III, 195–6.

[133] See the letters of Morley and Lady Pakington in Coventry MSS vol. 119, and in Hereford and Worcester Record Office, Microfilm of Pakington MSS in possession of Lord Hampton, vol. I, nos. 123, 159, 161, and vol. II, *passim*, and the letters of John Barwick in *ibid.*, vol. I, nos. 19, 174.

[134] D. T. Witcombe, 'The parliamentary career of Sir William and Henry Coventry', unpublished B.Litt. thesis, University of Oxford, 1954, p. 4; see also Coventry MSS, vol. 80, fol. 47v, Henry Coventry to Sheldon, 27 Sept. 1665, and see vol. 7, *passim*.

[135] Bodl., MSS Add. C. 303, fol. 124, Clarendon to Sheldon, 26 Nov. [1665]; Pepys, *Diary*, IX, 112.

[136] H.P., III, 565–6; Thynne's correspondence with Hammond and John Fell is in Longleat House, Thynne MSS vol. 12, fol. 143ff.; for Interregnum Oxford anglicanism, see William Wynne, *The life of Sir Leoline Jenkins* (2 vols., London, 1724), I, iv–vi.

[137] H.P., II, 312–24; see Finch's letters to his son, *Hist. MSS. Comm.*, MSS of A. G. Finch Esq. (4 vols., 1913–65), I, 208–9, 211–12, 216, 249.

shire.[138] Sir Justinian Isham, M.P. for Northamptonshire, had during the Interregnum maintained an acquaintance and correspondence both among the anglican clergy at the forefront of the Church's defence – including Bishop Duppa, Herbert Thorndike and Thomas Peirce – and with similarly minded royalist laymen, in particular Sir Charles Harbord, M.P. for Launceston from 1661, and surveyor-general from 1660.[139]

This list far from exhausts the close connections between the sequestered clergy and pious anglican royalists: but two more examples must suffice. Sir Philip Warwick, the earl of Southampton's secretary, and the treasury's spokesman in parliament, had begun his career as secretary to Bishop Juxon, lord treasurer in the 1630s. He had friendships with many of the most active anglican clergy: he sheltered Hammond, for a time, at his house in Clapham, and he corresponded a little with Hammond's other patron, Lady Pakington;[140] in 1666 he was named (with Dr Thomas Peirce and Orlando Bridgman, lord chief justice of the common pleas) as one of the executors of John Warner, bishop of Rochester;[141] and his marriage brought him as brothers-in-law Sir Thomas and Sir Richard Fanshaw, both dedicated anglican royalists, both members of the Cavalier Parliament, and the former king's remembrancer of the exchequer and a man of violently anti-dissenting opinion.[142] The earl and countess of Bridgewater were renowned *dévots* of the Church of England. Bridgewater was close to Peter Heylin, Laud's biographer; and Sir John Berkenhead, Laud's protégé, wrote verses to celebrate his tenth wedding anniversary in 1652.[143] After the Restoration Bridgewater was one of the government's workhorses in the house of lords, although the fact went unrecognised until his appointment in 1667 to the privy council.[144]

These men, and others like them, formed a body of opinion within parliament dedicated to preserving the integrity of the Church of England, its

[138] [N. Pocock], 'Illustrations of the state of the Church during the Great Rebellion', *The Theologian and Ecclesiastic*, VI–XV (1848–54); see also R. A. Beddard, 'An unpublished memoir of Archbishop Sheldon', *Bodleian Library Record*, X (1978–82), 45 and n. 11.
[139] *The correspondence of Bishop Brian Duppa and Sir Justinian Isham*, ed. Sir Gyles Isham, Publications of the Northamptonshire Record Society, XVII, 1955; see also the letters of Harbord, Isham, and Thorndike in the Northamptonshire Record Office, Isham papers, IC 348, 428, 538, 540.
[140] Packer, *The transformation of anglicanism*, pp. 29–35; Hereford and Worcester Record Office, Pakington MSS, vol. 1, no. 160, Warwick to Lady Pakington, 8 May 1660.
[141] Bodl., MS Eng. Hist. b. 205; see Bodl., MS Smith 29, fol. 46ff. for Warwick's own friendship with Peirce. See also *The correspondence of Isaac Basire D.D.*, ed. W. N. Darnell (London, 1831), p. 203, Mrs Basire to Dr Basire, 10 Nov. 1661.
[142] *H.P.*, II, 298–302.
[143] Hertfordshire Record Office, Ashridge collection, AH 1063, 1105, 1107, Bridgewater to John Halsey, 20 Oct. 1661, 2 and 12 July 1666; Thomas, *Sir John Berkenhead*, pp. 138, 194–5.
[144] See below, pp. 93–4, 305.

liturgy, ceremony, and government. They were not, any more than most of the churchmen with whom they associated were, 'arminians' or 'Laudians', determined to push the Church in a new, more catholic direction. Their theological interests were rather with the antiquity and legitimacy of the Church of England – interests encouraged by the Roman polemical assault of the Interregnum – than with its doctrine; their concern was purely for the restoration, in all their glory, of episcopacy and the Book of Common Prayer, the ancient worship of England; their arguments for unity rested on custom and law, the political necessity of uniformity, and an anxiety that the church should not again be betrayed, rather than on theology.

Indeed, they owed much of their success to that very abandonment of theological argument: it is unlikely that most Englishmen were any more enthusiastic about arminianism now than they had been twenty years before. For important as these intellectually committed anglican royalists were in parliament, they were insufficient by themselves to prevent a legislative compromise of the Church's purity. To succeed they needed the support of a wider section of the parliament. They gained it, in part, by their prominence and importance in either house, in part, because they could employ a persuasive rhetoric calculated to appeal to those gentry who were less dedicated to the cause of the Church of England, less passionate about its integrity, but were conservative, legalistic, and anxious to restore peace and stability. Sir Richard Temple, arguing for a policy of comprehending the presbyterians within the church in early 1668, claimed that few M.P.s were in favour of persecution, 'though being suitable to the interest of the cavalier party (in which most of them or their ancestors, have been engaged) and conformable to the former actings of the house, they know not how in decency to appear against it if set afoot': persecution, he claimed, was driven on only by a clique, the associates of Clarendon, the duke of York, and those connected with the Church.[145] Temple had a political axe to grind; and certainly conditions by 1668 were rather different from those of the early 1660s. Yet his remark is a useful hint at the way in which most M.P.s were led, a little reluctantly, to persecution and the reconstruction of the Church by a rhetoric against which they could scarcely argue used by politicians of standing and ability.

The Cavalier Parliament as a whole was not particularly 'zealous for the church': only a small part of it was. But the rest of it was anxious enough about security and stability to accept that part's leadership. The need for order and the need for unity, its energetic politicians asserted, demanded not just the restoration of a single, national Church, but of the national Church,

[145] C. Roberts (ed.), 'Sir Richard Temple's discourse on the parliament of 1667–8', *Huntington Library Quarterly*, XX (1956–7), 143.

the Church of England, and of the Church of England in all its glory. If the
dissenters, they argued, could not abide by that rule, then what rule would
satisfy them? Unity had to be ensured by some rule – so why not the already-
established rule of law? 'Unity was so precious', Sergeant Charlton told the
house of lords at a conference on the Act of Uniformity in May 1662, 'that it
served not only for the peace of the church, but of the kingdom also'.[146] Sir
Robert Pointz claimed that 'the best philosophers and lawgivers did ever
repute unity in religion the chiefest pillar that upholdeth human society, and
obedience to supreme authority, which cannot stand after religion is
fallen'.[147] In the settled, ordered world of the conformist, dissent seemed
disturbingly unsettled and disordered, even irrational; either a triumph of
opinion over sense, or a merely wilful determination to upset traditional
values. As in politics, so in religion, conservatives wanted confusion and
uncertainty to be replaced by authority, order, and predictability. Ultimately,
many concluded, dissent was an expression of political, not simply religious,
antagonism to the established order: the conscience to which dissenters
pretended was, asserted Sir John Denham in the debate on religion in March
1668, 'nothing less than spiritual pride'.[148] That debate – the only commons
debate on religion fully recorded in the 1660s – allows one to hear something
of the powerful tone of anglican polemic. Churchmen acknowledged that
most of the issues in debate between presbyterians, independents and
anglicans concerned matters accepted by both sides to be indifferent –
matters of ceremonies and organisation – but they insisted that the verdict on
them of a legal authority still ought to be binding: as Sir Philip Warwick said,

> the word of God and government were the greatest ties of conscience, and if authority
> can truly show the legality of a thing enjoined it ought then to be assented to out of a
> good conscience, and where a thing that is simply indifferent, that is neither com-
> manded nor forbidden by the word of God, the thing (that is so) being enjoined by a
> lawful authority is then more than indifferent to those that are subject to that
> command, and ought to be obeyed by them for conscience sake.[149]

The word 'conscience' immediately raised anglican hackles. Lord Fanshaw,
who succeeded to his father's estates and his virulent pursuit of dissent in
1666, claimed of the nonconformists that 'if their tender consciences were so
good as is pretended to them they should live without offence to God and

---

[146] *L.J.*, 449; cf. Spurr, 'Anglican apologetic and the Restoration Church', p. 98; the commons'
address against the 1663 Declaration of Indulgence, *Parliamentary history*, IV, 262–3; and
Holland's 1668 speech, printed in Milward, *Diary*, Appendix I, pp. 325–6.

[147] Pointz, *A vindication of monarchy*, p. 35.

[148] Milward, *Diary*, p. 216. For this line of argument, see Ashcraft, *Revolutionary politics and
Locke's 'Two treatises'*, pp. 39–74, Abrams, *John Locke: Two tracts*, pp. 63–81, and *The
genuine remains . . . of Samuel Butler*, II, 48–9.

[149] Milward, *Diary*, p. 217.

man, but what villainies did these men commit when they had the power in their hands is most notorious; let us not (said he) stand in fear of their number, of which there is so much noise, but let the laws be put in execution against them, and they will soon be brought under'.[150] 'When we remember the villainies that these men committed under pretence of conscience', insisted Sir John Berkenhead in the same debate, 'the younger sort of them unlearned and ignorant, and that no oath (of which they had taken many) would bind or hold the older, we may well be cautious that we be not again cheated and destroyed by indulging their conscience into a new rebellion.'[151]

Arguing the supremacy of authority over the individual conscience brought some anglican polemicists perilously close to giving the sovereign the complete power to interpret the word of God, as Hobbes had done: yet they found his uncompromising location of moral and religious authority solely in the will of the civil magistrate repugnant. Quite apart from the theological reasons for doing so, it was clear that the unchecked power of an absolute sovereign in matters ecclesiastical could be as unpleasant an experience as the anarchy of unbridled opinion: conservatives in religion, like conservatives in politics, tended to look to the law, a law as absolute and unchanging as possible, to guarantee stability. The Church's lay defenders cherished the notion of a Church 'as by law established', and insisted that relaxation of part of the law would destroy the whole.[152] John Vaughan argued in 1668 that the purpose of a projected bill for the comprehension of dissent within the Church was only to 'raise new troubles by destroying the laws'.[153] Any alteration or innovation could weaken the law and cause its collapse: 'the asserting the laws, and the religion established, according to the Act of Uniformity', stated the commons in their address of February 1663, 'is the most probable means to produce a settled peace and obedience throughout the kingdom'.[154] Churchmen themselves found this alliance with the law polemically useful: in 1662, defending the Act of Uniformity against an attempt to suspend it for a time, Sheldon was quoted in the government newsbook as linking its firm execution with the survival of all laws.[155] The best guarantee of stability was a firm adherence to the known laws, and a disavowal of innovation. In the hands of determined anglican politicians, law and conservatism became the weapons of the Church of England against all arguments for compromise. The simple claim that only a full reconstruction of the government and liturgy of the Church of England, and a rigid enforcement of uniformity could

---

[150] *Ibid.*, p. 221. [151] *Ibid.*, p. 220.
[152] Beddard, 'The Restoration Church', p. 162.
[153] Milward, *Diary*, p. 249. [154] *Parliamentary history*, IV, 262.
[155] *Mercurius publicus*, 1662, p. 581; cf. Ward's letter to Sheldon, urging enforcement of the law, Bodl., MSS Add. C. 305, fol. 142.

prevent the decay and fragmentation of the religious life of the nation, with all the disruptive consequences that would ensue, was, among the frightened conservatives of the 1660s, deeply plausible and polemically effective.

Cavalier and anglican though the parliament of 1661 may have seemed, its deepest instincts were not. All seventeenth-century parliaments, composed of men who saw change as difficult, disruptive, and probably unnecessary, were profoundly conservative; their function merely to check the abuses which might have entered into 'the admirable frame of our government', to curb the corruptions which might have sullied 'these excellent laws we are governed by, which are so fitted, and assimilated, to the interest and genius of the people of this nation, that as to this world, we cannot wish ourselves to be in a better condition than we are'.[156] The Cavalier Parliament was – had more reason to be – even more conservative than most, its members threatened by social, political and economic subversion; but that very desire to avoid change, which prevented them from wanting to build on parliament's Civil War achievements, made them equally suspicious of attempts to strengthen the monarchy too far. Above all else, above even the tempting possibility of absolute security from popular turbulence in a Hobbesian sovereignty, the royalist gentry longed for a return to order and predictability, the restoration of the old relationships by and through which the country was harmoniously governed, the recreation of the trust on which the system depended, the reconstruction of the unity of the old regime.

[156] Grimston's charge to the St Albans sessions, 1665: *Hist. MSS. Comm.*, Verulam MSS, p. 198.

4

The structure of parliamentary politics

However much it was resented, the fact of political change was hard to ignore, hardest of all in the way in which politics was conducted. The previous two decades had seen a level of popular participation, passion, and violence hitherto unknown in English politics, and an expansion of the power and competence of parliament until it had seemed transcendent. The Restoration of the monarchy without conditions guaranteed at least the institutional reconstruction of the old regime. But could the assumptions which lay behind it, of popular quiescence, of the gentry's co-operation in government, of harmony, of parliament's essentially advisory role, be so easily reinstalled?

The revolution had brought parliament under immense external pressures – from the army, a shadow over all its debates; and from London and country opinion, expressed in petitions, demonstrations, and intimidation. The peaceful disbandment of the commonwealth army in late 1660 and early 1661 removed the first incubus, although the country's rulers were still subject to the occasional bad dream concerning the number of trained (if disarmed) radical soldiers. The second – of widespread participation and interest in politics – could not be so simply banished. When Samuel Sorbières visited England in late 1663, he found its people far from politically apathetic. The English, he said, 'sont faineans, et passent la moitié du jour à prendre du tabac ensemble, ils ne cessent dans cette débauché d'exercer leur resverie sur les affaires publiques, de parler des nouveaux imposts, de la taxe des cheminées, de l'employ des finances, de la diminution du commerce'.[1] But if the government could not stop the people grumbling, it did its best to prevent their more effective involvement in politics. Political interest during the revolution had been sustained by preaching and an industrious press: in the Cavalier Parliament and outside it, the government took steps to curb

---

[1] Samuel Sorbières, *Relation d'un voyage en angleterre où sont touchées les plusieurs choses, qui regardent l'estat des sciences, de la religion, & autres matières curieuses* (Paris, 1664), p. 130.

both. At the opening of the first session, Clarendon warned of the 'seditious preachers . . . who, by repeating the very expressions, and teaching the very doctrine, they set on-foot in the year 1640, sufficiently declare that they have no mind that twenty years should put an end to the miseries we have undergone'.[2] The gradual removal of the unorthodox from the ministry of the Church, and the Act of Uniformity's provisions to ensure the conformity of preachers and lecturers, largely removed the fear that the Church might again be the engine of revolution.[3] Nevertheless, the sermons preached by the ministers whom the provisions of the Act ejected, at their departure from their livings, caused the government some alarm in the autumn of 1662, and provoked it into issuing further instructions, advising preachers to refrain from political or religious controversy.[4] Even after their ejection, the establishment of conventicles in which they continued to minister to their faithful congregations meant that preaching could be seen still as dangerous, and religiously motivated protest still powerful.[5]

The government made valiant efforts, too, to curb the liberty the press had assumed. With the decay of effective constraints in the political crisis of 1658–60, books and pamphlets had multiplied. The Restoration and the reimposition of authority brought a sharp fall in new publications, despite the lively religious controversies of 1660–2; the Licensing Act of 1662 and (more particularly) Roger L'Estrange's energetic assault on unauthorised printing as surveyor of the press from early 1663 produced a further drop, so that by the mid-1660s fewer works were coming from the presses than at any other time between 1649 and 1684.[6] Even L'Estrange, however, failed to suppress radical printing entirely; accounts of regicide and quaker trials, radical tracts and the farewell sermons of ejected ministers, continued to be published.[7] Limiting the circulation of news was simpler: from October 1660 there was no competition for the two government newsbooks, *Mercurius Publicus* and the *Parliamentary* (later the *Kingdom's*) *Intelligencer*, and under the editor-

---

[2] *Parliamentary history*, IV, 184.
[3] 14 Car. II, c. 4, paras, XV–XIX, S.R., 367–8.
[4] D. Wilkins (ed.), *Concilia Magnae Britanniae et Hiberniae*, 4 vols. (London, 1737), IV, 576–8.
[5] See Timothy Harris, 'The bawdy house riots of 1668', *Historical Journal*, XXIX (1986), 537–56, and *London crowds in the reign of Charles II* (Cambridge, 1987); and the evidence of Bristol's popularity among dissenters in Greaves, *Deliver us from evil*, pp. 172–4.
[6] W. G. Mason, 'The annual output of Wing-listed titles, 1649–84', *The Library*, 5th series, XXIX (1974), 219–20.
[7] For his efforts, see R. L'Estrange, *Considerations and proposals in order to the regulation of the press: together with diverse instances of treasonous, and seditious pamphlets, proving the necessity thereof* (London, 1663); J. Walker, 'The censorship of the press during the reign of Charles II', *History*, XXXV (1950), 219–38.

ship of Sir John Berkenhead they became little more than official gazettes; when L'Estrange took over in late 1663 the news content was reduced even further – L'Estrange made no secret of his opinion that the public had no business to be informed of political events.[8] The manuscript newsletters produced by Henry Muddiman and James Hickes from the office of the undersecretary of state, Joseph Williamson, were more informative, but went only to a sympathetic and co-operative few.[9]

The attacks on seditious printing and preaching were designed to limit the manipulation of opinion by those antipathetic to the government of its aims: ministers tried also to limit its expression. The Act against Tumults and Disorders, intended to prevent petitions from becoming – as they had been in 1640–2 – a instrument of organised political dissent, was one of the first bills to be introduced into the Cavalier Parliament.[10] The government was nervous of the opportunities for political association provided by the new coffee houses, the centres of informed gossip and discussion of current affairs. In late 1666 the court became especially concerned: they were 'the places where the boldest calumnies and scandals were raised, and discoursed amongst a people who knew not each other, and came together only for that communication, and from thence were propagated over the kingdom': it discussed their suppression, but eventually drew back.[11] The government of the 1660s clearly felt the pressure of public opinion, and recognised the power of the means of influencing it which had been so strenuously exercised during the war: it was perhaps more nervous of it than most pre-war governments would have been, as its reaction to the 1668 bawdy-house riots suggests.[12] Yet whether opinion was better-informed, its expression more effective, and whether the public at large evinced a greater interest in politics than they had before the Civil War, is far harder to assess. M.P.s, at least, were preoccupied not so much with a newly articulate public opinion, politicised by the events of the Civil War, but by more traditional pressures from their neighbours and electors, who expected them to represent their local interests and grievances at the centre of power, and to be at least cautious in granting away their money to a voracious court. M.P.s felt as embarrassed about voting heavy taxes as they had before the war, as conscious of the need to protect the rights of their communities against the encroachment both of individuals and the

---

[8] Thomas, *Sir John Berkenhead*, pp. 212, 214–15, 225–6; and see L'Estrange's editorial in *The Intelligencer*, 31 Aug. 1663.
[9] J. B. Williams, 'Newsbooks and letters of news at the Restoration', *Eng. Hist. Rev.*, XXIII (1908), 252–76.
[10] 13 Car. II, c. 5, *S.R.*, 308.
[11] Clarendon, *Life*, II, 298–9. [12] See Harris, 'Bawdy house riots of 1668'.

state, as eager to secure local popularity by energetic lobbying at Westminster and Whitehall.[13]

The most profound legacy of the Civil War and Interregnum was not, indeed, any growth in the political maturity and sophistication of the nation, but rather the enduring divisions that they had created within it. Such divisions, in particular religious divisions, had been obvious enough before the Civil War; but the war and its sequel had both aggravated and ossified them. The Act of Indemnity and Oblivion of 1660 had sought, in a famous clause, to suppress all such divisions, that 'all names and terms of distinction may . . . be put into utter oblivion'. It provided penalties for anyone who in the following three years 'shall presume maliciously to call or allege of, or object against any other person or persons any name or names, or other words of reproach tending to revive the memory of the late differences or the occasions thereof'.[14] But its penalties were scarcely punitive – ten pounds for gentlemen and forty shillings for those of lower rank – and it was rarely enforced: it was hardly worth incurring the odium of local cavaliers to sue for such a sum.[15] Subsequent legislation, particularly the Corporation Act, must have produced many infringements of the law; the government itself must frequently have breached it. Some were no doubt prepared tactfully to ignore the subject of Civil War allegiance: for others, old resentment made at least verbal revenge impossible to resist, particularly where the resentment had been renewed by royal promotion of old enemies.[16] M.P.s and peers themselves flung references to the past at one another: in a debate in the lords on the Council of the North Buckingham's implied insult concerning Northumberland's war record produced a furious scene;[17] when the Irish Cattle Bill was under discussion in 1666, Lord Orrery in an angry moment – one of many in the Bill's progress – referred to Ashley as one of Cromwell's councillors;[18] and the election of James Philipps for the Cardigan boroughs in 1661 provoked a long and vigorously fought investigation into allegations that he had been a member of the high court of justice that had sentenced the

[13] D. M. Hirst, *The representative of the people? Voters and voting in England under the early Stuarts* (Cambridge, 1975), pp. 178–88; see, e.g., Holland's speech to the commissioners for an assessment, Bodl., Tanner MSS 239, fol. 75; *Hist. MSS. Comm.*, Hastings MSS, II, 142, Salisbury to Huntingdon, 27 July 1663; and P.R.O., SP 29/139/78, Daniel Furzer to commissioners of the navy, 20 Dec. 166[4], for Sir Baynham Throckmorton's resistance to the navy's appropriation of timber from Gloucestershire on the day of his election as knight of the shire.

[14] 12 Car. II, c. 11, para. XXIV, *S.R.*, 230.

[15] Although cf. Hutton, p. 135, who argues that the fewness of prosecutions signified the Act's 'almost complete formal success'.

[16] See, e.g., B.L., Loan MSS 29/51 and 29/79 for the argument of Col. Harley and Capt. Lister, and the intervention of local (royalist) gentry.

[17] P.R.O., 31/3/110, D'Estrades to Louis XIV, 28 Jan./6 Feb. 1662.

[18] Carte MSS 217, fol. 354, Anglesey to Ormonde, 20 Nov. 1666.

royalist John Gerard to death in 1654.[19] Much political bitterness was sublimated into religious divisions, as orthodoxy in religion was regarded in the Corporation Act as the touchstone of affection to the regime. The Corporation Act itself helped to confirm and renew the war's polarisation of political society, with expelled members of corporations and their replacements and ejectors forming instantly identifiable factions in local society. Even so, pursuing the past and forming factions was largely a minority, and an unpopular, activity – among those who enforced the Corporation Act there were many who preferred connivance to conflict. In any case, as long as anglican royalism seemed so firmly in power, its opponents may have felt it futile to resist.[20] In such circumstances the real divisions in society in the 1660s were obscured.

Yet it was the Civil War's expansion of parliament's role and importance that was most extraordinary to contemporaries and most striking to posterity: from 1642 to 1653 parliament had taken a central position in the life and administration of the country; it was difficult to imagine that it could easily and contentedly revert to its former, subordinate position. Even royalist theorists had incautiously admitted that the king was not superior to, but 'co-ordinate' with the other two houses in the making of law. By placing the king on a level with the two houses, parliament, not the king, became legally and theoretically sovereign.[21] A whole new generation of politicians – anyone born after about 1625 – had grown up without personal experience of a 'normal' parliament, one called by royal writ, exchanging supply for the reformation of abuses, and peacefully dispersing. Nevertheless, those politicians appear to have drawn no new lessons from the war years, and if some at least were anxious not to lose the safeguard to the subject's liberty, property, and religion which frequent meetings of parliament – at least theoretically – provided, they gave little indication that they possessed any much more ambitious conception of parliament's role.[22] Besides, parliament's prestige was already, by 1660, badly tarnished. Memories of its power and importance in the 1640s had been clouded by the impression of its ineffectiveness, impotence, alleged corruption, and unrepresentativeness in the 1650s. The Rump Parliament was a creation, and a victim, of the army; Barebone's was condemned for the social inadequacy of its members; and the

---

[19] B.L., Egerton MSS 2979, fols. 112–18; *H.P.*, III, 239–40.
[20] For the enforcement of the Corporation Act, see Hutton, pp. 160–1, 338–9, and for connivance, see M. A. Mullett, 'Conflict, politics, and elections for Lancaster, 1660–88', *Northern History*, XIX (1983), 64–8.
[21] C. C. Weston and J. R. Greenberg, *Subjects and sovereigns: the grand controversy over legal sovereignty in Stuart England* (Cambridge, 1981); A. Browning, 'Parties and party organization in the reign of Charles II', *Trans. Roy. Hist. Soc.*, 4th series, XXX (1948), 21.
[22] See Miller, 'Charles II and his parliaments'.

protectorate parliaments had been more memorable for their disruption by royalists, radicals, and republicans than for any solid legislative or administrative achievement. The Convention's recall of the king, and re-establishment of his power, gave it at least momentary popularity: but not such as permanently to enhance parliamentary power. The parliaments of the Interregnum, as Clarendon pointed out at the opening of the Cavalier Parliament, had been illegal, bastard parliaments; 'when people came together by such exorbitant means, it is no wonder that their consultations and conclusions were so disproportioned from any rules of order of sobriety'.[23] Even those who had taken part in the Long Parliament seemed pleased to see the old ways restored: Lord Crew, one of its M.P.s until his sec-lusion by Pride's Purge in 1648, wrote to the earl of Sandwich in July 1661 to celebrate parliament's summer adjournment, 'thus the old and good way of parliaments, for the Crown to give relief and pardon, and to receive subsidies, and it is our happiness that the king delights in these paths'.[24] The govern-ment's embarrassment at the currency of the notion that the king was a merely equal part of the legislative trinity, and not its head, was clear enough in its vigorous efforts to contradict co-ordination theory; and the Conven-tion's declaration that England's government was, and ought to be, by king, lords and commons, and the Cavalier Parliament's resistance to the royal dispensing power, in 1662 and 1673, might indeed seem to confirm the steady march of the legislative sovereignty of parliament.[25] In reality, how-ever, the debate on whether the king was, or was not one of the three estates made little difference in practice or theory to the problem of sovereignty, or of limitations on royal power.[26] The question of the dispensing power was far from new, as was the conundrum concerning legislative sovereignty which it raised. Before the war, there had been contradictory opinions on the extent to which royal dispensations from statute might be allowed; the Restoration and the theory of co-ordination did not introduce the issue.[27]

Yet there were legacies of the war which seemed to have altered the relationship of Crown and parliament permanently to parliament's advan-tage. One was obvious, and clearly visible: the Triennial Act, passed in February 1641, had made mandatory a meeting of parliament at least once in every three years and had established a procedure to summon one in case the government failed to do so. Demolishing much of the royal prerogative of summoning and dismissing parliament, it gravely threatened the Crown's

[23] *Parliamentary history*, IV, 181.
[24] Carte MSS 73, fol. 543.
[25] Weston and Greenberg, *Subjects and sovereigns*, pp. 149–76.
[26] Sommerville, *Politics and ideology*, pp. 174–6. See also G. R. Elton, *The parliament of England, 1559–81* (Cambridge, 1986), pp. 17–22.
[27] Sommerville, *Politics and ideology*, pp. 177–8.

power and independence. The other was more of a matter of perceptions. Parliament's assumption of executive responsibilities and its open rebellion against the king had been powerful reminders of how easily parliaments could be led, by fear, conspiracy and demagoguery, into claims and actions which were unthinkable a few years before. Since the invention of parliaments, no administration can ever have enjoyed them: governments have rarely welcomed the intrusion of busy, ignorant or unsympathetic auditors into their counsels. Yet the Civil War experience may have reinforced that antipathy: it made the old advice, that the Crown should never be, or seem so necessitous that parliament might hold it to ransom, appear even more relevant. When the king's wants were greatest, warned Sir William Coventry in 1664, 'ill men may be most bold in opposing him'.[28] Bennet seems to have found parliaments particularly disagreeable: at the height of the factional crisis of 1663, he wrote to Ormonde that 'I cannot but observe to your grace by what we see here that the king's power is not so easily restored by parliaments as it is retrenched'. Even in the calmer session of spring 1664, he exchanged nervous pleasantries on the subject: 'although there be safety (as Solomon saith) in a multitude of councillors yet we cannot but think our selves at ease when we are fairly rid of them'.[29] Not all ministers were so timid: Clarendon possessed a robust attitude towards parliament and considered his colleagues to be pusillanimous. 'Modesty and moderation in words never was, nor ever will be, observed in popular councils, whose foundation is liberty of speech.'[30] In 1663 Clarendon, as Ormonde remarked, was much less troubled about parliament's temper than the secretary;[31] in 1666 the chancellor complained bitterly about the readiness of his fellow councillors to appease parliament over what he regarded as fundamentals.[32] But others, more concerned by the consequences of parliamentary failure, were far less ready to take risks, or to trust the force of reason and argument alone to carry the government's case.

The Restoration, indeed, saw important changes in the way in which the court tried to direct its affairs in parliament which historians have seen as vital to the development of the institution. 'There is nothing better than to govern by well-regulated parliaments', pronounced Newcastle in 1660: yet, it has been argued, the recurrence of parliamentary disorders in the early

---

[28] B.L., Add. MSS 32094, fol. 52, memorandum on war with the Dutch, late 1664 or early 1665; cf. Newcastle, in Clarendon MSS 109, pp. 57–8; Clarendon, *Life*, II, 450–1, and Southampton, quoted above, p. 40.

[29] Carte MSS 46, fols. 64, 195, Bennet to Ormonde, 27 June 1663, 14 May 1664, cf. fols. 274 and 353, same to same, 20 March 1666, Carte MSS 221, fol. 44, same to same, 5 May 1663; see Clarendon, *Life*, I, 620, for Bennet's reluctance to speak in parliament.

[30] Clarendon, *History*, I, 10.

[31] Carte MSS 47, fol. 45, Clarendon to Ormonde, 11 April 1663.

[32] Clarendon, *Life*, II, 319, 328–30, 361.

1660s showed the Cavalier Parliament to be anything but well-regulated, and the incompetence of government management forced the king to adopt the more sophisticated methods offered by Sir Henry Bennet.[33] What was begun in 1663 by Bennet was developed by the earl of Danby in the 1670s into the beginnings of a modern, 'party' system.[34] But in fact, while frustration with Clarendon's parliamentary management was partly responsible for the changes which occurred in the course of the 1660s, their origins and meaning were more complex: what was at stake was as much ministerial power as the court's effectiveness; and the difference between Bennet's methods and Clarendon's was – at least at first – one of style, rather than of substance.

The problems and techniques of parliamentary management were in 1660 little different to those described by an M.P., perhaps Thomas Norton, in a treatise of nearly ninety years before, his recommendations as apposite now, as then: to avoid confrontation, to use tact, and avoid opportunities for the airing of lofty generalities such as liberty and the privileges of parliament; to prepare complicated legislation in advance, and if anything controversial was to be done, at least to do it quietly.[35] Elizabethan practice conformed to his guidelines: legislative programmes were drawn up in detail before the session; parliament was gently led, often by the nose, but rarely brow-beaten.[36] Most of the court's business was conducted not through privy councillors, but through less official channels – councillors' friends and relations, professional lawyers and those who hoped that parliamentary prominence might lead to an official career. Such a system was of course not wholly reliable: these were men who had only future, not actual, benefits to lose if they failed to support the government when its policies clashed with their own deepest instincts and commitments; they could equally discover difficult conflicts of interest between their loyalty to the government and the private interests they were expected to represent.[37] Yet such problems were facts of parliamentary life, however strongly M.P.s were tied to the court's purse strings. The court had, too, at least the basis of a block vote in the courtiers and royal servants who held parliamentary seats; not, perhaps, a payroll vote,

---

[33] Clarendon MSS 109, pp. 57–8.
[34] See D. T. Witcombe, 'The cavalier house of commons: the session of 1663', *Bull. Inst. Hist. Res.*, XXXII (1959), 181–91 (although cf. his repudiation of the argument in *Charles II and the cavalier house of commons* (Manchester, 1966), pp. 21–2); J. R. Jones, 'Parties and parliament', in J. R. Jones (ed.), *The restored monarchy*, pp. 50–2; Browning, 'Parties and party organization', pp. 21–36, and *Danby*, I, 151–2, 166–73, 273–6.
[35] Elton, *The parliament of England*, pp. 156, 323–8.
[36] *Ibid.*, pp. 71–4, 155–8.
[37] M. A. R. Graves, 'The management of the Elizabethan house of commons: the council's "men-of-business"', *Parliamentary history*, II (1983), 11–38.

but men who were expected by Francis Bacon to be not merely 'well affected', but 'sure and zealous for the king'.[38]

Parliamentary management after 1660 followed Elizabethan practice closely, and Elizabethan theory even closer. Admittedly, there is little evidence of careful preparation before a session: for the 1660s there exists no collection of papers concerning parliamentary planning such as those left by Burghley, Salisbury, or, later, Danby.[39] Nevertheless, it is clear that preparing for a session occupied a large amount of the government's time. Clarendon describes several meetings to arrange business in the ensuing session;[40] Charles complained of the burden of work before parliament resumed.[41] But thanks to the well-known account of his methods which Clarendon set down, much more can be learned of the techniques he used in the day-to-day management of the affairs of the commons: his informal network of lawyers, friends and relations, governed by regular meetings; his insistence on the court's quiet, self-effacing guidance of the house, as invisibly as possible; his emphasis on tact, on avoiding the imputation of interference with the liberty and independence of the members. He and Southampton, he wrote,

had every day conference with some select persons of the house of commons, who had always served the king, and upon that account had great interest in that assembly, and in regard of the experience they had and their good parts were hearkened to with reverence. And with those they consulted in what method to proceed in disposing the house, sometimes to propose, sometimes to consent to what should be most necessary for the public; and by them to assign parts to other men, whom they found disposed and willing to concur in what was to be desired.[42]

More details are given further on, although in some points they contradict this passage. Since the beginning of the Cavalier Parliament he and the Lord Treasurer had chosen certain men with whom to confer for directing business in the Commons. These they met only when necessary, 'upon accidents and contingencies', but the M.P.s, who 'had a mutual confidence in each other, and every one of which had an influence upon others and advised them what to do', frequently met by themselves, at the chambers of Lord Chief Justice Bridgman, or the attorney general, Sir Geoffrey Palmer, who collaborated closely with Clarendon and Southampton. Most M.P.s of any reputation in

---

38 James Spedding (ed.), *The letters and the life of Francis Bacon* (7 vols., London, 1862–74), IV, 367.
39 See, however, the drafts in Clarendon MSS 76, fols. 120–2, 132, 136, 140, 156–64, Clarendon MSS 92, fols. 198, 200, 204, 273; and the notes and precedents in P.R.O., SP 29/24, 95 and 96, the two lists of bills uncompleted at the end of the 1662 and 1663 sessions at SP 29/54/62, and SP 29/75/119.
40 Clarendon, *Life*, II, 60–4, 94–5.
41 Hartmann, *Charles II and Madame*, pp. 70–1, 95, Charles to the duchess of Orleans, 16 Feb. 1663, 29 Feb. 1664. Cf. pp. 74, 96, 97–8, 100–1, 128.
42 Clarendon, *Life*, I, 609.

the house were on cordial terms with them: many, who did not regularly attend such meetings, were at least willing to agree to support the king's business in the commons, or were even ready, 'upon private insinuation', to 'propose any thing which would not have been so acceptable from any, who had been known to have relation to his service, or to depend upon those who had'.[43]

Clarendon gives only a few clues to the structure and membership of his parliamentary management committee; but his hints do allow the identification of some of those involved. Andrew Browning has pointed out the importance of the over-represented South-West as the basis of successive court factions in the house of commons; Clarendon relied for his influence there on Sir Hugh Pollard, one of the few of his managerial committee whom he mentions by name. Pollard 'had in truth a very particular influence upon all the Cornish and Devonshire men', and had 'a greater party in the house of commons willing to be disposed of by him than any man that ever sat there in my time'.[44] He owed the trust Clarendon placed in him, and the benefits which followed – in early 1662 he became comptroller of the household and a member of the privy council – to his staunch anglican royalism, his prominence in Cornish society, and perhaps to an old friendship with Monck, the duke of Albemarle.[45] His own electoral patronage was negligible, but he may have provided an important link between the government and some of the smaller borough patrons. Pollard had been elected at Callington in 1660 on the recommendation of John Coryton, and Coryton continued to use the borough to provide seats for court candidates – Clarendon's friend Brodrick, Sir Cyrill Wyche,[46] and Sir Henry Bennet. The election of the latter was arranged by Clarendon at the king's request.[47] The extent and precise nature of Pollard's influence among the South-Western M.P.s remains, however, very uncertain. Many court M.P.s sat for seats in Devon and Cornwall; there is no evidence to suggest that they owed their election to the mediation of Pollard, although this is possible. The Cornish Trelawnys, a family respected

[43] *Ibid.*, I, 618–19.
[44] Browning, 'Parties and party organization in the reign of Charles II', pp. 29–30; Clarendon, *Life*, I, 616, 619.
[45] See Pollard's biography in *H.P.*, III, 258–9, and for his friendship with Albemarle, see Clarendon, *History*, VI, 155.
[46] Wyche was brother-in-law of the earl of Bath, a powerful local grandee, and may have owed his election to this fact: but he was also a recipient of Clarendon's patronage; he was made one of the chancery six clerks in 1662. See also his brother, Sir Peter Wyche's, petition to Clarendon, Clarendon MSS 80, fol. 352; cf. Bodl., MSS Add. C 303, fol. 120, Clarendon to Sheldon, 18 Sept. [1665]; *H.P.*, III, 770–2.
[47] Clarendon, *Life*, I, 612; for Bennet's subsequent attempt to have his secretary elected for the same seat, see *H.P.*, I, 158, and for Coryton's influence in Launceston, which may have secured the election of Sir Charles Harbord, the Surveyor General, see *H.P.*, I, 165.

and patronised by Clarendon,[48] used their interest at Looe to secure the election of Secretary Nicholas's son, Sir John; Southampton's nephew, Sir Henry Vernon; and Sir Robert Atkins, a lawyer who quickly proved himself of great value to the court, and whose knighthood shortly before the beginning of the 1661 session may have been an earnest of government favour.[49] One of Clarendon's secretaries, Bulteel, found a seat at Lostwithiel with the aid of the declining duchy of Cornwall interest; another, Matthew Wren, was elected at Mitchell; and Daniel O'Neill, an associate of Ormonde, was chosen at St Ives. Thomas Clifford, mentioned by Clarendon as one of Pollard's group, was recommended to Totnes in 1661 by the duke of York.[50] Pollard's role was probably partly that of election broker: but he probably also played a large, though shadowy role in the management of business in the house itself. His own participation in the commons' business was small; he was appointed to few committees, and his name occurs rarely in the Journals. But in 1665, on learning that Clifford had been sent to join him in his embassy to Sweden, Henry Coventry wrote to Pollard that 'now I find, you have such plenty of parliament-men, that you can afford two chair-men to a Stockholm committee',[51] an indication, perhaps, of Pollard's responsibility for the day-to-day running of the court's organisation in the commons.

Pollard was not the only man who exercised influence over a regional group on Clarendon's behalf. Lord Townshend may have acted as Clarendon's agent in Norfolk and Suffolk. Townshend, created a baron in April 1661, was described by Clarendon as 'a gentleman of the greatest interest and credit in that large county of Norfolk'.[52] His leadership of county society enabled him to recommend the unopposed candidates in the shire election in 1661; he used his own interest at Thetford on behalf of Clarendon's associate Sir Allen Apsley; and he also had an influence on Henry Howard, an important local borough patron, who commanded the seats at Castle Rising, Thetford, and Aldeburgh – he may even have managed Howard's election interest on his behalf.[53] When in 1664 Clarendon was searching for M.P.s willing to propose an unprecedented supply with which

[48] For instances of Clarendon's favour to the Trelawnys, see *H.P.*, III, 593; Clarendon MSS 80, fol. 157, Sir P. Warwick to Clarendon, 24 Aug. 1663, Carte MSS 217, fol. 473, Clarendon to Ormonde, 11 Aug. 1663; *Hist. MSS. Comm.*, MSS of J. M. Heathcote Esq. (1899), pp. 89–90, Clarendon to Sir R. Fanshawe, 16 May 1663.

[49] *H.P.*, I, 167–9.

[50] *H.P.*, I, 169–70, 171–2, 175–6, 201–2, 209–10.

[51] Coventry MSS, vol. 80, fol. 62, Coventry to Pollard, 15 Nov. 1665.

[52] Clarendon, *History*, VI, 111.

[53] C. Robbins (ed.), 'The election correspondence of Sir John Holland of Quidenham, 1661', *Norfolk Archaeology*, XXX (1947–52), 130–9; *H.P.*, I, 323, 332; see also Bodl., MS Eng. Hist. b. 212, Clarendon's lieutenancy correspondence, for Townshend reporting to Clarendon, via Apsley, on Norfolk lieutenancy affairs.

to begin the war with the Dutch, he asked Townshend to contact some
Norfolk M.P.s including Sir Robert Paston, who was ultimately prevailed on
to undertake the task.[54] Subsequently Townshend worked hard to help
Paston to get his private bill through parliament, and to get him the court
preferment he thought he deserved.[55] Some notes made by Townshend in
1663 seem to make more sense if they are considered as those of a parliamentary manager bringing to the government the suggestions, grievances, and
worries of his backbench followers than as notes for his own speeches.[56]

But Clarendon's busiest agents – the work-horses of parliamentary
management – were the lawyers. They had an obvious interest in pleasing the
chancellor: his recommendation was an easy title to preferment in the profession. Some of the most important were apparently recruited among the
members of his former inn, the Middle Temple. A contemporary of his there
was Sir Geoffrey Palmer, one of the men at the centre of his management committee. He had soon become one of Clarendon's circle, and their association
continued through the early years of the Long Parliament, and at Oxford
during the war. In 1661 Palmer became treasurer of their old inn.[57] Sir John
Bramston, who had been admitted to the Middle Temple in 1627, had been
Clarendon's 'chamberfellow', and remained on friendly terms ever after.[58]
He guided the Hearth Tax Bill through the commons, as chairman of a committee of the whole house in early 1662, and was involved in much other
government parliamentary business.[59] Another contemporary and friend of
Clarendon's at the Middle Temple was Sir John Maynard; but Maynard,
although created king's sergeant after the Restoration and involved in some
government business, had been compromised by joining parliament in the
Civil War, and by his Interregnum service as Richard Cromwell's solicitor

[54]   Clarendon, *Life*, II, 64–5, cf. 69. The 'man who had interest with the chancellor' is probably
       Townshend; Clarendon MSS 83, fol. 422, Townshend to Clarendon, 23 July [1665].
[55]   *Hist. MSS. Comm.*, 6th report (1877), Part I, appendix, MSS of Sir H. Ingilby, p. 364, Paston
       to his wife, 14 Jan. 1665; B.L., Add. MSS 27447, fol. 329, Paston to his wife, 4 Feb. [1665];
       Clarendon MSS 83, fol. 422.
[56]   B.L., Add. MSS 41654, fol. 62. These notes, made on the back of a letter to Townshend dated
       2 April, relate to the events (such as the dismissal of Lord Middleton) of 1663; most of them
       concern a suggestion for a select militia to replace the standing troops raised in late 1662, but
       they also include a list of popular grievances (Lauderdale's pre-eminence in Scottish affairs,
       French and Dutch interference with English fishing, the judgements of the commissioners for
       the Irish land settlement). Fol. 63v includes similar notes of grievances, in particular the
       'designs' of 'the Papist & Presbyter'. See also fol. 65.
[57]   Clarendon, *Life*, I, 55; *D.N.B.*
[58]   *The autobiography of Sir John Bramston*, p. 103, cf. p. 117 for his complaint that Bridgman
       and Palmer had persuaded the king and Clarendon of the strength of the presbyterians: this
       may reflect an estimate of the importance of the two men derived from his knowledge of their
       part in the direction of parliamentary affairs. See also the correspondence of Bramston and
       Clarendon in Essex Record Office, Bramston MSS D/DEb 25/4–7.
[59]   *C.J.*, 378, 379, 380, 382.

general. Clarendon clearly remained on friendly terms with him, but was reluctant to trust him with a great deal.[60] Robert Milward had entered the Middle Temple in 1631, and achieved prominence as stand-in for Sir Heneage Finch as chairman of the grand committee on the public revenue in 1661–2. In 1662 Palmer recommended him to Clarendon for a vacant place in the council of the marches of Wales, perhaps because of his parliamentary service; and in 1664 Clarendon suggested him to Ormonde for the Irish lord chief justiceship.[61] William Montagu was admitted to the Inn in 1635, became bencher in 1662, reader in 1663, and treasurer from 1663 to 1664. Since the commons' Journals often fail to distinguish him from the several other Montagus in the House, it is impossible to estimate his parliamentary record accurately. However, it was perhaps he who was teller with Clarendon's son Lord Cornbury against a motion to reject the bill for executing the regicides in November 1661: Cornbury and William Montagu were soon after both appointed to offices in the household of the new queen, Cornbury as private secretary and chamberlain, Montagu as attorney general.[62] Sir Edmund Peirce, admitted to the inn in 1641, became, after the Restoration, a judge of the admiralty in the Cinque Ports and a master in chancery.[63] Three of these Middle Templars, Peirce, Montagu, and Bramston, were in 1662 together entrusted with bringing in a bill to repeal the Triennial Act.[64]

Government influence through the lawyers was, of course, not limited to the members of Clarendon's old inn. The solicitor general, Sir Heneage Finch, was the most prominent of court spokesmen, chairing many committees, and handling many conferences.[65] Sir Robert Atkins was little less active; his exertions were awarded, in 1662, with the post of solicitor general to the queen.[66] Others of the sergeants at law also figured largely: in the 1661–2 session, Sir Job Charlton, as well as being chairman of the committee of

---

[60] Clarendon, *Life*, I, 55–6; cf. Bosher, *The making of the Restoration settlement*, p. 197, for his friendship with George Morley; *H.P.*, III, 38–9; *D.N.B.*; for his few important appearances in government legislation, see *C.J.*, 255, 321, 370, 423.

[61] *C.J.*, 303, 371, 308, 309. See also 367–8 for other indications of his importance in government business this session. He may also have been a stand-in for Sir Job Charlton in the committee for privileges and elections, *C.J.*, 376; *H.P.*, III, 69; Gloucester Record Office, Badminton MSS, 600.3.1, Carbery's book of commissions, Clarendon to Carbery, 22 July [1662]; Carte MSS 47, fol. 92, Clarendon to Ormonde, 2 April 1664; cf. Kent Archives Office, U269/C333, Milward to Henry Coventry, 24 May 1664, for his friendship with Coventry, one of the managers named by Clarendon.

[62] *H.P.*, III, 90–1; *C.J.*, 320.   [63] *H.P.*, III, 216–17.   [64] *C.J.*, 395.

[65] E.g., in the 1661–2 session, for the Press Bill (*C.J.*, 312, 313, 315–16), the Corporation Bill (310, 312, 313), the Militia Bills (249, 258, 264, 267, 273, 274, 275, 280, 284, 296, 347, 349, 355, 363, 376, 381), Voluntary Present Bill (266), Assessment Bill (321), etc.

[66] See, e.g., the Militia Bill (*C.J.*, 343–4, 345), 1663 revenue committee (453–4, 455, 456, etc.); *H.P.*, I, 565; cf. B.L., Add. MSS 9828, fols. 14 and 15, for letters of Clarendon to Atkins in 1666.

privileges and elections, chaired committees of the whole on the revenue and on the Bill for an eighteen months' assessment, and worked on conferences and amendments in the Corporation and Militia Bills.[67] Sir John Kelyng, too, handled some major government business.[68]

Browning has described how members of Clarendon's family – his three sons and a cousin held seats between 1661 and 1665 – formed the inner core of the chancellor's influence within the commons.[69] To these may be added his servants – his secretaries Bulteel and Wren – and his close friends, in particular Sir Allen Brodrick, Sir Allen Apsley, and Henry Coventry.[70] Coventry was among the principal members of the management committee.[71] Sometimes appointments to committees can show this little group acting as a block, appearing consecutively on the list printed in the Journal: in the committee on the Bill for restoring the bishops to the house of lords, Henry Coventry, two of Clarendon's sons (Lord Cornbury and Lawrence Hyde), Bulteel, and Wren, are listed together, and there are several similar cases.[72]

Clarendon's account of his parliamentary management exists only because his control over it was challenged, and ultimately wrested from him, by Bennet. Bennet's competition, and the compromise which was ultimately forced on them by the king, were events in the history of court faction, as much as in the development of parties;[73] yet the circumstances of the dispute, the nature of Bennet's style of parliamentary management, and the terms in which Clarendon defended his, have made it seem part of a larger issue – the replacement of inefficient, stuffy, and unrealistic methods by a more modern (if less scrupulous) system, an important step on the way to the classical party system. Bennet, with his ally William Coventry, rapidly made contacts and friendships among second-rank M.P.s – not those directly consulted by Clarendon's managers, but others who were usually open to their guidance – and found them complaining that they were insufficiently involved in the government's plans. Clarendon claimed that they flattered their vanity, introducing them to the king, and making them unrealisable promises of favour and preferment. Clarendon's system, and those careful Elizabethan ideals of tact and quietness, were wrecked by such obvious canvassing: 'great and notorious meetings and cabals had been always odious in parliament: and

[67] See, for the elections committee, *C.J.*, 271–2, 276, 280; for the revenue and assessment committees, see 318, 321, 326, 333; for the Corporation Bill, see 310, 335; for the Militia Bill, see 418, 423, 424, 431.

[68] *H.P.*, II, 670–1; for his few important appearances, see *C.J.*, 255, 260–1, 321, 367–8.

[69] Browning, 'Parties and party organization in the reign of Charles II', p. 28.

[70] *H.P.*, I, 721–3, 541–3.

[71] Clarendon, *Life*, I, 618; and see Clarendon's letters to Coventry in Coventry papers, vol. 2.

[72] *C.J.*, 267; see, e.g., 274 (revenue committee), 274–5 (Hitcham's Charities Bill), 293–4 (Damage Clere Bill), 277 (Corporation Bill).

[73] See below, chapter 9.

though they might produce some success in one or two particulars till they were discovered, they had always ended unluckily; until they were introduced in the late ill times by so great a combination, that they could not receive any discountenance'.[74]

There was probably some justice in Bennet's criticism of Clarendon's leadership of the government's business: there were occasions in the 1661–2 session when his caution made the court seem weak and dilatory.[75] Clarendon was reluctant to reward many of his associates; as Sir George Carteret complained to Pepys in 1667, the chancellor was not accustomed 'to do any man any kindness of his own nature'.[76] There is certainly little evidence that Clarendon rewarded regular supporters of the court with government office. Sir Courtney Pole, who brought universal odium upon himself by proposing the hearth tax in 1662, received no tangible acknowledgement until 1665, when he became one of Bennet's sub-commissioners of prizes. Coryton, too, was rewarded for his local labours only in 1665, at the hands of Bennet.[77] Yet Clarendon, as much as Bennet, used office and the hope of office to invite parliamentary support for the government: legal positions were used to reward service in the house of commons. In fact Bennet, without so large a supply of institutional patronage in his hands, had to work harder, and much more visibly, to gain his parliamentary agents. His disregard for Clarendon's convention of invisibility was a result as much of his limited patronage as his new insights: and Clarendon's annoyance was as much against his interference as against his way of interfering – Bennet and his ally in 1664, Sir Charles Berkeley 'thought it but their due that the king should take his measures of the house of commons by no other report but theirs, nor dispense his grace through any other conduit'.[78] Bennet saw a means to influence in the court through the construction of an independent faction within the commons. In a period when the government was clearly relying on parliament to provide it with new powers and new finances, an interest group in the house was one way to make oneself indispensable.

Clarendon mentioned both William Coventry and Sir Charles Berkeley (later Lord Fitzharding and earl of Falmouth) as Bennet's associates in the commons.[79] Berkeley was a favourite with both York and the king; and both men were York's servants, Berkeley as captain of his life guards and groom of his bedchamber, Coventry as his secretary. There are a few other early indications of their alliance – Bennet and Berkeley shared the spoils at the retirement of secretary Nicholas in October 1662, Bennet moving to the secretaryship while Berkeley took Bennet's discarded place as keeper of the

[74] Clarendon, *Life*, I, 618, cf. 616–17, 620.
[76] Pepys, *Diary*, VIII, 418, cf. 185–6.
[78] Clarendon, *Life*, II, 68.

[75] See, e.g., below, pp. 107–8.
[77] *H.P.*, II, 136, III, 253–4.
[79] *Ibid.*, I, 614–20, II, 68–70.

privy purse – but only in 1664 and 1665 is there evidence of all three working closely together.[80] Indeed, the central figure in Bennet's parliamentary faction was neither of these, who quickly grew too powerful in their own right to be mere instruments of the secretary, but one of the two, Thomas Clifford and Winston Churchill, whom Clarendon had claimed had been seduced from their allegiance to Pollard by Bennet and Coventry.[81] Churchill, who sat for Weymouth, was quickly taken up. In December 1661 he received on the king's personal orders an augmentation of his arms for, among other things, 'his present loyalty as a member of the house of commons'. During the first session he and Clifford were already in collaboration, and by its end, Churchill had secured a past as one of the Irish land commissioners, and a letter of recommendation to Ormonde from Bennet.[82] But it was Clifford who became the central figure of Bennet's faction. Evelyn told Pepys of his rise to power through Bennet's patronage, 'whose creature he is and never from him'.[83] Bennet also recommended Clifford to Ormonde in the summer of 1662.[84] By the end of 1662, he was one of Bennet's closest political allies, and his most important, and tireless, aide.[85] Sir Solomon Swale was probably another of the earliest members of Bennet's group. An undated petition among the State Papers described how he had been 'spoken unto & desired by several of the chiefest to waive his practice in the law, and to be constant in parliament'.[86] On two of the five occasions in the 1661–2 session when Bennet was appointed to committees on public bills, Swale's name was next to his on the list.[87]

Bennet's appointment as secretary of state in October 1662 gave him much opportunity to widen his circle of acquaintance among M.P.s. In December

[80] Carte MSS 47, fol. 373, Nicholas to Ormonde, 11 Oct. 1662; cf. Kent Archives Office, U269/c.321 [Sir Henry Bennet to Berkeley], n.d. (but cf. Carte MSS 46, fol. 21, Bennet to Ormonde, 16 Dec. 1662, which seems to refer to the same matter). The Kent note, asking for Berkeley's collaboration in Bennet's attempts to secure James's favour, suggests a close political alliance. The first of Coventry's many letters to Bennet amongst the State Papers was written in November 1664, although there were no doubt earlier ones: P.R.O., SP 29/104/104; see also Berkeley's letters to Bennet among the same series, SP 29/118/99, 122, 119/17, 43; and for his relationship with Coventry, see Coventry's memoranda prepared for him, in B.L., Add. MSS 32094, fols. 28, 46, 48, 50, etc. See below, pp. 233–4.
[81] Clarendon, *Life*, I, 617, 619, 620.
[82] *H.P.*, I, 71; Carte MSS 221, fol. 3, Bennet to Ormonde, 14 July 1662.
[83] Pepys, *Diary*, VIII, 185; see also *The diary of John Evelyn*, III, 469–70, IV, 18–19; and Burnet, *History*, I, 402.
[84] Carte MSS 221, fol. 11, Bennet to Ormonde, 13 Sept. 1662.
[85] See P.R.O., SP 29/64/8, Bennet's notes of 2 December of business to be done; cf. SP 29/253/12, Clifford to Arlington, 2 April 1666, and the contents of Arlington's coach when it overturned in September 1667: himself, Clifford, Sir Henry Capel, and Sir John Trevor. B.L., Egerton MSS 2539, fol. 120, Sir John to Sir Edward Nicholas; see also Browning, *Danby*, I, 74.
[86] P.R.O., SP 29/142/219, cf. 218, 220.
[87] *C.J.*, 320, 423. Cf. 421 for Swale's association with Clifford as a teller on the Militia Bill.

Richard Legh wrote to him relying on 'that short & happy experience I had of your civil freedom to me since I had the good fortune to know you'.[88] In February 1663 Pepys was told that the new secretary had offered Edward Montagu a pension and a title, in an attempt to wean him away from the patronage of Clarendon.[89] Bennet already had relatives in the commons; two cousins, Sir Humphrey and John Bennet. The latter died in May 1663, but by then Bennet was influential enough to secure the election of his brother, Sir John, at Wallingford, vacant because of the death of George Fane.[90]

During the intervals between sessions, members of this growing group kept in touch through Bennet and his secretary, Joseph Williamson. Swale wrote to Bennet in October 1663, 'presenting my service to you, with my love and respect to honest Mr Clifford'.[91] Clifford wrote frequently to Williamson. In January 1664 he asked him for information about the upheavals at court because 'when some of our fellow members ask me about this and twenty such matters I am at a little loss but this advantage I have by my ignorance I appear cautious and reserved':[92] other Devon and Cornwall M.P.s evidently regarded him as a man with access to the best and the latest information. Clifford's other correspondents included Sir Jordan Crosland, M.P. for Scarborough, to whom he addressed letters via Williamson.[93] Crosland was probably another member of this parliamentary group; in August 1663 Bennet had recommended him and his own brother to Ormonde, as undertakers for setting up an Irish postal service.[94] In October 1664 Sir Thomas Strickland, who sat for Westmorland, was writing to Williamson to ask him to pass on a note for Clifford.[95] In November 1664 Clifford sent William Coventry a lengthy and epic account of the supply debate of the 25th.[96] Sir Edmund Poley, member for Bury St Edmunds and a distant kinsman of Bennet by marriage, seems to have been relying on his patronage in March 1663 or 1664.[97] Sir Geoffrey Shakerley, M.P. for Wigan, who had probably received his governorship of Chester at Bennet's solicitation,[98] was also a regular correspondent of Williamson, and frequently thanked him for his kindness and favours.[99]

---

[88] P.R.O., SP 29/65/25, 19 Dec. 1662.
[89] Pepys, *Diary*, IV, 47.   [90] *H.P.*, I, 622–4.   [91] SP 29/81/15, 4 Oct. 1663.
[92] SP 29/90/36, 6 Jan. 1664. Cf. SPO 29/81/47, 9 Oct. 1663, and 137, 17 Oct. 1663, SP 29/91/5, 20 Jan. 1664.
[93] SP 29/90/36.
[94] Carte MSS 221, fol. 75, Bennet to Ormonde, 18 Aug. 1663.
[95] P.R.O., SP 29/103/96, 21 Oct. 1664.
[96] B.L., Add. MSS 32094, fols. 24–6.
[97] B.L., Add. MSS 38015, fol. 65v, note by Sir R. Southwell, dated March 1663.
[98] *H.P.*, III, 426; although cf. SP 29/76/85, deputy lieutenants of Cheshire to Albemarle, 16 July 1663, in which it seems that the local gentry themselves were pressing for Shakerley's appointment.
[99] SP 29/100/78, SP 29/103/147, SP 29/124/19.

The evidence of correspondence with Bennet's secretary, and favours received from Bennet, is not of course a secure basis on which to claim the existence of a sophisticated parliamentary faction. But to some extent the fact that these men co-operated within the commons can be demonstrated by the pairing of tellers on divisions. During the sessions of 1661–5 Clifford acted as teller twenty-one times, more than any other M.P. In five of these, his partner was Edward Seymour, son of his companion M.P. at Totnes. Seymour also became a member of Bennet's group, although it is difficult to know when, or how permanently. In 1665 the secretary was probably responsible for his appointment as a sub-commissioner of prizes.[100] In a further four divisions, Clifford's partner was Swale, one of them in defence of the Declaration of Indulgence in February 1663.[101] He also told once with the earl of Bristol's client, Sir Richard Temple, in 1663 when Bennet and Bristol combined against Clarendon;[102] once with Poley, on the important supply bill of November 1664;[103] and once with Strickland.[104] One of Swale's three tellerships with another of Bristol's allies, Sir Thomas Tompkins, may also be explained by the Bristol–Bennet partnership of 1663.[105] Swale also told once with Edward Seymour.[106] Members of Bennet's group seem to be found less frequently in blocks on committees, as Clarendon's are, although there are instances in which Clifford, Swale, and Strickland, or Swale and Churchill are listed together on committee lists.[107]

Several of this Bennet–Clifford group either were, or later became catholics, which suggests that they may have been drawn in by the policy which Bennet supported in late 1662 and early 1663 of allowing catholics, and other nonconformists, freedom of worship. Crosland may already have been a catholic, and Strickland, Clifford, Swale, and Bennet himself were all converted later. Their conversions, however, can only in some cases be dated, and where they come in the 1670s, they perhaps owed more to the political circles in which they moved than to strong latent convictions, although Swale and Strickland had catholic relations. Clifford was a strong devotee of the Church of England in the early 1660s, as were Churchill and Sir Humphrey Bennet. Most of them were strong opponents of protestant nonconformity;

---

[100] *C.J.*, 272, 502, 577, 582; cf. SP 29/157/44, Seymour to Arlington, 29 May 1666. See below, pp. 89–90.
[101] *C.J.*, 421 (twice), 440, 464.
[102] *C.J.*, 474. For the factional troubles at court in 1663 see below, p. 9.
[103] *C.J.*, 568.
[104] *C.J.*, 528.
[105] *C.J.*, 486 (sale of offices bill), cf. 520, 508. Swale was perhaps assigned the functions of teller and committee man: in *H.P.*, it is pointed out that his prominence in these roles was not at all matched by the number of his recorded speeches: *H.P.*, III, 514–17.
[106] *C.J.*, 620.   [107] E.g., *C.J.*, 579, 606.

Churchill, Shakerly, and Crosland were all active persecutors.[108] Clifford and Swale were referred to in 1663 as 'two of the greatest proctors the bishops had' in the commons.[109] Yet if their spontaneous support for policies of toleration was unlikely, they were probably very responsive to Bennet's hints of preferment and reward; all were ambitious or penurious, anxious to obtain court careers or court pensions.

The amalgamation of Clarendon and Bennet's parliamentary managers in 1663, at the end of a confused session made more confused by their rivalry, did not, however, end Bennet's construction of an independent faction, and may even have aided it.[110] The opening of war with the Dutch in 1664–5 brought the beginnings of a change, albeit a tentative and temporary one, in his method of parliamentary management. War demanded an expanded administration, offering increased opportunities for patronage on one side and profit on the other. Bennet took full advantage. One of the arguments advanced in 1664 in favour of waging war was that it would make a profit, or at least pay for itself, through the proceeds of the sale of prizes. Bennet, William Coventry, and Lord Ashley were closely involved with the appointment of a commission to deal with them in November and December 1664.[111] It consisted of the navy committee of the privy council, with Bennet its comptroller, and Ashley its treasurer. The sub-commissioners, though (who were actually to handle the sales), were to be mostly M.P.s: in December Coventry told Pepys that 'he knew that the king and the duke had resolved to put in some parliament men that have deserved well and that would need to be obliged by putting them in'.[112] In January Williamson wrote that of the thirty-nine or forty sub-commissioners, only three or four were not M.P.s.[113] In fact this appears to be an exaggeration: a list of the sub-commissioners in the commission's minute book gives only thirty, of whom twenty-four were M.P.s.[114]

Of these, Strickland,[115] Clifford, Poley, Edward Seymour, Sir Humphrey

---

[108] *H.P.*, I, 620–3, II, 71–3, 91–4, 175–6, III, 426–7, 504–6, 514–17.

[109] *The Mather Papers*, Collections of the Massachusetts Historical Society, 4th series, VIII (1868), 208, William Hooke to John Davenport, 5 March 1663.

[110] See below, chapter 9.

[111] Clarendon, *Life*, II, 88–92; P.R.O., SP 29/104/104, William Coventry to Bennet, 14 Nov. 1664.

[112] Pepys, *Diary*, V, 327, 342; cf. 322, 333; cf. Sir Richard Braham's petition, P.R.O., SP 29/142/23.

[113] *Hist. MSS. Comm.*, Heathcote MSS, pp. 174–5, Williamson to Sir A. King, 16 Jan. 1665.

[114] B.L., Harleian MSS 1509, fol. 28r–v; cf. the list in P.R.O., SP 29/111/11, perhaps an earlier version, which adds Ashburnham, but omits Col. Edward Villiers, Sir Thomas Peyton, Sir John Coryton, and Captain John Strode. Both lists make no mention of the deputy-treasurers for prizes, of which Col. Reymes was one (*H.P.*, III, 323), and I have found no list of them elsewhere. Their existence may explain the difference between Williamson's report and the number of sub-commissioners in the two lists.

[115] See Strickland's request for office in October 1664, on the eve of the war, SP 29/103/96.

Bennet, John Ashburnham, and Sir Jordan Crosland were certainly or probably already linked to Bennet and his parliamentary group. Andrew Newport
had been an undergraduate at Christ Church, Oxford, while Bennet was a
student there, and from late 1664 was another of Williamson's correspondents.[116] Jonathan Trelawny had by late 1663 established close links with
Williamson, despite Clarendon's previous patronage.[117] Colonel Reymes was
already close to both William Coventry and Thomas Clifford.[118] If some
of them were not already in Bennet's coterie when they became sub-
commissioners, they were quickly drawn in. Sir Thomas Higgons by October
1665 was writing to Williamson as a 'person whom I have a particular
inclination to love & serve', and sent his service to Bennet, now Lord
Arlington: 'no man does love his lordship more faithfully than I'.[119] Sir
Thomas Peyton paid his respects to both of them in August 1665; and by the
end of the year was apparently advising Arlington on Kent elections.[120]
Colonel Kirby and Sir John Knight were also by late 1665 addressing
Williamson with great professions of service.[121] The remaining sub-
commissioners, Sir John Talbot, Sir Francis Clerke, Edmund Wyndham,
Massey, Prideaux, Ernle, Gilby, Marlay, Anderson, and Sir Henry North,
cannot be linked specifically to Bennet, although they were probably habitual
government supporters whom he wished to reward and retain. One sub-
commissioner who was not an M.P., Sir Francis Dodington, was a client of
Bennet's by 1669, and was in 1664 suspected by Clarendon of participating
in the earl of Bristol's plotting against him.[122]

Bennet may even have begun to encroach on Clarendon's closest friends.
Apsley wrote to him in April 1665, saying how ambitious he was of 'an
interest in your lordship.'[123] Clifford grew in importance. He was in constant
communication with the secretary's office,[124] and talk in 1665 of offering him
a barony seems to have progressed as far as discussing the title he should
have.[125] Bennet's own elevation, however, made Clifford's position in the
commons more essential still to the smooth running of the secretary's

[116] *H.P.*, III, 136; SP 29/104/71, 113/1, 129/30, 172/124; see the first of these letters for the
connection between Newport and Sir Philip Honeywood, one of the commissioners for
Portsmouth.
[117] SP 29/81/8, 83/67, 85/72, 86/22.   [118] *H.P.*, III, 323–4.   [119] SP 29/136/66.
[120] SP 29/128/47, 140/41 (Sir R. Southwell to Arlington, 29 Dec. 1665); cf. B.L., Stowe MSS
744, fol. 105, Arlington to Sir E. Dering, 20 March 166[6].
[121] SP 29/137/57, 139/103.
[122] *Hist. MSS. Comm.*, MSS in Various Collections, II (1903), MSS of Sir George Wombwell,
128–9, 139, 147; Clarendon MSS 81, fol. 226, Sir F. Dodington to Clarendon, 6 May 1664;
P.R.O., SP 29/76/96, John Dodington to Bennet, 17 July 1663; SP 44/16, p. 27.
[123] SP 29/119/14.
[124] SP 29/81/47, 137, 90/36, 91/5, 99/20, 103/96.
[125] P.R.O., SP 29/114/93, W. Godolphin to Williamson, 9 March 1665, although the syntax of
this letter makes it difficult to be certain whose title is being discussed.

parliamentary network. Clifford was teller in no divisions after January 1665, a development which might suggest that he began to take over Bennet's and Pollard's function as the chief director of the court's management in the house. After Pollard's death in 1666, Clifford's assumption of his role was signalled by his succession to Pollard's old office, the comptrollership of the household.

The 1665 prize commission indicates a propensity to use the expanding opportunities of patronage which the war presented to reward and retain loyal M.P.s. Nevertheless, the influence of the experiment was limited. Most of those appointed sub-commissioners were already Bennet's clients, or habitual supporters of the government; the commission was not used, apparently, to gain new and wider support. And in any event, in early 1666 the whole scheme was abandoned. In late March the sub-commissioners were all replaced, it was said, by three general commissioners: Poley, Ernle, and Wyndham. One of the sub-commissioners, Sir John Coryton, complained bitterly about their supercession.[126] But despite the system's abandonment, it had already helped to do some damage to the court's reputation: by 1667 the use of office and reward to secure the votes and attendance of M.P.s was a subject of grievance and satire,[127] and in the years after Clarendon's exile, with the increasing sophistication – or brazenness – in parliamentary organisation achieved by Bennet, then by the earl of Danby, the Cavalier Parliament became a byword for political jobbing and corruption.[128] In 1667 Evelyn told Pepys that 'of all the great men of England, there is none that endeavours more to raise those that he takes into favour than my Lord Arlington, and on that score, he is much more to be made one's patron than my lord chancellor'.[129] Clarendon's objections to Bennet's style of parliamentary management reflect the limits he placed on government policy: the government should behave in such a manner as to invite respect and thus to recreate the conditions for stability. Bennet's methods, he believed, did the opposite, propagating fears of governmental interference with parliamentary freedom: his attempts to bring more M.P.s in the court's orbit always 'lost more friends than were gotten by them'.[130] His friends shared his views: in 1679 Sir Allen Brodrick attacked Danby's style of parliamentary management:

---

[126] *Hist. MSS. Comm.*, 6th report (1877), part 1, appendix, MSS of Sir R. Graham, bart., p. 337, Sir Paul Neile to Henry Slingsby, 22 March 1666; B.L., Add. MSS 15857, fol. 186, Coryton to Sir Richard Browne, 9 March 166[6].

[127] 'The last instructions to a painter' in Margoliouth, II, 141–65, particularly 143–7; see also 'The alarum' of 1669, printed in part in A. Browning (ed.), *English historical documents, 1660–1714* (London, 1953), pp. 233–6.

[128] Browning, 'Parties and party organization in the reign of Charles II', pp. 23–5.

[129] Pepys, *Diary*, VIII, 185–6.   [130] Clarendon, *Life*, II, 70.

the revolutions since '67 have appeared to me and my thinking friends the inevitable consequences of my old lord's banishment . . . the house of commons debauched by committee to serve that turn were never afterwards true to their trust, and a new method of retaining pensioners dissolved the very essence of that assembly, who represented not those that chose them, but those that fed them.[131]

To Clarendon, Bennet's too obvious courtship and bribery of M.P.s with tempting prospects of favour and preferment would lead to the very dangers that he desired so much to avoid: the disillusion and alienation of people and parliament from the government.

For both Clarendon and Bennet, of course, these groups of personal allies and agents were only at the centre of a wider field of government influence, the king's servants and the government's employees. It is clear that these were expected – as they had been earlier in the century – to provide a fairly loyal backbone to the court's parliamentary activities. In 1665 Brodrick complained to Ormonde of the king's failure to command all the courtiers to attend the debates on the Irish Cattle Bill:[132] in 1666 he referred on several occasions to 'those that depend on the court', or 'we who depended on the king',[133] and it may be that the session of 1666–7, the most contentious of these years, saw a greater effort by the government to use its block vote. Yet this payroll vote had many inconveniences: indeed, of all M.P.s the government frequently found the courtiers themselves the most troublesome. Closely connected to prominent politicians and councillors, they might easily be led along other paths than those approved by Clarendon or Bennet; they were an excellent means for highly placed dissidents to promote their own policies or persons, and attack their rivals.[134]

In some ways this problem was most acute in the house of lords, where many of them sat, although, for the same reason, in the normal course of events the upper house presented far fewer problems of management: government influence had more straightforward channels.[135] In April 1661 there were twenty-one members of the privy council who had the right of sitting in the house – although some of them, such as the ex-Parliamentarians Saye and Northumberland, were not men on whom the government would have cared

---

[131] *Hist. MSS. Comm.*, MSS of the marquess of Ormonde, new series (8 vols., 1902–20), V, 95, A[llen] B[rodrick] to Ormonde, 13 May 1679.

[132] Carte MSS 34, fol. 448, Brodrick to Ormonde, 22 Oct. 1665.

[133] Carte MSS 35, fols. 118, 171, Brodrick to Ormonde, 3 Nov., 15 Dec. 1666. See also Pepys, *Diary*, VII, 399.

[134] See, for example, Sheldon's letters to Ormonde at the end of the 1666–7 session, Carte MSS 45, fols. 212 and 214.

[135] See Andrew Swatland, 'The house of lords in the reign of Charles II, 1660–1681', unpublished Ph.D. thesis, University of Birmingham, 1985.

to rely, and others, like Newcastle, were rare attenders.[136] There was a maximum of twenty-six bishops entitled to sit in the lords at any one time, and these were generally amenable to government guidance. Gilbert Sheldon, bishop of London, and from 1663 archbishop of Canterbury, worked hard on the behalf of both the government and the Church, in marshalling the attendance of the rest of the episcopal bench.[137] The proxies of absent members were also a useful resource for the court.[138] A letter of Clarendon to Sheldon just before the 1665 session of parliament suggests that Sheldon acted on Clarendon's behalf in organising the disposal of the episcopal proxies.[139]

Nevertheless, Clarendon seems to have used friends and associates as government managers in the lords as he did in the commons. When he advised Ormonde on whom he should trust with his proxy after the earl of Portland, who had originally held it, had died in Spring 1663, he recommended the earl of Bridgewater.[140] Portland was a close friend of Ormonde, Clarendon, and their circle,[141] and in April 1662 had been appointed to the privy council;[142] during the session of 1661–2 he chaired and managed many important committees and conferences.[143] Bridgewater's piety and his anglican connections had probably brought him to Clarendon's attention: he gained in importance

---

[136] For a list of the privy council, see James Heath, *The glories and magnificent triumphs of the blessed restitution of his sacred majesty K. Charles II* (London, 1662), pp. 211–12; for Newcastle's retirement, see Margaret Cavendish, duchess of Newcastle, *The Life of William Cavendish, duke of Newcastle*, ed. C. H. Firth (London, 1886), p. 131.

[137] See Bodl., Tanner MSS 48, fol. 69, archbishop of York to Sheldon, 6 Dec. 1662, MSS Add. C. 305, fol. 52, bishop of Chester to Sheldon, 16 Nov. 1665, fol. 338, bishop of St David's to Sheldon, 15 Sept. 1666, Tanner MSS 45, fol. 26, bishop of Lichfield and Coventry to Sheldon, 20 Sept. 1665.

[138] For the use of proxies see E. R. Foster, *The house of lords, 1603–1649* (Chapel Hill, 1983), pp. 19–22, 35, 201; for Ormonde placing his proxy at Clarendon's disposal, see Carte MSS 47, fol. 89, Clarendon to Ormonde, 21 March 1663; although cf. H.L.R.O., Proxy Books, H.L., vols. 1 and 2, which indicate that the government's use of proxies was not particularly systematic.

[139] Bodl., MSS Add. C. 303, fol. 120, 18 Sept. 1665.

[140] Carte MSS 47, fol. 89.

[141] *Ibid.*, fol. 39, Clarendon to Ormonde, 17 March 1663, cf. fols. 43, 52, 56, and Clarendon MSS 79, fol. 161v, Clarendon to Anglesey, 18 April 1663, Clarendon MSS 76, fol. 281, Portland to Clarendon, 19 May 1662 and fol. 228 same to same, 20/21 May 1662; P.R.O., SP 29/67/31, Portland to Brodrick, 10 Jan. 1663; Clarendon, *Life*, II, 132–3.

[142] P.R.O., PC 2/55, fol. 301.

[143] E.g., H.L.R.O., Committee Minute Book, H.L., King's Preservation Bill, 24, 25, 27 May 1661, Strafford's Attainder Repeal Bill, 27, 31 May 1661, Catholic penal laws, 1, 3, 18, 23, 24, 25 July 1661, confirmation of public acts, 3 July 1661, corporations, 10 Dec. 1661; *L.J.*, 266 (King's Preservation Bill), 297 (confirming public acts), 418 (Prize Goods Bill), 441 (Uniformity Bill), 318, 321, 349 (corporations).

as time went on, dealing with much government legislation.[144] In February 1667 he was appointed to the council and Clarendon tried hard to have him made Southampton's successor as lord treasurer.[145] These two peers were the most assiduous promoters of court legislation in the lords,[146] although government ministers themselves also handled much of the work; Ashley, Robartes and Anglesey were among the most important, and most of the others also shared the burden.[147]

The government was only one, albeit the biggest and most effective, of the network of factions, parties and interest groups in parliament. The arts of parliamentary lobbying were probably a good deal more sophisticated than there is hard evidence to prove: L'Estrange hinted at some of them in his 1662 *Memento*:

They have their contrivers, their speakers, their sticklers, their dividers, their moderators, and their blancks: (their I-and-NO men) by which method and intelligence, all debates are managed to the advantage of the party, and occasion. They know when to move, when to press, when to quit, divert, put off, &c and they are as skilful in the manner of moulding their business as they are watchful for the season of timing it.[148]

L'Estrange's point was that it was easy for cabals with enough skill and determination to incense the parliament against the court. There were indeed factions which operated against the government during the 1660s, although their composition was unstable and fluid. Central, in some way, to most of these combinations was John Vaughan, the most respected of the government's critics.[149] Vaughan, 'magisterial and supercilious', 'proud and insolent', was an old acquaintance of Clarendon, who wrote of him that he 'looked most into those parts of the law which disposed him to least reverence to the Crown, and most to popular authority; yet without any inclination to any change in government'.[150] Vaughan was involved in many attacks on government legislation: the court was sufficiently apprehensive of his opposition in 1664 to arrange the debate on the Triennial Act in order to exclude him; and in 1667 he became one of the principals in the impeachment

[144] H.L.R.O., Committee Minute Book, H.L., Poor Relief Bill, 10 July 1661, Printing Bill, 25 26 Feb., 13 March 1662; *L.J.*, 316 (Tax Arrears Bill), 353, 372, 395 (Quakers Bill), 406 421, 426, 441 (Uniformity Bill), 431, 453, 466 (Militia Bill), 443 (Customs Bill); see also Swatland, thesis, pp. 67, 75.
[145] Carte MSS 35, fol. 465, Brodrick to Ormonde, 8 June 1667.
[146] See the list in M. P. Schoenfeld, *The restored house of lords* (The Hague, 1967), appendix A pp. 226–30. This list is based on 'selected committees', which I take to mean those on majo public bills, rather than 'select' committees; and compare the more reliable lists in Swatland thesis, pp. 67, 75.
[147] For Robartes, see, e.g., *L.J.*, 389 (Quakers), 443 (Customs Bill), 441 (uniformity), 453, 454 466 (Militia Bill); for Ashley, 432, 443 (Customs Bill), 466 (Militia Bill); for Anglesey, 28 (Bishops Bill), 425 (Uniformity Bill), 466 (Militia Bill).
[148] *A memento*, p. 145.   [149] See above, pp. 47–8.   [150] Clarendon, *Life*, II, 30–?

proceedings against Clarendon.[151] Sir Thomas Littleton was described by Sir William Penn in 1666 as 'one of the greatest speakers in the house of commons, and the usual second to the great Vaughan'.[152] Littleton joined Vaughan in opposing much court legislation and in the impeachment of Clarendon; after Vaughan's own removal from the commons, and his own brief spell in government, he continued to oppose the court in conjunction with Vaughan's son Edward, in the 1670s.[153] Sir Richard Temple, M.P. for Buckingham, became one of Vaughan's and Littleton's chief allies, partly, perhaps, because he was disappointed in his hopes of place and favour in 1660;[154] but all of them seem to have been genuinely concerned with the preservation of English liberties under a reactionary government, even if they disagreed on other issues – Vaughan, unlike the other two, was among the most resolute of the Church's defenders.[155] Around this nucleus others – William Garraway, Sir Robert Howard, Thomas Thompkins, and Brome Whorwood in particular – came and went, some seconding them out of agreement with their opinions, others from more complex and murky motives. Sometimes wooed by factious courtiers – Bristol and Buckingham – who had different motives still, they nevertheless remained independent of them.[156]

There was another nucleus of opposition politicians, in parliament's 'presbyterian' members. Although they were few, commentators claimed to identify a distinct 'presbyterian' interest in either house: Sir Robert Paston blamed the 'presbyterians' in the commons for resisting his private bill in 1665; Robert Milward and Edward Gower complained about their proposal for a voluntary gift in 1661; and John Milward attributed to them the pressure for an assessment on land in 1666, and for comprehension in 1668.[157] Marvell, in his satire on the events of 1666–7, described a presby-

---

[151] See below, pp. 122, 138–9, 315; Milward, *Diary*, pp. 86, 102, 113, 121, 123, 129, 131, 133, 142, 143, 150–1, 155.

[152] Pepys, *Diary*, VII, 210. For Littleton's relation to Vaughan, see Tuck, ' "The ancient law of freedom" ', p. 139, and *H.P.*, II, 748–9.

[153] Burnet, *History*, I, 414–15, II, 92–3.

[154] For Temple, see E. F. Gay, 'Sir Richard Temple, the debt settlement, and estate litigation, 1653–75', *Huntington Library Quarterly*, VI (1942–3), 255–91; G. Davies, 'The political career of Sir Richard Temple, 1634–97', *Huntington Library Quarterly*, IV (1940), 47–83; C. Roberts, *Schemes and undertakings: a study of English politics in the seventeenth century* (Columbus, Ohio, 1985), pp. 57–9; *H.P.*, III, 536–44; and see his notes, speeches and essays in B.L., Stowe MSS 304, particularly 'an essay upon government', fol. 1ff.

[155] For Vaughan's religious position, see Milward, *Diary*, pp. 249–50, 282, and B.L., Add. MSS 4274, fol. 222, Morley to [Sheldon], 14 March 1669; for Littleton's, see Milward, *Diary*, pp. 216, 218, 225; for Temple's, see Stowe MSS 304, fols. 10v–14.

[156] For their connections with factions in the house of lords, see below, pp. 219, 223–7, 230, 298–301, 313.

[157] *Hist. MSS. Comm.*, 6th report (1877), part 1, appendix, MSS of Sir H. Ingilby, bart, p. 364, 5th report (1876), appendix, part 1, MSS of the duke of Sutherland, pp. 145, 203; Milward, *Diary*, pp. 25, 127, 153.

terian group in the excise debates of that session.[158] But many of these references suggest that its enemies – and even, perhaps, Marvell, its friend – made
little distinction between this 'presbyterian' faction and the commercial
interests they so readily identified with presbyterianism. In the lords,
'presbyterians' were still fewer; and some of those who had been associated
with political presbyterianism in the past – such as Manchester and Robartes
– were now, by their employment at court, effectively divided from it. The
most prominent of those that remained was perhaps the earl of Northumberland, a grandee who 'lived with all the greatness of the ancient nobility, and
under much form and high civilities kept himself on the reserve with all
people'.[159] The earl was a severe critic in the lords of the government's
actions: he resisted the expansion of the regular army, the re-establishment of
the council of the North, and the Act of Uniformity;[160] he seems, besides, to
have been the leading figure in a small group of lords – himself, the ex-
presbyterian M.P. Holles, and his own brother-in-law, Leicester, a man of
complicated and equivocal Civil-War allegiance – who in 1667 tried to come
to some sort of political bargain with Charles and James.[161]

Not all politics is opposition politics: factions and lobbies existed for
numerous political purposes – for individual trades, for individual localities,
for the City, for the navy, for and against private bills. Only one need be considered in detail here: that for the Church. It has already been argued that the
house of commons owed its prelatical legislation not to the overwhelming
anglicanism of the country gentry as a whole, but to the existence of an
influential group within the house: although there are only a few explicit
references to an 'episcopal party' or a high-flying version of it, in either house,
the importance of prominent anglican royalists – many of them well connected to the government – in the promotion of parliament's ecclesiastical
legislation can be demonstrated. Lord Fanshaw, Sir Job Charlton, Sir
Thomas Meres, Sir Edmund Peirce, Sir John Berkenhead, and John Vaughan
appear over and over again as the inceptors and managers of ecclesiastical
bills. Charlton and Fanshaw were the first two to be appointed to the committee for the Conventicle Bill of 1663; Fanshaw was the first on the committee on the 1664 Bill (and was probably the proposer of both bills) and was the

---

[158] Margoliouth, I, 147, ll. 283–4.
[159] H. C. Foxcroft (ed.), *A supplement to Burnet's history of my own time* (Oxford, 1903),
      pp. 77–8.
[160] *Ibid.*, P.R.O., PRO 31/3/110, D'Estrades to Louis XIV, 28 Jan./6 Feb. 1662; Clarendon,
      Life, I, 553.
[161] Clarke, *Life of James II*, II, 426–7; for his relationship with Leicester, see *Hist. MSS. Comm.*,
      MSS of the Rt Hon. Viscount De L'Isle at Penshurst, 6 vols. (1925–66), VI, 512–18, and
      Arthur Collins, *Letters and memorials of state*, 2 vols. (London, 1746), II, 701, 722–3.

first on that for the Bill of Uniformity in 1661.[162] Berkenhead and Peirce were those most involved in guiding the house through the discussions with the lords on uniformity in April 1662.[163] Berkenhead also defended the Church against a bill prepared by Prynne to restrict pluralism.[164] Sir Thomas Meres worked hard on the bill for confirming the 1660 Ministers Act, in which Fanshaw, Charlton, and Berkenhead were also prominent.[165] Sir Edmund Peirce was the chairman of the committee for the Bill of Uniformity in 1661, and for the companion bill for the restoration of ecclesiastical jurisdiction.[166] Many of those most frequently appointed to committees in the commons on religious legislation were members of the anglican cliques of the Interregnum, or had strong clerical and ecclesiastical connections, men such as Crouch, Finch, Burwell, Sir Robert Holte, Lord Bruce, and Sir Thomas Meres.[167] One of them, Bramston, may have helped Sheldon in extra-parliamentary ways as well, gathering information on livings in the gift of the see of London and on their incumbents, when Sheldon was its bishop:[168] Robert Milward and his cousin John were welcomed by Sheldon at Lambeth.[169]

In the lords, the fiercest anglicans were perhaps those who signed the protest against the lords' proviso to the 1663 Bill concerning subscriptions to the Act of Uniformity.[170] York was possibly their figurehead, and several of the other signatories, including Berkeley and Peterborough, were his associates. Most were prominent cavaliers, men such as Derby, Northampton, Mordaunt, Dorset, Gerrard, and Lucas. But it was Bridgewater who was undoubtedly the most active. He chaired the committees on the Quaker Bill, the Uniformity Bill, the 1664 Conventicle Bill, and the Five Mile Bill.[171] Gossip said that he was one of the most zealous in the lords for the Act of Uniformity.[172]

Many of these men were among those most trusted by the government to handle its affairs in parliament: Milward, Peirce, Bramston, Charlton, Warwick, and Finch were among its principal agents in the commons; Bridgewater was indispensable in the lords. Men such as Berkenhead, John Heath,

---

[162] *C.J.*, 539, 473, 288–9.
[163] *C.J.*, 402, 406, 409–10, 412–13, 417.
[164] B.L., Lansdowne MSS 958, fols. 17–26; for the bill, see *C.J.*, 436, 440, 461, 516, 527.
[165] *C.J.*, 322, 343, 358, 367, 415, 436.
[166] *C.J.*, 295, 296.
[167] For a list of those most frequently appointed to such committees, see the appendix, p. 328.
[168] Essex Record Office, Bramston MSS D/DEb 28/1–11; see also H. Smith and T. Hope, 'Essex clergy in 1661', *Transactions of the Essex Archaeological Society*, new series, XXI (1933/7).
[169] Milward, *Diary*, p. 33.
[170] *L.J.*, 573.
[171] H.L.R.O., Committee minutes, H.L., 10, 12 Dec. 1661, 21, 27 Feb., 3, 5, 7, 10, 20, 22, 24, 26 March 1662, 6, 9, 10 May 1664, 27 May 1665.
[172] Bodl., MS Eng. Lett. c. 210, fol. 69, Sir H. Yelverton to Archdeacon Palmer, 29 Jan. 1662.

Sir Charles Harbord, and Sir John Kelyng, while not the government's chief agents, were clearly enough identified with it; even Lord Fanshaw was described by Clarendon as a 'friend'.[173] Clifford and Swale, described as two of the Church's 'greatest proctors' in the commons, were essential members of Bennet's faction.[174]

Membership of committees does not, of course, mean whole-hearted support for every aspect of the legislation involved. Despite the rules of the house, Littleton, Temple, Atkins – opponents of persecution – were appointed to most of the major committees.[175] Moreover, the prominence in religious legislation of major government figures may reflect their general prominence in the house as much as their particular enthusiasm for persecution. Yet their consistency in the committees combines with what is known of their religious attitudes to suggest that most of these figures did, indeed, strongly support these acts, and were themselves largely responsible for them. Entrenched in government, and particularly in the court's parliamentary leadership, it was easy for high-flying prelatical anglicans to dominate the discussions on religion, and difficult for the government to introduce and support milder measures.[176] Clarendon's Elizabethan system of management had an Elizabethan problem – the government's parliamentary agents, along with some of the privy council, held a rather divergent view of religious policy from that of the monarch.

The existence of factions, the politics of the pressure group, were perennial features of parliamentary life: there was little that was distinctively different in the politics of the 1660s from the politics of, say, the 1620s. The legacy of the Civil War and Interregnum, if there was one, was less tangible: a more politically educated and mature membership, perhaps; in the government, perhaps a sharpened sense of the risks of parliament, a feeling that the penitent prodigal might turn prodigal once more, and a consequent decline in the court's willingness to play the parliamentary game by its old rules. As important as the legacy of 1640–60, were, however, the developments of the 1660s themselves: a decade of intense parliamentary activity, a large programme of government legislation, an enormous number of private bills from individuals anxious to sort out the legal confusion which the troubles had

---

[173] *Hist. MSS. Comm.*, MSS of the earl of Verulam (1906), p. 61, Clarendon to Grimston, 9 Aug. [1666].

[174] *The Mather papers*, p. 208.

[175] For the rules on the membership of committees, see W. Hakewill, *The manner how statutes are enacted in parliament by the passing of bills* (London, 1670), p. 146.

[176] Cf. the embarrassment of Henry Coventry and Sir Philip Warwick in describing the government's religious policy in 1663, and parliamentary opposition to it: *Hist. MSS. Comm.*, MSS of J. M. Heathcote Esq. (1899), pp. 77–8, Warwick to Sir R. Fanshaw, 12 April 1663; Carte MSS 47, fol. 397, Coventry to Ormonde, 28 Feb. 1663.

brought to their estates. Parliament sat every year, in lengthy sessions. Such conditions set a premium on the ability of all interests – the government, the Church, individuals – to manipulate it, and encouraged the development of new methods of doing so. Bennet's methods, although at first different from Clarendon's in style rather than in substance, became increasingly directed towards the artificial construction of a commons 'party'. In the later 1660s and 1670s, fuelled by the government's nervousness of a too loosely controlled parliament and by its need for legislation, they would be developed into something more systematic: the more tightly organised court faction of Danby. As Clarendon had predicted, and Brodrick confirmed, this more interventionist management, while providing occasional successes, changed parliament more fundamentally than had any of the developments of the Civil War, eroding the assumption of a shared interest between court and country, and replacing it with mutual mistrust.

Part Two

THE RECONSTRUCTION OF
THE OLD REGIME

5

Finance

Above all else, the survival of the restored regime depended on its financial security; without it, the government would risk following the example of its early Stuart predecessors, staggering from crisis to crisis at the mercy of parliament and the City, or else forced into unpopular expedients of dubious legality. That security was at risk from the vast debts left by the Interregnum powers, including the growing arrears of pay owed to the republican army and navy which threatened to choke the monarchy before it was even properly established. To function effectively, without constantly having to appeal to parliament for temporary taxes, the government would need to clear these debts, and to obtain the sort of settlement of a permanent annual revenue which had eluded James I and Charles I.

The Convention Parliament had responded handsomely to these necessities. Extraordinary taxes worth a total of approximately £800,000 were voted to pay the forces and to allow them to be disbanded. In its discussions on the permanent revenue, the commons' finance committee, headed by the solicitor general, had estimated average annual expenditure at £1.2 million a year. With the income from the court of wards replaced by the retention of half of the unpopular commonwealth excise, the traditional sources of Crown revenue would, they calculated, produce £819,398 a year. This could be increased by an expected improvement in the queen mother's jointure, and the addition of the forfeited estates of those excepted from the Act of Indemnity; to balance expenditure, the house added the rest of the liquor excise, estimated at £300,000.[1]

But by the beginning of the 1661 session it was plain that the Convention's settlement was far from adequate. The money for paying the troops' arrears came in slowly, and as they waited to be paid, the sums owed to them grew rapidly. Professor Chandaman has estimated at £375,000 the additional debt that was thus created. Worse still, it was soon pointed out that the assump-

---

[1] This figure should in fact have been only £150,000; for this mistake, see below, p. 104, and Chandaman, p. 202.

tions on which the Convention based its claim to have made up a sufficient permanent revenue had been founded on confused arithmetic. The committee had admitted that £45,699 included in the £819,398 was irrecoverable, and had therefore discounted it: but when the total revenue was supposedly made up, the figure was restored. The half of the liquor excise included in the £819,398 as compensation for the removal of the court of wards was also included in the estimate of £300,000 for the liquor excise added to bring the revenue up to the full amount. To add to Lord Treasurer Southampton's chagrin the excise, the queen's jointure and the forfeited estates had all been overvalued.[2]

Over the next few years, the government tried constantly to amend these errors, seeking more extraordinary grants to remove the remaining debt, and an increase in the permanent revenue which might allow financial stability and freedom from dependence on parliament. Southampton was particularly nervous of the need to rely on the goodwill of the house of commons.[3] Yet even in the early 1660s, when the relations of Crown and parliament were on the whole unusually harmonious, this was never achieved. To a large extent the reason was economic. Many sectors of the economy were severely depressed throughout the decade: war with Spain in the later 1650s had disrupted England's trade with one of her major partners, ruined the carrying trade in the Mediterranean, and dislocated the many industries which depended on Spanish raw materials; the political uncertainty of 1658–60 had added to the problems of commerce; the heavy taxation of the 1650s had spread the recession much more widely; and the dearths and consequent high food prices of 1658–62 produced distress among the poor and some smaller farmers – before, in the mid-1660s, agricultural production swung quickly into surplus, and the sudden abundance caused other difficulties.[4] Under these conditions, M.P.s, however loyal, remained reluctant to add to the country's burdens. But some saw a more political reason for the Crown's failure to achieve a satisfactory settlement: the concern of some M.P.s, and even, it was said, of ministers like Clarendon, that the Crown might become too well endowed, so much so that parliaments, no longer necessary, might be forgotten. A few M.P.s were influenced by such a fear. But there is little to suggest that it had any effect on Clarendon: the chancellor was no less

---

[2] Chandaman, p. 202; B.L., Harleian MSS 1223, fol. 203.
[3] See his comment in the 1663 report, *ibid.*, fols. 205v–6, quoted above, p. 40.
[4] For these problems, see Hutton, pp. 76–7; G. Davies, *The Restoration of Charles II* (London, 1955), ch. 10; R. A. Stradling, 'Anglo-Spanish relations 1660–68', unpublished Ph.D. thesis, University of Wales, 1968, ch. 1; Thirsk (ed.), *Agricultural history of England and Wales*, V, ii, 55–6, 59, 61–2, 75; for the bad harvests of 1661 see *The diary of Ralph Josselin 1616–83*, ed. A. Macfarlane, British Academy Records of Social and Economic History, new series, III (London, 1976), p. 483.

anxious than other ministers that the Crown's financial foundations should give it security and avoid the need to rely on parliaments. Yet the fact that such suspicions were aroused shows that for Clarendon the obtaining of money was not always a primary consideration: the reconciliation of the monarchy and the nation demanded that heavy taxation should be avoided as far as possible. At the beginning of the 1661 session he told the assembled houses that 'the monster Commonwealth cost this nation more, in the few years she was begot, born and brought up, and in her funeral (which was the best expense of all), than the monarchy hath done these six hundred years'.[5] The new regime could not be seen as similarly oppressive, if it was not to jeopardise its popular support.

It is indicative of Clarendon's main preoccupations that when the new parliament opened he was reluctant to press hard for an augmentation of the revenue. More important for him was a demonstration of the unity and harmony of the political nation. In mid-April he wrote to the French minister, Bastide, asking for a temporary loan, because although

we cannot have more reason to be confident of any thing, than of the good temper and great affection of the parliament . . . we have many matters of greater importance to settle with them than the procuring of money, which we shall defer (I mean defer the asking) till the other things are done, and yet you will easily believe, that the king before that time may be in some straits, which he will not willingly own.[6]

In his speech to parliament on 8 May, Clarendon mentioned the deficiency in the Convention's financial provision; yet his comments on the point were short and restrained, and he made no specific request for money.[7] A letter from Southampton in September confirms that it had been decided not to demand supply: 'had we had time, or rather had we not in this conjuncture supposed it fitter to decline pressing for taxes, I believe we had had a fuller coffer than now we enjoy, which you know is very natural for a treasurer to complain of'.[8]

The government may have resolved to avoid a direct appeal for taxation, but this did not prevent it from making less conspicuous efforts to obtain supply. Two weeks into the session, on 21 May, 'Mr Montegew', probably William Montagu, moved for a supply, and Sir Robert Atkins pointed out the deficiencies of the ordinary revenue.[9] Atkins and Montagu were to be frequent government agents in the commons, and it is possible that the motion

[5] *Parliamentary history*, IV, 206.
[6] *State papers, collected by Edward, earl of Clarendon*, ed. R. Scrope and T. Monkhouse (3 vols., Oxford, 1767–86), III, supplement, iv–v, Clarendon to Bastide, 18 April 1661.
[7] *Parliamentary history*, IV, 183.
[8] *Hist. MSS. Comm.*, Finch MSS, I, 154, Southampton to Winchilsea, 14 Sept. 1661.
[9] B.L., Egerton MSS 2043, fol. 9; *The notebook of Sir John Northcote*, ed. A. H. A. Hamilton (London, 1877), p. 129.

was made at the court's instigation in order to test the support for supply.[10] Certainly the opportunity was seized. On 30 May, when the subject was again discussed, Sir Philip Warwick, Southampton's secretary, grasped the opportunity to move 'some thing in behalf of a supply for the king'. Two resolutions were taken: that the house would attend both to the Crown's immediate needs and to making up the deficiencies of the permanent revenue; and secondly that a bill should be brought in for a benevolence, a 'free and voluntary contribution'.[11] The latter vote was, however, bitterly resented by cavaliers, who considered it to be a measure planned by rich presbyterians to allow them to demonstrate their loyal liberality: impoverished royalists could not hope to compete in the bidding for royal gratitude.[12] Marvell thought that Prynne was ordered to draft the Bill:[13] in fact, it was brought in by Finch, but Prynne, who was the chairman of the committee of the whole house on the Bill, may well have been one of the presbyterians supposedly pressing for it. The benevolence was quickly passed in both houses.[14] Presenting it for the royal assent, on 8 July, the Speaker fulsomely praised the king's moderation in not asking for money, and promised 'great frankness and cheerfulness in your present supplies'.[15]

The vote of 30 May encouraged the government to go further. On the same day as the Bill for the voluntary present was read for the third time, some steps were taken towards repairing the deficiencies of the permanent revenue. Sir Philip Warwick was commissioned to produce a report, which he read to the house on 18 June. The major branches of the revenue, he told it, fell short of the estimate made in 1660 by £265,000; customs, the queen's jointure, excise, Crown lands, forfeited estates, and wine licences were all less productive than had been allowed.[16] It was apparently with the full approval of the court that the commons proceeded to examine the defects for themselves: the committee appointed for the purpose was headed by Warwick and other court M.P.s: Pollard, John Ashburnham, Finch, the surveyor general Sir Charles Harbord, and Sir Allen Brodrick.[17] The committee appointed subcommittees to consider the better management of the customs, excise, and

[10] See above, p. 83.
[11] B.L., Egerton MSS 2043, fol. 11.
[12] *Hist. MSS. Comm.*, 5th report (1876), appendix, part I, MSS of the duke of Sutherland, p. 145, R. Milward to Sir R. Leveson, 30 May 1661, cf. p. 203, E. Gower to Sir R. Leveson, 30 May 1661; cf. Bodl., Tanner MSS 239, fols. 3–4, a speech made at Watton 'in advancement of the voluntary present to be made to the king Charles the 2*d*'.
[13] Margoliouth, II, 26, Marvell to Hull Corporation, 30 May 1661.
[14] *C.J.*, 266, 267, 268, 270; *L.J.*, 279, 281, 284.
[15] *Parliamentary history*, IV, 211–12.
[16] *C.J.*, 270, 273–4; Warwick's report includes several inaccuracies, particularly in the 1660 estimate of the values of the customs and excise.
[17] *C.J.*, 273–4.

Crown lands. On 4 July reports from both were read to the full committee: with new powers for their collection, they thought, the customs might raise the £400,000 at which they had been over-estimated in 1660, and the excise £250,000. The Crown lands, valued in 1660 at £265,000, even with improvements, could be made to yield only £100,000.[18] On the basis of these, and other unrecorded reports, the committee drew up an account of the amount the established revenue might be expected to bring in if suitable improvements were made. This it computed to be £854,586.[19] On 12 July, Sir Robert Atkins delivered the full report of the committee to the house. Even with the proposed improvements, an additional £300,000 per annum would be required to achieve a permanent revenue of £1.2 million.[20]

The commons appear to have accepted this conclusion with little argument. The problem was not, indeed, any reluctance to supply the Crown's deficiencies, but an enormous concern to supply them in such a way as might be least burdensome to an already heavily burdened people. When, on 13 July, Atkins's report was discussed in a committee of the whole house, the committee resolved with alacrity to meet the shortfall by extending excise duties to home brewed ale and beer, to be levied by a poll tax – a charge on each household. But alternative, more immediately attractive suggestions seem to have quickly diverted the house: in a second meeting of the committee of the whole, on 18 July, no further progress was made;[21] and on the 19th Clarendon wrote to Sir George Downing, the English ambassador in the United Provinces, that the commons had considered many different ways to make up the permanent revenue,

as giving new & larger powers for gathering the customs, which, they say, if well regulated, would be of themselves a vast revenue; others propose the foreign excise, others have a project upon sealed paper like that in Holland; and some propose a general excise, that is, that everybody in the kingdom (though they brew themselves) should pay so much the year by the poll, and this is the likeliest to take effect. Tomorrow the house is to be again in a grand committee upon this work, & I hope we shall draw it towards a head, though it's not possible it should pass this session.[22]

Clarendon's letter indicates no firm leadership from the government on which of these options to choose, and it is possible that the court was holding back, anxious not to appear to interfere with the decision. The danger of this,

---

[18] See the minutes of the committee, preserved with the Shaftesbury (Lord Ashley's) papers, P.R.O., 30/24/34/20, fols. 3–6.
[19] *Ibid.*, fol. 6v.   [20] *Ibid.*, fols. 7–10; *C.J.*, 299.   [21] *C.J.*, 301, 305.
[22] B.L., Add. MSS 22919, fol. 158, Clarendon to Downing, 19 July 1661; Downing appears to have interpreted Clarendon's letter as a request for advice on means of taxation: cf. his replies, Clarendon MSS 104, fols. 237–8, 252–8, Aug. 9/19 and 16/26, and see H. Roseveare, 'Prejudice and policy: Sir George Downing as parliamentary entrepreneur', in *Enterprise and history: essays in honour of Charles Wilson*, ed. D. C. Coleman and P. Mathias (Cambridge, 1984), pp. 140–1.

though, was that the impetus so far built up might be lost as M.P.s were attracted first by one solution, then by another. On 20 July, the committee of the whole house decided to increase the excise to the value of £400,000, but when at its next meeting it considered ways of doing so, it discussed not the general excise, but an imposition either on salt (which was rejected on a division), or on sealed paper and parchment.[23] Although on the 23rd the house endorsed the committee's decision to add to the excise revenue, it resolved at the same time that M.P.s and J.P.s were to inspect the revenue of the excise in their own districts, implying a suspicion that better collection of the tax could render some of the proposed augmentation unnecessary. Now opinion seemed to have swung decisively against the general excise that had at first been proposed, towards a bill for a charge on sealed paper and parchment, and ten M.P.s, including Finch, Harbord, and Bennet, were requested to draft a bill to be brought in after the recess. Shortly before the summer adjournment the house made another declaration of principle, that it would take into consideration the advance of the king's revenue 'to such a proportion as may be sufficient to support the grandeur of his Majesty & be suitable to his occasions'. This was perhaps a court attempt to have the matter placed at the top of the agenda when parliament resumed.[24]

In some respects, the government could draw plenty of encouragement from the progress made so far. The commons had appeared more than willing to repair the Convention's inadequate settlement and to vote an ample permanent revenue. On the other hand, it was clear that agreement on how to raise it was to be less easy, particularly if the court was unwilling to take a stronger lead. Moreover, as the commons endlessly discussed alternative projects, the royal debt increased; the small yield of the benevolence had done little to diminish it. When the houses reassembled on 20 November, the government pressed for more urgent action: the king reminded them of the 'crying debts which do every day call upon me', and this time requested an extraordinary supply. In doing so, he referred to the inspection of the summer, and invited the commons to extend it to expenditure as well as revenue. As he hinted, the court was already beset with allegations of corruption and extravagance, and the offer was plainly an attempt to pre-empt criticism.[25]

The tactic may have contributed to a notable government success. The invitation was not taken up, this session at least; and on the following day the commons voted an extraordinary tax of £1.2 million, which it subsequently accepted should be levied by the deeply hated but more efficient assessment – an innovation of the Interregnum – rather than by the traditional, and

[23] P.R.O., 30/24/34/20, fols. 10v–11.
[24] *C.J.*, 309, 313.   [25] *Parliamentary history*, IV, 222–4

naturally more popular, low-yielding subsidy.[26] In further meetings of the committee of the whole house, the rest of the details of the tax were settled; and on 4 December the Bill was brought in. It passed quickly, although with the addition of five provisos, including a declaration that in the future taxation should always be by subsidy, not by monthly assessment.[27]

While pleased,[28] the court still wanted improvements in the permanent revenue. On 18 January 1662 Sir Richard Ford brought in a bill against abuses in the customs.[29] Ford was one of the members of the recently created royal committee of trade which in February 1661 had considered corruption and inefficiency in the customs, and had reported to the privy council.[30] This Bill may have been the result of their deliberations. It had powerful government backing: after its second reading, on 29 January, Warwick, Pollard, Morrice, and John Ashburnham were the first names appointed to the committee, which was empowered not just to consider the Bill, but also to inquire into the conduct of officials and consider ways of improving the yield.[31] Private interests in the encouragement of certain sectors of trade made discussions on it lengthy; clothiers, tin miners, and the company of importers of logwood for dyeing all demanded a hearing, and it passed the commons only on 21 March.[32] While willing to help to combat fraud, the house had no wish to increase the powers of customs officers unduly, and it rejected a lords' amendment designed to strengthen them by calling those who obstructed them in the course of the duty before the court of exchequer.[33] The Bill also laid an additional discriminatory duty on Scottish salt.[34]

The discussions of the previous July had centred, however, on improvements and additions to the excise. Now, as before, progress was slow, obstructed by conflicting plans for its augmentation. On the same day as the Customs Bill was brought in, a committee was appointed, headed by the

[26] *C.J.*, 317, 317–18; B.L., Egerton MSS 2043, fol. 18v; for the relative merits of the subsidies and the assessment, see Chandaman, pp. 140–3.

[27] *C.J.*, 318, 321, 325, 326, 328–9, 331, 332–3, 333; *L.J.*, 352, 353, 354; B.L., Egerton MSS 2043, fols. 19r–v, 21r–v; 13 Car. II, stat. 2, c. 3, *S.R.*, 325–48.

[28] See, e.g., *Hist. MSS. Comm.*, Finch MSS, I, 173, Sir Edward Nicholas to Winchilsea, 5 Dec. 1661.

[29] *C.J.*, 347; B.L., Egerton MSS, 2043, fol. 39.

[30] P.R.O., SP 29/31/164 (fol. 128v), proceedings of the committee of trade, 14 Feb. 1661.

[31] *C.J.*, 353; for a glimpse of this committee at work, see *Hist. MSS. Comm.*, 8th report (1881), part I, appendix, MSS of the Corporation of Trinity House, p. 251, and Thomas Violet, *To the king's most excellent Majesty and to the lords spiritual and temporal; with the commons assembled in parliament*, dated 25 January 1662, and probably presented to the committee.

[32] *C.J.*, 387, 390, 391, 391–2.

[33] *L.J.*, 414, 416–17; H.L.R.O., Committee Minutes, H.L., 1, 14, 16 April 1662, Main Papers, H.L., 18 April 1662; *L.J.*, 432; *C.J.*, 415.

[34] 14 Car. II, c. 11, *S.R.*, 393–400.

Norfolk and Suffolk M.P.s Richardson, Duncombe, and Gawdy, to improve the excise and to bring it up to its assumed value.[35] On 18 February Robert Milward read its report, and the committee was further requested to take suggestions from M.P.s for the improvement of the excise: but the court received a setback when an attempt to renew the resolution of the previous summer, to make the excise general on all beer and ale, was rejected in a division by seven votes. Although there was a further discussion a few days later on raising the excise to £400,000, nothing appears to have come of it.[36] A bill for improving the excise revenue was brought in from the excise committee on 15 March, but was rejected by a small margin after its second reading. A new bill was to be drawn up by a group which included Warwick, but also Sir Roger Bradshaigh (who had been a teller with Sir Robert Brooke against the first Bill), and M.P.s such as Temple and Hussey who were to become well known for their frequent opposition to the court. Their bill received two readings, and was committed, but proceeded no further.[37] The court also attempted to revive the project for a duty on sealed paper and parchment, suggested, and apparently resolved upon, in July. On 18 February the Bill which had then been ordered was brought in, and on the following day read a second time and committed to the whole house. After this, however, no further proceedings are recorded.[38]

As in the summer of the previous year, the discussions on raising the permanent revenue had produced a gratifying acceptance in principle of the necessity of doing so, but a frustrating inability to settle on the means. This slow progress provoked the court into taking a firmer lead. On 1 March, the king addressed the commons, complaining of the fact that they were no nearer to settling the revenue than they had been at Christmas, and asked them to establish a 'real and substantial revenue upon me, as may hold some proportion with the necessary expenses I am at, for the peace, benefit and honour of the kingdom'.[39] As soon as M.P.s returned to their chamber, Sir Courtney Pole moved that a bill for a tax on hearths should be brought in.[40] The Bill, already drafted, was read the same day. The similarity of the tactics to those described by Clarendon as used in obtaining the 'royal aid' of November 1664, even down to the employment of a country gentleman with no known court affiliation to propose it, suggests that the motion was carefully set up by the court; Pole was M.P. for Honiton, and might perhaps have been one of Pollard's group of South-Western M.P.s.[41] In the next few days

[35] *C.J.*, 347, 352, cf. 309.
[36] *C.J.*, 367–8, 392; for Birch and Doyley, see *H.P.*, I, 654–5, II, 230–3.
[37] *C.J.*, 309, 367, 368.   [38] *C.J.*, 387, 414, 423.   [39] *Parliamentary history*, IV, 230–.
[40] Bruce, Thomas, earl of Ailesbury, *Memoirs written by himself*, Publications of th Roxburghe Club (2 vols., London, 1890), I, 97; Pole took the Bill up to the lords o 14 March, *C.J.*, 387.
[41] Clarendon, *Life*, II, 64–5.

this pressure was maintained, as the Bill was discussed in committee of the whole under the chairmanship of Sir John Bramston. There was plenty of opposition to it: on 10 March, when Bramston reported the amendments and provisos added to the Bill, Temple and Colonel Strangwayes supported a proviso designed to raise the threshold of exemption from the tax, but were defeated;[42] John Fowke, one of the London independent M.P.s, argued that it would produce widespread popular discontent;[43] and on the 12th, when the Bill received its third reading, Sir Thomas Littleton unsuccessfully proposed that it should be only temporary.[44] According to Sir Henry North the argument was advanced that the tax would mean that the king would have less need of parliamentary supply, or, it was implied, parliamentary sessions – although this, he said, merely 'inclined the major part to pass it the sooner'.[45] Sir Richard Temple was one of those who hinted at a reluctance to do any more for the Crown's permanent revenues; 'I cannot find one precedent, that ever any parliament have intermeddled therewith, their business being to provide for extraordinary aids and not things of constant revenue'.[46] He attacked the novelty and inequality of the tax: it was a tax on necessities, not on luxuries; it would fall heavily on the poor and penalise corporations while failing to tap the wealth of the landed. He exposed his own anti-clerical and anti-French political preoccupations by proposing two alternatives – the improvement of the first fruits and tenths of the clergy to their true value, and the imposition of additional customs on foreign commodities.[47] All this opposition could not, however, prevent the rapid passage of the Bill.[48]

The hearth tax was soon to become as unpopular as the excise; but it was perhaps accepted only because it would prevent the need for the excise's extension. Professor Chandaman has argued that this was a bad bargain for the court. But at the time it was thought to be rather a good one, and certainly capable of supplying the £300,000 deficiency in the annual revenue. Estimates of its value varied enormously; some, wrote North, calculated it to be worth £1 million, North himself believed it to be £500,000. Another M.P. put it at £300,000. Even Southampton wrote that it was worth 'at least' £300,000, and Sir William Morrice thought its value to be £4–500,000. But

---

[42] *C.J.*, 376, 378, 379, 380, 382, 383.
[43] *H.P.*, II, 353.
[44] *C.J.*, 383; Clarendon MSS 76, fol. 260, Thomas King to Clarendon, 15 May 1662.
[45] B.L., Add. MSS 32500, fol. 9, Sir Henry North to Sir Dudley North, 13 March 1661[62].
[46] Temple's speech on the hearth tax, B.L., Stowe MSS 304, fols. 70–1v, and cf. fols. 72–3, 75.
[47] *Ibid.*, fol. 71.
[48] *C.J.*, 385; *L.J.*, 408, 410, 411; Chandaman, p. 77, refers to a 'long unexplained delay' before its passage. In fact it took only two and a half weeks to pass through both houses, although it did not receive the royal assent until May.

these inflated expectations – however they were arrived at – were to be dramatically disappointed.[49]

The government's problems did not consist merely of insufficient taxation; its pressing debts meant that it needed access to money much faster than it flowed into the exchequer from taxes. In February the first of several efforts to improve government credit was made, coinciding with the government's approach to the common council of London for a loan of £200,000 secured on the new assessment. The maximum legal rate of interest, set by a 1660 statute, was 6 per cent, but in its dealings with the bankers the government generally had to offer 4 per cent above that figure as a gratuity, as the bankers themselves often paid 6 per cent on the money they borrowed. It was presumably in an attempt to remove the legal difficulties to adding the extra interest that a bill was introduced into the commons on 13 February 'to make it lawful for persons that lend monies to the king, to take interest at ten per centum'.[50] The measure aroused much opposition from gentry – and particularly from royalists trying to restore their fortunes – concerned that high interest rates attracted money away from land, driving down land values and prices, and made it more difficult for landowners to borrow to improve their estates. After three days' debate in committee of the whole house with Atkins in the chair, on 18 February Secretary Morrice announted to the house that the king had ordered the Bill to be withdrawn: 'having heard that the Bill might have some ungrateful relish in it, [he] resolved to put himself upon the greatest straits, rather than adventure upon any course that might in the least seem to disgust this house, or prejudice his good subjects'. The very public withdrawal – which may have contributed to the reluctance of the City to respond to the government's request for a loan – was perhaps intended to encourage the house to pass the Bill for a tax on sealed paper and parchment, read for the first time on the same day: if so, of course, it was to be in vain.[51]

Even so, the court had reason to be satisfied with the first session of the new parliament. It had at last secured a permanent revenue which it believed was sufficient for its normal needs; and with the tentative beginnings of an economic recovery, and hence expansion in its permanent revenue, the

[49] Chandaman, p. 81; B.L., Add. MSS 32500, fol. 9; Clarendon MSS 76, fol. 260; B.L., Harley MSS 1223, fol. 204; *Hist. MSS. Comm.*, Finch MSS, I, 188, Morrice to Winchilsea, 29 March 1662.
[50] *C.J.*, 362; H. Roseveare, 'The advancement of the king's credit, 1660–1672', unpublished Ph.D. thesis, University of Cambridge, 1962, pp. 36–41; for the loan of February and the difficulties experienced in raising it, see G. V. Chivers, 'The City of London and the state, 1658–1664, a study in political and financial relations', unpublished Ph.D. thesis, University of Manchester, 1961.
[51] *C.J.*, 362, 365, 366, 367; W. Letwin, *The origins of scientific economics* (London, 1963), pp. 7–9; cf. [James Ralph], *The history of England during the reigns of K. William, Q. Anne and K. George I* (2 vols., London, 1744–6), I, 60. Ralph says that the Bill failed because of the opposition of those 'who were most willing to oblige the king'.

government might be confident that the financial problem had been solved.[52] But if these expectations were entertained, they were rapidly to be disappointed. For one thing, expenditure was constantly increasing: at Easter 1662 the receipts covered only just over half of the expenditure. Court extravagance, Southampton complained, was partly to blame for the growing burden of debt and anticipations of the revenue.[53] Added to this, the hearth tax was a failure. Apart from being profoundly resented in the country at large, its yield was far below what had been anticipated. In each of the first two years of its existence, the tax yielded an average of £115,000 a year, well under half its projected value.[54] The sale of Dunkirk to the French in October 1662 at least provided the government with a contingency reserve (soon used up), and removed an expensive liability: but this, too, was deeply unpopular. The reaction to Ormonde's request in the winter of 1662–3 for £60,000 to help pay off part of the Irish army showed how serious the problem was. Southampton and Warwick insisted that such a sum was simply unavailable: the only possible hope for supply was from parliament, for English necessities as well as Irish.[55] But in 1663 the commons were unlikely to be as forthcoming as they had been hitherto. After such large taxes granted in the previous session, the continuance of royal penury seemed to indicate financial incompetence and extravagance; this was to strengthen immeasurably the arguments of those who in the previous session had unsuccessfully resisted the demands for increased taxation or a widening of the powers of taxcollectors.

In preparation for what was likely to be a troublesome session, the court made some moves towards financial reform. In his 1663 report on the revenue, Southampton referred to his two earlier reports of May and October 1662, the latter just when issues were beginning drastically to exceed receipts. He referred to a decision to cut expenditure taken after the latter report; and certainly, in late 1662 plans were drawn up to assign money from the main branches of the permanent revenue to the payment of regular expenditure, including a sum of £200,000 to be devoted to the navy.[56] But such reforms as there were were neither in time, nor obvious enough, to remove M.P.s' suspicions of waste and corruption; irritated by the conspicuous extravagance of the court, and by its new religious policy announced in the

[52] Chandaman, p. 207.
[53] B.L., Harley MSS 1223, fol. 202r–v, 205r–v; Chandaman, pp. 208–9.
[54] Chandaman, p. 318; Pepys, *Diary*, III, 127.
[55] Carte MSS 32, fol. 230, Lord Berkeley to Ormonde, 3 Jan. 1663, fol. 272, Warwick to Ormonde, 9 Feb. 1663.
[56] B.L., Harley MSS 1223, fols. 202r–v; *Cal. S.P. Dom.*, 1661–2, p. 577; *Calendar of treasury books*, ed. W. A. Shaw (London, 1904–), I, 456, Southampton to Long, 3 Dec. 1661; Pepys, *Diary*, III, 297 and n. 1, cf. IV, 36, 49, 81.

Declaration of Indulgence of December, M.P.s, for all their loyalism, were confirmed in their distrust and dislike of courts and courtiers. Some anglican royalists believed that the government's religious policy and its poverty stemmed from the same root, the prominence at court of presbyterians who used their position to further their own religion and wealth, with little regard for the health of the regime.[57]

Despite this colder atmosphere, the court did attempt to solve its problems by requesting a further addition to the permanent revenue. When Charles responded on 16 March to the commons' rejection of an indulgence for non-conformists by asking them to 'put the kingdom into such a posture of defence, as that if any disturbance or seditious designs arose, they might be easily suppressed', the commons did indeed consider an account of the royal finances which had been delivered in, according to which royal revenue stood at £965,000, and ordinary expenses alone, after recent economies and excluding extraordinaries, repayments on debts, and defalcations, exceeded it by £121,100.[58] According to Southampton a motion was then made for the general excise of beer and ale to be added to the permanent revenue, but 'there was undoubtedly with a great reverence and affection to your Majesty's service, yet perchance not without some prejudice towards your officers an inspection desired, that might more clearly discover the true value of your revenue, with a belief that the same was now, after the chimney money given fully 1200000 *l*'.[59] The inspection of the summer of 1661, encouraged and guided by the government, provided the precedent for this new inspection; and the king's invitation of November 1661 to the commons to make a thorough inquiry into the revenue's deficiencies justified it – and made it difficult for the court to refuse to co-operate.

On 19 March the house began work on the inspection, appointing a committee to examine the customs, and authorising a committee of the whole house to appoint further sub-committees on individual branches of the revenue. The revenue of Crown lands and fee farm rents was also referred to the customs committee, with an instruction to inquire into all grants and alienations made since 1649 and the charges made to officers in their receipts and payments of the revenue. Pepys heard a few days later that they were considering the resumption of all alienated Crown lands.[60] Other sub-committees were created to consider the hearth tax, and the post office and wine licence revenue.[61] On 13 April the surveyor general gave the first report, a preliminary one on Sir John Winter's Forest of Dean contract. Further

[57] *The autobiography of Sir John Bramston*, p. 118.
[58] *Parliamentary history*, IV, 266; C.J., 453; B.L., Add. MSS 34217, fol. 78. This account seems likely to be a copy of that presented: it is dated 19 March [16]62 [i.e. 1663].
[59] B.L., Harleian MSS 1223, fol. 204r–v.
[60] C.J., 453–4, 456; Pepys, *Diary*, IV, 87–8.   [61] C.J., 466, 471.

reports from the sub-committees were delivered after the Easter recess. On 8 May, Harbord reported on the values of the customs and Crown lands, in which he repeated the verdicts of the 1661 committee: the customs could yield £400,000, and Crown lands, if the lands and rents granted away by letters patents were included and the whole was improved, could reach £100,000.[62] The house settled in for a long investigation, as government hopes of supply dwindled. Bennet wrote to Ormonde that many were doubtful that any money at all could be obtained this session.[63]

One proposal for amending royal finances, though, may have come from the court itself. A resolution was taken, probably in committee, to bring in a bill 'for fixing the public charge of the kingdom, upon some particular branches of his Majesty's revenue'. It seems likely that the Bill read on 13 June, for 'ordering and improving of the king's Majesty's revenue', was the result, and that this Bill was in fact a measure for appropriating half of the customs to the use of the navy.[64] This early appropriation scheme seems to have matched Southampton's own plans of late 1662 to settle the ordinary expenditure of the navy at £200,000 a year and to put aside certain branches of the revenue to pay for it:[65] the proposal may have been made to parliament in the context of the discussions on the customs revenue, or a consideration of the debts of the navy, which was proceeding at the same time.[66] A bill among undated state papers 'for appropriating the duty arising by the customs for the use of the navy' may well be this one; it provided that money from the customs was to be paid directly into the exchequer, whose officers were only to issue it out to the treasurer of the navy or the lieutenant and paymaster of the ordnance.[67] After the Bill's second reading, on 18 June, Sir George Carteret, the treasurer of the navy, was the first member appointed to the committee, which also included other court M.P.s such as Finch, Warwick, Harbord, Coventry, Bulteel, Cornbury, and Downing.[68] Its similarity to Southampton's own plans of late 1662, and the strong presence of government M.P.s on its committee may suggest that this scheme for the statutory appropriation of some of the revenue to a particular item of expenditure was not, as it might seem, an attempt by the commons to win greater control over government spending, but a measure sponsored by the court itself. Indeed, Southampton may have hoped that it would prevent the

[62] *C.J.*, 471, 478.
[63] Carte MSS 221, fol. 35, Bennet to Ormonde, 14 April 1663.
[64] *Hist. MSS. Comm.*, Ormonde MSS, III, 52–3, Henry Coventry to Ormonde, 12 May 1663; Carte MSS 222, fol. 12; *C.J.*, 501.
[65] Pepys, *Diary*, III, 297, IV, 36, 49, 81, 152, 206; Coventry MSS, vol. 96, fols. 5–8, letters of the officers of the navy to the lord treasurer.
[66] See P.R.O., SP 29/75/73 and 74 (petition of navy creditors).
[67] P.R.O., SP 29/51/65.　　　　　[68] *C.J.*, 506.

anticipation and diversion of money that was desperately needed to pay the running expenses of the government and the accumulated debt.[69] But the Bill made no further progress, though for what reason is obscure. Further measures of this sort of reform were delayed until the beginning of the Dutch War.

In other areas the court was undoubtedly irritated by the inspection. Private interests were probably attempting to use it to further their own ends, and the house's request that the king should not pass Daniel O'Neill's contested grant of the post office until the committee had considered it was brusquely swept aside.[70] In further reports from the committee Harbord criticised the low rents paid for the duty on Newcastle coals and the farm of the post office revenue, recommended a bill to void all leases and grants of Crown lands made since the Restoration for longer than three lives or thirty-one years, and complained of Sir John Winter's Forest of Dean timber contract.[71]

On 4 June, Harbord brought in his full report on the total permanent revenue, which, he concluded, was worth £1,025,246 at present, and might, with improvements, be worth £1,081,710 – but still nearly £120,000 less than its projected value. But as Southampton subsequently pointed out in his report to the king, even this exaggerated its real value to the Crown, as the committee had reckoned many branches at what they produced for their farmers, rather than for the government itself. Direct collection of these branches had been proved to be unsatisfactory, and if they had to be farmed, the rents paid would need to be substantially lower than the actual yield in order to allow the farmers a worthwhile profit.[72] Harbord's revelation that the hearth tax had produced only £170,603 12s in the past year was a shock to those who believed that it was worth at least twice that sum.[73] Hoping that the house would be suitably impressed by the inadequacy of the revenue, on 5 June the government made the session's second attempt to secure an addition. As Bennet wrote to Ormonde, this too was unsuccessful, 'and made so by the industry of those who have more earnestly put his Majesty upon the persecution of dissenters, which is a hard case but parliaments hardly give money so we must have patience and shuffle again'.[74] So a week later, the court tried a third time. The king addressed the commons in the Banqueting Hall, admonishing them that 'the reputation I had from your concurrence

---

[69] See his comments in B.L., Harley MSS 1223, fols. 205r–v.
[70] *C.J.*, 481, 485–6.
[71] *C.J.*, 481, 489–90, 495; cf. *H.P.*, II, 482–3 for Harbord's interest in the improvement of the revenue from the Forest of Dean.
[72] *C.J.*, 498–9; B.L., Harleian MSS 1223, fol. 205.
[73] *C.J.*, 498–9; William, Lord Bagot, *Memorials of the Bagot family* (Blithfield, 1824), pp. 71–2, William Chetwind to Sir E. Bagot, n.d.; cf. Chandaman, pp. 318–19, which suggests that the yield was lower still.
[74] *C.J.*, 499; Carte MSS 221, fol. 52, Bennet to Ormonde, 6 June 1663.

and tenderness towards me, is not at all improved since the beginning of this session; indeed it is much lessened'. Answering the argument that he implied was now current, that parliament was accustomed to grant extraordinary supplies, but not to increase the permanent resources of the Crown, he pointed out that it had been willing enough to do so in 1660 and 1662, and had now admitted that the revenue did not yield as much as they had then assumed. He offered that they should inspect his expenditure as well as his income, but told them that time was growing short.[75]

When the commons returned to their house, a supply was voted, after a division on putting the question in which Temple and Hussey told against supply, and Apsley and Legge for it. But when the means of supply were discussed, it was an extraordinary grant, by the low-yielding subsidy, rather than an increase in the permanent revenue, that was resolved on.[76] On 19 June the government suffered another setback when at a division it failed to prevent the setting of debts and other expenses against the valuation of both lands and goods in the tax. On the 26th the Bill had its first reading, and passed quickly through both houses; although the lords' committee thought it more in accordance with precedent that the commissioners to assess those liable should be appointed by the king, rather than named in the Act itself, they were unwilling to make any alterations for fear of losing the whole Bill in a dispute between the houses.[77]

Several bills resulted from the inspection. Brewers from several towns had petitioned the commons against the excise farmers' oppressions, and on 4 April a subcommittee had been named to consider their appeal.[78] The Bill for the better regulation of the excise that was read after Harbord's report on 4 June probably came out of it; many of its leading members were also at the head of the committee to which the Bill was referred. Although the Bill as it was passed imposed penalties for concealment and other avoidance by brewers, it was also directed at the corruptions and oppressions of the commissioners and subcommissioners.[79] But the most dramatic revelation of the inspection had been the deficiency in the hearth tax revenue: a subcommittee was appointed on 6 April to consider how it might be amended. Many had rather it be removed altogether: 'there never was any revenue settled upon the Crown by act of parliament, that ever drew after it so loud clamours and so

[75] *Parliamentary history*, IV, 266–9.
[76] C.J., 500–1, 503; cf. National Library of Scotland, MS 3830, fol. 41, M. Fraiser to Lauderdale, 13 June 1663.
[77] C.J., 506, 511, 515, 517, 518, 519–20, 521, 523, 524; L.J., 562, 562–3, 564, 566; H.L.R.O., Committee Minutes, B.L., 18 July 1663.
[78] C.J., 460, 465; cf. H.L.R.O., Main Papers, H.L., 20 July 1663.
[79] C.J., 498, 514, 522, 527; L.J., 567, 568; C.J., 530, cf. 460; 15 Car. II, c. 11, S.R., 488–92; cf. Chandaman, pp. 43–4.

desperate discontentments as this of the hearth money have done', claimed Sir John Holland in a speech on the tax.[80] After Harbord's report from the sub-committee on 21 May, and the examination of each county's hearth tax returns by its M.P.s, on 15 July a bill was brought in and read; but after its second reading it was rejected in a division on its commitment, opposed by the 'country' M.P.s, Sir Thomas Tompkins and Brome Whorwood.[81] This Bill was perhaps similar to that introduced in 1664, for direct collection of the tax by officers of the central government (rather than by constables and sheriffs), something which it was felt would considerably improve the yield.[82] A replacement bill, probably drafted by Sir Robert Howard (who was first on the committee and carried it up to the lords), was read for the first time on 22 July. This was more limited in scope, directed mainly at obtaining a more accurate assessment of the numbers of hearths, and giving officers powers to enter households and check the accounts given by occupants. By 27 July, it had passed both houses.[83]

The session ended on the same day. As Sir Philip Warwick wrote, for a time the inspection had given the treasury some serious cause for worry:

I'll assure you the storm blew from all quarters, & malmanagement of treasure (& I confess it is to spend a great deal & have but a little though the expenses be upon necessary things for all things that are necessary are not absolutely necessary) made a great noise. And though my superior's integrity & innocency be such & his courage so great (for in this last session he hath eminently showed wisdom & courage) as he gave a defy to all reflexions, yet the noise that the king was poor & we were rich (which I assure you is as a shorn sheep) & inspections should do great things, made me almost cry to the Gods to take their honesty again.[84]

The government was lucky to come away with its four subsidies, and the inspection achieved little; the minor improvements in the rules for the collection of the excise and the hearth tax were its only concrete results.

Instead of the projects for financial reform which Southampton had proposed in 1662, after the end of the 1663 session the government resorted to a drastic attempt to cut its expenditure. In August, orders were issued for a stop on pensions and a retrenchment in household expenses, in order, as Morrice wrote to Lord Winchilsea, to prevent a repetition of the sharpness and petulancy of the 1663 inspection.[85] Retrenchment and a healthy increase in customs and other revenues during 1663 allowed Charles at least to avoid

---

[80] Bodl., Tanner MSS 239, fol. 69v. Holland's speech is difficult to date; it could belong to 1663, 1664, 1666, 1667 or even later.
[81] *C.J.*, 466, 489, 495, 524, 526.
[82] *Surrey hearth tax, 1664*, ed. C. A. F. Meekings, Surrey Record Society, XVII (1940), introduction, xxv–xxvi.
[83] *C.J.*, 528, 531, 533; *L.J.*, 570, 574; 15 Car. II, c. 13, *S.R.*, 493–5.
[84] Bodl., Tanner MSS 47, fol. 31, Sir Philip Warwick to Sir Richard Fanshaw [July 1663].
[85] P.R.O., SP 29/79/33 and 82; *Hist. MSS. Comm.*, Finch MSS, I, 274, 3 Sept. 1663.

a direct request for a further grant when parliament reassembled in March 1664.[86] He did, however, refer to his necessities: the yield of the subsidies was much smaller than had been expected. He complained too of avoidance of the customs and excise duties and the hearth tax, and particularly requested that (as in the abortive Bill of 1663) the collection of the hearth tax should be placed in the hands of his own officers.[87] On 1 April a bill to authorise this was read. The tax remained immensely controversial, and this Bill made it more so: hours were spent on it in committee of the whole house, many of them over attempts to challenge the clause allowing officers to enter and search houses and to add a proviso protecting the subject against their abuses. As a concession to these concerns, in the final Act J.P.s were entrusted with supervision of the officers' activities. In the lords the Bill was passed quickly, with few amendments.[88]

Some attempt was made, too, to improve the collection of the customs and excise; in April the commons appointed a committee to consider the Customs Act, but its purpose was rather to hear the complaints of those who considered themselves oppressed than to make any real improvements – no important officials were named to it.[89] On 29 April, however, a committee was appointed to draw up a bill against frauds and abuses in the excise, including many M.P.s with close government connections – Berkenhead, Charlton, Milward, Doyley, Sir Heneage Finch, and Sir John Shaw. No bill, however, emerged from this committee either.[90] Meanwhile the petitions of unpaid navy creditors and soldiers kept royal penury before the house.[91]

For after three years of hard bargaining in parliament, financial stability continued to elude the government. Yet the prospects for the future were far from hopeless. The mistrust of the session of 1663 seemed to have given way in 1664 to a renewal of the harmony and mutual confidence of 1661–2. Southampton's retrenchment schemes had done something to reduce expenditure, and a revival of trade was beginning to produce an expansion in the customs and excise.[92] The burden of debt remained, but if the expansion in the revenue and the reduction of expenditure continued, this would eventually be brought under control. These calculations did not completely sweep away financial anxiety: during the summer of 1664 the government continued to contemplate further additions to the revenue, including proposals

[86] Chandaman, appendix 3, p. 349, although cf. p. 351 for the concurrent increase in issues, and B.L., Loan MSS 29/180, fol. 94, Capt. J. Grant to Sir E. Harley, 19 Jan. 1664, for the treasury's continuing difficulties.

[87] *Parliamentary history*, IV, 291.

[88] C.J., 539, 541, 542, 544–5, 546, 547, 550; L.J., 604, 605, 606, 609; H.L.R.O., Committee Minutes, H.L., 5 May 1664; 16 Car. II, c. 3, S.R., 514–16.

[89] C.J., 550.   [90] C.J., 551.   [91] C.J., 547, 550, 552, 567.

[92] Chandaman, p. 209, cf. pp. 348–9.

for the replacement of the hearth tax with an extension of the excise, for the restoration of the court of augmentations, or for the much-admired stamp-duty. There were even some hints that the restoration of purveyance was planned.[93] But the hope that existed, as Professor Chandaman has observed, was shattered by the outbreak of the Second Dutch War, which had quite the opposite effect, wrecking the revival in trade and drastically reducing customs and excise revenue while massively inflating government expenditure.[94] The war was equally detrimental to the political aspects of the court's search for financial stability; it brought an increased dependence on the house of commons, greater parliamentary limitations on the government's financial freedom, and prevented any further work, for the time being at least, on the augmentation of the permanent revenue.

Parliament had itself had a share in the creation of the war. In April 1664, hoping that a declaration of support and a hint of belligerence from parliament might encourage the Dutch to make some serious concessions on a whole range of complex trade disputes, the government obtained from a carefully directed committee of the commons a resolution condemning the Dutch for their obstruction of English trade; both houses endorsed it, adding a commitment to support the king in any action he might take against them 'with their lives and fortunes'. The government had plainly caught a popular mood in a country which, though in a slow economic recovery, was still feeling in a battered and protectionist mood. Some, though, had demurred: Vaughan, Temple, Littleton, Sir Charles Hussey, and William Garraway, concerned about the possibility of war, the money which would be required to fight it, and the enormous opportunities for corruption that it could create, urged the revival of the proposal made in 1624, that the money voted for war in the Palatinate should be placed in the hands of a council of war and of treasurers appointed by parliament. The proposal shocked Brodrick, but had little other effect.[95]

For a while, parliament's vote did help to stimulate the negotiations to more serious progress. But the talks soon foundered as both sides took hostile actions against each other's commercial interests in Africa. By October, and the beginning of a new session, war was almost certain as distrust mounted on both sides. Its approach was regarded at court with very mixed feelings. Clarendon and Southampton vigorously opposed any war: war would wreck the fragile beginnings of the country's financial, economic, and political

---

[93] See P.R.O., SP 29/91/6, 96/9, 36, 109/84, 85, 86; B.L., Stowe MSS 744, fol. 81, Sir Heneage Finch to Sir E. Dering, 15 Sept. 1664.

[94] Chandaman, pp. 210–13.

[95] For the vote and the background to it, see Seaward, 'The house of commons committee of trade and the origins of the Second Anglo-Dutch War, 1664', *Historical Journal*, XXX (1987), 437–52.

recovery.[96] Yet they still believed, as earlier in the year, that the best means of avoiding it would be to show the Dutch how willing England was to fight – and as such pressure was placed on the Dutch, the whole question gradually seemed to become one as much of national honour as national interest. If parliament's resolution had failed to prevent the war, it had at least prepared the commons for requests for heavy taxes – and obliged them to accept. Fears that the Dutch were again flagging in the negotiations because of a revival of their scepticism about parliamentary open-handedness, as well as the need, if there was to be fighting, of rapid and extensive work in the naval dockyards, made a large grant seem essential.[97] At a meeting shortly before the opening of the session, Clarendon and Southampton pressed for one. The commons, they argued, should be asked for at least £2.5 million while it remained in its current generous and belligerent mood: later on in the war its temper might change. Bennet and Coventry, Clarendon claimed, disagreed, anxious not to invite opposition with so enormous a request; but a letter of Coventry to Bennet on the day the session began, makes it clear that he had no part in the decision, and suggests that he was rather of Clarendon's mind: 'I dare not oppose any resolutions taken by such an assembly as that which you tell me concluded of the terms to be demanded, nor do I think the sum greater than the war will require.' He did, though, advise against a decision to tell parliament that £800,000 had already been spent on naval preparations. The true sum was about £504,000 and probably less, and if parliament reached that conclusion itself, the lie would diminish for the future the government's credibility.[98]

The figure of £800,000 had been arrived at in several days of discussions between Warwick, Carteret, and Pepys, and the latter admitted that they had taken some pains to inflate the amount already spent as much as possible.[99] But Coventry's letter was sent too late to prevent the sum being mentioned in the king's speech on 24 October, when Charles requested the commons to use 'all possible expedition, that our friends and our enemies may see that I am possessed of your heads and that we move with one soul'. Charles and Clarendon both referred to the vote of April in the requests for supply that they each made at the opening of the session.[100] Yet more than this was needed to persuade the commons to agree to so large a sum as £2.5 million. Clarendon resorted to subterfuge; he asked three Norfolk gentlemen,

[96] Carte MSS 215, fol. 29v–30, Brodrick to Ormonde, 23 April 1664; for the 1624 scheme, see S. R. Gardiner, *History of England from the accession of James I to the outbreak of the Civil War*, 10 vols. (London, 1883–4), V, 192–3.

[97] Clarendon, *Life*, II, 7–8; for the revival of Dutch scepticism of parliamentary generosity, see Lister, *Clarendon*, III, 339, Downing to Clarendon, 2 Sept. 1664.

[98] Clarendon, *Life*, II, 60–4; P.R.O., SP 29/105/76.

[99] Pepys, *Diary*, V, 327–9.   [100] *Parliamentary history*, IV, 296–302.

respected M.P.s with no known affiliations to the court, if they would propose it. At length one, Sir Robert Paston, agreed, and the other two (whom Clarendon does not name) consented to support it.[101] On 25 November supply was debated in the commons, after the house had been prepared with votes of thanks to the king for his speech of the day before and to the City for their readiness to lend to the government. In the main business of supply, Paston's motion for a grant of £2.5 million was greeted with a rather shocked silence, followed by a debate which lasted from ten in the morning to four at night. Although gradually speakers accepted the scale of the grant required, many preferred the method of taxation to be agreed before the amount was specified, concerned that another assessment would be imposed (in contradiction of the declaration in the 1661 Act). But the suggestion, supported by (amongst others) Sir Edmund Walpole and Sir John Goodrick, was ultimately rejected, although Vaughan, Temple, and Garraway (who had opposed the vote of 21 April) did obtain a guarantee of the house's freedom to decide how the tax should be raised. The preliminaries completed, Vaughan attacked the war and proposed that a mere £500,000 should be given. A motion for £1.5 million, backed by the other Norfolk and Suffolk M.P.s, North, Holland, and Walpole, received more support, but in a division on whether to put the question on Paston's original motion, the court was victorious, by 172 votes to 102.[102] The motion itself was then accepted *nemine contradicente*. In the division, the tellers for the court had been Clifford and Sir Edmund Poley: Poley had dined the previous day with several officials, Warwick, Thomas Povey, Thomas Chicheley, and Pepys – perhaps being briefed for the debate on the 25th.[103]

Naturally, the court was delighted;[104] but it remained to be settled how to levy the tax. M.P.s – particularly those who had been horrified by the sum demanded – were anxious that the burden of so large a tax should be made as light as possible: and they pressed, vigorously, that it should be levied by subsidy, rather than by assessment. Holland urged the virtues of the subsidy. It was, he said, the 'good old English parliamentary way of levying the supplies of the Crown', and he reminded M.P.s of their commitment to end assessment taxation.[105] The government's dislike of the subsidy had, however, been confirmed by the low yield of the 1663 tax, and over the next week

[101] Clarendon, *Life*, II, 64–5; Clarendon MSS 83, fol. 422, Townshend to Clarendon, 23 July [1665]; for other government preparations for this debate, see Pepys, *Diary*, V, 330, and P.R.O., SP 29/105/82, William Coventry to Bennet, 25 Nov. 1664.
[102] B.L., Add. MSS 32094, fols. 24–6v, Clifford to William Coventry, 25 Nov. 1664; Coventry MSS vol. 44, fols. 38, 40, Bennet and Morrice to H. Coventry, 25 Nov. 1664; for Paston's speech, see Add. MSS 36988, fol. 88; Bodl., Tanner MSS 239, fols. 33–4v; *C.J.*, 568.
[103] *C.J.*, 568; Pepys, *Diary*, V, 329–30.
[104] P.R.O., SP 29/105/92, Sir W. Coventry to Bennet, 26 Nov. 1664.
[105] Bodl., Tanner MSS 239, fols. 36v–7v.

the Crown fought hard for the assessment in committee of the whole house, obtaining resolutions on the nature of the tax which were scarcely consonant with a subsidy.[106] The house's attachment to the subsidy remained strong, although members were willing to admit that the system required an overhaul: on 28 November it resolved to raise the money by a 'regulated subsidiary way, reducing the same to a certainty in all counties, so as no person for his real or personal estate be exempted'. But without much hope of producing a new, revised, rate on which to base the subsidy and thus to meet the government's objections to it, the house fell back on the government's own preference. It did, however, resolve to eliminate some of the much-resented inequities in the distribution of the 1661 assessment by calculating the proportion of the tax to be set on each county by taking the average of the sums set in that tax, the 1641 £400,000 subsidy, and the much admired 1639 ship money rate. Despite this and a few other differences from the 1661 tax, and the title of 'Royal Aid', the levy was in effect an assessment, setting a particular sum on each county.[107] Its acceptance by the commons was made easier by an offer by the court to remit £40,000 from the total to be divided among those counties which believed themselves over-rated. William Coventry thought that without this offer, the final resolution on the method of raising the tax could never have been achieved – 'by relinquishing a small sum the whole is settled which I think will be both profitable & of reputation, the delay being contrary to both'.[108] After the abatement had been divided among the counties the Supply Bill could be drawn up, and it received its first reading on 17 December.[109]

Before the session began, Warwick had mentioned the possibility that the tax should be continued only as long as the war lasted.[110] There was some discussion on this subject in government circles: when William Coventry wrote to the earl of Falmouth on 10 December in reply to the question 'how much money the king might save out of the supply now given for the Dutch War', he argued that if it ever became known that money voted for hostilities had been diverted for other purposes, M.P.s would be reluctant to make further grants; indeed, he claimed, 'I believe the king's servants have not been without fear that the parliament would have attempted the management of the war, or at least the money upon this last occasion' – perhaps a reference to the motion of the last session for parliamentary treasurers and a council of

[106] Coventry MSS vol. 44, fols. 46, 48, Bennet and Morrice to H. Coventry, 2 Dec. 1664.

[107] *C.J.*, 569, 570, 573, 574, 575, 577; Bodl., Tanner MSS 239, fols. 35–6; *Calendar of treasury books*, ed. W. A. Shaw (London, 1904–), I, 715, Southampton and Ashley to Henry Brabant, 25 Jan. 1666; see the papers in which the new rate was worked out, Add. MSS 35865, fols. 238–46.

[108] *C.J.*, 577, 578, 579; Carte MSS 75, fol. 282v, W. Coventry to Sandwich, 14 Dec. 1664.

[109] *C.J.*, 580.   [110] Pepys, *Diary*, V, 328.

war.[111] There is no evidence that anything as much as this was demanded in the 1664–5 session; yet there is evidence, in a speech of Sir John Holland against it, of a proposed proviso that if a peace was concluded within the first year of the tax, the last year of it would be remitted.[112] The proviso seems not even to have been voted on: but it was not the only attempt to limit the government's freedom to dispose of the supply. An addition which was made to the preamble of the Bill in the committee of the whole house on 12 January smacked of appropriation – the tax was 'to be applied for the righting of your Majesty, and your Majesty's subjects, against the Dutch' – but the words 'to be applied' were subsequently removed in the house itself.[113] Southampton, despite his support for an appropriation scheme in 1663, was now anxious to avoid anything of the sort. If war, as he hoped, did not result from the current tension, then the present supply could be used to pay off some of the government's pressing debts and anticipations: in March he urged that as much of it as possible might be considered as repayment of the £800,000 the government was supposed to have already laid out in preparations, and used to pay off anticipations of the revenue, instead of being devoted directly to the war.[114]

Much of the rest of the session was spent in discussing the details of the Bill, and it did not finally pass both houses until 9 February.[115] The huge effort which had been required to get it accepted, and the ability of M.P.s to stomach only a certain amount of supply at a time, precluded the repetition of the earlier efforts to augment the permanent revenue. In any case, it was of more immediate importance to ensure that the City could cope with the enormous loans that would be required of it during the coming war: its resources had already been strained by the two loans requested of it in the summer and autumn of 1664, of, altogether, £200,000; the second loan came in slowly and was undersubscribed.[116] The government tried, as it had in 1662, to improve its credit with a bill 'for permitting persons that shall lend money for supply of his Majesty's occasions, to take above six pounds per cent interest', probably on the lines of the 1662 Bill. The treasurer of the navy, Sir George

---

[111] B.L., Add.MSS 32094, fol. 28; cf. Carte MSS 215, fols. 29v–30, Sir A. Brodrick to Ormonde, 23 April 1664.

[112] Bodl., Tanner MSS 239, fols. 39–40. Although a proposal similar to this was rumoured, at least in the 1666–7 session, the reference to the 'Royal Aid' must mean that Holland is speaking to the 1665 Bill. (See below, p. 292, for the 1666 proposal.)

[113] C.J., 581.

[114] B.L., Harleian MSS 1223, fol. 235.

[115] C.J., 581–2, 583, 584, 585, 586, 586–7, 587–8, 589–90, 590, 591–2, 592–3, 594; L.J., 651, 652, 653; B.L., Harleian MSS 7001, fol. 256 [Sir Justinian Isham] to ?, 17 Jan. 166[5].

[116] Chivers, 'The City of London and the state', pp. 267–73.

Carteret, who had a personal as well as an official interest in government borrowing, was the first to be nominated to the committee on 20 February.[117] But the Bill was defeated in a division after Sir Job Charlton's report on the 22nd, in which one of the earliest members of Bennet's group, Sir Winston Churchill, told against it. Again, the concern that high interest rates would ruin the prices of land and English goods was enough to prevent government attempts to regularise their payments of 10 per cent to the bankers, and so opened the way to Downing's proposals of the next session.[118]

By the end of the 1664–5 session it was evident that war could not be avoided, and in its closing days, on 22 February 1665, came the official declaration. The war's first large-scale action seemed to confirm the hopes of the most belligerent: in the summer the news of York's success over the Dutch at Lowestoft was received with rejoicing, though the subsequent fiasco of the attack on Bergen harbour restored a sense of proportion. But there were much greater difficulties ahead: the French, who had made great efforts to avoid having to honour their treaty obligations to the Dutch and stay out of the war, seemed increasingly likely to be forced into it; the plague which had broken out in London in the early summer quickly became a serious epidemic, and began severely to affect the nation's trade. The navy devoured money, and the revenue was anticipated far ahead.[119] The court needed new taxes, but it also needed better credit; and it was difficult to see, with the failure in the previous session of the Bill on government loans, how it might be raised. The City was already having difficulty in coping with the government's demands. At the beginning of the new session on 10 October 1665 – in Oxford, rather than Westminster because of the plague – both the king and the chancellor appealed for more supply.[120] In the following debate low attendance, coupled with anger against the Dutch and particularly the French (fomented especially by the speeches of Downing and Sir Robert Howard), helped to bring rapid agreement, although Sir Richard Temple made another attempt to force the abandonment of the assessment. In a remarkably short time, a tax of £1.25 million by a continuation of the 1664 assessment was settled, the motion being made probably by James Scudamore, a country gentleman with few political connections, perhaps put up to making the

---

[117] *C.J.*, 604, 606; for Carteret's importance in raising loans for the navy on his own credit, see Roseveare, 'The advancement of the king's credit', p. 38.

[118] *C.J.*, 606; cf. Downing's letter to Arlington, bitterly opposing the Bill, P.R.O., SP 84/174, fols. 114–15.

[119] Pepys, *Diary*, VI, 72, 75, 78; *Calendar of treasury books*, I, 680; cf. Coventry MSS, vol. 96, fol. 108, officers of the navy to the duke of York.

[120] *Parliamentary history*, IV, 317–27.

proposal as Paston had been in 1664.[121] On the 13th the solicitor general brought in the Bill and on the 14th it was committed.[122]

It was at this point that Sir George Downing introduced several provisos to the Bill, reflected in the instructions to the committee 'to ease his Majesty in the payment of interest; & to enable him to take up money to supply his occasions, upon security of the Bill'.[123] Downing had for long been severely critical of the way government credit was managed, and now proposed to end the confusion of anticipations of the incoming revenue, which had made it impossible to produce accurate accounts and prevented a fully reliable basis for government borrowing. In its place, he suggested a system in which advances of money and goods could be secured on the incoming revenue by a commitment to repay them in the order in which the debts were incurred. Downing's proposals took up paragraphs V to X of the Bill as it was engrossed and finally passed. They created a procedure by which lenders of money and suppliers of goods could be registered in the order in which they had made their payments or deliveries, and repaid, as the money came in, in the same order. Depositors of money were to be paid 6 per cent interest half yearly. The treasury orders given as receipts for the money or goods were to be negotiable, and the money which was to come in by the Act was to be directed exclusively to the satisfaction of the registered creditors – in effect, all the money was to be appropriated to the war. All the money would go through the exchequer, making accounting simpler; and, it was hoped, the certainty of repayment might encourage smaller investors and so reduce the increasingly strong grip over Crown finances held by a few major bankers – most notably Edward Backwell.[124]

Downing's plan attracted the king and several others, particularly Arlington and Sir William Coventry, but it horrified Clarendon and Southampton – both of whom had been kept ignorant of the proposals until they were revealed in parliament. The treasury disliked it for several reasons: one, no doubt, was pique at Downing's direct appeal to the king without consulting it; but more important, probably, was the prospect of the loss of the treasury's discretion over payments, and the damage it would do to its rather cosy relationship with the main City financiers. Southampton disliked antici-

---

[121] Carte MSS 34, fol. 429, Brodrick to Ormonde, 12 Oct. 1665, fol. 431, Southwell to Ormonde, 12 Oct. 1665; B.L., Add. MSS, 11043, fol. 115, ? to Sir James Scudamore, 18 Oct. 1665; Longleat House, Coventry MSS vol. 44, fol. 246, Morrice to Henry Coventry, 12 Oct. [1665]; for Scudamore, see P.R.O., SP 29/159/111, Scudamore to James Hickes, 25 June 1666, which may indicate his acknowledgement of Williamson's patronage.
[122] C.J., 615, 616.
[123] C.J., 616.
[124] Roseveare, 'The advancement of the king's credit', pp. 18–22; 17 Car.II, c. 1, S.R., 570–4, paras. V–X; Chivers, 'The City of London and the state', chs. 8 and 9; for Downing's animus against the bankers, see Clarendon, *Life*, II, 215, 229.

pations and assignments as much as Downing, and had tried in 1663 to control them and bring the receipts and payments of the exchequer into some order. Yet Downing's proposals went further, instituting a rigid system which would remove much of the treasury's freedom to dispose of its incoming revenues, and might prevent Southampton from using the profits of the new taxes to pay back old debts. It was just this, as Lord Ashley pointed out in one of several meetings with the king and his foremost advisers over the proposals, that threatened to wreck the treasury's relationship with its bankers. The bankers had already loaned much on the credit of this Act before Downing had introduced his provisos, and if the tax was to be appropriated to repayment only of future loans, they would be dangerously exposed, without a certain means of getting their money back. The probable result might be a run on their banks, their ruin, and the closure of the main channel of government borrowing.[125]

Despite the arguments of Clarendon, Southampton, and Finch, the king continued to be convinced by Downing's belief that the scheme would encourage loans 'by making the payment with interest so certain and fixed, that there could be [no] security in the kingdom like it', and would ultimately make the exchequer into the greatest bank in Europe; Downing's critics were silenced, and after its third reading, the Bill passed up to the lords with the provisos.[126] Ashley's more effective arguments against the scheme, presented at a second meeting at Clarendon's lodgings in the presence of the king and its proponents and opponents, made more impression. However, it was too late to make substantial alterations to the Bill, now passing through the lords, without jeopardising its passage altogether, and on 23 October it passed unamended. The subsequent history of the war showed that Downing was right in wanting to extend the credit facilities at the government's disposal. Taxes were collected over a long period: the government, especially in wartime, needed funds immediately. The gap was filled by loans from the City; but the City's resources were quite rapidly exhausted, particularly when investors became concerned about the ability of taxation to cover their loans. England's defeat and Dutch victory in 1667 was due less to the inadequacy of parliamentary supply, than to the superiority of the Dutch financial system, which Downing wanted to emulate: but Downing's reforms, produced too hastily and motivated to some extent by a dislike of the banking élite, were to add (at least in the short term) to the problem.[127]

One other supply bill was passed this session. The day after the Assessment Bill was passed by the lords, Sir John Goodrick moved for a grant to the duke of York, the victor of Lowestoft, of one month's assessment of £125,000.

---

[125] Clarendon, *Life*, II, 216–30.   [126] *C.J.*, 616–17, 617–18, 618–19, 619.
[127] Clarendon, *Life*, II, 223–30; *L.J.*, 693, 693–4; see also below, pp. 239–41, 303–4.

Although there was little enthusiasm for the tax, there were few who would openly oppose it, and Finch was ordered to draft it.[128] Goodrick was a Yorkshireman – perhaps one of those charmed by James when he had stayed at York during the summer – and he was seconded by a few other northern members. It was, however, Sir Edward Thurland, James's solicitor general, who was the chairman of the committee of the whole house to which the Bill was referred on 26 October.[129] It passed quickly through both houses, and ultimately most of the tax was devoted to the war, rather than to James himself.[130]

Both supply bills had passed with little difficulty except that which the government, by its division over Downing's provisos, had caused itself. The war's popularity, and the popularity, in particular, of war against the French; the thinness of a parliament summoned to a crowded Oxford which afforded little accommodation; and the absence from the session of John Vaughan, all contributed to greater than usual harmony over supply.[131] But the concerns of 1663, the suspicion of government corruption, had not gone away. If anything, they were increased as the opportunities for corruption had expanded, with the vast sums of money passing through the hands of ministers, officials, and naval contractors for the purposes of the war. George Sitwell in May 1665 reported his county's Royal Aid commissioners' jaundiced belief that the interest on any cash advances on the credit of the act would find its way into the purses of the revenue officers.[132] In 1664 the house had rejected the suggestion that the financing of the war should be handled by parliamentary treasurers; but in the 1665 session a more moderate proposal was accepted with ease. It was probably Temple who proposed on the last day of the session that the king should be requested to order his officers of the navy, ordnance, and stores to prepare an account of their disbursements for presentation to the commons in the next session. The house agreed, and Temple and Whorwood were entrusted with the message.[133]

So far, such suspicions had not prevented the extraordinary open-handedness of a loyal and belligerent commons. But signs of future problems already existed in that open distrust of government corruption, and in a general concern that the weight of taxation would force the country further

---

[128] *C.J.*, 621; C. Robbins, 'The Oxford session of the Long Parliament of Charles II, 9–31 October 1665', *Bull. Inst. Hist. Res.*, XXI (1946–8), 218, the 'Minnesota fragment'; Carte MSS 34, fol. 452, Southwell to Ormonde, 24 Oct. 1665.
[129] *C.J.*, 621; Browning, *Danby*, III, 13, Sir Thomas to Lady Osborne, 25 Oct. 1665.
[130] *L.J.*, 696; Chandaman, p. 211.
[131] For Vaughan's absense, see above, p. 48 and n. 63.
[132] Sitwell (ed.), *Letters of the Sitwells and Sacheverells*, I, 62, George Sitwell to Capt. Mazine, 13 May 1665.
[133] *C.J.*, 623.

into recession. Holland had spoken desperately against the scale of the wartime grants:

for what from the great scarcity of money in all places, what from the general declination of the inland trade, what from the low and mean prices of all our nation's commodities especially of wool and worn, the staple commodities of the kingdom, and the chief support of those that must bear the greatest part of the burthen, the land-lord and tenant, and what from a general infection that have almost overspread the whole nation by the corruption of the late times, and the vanity of these, of pride and idleness in the meaner sort of people, and of the excessive expense and liberality (to give it the best term I can) in the better, poverty is breaking in upon us, as an armed man against whom there is no resistance.[134]

In his own speech on the £2.5 million proposal, Finch had dismissed all such fears as 'tragical complaints of the miseries of their counties',[135] and it is no doubt true that they were standard features of all supply debates; but by 1665 M.P.s had much reason for their concern. The war, the plague, and a new agricultural crisis were already beginning to obliterate the few signs of a fragile economic recovery; further taxation would inevitably destroy them entirely. M.P.s found themselves unhappily divided, as ever, between the demands of the court and the cries of the country. M.P.s were like – and often themselves were – those J.P.s who were pressed on the one hand by the poor to shield them from the hearth tax, and on the other by a government which if they succumbed would brand them as 'obstructors of the king's revenue, and such as seek popularity with their neighbours'.[136] Arguments such as that mentioned in 1661 by Temple and Henry North – that the commons were not accustomed to augment the permanent revenue, or that in doing so they were effectively consigning themselves to impotence and decay – were not, at the moment, influential; but under the pressure of an economic crisis a larger group of M.P.s, not just the little knot of members around Vaughan, Temple, and Littleton, might become more truculent.[137]

The distress of a country subjected to years of burdensome taxation and experiencing difficulties in its international trade and its agriculture had already limited the government's success in obtaining a larger permanent revenue. If the government had not always pressed as hard as it might have done for a settlement, it was not because of its reluctance, but rather because of its recognition of and respect for M.P.s' concerns. The administration headed by Clarendon was careful to avoid alienating them: it refrained, whenever possible, from direct appeals for money; when large demands were essential, it took pains that it should not seem to be imposing them, seeking

[134] Bodl., Tanner MSS 239, fol. 33v. I have added some punctuation in this passage for the sake of comprehension.
[135] Leicester Record Office, Finch MSS, Box 4965, P.P. 15.
[136] Bodl., Tanner MSS 239, fol. 69v. [137] See below, pp. 296–301.

to have them proposed by members without court affiliations, like Sir Courtney Pole, Paston, and Scudamore, or (as in 1662) allowing the house to come to its own decisions, rather than demand a particular solution. The government was cautious rather than indecisive or reluctant in its dealings concerning the revenue; a firmer approach might have produced quicker solutions, but not necessarily (from the court's point of view) any better ones.

Financial stability, however, had still not been achieved: the revelation of the insufficiency of the hearth tax in 1662 had not led to its augmentation or its replacement, and the government was still bedevilled by the annual excess of its expenditure over its income. Yet that situation need not have been permanent. With an economic recovery and retrenchment, the existing revenue might have expanded and the debt reduced; with time, patience, and some action against corruption, parliament's reluctance to accept further ordinary taxes could have been overcome. It was the war that cleared away any such expectations. The government was forced to concentrate on obtaining extraordinary grants, not increases in ordinary taxes. As the war went on, other revenues declined with trade; and as the distress of the country and its contrast with the luxury and corruption of the court became ever more starkly apparent, M.P.s became ever less willing to consider increases. The advent of war in 1665 had ended for some time the Crown's opportunity to obtain financial solvency.

6

Government

The government's financial health formed the basis of its survival and its stability; but the most profound issues concerning the nature of the State under the restored monarchy were to be raised over legislation which affected the constitution and the security of the nation. Such legislation involved questions of political theory and the assessment of the past, the legacy of the Civil War, and the Restoration's own legacy to posterity. Two closely linked questions dominated the constitutional politics of the early 1660s: first, what was to be the constitutional nature of the State? In 1641–2 legislation had been passed, with royal assent, which had drastically reduced the power of the royal prerogative, and had, in the Triennial Act, made parliament an unavoidable and permanent feature in the political landscape: did it remain, now, as popular as it had undoubtedly been then? Secondly, how far might local autonomy and individual rights be sacrificed to ensure the absolute security of a frightened government? How far could M.P.s be brought to accept a greater centralisation as the price for removing the danger of rebellion and anarchy?

On neither subject could the government be said to have been in complete unanimity. Several contemporaries pointed out that both Clarendon and Southampton had participated in the creation of the 1641–2 legislation, and hinted that they were reluctant, now, to see it too easily overturned. Some of the government's hesitancy on the subject, and the half-heartedness of some of the measures it introduced, may indicate an unwillingness to extend the bounds of royal power much further than the limits then established. But Clarendon himself in writing his *History* in 1646 had plainly disavowed some of the laws passed five years before: the Triennial Act contained many clauses 'derogatory to majesty and letting the reins too close to the people'; the Act for removing the court of high commission 'comprehended much more than was generally intended', and the court itself – as long as it was 'exercised with moderation' – was 'an excellent means to vindicate and preserve the dignity and peace of the Church'; the Act for removing star chamber had been 'an act very popular', but the court itself 'whilst it was gravely and moderately

131

governed was an excellent expedient to preserve the dignity of the king, the honour of the council, and peace and security of the kingdom' – its removal was 'not then more politic than the reviving it may be thought hereafter, when the present distempers shall be expired'.[1] Clarendon was unlikely to be squeamish in restoring at least regulated versions of these prerogatives. The slow pace of reconstruction was indeed the effect not of unwillingness, but of caution: a reluctance to provoke alarm, or allegations that the government was aiming to restore institutions which could ride roughshod over English laws and liberties. The prerogative had to be fully restored – but reassuringly.

But however much the government wanted to secure some re-examination of this legislation, Clarendon made it plain that he, at least, did not share the feeling of some royalists that all those acts were invalidated because of the way they had been passed. On 13 May 1661 a bill for the repeal of the 1641 attainder of the earl of Strafford was introduced into the lords, perhaps by the government to test parliamentary opinion on repeal, or perhaps by the ultra-royalists who strongly backed it during its passage. The long, complicated, and passionate debate seems, from the discussions and the amendments made in committee, to have been concerned chiefly with two points: the recital of the circumstances of the Act's passage, and whether it should be made 'null and void', or simply repealed. These two issues were closely related. In the original draft of the Bill it was claimed that the conditions under which the Act had been passed – the pressure of the London mob and intimidatory tactics of the 'turbulent party' – had made it *ipso facto* null and void. According-ing to Clarendon, one of the arguments that had been put forward to per-suade Charles I to assent to the Bill to remove the bishops from the house of lords had been that an Act passed under the threat of violence was invalid, and the king's confirmation did nothing to validate it: it was null and void. In advancing the same claim now, the authors of the Bill – perhaps ultra-royalists like the earls of Dorset and Northampton,[2] both at various times chairmen of the committee on the Bill – may have intended to open a way to the simple removal of all the limitations placed on the Crown in 1641–2, without the need for a formal repeal. But Clarendon disavowed any such course: statute could not be voided simply in this way. If ever it was possible for the king so easily to overturn an act of parliament, then 'the making and declaring law will be of equal facility, though, it may be, not of equal justice': many men, he wrote, 'who abhorred the thing when it was done for the manner of doing it, will be of the civilian's opinion, *fieri non debuit, factum*

[1] Clarendon, *History*, I, 371–8.
[2] Both men, as M.P.s, had voted against Strafford's attainder: see *G.E.C.*; cf. Dorset's argu-ment on the Bill for restoring the bishops to the house of lords, Kent Archives Office, U269/O36, and see below, p. 165.

valet, and never consent to the altering of that which they would never have consented to the establishing'.[3] Enough peers shared Clarendon's opinion eventually to remove the phrase 'null and void' and make the Bill merely 'reverse' the Act; but it was not until 17 February that the repeal finally passed the lords.[4]

The debates on the Bill in January prompted the examination of the other Acts. After the second report of the committee on the Bill, on 22 January 1662, the house voted to debate these as well. Two days later it agreed to repeal the Triennial Act, and a committee was appointed to consider the repeal of the others. This included many ministers – Southampton, Robartes, Ormonde, Manchester, Albemarle, Anglesey, Ashley, Clarendon's ally Portland, and Prince Rupert – and the two rival claimants to the presidency of a restored council of the North, Strafford and Buckingham.[5] On the 28th the committee met in earnest for the first time. The confusion of the record of their meeting suggests a heated debate, which settled little more than had already been decided in the house on the 22nd. When it met again, however, there was further progress on the Triennial Act: it was to be replaced by a measure which would reiterate the vague commitment of an old statute of Edward III to meet parliament once in every three years (although the statute had in fact specified annual parliaments).[6]

On 6 February the committee went on to discuss the re-establishment of a court similar to star chamber. Lord Mohun, a rather equivocal and unenthusiastic royalist during the war, offered some guidelines for a new court based closely on the criticisms made against the old in 1641: its judges would be on oath; it would determine no titles to land; it was to be restricted to the causes specified in the 1487 Star Chamber Act, and it might impose no corporal punishment other than imprisonment, and only limited fines.[7] After the committee had unsuccessfully appealed to the house for more precise directions, Lord Chief Justice Bridgman on 1 March presented it with some guidelines of his own for a revival of the court. These were similar to

---

[3] Clarendon, *History*, I, 569–70.
[4] *L.J.*, 252, 254, 261, 368, 381, 387; H.L.R.O., Committee Minutes, H.L., 16, 27, 30 May, 8 June 1661, 4 Feb. 1662; for its passage in the commons, see *C.J.*, 368, 373, 374. Compare the two versions of the Bill in H.L.R.O., Main Papers, H.L., 13 May 1661, with the Act as passed (14 Car. II, c. 29, *S.R.*, 424); for the word 'repeal' see H.L.R.O., Committee Minutes, H.L., 1 Feb. 1662; cf. H.L.R.O., Braye MSS, vol. 53, no. 56, notes of the debate on 22 Jan. 1662.
[5] *L.J.*, 368, 369, 369–70.
[6] H.L.R.O., Committee Minutes, H.L., 27, 28 Jan., 1 Feb. 1662; cf. H.L.R.O., Braye MSS, vol. 53, no. 56, notes of the debates on 23 and 24 Jan.
[7] H.L.R.O., Committee Minutes, H.L., 6 Feb. 1662; compare Mohun's limitations of the court's competence and powers with Clarendon, *History*, I, 374–5, and the 1641 Act itself, S. R. Gardiner, *The constitutional documents of the puritan revolution 1628–1660* (Oxford, 1889), pp. 107–8.

Mohun's, but with some further limitations. The committee added a few more details. But all this work came to nothing: no more was heard of the Bill and there is no record of another meeting of the committee.[8] During the next session, in 1663, the house returned to the subject: on 19 March the lords appointed a committee to prepare a bill for repealing the acts of the Long Parliament. Most of those on the 1662 committee (except those now in Ireland or dead) were appointed to this one, and the new committee began where the old had left off. By 8 April it had accepted most of a draft bill for the re-establishment of star chamber along the lines laid down by Bridgman in 1662. Yet again, it never emerged from the committee.[9] This failure to bring any measure forward from the committee must reflect a lack of official enthusiasm, even if the proposals of Bridgman – a central figure in the government's parliamentary management – presumably came from the court. Possibly, in the end, the government was reluctant to have a court with wider powers, but a court with such limited powers was scarcely worth having.

The Act abolishing star chamber had also removed star chamber jurisdiction from the marcher, northern, duchy, and county palatine courts, and had prohibited the establishment of courts with a similar jurisdiction in any place in the kingdom.[10] Clarendon himself had been closely involved in the attack on the courts' abuses. But while star chamber had aroused little public enthusiasm, the regional courts were a different matter; petitions flooded in from both provinces complaining of the great costs of travelling to London for litigation – a local court could provide more speedy and inexpensive justice.[11] In January and February 1661 the government devoted much time to the problem. On 18 January, according to the petitions from Yorkshire read in the lords in July 1661, it was resolved in the privy council that in the case of the northern council a court should be erected by parliamentary statute.[12] At about the same time, however, a decision was taken to establish the Welsh court with only common-law jurisdiction (and thus not infringing the 1641 Act) without reference to parliament.[13]

Why the two should have been treated differently is uncertain. The North may have been considered to require a stronger court; or possibly the government was concerned about possible opposition in parliament to the

[8] *L.J.*, 382; H.L.R.O., Committee Minutes, H.L., 15 Feb., 1 March 1662.
[9] *L.J.*, 494, 499, cf. 369–70; H.L.R.O., Committee Minutes, H.L., 30 March 1662, 7, 8 April 1663.
[10] 17 Car. I, c. 10, para. II, *S.R.*, 111.
[11] P.R.O., SP 29/1/151, 37/69, 39/39–47: 30/24/4/124/1, 2 and 3; *L.J.*, 293–4.
[12] *L.J.*, 293–4.
[13] P.R.O., SP 29/41/31. These instructions to the lord president and the court were 'examined' by the attorney general on 11 February 1661. Carbery was already referred to as 'lord president' in February, PC 2/55, fol. 74; see C. A. J. Skeel, *The council in the marches of Wales* (London, 1904), pp. 166–71.

restoration of the Welsh council's jurisdiction in the marcher counties from the M.P.s and gentry of those counties, whose assault on the court in 1641 had helped to secure its downfall.[14] There was less formal opposition to a council in the North, and much pressure for it from local men and one court grandee in particular, the duke of Buckingham, who was furiously agitating for the post of president.[15] The main obstacle to the re-establishment of the northern court may indeed have been rivalry among northern lords for its presidency, potentially a position of enormous power. In December 1661 Charles scribbled a note to Clarendon about 'the great alarm amongst the Yorkshire gentlemen' at a rumour that the earl of Strafford was to be made president. Clarendon scribbled back 'I believe you can hardly choose any body, with whom the rest would be pleased, there be three or four would have it for themselves, and sure he is as fit as any of them'.[16]

The campaign to restore the court opened on 1 July, when two petitions from the northern nobility, gentry, and freeholders, which had been read and approved in council on 7 June were presented in the house of lords by the earl of Carlisle, the only privy councillor among the petitioners. A committee was appointed, including the dukes of York and Buckingham, and the earl of Strafford (the last two already vying for the presidency of the court).[17] A fortnight later the earl of Portland reported their recommendation for restoration by a bill to be brought in after the summer adjournment.[18] In fact, a bill was brought in much sooner – a short measure of only three sheets was read for the first, and only time on 19 July, which merely re-enacted the court 'as formerly, with such power, restrictions, and limitations as shall be directed by the king's most excellent Majesty with the consent and advice of the lords and commons, now in parliament assembled'.[19] Why this bill was presented, or by whom, is unknown: it may have been a move by those pressing for the re-establishment of the court to obtain a firmer guarantee that the question would receive further consideration.

---

[14] Copies of these petitions are at B.L., Add. MSS 11053, fol. 180, and Loan 29/88 Misc. 75; for the appearances of the petitioners at the council, see P.R.O., PC 2/55, fols. 74, 150, 2/56, fol. 150v. John Vaughan was one of the signatories of the petition from M.P.s.

[15] P.R.O., PRO 31/3/110, D'Estrades to Louis XIV, 28 Jan./6 Feb. 1662, cf. Carte MSS 49, fol. 300, Ormonde to Buckingham, 10 April 1665; for Buckingham's leadership of Yorkshire affairs, see P.R.O., SP 29/26/72.

[16] W. D. Macray (ed.), *Notes which passed at meetings of the privy council between Charles II and the earl of Clarendon*, Publications of the Roxburghe Club (London, 1896), p. 49.

[17] L.J., 293–4; H.L.R.O., Main Papers, H.L., 1 July 1661; for Strafford's ambitions to become President, see Carte MSS 33, fol. 716, Strafford to Ormonde, 26 Nov. 1664; but see Nottingham Record Office, Savile of Rufford MSS, DD SR 221/96/29, R. Turner to Sir George Savile, 23 Nov. 1661, for the current assumption that Buckingham would be president.

[18] H.L.R.O., Committee Minutes, H.L., 2, 3 July 1661; L.J., 310.

[19] L.J., 314; H.L.R.O., Main Papers, H.L., 19 July 1661.

The proper Bill, brought in on 18 January 1662, was a much more comprehensive measure. The king was empowered to issue out commissions for the court, and to appoint its lord president and assistants. These were to have extensive powers to investigate and to try all cases: it was to be a court of record, and to have both equity and common law jurisdiction.[20] On the 25th it was read again. In the following debate the earl of Northumberland, the northern magnate and ex-parliamentarian, argued vigorously against it, claiming that it was against the royal interest and that only a few northern justices were pressing it for their own advantage. Buckingham angrily refuted the charge, saying that there was a general desire for the court, and that he had noticed only a few individuals – those who had fought against the king, he hinted – to oppose it. The remark provoked a general turmoil, Northumberland believing that it had been directed at himself, and the subsequent quarrel between them divided the house: all the presbyterians, wrote the French ambassador, supported Northumberland, all the royalists supported the duke.[21]

The uproar of 25 January apparently prevented any further proceeding on the Bill in this session, but it did not kill the issue entirely. On 18 or 19 May 1663, leave was sought in the commons to bring in a bill for settling the court, which 'gave much debate among the Yorkshire gentlemen'.[22] Sir John Holland strongly approved of the court – he was convinced that it would bring justice more easily to the northern counties – although he also noticed the vehemence of some M.P.s from the North against it.[23] The Yorkshire plot in late 1663 gave fresh cogency to the arguments for a council, and among the several petitions sent in 1664 appealing for its establishment was one from northern deputy lieutenants.[24] According to a letter of Sir George Fletcher, the proposal was rejected this time because the king was against it.[25] In autumn 1664, however, there were new rumours. In September, Lord Mansfield believed that Buckingham had just been made president, and in November, Strafford wrote to Ormonde, bitterly complaining that although he, Clarendon, and Southampton had over two years ago promised him the presidency, yet now it appeared that it would go to 'one that is of late related

[20] *L.J.*, 366–7; H.L.R.O., Main Papers, H.L., 18 Jan. 1662.
[21] *L.J.*, 370; P.R.O., PRO 31/3/110, D'Estrades to Louis XIV, 28 Jan./6 Feb. 1662; H.L.R.O., Braye MSS, vol. 53, no. 16.
[22] Margoliouth, II, 36, Marvell to Mayor Wilson, 19 May 1663; see also *C.J.*, 486.
[23] Bodl., Tanner MSS 239, fols. 76–7. For a new rumour that Buckingham would be made president, see Carte MSS 222, fol. 15.
[24] P.R.O., 30/24/124/2, see the other one at 30/24/124/3, and notes on the subject, probably from 1664, at 30/24/6B/437, and 30/24/30/a and b.
[25] *Hist. MSS. Comm.*, 12th report, Le Fleming MSS, p. 32, Sir George Fletcher to Le Fleming, 21 Jan. 1664.

to your lordship'.[26] Again in January 1665 it was believed that 'the king hath again declared his pleasure to establish the courts by his prerogative, though some of our own country men would have had it by parliament, meaning thereby to defer if not prevent the establishing it, but the king is resolved to do it'.[27] A few months later, however, Buckingham was incensed that still nothing had been done, and blamed Ormonde.[28]

Ultimately, of course, no court was established. There are several possible explanations for this failure. The eighteenth-century historian of York believed that Clarendon had opposed it, as he had the original council in 1641.[29] Certainly there is some evidence that he supported the four marcher counties in their objections to the jurisdiction of the council of Wales, as he had done in the Long Parliament.[30] He may have felt that the restoration of the regional councils, like the revival of star chamber, would reawaken the fears for liberty and property which had caused its abolition. The opposition of Northumberland and some northern M.P.s may also have dissuaded the government from the project. Yet at several times the government sufficiently overcame these worries to be on the brink of re-establishing the northern council; perhaps the most likely reason for its failure to do so was the bewildering factionalism of northern politics. The fierce competition for the post of president, and the offence which would be caused by any decision may have been the most powerful argument against settling a court at all.

The repeal of the Triennial Act was more vital to the government. In January 1662 the lords had voted to repeal the Act, and some progress towards the drafting of a bill had been made in their committee;[31] but in April the commons also ordered that a bill be prepared and brought in for repeal. Associates of Clarendon and the government, Sir John Bramston, Sir Edmund Peirce, and 'Mr' (probably William) Montagu were asked to prepare it. But no bill was presented. In March 1663 it was again ordered that a bill be prepared; again, none resulted.[32]

In 1662 and 1663 the government was perhaps testing opinion. It seems to

[26] H. C. Foxcroft, *The life and letters of Sir George Savile, bart., first marquis of Halifax* (2 vols., London, 1898), I, 33, Mansfield to Sir G. Savile, 16 Sept. 1664; Bodl., Carte MSS 33, fol. 716, Strafford to Ormonde, 26 Nov. 1664; for the relationship of Ormonde and Buckingham, and their mutual dislike, see Clarendon, *Life*, II, 323.

[27] B.L., Add. MSS 18979, fol. 283, B. Fairfax to H. Fairfax, 5 Jan. 1664[5].

[28] Carte MSS 49, fol. 300, Ormonde to Buckingham, 10 April 1665.

[29] F. Drake, *Eboracum, or the history and antiquities of the city of York* (London, 1736), p. 238.

[30] Skeel, *The council of the marches of Wales*, p. 174.

[31] *L.J.*, 369–70; H.L.R.O., Committee Minutes, H.L., 1 Feb. 1662.

[32] *C.J.*, 395, 447; see the report of the Venetian resident in June (*Cal. S.P.Ven.*, p. 249, Sagredo to doge and senate, 2/12 June 1663), which may indicate that there were some further proceedings on the Bill then, which have left no trace in the Journal.

have concluded that repeal could be obtained, but only with great effort: in 1664 it decided to seek it more determinedly. At the opening of the session, the king told the assembled houses how the conspirators in the Northern plot which had come to light in the autumn believed that the Triennial Act meant that the present parliament, which had run for three years already, was now legally dissolved.[33] He asked them to consider 'the wonderful clauses in that bill, which passed in a time very uncareful for the dignity of the Crown, or the security of the people'.[34] As soon as the commons returned to their own chamber they voted to consider the Act the next day: in the consequent debate, Secretary Morrice told them that parliaments 'were the physick of the nation not the food, to be summoned but in time of sickness and want of help in affairs not at any fixed periods'. Prynne also spoke in favour of repeal, but Sir Richard Temple declared that the Act was the right of the people, who might demand annual Parliaments, as laid down in the Act of Edward III, not just triennial ones.[35] The government was more worried about John Vaughan – who had not yet arrived in London – than about his ally, Temple. As Morrice wrote to Downing on 1 April, 'there was more haste made with it that it might be expedited & dispatched before Mr Vaughan came to town which some having unadvisedly blabbed & perchance coming to his notice might occasion him to speake so long & so sharply against the passing thereof'.[36] Temple and others tried to delay the Bill until Vaughan could arrive: on 23 March, after its first reading, they tried to postpone discussion, but were defeated in a division. On the next day it was read a second time. While Holland (and presumably most others) argued for a commitment to the whole house, Temple again urged an adjournment.[37]

On Saturday the 26th, the Bill was discussed in the committee of the whole house; later the same day Vaughan arrived in London, and the most dramatic debates came on the following Monday, 28 March. Vaughan defended the Act: its repeal, he argued, would remove one of the most valuable safeguards of the subjects' rights. If the Act was a creation of evil times, so too had been most reforms beneficial to the subject:

if it be ground enough to repeal a law, because made in bad times, what will become of most of the best laws that were made in former ages, nay, what will become of those

[33] For this idea in the rebellion of 1663 (and for the interest of Henry Neville in it), see Greaves, *Deliver us from evil*, p. 198.
[34] *Parliamentary history*, IV, 289–90; see the government's preparations for repeal, at P.R.O., SP 29/95/24, and SP 29/109/89, and J. R. Jones, 'Court Dependents in 1664', *Bull. Inst. Hist. Res.*, XXXIV (1961), 81–91.
[35] *C.J.*, 534, 535; B.L., Add. MSS 38015, fol. 77, R. Southwell to ? [22 March 1664], M 636/19, Dr Denton to Sir R. Verney, 25 March 1664.
[36] *C.J.*, 536–7; B.L., Add. MSS 22920, fol. 33.
[37] *C.J.*, 536; Bodl., Tanner MSS 239, fols. 49–51, Holland's speech; B.L., Stowe MSS 180, fols. 88–90, Temple's speech.

other good laws & resolutions made in this very time concerning star chamber, high commission court, council table, & the condemnation of the strange judgment in ship moneys. All such were grounded upon former grievances under which the people had long groaned, & yet this argument will hold against them also.

The Act, he said, reflected neither on the memory of Charles I nor on the reputation of his son: the need for this Act and the others, on the contrary, had demonstrated that even under the best of kings, ministers might pervert justice and take away the liberty of the laws.[38] Finch answered him, in a lengthy speech: the usefulness of parliaments, even the regularity of their meetings, he pointed out, was not in question; the new Bill, while it repealed the old Act, incorporated a declaration that parliaments were to be held every three years. But the 1641 Act had laid down a procedure for the meeting of parliament if the king failed to summon it, and allowing one to be summoned if he or his officers failed to do so: and the latter, allowing it to be called by freeholders themselves, was more than a monarchy could bear. It was 'dethroning the king by act of parliament', it was 'sedition established by a law', if all its provisions came into effect, it would mean 'the state had been set up by act of parliament'; the Act had taken from the king a prerogative as inalienable as the command of the sword – so inalienable that it was void in itself, an infringement of the fundamental law.[39] Finch's arguments, and the court's pressure, were the more effective. Even a moderate amendment backed by Temple and Meres which aimed to prevent long prorogations was rejected, though it had more support in a division than had Temple's earlier attempts to delay the Bill. Another proviso was also rejected, and the Bill was passed.[40] In the lords the Bill passed quickly, with little debate and no amendment: although many had reservations, alterations were avoided, to prevent Vaughan and Temple from having further opportunity to speak on it.[41]

Pepys wrote that among those taking the court line there was little spontaneous enthusiasm for repeal; they had supported it 'purely, I could perceive, because it was the king's mind to have it', although he thought there was plenty to be said for it:[42] indeed, the arguments put forward for the repeal addressed many of the most basic anxieties of the English gentry. Finch had stressed how the Act had provoked conflict and Civil War, how it had swept away the constitution, and given sovereign power to the people. Henry Coventry agreed that the Act had removed sovereignty from the Crown: 'where the appeal is, there's the government'. Holland and Morrice concurred in telling the house that regular parliaments at fixed times were foreign

---

[38] P.R.O., SP 29/53/7; cf. Temple's speech, B.L., Add. MSS 35865, fols. 212r–v.
[39] Leicestershire Record Office, Finch MSS, Box 4965, P.P. 14.
[40] C.J., 537, 538; B.L., M636/19, Dr Denton to Verney, 25 March 1664.
[41] L.J., 588, 589, 590; B.L., M636/19, Sir N. Hobart to Sir R. Verney, endorsed 3 April 1664.
[42] Pepys, *Diary*, V, 102–3.

to the English constitution.[43] Many M.P.s were perhaps divided in their own minds on the subject, as appeals to the tradition of English liberty conflicted with appeals to loyalty, hierarchy, tradition, and the maintenance of order. But one argument was decisive: behind most of the speeches for repeal lies a distrust of change, a fear of innovations which, in pursuit of absolute security, produced only turbulence and misery. Holland drew on a common sentiment when he reminded M.P.s of 'the sad & dear experience of that which was then incredible I think to most Englishmen (I am sure it was so to me) that through the long sitting of a parliament contrary to the good will of the king greater & more desperate mischiefs have arisen both to king & people than ever have or possibly can arise through the long intermission of parliament, though these inconveniences be very great'.[44] As Finch said, 'when we have done all we can a mathematical security is not attainable'.[45] The pursuit of the most certain safeguards was chimerical: better, by far, to trust only to the ancient standards and laws of the constitution, and the goodness of the king.

The logical conclusion – or *reductio ad absurdum*, depending which way one looked at it – of this disavowal of innovations was the restoration of feudalism, whose last dying squeals had been extinguished when the abolition of the court of wards and the Crown's right of purveyance in the Interregnum was confirmed in 1660 by the Convention. There were some regrets at their abolition, not all from unemployed officials of the court of wards or from those who felt that the excise, which replaced them, was worse.[46] The government toyed with the idea of re-introducing at least purveyance: in 1664, shortly after the passage of the Triennial Act's repeal, the restoration of both purveyance and the court of wards was rumoured; and a few months later Sir Heneage Finch hinted that the partial restoration of purveyance was being contemplated.[47] But no more appears to have been done; and although a few appear to have accepted that somehow the decay of feudalism was related to the decline of the nobility, there were perhaps not enough of the gentry to agree with them to produce any real enthusiasm for institutions which in 1641 had been so deeply resented.

In some ways, the consideration of royal prerogatives removed since 1640 was a matter of philosophical importance as much as of political reality: the repeal of the Triennial Act had been thought of as necessary from a constitutional and ideological, as well as a practical, point of view. There were

---

[43] B.L., Add. MSS 35865, fol. 212; Bodl. MSS 239, fols. 49–51; B.L., Add. MSS 38015, fol. 77, Southwell to ? [22 March 1664].
[44] Bodl., Tanner MSS 239, fol. 50v.   [45] Finch MSS, Box 4965, P.P. 14.
[46] See above, p. 43.
[47] B.L., M636/19, Dr Denton to Verney, 27 March 1663; B.L., Stowe MSS 744, fol. 81, Finch to Sir E. Dering, 15 Sept. 1664.

other matters which more immediately affected the survival of an insecure regime: above all, its control over military power. The government was acutely aware of the need for an adequate military force to guarantee its security. By the end of 1660 most of the old army had been disbanded, but rumours of conspiracies and Venner's rebellion in the last few days of 1660 alarmed the government into forming a new regiment of guards in November, retaining Albemarle's regiment in February, and amalgamating the remnants of Charles's small army of royalist exiles with Cromwell's life guard to make three troops of horse – creating a force of about 3,500 men.[48] But a permanent army was unpopular, even among ministers: Southampton, wrote Burnet, feared it could be used as an instrument of despotism, and Clarendon, partly convinced by his arguments, persuaded Charles to keep only a few soldiers.[49] More important – and probably as relevant for Southampton's rejection of a professional army – was its expense: as Charles was frequently to explain to the French resident during early 1661, paying for the few troops he had already was virtually impossible.[50] An establishment of June 1661 shows that the annual cost of the army and the provincial garrisons was £189,724, a heavy drain on an ordinary revenue not designed to bear it.[51]

The burden of defence and the maintenance of public order would inevitably, therefore, fall – as it had always done – on the militia. But the militia's legal foundations, let alone its organisation, were hopelessly confused. Since the repeal in 1604 of the 1558 Militia Act, the militia was based either (according to one view) on a miscellany of statutes dating back to the thirteenth-century Statute of Winchester, or (according to another) simply on the royal prerogative. When the government tried in 1660 and 1661 to reorganise the militia by the authority of the prerogative, along its old, unreformed lines, its inadequacies were obvious.[52] A better instrument did, however, lie easily to hand and the government had little hesitation in grasping it, despite its origins: the parliamentary, commonwealth, and protectorate regimes in response to need had gradually evolved a more regular

---

[48] J. Childs, *The army of Charles II* (London, 1976), pp. 11–16.
[49] Burnet, *History*, I, 279–80; cf. Clarke, *Life of James the Second*, I, 391.
[50] P.R.O., PRO 31/3/109, Bartet to Mazarin, 20/30 Jan. 1661, 28 Jan./7 Feb. 1661.
[51] Childs, *The army of Charles II*, p. 17.
[52] A. Hassell Smith, 'Militia rates and militia statutes, 1558–1663', in *The English commonwealth, 1547–1640: essays in politics and society presented to Joel Hurstfield*, ed. P. Clark, A. G. R. Smith, and N. Tyacke (Leicester, 1979); Tuck, ' "The ancient law of freedom" ', *passim*; for the problems which faced those organising the militia, see Fletcher, *Reform in the provinces*, pp. 318–19, and D. P. Carter, 'The Lancashire Lieutenancy', unpublished M.Litt. thesis, University of Oxford, 1981, pp. 80–3; J. R. Western, *The English militia in the eighteenth century* (London, 1965), pp. 10–11; J. G. Ive, 'The local dimension of defence: the standing army and militia in Norfolk, Suffolk and Essex, 1649–1660', unpublished Ph.D. thesis, University of Cambridge, 1986, p. 253.

system of militia organisation, codified in the Rump's ordinances of 1650 and (rather more elaborately) of 1659.[53]

The government's original intentions in 1661 appear to have been to re-enact the 1659 ordinance as statute. One of the first bills to be discussed in parliament in 1661 was for the reform of the militia, brought in by the solicitor general and Sir Job Charlton, and read for the first time on 17 May.[54] No copy of this Bill has been found, but comments on it suggest that it was similar to that finally passed in 1662; like that Act, it must have closely followed the 1659 ordinance, setting comparable rates for contributions, similar rules for musters and exercises, and allowing – as the ordinance had done – a month's assessment to be levied in times of emergency to defray extraordinary expenses.[55]

The length of debates on the Bill in committee of the whole – perhaps unavoidable in a measure which so closely concerned county administration – thwarted any hope of passing it before the summer recess;[56] on 16 July, aware that it could not be finished before the house rose, the commons decided instead to pass an interim measure to confirm the legality of the present militia arrangements until the new act could be completed. This Bill was read twice on the 16th, and committed to the whole house, chaired by Robert Milward. One proviso then added suggests that difficulties over rating were largely responsible for the slow progress on the original Bill: the temporary Act was not to mean that current rates could not be altered after its expiry.[57] It was quickly passed by the lords, rejecting their own committee's recommendation of a proviso saving peers' privileges, which might have caused a lengthy dispute between the houses.[58] Declaring that the king had the sole right and command of the militia, that the militia and land forces were to continue in being as they were now until 25 March 1662, and

---

53 Ive, 'The local dimension of defence', *passim*. I am most grateful to Dr Ive for discussion on this subject.
54 *C.J.*, 249, 254.
55 Compare *The notebook of Sir John Northcote*, p. 135 with paragraphs III and IV of the 1662 Act, and *Hist. MSS. Comm.*, 5th report, Sutherland MSS, p. 160, Andrew Newport to Sir Richard Leveson, 21 May 1661, with paragraphs I and VI, *S.R.*, 358–63; see also Higgons's speech on the Bill, B.L., Add. MSS, 10116, fols. 202–3v, and B.L., Egerton MSS 2043, fol. 38v, in which Reymes refers to the Bill to which the House turned after the abandonment of an alternative measure, and which eventually became the 1662 Militia Act, as the 'old bill for the militia'; compare the provisions mentioned in these sources, and the later paragraphs of the Act itself, with the two ordinances, especially the 1659 one: C. H. Firth and S. R. Rait (eds.), *Acts and ordinances of the Interregnum* (3 vols., London, 1911), II, 397–402, 1320–42.
56 *C.J.*, 257, 258, 264, 267, 273, 274; *The notebook of Sir John Northcote*, pp. 130, 131, mentions debates on the Bill also on 25 and 27 May.
57 *Hist. MSS. Comm.*, 12th report, Beaufort MSS, p. 50, Lord Herbert to Lady Herbert, 16 July 1661; *C.J.*, 303, 304.
58 *L.J.*, 313, 314, 317; H.L.R.O., Committee Minutes, H.L., 19 and 20 July 1661.

indemnifying all proceedings under militia commissions between 24 June 1660 and 20 July 1661,[59] the Bill cleared up – for the moment – all the doubts about the legal status of the militia.

The main Bill was adjourned until parliament met again in November. But during the autumn there were renewed fears of republican and 'fanatic' unrest: in September Sir John Pakington revealed to Secretary Nicholas the details of a plot of which he had received information, and the Venetian ambassador reported that a conspiracy among members of the disbanded army had spread to soldiers of the new army.[60] These rumours resulted in a reconsideration of the whole question of the militia in the winter session. Pakington disclosed his information to the commons, either at the re-opening of parliament on 20 November, after M.P.s returned from listening to the king's speech, or more probably on 3 December, when Sir Roger Bradshaigh and Sir Philip Musgrave both spoke of plots in Lancashire and Carlisle, and several others members told similar stories. This display of M.P.s' fears of rebellion led to the appointment of a committee, with Sir Job Charlton at its head, and including government representatives such as Finch, Pollard, Warwick, and Henry Coventry, to bring in a new militia bill.[61]

The government seems to have seized the chance of M.P.s' fears of fresh rebellion to obtain their support for a force rather different from that planned in the spring, although there is not enough evidence to prove that it had itself orchestrated the revelations on the 3rd. On 5 December, Sir Edward Nicholas reported to Winchilsea that the commons (presumably, their committee) had 'resolved to raise twelve hundred good horse for the public security on all emergencies, which they will constantly maintain at the public charge'.[62] On 6 December Vaughan reported from the committee a request that M.P.s should bring in estimates of the numbers of the militia, and its cost in each county.[63]

Although these hints are insufficient to reconstruct the committee's proposals in detail, it is clear that they planned a temporary, 'select' militia, along

[59] 13 Car II, c. 6, *S.R.*, 308–9.
[60] B.L., Add. MSS 10116, fols. 257, 261, 262v; *Mercurius publicus*, 1661, pp. 581, 672, 696; P.R.O., SP 29/44/39, 40, SP 44/1, p. 14; *Cal. S.P. Ven.*, pp. 63–4, Giavarina to doge and senate, 4 Nov. 1661.
[61] *C.J.*, 324; *Parliamentary history*, IV, 224, says that Pakington's revelations were made on 20 November, yet there is no trace in the commons' Journal of any resolution made as a result on that date, nor does Reymes mention a speech by Pakington: B.L., Egerton MSS 2043, fol. 23v; for the accuracy of the rumours, see Greaves, *Deliver us from evil*, pp. 70–7.
[62] *Hist. MSS. Comm.*, Finch MSS, I, 173; cf. 15th report, appendix, part VII (1898), MSS of the duke of Somerset, p. 93, J. Kelland to Sir Edward Seymour, 21 Jan. 1662.
[63] *C.J.*, 326; cf. the proposals of Yorkshire M.P.s for their own county's militia, P.R.O., SP 29/26/72, and Clarendon MSS 106, fol. 24, Dutch Ambassadors to states general, 13/23 Dec. 1661.

the lines of that raised by Cromwell's major-generals of 1655; a force of volunteer horse divided into regionally-based groups.[64] Earlier in the year, the government had drawn up plans for such a force. The state papers of March 1661 contain a scheme of ten regiments of horse of 500 each to be raised at the yearly rate of £70,000, each of the regiments to be based and paid for in one of ten regions. The officers, who were listed, were all to be local lords and gentlemen. One of the papers associated with the draft is in Secretary Nicholas's hand.[65] Another plan, drawn up by Albemarle's secretary, Sir William Clarke, provided for 7,213 horse rated on twenty-three areas, also at a cost of £70,000 a year.[66] A 'select' militia such as this had a particular attraction for royalists: few were confident of the ordinary militia's reliability if it should come to fighting, and there were many reasons to doubt the loyalty of both militia and the regular army. Volunteer troops could be more easily vetted, more easily trained, and would be consequently more professional and more reliable.

But two weeks after Vaughan's report, the committee's plans (whatever they were) were apparently set aside as the government attempted to go still further: encouraged, perhaps, by the success of the 'select' militia proposal, ministers seem to have tried to obtain the commons' approval for an even more ambitious project, a standing army funded by parliament. On 19 December Clarendon delivered to the lords a message from the king disclosing a new republican conspiracy. Their response was to nominate a committee of twelve to meet with a 'proportionable' number of M.P.s during the Christmas adjournment to consider the dangers arising from the plots, and to propose remedies for the country's security. The committee included eight privy councillors – York, Cumberland, Clarendon, Southampton, Robartes, Albemarle, Ormonde, and Ashley; one of James's confidants, Lord Berkeley of Stratton; the royalist commanders Lucas and Belasyse; and two bishops closely connected to the court, Sheldon and Gauden. On the same day, at a conference with the commons, Clarendon repeated his account. He revealed that what M.P.s were to assume was a well organised and desperate association of various radical groups had held several meetings – including one chaired by Harrington – in which they had planned the remarkable success of presbyterians and independents in the London election of 1661;

---

[64] See Reymes's reference to the 'temporary militia', B.L., Egerton, MSS 2043, fol. 24v; Ives, 'The local dimension of defence', pp. 250–3; Western, *The English militia in the eighteenth century*, pp. 8–9.

[65] P.R.O., SP 29/33/105–7.

[66] B.L., Add. MSS 37425, fols. 48–53. See also the plan apparently proposed by Lord Townshend, although in what context, or when (probably some time in 1663) is unclear, B.L., Add. MSS 41654, fol. 62; cf. Clarendon MSS 109, pp. 5–6, 49.

they had more recently been preparing to petition parliament, and also, more sinisterly, organising the return to London of the disbanded soldiers.[67]

Whether the plot was genuine or not, and whether the government itself believed it, is difficult to judge; but the attempt to manipulate parliamentary opinion was quite evident. Joint committees of both houses which were not simply conferences under another name occurred occasionally in the early Stuart period, although they were unusual enough to be opposed as 'unparliamentary' in 1628.[68] After the Restoration, though, they became rare: few more are recorded until the device was revived and refurbished in 1864.[69] Even rarer were joint committees appointed to meet during a recess:[70] that appointed on 9 September 1641 to meet during a few weeks' adjournment was apparently the first. Clarendon had called the proceeding then 'irregular', disapproved of the innovation, and even more of the use to which it was put – gathering evidence 'to amuse the people, as if the parliament was in danger'.[71] In 1641 it had enabled Pym to keep up the momentum of suspicion and fear which he had created in parliament during a recess which might have dissipated it.[72] Despite his earlier censure, in 1661 Clarendon imitated Pym's tactic for a similar purpose.

The commons' reaction to Clarendon's message shows how unusual it was. At four in the afternoon the house met again, and for four hours debated how to choose the members of its committee to join with the lords'. Finally there was a division on a motion that it should be nominated in the normal way: the identity of those who told against the motion, Sir Richard Temple and Edward Seymour, suggests that 'country' members, fathoming the government's intentions, hoped that by debating the method of nomination they might prevent the commons' side of the committee being dominated by privy councillors and ministerial associates. In the event, they lost. The committee was headed by Sir Hugh Pollard and included the councillors Carteret and Finch, and Clarendon's clients Apsley, Bramston, and Charlton, besides strong haters of dissent and men with government connections such as Lords Bruce, Fanshaw, and Falkland, Thomas Clifford, Duncombe, and Sir John Goodrick. Only a few, such as Sir Thomas Littleton, Sir Richard Onslow, and

[67] *L.J.*, 355; *C.J.*, 339; Reymes supplies the details of Finch's report of the conference, omitted in *C.J.*, B.L., Egerton MSS 2043, fols. 29–30v; for the details of the 'plot', see Greaves, *Deliver us from evil*, pp. 78–81, and Hutton, p. 164.
[68] Foster, *The house of lords*, pp. 116–18.
[69] T. Vardon and T. Erskine May, *General index to the Journals of the house of commons* (London, 1852), pp. 201–9; M. Bond, *The records of parliament* (London, 1971), p. 57; J. Hatsell, *Precedents of proceedings in the house of commons*, new edn, 4 vols. (London, 1818), III, 38–45.
[70] But see the remarks of Foster, *The house of lords*, pp. 95–6.
[71] Clarendon, *History*, I, 386, 389, 395.
[72] A. Fletcher, *The outbreak of the English Civil War* (London, 1981), pp. 126–31.

George Montagu, were unconnected with the court, or sympathetic to nonconformists.[73]

It was clearly hoped that the committee would recommend to parliament the augmentation of the regular army. That evening one of the M.P.s on it, Lord Herbert, wrote to his wife that its purpose was to 'sit and consider what proposals should be made to parliament at their meeting again for such a force to be constantly, at least for some time, upon duty as a security to the king and kingdom, and the trained bands to be relieved from the continual duty they are now on'.[74] Another of the committee's members, George Montagu, told Pepys that what was intended was the establishment of a standing army under the duke of York, and there were several other similar reports.[75] But in fact the committee scarcely met, because, as Morrice told Downing, its appointment had 'started great jealousies, fomented chiefly by such of the house as were ambitious of being of that number & were defeated of their hopes, nothing is come into more light concerning the plot, which hath set many into an ambiguity & suspense of judgment on which side the plot lies'.[76] Morrice's hint points towards Sir Richard Temple and Edward Seymour, the tellers for the opposition on 19 December. In the face of such hostile public reaction, the government hastily abandoned its plans, not even daring to put parliamentary opinion to the test: as William Coventry delicately, if inelegantly, put it on the 17th, the attempt had been 'declined by one party out of jealousy by the other to avoid the occasion of it'. On the day that parliament reconvened Clarendon reported the decision of the committee to leave the whole business to parliament itself, because of the 'jealousies' raised 'of the end and intent of the committee's meeting'.[77] On the 11th and 14th the commons revived their debate on the militia in committee of the whole, and on the 14th they resolved that temporary additional forces should be raised out of the 'trained bands & auxiliaries', a return to the proposals of early December.[78]

Despite this decision, at the next meeting of the committee of the whole on 17 December, this plan was also dropped, and the house reverted to the

[73] C.J., 339.
[74] Hist. MSS. Comm., 12th report, Beaufort MSS, p. 51, Lord Herbert to Lady Herbert, 19 July 1661.
[75] Pepys, Diary, III, 15; Cal. S.P. Ven., pp. 91–2, Giavarina to doge and senate, 28 Dec. 1661/ 6 Jan. 1662; Bodl., MS Eng. Lett. c. 210, fol. 65v, Sir Henry Yelverton to Archdeacon Palmer, no date [Jan. 1662].
[76] B.L., Add. MSS 22920, fol. 1, 3 Jan. 1662, cf. Add. MSS 22919, fol. 178, Cornbury to Downing, 27 Dec. 1661; cf. the charge against Clarendon in 1667, Milward, Diary, p. 100.
[77] L.J., 359; C.J., 342; B.L., Add. MSS 22919, fol. 186, W. Coventry to Downing, 17 Jan. 1662.
[78] C.J., 343–4, 345; B.L., Egerton MSS 2043, fols. 35, 37; Bodl., MS Eng. Lett. c. 210, fol. 81, Yelverton to Palmer, [15 Jan. 1662].

original Bill of the previous spring.[79] The reason was perhaps that the temporary Militia Act was due to expire on 25 March, and it may have seemed wiser to settle for the Bill which was already half finished rather than to enter into lengthy discussions on an entirely new one. But the government's hasty retreat plainly showed its recognition that it had overreached itself: encouraged by the anxiety that M.P.s expressed about radicals, it too easily persuaded itself that it indicated sufficient support for a stronger professional army. Ministers and their advisers had failed to recognise the very conservative – and especially anti-militarist – nature of gentry opinion, even of much royalist gentry opinion. In April 1662 the royalist journalist Roger L'Estrange contributed, from outside parliament, to the current debate on the militia. He appealed to kings in general (and by implication, Charles in particular) not to seek to ensure their rule with force, but with law and good government. He wrote of the dangers of relying too closely on a standing army, and hinted at the proposals of the winter in showing how easily the commonwealth army, 'a slight temporary force raised (in pretence at first) as an expedient against plots', was 'increased, continued, and carried on, by policy and power': such an army could easily turn on its makers and destroy them, as the New Model had destroyed parliament.[80] George Montagu put the point more directly to Pepys: 'the house did in very open terms' he told him, 'say they were grown too wise to be fooled again into another army; and said they have found how the man that hath the command of an army is not beholden to anybody to make him king'.[81] A standing army brought a dangerously unpredictable element into the political system: far from allowing the king more power, it could easily deprive him of his throne, and the people of their liberties.

But the government had not entirely abandoned its hopes at least of improving the professionalism and commitment of the militia itelf. When the revived 1661 Bill was sent up to the lords, they made several amendments in committee of the whole giving lord lieutenants much greater control over the militia;[82] then, on 14 April, a proviso was agreed, wehich would have permitted persons charged with providing horse, soldier, and arms, to compound in money instead. The draft of the proviso is headed 'l[or]d trea[sure]r', and may therefore have been Southampton's project; but the idea was not his own, nor a new one. The 1659 militia ordinance had included a similar measure, although it had been omitted in the subsequent

---

[79] *C.J.*, 347; B.L., Egerton MSS 2043, fol. 38v.
[80] L'Estrange, *A memento*, p. 64, cf. pp. 61–85, 224, 233.
[81] Pepys, *Diary*, III, 15.
[82] For the Bill's completion in the commons, see *C.J.*, 349, 355, 363, 371, 373–4, 378, 381, 384, 386. *L.J.*, 407, 413; H.L.R.O., Main Papers, H.L., 13 May 1662, papers 4 and 5, Committee Minutes, H.L., 22 March 1662.

ordinance of March 1660. The intended effect, then as now, would have been to convert the general local militia into a more select force whose members could be more easily chosen and more effectively drilled and commanded.[83] The committee also added limitations on the powers of search, particularly of the houses of peers.[84] On 17 April the earl of Bridgewater reported to the house. Although the lords conceded a point in agreeing to be charged for the militia, which they had in 1660 refused, they insisted on being assessed by their peers. A proviso was added accordingly, and the Bill was passed and returned to the commons.[85]

When the lower house debated the lords' amendments, they rejected the measures to strengthen the powers of the lord lieutenant over the militia, and watered down the special arrangements for the assessment of peers and searches of their houses.[86] They also threw out Southampton's proviso. Sir John Holland was probably not the only man to feel that the suggestion concealed another attempt to introduce a standing army by the back door:

I cannot forget that in the late usurping time that the ancient militia raised out of the freeholders and persons of interest of this nation was laid by and a troop of eight pound men raised in every county who were to be in readiness at all times and upon all occasions to be executors of that tyrant's will. Truly, sir, methinks on one side of it it looks too much like that.[87]

Like others he found the proviso's removal of the direct link between the property-holders who paid for the militia and the soldiers they provided disturbing: a step towards the breaking of tried and tested constitutional habits, cutting away the participation of the gentry in the government. Southampton's proviso received considerably shorter shrift than the analogous proposals of early December 1661: the decline of interest was perhaps due to the furore of January; perhaps simply to diminished concern about radical plotting; even, perhaps, to irritation at the lords' technical usurpation of the commons' sole right of voting taxation.

After reluctantly compromising on their privileges, the lords accepted most of the amendments. Several more conferences were required before final agreement on the Bill was reached and it was passed on 17 May.[88] Sweeping

[83]   *L.J.*, 427, 429; H.L.R.O., Main Papers, H.L., 13 May 1662, papers 6, 17 and 18; Ive, 'The local dimensions of defence', pp. 314–17.
[84]   *L.J.*, 430; H.L.R.O., Main Papers, H.L., 13 May 1662, papers 7 and 8.
[85]   *L.J.*, 430, 431; H.L.R.O., Main Papers, H.L., 13 May 1662, paper 23, the second proviso, and 24; Western, *The English militia*, p. 14.
[86]   *C.J.*, 418, 421, 426; *L.J.*, 454–6; H.L.R.O., Main Papers, H.L., 13 May 1662, papers 25, 26, 27.
[87]   *C.J.*, 423; Robbins, 'Five speeches by Sir John Holland', pp. 198–200; see also Charlton's speech to the lords, *L.J.*, 454–6.
[88]   *C.J.*, 429, 431, 432–3; *L.J.*, 457–8, 459–60, 463–4, 466.

away the complexity and confusion of the pre-war system, the new Act thoroughly reorganised the militia. It reformed the setting of rates for contributions towards finding soldiers, horses, and arms; it placed the militia entirely under the command of the lieutenancy; it allowed for the payment by the contributors of the troops while on exercises, and the defrayment of other expenses by a county rate; and in cases of danger, it empowered the king to raise an extra month's assessment in each of three years, in order to keep the force in being.[89] Nevertheless, it was far from an instant success. As reorganisation proceeded throughout late 1662 and early 1663 there were plenty of complaints: the Act drastically reduced the militia's total strength;[90] there were delays in its implementation; and because of the fewness and dispersion of the soldiers it was difficult to collect them together quickly.[91] Later in the year the government demonstrated its own doubts of its adequacy. Although there were none of the expected disturbances accompanying the ejection in August and September of ministers who failed to subscribe to the new Act of Uniformity, strong rumours of plots and rebellions continued throughout the autumn, and to counter any possible insurrection the government issued commissions for three new regular regiments of cavalry and two of foot, provoking some criticism. It had become, according to one M.P., 'the general report of the whole town, strange censure being passed of it'.[92]

Both the new troops and the defects in the Act came in for some muted criticism in the session of 1663. On 3 April Sir Thomas Meres reported a bill to amend the Act.[93] Supporting it, Sir John Holland argued that any improvement in the effectiveness of the militia would make the arguments for a standing army less powerful. He told the house that he recognised the necessity of the king's guards, retained in 1660 and 1661, but bemoaned the recent expansion: 'truly, sir, when these commissions were issued out, there seemed some necessity for it, for it was at a time when his Majesty had certain intelligence of a dangerous plot, dangerous both to his person and government . . . But sir, these commissions being still on foot, it is now incumbent upon us to take notice of these commissions and humbly to present his

---

[89] 14 Car. II. c. 3, *S.R.*, 358–63; see A. Hassell Smith, 'Militia rates and militia statutes', pp. 109–10, and Western, *The English militia*, pp. 16–29.

[90] Carter, 'The Lancashire lieutenancy', pp. 81–3.

[91] P.R.O., SP 29/57/25, 42, 70, 62/84.

[92] Childs, *The army of Charles II*, p. 19, cf. appendix A, pp. 233–4; B.L., Lansdowne MSS 525, fol. 56, William Haward to 'my Lord', 16 Sept. 1662.

[93] *C.J.*, 437, 439, 454, 462, 464; see the king's speech on 16 March, hinting at the need to amend the Act, *Parliamentary history*, IV, 263, cf. 264; the lords – presumably moved by the king's speech – also debated problems of security on 30 March: see *L.J.*, 502.

Majesty with our advice touching these commissions'.[94] Holland took his argument much further in a debate apparently on a motion for such a petition. In one of his longest and most strongly-argued speeches, he desperately appealed against this expansion of the government's military force. In a passage that was marked as 'upon consideration not spoken' he described the rumours current in the country that 'there is a design, and an intention to change the constitution of the government of this kingdom and to reduce us after the model of France'. Such rumours were, he said, fomented by radicals, and Holland distanced himself from them: yet it was clear that he was worried not merely about provoking revolt, but was himself genuinely concerned about the state of English liberties. The motion, if it was made, was clearly not accepted – only a minority in parliament can have felt that there was all that much cause for alarm – yet it shows how early in the Restoration fears of military and arbitrary rule were aroused.[95]

The Bill itself, after much debate in committee of the whole house, was read the third time and passed on 16 July.[96] In the lords, it passed quickly, with only a few amendments.[97] Most of its provisos were improvements or adjustments of the 1662 Act: those then exempted were made capable of contributing towards the cost of the militia, considerably increasing the funds, and thus the number of troops, available; lieutenance were enabled to keep their forces together for longer; and some of the limitations on the frequency and duration of musters and exercises were removed. The new Act completed the 1663 settlement to create a lasting and effective militia system, a useful bulwark against internal disorder.[98]

The shape of the militia settlement, it has been said, represented the desire of the Restoration gentry to establish their power in government and their hegemony within their counties.[99] Undoubtedly, the desire to retain gentry oversight of local forces was a powerful motive in the rejection of the alternative schemes, and made the Militia Acts more acceptable to members: yet the settlement was, in effect, a creation not of the Restoration gentry but of the Rump Parliament, and one which was introduced by the government, not by

---

[94] *C.J.*, 464, 469; Robbins, 'Five speeches by Sir John Holland', pp. 201–2; cf. B.L., Add. MSS 41654, fol. 62; Holland's speech suggests that the new regiments were not actually raised, only commissioned.

[95] Bodl., Tanner MSS 239, fols. 53–9v; the speech is clearly connected with that previously mentioned, supporting the motion there suggested. References in the speech seem to place it shortly after the 1662 Declaration of Indulgence: but there is no other evidence of the motion.

[96] *C.J.*, 480, 484, 493, 495, 516, 518, 523–4, 525.

[97] *L.J.*, 563, 564, 567.

[98] 15 Car. II. c. 4, *S.R.*, 443–6; for a discussion of the militia under the new Act, see Fletcher, *Reform in the provinces*, pp. 323–32.

[99] E.g. Fletcher, *Reform in the provinces*, pp. 322–3.

ordinary members. The attitudes that lay behind the opposition to the alternatives were rather conservative than anything else – a deep feeling, certainly, for the English tradition of popular defence,[100] but mostly a profound antipathy to the confusion and unpredictability that the dark shadow of military power would bring to political affairs. That is not to say that there was absolutely no support for a professional army: many anglican royalists, and indeed others, were convinced that only professional soldiers could guarantee the country's security from dangerous conspiracies.[101] But rather more M.P.s – especially those whose past politics and current positions made them less vulnerable to contumacious nonconformists – were more prepared to draw firmly the line between greater security and irresistible power. If M.P.s were concerned, as Holland said, that the militia be 'raised out of the freeholders and persons of interest in the nation',[102] it was not so much because of their desire to expand the role and authority of the gentry in local administration, as to preserve their existing role; and because drastic change would only increase, not diminish, the likelihood of disaster.

Government control in the counties could be exercised easily through the lords lieutenant, the deputy lieutenants and the justices of the peace, whom it commissioned. But its power in the towns – among them the most vexatious centres of political and religious dissent – was more circumscribed. The little self-perpetuating oligarchies that ran the town corporations and elected their principal officers, and often their members of parliament as well, were largely (depending on the terms of each charter of incorporation) independent of royal control. Ministers undoubtedly conceived the power and independence of the corporations as a problem. Clarendon referred to their 'natural malignity', and at one lords' committee meeting Lord Ashley remarked that 'the greatness of corporations [is] inconvenient to monarchy'.[103] Hobbes called corporations 'many lesser common-wealths in the bowels of a greater, like worms in the entrails of a natural man'.[104] One author of a paper of advice sent to the king recommended the alteration of all charters so that the Crown, rather than the people, would have power to elect and constitute the mayor and chief officers, and the election of M.P.s would be entirely removed

[100] L. G. Schwoerer, *'No standing armies!': the antiarmy ideology in seventeenth-century England* (Baltimore, 1974).
[101] E.g., P.R.O., SP 29/81/94, Peterborough to Williamson, 14 Oct. 1663; SP 29/62/84, Sir J. Crosland to Bennet, 10 Nov. 1662, SP 29/81/16, Sir T. Bridges to Bennet, 5 Oct. 1663; Bodl., Tanner MS 47, fol. 50, Bishop of Chester to ?, 3 Oct. 1663; Clarendon MSS 109, pp. 5–6, 49; B.L., Add. MSS 21922, fols. 251v–2, Sir Richard Norton and Sir Humphrey Bennet to Southampton, 18 Aug. 1662.
[102] Robbins, 'Five speeches by Sir John Holland', p. 198.
[103] Clarendon, *History*, II, 226; H.L.R.O., Committee Minutes, H.L., 4 Feb. 1662.
[104] *Leviathan*, ed. C. B. Macpherson (Harmondsworth, 1968), pp. 374–5; cf. Clarendon MSS 109, p. 47; P.R.O., SP 29/1/81.

from their hands.[105] Southampton's complaint of the influence of merchants, traders, and yeomen in parliamentary elections hints at an ambition to limit corporation franchises.[106] To make the corporation problem worse, the Interregnum regimes had forced many of them to renew their charters and by that means had stuffed them full of their own supporters. It was obvious that the king, by recalling all existing charters, might do the same: and it was equally clear that he might, simply by altering the terms of those that replaced them, reduce the freedom of corporations for good. The first was essential if the monarchy was to rest secure: the second desirable, but provocative. In its subsequent actions, it has for long been held, the government demonstrated its desire to achieve the latter, as well as the former. But in a recent article John Miller has argued that this was far from the government's intention; in common with most royalists it aimed only to ensure that the powers of local officials and magistrates were exercised by loyal men.[107]

As Miller has pointed out, although in early 1661 the government did draw up some far-reaching proposals for the drastic alteration of borough charters, these were never properly implemented;[108] and when, in June 1661, a bill for regulating corporations was brought into the commons, it was presented – apparently – not by the court itself, but by anglican royalists, seeking to chase Cromwellians, presbyterians, and collaborators with the Interregnum regimes from town governments. The Bill's sponsor was probably Sir John Duncombe, a strong anglican royalist; he was teller in several of the divisions on it, he was named first to its committee, and was involved in the several conferences on it.[109] It was read for the first time on 19 June.[110] In the vote on its commitment, Duncombe was partnered as teller by the younger Sir Thomas Fanshaw, renowned for his vehement persecution of dissenters. The tellers for the noes included Sir Edward Massey, a presbyterian royalist.[111] After several fruitless attempts to add provisos, the Bill was engrossed on 2 July, with a clause allowing the king to appoint commissioners for London – the City's four presbyterian and independent M.P.s, repudiating the Bill, had evidently refused to co-operate in nominating any. On 5 July the Bill was read for a third time, two provisos were added, and after a division on its

---

[105] Clarendon MSS 73, fols. 359–60.
[106] B.L., Harleian MSS 1223, fol. 205v.
[107] J. Miller, 'The Crown and the borough charters in the reign of Charles II', *Eng. Hist. Rev.*, C (1985), 53–84; cf. J. H. Sacret, 'The Restoration government and municipal corporations', *Eng. Hist. Rev.*, XLV (1930), 232–59.
[108] Miller, 'The Crown and the borough charters', pp. 57–9.
[109] For Duncombe, see *H.P.*, II, 243–4. In February there had been a dispute about the membership of the borough for which he was M.P., Bury St Edmunds. See Sacret, 'The Restoration government and municipal corporations', p. 239.
[110] *C.J.*, 275.   [111] *C.J.*, 276–7, 291, 335, 336–7, 339–40.

passage, in which the tellers against it were the presbyterians Prynne and Sir Ralph Ashton, it passed up to the lords.[112]

In so far as it can be reconstructed, the commons' Bill appears to have been a relatively simple measure. It empowered named commissioners to displace any member of a corporation who refused to take the Oaths of Allegiance and Supremacy and a declaration against taking arms against the king or his officers. The commissioners were also authorised to restore members ejected from corporations during the Interregnum. It is likely that, as in the final Act, they were enabled if they thought fit also to displace members who were willing to take the oaths and the declaration if they suspected their good faith.[113] In an anonymous pamphlet published soon after the Bill's passage in the commons, it was passionately attacked: the tyranny and injustice of the measure, it was claimed, exceeded the 'late arbitrary powers, proceedings of sequestrators, decimators, and committee-men during our wars, and sad confusions'; the procedure allowed no appeal or trial by jury; it ejected men from an office which was considered to be a freehold; and the commissioners who were to carry it out were compelled to take no oath to see that justice was done.[114] The Bill's promoters were incensed by the attack: a committee headed by Sir John Duncombe and Sir Thomas Fanshaw soon discovered the identity of its author, William Prynne; and Prynne, in uncharacteristic tears, received the reprehension of the house from the speaker.[115]

But in the lords, Prynne's arguments shortly became largely irrelevant, because the Bill was so completely altered as to become almost an entirely different measure; and although little can be learned of their proceedings on it, it seems likely that the changes were made with the blessing, and perhaps at the behest, of prominent ministers. The alterations were worked out by a committee which included York, Southampton, and Robartes; they were reported to the house on 23 July by the earl of Portland, and on the 24th the Bill was returned to the commons.[116] They were horrified. The lords had left out a large part of the Bill, including all that referred to the commissioners and their powers. Instead, all corporations by 24 June 1662 were to renew

---

[112] *C.J.*, 279, 288, 291, 254.
[113] Compare the Act as printed (13 Car. II. stat. 2. c. 1, *S.R.*1, 321–3) with the lords amendments in *C.J.*, 336–8, and [W. Prynne], *Summary reasons, humbly tendered to the most honourable house of peers by some citizens and members of London, and other cities, borough corporations, and ports, against the new intended Bill for Governing and Reforming Corporations* [1661], B.L., C 112 h.4/92; but cf. the certainly inaccurate report of the Bill's contents in Marvell's letter of 20 June (Margoliouth, II, 31).
[114] [Prynne] *Summary reasons.*
[115] *C.J.*, 299, 301–2; *Hist. MSS. Comm.*, 12th report, appendix, part IX (1891), MSS of the duke of Beaufort, pp. 50–1, Lord Herbert to Lady Herbert, 16 July 1661; B.L., Add. MSS 10116, fols. 229r–v.
[116] *L.J.*, 309, 311, 313, 318, 319.

their charters: those which replaced them would allow the king to nominate and appoint recorders and town clerks, and to select mayors from a list of six men provided by each corporation. County J.P.s were to be allowed to act in towns within their jurisdictions.[117] This was a drastic curtailing of municipal independence (if not quite as drastic as some of the measures which had been suggested before the session): the government would obtain a wide and uniform measure of control over the officers of the boroughs. Rather than – as Sacret has suggested – representing only the ultra-royalist policy of the duke of York, the alterations seem to have had wide ministerial backing: Portland's involvement probably indicates Clarendon's support for the measure; Southampton and Ashley both commented on the need for the power and independence of corporations to be curbed; and even some ex-presbyterian government members may have supported the amendments which omitted the wholesale purges certain to result from the commons' Bill.[118]

What is most extraordinary about these bold amendments is that those who promoted them could believe that the commons would accept them. Still ignorant, perhaps, of the nuances of royalist opinion, ministers carelessly assumed that the commons' spontaneous enthusiasm for crushing the political power of the regime's enemies indicated as well a more general willingness to extend royal control over the bases of that power. Predictably, the commons rejected all but one of the lords' amendments. At a conference on 26 July Sir Heneage Finch delivered their reasons: the original Bill, he said, had been directed towards 'placing the government in right hands'. Rather than achieving this, the Bill would now make a 'perpetual change'. No borough members, he added, could possibly agree to the amendments 'without breach of trust reposed in them by those corporate towns they serve for; as conceiving these alterations tend to the destroying the charters of all corporations' – although some anglican royalists were possibly as irritated by the removal of their opportunity to sweep their opponents from local administration. For a day or so, the commons' reaction to the Bill seems to have seriously alarmed the government: Lord Falkland even proposed (though with little support) that they should print a remonstrance in protest against the peers' action. Ultimately the lords resolved to send a placatory message. At a conference later in the day, Southampton thanked the commons for their 'care and fair carriage', and emphasised the points of agreement between the houses: the matter, he suggested, should be adjourned until after the recess. The commons readily accepted. On the evening of the 26th Finch was thanked by the king and the duke of York for his part in calm-

---

[117] C.J., 310–11.
[118] Sacret, 'The Restoration government and municipal corporations', p. 249.

ing the storm. Southampton's conciliatory message is perhaps a measure of how seriously it was taken: in the other inter-house disputes, on the militia and the highways Bill, the government did nothing to defuse the situation.[119]

The lords' amendments to the Corporation Bill suggest that the government in July 1661 was as interested in securing central control over the boroughs as in purging them (as anglican royalists in the commons hoped simply to do). But during the winter meeting of parliament the lords recommitted it. When the committee met on 10 December, with Portland in the chair, the attorney general presented a new version of the commons' original Bill. This the house passed, and it was delivered to the commons at a conference on the 17th.[120] Palmer's amendments made large concessions to cavalier opinion. The clauses requiring the surrender and alteration of charters were dropped, and it returned to the principle of the commons' original Bill of regulation by commissioners, although these were to be appointed by the king, not by parliament. The original Bill's provision that all members of corporations should take the Oaths of Allegiance and Supremacy was retained, but the declaration against taking arms against the king was converted into an oath, and a new declaration, against the Covenant, was added. Not only those who refused to take these oaths and declarations were to be ejected, but also any whom the commissioners suspected; they were also permitted to put into the corporations any whom they thought fit. In addition, the important sacramental test was now added: no one was to be elected to municipal office unless he had received the sacrament within the last year.[121] The commons accepted these changes with little alteration, save a clause preventing the surrender of corporation charters as a penalty for actions during the war (an unusual instance of the commons standing by the Act of Indemnity), and a limitation of the operation of the Bill to three years. On the 20th it received the royal assent.[122]

As John Miller has remarked, the amendments to the original Bill in the summer, and now the substitution of commissioners appointed by the Crown for those appointed by parliament demonstrate the government's concern to avoid a royalist purge of the corporations, which might arouse charges of arbitrary behaviour (such as those of Prynne's pamphlet) and even rebellion.[123] The government itself was probably as anxious that some sort of purge should take place, but hoped to make one with less publicity and less

---

[119] *C.J.*, 312, 313; *L.J.*, 321–3; B.L., Add. MSS 23215, fols. 40r–v, John Finch to Lord Conway, 27 July 1661; for the other inter-house disputes at the end of July, see B.L., Egerton MSS 2717, fols. 209–10, J. Holland to W. Gawdy, 31 July 1661.

[120] *L.J.*, 346, 349, 353; H.L.R.O., Committee Minutes, H.L., 10 Dec. 1661.

[121] *C.J.*, 336–8; compare with the Act as printed, *S.R.*, 321–3.

[122] *C.J.*, 336–8, 339; *L.J.*, 356, 358.

[123] 'The Crown and the borough charters in the reign of Charles II', p. 62.

rancour in its renewal of the charters of all the country's boroughs. Yet the amendments of the summer indicated that its ambitions went further, an increase in the government's own powers at the expense of local privileges, principally in its control over the senior permanent officials of the corporations: not, perhaps, as thorough a control over the corporations as might have been suggested, but at least an attempt to enhance the importance of unelected officials and draw the towns – by their means – into a closer relationship with Whitehall.

The commissioners who were to administer the Act soon ran into difficulties. An additional bill on corporations, read twice in May 1662, suggests that there was already an awareness of some defects in the Act, but the intent of the Bill is unknown.[124] In early 1663 these defects were discussed in the commons: the commissioners' decisions were being challenged, and overruled, in the king's bench; people were refusing to take the oaths and declaration in order to escape the burden of local office; and the Bill's expiry in another year's time threatened the return of the ejected members.[125] A bill was brought in in July, but its provisions are unknown.[126] By the following year, after the rebellion in the North, the government may have been rather more concerned by reports of the undisturbed re-election of many ejected corporation members. A bill concerning corporations read in April 1664 was probably government-inspired: the tellers in a division for its commitment were both members of Bennet's group, Swale and Coryton, and the first few members of the committee, Clifford, Finch, Sir Thomas Strickland, Reymes, Hyde, and Heath (the committee also included Lord Cornbury and Bulteel), were closely connected with the government. This Bill was probably that identified by John Miller among undated state papers, a measure that, describing the danger that would arise by the return of the ejected members, renewed the Corporation Act for the rest of the reign, and provided for the Crown to appoint new commissions to exclude from municipal office any whom the commissioners believed to be of disloyal principles (even if they had taken the oaths and the declaration), all who had served on the Interregnum county committees, or had been sequestrators or purchasers of Crown, Church, and royalist land; the commissioners were themselves empowered to replace those they removed.[127] But the Bill was never passed, perhaps a victim of the government's other main objectives of the session – the repeal of the Triennial Act, and the declaration against the Dutch.

The Crown's interference with municipal privileges drifted rather uneasily between two aims: first, to ensure that loyalists were firmly in control of the

[124] *C.J.*, 424, 426.   [125] *C.J.*, 445, 446.   [126] *C.J.*, 517.
[127] *C.J.*, 551, 553–4; Miller, 'The Crown and the borough charters in the reign of Charles II', p. 63, citing P.R.O., SP 29/440/93.

towns; and secondly, and more controversially, permanently to exercise greater influence in corporation affairs. In many ways the two aims were complementary; but when the government, counting on the enthusiasm of anglican royalism for the destruction of their enemies' power, tried to make the second aim more explicit and more central in the Corporation Bill, royalists, sensing too radical a change – and also, perhaps, an attempt by the presbyterians within the government to limit its partisan effect – reacted violently against it.

Not all of the government's attempts to obtain legislation to increase its security were so controversial. The second bill read in the commons at the opening of the 1661 session was one 'for the securing and preserving of his Majesty's person and government', based on the 1571 second Treasons Act of Elizabeth. It confirmed the customary definitions of treason, and added a second group of offences which were to entail dismissal and disablement from office – calling the king a heretic or papist, or saying that he intended to introduce popery – and a third group which would incur a praemunire – claiming that the Long Parliament was not legally dissolved, or that an obligation from Interregnum oaths or the Covenant 'to endeavour a change in government either in Church or State' still remained.[128] It was the first appearance of the clause against the Covenant which was later to be made into a declaration and incorporated into the Bill for confirming the Act confirming ministers, the Act of Uniformity, the Corporation Act, and several others. Three provisos were added in the commons: for ensuring that the Bill did not conflict with the Act of Indemnity; for treason to be proved by two witnesses in the presence of the accused; and for freedom of debate in parliament.[129] The lords added to those opinions that the Bill condemned the idea that 'both houses of parliament, or either of them, have a legislative power without the king', and provoked a dispute between the houses by attempting to insist on the trial of lords by their peers, before the Bill was finally passed.[130] On the same day as it had received a first reading in the commons, a bill 'against tumults and disorders' was presented in the lords. Clearly influenced by memories of the petitioning of 1640–2, to which reference was made in its preamble, it limited the numbers allowed to sign a petition to the king or to parliament unless it had first received the consent of

[128] *C.J.*, 247, 249; 13 Eliz. I. c. 1, *S.R.*, IV, 526–8; *S.R.*, 304–6.
[129] *C.J.*, 252, 255, 256; 13 Car. II, c. 1., paras. III, V, VI, *S.R.*, 305–6; the London aldermen, Fowke and Love, were probably responsible for the first of these. See B.L., Egerton MSS 2043, fol. 8v; *Hist. MSS. Comm.*, 5th report, Sutherland MSS, p. 196, Sir Thomas Gower to Sir Richard Leveson, 21 May 1661.
[130] *L.J.*, 266, 267, 269, 270–1, 274–5, 276; *C.J.*, 260–1, 265, 265–6, 266, 267, 268; *S.R.*, 306, para. VII. In fact the lords' proviso was in the end left in the Bill, presumably by an oversight, since the lords had agreed to its omission.

a county grand jury, or of the common council of the City of London, and forbade the gathering of large crowds to present it. By 11 July it had passed both houses.[131]

The regulation of the press was rather more contentious, largely because of the special interests it concerned. In the past, the legal authority for censorship rested on the treason laws, proclamations, the royal injunctions of 1559, and star chamber decrees of 1586 and 1637. The removal of star chamber and high commission in 1641 demolished the main agencies of enforcement, so while it was still possible to authorise licensing, how penalties could be inflicted for avoidance was unclear.[132] The lawyers Maynard, Kelyng, and Swale were asked on 3 July to prepare a bill to prevent the publication of 'traitorous, schismatical, and scandalous pamphlets'. This was never brought in, however, and instead on 25 July the solicitor general was asked to produce a bill 'to impower his Majesty to regulate the press, till it be otherwise provided for'.[133] This, then, was to be a temporary measure, and it was clearly intended that when time would allow, some more comprehensive regulation of the industry should be set up. The Bill passed swiftly through both houses, the lords ignoring petitions for the inclusion of individual copyrights and adding just two amendments.[134] But the second of these, a proviso to exempt peers' houses from search, was enough to ruin its chances of passing. The commons immediately rejected it, as being both an undue extension of the privileges of the peerage and an alteration liable to render the Bill nugatory. Even after several conferences the houses were unable to reach a compromise, and by the fourth conference of the day tempers had run so high that Lord Robartes flung the original proviso down on the table in the painted chamber, refusing to make any alteration, 'where we left it' wrote Sir John Holland, '& where possibly you may find it the 20th of [Novem]ber to which day the parliament is adjourned'.[135]

When printing was again discussed during the autumn, this Bill was abandoned, and a new one was ordered by the lords from the attorney general on 17 December.[136] Colonel Atkins commented that the new Bill was 'the very transcript of the decree of star chamber'; and indeed much of it was lifted directly out of the 1637 regulations. It imposed the same rules for licensing,

---

[131] *L.J.*, 252, 254, 257, 262, 267; H.L.R.O., Committee Minutes, H.L., 16, 17 May 1661, Main Papers, H.L., 13 May 1661; *C.J.*, 263, 279, 291, 294, 294–5, 297; 13 Car. II. c. 5., *S.R.*, 308.
[132] Walker, 'Censorship of the press during the reign of Charles II'; F. S. Siebert, *The freedom of the press in England 1476–1766 (Urbana, 1952), pp.* 21–87, 127–46.
[133] *C.J.*, 288, 312.
[134] *C.J.*, 313, 314; *L.J.*, 324, 325; H.L.R.O., Main Papers, H.L., 27 July 1661.
[135] *L.J.*, 325–6; *C.J.*, 315–16; B.L., Egerton MSS 2717, fol. 209, Sir John Holland to Sir William Gawdy, 3 July 1661; P.R.O., SP 29/40/19, Sir Thomas Baines to Lord Conway, 3 Aug. 1661.
[136] *L.J.*, 351, 353.

the same limitations on the number of master printers, and, as the decree had done, confirmed the responsibility of the stationers' company for enforcing it.[137] Palmer's Bill was read on 16 and 17 January and spent months in committee. The delay is mostly attributable to the important interests at stake: much of the time was taken up with reading the petitions and hearing the counsel of both the stationers' company and of individuals who claimed exemption from the company's monopoly. But when finally Lord Hunsdon reported the amendments on 22 April there were none which altered the main provisions of the Bill.[138] In the commons its passage was speeded by the king's message that the Bill 'did most conduce to the securing of the peace of the kingdom'. The house made two important amendments: the requirement that searches of peers' houses could be carried out only by immediate warrant from the king was extended to commoners not involved in the trades mentioned in the Bill – thus gaining the point disputed the previous summer, and allowing the peers no extra privilege; and the operation of the Act was limited for two years from 10 June 1662. Such a short time suggests that the commons regarded the Bill as only a short term measure, and considered that a full overhaul of the operation of the press remained necessary.[139]

The Act was a temporary victory for the stationers, who had escaped any serious incursion on their monopoly. Their campaign had evidently been a hard one – they had spent heavily on legal counsel, including Sergeant Kelyng, and on dining the commons' committee.[140] But there were further challenges to their control of the industry. The committee for revising various acts was asked to look at the Press Act on 23 February 1663, although no report is recorded. A bill was read, for 'better regulating the press', on 10 July, although it got nowhere.[141] Colonel Atkins, on behalf of the printers, vigorously attacked the stationers' monopoly.[142] Roger L'Estrange, obsessed with the unlicensed printing of subversive pamphlets, urged that the industry should not be entrusted with its own regulation, and that a royal officer, equipped with much wider powers than at present were authorised, should be appointed to enforce the Act. Both stationers and printers should be subject

[137] P.R.O., SP 29/88/132; compare 14 Car. II. c. 33, *S.R.*, V, 428–33 with the 1637 decree printed in *A transcript of the registers of the company of stationers of London, 1554–1640*, ed. E. Arber (5 vols., London, 1875–94), IV, 528–36; H.L.R.O., Main Papers, H.L., 19 May 1662, list of lords' amendments to the Bill; see *C.J.*, 435 for the commons' amendments.

[138] *L.J.*, 365, 366, 435, 439; H.L.R.O., Committee Minutes, H.L., 27 Jan., 3, 6, 15, 20, 21, 25 Feb., 1, 6, 13, 15, 18, 22 March, 1, 4, 9, 12, 16 April 1662, Main Papers, H.L., 16, 17 Jan., 19 May 1662; see also Col. Atkins's proposals, P.R.O., SP 29/88/132; Siebert, *Freedom of the press*, pp. 244–9.

[139] *C.J.*, 417, 418, 425, 429, 434, 435.

[140] B.L., M455/27, Journal book of the stationers' company for money disbursed, 1656–98.

[141] *C.J.*, 439, 520.

[142] P.R.O., SP 29/88/132 (Atkins's proposals); for the stationers' revenge on Atkins, see below, p. 270 and n. 164 and Bodl., Tanner MSS 239, fol. 68v–9.

to the same rules, and under the same control. L'Estrange himself was soon appointed surveyor of the press and given wide powers, but his proposals were not included in any bill.[143]

When it became necessary to replace the Act, due to expire after 10 June 1664, all that was done was to pass a simple short bill renewing it, but only until the following session.[144] But neither was there any serious debate then, and in early 1665 the Act was again extended for another session.[145] In the session of Autumn 1665 it was perhaps recognised that the onset of the war made further consideration of the press unlikely for the moment, and a new bill renewed the Act until the end of the first session of the next parliament.[146] The rather inadequate arrangements of the 1662 Act thus remained in force until 1679, not because of an unwillingness to draw up any more efficient system of censorship, but because any plans to do so were defeated by a lack of time, and probably by the powerful opposition of the stationers' company.

Throughout the early 1660s the government had tried – albeit tentatively – to claw back some of the power that its principal members felt had been lost since the Civil War, or even before. 'The late rebellion could never be extirpated and pulled up by the roots', Clarendon reported himself as telling Charles, 'till the king's regal and inherent power and prerogatives should be fully avowed and vindicated; and till the usurpations in both houses of parliament since the year 1640 were disclaimed and made odious; and many other excesses, which had been affected by both before that time under the name of privileges, should be restrained'.[147] Yet Clarendon's concern to make clear the regime's respect for property, liberty, and for law, their guarantor, meant that there were strict limits to the government's ambitions. There had been no attempt to repeal those Acts passed in 1641 which had outlawed the arbitrary impositions of the 1630s – ship money, knighthood fines, the extension of the forest laws; and although the revival of star chamber was discussed, it was clear that any restored version of the court would not be endowed with the powers that had made the original seem so burdensome to the subject. There remained plenty of scope, though, for an expansion in royal power and authority, for increasing the government's military security, and for reducing the power of institutions – parliament and the corporations – whose independence and privileges could limit the Crown's own freedom of action.

[143] L'Estrange, *Considerations and proposals in order to the regulation of the press*; cf. SP 29/68/102, 39/92 and 94; Siebert, *Freedom of the press*, pp. 249–60; Williams, 'Newsbooks and letters of news of the Restoration', pp. 260–4.
[144] 16 Car. II. c. 8, *S.R.*, 524; *C.J.*, 556, 557, 559; *L.J.*, 611, 611–12, 614.
[145] 16/17 Car. II. c. 7, *S.R.*, 556; *C.J.*, 602, 604, 605; *L.J.*, 663, 664, 667.
[146] 17 Car. II. c. 4, *S.R.*, 577; *C.J.*, 615, 618, 620, 622; *L.J.*, 696, 696–7.
[147] Clarendon, *Life*, II, 347.

But parliamentary opinion further restricted the powers the government might obtain. Anglican royalists and conservatives of all political complexions could appreciate the government's fears of subversion and insurrection and (to various extents) support them. Yet none saw the situation precisely in the government's terms. Anglican royalists might feel that the increased control given to the Crown in the lords' amendments were designed by ex-presbyterians in the government to protect dissenters, former parliamentarians, and Interregnum officeholders; conservatives could accept the government's intentions to remove dangerous innovations such as the Triennial Act, but were equally horrified by the other changes it proposed. The government was not too weak, nor parliament unwilling, to reassert royal power in some degree; but the conservatism of parliament, and the government's recognition (although in some cases belated) of that conservatism, set bounds both to the government's intentions and its achievement.

Religion

In April 1660, in the Declaration of Breda, Charles had pleaded that 'all notes of discord, separation and difference of parties be utterly abolished among all our subjects whom we invite and conjure to a perfect union among themselves'.[1] Most contemporaries took it for granted that the reconstruction of national unity was a prerequisite for the restoration of political stability, and it was clear that religious divisions were the greatest causes of disunion. But could religious unity be best obtained by rigorously enforcing obedience to the established Church, or by relaxing its laws a little to encourage moderate dissenters to conform? Or should, as a few argued, the search for religious unity as an end in itself be abandoned, and national harmony, and hence stability, be instead ensured by allowing nonconformists to worship according to their own practices outside the national Church?

Naturally, the court was far from united: Charles's theological indifference accorded ill with the concern of men like Sheldon for the doctrinal purity of the Church of England. Clarendon's considerable influence would be employed on behalf of a firmly anglican settlement, yet one which made enough concessions in the inessentials of ceremony and liturgy which might allow moderate presbyterians, at least, scrupulously to conform. But the king's own preferences in ecclesiastical policy wavered between this, and the more liberal suggestions of a wider freedom of conscience for dissenters: Charles himself, and a powerful catholic lobby at court, tended to see toleration as a means of achieving the freedom of the catholics from the penal laws if it could not be obtained in any other way. But for some at court, any significant departure from uniformity or the old standards of religion was unthinkable, threatening the Church's destruction and the monarchy's fall: resolution, not compromise, was the only means to combat the political threat of dissent.

But parliament, not the court, has usually been seen as the real initiator of the legislative offensive against nonconformity in the early 1660s: backbench

[1] Kenyon, *The Stuart constitution*, pp. 357–8.

anglican squires, anxious to erase the unpalatable political and social implications of dissent, eagerly enacted a series of laws intended firmly to coerce
all back into the established Church.[2] In fact, however, parliament was as
divided as the government: admittedly, there were few who wanted a full
toleration; but few were enthusiastic about persecution, either, and all
aspects of the religious legislation of the 1660s were fiercely disputed. Some
of the most virulent arguments for persecution came not from the back-
benches, but from courtiers, officials, and royal spokesmen; for it was the
court's own confusions and divisions over ecclesiastical policy, rather than
parliament's single-mindedness, that was the principal cause of the uncompromising legislation that was ultimately enacted.

Already in 1660, the ambiguities of court policy were evident in the differences which emerged on the scale of the concessions that the presbyterians
were to be offered: those originally put forward by Clarendon during the
negotiations that led to the Worcester House Declaration of October were far
from generous. The terms that the Declaration finally granted were much
more satisfactory to the presbyterians – a full consideration of the future of
the Church by a synod, and a review of the Book of Common Prayer, so that
new laws could be made 'as may best provide for the peace of the Church and
State' – but some principal members of the government plainly considered
this as only an interim settlement and a means of cooling presbyterian feeling.[3] An attempt by the presbyterians to have the Declaration enshrined in
statute was rejected by courtiers and their allies.[4] But in May 1661, with a
newly elected anglican and royalist parliament, the court was in a position to
impose the settlement it wanted on the presbyterians, rather than *vice versa*:
and Clarendon's predilections guided it. During the summer the court
attempted to enact legislation which would complete the restoration of
Church institutions, thoroughly re-impose uniformity, attack the basic
religious and political principles of the sects and dissenters, but which would
also, by slightly lowering the standard of conformity in inessentials, allow
those whose differences with the Church of England were not more fundamental to become gradually reconciled to it.

Some historians have given the impression that the government wanted to
keep the religious question out of parliament during the summer session, and
preferred to leave such matters to the conference of anglican and presbyterian

[2] See, e.g., Green, *The re-establishment of the Church of England*, ch. 9; Abernathy,
'Clarendon and the Declaration of Indulgence'; Witcombe, *Charles II and the cavalier house of commons*, pp. 22, 173.
[3] E. Cardwell, *A history of conferences and other proceedings connected with the revision of the Book of Common Prayer*, 3rd edn (Oxford, 1849), pp. 286–98; Green, *The re-establishment of the Church of England*, pp. 210–11.
[4] Bosher, *The making of the Restoration settlement*, pp. 185–9, 195–9.

divines to revise the liturgy which assembled on 15 April, or to convocation, which opened on the same day as parliament.[5] In fact Clarendon included in his speech to parliament at the beginning of the session a specific request for a revision of the ecclesiastical laws, and guidance on the form that revision should take. Reminding the assembled houses of the Declaration of Breda's reference to parliament of religious matters, he asked them to use compassion in their attempts to heal the ills of the nation:

if the good old known tried laws be for the present too heavy for their necks which have been so many years without any yoke at all, make a temporary provision of a lighter and easier yoke, till, by living in a wholesome air, by the benefit of a soberer conversation, by keeping a better diet, by the experience of a good and just government, they recover strength enough to bear, and discretion enough to discern, the benefit and the ease of these laws they disliked. If the present oaths have any terms or expressions in them that a tender conscience honestly makes scruple of submitting to, in God's name let other oaths be formed in their places, as comprehensive of all those obligations which the policy of government must exact: but still let there be a yoke: let there be an oath, let there be some law, that may be the rule to that indulgence, that, under pretence of liberty of conscience, men may not be absolved from all the obligations of law and conscience.[6]

A strict conformity to the rules was to be demanded; but the rules themselves could be moderated – albeit only by a few, rather small and temporary concessions – to coax moderate presbyterians back to conformity. Meanwhile, he made it clear, the religious and political principles of the sects and the presbyterians were to be thoroughly disavowed, whatever concessions were offered on inessentials; in the same speech he called for laws against seditious preachers, and four weeks before parliament opened, he had asked the earl of Orrery that the Irish Parliament should 'abhor the covenant, & never suffer anybody to think well of it'.[7] The attack on the Covenant in the English parliament may also have been government inspired. When on 17 May the commons voted that it should be burnt by the common hangman, the ex-presbyterian secretary of state Sir William Morrice bitterly resisted: yet he seems to have received little support from the lords, where official influence was stronger – they repeated the commons' vote.[8] In subsequent editions of the newsbook, Berkenhead appears to have received no discouragement for printing in exuberant detail accounts of the burnings of the Covenant throughout the provinces.[9]

---

[5] E.g. Abernathy, 'The English presbyterians and the Stuart Restoration', p. 81; Bosher, *The making of the Restoration settlement*, p. 239.

[6] *Parliamentary history*, IV, 191–3.

[7] Clarendon MS 74, fol. 297, Clarendon to Orrery 31 March 1661.

[8] *C.J.*, 254; *Hist. MSS. Comm.*, 5th report, Sutherland MSS, p. 170, S. Charlton to Sir R. Leveson, 18 May 1661, p. 160, Andrew Newport to Sir R. Leveson, 18 May 1661; *L.J.*, 260.

[9] *Mercurius publicus* 1661, pp. 337–8, 352–6, 429–30.

The most pressing issue was not, perhaps, the ecclesiastical settlement itself, but the constitutional position of the bishops, excluded from parliament by statute in 1641. As one contemporary pamphleteer, claiming to be an 'anti-hierarchical divine', pointed out, unless the bishops were restored before the Act of Indemnity was confirmed it would be easy for them to claim that their restoration invalidated the confirmation.[10] The point was, presumably, even more apposite to the ecclesiastical settlement: some defenders of the episcopal order had for long held that the exclusion of the bishops from the house of lords had been against the fundamental laws; anything done in their absence could be held to be illegal.[11] Certainly in debates in both houses on the restoration of the bishops, claims were made that their exclusion had been an alteration 'made prejudicial to the constitution and ancient rights of parliament and contrary to the laws of this land' – a statement ultimately included in the statute re-admitting them.[12]

The government's hand can be detected clearly in the motion made in the commons on 30 May for their restoration. Clarendon describes it as being proposed 'by a gentleman who had been always taken to be of a presbyterian family': this was Sir Henry Worsley, who was also placed at the top of the committee list for the Bill. But Worsley's motion was perhaps not as spontaneous as Clarendon's comment was intended to suggest: the proposal of a potentially unpopular motion (and the court, although aware of anglican strength in the commons, was perhaps still not entirely certain of how such a motion might be taken) from an unexpected quarter was precisely the tactic which Clarendon used to aid the passage of the supply vote of November 1664. In that instance, a country gentleman proposed an unprecedentedly large tax; in this, a presbyterian proposed the restoration of bishops to the lords.[13] Certainly the Bill received much attention from those close to the chancellor: when it was passed in the commons on 13 June, it was

---

[10] P–.S–., *A letter from an anti-hierarchical divine in the country, to a member of the house of commons, concerning the bishops being restored to their votes in parliament* (London, 1661), p. 1.

[11] For Heylyn's defence of the bishops' rights, see P[eter] H[eylyn], *The stumbling block of disobedience and rebellion cunningly laid by Calvin in the subject's way, discovered, censured and removed* (London, 1658).

[12] 13 Car. II, c. 2, *S.R.*, 306; cf. the argument of Holland's speech in Robbins, 'Five speeches by Sir John Holland', pp. 193–5, and Dorset's speech on the subject, Kent Archives Office, U 269/036.

[13] Clarendon, *Life*, I, 529; B.L., Egerton MSS 2043, fol. 11v; *C.J.*, 261, 266–7; some with presbyterian backgrounds were not, however, so amenable (if amenable he was) as Worsley: see Holland's speech on the occasion, Robbins, 'Five speeches by Sir John Holland', pp. 193–5; for Worsley, see *H.P.*, III, 758.

Clarendon's son, Lord Cornbury, who was given the honour of carrying it up to the lords,[14] where it was quickly agreed.[15]

The origins of the Act of Uniformity are more obscure. Bosher has argued that its introduction in the commons was due to the impatience of anglican royalists anxious to prevent any compromise in the current Savoy negotiations.[16] Yet there is no evidence that the government considered the original Bill to be contradictory to its religious policy, and its introduction was entirely in accordance with Clarendon's words at the beginning of the session. Nevertheless, it was not until 25 June that the commons established a committee to draw up a bill. The delay may have been because the government, despite originally requesting a revision of the ecclesiastical laws from parliament, wanted to hold back until it had some idea of the result of the Savoy conference; by mid-June it was fairly clear that the parties were too irreconcilable for it to have any successful result: or it may have been because the government waited until it was certain of the restoration of the bishops to the lords, and thus of creating an acceptable settlement.[17] The instructions given to the committee on the 25th show that Clarendon's guidelines were to be followed. The committee was to review the laws confirming the liturgy, 'and to bring in a compendious bill to supply any defect in the former laws & to provide for an effectual conformity to the liturgy of the Church of England for the time to come'; but it was also particularly requested to look for the Book of Common Prayer that had been annexed to the 1552 Act of Uniformity. If the settlement was to be based on this most protestant of the versions of the Prayer Book, it might meet some, at least, of the presbyterians' objections to the liturgy. But the book was not found, and the Bill, drawn up by the strongly anglican John Kelyng and a committee of lawyers, endorsed the 1604 book.[18]

By 3 July the Bill had been read twice and entrusted to a committee whose first member was Sir Thomas Fanshaw, the king's remembrancer of the exchequer and a prominent Hertfordshire cavalier, with a renewed instruction to look for the 1552 Book of Common Prayer.[19] At this stage, the Bill

[14] C.J., 261, 266–7, 268, 270, 275.
[15] L.J., 279, 281, 283, 284; Clarendon, *Life*, I, 530–1; for a discussion of Clarendon's account of the Bill in the lords, see Bosher, *The making of the Restoration settlement*, p. 223.
[16] *Ibid.*, pp. 223–35.
[17] E. C. Ratcliff, 'The Savoy Conference and the revision of the Book of Common Prayer', in *From uniformity to unity, 1662–1962*, ed. G. F. Nuttall and O. Chadwick (London, 1962), pp. 91–148; B.L., Add. MSS. 28053, fols. 1–2; Bosher, *The making of the Restoration settlement*, p. 228.
[18] C.J., 279–80.
[19] C.J., 285, 288–9. It is perhaps significant that the preamble of the Bill closely followed that of the 1552 Act of Uniformity. See C. A. Swainson, *The parliamentary history of the Act of Uniformity* (London, 1875), pp. 28–31.

enjoined the use of the Book of Common Prayer by all ministers, and ordered that any incumbent of an ecclesiastical benefice was on some Sunday before Michaelmas 1661 publicly to read Morning and Evening Prayer, and declare his 'unfeigned assent and consent' to the use of everything prescribed in the Book on pain of deprivation. Anyone subsequently presented was to do the same, and similar declarations were to be made by lecturers and preachers. All former laws concerning uniformity and the Book of Common Prayer were confirmed.[20] The Bill did not, indeed, offer any concessions; but at least it did little more than renew the legal requirements of uniformity of before the Civil War.

On 8 July the Bill was reported from committee by Sir Edmund Peirce, and on the 9th, after the defeat of a further attempt to have the Act refer to the 1552 Book of Common Prayer, and after minor alterations to the 1604 Book, it was passed, and taken up to the lords by Fanshaw.[21] Even if the government had not itself drafted it, it did not find the Bill unwelcome. Clarendon later described with some sympathy the objections to the clauses added in the lords (for ordination and forswearing of the Covenant) but dismissed those against the assent and consent clause, the heart of the commons' original Bill.[22] The attempt to revive the 1552 Common Prayer had failed; but now the court may have been considering using the Bill as a vehicle for a new liturgy instead. By the time the Bill passed in the commons, the bishops had already been entrusted with the revision of the Book of Common Prayer.[23] Certainly, by the end of November Secretary Nicholas was assuming that it would become law, even though it had not yet received a first reading in the lords.[24]

As well as re-imposing ecclesiastical uniformity, the commons sought to restore the means of enforcing it. The Bill for the repeal of the 1641 Act abolishing the coercive powers of Church courts emerged from the same committee which produced the Bill of Uniformity, received its first reading on the same day, and was referred to the same committee, from which Sir Edmund Peirce reported on 9 July.[25] Not all the courts were restored, however; as it was sent to the lords on the 13th the Bill seems already to have contained the

---

[20] The Bill as received by the Lords is printed in Swainson, *Parliamentary history of the Act of Uniformity*; cf. Lord Wharton's copy of the Bill, Carte MSS 81, fols. 102–6. The last proviso allowed for alterations to be made to the translations of the Gospels, Epistles, and Psalms to bring them in line with the Authorised Version of 1611, one of the few points of agreement to emerge from the Savoy Conference; cf. the 'bishops' answer to the ministers' exceptions' at the Savoy Conference, Cardwell, *History of conferences*, p. 362, 'The concessions', para. 1.

[21] C.J., 295, 296.

[22] Clarendon, *Life*, I, 554–61.

[23] Bosher, *The making of the Restoration settlement*, p. 228. The precise timing of the decision is uncertain.

[24] P.R.O., SP 44/1, p. 21, Sir Edward Nicholas to Henry Coker, 28 Nov. 1661.

[25] C.J., 279–80, 286, 291, 296.

clause which confirmed the abolition of high commission.[26] Burnet believed
that it was Clarendon who prevented the court's restoration: but there is no
other evidence to prove this, and although Clarendon had criticised the
abuses of the court in his *History*, he had disapproved of its complete
abolition.[27] The clause more probably reflects the fact that the commons' out-
look – despite their anglicanism – was far from excessively clerical. The Bill
had a far rougher passage through the lords, where presbyterians determinedly tried to obstruct it: their most effective argument was to claim the
invalidity of the ecclesiastical laws, because they were not made in the king's
name. On 19 July the Bill was committed, on the 22nd recommitted.[28] For
three days after Lord Lucas's second report on the 25th, it was lengthily
debated. On the 26th, the duke of York, impatient with the opposition of the
presbyterian lords, told them that 'the Bill should pass on the morrow and
that they were resolved to sit it out with them'.[29] As he predicted, the Bill
passed on the 27th, although with a proviso which denied any validity to the
canons of the 1640 convocation, and echoed the presbyterians' argument in
adding that the Act 'was not to abridge or diminish the king's supremacy in
ecclesiastical matters and affairs'.[30] But it was a catholic, Lord Stafford, who
was the only peer to enter a protest against the Bill in the Journal.[31]

Despite Stafford's support for the presbyterians on this issue, in the first
session the Catholics pursued their own attempts to obtain relief without any
reference to protestant nonconformists. Nor, it seemed, did they need such
allies, for their cause was strongly supported by the king. Discussions had
already been held in 1660 and probably continued into 1661.[32] In June, the
catholics put their case before the house of lords, during debates already proceeding on the Oaths of Supremacy and Allegiance. In their petition, they
asked not to be excluded from the benefit of the Declaration of Breda, and
requested a modified oath of allegiance and the removal of the penal laws.

---

[26] *C.J.*, 300.
[27] Burnet, *History*, I, 276; Clarendon, *History*, I, 124–5, 372–4.
[28] *L.J.*, 313, 314, 317; H.L.R.O., Committee Minute Book, H.L., 20, 23 July 1661; cf. Sir
Edward Lake, *Memoranda: touching the oath ex officio, pretended self accusation, and
canonical purgation* (London, 1662), pp. 14–15.
[29] *L.J.*, 320, 321; H.L.R.O., Manuscript Minutes, H.L., 25 July 1661; B.L., Add. MSS 23215,
fol. 40, John Finch to Lord Conway, 27 July 1661.
[30] *L.J.*, 323; 13 Car. II, c. 12, para. V, *S.R.*, 316. The proviso is one annexed to the commons'
engrossed Bill, and therefore added in the lords.
[31] *L.J.*, 323; *C.J.*, 314.
[32] J. Miller, *Popery and politics in England, 1660–1688* (Cambridge, 1973), pp. 97, 99,
mentions negotiations in 1660 and 1662, but Clarendon, *Life*, I, 538–9, seems to place these
discussions well in the context of the moves in the lords in summer 1661. See also Clarendon,
Religion and policy and the countenance and assistance each should give to the other
(2 vols., Oxford, 1811), II, 669–71; and see Heneage Finch's draft and amendments on a
revision of the Oath of Allegiance, Leicester Record Office, Finch MSS, Box 4965, P.P. 8.

When their proposals were discussed, the house showed some willingness to remove the death penalty from the laws against them, but much more reluctance to make modifications of the Oath of Allegiance which might make it possible for catholics to hold office.[33] But the catholics continued to press for fuller liberties: on 21 June Samuel Tuke and Lord Arundell of Wardour presented their objections to all the penal laws.[34] The ensuing debate showed how catholics were caught in a circular argument. As the earl of Bristol said, either on the 21st or on the 28th when the debate was resumed, he realised that 'there is little hopes for us to obtain any ease from penalties till your lordships be satisfied what security we will give by oath of our duty & allegiance to his Majesty'.[35] But Wharton's speech on Arundell's reasons made it plain that he doubted that catholics could be bound to any oaths which conflicted with those they had taken to the pope. Wharton presented a further argument for retaining the penal laws (though he accepted that they might be leniently administered): they would remain a bargaining counter to be used against catholic persecution of protestants abroad.[36] When, finally, a committee was appointed to consider the repeal of some of the anti-catholic laws, it was instructed to consider only those laws which imposed the death penalty. The government was well represented; the committee included York, Southampton, Robartes, Ormonde, and Manchester, and Portland was its chairman.[37] The results of their deliberations were presented to the lords on 5 and 16 July,[38] and they were asked to produce a bill. After detailed discussion in the following week, they sent their proposals to the attorney general for him to draft one.[39]

These proposals were considerably more liberal than the directions given to the original committee might suggest. Catholics would still be banned from office, but would suffer no other penalties for their refusal to take the Oaths; priests (except jesuits) would be allowed to minister to them, and live among families, as long as they registered with the secretary of state; 'an' oath of

---

[33] *L.J.*, 273, 276–7, 277; see also A— G—, *Some few questions concerning the Oath of Allegiance propos'd by a catholic gentleman in a letter to a person of learning and honour* (London, 1661), dated 23 April; B.L., Harleian MSS 1579, fol. 114, first speech of the earl of Bristol on the catholics.

[34] *L.J.*, 281, 286; H.L.R.O., Main Papers, H.L., 10 June 1661. See also Clarendon, *Life*, I, 537, and J— H—, *A letter from a person of quality to a principal peer of the realm, now sitting in parliament. Occasioned by the present debate upon the penal laws*, signed and dated 17 June 1661, no place or date of publication.

[35] B.L., Harleian MSS, 1579, fols. 114v–20.

[36] Bodl., Carte MSS 81, fol. 183, copy of Arundell's paper with marginal comments by Wharton, and fols. 187–8, Wharton's answer. Cf. his first draft of this, fols. 185–6; *L.J.*, 286; H.L.R.O., Manuscript Minutes, H.L., 28 June 1661.

[37] *L.J.*, 291–2; H.L.R.O., Committee Minutes, H.L., 1 July 1661.

[38] H.L.R.O., Committee Minutes, H.L., 1, 3 July 1661; *L.J.*, 295, 299, 310–11.

[39] *L.J.*, 310–11; H.L.R.O., Committee Minutes, H.L., 18, 23, 24, 25 July 1661.

allegiance was to be taken by the catholic clergy and laity; and catholics were not to be forced to abjure the realm for not attending church, but there were to be provisions for the education of their children in the protestant faith. This still left, however, the laws against conversion and converts, those against the hearing or saying of mass, the other penalties – both fines and imprisonment – for not coming to church, the laws against the acknowledgement of papal jurisdiction, and the law which forbade catholics to move more than five miles from home without licence.[40] Their freedom was still to be severely circumscribed.

The committee's bill was never brought in. One strong tradition suggests that it was killed by the jesuits; Clarendon wrote that divisions among catholics themselves were responsible for its failure.[41] The catholics, however, blamed Clarendon, suspecting that he had suppressed it. The king seems to have shared their view, registering his displeasure and delighting Clarendon's enemies by snubbing him in passing over his candidate for promotion to a court post in August. The French ambassador thought that Clarendon had opposed the catholics' measures merely because of his enmity with their patron, Bristol.[42] Clarendon may well have aroused the catholics' anger by opposing their pleas for the widest liberties in the debates of July:[43] but if he was responsible for suppressing the Bill, it may have been because he was worried about provoking a political furore. The 1641 Act for their exclusion having been repealed in June, the bishops were due to return to the house of lords when it resumed in November. As William Fuller wrote to Archbishop Bramhall, it had originally been intended that the Bill should be brought in then, shortly after parliament returned, perhaps accompanied by a royal message in support. But this plan had been dropped: 'fain would they cast the odium of taking off the sanguinary laws of the papists upon the bishops, it being to be proposed suddenly upon their entrance into the house'.[44] Whatever the cause, the catholics' failure to achieve their hopes in 1661 pushed some of them back to the alliances with other opponents of the Church of England which had been contemplated during the Interregnum.

---

[40] I.e., repeal of 5 Eliz. c. 1, 27 Eliz. c. 2, 35 Eliz. c. 1 (although the committee must have overlooked para. IX of this Act, by which catholics were not forced to abjure the realm for not coming to church anyway), some clauses of 3 and 4 Jac. I, c. 4, and 2 Hen. IV, c. 15. It left unrepealed 23 Eliz. c. 1, 13 Eliz. c. 2, 35 Eliz. c. 2, 28 and 29 Eliz. c. 6, most of 3 and 4 Jac. I, c. 4, and 3 Car. I, c. 2; H.L.R.O., Committee Minutes, H.L., 18, 23, 24, 25 July 1661.

[41] Miller, *Popery and politics*, p. 99.

[42] J. Corker, *Stafford's memoires* (London, 1681), p. 53; P.R.O., PRO 31/3/109, D'Estrades to Louis XIV, 15/25 July 1661, 19/29 Aug. 1661.

[43] See, for example, the attitudes he describes in detail in the *Life*, I, 537–9, which may well have matched his own; see also Clarendon, *Religion and policy*, II, 669–71.

[44] *Hist. MSS. Comm.*, Hastings MSS, IV, 118 (19 Nov. 1661).

The earl of Bristol emerged as the principal exponent of such a policy, over-coming his previous antipathy to nonconformists: with such support, a wider toleration – so far a rather remote possibility – seemed a serious alternative to Clarendon's plans; it rapidly dissolved the court's fragile unity on religion.[45]

How remote a prospect toleration was without greater government support was amply demonstrated by the other petitions for a wider religious liberty presented to the lords in the summer of 1661. Quakers, 'good christians' and anabaptists all petitioned, and the quakers were even given some hopes of an alternative to the oaths by a slightly sympathetic committee, chaired by the earl of Pembroke (who was, by 1665, a quaker himself). Few others, however, cherished any such sympathy, and the proposal was ignored by the house.[46] Parliament's instinct – stimulated (if it needed to be) by Venner's rebellion of January – was not for toleration, but for repression: at the same time as the sects were making their appeals to the lords, the commons were preparing legislation to suppress them.[47] It was the committee on the Bill for the safety and preservation of the king's person and govern-ment that recommended on 16 May a bill against quakers, baptists, and 'fanatics' in general. Presbyterians were among its most enthusiastic supporters: Prynne and Sir Ralph Ashton were prominent in the committee for the Bill.[48] Both committee and the house were addressed by quakers, and a few M.P.s showed some sympathy for their cause; but most were openly hostile.[49] The Bill's progress in the lords was slow; it was committed four times, and several alterations were made, including the addition of a clause which limited its scope to quakers alone. This was probably an attempt to protect catholics, who might themselves refuse the Oaths of Allegiance and Supremacy and thus become liable to the heavy penalties – including trans-portation for a third offence – which the Bill prescribed for attendance at a

---

[45] For Bristol's previous attitude to protestant nonconformity, see his remarks in his speeches in B.L., Harleian MSS 1579, fol. 116, and Add. MSS 12510, fols. 32–7, esp. fol. 34r–v.

[46] For the quakers, see *L.J.*, 263, 267, 268–9, 273; H.L.R.O., Main Papers, *H.L.*, 6 June 1661, Committee Minutes, H.L., 30 May 1661; *Hist. MSS.Comm.*, 5th report, Sutherland MSS, p. 151, Francis Newport to Sir Richard Leveson, 28 May 1661; for Pembroke, see *Hist. MSS. Comm.*, Hastings MSS, II, 150–1, J. Jaques to Lord Huntingdon, 27 April 1665; for the anabaptists and 'good christians' see *L.J.*, 299, 306–7; H.L.R.O., Manuscript Minutes, H.L., 12 July 1661, Main Papers, H.L., 5 July 1661, annexe to the petition of the 'good christians'.

[47] See Clarendon's remarks in his speech on 8 May, *Parliamentary history*, IV, 194–6.

[48] *C.J.*, 252, 273, 285; for Ashton's efforts in rounding up quakers after Venner's rebellion, see P.R.O., PC 2/55 fol. 53v.

[49] *C.J.*, 305; G. Whitehead, *The christian progress of that ancient servant and minister of Jesus Christ, George Whitehead* (London, 1725), p. 262.

conventicle by those who refused to take a lawful oath.[50] To all of the lords'
amendments the commons demurred; but while the lords accepted many of
their objections, they remained concerned about the scope of the Bill, and
clarified the point by adding a clause that it referred only to those who both
refused to take the Oaths and held 'that the taking of the oath in any case
whatsoever, although before a lawful magistrate, is altogether unlawful, &
contrary to the word of God'. To this the commons agreed, and the Bill was
passed on 2 May 1662.[51]

During the summer, despite the failure of the attempt to revive the 1552
Common Prayer, there had been no irrevocable setback to the government's
object of retaining moderate presbyterians within the Church. Yet there were
early signs that anglicans in the commons were frustrated by the slow
proceedings on the settlement. The Convention's Act for confirming and
restoring ministers had restored to their livings anglicans who had been
sequestered, or whose entry to benefices to which they had been presented
had been blocked by the triers; but it had allowed all the Interregnum incumbents not displaced by these restorations, or disqualified because they had
petitioned for the trial of Charles I or opposed the Restoration, to retain
theirs.[52] Some resented the Act's generosity to presbyterians, and as early as
16 May Robert Milward wrote that it was unlikely to be confirmed without
alteration. When considering the confirmation of the acts of the Convention,
the house of commons separated this and a few others from those which were
to be confirmed with the Act of Indemnity, and included them in a second Bill
for confirming public acts which was given a first reading on 19 June. The
report from the committee was not heard until after the summer recess, on
29 November; then Sir Thomas Meres reported a set of amendments entirely
destructive of the original Act.[53]

In the hostile atmosphere which followed the revelations of presbyterian
and fanatic plots on 3 December, the house considered the Bill – now limited
to confirming only three Acts – and particularly the committee's drastic alterations to the Ministers Act. It rejected few of them: the effect of the Bill which
resulted would have been to demand from ministers many more tokens of

---

[50] *L.J.*, 318, 338, 340, 353, 365, 372; H.L.R.O., Committee Minutes, H.L., 28 Nov. 1661,
12 Dec. 1661, 9, 16, 21 Jan. 1662. There is little evidence of much support for a proposal of
Gauden's, apparently made in a speech in the lords, for the Bill's operation to be delayed by
some months: John Gauden, *A discourse concerning publick oaths*, dated 20 March 1662
(London, 1662); 14 Car. II, c. 1, *S.R.*, 350–1.

[51] *L.J.*, 388, 389, 390–1, 395, 397, 443; *C.J.*, 353, 355, 356, 367, 376; H.L.R.O., Committee
Minutes, H.L., 25 Feb. 1662.

[52] 12 Car. II, c. 17, *S.R.*, 242–6.

[53] *Hist. MSS. Comm.*, 5th report, Sutherland MSS, p. 207, R. Milward to Sir R. Leveson,
16 May 1661; for Milward, see above, p. 83.

their conformity than did (at present) the Bill of Uniformity.[54] All incumbents not legally instituted, inducted, and ordained according to the forms of the Church of England would be ejected; any minister who had held a sequestered living was made liable to pay his predecessor a full fifth of the profits of his incumbency; ministers who had procured the sequestration of their predecessors were to be ejected; and sequestered pluralists would be restored to all their livings. But one of the most important amendments has been overlooked, because unlike most of the others, it was not printed in the commons' Journal; Wharton's copy of the Bill, however, fills the lacuna. Before 1 March 1662 every minister was to take the same declaration and acknowledgement against the Covenant and admitting the unlawfulness of resistance to the king which the Corporation Bill demanded of the members of town governments, and was to make public declaration of the fact the following Sunday in his parish church. Although it is difficult to tell from the Journal whether this proviso was retained or rejected by the house, contemporary comment indicates that it was accepted.[55] Despite stiff opposition, the Bill passed the house on 8 January.[56]

This was a much greater threat to the government's religious policy than the Uniformity Bill: far from retaining moderate presbyterians within the Church it would have led to their wholesale removal. Debate in the lords was as fierce, if not fiercer, than it had been in the commons. On 29 January it was decided to consider the Bill in committee of the whole house on 1 February. A vote that the reference to the committee should restrict it to a confirmation of the original Act, omitting the commons' amendments, was tied with forty on each side, and was thus rejected.[57] On the 3rd, however, the committee resolved anyway to confirm the Act without the amendments: during the interval between the two votes, according to Dr Pett, Clarendon had got seven of the bishops, including Sheldon, Reynolds, Gauden, Sanderson, and Morley, and the duke of of York to oppose the commons' amendments, while Bristol and other catholics signalled their alliance with the nonconformists by

[54] *C.J.*, 275, 278, 322; B.L., Egerton MSS 2043, fol. 22v; the account of the amendments in the commons' Journal can be supplemented by Wharton's copy of the Bill, as it was sent from the commons to the lords; Carte MSS 81, fols. 152–5, see the endorsement on fol. 155v; *C.J.*, 322, 324–5, 330–1, 332.

[55] Carte MSS 81, fol. 154v. The declaration against the Covenant was not in the original Corporation Bill, but in the amendments presented in the lords in November, when the declaration against resistance to the king was also converted into an oath; *Hist. MSS. Comm.*, Hastings MSS, IV, 123–4, Parker to Bramhall, 14 Dec. 1661; cf. H.L.R.O., Committee Minutes, H.L., 5 March 1662; *C.J.*, 333; cf. Newcome's comment, quoted by Bosher, *The making of the Restoration settlement*, p. 241 and n. 5.

[56] *C.J.*, 333, 334, 340, 341; B.L., Egerton MSS 2043, fols. 27, 32v.

[57] *L.J.*, 364, 373; Bodl., MS. Eng. Lett. c. 210, fol. 69, Sir Henry Yelverton to Archdeacon Palmer, 29 Jan. 1662; but cf. R. Davis, 'The "presbyterian" opposition and the emergence of party', pp. 5–6.

joining them. When the Bill was returned to the commons, they (predictably) angrily objected to the amendment, and demanded a conference.[58] None was apparently had, perhaps because the commons were pacified by other means. In a committee of the lords on the Bill of Uniformity on 27 February it was ordered 'that what was lately promised to the house of commons to be provided for by way of conformity may be done accordingly'.[59] The nature of this promise is obscure; but from the sequel, it seems that the lords agreed to add to the Bill of Uniformity amendments similar to those in the Ministers Act.

The Uniformity Bill itself, sent up from the commons in July, was not read in the lords until 14 January. It was committed three days later.[60] The revision of the Book of Common Prayer had been completed by 20 December; Clarendon had probably held back the Bill until it was likely that the Book could be added to it, but despite his own sense of urgency there were many last minute delays. The new Book of Common Prayer was not presented to the council until 21 February, and the council itself demanded alterations: Bishop Gauden, with the support of Southampton and Bishop Morley (according to Burnet) or Clarendon (according to James) requested that the 'Black rubric', explaining the requirement that communicants kneel at receiving the Sacrament, which had been added to the 1552 Book but omitted from subsequent versions, should be restored. Despite the opposition of Sheldon, and the disapproval of the duke of York, it was added, perhaps because, as James alleged, some dissenters had promised Gauden and Clarendon that this might enable them to accept it.[61] The Book was finally sent to the lords on the 25th, with the king's recommendation.[62] Presbyterians immediately attacked it: most of their objections to the anglican liturgy had been rejected in its composition. The earl of Northumberland requested that the old 1604 Book be confirmed instead, and the Book was referred straight to the uniformity committee.[63] But the committee – eight of whom were bishops, including Cosin, the man most responsible for the revision – made no changes to it, and set about marrying the Book to the commons' Bill; at the same time they added to the Bill several of the provisions of the commons' amendments to the

---

[58]   L.J., 376, 377; C.J., 358, 367; *The Rawdon papers consisting of letters . . . to and from Dr. John Bramhall*, ed. E. Berwick (London, 1819), pp. 136–8, Dr Pett to Archbishop Bramhall, 8 Feb. 1662.

[59]   H.L.R.O., Committee Minutes, H.L., 27 Feb. 1662.

[60]   L.J., 364, 366.

[61]   Cardwell, *History of conferences*, p. 372; P.R.O., PC 2/56, fols. 281v, 282v; Foxcroft, *Supplement to Burnet's History*, p. 71; Burnet, *History*, I, 324; Macpherson, *Original papers*, I, 25. For Clarendon's concern about the need for speed, see *Notes which passed at meetings of the privy council*, pp. 59, 62.

[62]   L.J., 383, 390, 393; H.L.R.O., Committee Minutes, H.L., 29 Jan., 3, 8, 15 Feb. 1662.

[63]   Clarendon, *Life*, I, 553.

Ministers' Act, particularly those which demanded of ministers anglican ordination and abjuration of the Covenant.

The incorporation of these amendments drastically altered the character of the Bill; it ignored Clarendon's appeals for moderation, and aimed simply to cast out any but the unimpeachably orthodox and loyal from the Church. Clarendon made no effort to prevent their addition – the mysterious 'promise' to the commons perhaps prevented him – but he did try to mitigate them. Sometime in March he interviewed the independent divines Thomas Goodwin and Thomas Mallory and assured them of his goodwill and commitment to liberty of conscience.[64] One attempt was made in the committee to lighten the Bill's provisions: a proviso 'for avoiding re-ordination' was added, probably that mentioned by Clarendon enabling priests who had been ordained by presbyters to accept re-ordination into the Church of England. Although Clarendon believed that this remained in the Act, and it does seem at first to have been accepted by the committee, their minutes make it clear that they later changed their minds and left it out. The Bill was completed by the committee after a long debate on 10 March, and reported to the house on the 13th.[65] When the house came to debate it, Clarendon made his own attempt to soften its harshness. On the 17th, he offered a proviso with the king's recommendation, allowing the Crown to dispense with the Act in order to allow individual ministers exemption from wearing the surplice and signing with the cross in baptism, as required by the Book of Common Prayer.[66] On the 17th, according to a letter of Sir William Morrice, the proviso 'past smoothly'. Next day, however, Bristol attacked it. He first complained that the privileges of the house had been breached in the recommendation of a proviso directly from the king; but a motion to enter a salvo in the Journal was defeated, and Bristol turned to a second line of argument: that the proviso did not represent Charles's own policy on ecclesiastical matters. Ormonde, York, and Clarendon contradicted him, and an angry debate followed.[67] Clarendon was supported by the court and moderate

[64] Spalding, *Improbable puritan*, pp. 234–5.
[65] H.L.R.O., Committee Minutes, H.L., 27 Feb., 3, 5, 7, 10 March 1662; Swainson, *Parliamentary history of the Act of Uniformity*, pp. 29–46. Most of the committee's additions are easily identifiable in Swainson's Bill; *L.J.*, 406; Clarendon, *Life*, I, 555–6.
[66] *L.J.*, 406, 407, 408, 409; Swainson, *Parliamentary history of the Act of Uniformity*, pp. 44–5, lines 518–55; cf. the several draft provisos in Clarendon MSS 76, fols. 156, 158, 160, 162. The last, in Clarendon's own hand, is that presented on the 17th. See also Carte MSS 81, fols. 112, 113, 120, 121, 131, 133, for other suggestions drawn up by Wharton, probably around this time; both of the proviso's concessions were among those which the bishops had been prepared to accept in 1660: see F. Procter and W. H. Frere, *A new history of the Book of Common Prayer*, 3rd impression (London, 1929), pp. 166–8.
[67] B.L., Add. MSS 22919, fol. 203, Sir William Morrice to Sir George Downing, 21 March 1662; *L.J.*, 409, 410; H.L.R.O., Braye MSS, vol. 53, no. 17; P.R.O., SP 84/165/162 [Dutch ambassadors to states general], 21/31 March 1662.

bishops, Sheldon, Morley, Reynolds, and Gauden, while Bristol was backed by Buckingham and by the ardently anglican Bishop Cosin of Durham, the latter intent on preventing any concessions being included in the Act.[68]

Bristol's intentions in opposing the Clarendon proviso became clear on the following day when he presented his own. This, although a copy of it probably exists, is difficult to identify – there are several provisos relating to the Bill among Clarendon's papers several of which might be Bristol's – but it seems likely that it was one sent to 'B' or 'LB' with a covering letter on 26 February by an unknown adviser. The proviso itself is lost; but the letter indicates that it was intended to confirm the prerogative powers of the king in ecclesiastical matters, and implied a much wider latitude for royal dispensation than that which Clarendon's would have allowed.[69] According to Morrice, it was rejected because it was obvious that its real purpose was to release catholics from the penal laws. There was an extraordinary debate in which Cosin argued against both provisos that it was not in the king's power to dispense with ecclesiastical laws, which was rapidly denied by four bishops and by Clarendon. Bristol hurried to Cosin's defence, now more anxious to score points than to try and rescue his case; his heavy hints that Clarendon was suppressing his right to speak provoked a furious row between them.[70] Despite the incident the royal proviso was ultimately accepted, and the Bill was recommitted so that it could be added. But Bristol's motion showed how weak was any court consensus on religion; most ominous of all were the signs, flaunted by Bristol in the debate on the 17th, of the king's own divided mind on the issue. Later, he told Gauden that he had a 'key to the cabinet': Clarendon's hold over the king's opinions and the government's religious policy was beginning to be effectively challenged.[71]

The consequences of this division lay some months ahead, however. For the moment, Clarendon continued his efforts to ease the presbyterian path to

---

[68] *Hist. MSS. Comm.*, 15th report, Somerset MSS, p. 94, Sir Edward to Lady Seymour, 22 March 1662, Hastings MSS, IV, 129–30, Dr Lake to Archbishop Bramhall, 4(5?) April 1662; *Cal. S.P. Ven.*, p. 124, Giavarina to doge and senate, 21/31 March 1662; P.R.O., PRO 31/3/109, Comminges to Louis XIV, 12/22 Jan. 1663; *The Rawdon papers*, pp. 140–4, Dr Pett to Archbishop Bramhall, 21 March 1662.

[69] B.L., Add. MSS 27382, fols. 256–8v; Bristol's proviso may be Clarendon MSS 92, fol. 273 for the king's power in matters ecclesiastical, cf. fol. 273v, which outlaws proceedings against non-attenders at church services except by special order of the king, and Carte MSS 81, fol. 105, where a draft amendment makes the confirmation of all former laws on uniformity relate only to ecclesiastical persons; cf. Clarendon MSS 76, fol. 158, which might also be the proviso.

[70] B.L., Add. MSS 22919, fol. 203; *L.J.*, 411.

[71] *State papers collected by Edward, earl of Clarendon*, III, appendix, xcvi, Gauden to Bristol, 20 March 1662, xcviii–xcix, Gauden to Bristol, 1 May 1662. It would be interesting to speculate how copies of these letters (the originals are in Lambeth Palace Library) came into Clarendon's possession.

conformity. When, on 4 April, the committee reported back to the house, having added the royal proviso and brought forward the date of the Act's coming into effect,[72] Clarendon tried to mitigate it further, urging that the renunciation of the Covenant might also be dispensed with by royal licence, or even expunged from the Act. Only a year before, Clarendon had condemned the Covenant in the firmest terms: but in his *Life* he described the reasons which had induced 'many who had never taken it, and always detested it, and paid soundly for being known to do so' to oppose the abjuration of the Covenant. Clarendon may have shared their views. Disavowing the Covenant was one thing; forcing presbyterians to forswear it was another. Many presbyterians otherwise willing to accept most of the discipline and doctrine of the Church of England were reluctant to reject the Covenant; a demand for abjuration would force them, unwillingly, out of the Church and into the arms of the sects. As a result of Clarendon's motion, the Covenant was committed to the bishops; but they would recommend nothing less than a complete renunciation. Despite this, Clarendon and others continued to urge that it should not be renounced, but on a vote they were defeated by 39 votes to 26.[73] If abjuration could not be avoided, it could perhaps be made easier for presbyterians to accept it. On the 7th Morley offered a clause which would have slightly weakened the declaration that no obligation remained from the Covenant itself; but on the 8th this, too, was laid aside.[74] On the 8th one further concession was achieved, a vote that the king might allow a minister ejected from his benefice by the Act to receive one fifth of its profits for the rest of his life. Those appointed to draft the clause were perhaps its proposers: Bristol; the ex-presbyterians Anglesey and Holles; Wharton, Buckingham, and Lucas; and three bishops, Morley, Gauden, and Croft. With this clause added, the Bill was finally passed on the 9th.[75]

Clarendon may have hoped that the king's recommendation of the royal proviso might guarantee its passage in the commons, but he must have realised that it would be vigorously opposed. Nevertheless, presbyterians and their supporters struggled hard to preserve the lords' concessions and to win

[72] H.L.R.O., Committee Minutes, H.L., 20, 22, 24, 26 March 1662.
[73] Clarendon, *Life*, I, 561; *Hist. MSS. Comm.*, Hastings MSS, IV, 129, Lake to Bramhall, 4 April, 1662. This letter was probably in fact written on the 5th, when the vote it mentions is recorded in the Journal; *L.J.*, 421, 422.
[74] *L.J.*, 423, 424; cf. Clarendon, *Life*, I, 557–61. See Morley's speech on the Five Mile Bill in 1665 for his conviction that the Covenant was the sticking point for many presbyterians: Robbins, 'The Oxford session of the Long Parliament of Charles II', pp. 223–4. At the same time, there seem to have been some unsuccessful attempts to 'revive' the Covenant in the Commons; see *Cal. S.P. Ven.*, p. 133, Giavarina to doge and senate, 11/21 April 1662, and *C.J.*, 400.
[75] *L.J.*, 424, 425, 526.

more. The commons spent much of the next three weeks examining the lords' amendments to their original Bill: the debates were long and far from one-sided; the Book of Common Prayer was studied by a committee, and presby-terian efforts to call into question convocation's work were thwarted by a mere five votes;[76] an attempt to put back the date of the implementation of the Bill to Michaelmas (which would have allowed ejected ministers the benefit of rents which then fell due) was lost by nine votes. On 22 April the king's proviso, and on the 26th the proviso for allowing fifths to expelled ministers were struck out, the latter by only seven votes.[77] But defeat by so small a margin remained defeat. At a conference on the 30th Sir Job Charlton told the lords that the phrase 'tenderness of conscience' (which the commons had omitted from the preamble) had been 'much abused', and proceeded to underline the point: the royal proviso was without precedent; it would estab-lish a schism by creating a Church within a Church; and it would not satisfy those for whom it was intended, 'for such chiefly reject it upon these grounds, that things indifferent ought not to be enjoined; which opinion . . . took away all the weight of human authority, which consists in commanding things otherwise indifferent'. As to the proviso for fifths, he argued, 'what could be more repugnant, at the same time, to enact uniformity, and to allow the fifth of an ecclesiastical living to a non-conformist for not conforming?'[78]

The amalgamation of the commons' amendments to the Ministers' Act with the Bill of Uniformity had created a measure far in excess of the govern-ment's intentions, which rather than coaxing presbyterians back to the Church would expel many even of the most moderate. Ministers must have been at a loss what to do next: the end of the session was approaching, and could not be long delayed after the imminent arrival of the new queen at Portsmouth; but withholding assent would leave the ecclesiastical settlement dangerously doubtful until the next session. Clarendon fell ill on 2 May, and this may have caused the pause before the discussion of the commons' amend-ments by the lords, but there may equally have been some debate within the government about what best to do with the Bill.[79] In the end some form of compromise was reached. The Bill as it stood was accepted, but Clarendon included in his valedictory speech to parliament a clear hint that the Act would be liberally interpreted.

[76] *C.J.*, 403, 404, 405, 406, 407–8, 408–9, 409–10.
[77] *C.J.*, 410–11, 411–12, 412–13, 413, 414, 415; compare Swainson's copy of the Bill with the Act as printed, and Robartes's report of the conference, *L.J.*, 446–50, for all these amend-ments; P.R.O., SP 29/448/18, John Wandesford to [Richard] Norton, 21 April 1662.
[78] *L.J.*, 446–50.
[79] 14 Car. II, c. 4, *S.R.*, 364–70; *L.J.*, 443, 446–50; Carte MSS 31, fol. 485, Sir Edward Nicholas to Ormonde, 4 May 1662.

You have done your part like good physicians, made wholesome prescription for the constitution of your patients; well knowing, that the application of these remedies, the execution of these sharp laws, depends upon the wisdom of the most discerning, generous, and merciful prince who . . . can best distinguish between the tenderness of conscience and the pride of conscience.[80]

The Act's passage placed the government in an awkward position. Some nonconformists, aware of the government's previous attempts to moderate the Act, began to look towards the king to help them by means of the prerogative.[81] Others were openly defiant, and some anglican royalists became worried about the possibility of violence and rebellion.[82] Clarendon later claimed that despite his concern about those new clauses in the Act 'which he foresaw might produce some inconvenience', after it had been passed he believed it had to be firmly administered.[83] Clarendon's commitment to the rule of law would undoubtedly have been compromised by prerogative tinkering with the Act of Uniformity; yet it was difficult to see how an explosion of discontent, widely predicted on the Act's enforcement, might otherwise be avoided. In his account of negotiations with the presbyterians in the *Life*, Clarendon appears to have conflated two sets of discussions on moderating the Act. It was, he claimed, through the duke of Albemarle that the dissenters made their first approaches to the king; and although Clarendon felt unhappy about the king's promise – made without his advice – to do his utmost for them, he felt that Charles was bound, in honour, to keep it.[84] But it was Clarendon whom the nonconformists identified as their patron in all the discussions of the summer. Sometime before 2 June some of them presented him with a petition, which may have been discussed later in privy council. Abernathy is probably correct in arguing that Clarendon's account of an attempt to secure a suspension of the Act for three months relates to the result of this petition in June, rather than to a later one. On this occasion, the plan was defeated by the lawyers, who argued that the king's suspension of the Act could not abrogate the rights it gave to patrons to present to livings whose incumbents had not fulfilled its terms.[85] But this did

---

[80] *Parliamentary history*, IV, 252.
[81] P.R.O., SP 29/56/6, ? to Nicholas, 2 June 1662.
[82] E.g., SP 29/55/16, Sir T. Leigh to Col. Leigh, 30 May 1662, 56/1, William Williamson to Joseph Williamson, 1 June 1662, 57/70, Lord Fauconberg to Williamson, 16 July 1662; Carte MSS 47, fol. 334, Nicholas to Ormonde, 15 July 1662.
[83] Clarendon, *Life*, I, 568.
[84] *Ibid.*, I, 564–70.
[85] P.R.O., SP 29/56/6; Bodl., MS Eng. Lett. c. 210, fol. 73, Sir Henry Yelverton to Archdeacon Palmer, 5 July 1662; cf. Abernathy, 'Clarendon and the Declaration of Indulgence', p. 61; Clarendon, *Life*, I, 569–70; cf. Carte MSS 59, fol. 576, Thomas Pares to ?Lord Massarene, n.d., but read in Irish privy council, 16 June 1662: the letter describes Clarendon's annoyance with Baxter, apparently caused by his precipitate action in resigning his benefice before the Act came into force, and before there had been any discussions on moderating it.

not put an end to the discussions on some sort of indulgence, and there was some nervousness among anglicans about Charles's and Clarendon's will to enforce the ejections as the date for their enforcement approached.[86] A few days before it was due to come into effect, a new initiative from Clarendon produced another petition, discussed in council on 28 August.[87] According to the account published by Berkenhead – probably at Sheldon's instance – in *Mercurius Publicus*, the plan put forward was to allow non-subscribing ministers to retain their benefices and preach, so long as the Common Prayer was read in their churches by some other priest – a suggestion similar in effect to one of the draft provisos to the Act of Uniformity among Clarendon's papers. But in council Sheldon stoutly resisted it, and York supported him. Sheldon even appropriated Clarendon's own arguments: suspension of the law, he was said to have argued, 'would not only render the parliament cheap, and have influence upon all other laws, but in truth let in a visible confusion upon Church and State'.[88] Clarendon's claim that he supported the presbyterian appeal only because he considered the king bound by his previous engagement was either disingenuous or forgetful: the chancellor's correspondence with others during the summer, the nonconformists' acknowledgement of his personal involvement in the attempts to help them – even his anger with Sheldon now – all show that Clarendon was worried enough about the possible effects of the Act's enforcement to sponsor the plans for its suspension, or for dispensation from it.[89] But now, Charles himself was convinced enough by Sheldon's argument that the consequences of indulgence would be worse than those of enforcement to go back on his former resolve: no indulgence, he decided, would be permitted.

In fact the ejections caused by the Act of Uniformity occasioned few disturbances, and the recruitment of the new regiments raised during the autumn was probably unnecessary; but this was as much because of the hesitant and piecemeal way in which they were effected as the quiescence of the nonconformist population. The danger of insurrection remained, and during the Autumn Charles came under strong pressure to meet noncon-

---

[86] Clarendon MSS 77, fol. 157, Bishop Sanderson to Sheldon, 5 Aug. 1662, fol. 222, Archbishop Frewen to Sheldon, 13 Aug. 1662, fol. 236, Northampton to the king, 18 Aug. 1662.

[87] Bodl., MSS Rawlinson Letters 109, fol. 87, [John Owen] to John Thornton, n.d.; B.L., Add. MSS 10117, fol. 42v; B.L., Add. MSS 45538, fol. 97, the petition of the ministers.

[88] *Mercurius publicus*, 1662, no. 35, pp. 578–82; Clarendon MSS 76, fol. 160. See also Carte MSS 47, fols. 359–60, Sir Edward Nicholas to Ormonde, 30 Aug. 1662; Carte MSS 32, fol. 3, O'Neill to Ormonde, 2 Sept. 1662; the earlier objections of the lawyers would presumably mean that this plan could have applied only to royal benefices, and those where the patron would waive his right to present.

[89] See, e.g., Morley's letter to him, shortly after this meeting, 3 Sept. 1662, Clarendon MSS 77, fol. 340; for his irritation with Sheldon, see *ibid.*, fol. 319, Sheldon to Clarendon, 30 Aug. 1662.

formist discontent. But now it came from a different quarter. Since his failure to have his scheme for a wider toleration accepted in parliament in March, Bristol had been canvassing for support for it. His comments then indicated that the king might easily be convinced of its desirability; and the return of the queen mother to England in July gave him an influential ally in convincing him. Bristol sought wider backing, too, from the catholic community, calling on them shortly after the passage of the Act of Uniformity (according to Burnet's informant, Lord Stafford) to join the nonconformists and procure a general toleration.[90] Bennet, his protégé, was naturally his ally; so was Lord Ashley, anxious to secure liberty of conscience and to strike at the power of the Church. Strengthened by Bennet's replacement of Nicholas in the secretaryship, by December they had secured Charles's agreement to a scheme for a limited toleration, to be endorsed by parliament when it met in the spring. This policy was only cautiously expressed in the Declaration of Indulgence, published on 26 December.[91] The policy itself was a radical departure from the comprehension which Clarendon had so far sought, and the question of whether he supported or opposed it has been the subject of much controversy.[92] Certainly neither the Declaration nor its companion Bill of Indulgence, introduced into parliament in February 1663, was Clarendon's creation. He was incapacitated by illness from November to March, and was prevented from taking a leading role in making government policy. Nevertheless, as Ormonde heard from Bennet, the secretary had read the Declaration to Clarendon, who had suggested some alterations. These Bennet adopted, returning with the revised document for his approval.[93] It is as obvious from Clarendon's own careful letter to Ormonde, as it is from Bennet's, that the chancellor did not fully oppose it on either occasion, although he did raise some doubts as to its 'seasonableness' the first time it was shown to him.[94] For the Declaration as published can have given Clarendon little cause for alarm. It announced an intention of seeking during the next session an act to enable the king 'to exercise with a more universal satisfaction that power of dispensing which we conceive to be inherent in us', and promised to avoid any invasion of parliamentary freedoms, of which Bristol had complained when the royal proviso had been introduced in March. This seemed to confirm Clarendon's own policy of the last few

[90] Burnet, *History*, I, 344–5; cf. B.L., Add. MSS 61483, fol. 231, W. Montagu to Bristol, 8 Dec. 1662.
[91] See above, pp. 31–2; Carte MSS 47, fol. 24, Clarendon to Ormonde, 31 Jan. 1663.
[92] E.g., Witcombe, *Charles II and the cavalier house of commons*, p. 8; Green, *The re-establishment of the Church of England*, pp. 220–6; Abernathy, 'Clarendon and the Declaration of Indulgence', pp. 64–73.
[93] Carte MSS 221, fol. 19, Bennet to Ormonde, 13 Jan. 1663.
[94] Carte MSS 47, fol. 24, Clarendon to Ormonde, 31 Jan. 1663.

months, of a moderate comprehension by a dispensation from the Act of Uniformity, rather than to promise anything more sinister. Even the Declaration's other promise of securing some relief for loyal catholics threatened nothing more than what Clarendon had already attempted in 1661.[95]

But when, sometime in February, the Bill to give force to the proposals of the Declaration was read at a meeting at Worcester House, Clarendon and Southampton were horrified.[96] It enabled the king to dispense with the Act of Uniformity and any other laws 'which do enjoin conformity to the order, discipline and worship established in this Church', and to grant licences to protestants to use their own forms of worship. There were a few exceptions: no minister who could not subscribe to the Thirty-nine Articles was to hold an ecclesiastical benefice; the Bill did not dispense with the requirement that the Book of Common Prayer should be read in churches, nor did it permit publication or preaching derogatory to the Book of Common Prayer; neither would it enable anyone to hold office who on 8 May 1661 would have been excluded. But these provisos merely indicated more clearly the drastic nature of the Bill's provisions; the latter exception made it clear that the Corporation Act could also be dispensed with, perhaps the Bill's most unwelcome aspect for many cavaliers. The Bill was not, however, to be taken to allow the exercise of the catholic religion in the kingdom; yet the prominence of catholics in promoting it made it clear that they expected it to favour them in some way.[97] Clarendon's own objections were not so much religious ones, as legal and constitutional: the Bill conjured up a Hobbesian vision of a religion governed by royal decree. Abolishing many of the ecclesiastical laws, it left the Church almost the creature not of law, but of the sovereign's will.[98] In the country at large the Declaration had already been greeted with jubilation by catholics and sectaries, rejection by many presbyterians, and alarm by anglicans. Presbyterians took it to be a catholic device, but anglicans saw in it the sort of combination of papist and presbyter which some believed to have been responsible for instigating the Civil War. Certainly it seemed to indicate a preponderance of men of both creeds at court which threatened

---

[95] Kenyon, *The Stuart constitution*, pp. 403–6; cf. Sheldon's remark on the Declaration: *The correspondence of John Cosin*, II, 101–2, Sheldon to Cosin, 26 Dec. 1662.
[96] Clarendon, *Life*, II, 94–5.
[97] The Bill is printed in W. D. Christie, *A life of Anthony Ashley Cooper, first earl of Shaftesbury* (2 vols., London, 1871), appendix VI, pp. lxxix–lxxxi; the original Bill is H.L.R.O., Main Papers, H.L., 23 Feb. 1663.
[98] Cf. his remarks on Part II of Hobbes's *Leviathan*, in *A brief view and survey*, pp. 195–287, and on the Scottish canons of 1637 in *History*, I, 140–2.

their own dominance. It was even widely believed, Pepys reported, that the indulgence was not at all the king's own policy.[99]

In his speech at the opening of the session, on 18 February, the king himself refuted the idea that he would favour popery, and indeed recommended that laws should be prepared to prevent its growth. Yet he did request some relief for catholics, and 'such a power of indulgence, to use upon occasions, as might needlessly force [dissenters] out of the kingdom, or, staying here, give them cause to conspire against the peace of it'.[100] The lords voted thanks for his speech, and on 23 February Lord Robartes, the Speaker in Clarendon's and Bridgeman's absence, presented the Bill.[101] But the dissenters' wilder hopes were quickly dashed; on 5 March the house resolved that it was to refer to the Act of Uniformity alone.[102] After a debate on the 6th the Bill was put off and the house adjourned until the 12th. Its reception showed how unlikely it was to succeed, and the adjournment was perhaps to give the government time to decide on its next move. Accepting the inevitable, it resolved to abandon the measure. When the house sat once more, on the 12th, Clarendon attended for the first time this session, commissioned by the king to suppress it. The Bill was referred to a sub-committee, which spent three further afternoons on it, and was then quietly dropped.[103] According to Clarendon's own account, his carefully neutral speech on the 12th was marred by a passage in which Ashley taunted him into speaking his mind about the Bill. He bitterly attacked its 'wildness and illimitedness', and compared it to ship money. The parallel is suggestive. In his *History*, Clarendon had pointed out how the judges' decision on the legality of ship money had converted a tolerable stretching of the prerogative into an intolerable burden on the subject. This Bill, similarly, changed the nebulous royal prerogative in ecclesiastical matters into a definite and powerful instrument by which the Crown could

[99] For these reactions, see Pepys, *Diary*, IV, 44, 48, 58; P.R.O., SP 29/67/36, Sir P. Musgrave to Williamson, 12 Jan. 1663; Carte MSS 47, fol. 385, Nicholas to Ormonde, 13 Jan. 1663; *Hist. MSS. Comm.*, 12th report, Le Fleming MSS, p. 29, Smith to Fleming, 6 Feb. 1663. And see the works expounding the thesis of the alliance of papist and presbyter published in 1663, in particular Sir John Berkenhead's *Cabala, or an impartial account of the nonconformists' private designs*, and the republication of David Owen's *Herod and Pilate reconciled*, first published in 1610; cf. Goldie, 'John Locke and anglican royalism', pp. 81–5.
[100] *Parliamentary history*, IV, 258–60.
[101] *L.J.*, 479, 482; Clarendon, *Life*, II, 95; Abernathy, 'Clarendon and the Declaration of Indulgence', p. 69, believes that it was York who introduced the Bill (apparently from Hooke's letter to John Davenport of 5 March 1663, *The Mather Papers*, p. 208). See also P.R.O., PRO 31/3/111, Comminges to Lionne, 27 Feb./8 March 1663; Clarendon, *Life*, II, 98, insists that York was strongly opposed to the Bill.
[102] *L.J.*, 484, 485, 486, 487; H.L.R.O., Committee Minutes, H.L., 27, 28 Feb. 1663, 5 March 1663; see Dorset's speech on the Bill in Kent Archives Office U269/036.
[103] *L.J.*, 489, 491, 492; H.L.R.O., Committee Minutes, H.L., 12, 13, 16, 19, 24 March 1663; *Cal. S.P. Ven.*, p. 283, Giavarina to doge and senate, 19/29 March 1663; P.R.O., PRO 31/3/111, Comminges to Lionne, 12/22 March 1663.

control the Church. It was possible to accept occasional and temporary irregular alterations to the law, but not something which would make irregularity regular.[104]

Meanwhile the commons had demonstrated their own concern about government policy by investigating the release from the Tower on Bennet's orders of the prominent presbyterian Edmund Calamy. Calamy, an ejected minister, had been arrested for his breach of the Act of Uniformity by preaching. A committee appointed by the house on 9 March reported that they could find no loophole in the Act which could have permitted his release, implying that it was illegal.[105] The commons had already debated the proposed indulgence as well: on 25 February the court had tried to suppress discussion of the king's speech and Declaration until the Bill was sent from the lords, but was defeated by 269 votes to 30, Bennet's agents in the commons, Clifford and Swale, telling for the minority. The house resolved to request the king to grant no indulgence.[106] Its message, drawn up by a committee and reported to the house on the 27th by the solicitor general, pointed out that the dissenters had no right to liberty of conscience from the Declaration of Breda since parliament had passed the Act of Uniformity (although the king had spoken in terms of his own duty, rather than their right), and argued that the proposed indulgence would establish a schism by law and rather increase than diminish the number of dissenters. If they were tolerated, they might come to realise their power and some prevalent sect might even ultimately 'contend for an establishment'. In the house two important amendments were added which made much larger claims against the royal dispensing power than had the committee's original draft. One retrospectively criticised both the Declarations of Breda and Worcester House because 'there were laws of uniformity then in being, which could not be dispensed with, but by act of parliament'. Another attacked the Declaration and Bill of Indulgence on the grounds of custom and law: it was 'inconsistent with the methods and proceedings of the laws of England'.[107] The feeling against so wide an indulgence was strong. Anglican royalists – including those with such strong court connections as Henry Coventry and Sir Philip Warwick – justified the commons' actions; and even those anxious that some relief should be offered to the presbyterians opposed the Bill: as Sir John Holland said, if it had passed 'then the doors would have been set so wide open, that no man could foresee

[104] Clarendon, *Life*, II, 98; *History*, I, 86–8; cf. above, pp. 17–21.
[105] The sermon that provoked his arrest was *A (farewell) sermon preached at Aldermanbury church Dec 28 1662* (London, 1662); *Mercurius publicus*, 1663, no. 1, pp. 15–16; P.R.O., SP 44/9, p. 244, the order for Calamy's release, 13 Jan. 1663; B.L., Add. MSS 10117, fol. 61; *C.J.*, 437, 446–7; see below, pp. 188–9, for the loophole they perhaps suspected.
[106] *C.J.*, 440; Carte MSS 47, fol. 397, H. Coventry to Ormonde, 28 Feb. 1663.
[107] *C.J.*, 441, 442; *Parliamentary history*, IV, 260–3.

what might or might not be brought in thereby'.[108] M.P.s felt – like Clarendon
– that such radical change opened the way to political disaster. The reaction
against the Declaration and Bill was so powerful not so much because of the
strength of religious sentiment, but because of an unease against the consequences of so drastic and so dangerous an alteration in the law.

On the 28th the address was presented to the king, and he returned a bland
and non-committal answer, saying that he would make a fuller reply later.[109]
At first the intention may have been to stand by the Bill: a draft answer was
prepared, which thanked the house for its address, but answered point by
point their reasons against indulgence. This draft, now in the British Library,
has been claimed by Abernathy to be the work of Clarendon, in his own hand,
and forms the heart of his argument that Clarendon supported the 1663 Bill.
In fact it is not in his hand, and clearly not of his authorship.[110] Clarendon
may have consented to save the government's face in the lords; but he would
scarcely have defended so comprehensively a policy of which he fundamentally disapproved. Who did write the British Library manuscript, and
whose policy it represented, remains a mystery. It was anyway never sent and
instead, after the government's retreat in the lords, a short reply drafted by
Bennet was given in which the subject was dropped.[111]

The committee which had drawn up the commons' address had also been
directed to draw up a bill against the growth of popery, in accordance with
the king's suggestion. On 6 March Sir Robert Atkins reported the committee's proposals of measures to encourage recusancy convictions and to
discourage new conversions.[112] On 12 March a bill was presented and read
the first time: on the 17th it was referred to a committee which included
Bennet, and several of his associates; Clifford, Crosland, and Sir Humphrey
Bennet. The government perhaps hoped to win back some popularity by
making obvious its support of the measure, and it may also have been trying
to limit its scope. But although there was much debate on the Bill over the
next few days, its cause is impossible to discover. Not until 27 June did it pass

[108] Robbins, 'Five speeches by Sir John Holland', p. 196: the speech clearly refers to the
Declaration Bill, and to this debate, and must date not to 9 or 19 Aug. 1662 (as it is variously
dated by Robbins, pp. 191, 195), but to late in the session of 1663. The MS indicates no particular date for the speech (Bodl., Tanner MSS 239, fol. 45v).
[109] *C.J.*, 444.
[110] B.L., Sloane MSS 4107, fols. 260–4v; Abernathy, 'Clarendon and the Declaration of
Indulgence', pp. 71–2, and p. 72, n. 1; compare the endorsements and corrections on B.L.,
Add. MSS 27382, fols. 256–8v, with the hand of this MS; for Add. 27382, see above, p. 176
and n. 69; see also the defence of the royal dispensing power drawn up by Bulstrode
Whitelocke in response to the king's request on 13 March: Spalding, *Improbable puritan*,
p. 237, B.L., Add. MSS 21099.
[111] *C.J.*, 451; P.R.O., SP 29/69/79, Bennet's draft; *Parliamentary history*, IV, 263.
[112] *C.J.*, 441, 445; P.R.O., SP 29/69/30.

the commons, after the rejection ten days earlier of a proviso on behalf of catholics who had been in arms for the king or his father.[113]

This was not the sole symptom of the backlash in the commons against the catholics that the Declaration and the Indulgence Bill had caused. On 17 March the commons had resolved to request the king to issue a proclamation expelling all catholic priests, particularly jesuits: two days later the resolution was taken to the lords for their concurrence. The court was placed in an embarrassing situation, and tried to save catholics from the consequences of its error. On the 23rd the lords appointed a committee including Clarendon, Southampton, Robartes, Manchester, Ashley, Sheldon, and Morley. When they met the next day, Clarendon presented a new version of the address, which asked the king merely to ensure the departure of any catholic priests 'of whose modesty and peaceable behaviour you are not, upon some observation and experience of your own, or other good testimony, well assured'.[114] But although the lords passed the new petition (albeit after a long debate), the commons rejected most of it, retaining only its preamble to add to their version, and insisted that the king should be asked for a proclamation, not a mere assurance.[115] Finally the lords had to agree, and the petition was presented to the king by both houses on 31 March.[116] His reply, given on 2 April, assented to a proclamation, for which both houses voted thanks.[117] But when it appeared it fell far short of expectations. The commons had wished to allow only the queens' foreign priests to remain; the proclamation permitted both native and foreign priests in their service to stay, 'by which', wrote Daniel O'Neill, 'we are defeated of all our expectation of having all these his Majesty's subjects banished'.[118]

On 29 April the commons turned to protestant dissenters. Lord Fanshaw, one of the strongest advocates of persecution in the house, produced a letter from Hertfordshire J.P.s and gentry complaining 'of the frequent and numerous conventions of quakers, anabaptists and other dissenters from the Church of England'. A committee was appointed to consider whether the

[113] *C.J.*, 449, 452, 460, 462, 464, 466, 477, 478–9, 499, 503, 504, 512; see also Pepys, *Diary*, IV, 95, and P.R.O., PRO 31/3/111, Comminges to Lionne, 22 March/2 April 1663; H.L.R.O., Parchment Collection, H.L., 25 July 1663.
[114] *C.J.*, 449, 452, 453; *L.J.*, 495, 497, 498; P.R.O., SP 29/71/56, draft of the new version; H.L.R.O., Committee Minutes, H.L., 24 March 1663, Main Papers, H.L., 24 March 1663.
[115] *L.J.*, 499; B.L., M636/19, Dr Denton to Sir R. Verney, 26 March 1663; *Cal. S.P. Ven.*, p. 241, Giavarina to doge and senate, 2/12 April 1663; Clarendon's protection of the catholics may have caused a clash in the lords between him and Southampton: see Clarendon MSS 79, fol. 150, Ormonde to Clarendon, 8 April 1663; *C.J.*, 458, 459.
[116] *L.J.*, 502.
[117] *L.J.*, 500, 501, 502; B.L., M636/19, Dr Denton to Sir R. Verney, 29 March 1663.
[118] *C.J.*, 462, 463, 466; *L.J.*, 503, 505; Carte MSS 214, fol. 471, O'Neill to Ormonde, 18 April 1663; P.R.O., PC 2/56, fols. 191v, 193; see also Carte MSS 32, fol. 347, O'Neill to Ormonde, 4 April 1663, and fol. 357, O'Neill to Ormonde, 14 April 1663.

Elizabethan Conventicle Act required further strengthening, and to provide further remedies against sectaries. On 21 May a bill was brought in and read, and on the 23rd committed. This followed the Elizabethan Conventicle Act quite closely, particularly in causing obstinate offenders (those who did not make submission and conform within three months of their conviction) to abjure the realm, and making it a felony to return. A proviso which excluded from office those who refused to take the Oaths of Supremacy and Allegiance and the declaration of abjuration of the Covenant in the Act of Uniformity was probably added as a result of Lord Bruce's motion of 5 May, that all offices should be in the hands of 'such persons as have been loyal subjects and conformable to the Church of England'.[119] The Bill was directed not merely against the sectaries and the fanatics, but it confirmed the expulsion of the presbyterians from the Church by drawing no distinction (as had the Quaker Act) between them and the more radical: all dissenters were classed as equally dangerous and seditious. Only such treatment, it was argued, could drive the presbyterians back to the Church.

At John Heath's report on 3 June, the house made the Bill yet more severe by changing expulsion to transportation.[120] On the 30th it was given a third reading; but this was the occasion for a determined effort to win concessions for the presbyterians. A proviso, apparently to exempt from the Act 'occasional conformists', those who attended Church and received the sacrament three times a year, was defeated by only a few votes; another, to exempt those 'as were aiding and assisting to the duke of Albemarle and the earl of Sandwich' was more easily rejected (perhaps because of royalist indignation at the implication that the Restoration had been the achievement of the presbyterians).[121] After another long battle over a clause allowing the offender to return it he conformed after transportation, and a further failed attempt to liberalise its provisions by making transportation depend on royal licence, the Bill passed by a large majority, and Fanshaw took it up to the lords.[122] As engrossed it would have led to the transportation of anyone who denied the king's power and authority in ecclesiastical causes (meaning the authority of statute), who tried to dissuade people from coming to church, or who attended an unlawful conventicle, if they refused within a month to conform to the church and take the Oaths and declaration in the Act of

---

[119] Carte MSS 81, fols. 172–6, with the clauses added in the commons removed; cf. another copy of the Bill at Carte MSS 77, fol. 555; *C.J.*, 473, 489, 491, 497, 505, 508, 510, 513–14, 476; Carte MSS 32, fol. 390, O'Neill to Ormonde, 5 May 1663; Pepys, *Diary*, IV, 136.

[120] *C.J.*, 497, 505, 508, 510; Carte MSS 81, fols. 172–6.

[121] *C.J.*, 513–14; Carte MSS 81, fol. 178; for the presbyterians' efforts to delay, or talk out the Bill, see B.L., Add. MSS 23119, fol. 56, Moray to Lauderdale, 25 June 1663.

[122] *C.J.*, 513–14.

Uniformity. Costs were, if necessary, to be defrayed by contracting the convict for five years as a labouring servant on the plantations.[123]

The Bill had a first and second reading in the lords on 3 and 11 July, and Wharton prepared to fight it, clause by clause. But after the debate in committee of the whole on the 22nd, no further progress on it was recorded:[124] the government may have found it easy to suppress both this and the Popery Bill amid the excitement of Bristol's attempted impeachment of Clarendon.[125] At the end of the session, the king responded to the commons' request that the laws should be put into force with promises for bills against both popery and conventicles in the next session.[126] But it is doubtful whether this was sincere: no popery bill was discussed in 1664, and the Conventicle Act of that session seems to have come not from the court, but from the same M.P.s who were behind the Bill of 1663.[127]

One other bill occasioned a further attempt to make the Act of Uniformity more acceptable to presbyterians. The 'Act for relief of such persons as by sickness or other impediment were disabled from subscribing the declaration in the Act of Uniformity' began in the commons as a routine measure, mainly directed at those who were abroad when the Act came into force, and had thus been unable to subscribe in time – particularly those who held benefices in both the English and the Irish Church. It was probably brought in by Thomas Crouch, the Cambridge University M.P., who reported it on 3 July. On 18 July it was read for the third time.[128] At this point a clause was added which removed a loophole in the Act of Uniformity. It had been argued that the wording of the Act disabled only lecturers from preaching if they refused to take the Oaths and declaration, and so could not apply to casual preachers; this may have been the defect in the Act which had earlier been thought to have led to the release of Calamy.[129] The new clause made it clear that the Act referred to all preachers. In the lords the Bill was sent on 24 July to a committee which included Southampton and Manchester; several government

123 Carte MSS 81, fols. 172–6.
124 *L.J.*, 549, 558, 561, 563, 567; Carte MSS 81, fols. 170, 178, 240–1; Carte MSS 77, fol. 555, for Wharton preparing material to oppose the Bill.
125 For the Popery Bill, see *L.J.*, 547, 550, 557; see also B.L., Lansdowne MSS 841, fol. 37, R. Pugh, to Capt. W. Pugh, 7 July 1663, and fol. 39, same to same, 5 July 1663; Carte MSS 32, fol. 737, O'Neill to Ormonde, 15 July 1663.
126 *Parliamentary history*, IV, 287–8.
127 But cf. Clarendon, *Life*, I, 624–8; but this account is so confused, and events in it so conflated, that it is difficult to make sense of it.
128 *C.J.*, 502, 512, 516, 526.
129 *C.J.*, 526; 14 Car. II, c. 4, para. XV, *S.R.*, 367–8; see F— A—, *A letter from a gentleman in Grays Inn, to a justice of the peace in the country, explaining the Act of Uniformity, in that part which doth concern unlicensed preachers*, dated 30 Oct. 1662, no place or date of publication; for the discussion on Calamy, see *C.J.*, 437, 446–7; 15 Car. II, c. 6, para. VI, *S.R.*, 448.

supporters of indulgence (Anglesey, Sandwich, and Ashley); the court bishops, Sheldon, Morley, and Earles; and Bridgewater as its chairman. On the 25th they added a clause to ensure that those who were likely to remain absent in Ireland would provide for the serving of their English benefices by curates.[130] More important, they also added 'that the declaration and sub-scription of assent and consent in the said Act mentioned shall be understood only as to the practice and obedience to the said Act, and not otherwise'.[131] Nonconformists had vigorously objected to the assent and consent clause: they were prepared to read the Common Prayer as they were obliged, but reluctant by declaring their assent and consent to imply that they believed it perfect.[132] Southampton, Manchester, and Earles may have had much to do with the introduction of the clause, since in 1665 they raised similar objec-tions to forcing oaths and declarations on nonconformists.[133] Although the house accepted it, zealous anglican royalists, including York, Peterborough, Derby, Northampton, Dorset, Lucas, and Bridgewater protested against it, and in the commons it was thrown out on a division in a thin house on the same day.[134]

The failure of the Bill of Indulgence in the 1663 session had shown, definitively, that this parliament was unlikely to be persuaded to countenance toleration: it was, as Holland had suggested, too much of a step in the dark, too great an uncertainty, too hazardous a risk. Bristol's fall from grace in July removed, too, much of the pressure for it. Yet there still seemed to be a possi-bility of obtaining some relief for presbyterians: no vote in the house of commons for measures against them had received an overwhelming majority, and Clarendon had before been able to extract concessions from the lords. The chancellor was still interested in moderating the laws against them: in early August he discussed with Lord Anglesey how to extend 'such liberty as may be safe to men of peaceable spirits, though they differ in judgement'. They could agree that 'time with wisdom may do that which haste and violence will never compass'.[135]

But if such intentions still existed, they were destroyed by the discovery of

---

[130] L.J., 570, 572; H.L.R.O., Committee Minutes, H.L., 25 July 1663; 15 Car. II, c. 6, para. V, S.R., 448; this clause was perhaps Sheldon's suggestion: see Carte MSS 45, fol. 169, Sheldon to Ormonde, 22 Aug. 1663, and fol. 177, Ormonde to Sheldon, 25 Oct. 1663, for his dis-approval of ministers holding benefices on both sides of the Irish Sea.

[131] H.L.R.O., Committee Minutes, H.L., 25 July 1663; L.J., 573.

[132] Clarendon, *Life*, I, 556–7; see also Bodl., Tanner MSS 48, fol. 48, Bishop Ward to Sheldon, 27 Sept. 1663.

[133] Burnet, *History*, I, 400–1; cf. below, pp. 192–3.

[134] L.J., 573–4; C.J., 533; L.J., 575, 577; the Bill may also have been the occasion for an attempt to remove (or allow dispensations from) the declaration against the Covenant in the Act of Uniformity, and for Holland's speech on the subject – certainly some time in the 1663 session. See above, p. 185 and n. 108, and see also *Reliquianae Baxterianae*, part II, 433.

[135] *Hist. MSS. Comm.*, Ormonde MSS, III, 71, Anglesey to Ormonde, 11 Aug. 1663.

the Yorkshire plot in the autumn. The risings, which eventually occurred in mid-October, were small, scattered, and ineffective. Some – though not the government, for whom it was the largest and most worrying rebellion since the Restoration – regarded them as merely comical. But as the investigations and the trials of those involved proceeded it was clear that it was much wider and more dangerous than had at first been thought. They also showed that the conspirators included – as well as the wilder radicals – a fair scattering of presbyterians.[136] The government quickly withdrew from any plans for moderating the religious laws. From 1664 Clarendon seems to have closed his doors to the presbyterian and independent leaders whom he had welcomed before;[137] the king withdrew his protection from quakers;[138] and Anglesey was warned that Charles would view with disfavour his further advocacy of their cause.[139] Sir Brian Broughton reported on 16 January 1664 that the non-conformists' 'grandees about the court fail them and prove enemies, so that they are terrified and find more difficulties than formerly'.[140] Anglican royalist opinion was naturally inflamed, and the gentry in general concerned. L'Estrange filled his newsbooks with accounts of conventicles to frighten the gentry, and deputy lieutenants complained of the leniency of the judges over the past two years.[141] It was evident that there would be great pressure for the passage in the next session of the Conventicle Bill, and unlikely that the government would this time do much to prevent it. At his speech at the beginning of the new session the king made much of the plot, although he recommended no specific new laws against nonconformity despite his promise at the end of the previous session.[142] When a bill to suppress conventicles was proposed, on 29 March, it was the work of the same men who backed the 1663 Bill, most notably Lord Fanshaw and Sir Job Charlton, who headed the committee to which it was referred.[143] The new Bill was similar to the old, although a scale of penalties from the first to the third offence was now introduced, and the clauses requiring office holders to take the oaths and declaration had been removed – perhaps to make it more acceptable to the court.[144] After the report by Charlton and the third reading on the 27th, debate continued; a clause restoring the abjuration in the original 1663 Bill, instead of

[136] Greaves, *Deliver us from evil*, pp. 165–206.
[137] The Diary of Bulstrode Whitelocke (see above, p. 29, n. 86).   [138] Hutton, p. 208.
[139] *Hist. MSS. Comm.*, Ormonde MSS, III, 131–2, Ormonde to Anglesey, 26 Dec. 1663, cf. p. 140, Anglesey to Ormonde, 23 Jan. 1664.
[140] P.R.O., SP 29/90/10, Sir Brian Broughton to Joseph Williamson, 16 Jan. 1664.
[141] *The Intelligencer*, 1664, pp. 57, 129–30, 152, 168, 182–4, 199, 231, 249–53, 257, 264, 265, 268, 273, etc.; Bodl., MS Eng. Hist. b. 212, fol. 16, Oxfordshire deputy lieutenants to Clarendon, 9 Feb. 1664; Hutton, pp. 206–7.
[142] *Parliamentary history*, IV, 289–90; cf. 288–9. See also Clarendon, *Life*, I, 623–4.
[143] *C.J.*, 539.
[144] *C.J.*, 541, 542; Bodl., Tanner MSS 47, fol. 115, newsletter of 7 May 1664.

transportation, was rejected, as were a proviso for those who recanted and an attempt to widen the number allowed at a conventicle. On the 28th the Bill passed and Fanshaw took it up to the lords.[145]

The upper house spent much time on it in committee of the whole. Some of their alterations mitigated it: they enlarged the numbers permitted at a conventicle by including the offender's family and servants, and allowed a heavy fine to be imposed as an alternative to mandatory transportation for the third offence. Two provisos were also added for the peers' privileges. Clarendon himself offered another proviso, which reflected both the government's concern about quakers, and his own irritation with the disruption they caused in legal proceedings: anyone who refused to take a lawful oath in any court of law would be automatically liable to transportation. Lord Ashley may have tried to make the Bill less harsh with a proviso 'for reparation without just cause', but this was rejected and after Clarendon's proviso was accepted (following further debate) the Bill was read a third time and passed.[146]

For once, the commons were more moderate than the lords. They accepted many of the lords' alterations, but rejected the clause concerning oaths and the two provisos for peers' privileges. A compromise proviso was eventually worked out on the privilege issue, although Temple and Tanner, who both had strong sympathies with the dissenters, attempted to secure its rejection and perhaps by forcing a dispute between the two houses to wreck the Bill's chances of passing.[147] The commons' deepest objections were to Clarendon's proviso: they thought that it did not properly belong in the Bill and that it was too harsh, and probably most disliked the inclusion of all courts – not just Common Law courts – among those in which refusal to swear would incur the penalty.[148] Eventually, however, they accepted defeat, although the retention of ecclesiastical courts in the proviso was won only after a close division in which two ex-presbyterians, Birch and Swinfen, were tellers for leaving them out.[149]

In accepting the Conventicle Act in 1664, the government finally abandoned the attempt to lift the laws of uniformity to encourage presbyterians to

---

[145] *C.J.*, 551, 551.
[146] *L.J.*, 605, 606, 609, 611, 612, 614; H.L.R.O., Committee Minutes, H.L., 6, 9, 10 May 1664, Main Papers, H.L., 6 May 1664, which includes many papers relating to Anglesey's work on the Bill in subcommittee; Bodl., Rawlinson MSS A 130, fol. 15v; see also Wharton's notes on the 1663 Bill in Carte MSS 81, fol. 170.
[147] *L.J.*, 614, 616, 617–18; *C.J.*, 562–3, 564; Pepys, *Diary*, V, 147–8; Bodl., Rawlinson MSS A 130, fol. 17v; H.L.R.O., Main Papers, H.L., 6 May 1664, for the lords' rejected clauses, and the working out of new ones.
[148] Bodl., Rawlinson MSS A 130, fol. 18v; *C.J.*, 564–5.
[149] *C.J.*, 564–5; *L.J.*, 617–18, 618–19; Bodl., Rawlinson MSS A 130, fol. 19; H.L.R.O., Main Papers, H.L., 6 May 1664, for the smaller amendments to the proviso, including the addition of a short preamble.

conform: the new Act was designed to force them to do so. The plot of 1663 had – for the moment at least – convinced the government that lenity was not, at present, the best solution to the religious problem: by May 1665 Clarendon was echoing what Sheldon said in 1662 when he told Bennet (now the earl of Arlington) that 'without doubt without a severe execution at present, the law and the government will fall into great contempt'.[150] Yet the chancellor remained hopeful that, if their leaders were irreconcilable, most nonconformists might be persuaded rather than coerced back to the Church. He endorsed severity against the leaders of conventicles, but suggested that their misguided followers should be dealt with more leniently.[151] In 1664 he appears to have tried to persuade John Owen to accept preferment in the Church.[152]

The session of 1664–5 was the first in which religion was not discussed, but by that of late 1665, with the war properly joined and the plague raging in London, religious dissent seemed more than ever to be a potential source of dangerous political unrest. In July and August the government was concerned that in London particularly, ejected ministers were preaching to congregations deserted by incumbents who had fled the town.[153] There was already some pressure from anglican royalists for a measure to banish them from the towns, and it was they, rather than the government itself, who were responsible for introducing a new bill against dissenting ministers into the commons: nevertheless, Clarendon's speech at the beginning of the session had included strong hints against internal as well as external enemies, and the Bill received much support from ministers and officials.[154] It was probably introduced in the commons by Sir William Lowther or Giles Strangwayes (who were first and second on the committee list), and passed quickly; in the lords it was committed on 27 October, and reported by Bridgewater on the 30th.[155] The ensuing debate is one of the few of which there is a full account, from notes taken by Wharton. The Bill imposed an oath – the same as that in the 1662 Militia Act – on all ejected ministers: those who refused to take it were banished to five miles away from any corporate town. Southampton

---

[150] Note at the foot of the petition of Thomas Fraser and Richard Baddeley, P.R.O., SP 29/121/95.

[151] Clarendon MSS 81, fol. 199, Sir William Armourer to Clarendon, 12 April 1664; see also the note at the foot of the letter of W. Portman and Sir J. Warre to Arlington, dated 15 July 1665, P.R.O., SP 29/126/109.

[152] *A complete collection of the sermons of . . . John Owen*, xxiii–xxiv; Diary of Bulstrode Whitelocke, April 1664 (see above, p. 29 and n. 86).

[153] See P.R.O., SP 29/127/136, Arlington to Henchman, no date; SP 29/127/63, Henchman to Arlington, 19 Aug. 1663; and Sheldon's letter to Henchman of 7 July, and his more general letter of inquiry in Wilkins, *Concilia*, IV, 582.

[154] *Parliamentary history*, IV, 326–7.

[155] *C.J.*, 616, 617, 619; *L.J.*, 695, 697; H.L.R.O., Committee Minutes, H.L., 27 Oct. 1665.

forcefully objected to the oath which promised not 'to endeavour any change or alteration in Church or State': this, he argued, was an unduly complete removal of a right to peaceful political action. Manchester and Lucas supported him, but Sheldon, York, and Northampton were irritated by the objection; for them it was perhaps fortunate that Wharton turned the debate back to the loyalty of the nonconformists, allowing Bridgewater and Morley to speak on much stronger ground. Southampton and Lucas failed in their attempt to have the Bill recommitted, and it passed, completing the 'Clarendon Code'.[156]

In the creation of this series of Acts, anglican sentiment in the house of commons was clearly decisive. The commons rejected appeals for lenity to dissenters with embarrassing regularity, and relentlessly pressed for legislation designed to crush dissent. But the passage of that legislation concealed the very real doubts of many M.P.s about the persecution of presbyterians. Divisions in the commons on attempts to ease the lot of the ministers ejected by the Act of Uniformity or to permit occasional conformity produced extraordinarily and consistently close results: the Church vote hovered just above ninety, the pro-presbyterian vote just below it. There were, for sure, far fewer M.P.s who were willing to support other nonconformists. In June 1663 a clause for occasional conformity was rejected by only ninety-four votes to eighty-nine, but in the vote on the passage of the Conventicle Bill just afterwards, the pro-nonconformist vote had dropped to sixty-one and the other side had correspondingly risen to 125.[157] In the absence of lists of those voting in these divisions, it is impossible to be sure of what they indicate: but it at least seems certain that while many in the house saw the suppression of the sectaries as essential, far fewer were eager for the persecution of moderate presbyterians. Indeed, the government's repeated efforts to achieve their relief in parliament testifies to its own belief that the majorities were narrow enough to be eventually reversed.

Action against the presbyterians was the preoccupation not of the house as a whole, nor even of the country gentry within it, but of a determined minority, a few anglican royalists who were always in the forefront of the attacks on dissent: Lord Fanshaw, Charlton, Finch, Berkenhead, Robert

[156] *L.J.*, 697; Wharton's notes are printed by C. Robbins in 'The Oxford session of the Long Parliament of Charles II', pp. 221–4; see also Bodl., Rawlinson MSS A 130, fol. 56; B.L., M636/20, Sir N. Hobart to Sir R. Verney, 1 Nov. 1665; Burnet, *History*, I, 400–3; and see Wharton's notes for his own speech on the Bill, Carte MSS 81, fol. 260.

[157] These votes are: 16 April 1662, whether to admit debate to the amendments to the Book of Common Prayer (90–6); 17 April 1662, to adhere to the words Michael the Archangel, i.e., to postpone the date of the Act's coming into force (87–96); 26 April 1662, to put the question on permitting the allowance of fifths to ejected ministers (87–94); 30 June 1663, to read again a proviso on behalf of those who go to church and receive the sacrament every year (89–94).

Milward, and others. Such men, whose dislike of presbyterianism had both religious and political roots, possessed the standing in parliament always to be heard; they also possessed powerful arguments which could bring the less enthusiastic country gentry to support persecution. They did not oppose presbyterians on purely religious grounds, they might argue: if it was solely a matter of religion, they would be as eager as anyone to see peaceable dissenters peaceably dissenting. But it was not solely a matter of religion: presbyterians differed not out of genuine conscience, but out of spiritual pride; their principles in Church and State led them into dangerous anti-monarchical positions; for all their protests, they were no better than the other, more obviously pernicious sectaries; and what better proof was there of their undesirability than their part in beginning the Civil War, from which so much confusion had followed? Better, they might say, to show that they would be utterly discountenanced than risk once more civil strife and social chaos. All the arguments that presbyterians and their sympathisers could use against these were weak ones, demolished by the single, incontrovertible statement, and its inevitable corollary: the presbyterians had rebelled before; they might do so again. The government had endowed the anglican royalists with power and prestige, a power and prestige which they used to thwart every attempt of some of its ministers to obtain any relaxation of conformity. The stability of Church and State depended, they believed, on uniformity: any policy which failed to recognise that, they felt bound to oppose. There are many reasons why concern about dissent would gradually decline, and be replaced with a grudging toleration: but one of the most important was perhaps that the rhetoric against dissent was the dialect not of the average backbench country gentleman, but of a powerful minority, a minority whose power lay in its dominance within the government and its dominance of parliament. Within the wider political nation, among the country gentry as a whole, there was, it is true, concern about the political and social effects of nonconformity and anxiety about the collapse of unity: but much less of a feeling that any compromise was undesirable.

All this placed policy-makers in an embarrassing, and contradictory position: their own agents in parliament had engineered the rejection of their own policies for reasons with which some ministers themselves sympathised; their deep commitment to the survival of the Church of England. Yet this did not mean that the commitment really (in their view) conflicted with their loyalty to the monarchy. They saw the Church and the monarchy as two parts of one institution, joined together by tradition, history, and excellence, their union consecrated by the blood of Charles I. Neither part could survive without the other. In the wake of the 1663 rising, the government abandoned – in some quarters, perhaps with relief – its attempts to lighten the requirements of conformity. Their abandonment indicated some disillusion over the possibility, and even the necessity, of bringing the presbyterians back into the Church: 'the truth is', Clarendon wrote to his son in 1671, 'they are a pack of knaves'.[158] Presbyterian dissent, he claimed, was kept alive only by the belief that concessions would be forthcoming; but there was no concession, short of the most radical, that could ever satisfy all of them. In retrospect, the 1663 rising, by showing both that there were some presbyterians who were so irreconcilable to the regime that it was pointless trying to reconcile them, and by exploding the idea that there were enough presbyterians willing to rebel to protect their religion, had greatly weakened all the arguments for comprehension. Although there were, throughout the reign of Charles II, further attempts towards comprehension, none received any more than luke-warm support from the government, and presbyterians themselves drifted into an acceptance of separation. Instead, the government persevered with its attempts to link the plight of catholics with that of protestant dissent, and to suppress the objections to the toleration of the former with the toleration of the latter.[159] In doing so, it was again thwarted not by the overwhelming anglicanism of parliament, but, as in 1663, by its conservatism and its legalism; its desire to preserve the laws, and to eschew radical change.

---

[158] Lister, *Clarendon*, III, 483, Clarendon to Cornbury, 10 June [1671].
[159] See R. Thomas, 'Comprehension and indulgence', in *From uniformity to unity, 1662–1962*, eds. O. Chadwick and G. F. Nuttall (London, 1962), pp. 189–253.

8

Indemnity

'My lords and gentlemen,' Charles said to parliament on passing the Act confirming the Convention's Act of Indemnity and Oblivion, 'let it be in no man's power to charge me or you with breach of our word or promise, which can never be a good ingredient to our future security'.[1] If the reconstruction of certainty and the rule of law was the basic principle of government policy, the preservation of the letter and the spirit of the Act of Indemnity was its essential corollary: stability might only be preserved and nurtured by assuring the former opponents of the monarchy that their lives and their property were safe in the protection of the law. But for royalists, the firmness of the government's commitment to the Act of Indemnity seemed less statesmanlike than foolish, a little suspicious, and above all insulting. The Act, as Sir Edward Lake pointed out, drew little distinction between loyalty and treason; the service and sufferings of royalists seemed to be ignored or undervalued.[2] Their attempts to change or infringe it were defeated by the government's resolute defence of its principles; and the bitterness this and other quarrels exacerbated helped to confirm and propagate the 'country', anti-court instincts of cavalierism.

Apart from the casual attitude to their sufferings which the government's whole policy suggested (and which Clarendon's behaviour particularly exemplified), cavaliers had two more specific grievances – although both possessed much wider implications. First, they resented the way in which (as they saw it) the Act of Indemnity had perpetuated the results of the war by impoverishing royalists and enriching their enemies. Many royalist families had been temporarily crippled by the financial consequences of defeat: but it is now known that few estates were permanently lost because of composition fines, confiscation or decimation; and those families which were forced to sell were often already heavily burdened with pre-Civil War debts. Nor were royalists the only ones affected: the war severely damaged the finances of neutral and even parliamentarian gentry, as well. Nevertheless, it remains

---

[1] *Parliamentary history*, IV, 213.   [2] Lake, *Memoranda*, pp. 109–11.

true that some families suffered difficulties, even hardship and penury, during the 1650s and 1660s because of the additional burdens imposed by the revolutionary regimes.[3] The compositions which had been charged to about 3,225 royalists to free their estates from sequestration had often forced them to mortgage, and sometimes to sell land. In many cases they were compelled to convey lands to their creditors, or creditors and trustees entered into property which had been assigned for debt before the Civil War, or took possession of mortgages to safeguard their rights.[4] Many of the 780 who had lost their lands in the three acts of sale of 1651–2 had contrived to recover them piecemeal over the rest of the Interregnum period, though often at considerable expense through repurchase. But often shortage of money had forced royalists to trade confirmations of title for immediate cash, and such confirmations – fines, conveyances, and recognisances – were left good and valid in law by the Act of Indemnity's sibling, the Act of Judicial Proceedings, because they legally represented a voluntary agreement between two parties.[5] In addition, no compensation was to be paid for the profits made by Interregnum purchasers while royalists' lands were in their possession. For many royalists, the Restoration simply accelerated the decline of the old nobility and gentry into poverty and the rise of a set of brash, unprincipled men, newly rich from the profits of the City and from trading in royalist property.[6] Insult was added to injury by the fact that although members of the parliamentary, Commonwealth, and Protectorate armies had long ago received compensation from those regimes for their wounds, and had since been properly paid off by the present government, royalist troops, for their arrears of pay, their wounds, and sometimes loans to the royalist war effort, had so far received nothing.

Royalists could have understood the government's caution and parsimony if they had not suspected something more sinister: beneath their financial worries lay their second grievance: a belief that their old enemies, having inveigled themselves into some of the best jobs in the new administration, were using them to block the path of preferment for cavaliers. With presbyterians entrenched in government and using their patronage to fill other posts

[3] J. Thirsk, 'The sales of royalist land during the Interregnum', *Econ. Hist. Rev.*, 2nd series, V (1952–3), 188–207; H. J. Habakkuk, 'Landowners and the Civil War," *Econ. Hist. Rev.*, 2nd series, XVIII (1965), 130–51; P. G. Holiday, 'Land sales and repurchases in Yorkshire after the Civil Wars, 1650–1670', *Northern History*, V (1970), 67–92; B. G. Blackwood, *The Lancashire gentry and the Great Rebellion 1640–1660*, Chetham Society, 3rd series, XXV (1978), 111–58; J. Broad, 'Gentry finances and the Civil War: the case of the Buckinghamshire Verneys', *Econ. Hist. Rev.*, 2nd series, XXXII (1979), 183–200; Roebuck, *Yorkshire baronets*, pp. 46–52, 112–15, 157–61.
[4] Habakkuk, 'Landowners and the Civil War', pp. 132–45.
[5] Holiday, 'Land sales and repurchases in Yorkshire', pp. 82–4.
[6] See above, pp. 40–1.

with their friends, it was difficult to see how royalists could ever return to high office – or hope for its emoluments to help them reverse their economic decline. Anglican royalists suspected too that presbyterians used their power to shelter nonconformists, even radicals, from the rigour of the law, and acted as advocates for them at court: the more virulent believed that their purposes remained (as they thought they had always been) their own profit and the ruin of the regime.[7] Some – such as the earl of Northampton – appealed to the king to abandon his reliance on their counsels; the presbyterians, they claimed, had merely 'connived at your Majesty's Restoration, as a degree to their rise, & yours & the monarchy's eternal destruction, & the Church's fall'.[8] While presbyterians had rebelled against the king once already, they pointed out, none could be trusted more than those who had already thrown in their lot with the monarchy and whose losses had set a seal on their loyalty.[9] Some of their anger, inevitably, was directed against those who had kept them from office – against Clarendon, in particular, who also upheld the government's refusal to compromise on the Act of Indemnity – and some sought the reason for their exclusion in corruption: the conspicuous wealth of presbyterians gave them obvious advantages in the race for favour and preferment.[10]

Although most at least paid lip-service to the basic premises of the Act of Indemnity – the stilling of partisan strife – many in the Cavalier Parliament and outside it believed much in it was capable of improvement. The famous jibe that it was an Act of Indemnity for the king's enemies and of Oblivion for his friends gained wide currency.[11] Clarendon commented that

men were well enough contented, that the king should grant indemnity to all men that had rebelled against him; that he should grant their lives and fortunes to them, who had forfeited them to him: but they thought it very unreasonable and unjust, that the king should release those debts which were immediately due to them, and forgive those trespasses which had been committed to their particular damage.[12]

Sir Edward Lake urged that goods which had been plundered or removed by reason of sequestration, should be forcibly restored to their original owners; royalists faced every day with the sight of their possessions remaining in the

---

[7] See above, pp. 52–6.
[8] Clarendon MSS 77, fol. 236, Northampton to the king, 18 Aug. 1662.
[9] E.g., B.L., Lansdowne MSS 525, fol. 56, Will. Haward to Lord Oxford or Northampton, 16 Sept. 1662; see 'The cavalier's complaint', and 'An echo to the cavalier's complaint' in *The cavalier songs and ballads of England*, ed. C. Mackay (London, 1863), pp. 209–12.
[10] See *The autobiography of Sir John Bramston*, p. 117; Ailesbury, *Memoirs*, I, 6–7; Lister, *Life of Clarendon*, III, 532–5, narrative of Sir Philip Monckton; see also Monckton's other (rather deranged) papers in the Nottingham University Library, Galway MSS 12631/1a.
[11] *Hist. MSS. Comm.*, 5th report, Sutherland MSS, p. 205, W. Smith to J. Langley, 30 June 1660.
[12] Clarendon, *Life*, I, 448–9.

hands of their former oppressors had reason to feel aggrieved. 'Surely', wrote Lake, 'this looks like a continued triumph after the War.'[13]

At the opening of the new parliament, Charles and Clarendon hoped to avoid a re-examination of the Act of Indemnity by recommending its confirmation in the strongest terms possible. Charles spoke against anyone 'who would endeavour to undermine or shake that foundation of our public peace, by infringing that Act in the least degree', and told the assembled houses that he had had two bills prepared for the confirmation of everything passed in the Convention.[14] On the first full day of business one of these, for the confirmation of all public acts, was read in the commons. The committee for the Bill was instructed to check the Act of Indemnity, the Act for Judicial Proceedings, the Act for taking away the court of wards, and all those acts to do with the revenue, only to make sure that they agreed with their titles; as to the other acts, however, including the Act for Confirming Ministers, the committee was left free.[15]

Ultimately, after John Vaughan's report from the committee, the Bill was divided into two: one to confirm the Acts of Indemnity, Judicial Proceedings, abolition of the court of wards, and the financial acts, the other to confirm all the other statutes which were more likely to be amended. Even so, the first Bill was held up: not until 14 June was it read for the third time; then the house was kept until well into the afternoon – despite the Speaker's attempts to adjourn – by a proviso presented by Edward Seymour, seeking to alter part of the Act of Indemnity, and seeming, as Marvell said, 'to open the way for many provisos more'. The Speaker prevented a vote on the proviso then, which one observer believed might have been successful; and the following morning (after the king had made known his disapproval of the proviso) Seymour was defeated in a division.[16] The Bill was debated again on 19 June, but on the 22nd a further reminder of his commitment to the Bill from the king ensured its speedy passage.[17] In the lords it passed quickly without any attempt at amendment.[18]

Seymour's proviso seems to have been limited in scope: more general efforts to infringe the Act had less support. On 21 May, Sir Richard Spencer presented a bill 'for supplying the Bill of Indemnity', probably the same as that noted by Reymes 'for securing the subject according to the 11th of

[13] Lake, *Memoranda*, pp. 110–11.
[14] *Parliamentary history*, IV, 179, 182.
[15] *C.J.*, 247, 249–50; see *Hist. MSS. Comm.*, 5th report, Sutherland MSS, p. 207.
[16] *C.J.*, 260, 271, 272; Margoliouth, II, 30, Marvell to Hull Corporation, 15 June 1661, cf. p. 31, same to same, 17 June 1661; Clarendon, *Life*, I, 528; B.L., Add. MSS 11324, fol. 27, ? to ?, 18 June 1661.
[17] *C.J.*, 275, 278.
[18] *L.J.*, 295, 296, 297–8; 13 Car. II, c. 7, *S.R.*, 309–10.

H: 7'.[19] The 1495 '*de facto*' act had been intended to reassure Henry VII's late enemies, indemnifying all who claimed allegiance to any king, including Richard III.[20] But its terms could adroitly be turned to cavalier advantage, discharging all who had been loyal to any king from all forfeitures resulting from their allegiance. The effect of the Bill would probably have been to restore cavalier lands to the position before the war. Spencer had himself suffered much in the war; he had lent large sums to Charles I and had been imprisoned twice.[21] His Bill was read but not passed, according to Reymes, 'by reason of some things therein contained not fit to pass the house'.[22] In such general cases, the commons showed respect for the king's desire to avoid a comprehensive reversal of the Act of Indemnity, or anything approaching it: but in particular cases they and the lords were more willing to demonstrate their appreciation of the sacrifices of individual cavaliers. 'The king is most gracious & resolved for the Act of Indemnity', wrote Roger Pepys in June, 'was it not for his Majesty, that would be shaken: here will be some endeavour to pare its nails till the blood come, by private bills, which cannot be kept off unless the king hath notice of it.'[23]

As so many private bills are now lost, and because a bill's title is often uninformative, it is difficult to discover exactly how serious this problem was. There were, however, a few notorious bills which were considered to entrench upon the Act of Indemnity, and raised in a more urgent form old questions concerning the inviolability of the firmest legal instruments. To these cases Charles referred, when at the end of the first session he complained about the numbers of private bills presented for his agreement.

It is true, these late ill times have driven men into great straits, and may have obliged them to make conveyances colourably, to avoid inconveniences, and yet not afterwards to be avoided. And men have gotten estates by new and greater frauds than have been heretofore practised; and therefore, in this conjuncture, extraordinary remedies may be necessary, which hath induced me to comply with your advice, in passing these bills.[24]

Royalists who had entered into fines, conveyances, and recognisances which confirmed their sales of land to Interregnum purchasers could claim that they had been forced into them by the circumstances of the time, and thus bring their validity into doubt. Naturally, lawyers were disturbed by the impli-

[19] *The notebook of Sir John Northcote*, p. 129; B.L., Egerton MSS 2043, fol. 9; *C.J.*, 256–7.
[20] G. R. Elton, *The Tudor constitution* (Cambridge, 1960), pp. 2, 5; although for an interpretation of the intent of the original Act which rather closely accords with this hypothetical cavalier reading of it, see D. E. C. Yale, 'Hobbes and Hale on law, legislation and the sovereign', *Cambridge Law Journal*, XXXI (1) (1972), 153–5.
[21] *H.P.*, III, 465.
[22] B.L., Egerton MSS 2043, fol. 9.
[23] Bodl., Tanner MSS 49, fol. 101, Roger Pepys to Sir John Hobart, June 1661.
[24] *Parliamentary history*, IV, 247.

cations: if such confirmations could so easily be annulled by this argument, it would weaken the strongest assurances the law could give; if the annulment was done by act of parliament, it would provide a further instance of the supremacy of statute over the fundamentals of the common law; and any such annulment would show that the Act of Indemnity could do little to protect individuals from royalist vengeance. As Clarendon had insisted, the best guarantee of stability was 'firmness and constancy, by every man's knowing what is his right to enjoy and what is his duty to do'.[25] By allowing parliament to deny at will what were otherwise considered to be excellent titles of ownership, the whole foundation of the country's peace and security might be rocked.

Every man had raised an equity in his own imagination, that he thought ought to prevail against any descent, testament, or act of law; and that whatever any man had been brought to do, which common reason would make manifest that he would never have done if he could have chosen, was argument sufficient of such a force, and ought to find relief in parliament, from the unbounded equity they were masters of and could dispense, whatever formalities of law had preceded or accompanied the transaction. And whoever opposed these extravagant notions, which sometimes deprived men of the benefit of the Act of Oblivion, was thought to be without justice, or, which to them was worse, to be without any kindness to the king's party.[26]

The government's commitment to the principles of the Act, and to the certainty of the rule of law was demonstrated in a number of *causes célèbres* in which the efforts of cavaliers to recover their lands in parliament were stiffly resisted by the government, provoking much royalist bitterness. The greatest of these was the earl of Derby's attempt to recover land sold in the first of the 1651 acts of sale, which he had failed to repurchase. Among this was property in Flintshire, bought from the treason trustees by George Twistleton (then governor of Denbigh), Humphrey Ellis (then governor of Hawarden), and Sir John Trevor of Trevallin, who together paid Derby £1,700 in return for his legal recognition of their title to the land and any subsequent conveyances they made. In 1660 Derby made a concerted effort to reclaim all his lands through parliament, but could get neither of the bills which he had introduced for the purpose passed.[27] In May 1661 he presented a new bill: all his land was to be restored, but in the single case of the Flintshire property he was to repay the purchase price, plus 6 per cent interest, although all the rents the purchasers had received from it were to be deducted: they were to be allowed no final profit.[28] They petitioned against

[25] Clarendon, *Brief view and survey*, p. 124.
[26] Clarendon, *Life*, I, 574; see also *Parliamentary history*, IV, 247.
[27] B. Coward, *The Stanleys, Lords Stanley and earls of Derby, 1385–1672: the origins, wealth and power of a landowning family*, Chetham Society, 3rd series, XXX (1983), 72–5.
[28] *L.J.*, 265, 271; H.L.R.O., Main Papers, H.L., 25 May 1661.

the Bill, and in committee, their counsel (one of whom was Francis Goodrick, who had been prominent in 1660 in urging as wide an indemnity as possible) argued that because it reversed a fine, the Bill infringed both the Act of Indemnity and the Act of Judicial Proceedings. The judges declared for Derby, but on 20 June, after the hearing of the counsel for the other purchasers, the committee accepted that Derby should be restored only to the Flintshire estates, as they could find 'no fraud or force' in the other cases.[29] Although counsel were later heard at the bar of the house, however, there was no further progress in the bill, perhaps because of several complaints from the purchasers of the earl's illegal entry into their lands.[30]

In December Derby tried again, with a similar bill, this time limited to the Flintshire property and deducting from the compensation which he offered the rents the purchasers had received, and the £9,000 which they had had from John Glynne for the purchase of Hawarden. This time sentiment ran decisively in favour of Derby, and despite some strong opposition on 6 February the Bill passed.[31] A protest was entered against it, claiming that it was against the Acts of Indemnity and Judicial Proceedings, because it overrode the fines and recoveries that they had made good. Breaking such excellent and legal assurances was dangerous, particularly as the fraud of the purchasers which provided the pretext for doing so had not been proved. Clarendon, one of the protest's chief signatories, may have been behind it: the others who signed it included several of his associates – Ormonde, Bridgewater, and Portland – as well as ex-presbyterians and ex-Cromwellians several of whom now held high office – Robartes, Anglesey, Manchester, Carlisle, Bedford, Northumberland, Wharton, Warwick, Scarsdale, and Grey of Warke.[32] For cavaliers, the protest must simply have confirmed their suspicions about Clarendon's support for and association with presbyterians, and his disregard for themselves. In the commons the Bill was extensively discussed, and debated by counsel; evidently they, too, were troubled by the overriding of fines and recoveries. But on 17 March, after it was reported by Sir John Berkenhead (who had some connections with the house of Derby), the Bill passed there as well.[33]

Shortly after its passage in the commons, Derby appealed to the king to allow the Bill to pass: in his petition he stressed the judgement of Lord Chief

[29] H.L.R.O., Main Papers, H.L., 19 June 1661, Committee Minutes, H.L., 11, 14, 20 June 1661; *H.P.*, II, 409–10.
[30] *L.J.*, 301; H.L.R.O., Main Papers, H.L., 15 July 1661.
[31] *L.J.*, 347, 348, 361–2, 363–4, 372, 378–9; H.L.R.O., Main Papers, H.L., 10 Dec. 1661, Committee Minutes, H.L., 18, 21 Jan. 1662.
[32] *L.J.*, 379.
[33] *C.J.*, 363, 366, 372–3, 375, 388; for Berkenhead's Stanley connections, see Thomas, *Sir John Berkenhead*, pp. 4, 6, 9.

Justice Bridgman that the Bill did not infringe the Acts of Indemnity or Judicial Proceedings.[34] The matter was discussed at council, all parties were heard, and a compromise was reached, to refer the whole matter to the king: at the end of the session, the Bill was one of two which were vetoed; Clarendon, in his closing speech on 19 May, informed the houses of the king's decision, and was careful to commend 'that noble family, which hath served him so faithfully, and suffered so much for so doing'. But this failed to mollify some cavaliers. The earl of Ailesbury was probably repeating his father, Lord Bruce's reminiscence, when he wrote of the fury the decision aroused: when the veto was announced the two houses 'fetched a deep sigh'; Clarendon, he claimed, had pursued a vendetta against the Stanleys, and had deliberately favoured the Interregnum purchasers. Two of them, Maynard and Glynne, had held office under the usurped powers, and now received high legal preferment from the chancellor's hands.[35]

Derby was not the only one to seek to avoid fines and conveyances made during the Interregnum. On 17 May a bill was read in the commons to break the conveyances of some lands near Aylesbury made during the war by Sir John Pakington. When the house ordered that it should be read again, Reymes noted that Sir Thomas Fanshaw 'took occasion to thank the house for showing so much kindness to a cavalier it being the first time he ever saw any'.[36] But ten days later Pakington's wife wrote to Bishop Morley to tell him of the Bill's withdrawal. It was, she wrote, an 'act of obedience', presumably of obedience to royal command. The king appears – as he had for Derby – to have offered to arbitrate in the case himself instead.[37] In 1664 a similar bill was ultimately allowed to pass, despite the purchasers' appeal to the fine: Pakington's counsel argued that he had received no money from the transaction, only an abatement of his composition, and this may have given him a better case than Derby; royal arbitration may have concluded that Pakington had justice on his side; or else by 1664 the government was perhaps less nervous of minor infringements of the Act of Indemnity.[38]

Several other bills were of similar intention: one 'to enable John Newport to enter into certain messuages lying in Westminster' involved fines, and was declared by Lord Chief Justice Foster to be against the Act of Judicial Proceedings.[39] Another read in 1663 was for avoiding conveyances entered into

---

[34] P.R.O., SP 29/52/95, PC 2/55, fols. 295, 297v.
[35] *Parliamentary history*, IV, 254; Ailesbury, *Memoirs*, I, 5–6.
[36] *C.J.*, 253; B.L., Egerton MSS 2043, fol. 6v.
[37] Coventry papers, vol. 119, fol. 29, Dorothy Pakington to Morley, 27 May 1661.
[38] *C.J.*, 536, 537, 544, 545; *L.J.*, 595, 596, 601, 602, 603, 605; H.L.R.O., Main Papers, H.L., 19 April 1664, Committee Minutes, H.L., 29 April 1664; Bodl., Rawlinson MSS A 130, fol. 12.
[39] *L.J.*, 531–2; H.L.R.O., Parchment Collection, H.L., 15 May 1663.

by Lord Mollineux: despite the fact that it had been consented to by all parties concerned, a division was still forced on it in committee.[40] The marquis of Worcester, a catholic whose estates had been sold during the Interregnum, had two bills read for settling lands on foeffees in trust for the payment of his debts, the second of which was appealed against by purchasers of his land, 'for which', it was claimed, 'they have as good assurances as the law can give'.[41] But in fact the most vehement debates on fines came over a case whose details had little to do with the hazards of Civil War allegiance: the case of the fines levied by Sir Edward and Lady Powell during the 1650s, to which Lady Powell's agreement (so it was alleged) had been wrung from her by force, had already caused immense controversy in the Convention. Part of the argument was over the matter of fact, the authenticity of the allegations advanced by those who wanted the fine to be vacated. But the more important matters in dispute concerned the inviolability of the Common Law: lawyers claimed that there were some assurances in Common Law (and fines were amongst them) which even statute could not vacate; vacating a fine would lead, as Bristol ridiculed their argument, to 'earthquakes . . . shaking of foundations . . . confusion through insecurity in all the tenures in England'.[42] In 1661 a second bill was presented for vacating the fines: in the commons it was opposed by the lawyers; and in the lords, several of those who had protested against Derby's Bill also protested against this one.[43] One speech, arguing strongly against the vacating of fines, hinted at the possible results of the precedent; 'how can men know or with whom advise to be safe in bargaining if the legislative power shall become a court of pleas? Will not bills here be as frequent as in Chancery? . . . You have all eyes upon you, men's expectations are big to see the issue of this cause which hath a chain of consequences that will reach through the whole realm.'[44] If a cavalier parliament was enabled to override many of the conveyances executed over the Interregnum, the guarantees of law on which the stability of the regime rested were unlikely to survive for very long.[45]

Derby's case had been an unusually clear example of the exploitation of straitened cavalier circumstances by unscrupulous Interregnum speculators –

---

[40] C.J., 516, 517, 530; L.J., 574, 577; H.L.R.O., Committee Minutes, H.L., 27 July 1663.
[41] L.J., 348, 386, 396, 404; H.L.R.O., Main Papers, H.L., 10 March 1662.
[42] See Bristol's speech (presumably of 1660, as it refers to the lords' judicial decision on the case as occurring in the same parliament) in Hertford Record Office, Verulam MSS XII, B7. I am grateful to Dr Swatland for drawing my attention to this speech.
[43] L.J., 265, 279, 282, 287, 293, 296, 298, 304, 311–12; C.J., 306, 311–12, 318, 333, 344, 348, 350–1, 352–3; B.L., Egerton MSS, 2043, fol. 44.
[44] Bodl., Rawlinson MSS D. 922, fol. 309v.
[45] It was perhaps the topicality of the issue which provoked the publication in 1662 of a Tudor reading on the 1488–9 Statute of Fines; *Le Reading del Monsieur Denshall sur l'Estatute de Finibus fait anno 4. H. 7.* (no place of publication, 1662).

men who were also agents of the usurping government. Few other cases were quite so obviously iniquitous. In many, the purchasers had been tenants, exercising their rights of pre-emption to avoid losing the land: in others, pre-war creditors had attempted during the War and Interregnum to recoup their money by taking possession of mortgages or entering into land held on trust, and often the bitterness that resulted from such cases divided those who had fought on the same side or were even in the same family, as much as it confirmed the divisions of the war.[46] The spectacular family quarrels of the Pawletts over the settlement of the marquis of Winchester's estate, complicated by the confiscation and sequestration it had undergone during the Interregnum, were dragged through parliament several times in the early 1660s.[47]

But royalists might have expected a more sympathetic response to their demands for reparation where the guilt of those who had benefited from their lands had been clearly acknowledged by their exception from the Act of Indemnity.[48] The marquis of Winchester, whose defence of his house at Basing had become a legend of cavalier tenacity, had been excepted from parliament's pardon, and from 1649 was imprisoned, his estate sequestered and vested in Robert Wallop in reparation for £10,000 in damages inflicted on his own property by royalist forces. In 1660 Wallop had himself been excepted from pardon and reserved to pains and penalties not extending to life; in May 1661 Winchester took the opportunity of his as yet undetermined punishment by presenting a bill in the lords to allow him £15,000 in compensation out of Wallop's estate – although this was rejected immediately.[49] In the following month he presented a similar bill in the commons, and, backed by such well-known royalists as Sir John Strangwayes and George Fane (first and second on the committee list), it passed with little apparent difficulty. In the lords, however, it was again thrown out, when the judges reported that the Bill was against the Act of Indemnity.[50] Two similar bills were read in the commons, one for taking £3,000 out of the lands of Sir John Danvers, for the benefit of Angel Gray,[51] and another for levying £2,690 out of the lands of Colonel John Hutchinson: neither, however, was passed.[52]

[46] See Habakkuk, 'Landowners and the Civil War', pp. 143–7.
[47] *L.J.*, 400, 401, 432, 435, 436, 529, 531; *C.J.*, 462, 464, 489, 493; H.L.R.O., Main Papers, H.L., 6 March 1662, 1 June 1663, Committee Minutes, H.L., 3, 16, 27 June, 2 July 1663.
[48] 12 Car. II, c. 11, paras. XXXIV–XLII, *S.R.*, 231–2.
[49] *L.J.*, 254; H.L.R.O., Main Papers, H.L., 15 May 1661.
[50] *C.J.*, 269, 272, 287; *L.J.*, 299, 307; H.L.R.O., Parchment Collection, H.L., 2 July 1661; see 12 Car. II, c. 11, para. III, *S.R.*, 227 for their probable reason.
[51] Fane was also first on the committee list for this bill, and Sir John and Giles Strangwayes, William Legge, and Winston Churchill were included. *C.J.*, 299, 306; cf. *Calendar of the proceedings of the committee for compounding*, ed. M. A. E. Green, 5 vols. (London, 1889–92), II, 1563.
[52] *C.J.*, 267, 283; Lucy Hutchinson, *Memoirs of the life of Colonel Hutchinson*, ed. J. Sutherland (London, 1973), p. 239, cf. pp. 184–6, 231, 233.

Other attempts on the regicides' estates were made when the Bill to declare the penalties to be imposed on those excepted from the Act of Indemnity was discussed. On 1 July the evidence against them was considered in the commons. All their estates, the house resolved, should be confiscated; those whose lives had been pardoned were to be imprisoned, degraded, and to suffer humiliation. Those who had been excepted utterly from pardon, but who had voluntarily surrendered themselves, whose deaths had been suspended in the Act of Indemnity were now to be executed.[53] A bill for the pains and penalties not extending to life was read twice on 4 July and referred to a committee dominated by government associates and legal counsel. Progress in the committee was hampered by the presentation of petitions claiming interests in the offenders' estates; and on 15 July, after Bramston's report, three provisos were added, one for the marquis of Winchester, probably again for his reparation from Wallop's estate, another on Lord Craven's behalf, and a third for Sir William Lewis. On the 19th there was an attempt by Angel Gray to follow suit; but his proviso was rejected in a division, although his Bill received a second reading the following day.[54] In the lords, however, there was vehement criticism of the provisos: Craven withdrew his, but Winchester refused to do the same, despite Southampton, Wallop's brother-in-law, pointing out that he had no right to reparation, since the treason for which the penalty was imposed had not been committed against him, but against the king. The proviso was rejected, although the house, recognising Winchester's grievance, agreed instead to petition the king on his behalf.[55] Angel Gray and the other petitioners were also referred to the king by the committee, and on the 27th the Bill was returned.[56]

But the commons refused to accept the rejection of Winchester's proviso. What followed was something like a cavalier revolt: Clifford, Ryve, Churchill, Fane, Strickland, Duncombe, Meres, and Henry Coventry were appointed to ask for and manage a conference with the lords on the proviso. They told the lords' managers – Southampton, and three ex-Cromwellians and ex-presbyterians, Manchester, Robartes, and Ashley – that it 'did appear to be a just thing ... they conceive this proviso did not intrench upon the Act of Oblivion; & they look upon the marquis of Winchester to have done much service for the king, & suffered much in his estate for him; & nothing hath been yet given him by way of recompence & this proviso gives him nothing but his own'.[57] The lords answered that they had received a message from the king that the proviso should be omitted, because it intrenched on his own

[53] C.J., 286–7; S.R., 231–2.
[54] C.J., 290, 297, 301, 306.
[55] L.J., 318, 320–1; B.L., Add. MSS 23215, fol. 40, John Finch to Lord Conway, 27 July 1661.
[56] H.L.R.O., Committee Minutes, H.L., 26, 27 July 1661; L.J., 323–4.
[57] C.J., 314; L.J., 323–4.

prerogative: as they pointed out, 'pains & penalties upon crimes of so high a nature do absolutely belong of right to the king; & that their lordships cannot admit the taking away any of them from his Majesty without a manifest violation of justice, and his Majesty's just & legal right', adding from themselves that it was completely against the Act of Indemnity. These arguments the commons seem to have been willing to accept; instead of the proviso a petition to the king on behalf of Winchester was drawn up and taken to the lords by Lord Bruce, and the Bill was passed.[58]

Such bills affected only a few individuals – although the impression they gave of the court's insensitivity and disregard for cavalier distress was spread much wider. Yet many more royalists had interests in recovering other rights. Since the king's return, royalists had been anxiously expecting the introduction of a bill to restore to them the advowsons and impropriate rectories confiscated as part of their composition fines. These had been vested in the trustees for the maintenance of ministers, for making grants to poor clergy and augmenting the stipends of impoverished livings; at the Restoration this fund reverted to the Crown. A bill to restore the advowsons and tithes to their original owners had been rejected in 1660; another was apparently presented in the commons in May 1661, although there is no record of it having been read until 4 July.[59] On 6 July it was referred to a committee the first member of which was John Freschville, who had himself been forced to endow a local chapel as part of his composition. The committee was instructed to ensure that arrears of rent would be paid to the original owners, not to the clergy who had benefited from the trustees' augmentations, and to annul the bonds into which many royalists had entered – principally after Penruddock's rebellion in 1655 – which encumbered several estates.[60] The latter provision seems to have been dropped in the commons, but when the Bill came to the lords the committee's clause concerning rent arrears was declared by Sir Robert Foster, lord chief justice of the king's bench, to be against the Act of Indemnity. He also pointed out that many advowsons, rectories, and impropriate tithes had been bought with the consent of the former owners, and when their value had exceeded the amount of composition charged they had been paid for the excess: in these cases, the Bill might be against both the Acts of Indemnity and the Act for Judicial Proceedings. In any event, he

[58] *L.J.*, 323–4, 325–6; *C.J.*, 314, 315; cf. the Bill to confirm the royal arbitration in Winchester's affairs: *L.J.*, 400, 401, 436; H.L.R.O., Main Papers, H.L., 6 March 1662.

[59] *Hist. MSS. Comm.*, 5th report, Sutherland MSS, p. 150, F. Newport to Leveson, 16 June 1660, p. 154, A. Newport to Leveson, 26 June 1660, p. 158, same to same, 6 Dec. 1660, p. 151, F. Newport to same, 28 May 1661, p. 145, R. Milward to same, 30 May 1661; *C.J.*, 290.

[60] *C.J.*, 293; *H.P.*, II, 368; see also *Hist. MSS. Comm.*, 5th report, Sutherland MSS, p. 150, F. Newport to Leveson, 16 June 1660; P. H. Hardacre, *The Royalists during the Puritan Revolution* (The Hague, 1956), pp. 128–30.

argued, the advowsons and impropriations were now vested in the king, and the Bill would require his prior consent. The lords' committee accepted the first part of Foster's report and removed the reference to the payment of arrears, but they rejected the relevance of his other comments – although they did allow to stand all changes in ownership which had been confirmed by fines and recoveries.[61] During a recommitment, when the king's title to the impropriations which had been thus confirmed or had been sold to persons excepted from the Act of Indemnity was discussed and rejected, this clause concerning fines and recoveries was removed.[62] Although the Bill passed and cavaliers were returned to their advowsons and impropriated rectories, the arguments on the king's right to retain them, defended in the committee by the attorney general, might even have made it look as if the government itself was trying to profit from cavalier misfortune.

The reconstruction of royalist estates demanded more than the return of confiscated land and property rights: many of the cavaliers had other difficulties besides, among them the problems of overcoming a burden of debt while interest rates were high. Sir John Habakkuk has pointed out the connection between the sufferings of indebted royalists and the agitation for a reduction in the legal maximum interest rate in the 1660s and 1670s: this was made explicit in the Bill passed in the commons in July 1661, but rejected – partly, perhaps, because of the government's dependence on the City – in the lords, for abatement of interest to 3 per cent for debts contracted before the wars by those who had fought for the king. The Bill was probably sponsored by Fane, Churchill, and perhaps Bramston, the first three M.P.s on the committee list – all members deeply involved in other cavalier legislation.[63]

Then there were the soldiers, the officers and soldiers of the royal armies who had received none of their vast arrears of pay, nor any compensation for their wounds and sufferings, nor even support for their widows. Shortly before the new parliament opened, they were organising petitions:[64] that of the 'king's party' was printed, urging their claim on the country's generosity; their courage, constancy, and integrity, they hoped, 'how it engaged us in attempts, which, perhaps were more honest than prudent, by opposing plots to counsels, and tumults to the best armies, will not (I trust) be forgotten by English men in our days'. They accepted the Act of Indemnity, but pleaded for recompense in offices and in reversions, in favourable leases of Crown and

[61] *L.J.*, 313, 314, 412, 442; H.L.R.O., Committee Minutes, H.L., 2 May 1662.
[62] *L.J.*, 451; H.L.R.O., Committee Minutes, H.L., 7 May 1662; *C.J.*, 424, 429, 432.
[63] Habakkuk, 'Landowners and the Civil War', p. 149; *C.J.*, 290, 307, 308, 311; *L.J.*, 323; cf. above, p. 112, for cavalier opposition to a rise in interest rates proposed by the government.
[64] *Hist. MSS. Comm.*, 5th report, Sutherland MSS, p. 203, E. Gower to Leveson, 11 May 1661.

Church lands, and in provision for the maimed and wounded in hospitals.[65] But by 30 May the soldiers had abandoned their plan to petition parliament – perhaps asked by the government to wait until after the confirmation of the Act of Indemnity had been secured; so all that had been done for their relief before the summer recess was a collection in the lords for poor men crippled in the service of Charles I.[66]

Over the summer, the dissatisfaction of some royalists became more marked. Rugge noticed in August many unrewarded poor cavaliers walking 'sadly up and down the streets'; and a few days before the reopening of parliament in November a correspondent of Sir Job Charlton was concerned that cavalier discontent might get out of hand.[67] The government was not entirely blind to the political dangers of ignoring cavalier complaints, and Charles hinted in his speech at the resumption of parliament that measures for their satisfaction would not be unwelcome, but could come only with the augmentation of the royal revenue.[68] In November Prynne's appeal in the commons for £160,000 to complete the paying off of the Interregnum army and navy provoked indignation and counter-proposals for the relief of royalists. On the 27th it was decided that £60,000 out of the assessment just voted by the house should be devoted to the cavaliers, and a committee was appointed to consider ways of augmenting this sum.[69] A group calling themselves the 'loyal society' wrote to Clarendon on 30 November, asking if they might present the king with an address containing the royalists' desires, and if he thought fit, to offer parliament some suggestions for the further supply of the cavaliers. Their request was received sympathetically, and the group, which included the prominent cavalier officers Colonel Francis Lovelace, Lord John Poulett, Sir Philip Monckton, Sir William Courtenay, Sir John Boys, Sir Robert Carr, Sir Edward Broughton, Lord Byron, and Sir William Throckmorton, reported again to Clarendon a few days later.[70]

A Bill for charging a parish rate for the relief of poor and maimed soldiers was probably the work of the committee appointed on 27 November: it was sent on 5 February to the same committee, chaired by Lord Bruce. By

---

[65] *An humble representation of the sad condition of many of the king's party* (London, 1661), and cf. *The history and proceedings of the house of lords from the Restoration to the present time* (2 vols., London, 1742–3), I, 46–50.

[66] *Hist. MSS. Comm.*, 5th report, Sutherland MSS, p. 160, A. Newport to Leveson, 30 May 1661; *L.J.*, 295.

[67] B.L., Add. MSS 10116, fol. 237v; P.R.O., SP 29/44/61, B—.A—. to Sir Job Charlton, 16 Nov. 1661.

[68] *Parliamentary history*, IV, 223; see also Clarendon MSS 76, fol. 170, the lord treasurer's report on a petition of Civil War royal creditors.

[69] *C.J.*, 318, 321; B.L., Egerton MSS 2043, fols. 19v, 21v; the figure was the amount in excess of the £1.2 million that the commons had voted, produced by an assessment of £70,000 a month for eighteen months.

[70] Clarendon MSS 76, fol. 337, and 93, fol. 156.

12 March it had passed both houses.[71] This, however, was probably seen as a temporary measure: the main Bill, for the distribution of the £60,000, was also to include a further tax for the cavaliers' benefit. It was much longer in preparation: it had its first reading only on 19 March, and was reported, by Bruce, on 4 April. As the further supply, the Bill imposed a tax of 12 per cent a month for eighteen months on all offices worth over £5 a year not already rated in the assessment, an imposition perhaps suggested by royalists who were convinced that presbyterians held the cream of government offices.[72] When the Bill reached the lords, some criticised its preamble, a brief but partisan account of the unfailing constancy of the 'loyal party' throughout the 'barbarous rebellion' raised by 'certain men then sitting at Westminster'. The latter phrase and the word 'party' were heavily debated in an unusually full committee meeting on the Bill, and accepted only after two divisions.[73] But in the house – perhaps less dominated by cavaliers than the committee – 'by certain men' was altered to 'by some of the men', presumably allowing those who had sat in the lords after 1642 to make their own construction of the phrase's meaning.[74] The Bill passed only after a dispute between the two houses on the assessment of the lords for their offices.[75]

The loyal soldiers' problems were not over, however: on 12 March 1663 some of the officers presented a petition to the commons, and supported it with a pamphlet, dated two weeks later, addressed to both houses. They complained both of the fraudulent claims of many applicants to the fund and of corruption in the distribution of the money.[76] The petition was referred to a committee, of which Bruce was again the first member, and out of this came an act tightening the rules for distributing the money, allowing commissioners to examine claimants on oath, and laying down criteria for deciding eligibility.[77] Another bill was read the same session, perhaps sponsored by Thomas Tompkins, the first M.P. named to the committee on it, to allow loyal soldiers to exercise trades presumably by bypassing corporation laws on apprenticeship.[78] But still in 1664 the cavaliers' problem remained unsolved: a tract by Charles Hammond complained again of fraud and corruption, another petition was presented in the commons, and the consequent inquiry

[71] C.J., 350, 358, 368, 376; L.J., 399, 400, 405; 14 Car. II, c. 9, S.R., 389–90.
[72] C.J., 381, 384, 389, 391, 397; 14 Car. II, c. 8, paras. IX, XIV, S.R., 387, 388; see Chandaman, *The English public revenue*, p. 161.
[73] L.J., 433, 436–7; H.L.R.O., Committee Minutes, H.L., 28, 29, 30 April 1662.
[74] L.J., 444, 445, 446.
[75] C.J., 426, 430, 432, 433; L.J., 453, 454, 459, 460; 14 Car. II, c. 8, S.R., 380–8.
[76] C.J., 448–9; *The plea, case and humble proposals of the truly-loyal and suffering officers* (London, 1663).
[77] C.J., 500, 501, 519, 520, 531; L.J., 558, 563, 570; 15 Car. II, c. 3, S.R., 442–3.
[78] C.J., 512, 518.

continued into the following session under the chairmanship of Sir John Berkenhead and Sir Thomas Littleton.[79]

Most of the impetus for measures for cavalier relief had come not from the government, but from a small group of M.P.s interested in the issue, particularly Lord Bruce, Lord Fanshaw, Sir Bainham Throckmorton, George Fane, John Freschville, and a few others. It was clear that royalists resented the government's apparent lack of interest in their condition, were deeply hurt by allegations that they were trying merely to upset the reconciliation brought by the Act of Uniformity, and felt that part of the reason for their failure to obtain relief was attributable to the power of their former enemies about the court.[80]

As a result, some royalists felt their problem needed to be addressed at a more fundamental level than mere charity; and some anglican royalist politicians, who believed that ex-presbyterians and ex-Cromwellians exercised a pernicious influence in local and national government, tended to agree with them. The power of presbyterians could not be broken, and the grievances of impoverished cavaliers could not be attended to, until they were thoroughly eradicated from all levels of the administration. In February 1664, William Legge spoke for many royalists when he urged that in the next meeting of parliament

the king has no way, or counsel so good, as wholly to countenance, own and trust the old royal party, and truly besides my interest there, I am of opinion, it will be best for his service, the major part of that assembly being composed of that body, and their opposite still plotting and contriving disturbances, besides that, we observe, all considerable persons now in trust that formerly opposed the Crown (three or four only excepted) to carry on a bias still to their old partners, and endeavour to preserve a faction among them, and I could wish my friends would lay by their mask of policy, and declare frankly for the old honest party.[81]

In June 1663 Sir Edward Nicholas wrote that 'until there shall be a law made & executed that no person shall hold any office or place in Church or State, that shall not abjure the Covenant, I am persuaded that neither this, nor any of his Majesty's kingdoms will be secure from treasonable practices'.[82]

Royalists made several efforts to procure the expulsion from the administration of all collaborators with the Interregnum regimes. The commons'

---

[79] C. Hammond, 'Truth's discovery, or the cavaliers' case clearly stated by conscience and plain dealing', in *A collection of scarce and valuable tracts ... selected from ... public as well as private libraries, particularly that of the late Lord Somers*, ed. W. Scott (13 vols., London, 1803–15), VII, 557–65; *C.J.*, 540, 543, 559, 569, 571, 580, 600, 609, 612; cf. *L.J.*, 592, 594.

[80] *The plea, case, and humble proposals of the truly-loyal and suffering officers*, pp. 9, 13; Hammond, 'Truth's discovery', p. 563.

[81] Carte MSS 232, fol. 19, Legge to Ormonde, 1 Feb. 1664.

[82] Carte MSS 32, fol. 566, Nicholas to Ormonde, 10 June 1663.

original version of the Corporation Bill was described by one commentator as designed to enforce some part of the proviso which Seymour had tried to have added to the Act of Indemnity, but extending, unlike the proviso, 'only to some corporation men': Seymour's proviso may therefore have been intended to remove presbyterians from government.[83] In December 1662 Lord Crew told Pepys of rumours that during the next session a bill would be brought in to exclude from office those who had been in arms for parliament.[84] The need for such a bill may have seemed even more pressing by the Spring of 1663, with Ashley and Robartes involved with Bristol in supporting an attempt to introduce a general toleration of dissenters, and cavaliers deeply troubled by the impending victory of the ex-presbyterian Lauderdale over one of the doyens of the anglican royalists, Lord Middleton, in a struggle for power in Scotland.[85] On 5 May Lord Bruce proposed a bill for putting all offices into the hands of those who had been 'loyal subjects, and conformable to the Church of England'.[86] Daniel O'Neill described it as imposing the oaths in the Act of Uniformity on all who held office, 'which troubles extremely the presbyterians, who are bringing in a bill to distinguish Commonwealthmen and the monarchical'.[87] Bruce's bill never emerged from committee, but a clause to the same effect was incorporated in the Conventicle Bill which had its first reading on 21 May. This clause linked the need to prevent conventicles being encouraged from above with the need to ensure that all offices were in loyal hands: no-one was in future to hold office unless he had taken the Oaths of Allegiance and Supremacy, and had subscribed to the declaration and acknowledgement in the Act of Uniformity.[88] In 1663 the Conventicle Bill did not pass, and when a similar bill was accepted by the government in 1664, the clause was omitted.

In the Oxford session of 1665, however, an even more far reaching bill was proposed, 'to enjoin the taking of the oath and declaration therein mentioned'. According to a speech of Southampton in the lords, this would have extended to the whole nation the oath imposed on ministers by the Five Mile Bill, not to endeavour any alteration of government in Church or State.[89] The Bill appears to have had the same sponsors as the Five Mile Bill itself – Giles Strangwayes had been second on the committee of the latter, and had taken it up to the lords, and he was probably the Colonel Strangwayes who

[83] B.L., Add. MSS 11324, fol. 27.
[84] Pepys, *Diary*, III, 290–1.
[85] Carte MSS 47, fol. 403, Henry Coventry to Ormonde, 18 June 1663; cf. Carte MSS 32, fol. 391, O'Neill to Ormonde, 5 May 1663.
[86] *C.J.*, 476.
[87] Carte MSS 32, fol. 390, O'Neill to Ormonde, 5 May 1663.
[88] *C.J.*, 489; Carte MSS 81, fol. 176r–v, paras. S and T.
[89] *C.J.*, 622; Robbins, 'The Oxford session of the Long Parliament of Charles II', pp. 221–2.

was one of the tellers for the Oath and Declaration Bill's commitment. The division was lost, and the Bill rejected, but by only six votes.[90]

Despite such attempts, the government was remarkably successful in stemming cavalier revanchism. Only in the religious issue did cavalier partisanship really pose a threat to the royal policy of reconciliation: elsewhere royalists appear to have accepted, albeit a little reluctantly, the king's injunctions against infringements of the Act of Indemnity. The strength of the law, its power as a guarantee of individual rights and national order, rested – as Clarendon well recognised – not just on the government's behaviour, but also on parliament's. If parliament once began to undermine the basic standards of the settlement in particular cases, chaos could follow.

There was no doubt of the political virtue and practical merit of such a policy. But for royalists, starved of offices and honours, eager for the spoils of victory, and anxious to ensure their enemies were put firmly in their places, it was both offensive and incomprehensible. In handling their concerns the court often seemed brusque and insensitive, taking too little action, too late, to dispel royalist worries about the prevalence of presbyterians, and others, at court. At best, the royalist attitude to the court became cynical: a satirical 'catalogue of books printed at Oxford in the year 1666' included 'How to look backwards, and forwards, of this side, and that side and every, written by the Lord Ashley Cooper, and dedicated to the major part of the council'.[91] At worst, royalists became bitter opponents of the court in general, and Clarendon's administration in particular. When in 1663 the earl of Bristol attempted to impeach the chancellor, he received strong support from renowned cavaliers: Derby, who counted himself to have suffered at his hands, the earl of Northampton, and Lord Lucas. Both the latter became the chancellor's implacable enemies. But cavalier resentment had wider objects, as well. Lord Bruce – not exactly a cavalier but one of the strongest advocates of their cause – was described by his son as 'ready to lay down his life for his king, but at the same time a true patriot, and manifested it greatly in parliament in opposition to pernicious projects of double-dealing ministers, retaining at the same time a most dutiful behaviour to his sovereign'.[92] The belief that presbyterians owed their preferment to corruption – corruption paid for by the wealth they had accumulated during the Interregnum – turned many of them into violent critics of ministerial peculation, extravagance, and bribery. Even one of Clarendon's friends, Sir John Bramston, thought that the ex-parliamentarian ministers, Manchester in particular, 'sold all offices, and

---

[90] *C.J.*, 617, 621, 622; see also 'A letter from a person of quality to his friend in the country', in *Parliamentary history*, IV, appendix, p. xi.
[91] Bodl., MS Eng. Hist. e. 87, fol. 20 (no. 81): cf. fol. 17 (no. 31), fol. 11 (no. 13), fol. 8.
[92] Ailesbury, *Memoirs*, I, 11.

the presbyterians purchased them', and indeed, although the motion for an inquiry into the sale of offices in 1663 was principally directed at Clarendon and was an episode in the struggle between him and Bristol, it was also said to be aimed at Manchester.[93] Cavaliers were among those most prominent in the inspection of the revenue in 1663;[94] in 1667 Sheldon complained of the part they had played in the parliamentary difficulties of that year;[95] and in a famous speech later, in 1671, Lord Lucas had encapsulated the causes of royalist anger, contrasting cavalier poverty with the wealth of men who had profited by government corruption.[96]

In 1660 the marquis of Newcastle had returned from his long exile with the king and the duke of York: enraptured by the miracle of the Restoration he asked a companion to 'jog and awake him out of his dream, for surely, said he, I have been sixteen years asleep, and am not thoroughly awake yet'. But as Newcastle himself found, the seemingly bright dawning of royalists' hopes and prospects after the dismal long night of banishment and deprivation proved little more than a trick of the light: royalists failed to inherit the earth; some had difficulty enough in inheriting their own estates.[97] Like other colleagues, Newcastle was soon forced to abandon the court, and return to the country to sort out his own financial affairs. In the Interregnum, royalists had despised and loathed the City and the government, a centre of presbyterians, independents, corruption and hypocrisy – no place for virtuous royalism to survive. After the Restoration, some royalists came to feel that little had changed.

[93] *The autobiography of Sir John Bramston*, pp. 117–18; P.R.O., PRO 31/3/111, Comminges to Louis XIV, 4/14 May 1663; *L.J.*, 471, 474, 480, 483.
[94] Carte MSS 32, fol. 597, O'Neill to Ormonde, 20 June 1663, Carte MSS 221, fol. 52, Bennet to Ormonde, 6 June 1663.
[95] Carte MSS 45, fol. 222, Sheldon to Ormonde, 16 March 1666[7].
[96] *State tracts: being a collection of several treatises relating to the government* (London, 1693), pp. 454–6.
[97] Margaret Cavendish, duchess of Newcastle, *The life of William Cavendish, duke of Newcastle, to which is added, the true relation of my birth, breeding, and life*, p. 126. Cf. pp. 131, 133–4.

Part Three

THE END OF RECONSTRUCTION

9

Faction: 1661–September 1665

Of the several mortifications, wrote Clarendon, that detracted from the rejoicing of the Restoration, the disunity, rivalry, and squabbling of the royalists was that which most profoundly depressed the king. He found his loyal party demoralised and divided: 'all men were full of bitter reflections upon the actions and behaviour of others, or of excuses and apologies for themselves for what they thought might be charged upon them'. The Restoration offered an opportunity to recoup fortunes and to restore reputations; but with the limited number of offices and rewards at the Crown's disposal, competition was bound to be intense, and corruption rife.[1] Nowhere was the competition more savage than in the court itself, among the most prominent of the exiles. While abroad, they had spent as much time quarrelling amongst themselves as working for the defeat of their real enemies, and now that the fruits of office were again rather tangible than vainly promised, the jealousy of those excluded from real power and wealth for those who now obtained it could be unbounded. For those excluded, it was a matter as much of honour as of profit; they were forced to bear the sight of men they considered much beneath them in qualities both of birth and of mind established in the great offices of state. But the quarrels of the exiled court had concerned policy, as well as office; and exclusion from power meant exclusion, too, from policy-making – particularly vexatious for those whose views of religious policy differed markedly from that propounded by Clarendon. The struggle of court factions for office and policy was inevitable; and until the advent of war in 1665 it was faction, allied with religion, which brought the government the worst of its parliamentary difficulties.

Clarendon was the focus of most jealousy: so much power concentrated in a single adviser was bound to attract it, and he did little to discourage it, behaving with an easy grandeur and a serene sense of righteousness that infuriated his enemies and irritated his friends. For the moment, Charles was loyal to him: Clarendon basked in his master's favour, sharing high office

---

[1] Clarendon, *Life*, I, 300–2, cf. 286–306.

with friends and old companions, his judgement and experience seemingly indispensable in all government affairs. But Charles never gave his favour unreservedly to anyone. Although, for the moment, he was content to leave much business in his chancellor's capable hands while he spent his time in more pleasant and more princely pursuits, he was deeply sensitive to any usurpation of his own authority: Charles was jealous of his own power but reluctant to exercise it, and those who presumed too far on their indispensability were always liable to a sharp rebuke. The king spent much of his time in the society of his mistresses and the *beau monde* that hung around the court, whose cordial loathing of Clarendon and his allies who blocked their preferment, their honours, and their pensions, was just as cordially returned. Their much quoted ridicule of the stately and weighty chancellor amused the king, but had little effect on the value in which he held him: but their insinuations about Clarendon's power, his wealth, and his ambition did. The marriage of the chancellor's daughter, Anne, to the duke of York seemed to some (who rejected as palpable fiction Clarendon's horror when it was revealed) obvious evidence of his presumption.[2] Clarendon's pursuit of power and honour seemed to aim even at the foundation of a new royal dynasty.

In 1661 there were already some signs of a slackening of Charles's support for his chief minister. The earl of Bristol, with whom Clarendon had had cool relations since Bristol's reception into the Church of Rome and their disagreements during the negotiations with Spain in 1659, opposed his plans for the king's marriage and, with Charles's approval, began discussions for alternative brides.[3] In the summer of 1661 their relations cooled still further, when they clashed over the removal of the penal laws on catholics.[4] Clarendon's position seemed no longer impregnable. Although at the end of July George Montagu told Pepys that Clarendon was safe from the envy of others (in particular Bristol and the duke of Buckingham) because the king depended too much on him,[5] in August the French Ambassador reported that Charles had been offended by Clarendon's handling of the catholic issue in parliament, and had bestowed the keepership of the privy purse on Bristol's client and former secretary, Sir Henry Bennet, rather than on Clarendon's friend Lord Newburgh, to whom he had originally promised it.[6] Courtiers began to look for further signs of the eroding of Clarendon's position. George Montagu noticed that Buckingham had been admitted as a gentleman of the

---

[2] For the marriage, see Clarendon, *Life*, I, 315–47, II, 582–3; see also Dartmouth's note to Burnet, *History*, I, 461.

[3] Clarendon, *Life*, I, 424–32.

[4] See above, pp. 168–70; Clarendon, *Life*, I, 530–2.

[5] Pepys, *Diary*, II, 142.

[6] P.R.O., PRO 31/3/109, D'Estrades to Louis XIV, 19/29 Aug. 1661.

bedchamber, and 'waits close'.[7] The Spanish ambassador, de Vatevile, believed and ardently hoped that Clarendon's credit was declining: Bristol and Bennet were well known for their pro-Spanish sentiments.[8] Nevertheless, their faction failed in an attempt to have Bennet made ambassador to France in February 1662. Clarendon's candidate, Lord Holles, went instead.[9]

Bristol's intention in weakening Clarendon's power was not simply a wish to supplant him, nor a desire for revenge after Clarendon had insisted on his removal from office after his conversion. Since his conversion, Bristol, a passionate supporter of hopeless causes, had agitated determinedly for the removal of the penal laws from the English catholics. In 1661 and 1662 he had been frustrated – he suspected by Clarendon – and his failure showed how little he could expect any success without stronger support in both court and parliament. During the summer of 1662 he made efforts to amend this: the queen mother's return to England in July brought him the assistance of another zealous advocate of the catholic cause; his suggestion of a toleration scheme in the lords in May had brought some interest and sympathy from one of the bishops, Gauden, and perhaps suggested an alliance with Ashley, the chancellor of the exchequer and proponent of liberty of conscience. But Bristol gained most from his association with Bennet and from Bennet's industrious courting of members of the commons. If Bristol had any followers in parliament, they were few and obscure. William Russell, the son of the earl of Bedford, was closely associated with him: Bristol had married his aunt, and in June 1663 Russell nearly fought the earl of Sunderland because Sunderland had jilted Bristol's daughter shortly before they were due to be married.[10] But Russell was as yet politically inactive. During the 1663 session Bristol was to work closely with Sir Richard Temple – like himself, a political maverick – but there is no means of knowing how early their association began.[11] Bennet's creation of a faction in the commons opened the prospect of a wider parliamentary influence than Bristol could achieve on his own: and Bennet could himself be seen as an administrator, able, energetic, and eligible enough to challenge the grip Clarendon and his friends had over affairs.

During the summer of 1662, Clarendon's adversaries gained ground. In May Charles's bride, Catherine of Bragança, arrived from Portugal. At first, the king seemed satisfied with his wife; but his attempt to provide for his mistress, the countess of Castlemaine, by making her a lady of her bedchamber, was thwarted by the absolute, and furious, refusal of Catherine.

---

[7] Carte MSS 73, fol. 581, Montagu to Sandwich, 24 Aug. 1661.
[8] Clarendon MSS 75, fol. 231, intercepted letter of 30 Nov./10 Dec. 1661.
[9] P.R.O., PRO 31/3/110, D'Estrades to Louis XIV, 28 Jan./6 Feb. 1662, and 10/20 Feb. 1662.
[10] J. P. Kenyon, *Robert Spencer, earl of Sutherland* (London, 1958), p. 6.
[11] See B.L., Stowe MSS 304, fol. 16, for an indication of their association on other matters besides the 'undertaking' affair of 1663.

The trivial issue became for Charles a wider one, a token of his will to impose his own authority over his court. Clarendon, who attempted to dissuade him from his resolution, received a tart warning, and his enemies ranged themselves on the side of Castlemaine. Towards the end of August the queen finally gave in.[12] Clarendon felt his power in decline: Ormonde's departure for Ireland in July, and Nicholas's serious illness in August deprived him of two of his greatest friends at a crucial time,[13] and on 30 August he had a row over the Act of Uniformity with another, Gilbert Sheldon, the bishop of London.[14] Clarendon was becoming isolated, his enemies more and more in favour with the king. In early September Daniel O'Neill, Ormonde's court informant, told him that Castlemaine's power and influence were now at their height, and that she and the king regularly visited Bristol's house at Wimbledon, 'the master of which is much in grace'.[15] When they were not at Wimbledon, the royal entourage spent much time with the queen mother, an old, if respected enemy of the chancellor's, at her home in Somerset House.[16] Clarendon's opposition to a grant to Bennet of the office of postmaster-general was said to have further incensed the king, and to have put him 'on a design that Bennet will find more to his advantage'.[17]

The 'design' was to make him secretary of state in succession to Nicholas, who was over sixty and had recently been incapacitated by illness. In fact Bennet had been promised the secretaryship in succession to Nicholas a long time before, but the easing out of Nicholas against his will was widely recognised as an effect of the growing strength of the Bristol–Bennet faction. Nicholas himself believed it had been engineered at the queen mother's by her chamberlain, the earl of St Albans, and Bristol and Bennet, with the powerful aid of Sir Charles Berkeley, who thereby received Bennet's old office, the keepership of the privy purse.[18] Bennet was sworn into the secretaryship on 15 October, and it was not long before rumours began to circulate of further changes: Southampton, it was said, was to go, to be replaced by Sheldon or St Albans, although all these stories were vigorously

[12] Clarendon, *Life*, I, 584–604; B.L., Lansdowne MSS 1236, fol. 128, Charles to Clarendon, n.d.; Carte MSS 31, fol. 602, O'Neill to Ormonde, 28 Aug. 1662.
[13] Carte MSS 217, fol. 460v, Clarendon to Ormonde, 11 Aug. 1662, Carte MSS 47, fol. 351, Nicholas to Ormonde, 12 Aug. 1662.
[14] See above, pp. 179–80.
[15] Carte MSS 32, fol. 3, 2 Sept. 1662, Carte MSS 33, fol. 9, 6 Sept. 1662.
[16] Pepys, *Diary*, III, 191; Carte MSS 32, fol. 107, Sir Herbert Price to Sir George Lane, 4 Sept. 1662.
[17] Carte MSS 32, fol. 25, O'Neill to Ormonde, 13 Sept. 1662.
[18] Clarendon, *Life*, I, 633–5; Carte MSS 47, fol. 371, Nicholas to Ormonde, 7 Oct. 1662, fol. 373, Nicholas to Ormonde, 11 Oct. 1662.

denied at court.[19] At the same time, Clarendon was being heavily criticised for the sale of Dunkirk. The offer of Dunkirk and a strict alliance to the French in the summer of 1662 led to lengthy negotiations mainly conducted in secret by Clarendon and the special French envoy D'Estrades. But by September the purpose of D'Estrades's visit was widely known, and the pro-Spanish councillors attacked the proposed treaty and particularly Clarendon's part in it. D'Estrades reported that Bennet had even threatened the chancellor with impeachment.[20] Certainly the sale of Dunkirk was deeply unpopular, and ideal material for an attack on the man who was apparently responsible for it.[21] Pepys and the Venetian Resident also heard rumours of an impeachment.[22]

During the autumn of 1662 Bristol and his allies persuaded Charles to accept their plans for a wider toleration than Clarendon's suggestions for a suspension of the Act of Uniformity would achieve. On 26 December the Declaration of Indulgence was published, heralding the introduction of a bill in the following session. It provoked an immediate outcry among Anglicans, and Bennet realised that it had sadly misfired.[23] Clarendon and Southampton's violent disapproval of the Bill when it was shown to them made ministerial relationships even frostier than they already were. The possible consequences of that coldness were plain enough as the session approached.[24] The unpopularity of the sale of Dunkirk, and of the Declaration; widespread rumours of corruption and misdemeanours in government circles that 'country' members were anxious to invesgigate; and anger (fomented by protestant settlers in Ireland) at the alleged bias among the commissioners of claims for the settlement of Ireland towards the catholic ex-rebels – arousing suspicion of catholic influences at court – all suggested that the session would be particularly difficult to manage.[25] But worse was the fact that all these issues gave ministers an armoury of popular causes with which to assault their rivals. Bennet and Clarendon were nervous of their own support and apparent defections to the other camp were treated with touchy

---

[19] P.R.O., PC 2/56, fol. 91v; B.L., M636/18, Dr Denton to Sir R. Verney, 10 Oct. 1662; Carte MSS 32, fol. 82, O'Neill to Ormonde, 18 Oct. 1662, Carte MSS 47, fol. 11, Clarendon to Ormonde, 25 Oct. 1662.

[20] P.R.O., PRO 31/3/110, D'Estrades to Lionne, 19/29 Sept. 1662, D'Estrades to Louis XIV, 17/27 Oct, 27 Oct./6 Nov. 1662.

[21] E.g., *Hist. MSS. Comm.*, 11th report, appendix, part V (1887), MSS of the earl of Dartmouth, pp. 10–11, G. Wharton to Legge, 14 Oct. 1662.

[22] *Cal. S.P. Ven.*, p. 206, Giavarina to Doge and Senate, 3 Nov. 1662; Pepys, *Diary*, III, 290–1, 303.

[23] Carte MSS 221, fol. 15, Bennet to Ormonde, 30 Dec. 1662.

[24] See above, pp. 180–3.

[25] Pepys, *Diary*, IV, 66, 80; Carte MSS 46, fol. 37, Bennet to Ormonde, 11 April 1663, Carte MSS 221, fol. 27, Bennet to Ormonde, 10 March 1663.

anger.[26] The king, it was reported, tried to defuse the growing factional tension by suggesting a marriage between Bristol's daughter and Clarendon's eldest son,[27] but nothing came of it, and each side prepared itself for the forthcoming session. Clarendon had for a while been asking Ormonde if Henry Coventry could be spared from his duties as one of the Irish commissioners for claims: now he sought Sir Allen Brodrick's return as well.[28] Bennet requested that Ormonde should send Churchill back, and was also courting other M.P.s: Pepys was told on 17 February that Bennet had offered Edward Montagu a pension and a title.[29]

When the new session opened, the Declaration was swiftly attacked in the commons, and the Bill had to be dropped in the lords. The chancellor's enemies blamed him for their failure – the indulgence had been attacked in both houses by himself and his friends – and did their best to arouse the king's own anger.[30] Clarendon wrote to Ormonde that Bennet

hath credit enough to persuade the king that because I did not like what was done I have raised all the evil spirit that hath appeared upon and against it which, I think, you will absolve me from, for without doubt, I could as easily turn turk as act that part. On the contrary, God knows I have taken as much pains to prevent those distempers as if I had been the contriver of the counsels.[31]

Rapidly, he came to suspect that his position was being threatened: a grant of Irish money arranged some time before and on which he was relying for the half-completed purchase of land in Wiltshire, was suddenly withheld.[32] For a while it seemed as if the king would at last reject him.

On 19 March, however, Clarendon and the king had a long interview which seemed to indicate a renewal of confidence, and a few days later the duke of York appeared to have managed to bring the queen mother, as well, to some sort of reconciliation with the chancellor.[33] Some attempt was made to mollify anglican royalists with the appointment of Juxon, the archbishop of Canterbury, and Sheldon to the privy council early in April, although the

[26] P.R.O., PRO 31/3/110, Batailler to Lionne, 4/14 Dec. 1662, Comminges to Lionne, 29 Dec. 1662/8 Jan. 1663.
[27] *Ibid.*, Comminges to Louis XIV, 12/22 Feb. 1663; P.R.O., SP 29/67/31, Lady Anglesey to Lord Anglesey, 10 Jan. 1663.
[28] Carte MSS 47, fol. 18, Clarendon to Ormonde, 18 Dec. 1662, fol. 32, Clarendon to Ormonde, 28 Feb. 1663.
[29] Carte MSS 221, fol. 19, Bennet to Ormonde, 13 Jan. 1663; Pepys, *Diary*, IV, 47.
[30] *C.J.*, 441, 442; Carte MSS 47, fol. 397, Coventry to Ormonde, 28 Feb. 1663; *Hist. MSS Comm.*, Heathcote MSS, pp. 77–8, Sir P. Warwick to Sir R. Fanshaw, 12 April 1663 Clarendon, *Life*, II, 97–8.
[31] Carte MSS 47, fol. 45, Clarendon to Ormonde, 11 April 1663.
[32] *Ibid.*, fol. 39, Clarendon to Ormonde, 17 March 1663.
[33] *Ibid.*, fol. 91, Clarendon to Ormonde, 21 March 1663; *Hist. MSS. Comm.*, Ormonde MSS III, 46, H. Coventry to Ormonde, 20 March 1663; P.R.O., PRO 31/3/111, Comminges to Lionne, 30 March/9 April 1663.

inquiry into the conduct in Scotland of Lord Middleton, a particular favourite with cavaliers now engaged in a struggle for power with Lauderdale, was more likely to alienate them.[34] Comminges thought that the reconciliations had caused 'la cabale contraire' to take alarm. Bristol and his allies tried to regain their lost ground by mounting an attack on Clarendon in parliament. Clarendon's growing popularity because of his apparent opposition to the indulgence scheme may also have caused them some concern: but he soon lost this by his efforts to evade the commons' request for a proclamation ordering the expulsion of all catholic priests.[35]

Clarendon's antagonists grasped the opportunity of this new drop in popularity.[36] Bristol sought to widen his appeal and to find new allies against the chancellor: he looked for support to 'country' M.P.s – Thomas Tompkins, member for Herefordshire, was hinted at in a letter written after the end of the session as one of those who joined him – and to old cavaliers, indignant at their treatment by Clarendon, as well as to catholics and non-conformists. His allies spread the message of his intentions in order to secure these (rather contradictory) alliances: 'in respect of his accomplishments, courage and prudence', they were said to have claimed, Bristol 'might be of great use to assist the discontented officers and to help him [i.e., those] to a livelihood who were nearer desperation, & likewise to moderate the rigour of uniformity, if not to procure a toleration, & that although he was a catholic, yet he was of a public spirit & rather a statesman in his religion than a devotary'.[37] Bristol's new allies began their attack on Clarendon by moving in the house of commons for an inquiry into the sale of public offices. Henry Coventry wrote that the inquiry was proposed 'by one that hath so often made extravagant propositions, that it was neglected at first, but afterward seconded by one of a more cunning & less zealous temper': according to another account, it was Tompkins who had made the motion, although when a committee was appointed to consider whether the current laws against the sale and purchase of offices were inadequate, it was another of Bristol's associates, Sir Richard Temple, who was its first member; Tompkins was also on the committee. There was a suggestion that the penalties would be made retrospective, and Coventry added darkly that 'by some men's appearing in it, it is conceived backed from some at Whitehall, & a design against some

---

[34] Carte MSS 32, fol. 346, O'Neill to Ormonde, 4 April 1663, Carte MSS 33, fol. 368, O'Neill to Ormonde, 28 April 1663, fol. 390, O'Neill to Ormonde, 5 May 1663, Carte MSS 47, fol. 403, H. Coventry to Ormonde, 18 April 1663.

[35] P.R.O., PRO 31/3/111, Comminges to Lionne, 30 March/9 April 1663; see above, p. 186.

[36] P.R.O., PRO 31/3/111, Comminges to Lionne, 9/19 April 1663.

[37] Clarendon MSS 80, fol. 223, N. Hodges to Dr Hodges, 10 Oct. 1663.

particular great persons in it'.[38] The French ambassador believed that it was directed at Clarendon and Manchester, and later in the year it was reported that at the time it had been said to have been aimed against Ormonde and Clarendon – by the latter's fall it was hoped that 'such a scramble of preferment would happen that all their friends might be satisfied'.[39]

Proceedings in parliament were temporarily halted by the Easter recess, but meanwhile commentators continued to report the destructive effect of court faction on the effectiveness of the king's ministers: they were 'si acharnez à se destruire', wrote Comminges, 'que je croy que le ciel tomberoit sans qui'ilz s'aperçussent'. Amidst all this, they noticed, the king seemed to have given up caring, and devoted himself only to his pleasures, spending most of the time with Castlemaine. 'God help us', wailed O'Neill.[40] Coventry lamented that 'for the condition of our affairs, as one troubled with the yellow jaundice sees all things yellow, so it may be my melancholy temper, maketh them look so. But this much I must freely tell your Grace, which way particular men intend their owne advancement & their adversaries' destruction, was never more visible, but which way the king's preservation, & his enemies' destruction is intended, was never less visible, I hope it is the secrecy of our counsels not the ambiguity.'[41] Most observers felt that Clarendon was again losing ground. On 25 April Ormonde wrote warily to O'Neill that 'contrary to my lazy custom & nature, I begin to wait & prepare for a change'.[42] From 29 April, Pepys began to hear that Bennet and Bristol were overcoming Clarendon, who, William Coventry told him on 4 May, was 'falling past hopes'.[43]

When parliament resumed, the campaign against Clarendon continued smoothly. On 2 May Temple reported from the committee on the sale of offices the recommendation that a bill be prepared for action against offences committed since the Restoration. In the following division Temple and Bennet's agent Clifford were the tellers for agreeing to the proposal: they were successful, and on 18 May a bill was brought in and read. Despite two divisions on it, the retrospective clause for punishment of past offences was retained. The membership of a committee appointed to add a clause against the sale of honours shows the importance each faction attributed to the debate – exceptionally, both secretaries of state were present, as were Clifford

[38] Carte MSS 47, fol. 403, Coventry to Ormonde, 18 April 1663; Clarendon MSS 80, fol. 223. *C.J.*, 471.
[39] P.R.O., PRO 31/3/111, Comminges to Lionne, 4/14 April 1663; Clarendon MSS 80, fol. 223.
[40] P.R.O., PRO 31/3/111, Comminges to Lionne, 20/30 April 1663; Carte MSS 32, fol. 390, O'Neill to Ormonde, 5 May 1663, Carte MSS 214, fol. 471, same to same, 18 April 1663.
[41] Carte MSS 47, fol. 403, Coventry to Ormonde, 18 April 1663.
[42] Carte MSS 49, fol. 169.   [43] Pepys, *Diary*, IV, 115, 123, 137–8.

and Sir Charles Berkeley, and of Clarendon's group, Wren, both the Lawrence Hydes, Henry Coventry, and Sir Allen Apsley.[44]

But during May, there were at last signs of an improvement in the situation at court. Castlemaine's influence was beginning to wane as Charles began to turn his affections instead towards Frances Stuart, a protégé of the queen mother, but aligned with no particular faction.[45] Bristol's power declined with Castlemaine's; but more important, perhaps, was the king's belated recognition of the need to assert his own authority, to end the warfare of his ministers which was threatening to drag his government into confusion. Bennet evidently noticed the trend, and painfully, but in the normal spirit of *sauve qui peut* which surrounds such matters, decided to repudiate his old alliance with Bristol. On 26 May O'Neill wrote that the king was to bring the secretary and the chancellor to a reconciliation the following day. The first *rapprochement* quickly broke down; on 30 May Bennet himself was writing that he expected to be called to a new reconciliation.[46] But on 1 June, Comminges told Lionne that the two ministers 'sont apparement dans la meilleure intelligence du monde', and on 6 June even Clarendon was cautiously optimistic:

I can only say, that a man who hath not been deceived so much as I have been, would think that opinions are much changed, and that another course will be steered, than hath lately been, I have stood still, and looked on only, so that I am sure there is no thought of alteration in me, yet the countenances are not the same as they have been, and the secretary makes great professions.[47]

Reconciliations at court meant reconciliations in parliament as well. The account in Clarendon's autobiography of the king's insistence that the chancellor's parliamentary management committee be joined by Bennet, Clifford, and Churchill should probably be dated to early June 1663. Clarendon attempted to avoid having them added, but, on the king's order, acquiesced.[48] This event has been magnified into the 'first decisive step to initiate a new type of political management that was to change the character of parliamentary politics': certainly Bennet's style of management differed a little from Clarendon's, and may have been in some ways more efficient. But Charles had no such idea in mind: his attempt to unite the factions was rather

---

[44] *C.J.*, 474, 483, 486; for Bennet's alliance with Temple, as well as Bristol, see Bennet to Temple, 3 Sept. 1663, Huntington Library, Stowe MSS, quoted in C. Roberts, *Schemes and undertakings: a study of English politics in the seventeenth century* (Columbus, Ohio, 1985), p. 63.

[45] Carte MSS 214, fol. 471, O'Neill to Ormonde, Carte MSS 32, fol. 390, same to same, 20 June 1663; Hartmann, *Charles II and Madame*, p. 42.

[46] Carte MSS 32, fol. 477, O'Neill to Ormonde, Carte MSS 221, fol. 48v, Bennet to Ormonde.

[47] P.R.O., PRO 31/3/111, Comminges to Lionne, 1/11 June 1663; Carte MSS 47, fol. 52, Clarendon to Ormonde, cf. fol. 55, same to same, 13 June 1663.

[48] Clarendon, *Life*, I, 617–21.

intended simply to avert the consequences of ministerial division in parliamentary business.[49]

The new alliance had rapid results. At last, on 12 June, the court obtained a vote in the commons in favour of a supply. Bristol's distance from the court was symbolised by the opposition to the vote on supply of Sir Richard Temple, his ally, in conjunction with the 'country' M.P., Sir Charles Hussey; in charges the government later drew up against Bristol it was alleged that the earl had

laboured to alienate the affections of the members of both houses and other his Majesty's liege people by aspersing his Majesty's person and government and by persuading them to give no supply to his Majesty until such time as his ministers and his servants were removed using these words or to this effect you are mad if you give any money whilst the king is in these men's hands and by God I will have them removed.[50]

But the attacks on Clarendon continued: on 20 June O'Neill reported other motions supporting that against the sale of offices, including one against Lord Mordaunt's grant of the duty on coal. As the impeachment of Mordaunt in 1666–7 was generally assumed to be the precursor to an attack on Clarendon himself, this may have been another effort to strike at the chancellor through one of his friends.[51] Meanwhile, Bristol was busy gathering further information against Clarendon. Associates of his visited the man who had handled much of the financial negotiations concerning the king's marriage, Sir Augustine Coronel, in order to discover something 'against the carriage and deportment of the lord chancellor'.[52] But Clarendon and his allies were now capable of fighting back. The day following Temple's vote against supply several of them, particularly Henry Coventry, persuaded the king to allow a complaint against Temple to be delivered to the commons in his name. Temple, it was revealed, had made an offer to the king through a 'person of quality' to arrange matters in the house in order to secure supply.[53] With the guaranteed neutrality of Bennet's group – Bennet appears to have unhappily washed his hands of the whole affair – Clarendon's friends turned their counter-attack onto Bristol.[54] On 13 June Temple denied offering to undertake the management of the house, and was allowed to petition the king for the name of the 'person of quality'. Not until 26 June, however, was Bristol's name given to the commons. In the meantime Bristol had been banished from the court. Yet the attack on Temple went wrong: somehow his allies

[49] Jones, 'Parties and parliament', p. 51; see above, pp. 85–9.
[50] Clarendon MSS 80, fol. 73.
[51] *C.J.*, 501; Carte MSS 32, fol. 597, O'Neill to Ormonde.
[52] Clarendon MSS 79, fols. 287–8; cf. Clarendon MSS 80, fols. 69, 81.
[53] Carte MSS 32, fols. 597v–8, O'Neill to Ormonde, 20 June 1663.
[54] Carte MSS 221, fol. 57v, Bennet to Ormonde, 20 June 1663.

succeeded in dominating the committee appointed by the house to examine the affair. Hussey, the other teller with Temple in the division of the 12th, was its chairman, and Vaughan and Garraway, both prominent 'country' members, were the men chosen to request Bristol's answer to the charges made against him.[55]

Bristol's response was to request permission from the commons to address them on 1 July. This was granted, and in a long speech he pointed out his dilemma: he could either completely deny the charge and offend the king, or admit the attempt at undertaking, and infuriate the commons. His solution was to accept only that he had advised the king on the conduct of the session, and that the intervention of Temple and himself had been a well-intentioned attempt to destroy the 'false and self-interested measures of some courtiers'; he had, he claimed, argued against pressing for supply, or if supply was absolutely necessary, that it should be made acceptable by reforming abuses; he vindicated himself from being a 'dangerous driver of the papistical interest' by distinguishing between his religious and political allegiances, and he adroitly suggested that the real catholic danger came from another quarter, hinting at Clarendon's negotiations with the pope for a cardinalate for Lord D'Aubigny, the king's cousin and almoner to the queen mother. He rebutted with dignity any charge that he had been involved in the corruption of the court. With the deep respect he showed to the commons, and his hints at his own enormous services to the Crown, he won votes clearing both himself and Temple.[56]

Charles was furious. On 5 July, Bristol himself read him the speech, which the king said was even more mutinous and seditious than he had heard it to be. In the argument that followed, Bristol said that his enemies had prejudiced Charles against him, and that 'since his ruin was their design, it was natural for every man to defend himself, and that before his fall he would make such a bustle as would trouble his peace and the prosperity of others'. But Charles was unmoved, and the efforts of Bristol's cousin Sir Kenelm Digby and the queen mother to mediate were equally unsuccessful.[57] While Bristol spent the next few days in preparing new material with which to charge Clarendon, and in consulting with members of the house of commons, there was an air of expectancy in the capital. On 9 July Bristol made ready to accuse Clarendon the following day and the duke of York canvassed his friends to oppose the expected charges.[58]

[55] *C.J.*, 503, 507, 511; Carte MSS 32, fol. 598.
[56] *C.J.*, 512, 514–15; *Parliamentary history*, IV, 270–6.
[57] Carte MSS 32, fols. 708–9; O'Neill to Ormonde, 11 July 1663, cf. Clarendon MSS 80, fol. 73; it is possible that Bristol's finances were being threatened by his loss of position, as Clarendon's had been earlier. See Clarendon, *Life*, II, 22–4.
[58] Carte MSS 77, fols. 524–5, earl of Salisbury to earl of Huntingdon, 13 July 1663.

On 10 July Bristol delivered them. Broadly, Clarendon was accused of trying to alienate the affections of the people from the king by favouring catholics (and particularly by organising the mission to Rome on D'Aubigny's behalf) and then seeking popularity by setting himself up as the chief bulwark of the protestant religion; of making the king suspicious of parliament; and of enriching himself and his friends by selling offices. Bristol requested that the Crown's legal counsel should draw up a proper indictment, and that he should be allowed to bring in additional charges and call witnesses from Scotland and Ireland.[59] Clarendon's brief speech in his own defence was followed by York's intemperate attack on Bristol as a 'sower of sedition'. Southampton, more moderately, pointed out that the matter contained in the charges did not seem to amount to high treason – his motion that the judges and royal counsel should consider whether they did, and whether they were correctly brought in, was accepted.[60]

Bristol appears to have soon realised his blunders in drawing up the charges. On the following day he attempted to get the words of the order of commitment to the judges altered, and later on he interfered at their meeting.[61] He was unsuccessful, however, and when Bridgman reported from the judges on the 13th, the consequences of his mistakes became obvious: a charge of high treason, they ruled, could not be exhibited by one peer against another in the house of lords, and therefore the charges were irregularly and not legally brought in. Even if they were true, and had been allowable, they did not amount to high treason.[62] Bristol and his allies attempted to contest this verdict, but when on the next day the judges delivered their reasons, the house accepted them, in spite of Lord Ashley's argument that their opinion in no way bound it. In the following debate, Clarendon appears to have dropped his insistence on an immediate trial of the 'misdemeanours' (which the charges amounted to if they were not high treason), and allowed these to be carried over to the next session; and meanwhile a committee was appointed to draw up a declaration vindicating Clarendon from treason.[63] After his

---

[59] *L.J.*, 555–7; cf. Carte MSS 130, fol. 276, Sir J. Talbot to Lord Herbert, 11 July 1663, Carte MSS 77, fol. 524–5; Pepys, *Diary*, IV, 223–4, all of which mention charges or add detail not included in the list given in the lords' Journal.

[60] Carte MSS 77, fol. 525; cf. B.L., RP 409, ? to Carlingford, 11 July 1663, describing York's speech.

[61] B.L., Stowe MSS 302, fol. 125; Carte MSS 130, fol. 276.

[62] *L.J.*, 599; Carte MSS 32, fol. 716, O'Neill to Ormonde, 14 July 1663, Carte MSS 81, fols. 226–7, notes of the debates on 13 and 14 July. These are virtually illegible; for some attempt at decipherment, see G. F. T. Jones, 'The Bristol affair, 1663', *Journal of Religious History*, V (1968–9), 17, 25–8; see also the notes of the debates on the 10th and 13th in Northamptonshire Record Office, Finch-Hatton MSS 2892B.

[63] B.L., Stowe MSS 302, fols. 125–31; Carte MSS 32, fol. 716, and fol. 737, O'Neill to Ormonde, 25 July 1663, Carte MSS 36, fol. 69, Bellings to Ormonde, 18 July 1663, Carte MSS 81, fol. 233; Pepys, *Diary*, VIII, 445; *L.J.*, 560.

defeat Bristol turned his energies to securing parliamentary privilege for the recess to escape the king's anger or Clarendon's personal action at law. Lord Wharton tried to help him, moving 'that no lord should be questioned, during the prorogation, or session of parliament, for any thing that he had done in parliament, that was not treason', and was seconded by Buckingham, but Clarendon deftly avoided hearing their motion when it was first proposed, and Bristol and his allies, despite their efforts, never succeeded in bringing it up again.[64] Without this guarantee at the end of the session Bristol vanished.

Many contemporaries found Bristol's charges incomprehensible. Several wondered why a papist should make allegations of popery; Pepys thought it was 'all very strange'.[65] But G. F. T. Jones has argued that Bristol's motion was far from a piece of lunacy, as it was widely regarded at the time: he had a large body of support in the lords, most of it from catholics, ex-presbyterians, and ex-Cromwellians. Clarendon's support, he argued, came almost exclusively from cavaliers and anglicans: the attempted impeachment of Clarendon was in reality 'an episode in the long struggle for religious toleration', its purpose the destruction of the most prominent opponent of toleration by those most deeply interested in it.[66] Most of the evidence for this view comes from a list of lords drawn up by Wharton, dated 13 July 1663. The lords included in it are arranged in five columns, explained by Jones as one of forty-four expected to support Bristol; another of fifteen proxies they held; one of twenty-six expected to support Clarendon; another of the proxies he held; and one of fifteen uncommitted lords.[67] This gloss is not borne out by an examination of the names themselves. Bath and Bridgewater are in both 'Bristol's' and 'Clarendon's' lists. Derby (said by the earl of Salisbury to be one of Clarendon's fiercest opponents),[68] Northampton and Lucas (Bristol's only real supporters in the debate at the beginning of the 1664 session) are all down as Clarendon's allies. The so-called 'uncommitted' list is headed by York, Clarendon's most passionate defender. The only bishops included in the list are those who were represented only by their proxies, which Jones has taken to mean that all were supporters of Clarendon. What the list exactly does represent is far from clear: rather than the actual record of a vote, it may simply be Wharton's expectations of support for Bristol. If so, it shows how atrocious a political commentator Wharton was.

Certainly, Bristol's attack on Clarendon was related to the struggles at court and in Parliament over the religious issue. Those who supported Bristol

[64] Carte MSS 32, fol. 737, Carte MSS 33, fol. 34, O'Neill to Ormonde, 7 Aug. 1663.
[65] Pepys, *Diary*, IV, 224.
[66] Jones, 'The Bristol Affair'; see also R. Davis, 'The "presbyterian opposition" and the emergence of party in the house of lords in the reign of Charles II', pp. 6–8.
[67] Jones, 'The Bristol affair', pp. 24, 29; Carte MSS 81, fol. 224.
[68] Carte MSS 77, fol. 524v.

included several who were, or became, strong exponents of toleration –
Buckingham, Ashley, and Wharton.[69] Bristol's quarrel with the chancellor
was in part over religious policy. Yet it is clear that Bristol sought, and found,
backing from men of all political and religious groups in order to mount his
attack on Clarendon. The charges he drew up, his speech on 1 July to the
commons, and his activities beforehand were all directed towards gaining the
goodwill of 'country' and backbench M.P.s.[70] He castigated the corruption
and evildoing of the king's ministers, and sought popularity in pursuing them.
O'Neill told Ormonde of Bristol's endeavours to excite more widespread
interest in his cause: on the day before he produced his charges, and for
several days afterwards

> he quitted his ordinary way of going to the lords house, and came through the great
> hall and exchequer chamber, with his hat in his hand saluting with a sad and humble
> countenance all the crowd that followed, wishing him all success, he showed himself
> several days upon the exchange, and told many considerable merchants his story
> which is but too well received and credited.[71]

In London there were some reports of a planned riot of apprentices in his
support.[72]

It was perhaps the revelations of Clarendon's negotiations with Rome, and
the other indications of the favour shown to catholics at court and in Ireland
which aroused most interest, and particularly the interest of those sympathetic to dissent. Salisbury believed that Bristol's charge could only be the effect
of divine providence, 'which watcheth to be gracious to this poor Church,
even when the watchmen not only sleep but wink at the approaching enemies
therof',[73] and it was no doubt these charges that induced Wharton, an
opponent of granting liberty of worship to the catholics, to support Bristol.[74]
Some of Bristol's greatest allies, though, were cavaliers, discontented
royalists, many of them perhaps old friends and companions in arms.
Salisbury mentions among Bristol's allies in the lords the earl of Derby, 'now
persecuted for life & estate', the duke of Newcastle, Lord Hatton, and Lord
Gerrard.[75] In 1664 the earl of Northampton and Lord Lucas were almost the
only men to stand by Bristol. It is evident that he owed what allies he had
managed to muster not to his struggle for religious toleration, but to his
assiduous courting of a mixture of 'country', anti-popery, and cavalier
opinion.

[69] Carte MSS 32, fol. 708v, Carte MSS 33, fol. 34, Carte MSS 77, fol. 524v.
[70] See Clarendon MSS 80, fol. 223.
[71] Carte MSS 33, fol. 34.
[72] Clarendon MSS 80, fol. 75, information against J. Dodington.
[73] Carte MSS 77, fol. 524v.
[74] For his opposition to liberty for catholics, see above, p. 169.
[75] Carte MSS 77, fol. 524v.

The failure of Bristol's last desperate effort to regain power produced temporary tranquillity at court. Castlemaine's power seemed at last to be ended; Clarendon appeared to have fully regained Charles's favour, and his new *modus vivendi* with Bennet was still secure.[76] Bristol remained popular, though, and Anglesey felt that the mood in London was disturbingly restless.[77] Despite all attempts to find him, he eluded his arrest, ordered by the king, and escaped, apparently to Brussels. Temple also went to ground.[78] The earl continued nevertheless to pursue his intention of carrying his attack on Clarendon into the next session; Sir Augustin Coronel was again approached for information, and Bristol's friends at court, including Buckingham and Lord Crofts, tried to win back the king's favour through the new favourite, Frances Stuart.[79] But Bristol's chances of quickly regaining royal favour were ended by the Northern rebellion of autumn 1663: although small, badly organised, and penetrated by government agents from the start, the court attached great significance to this rendezvous of armed political and religious radicals around Leeds and other places in Yorkshire and Westmorland during October; all the indications were that the rebels possessed contacts throughout the three kingdoms and abroad, and a much greater appearance had been expected.[80] There was little obvious connection with Bristol apart from his general popularity, particularly among nonconformists; but some was clearly assumed. In an impromptu speech shortly before the opening of the 1664 session of parliament, Charles claimed a collusion between the earl, the only M.P. arrested on suspicion of involvement in the plot, and his accomplices.[81] Charles's speech was part of a plan by the government to limit Bristol's ability to create havoc in the following session: the earl was known to have returned to England and to be preparing charges,[82] and the king took hasty action to crush any rumour that he retained any favour for him and to

---

[76] Hartmann, *Charles II and Madame*, p. 80; Bodl., Tanner MSS 47, fol. 38, Bennet to Fanshaw, 25 July 1663; P.R.O., SP 29/78/19.

[77] P.R.O., SP 29/95/58; *Hist. MSS. Comm.*, Ormonde MSS, III, 67–8, Anglesey to Ormonde, 4 Aug. 1663.

[78] *Hist. MSS. Comm.*, 15th report, appendix, part VII (1898), MSS of the marquis of Ailesbury, p. 170, dowager countess of Devonshire to Lord Bruce, 21 Aug. 1663; P.R.O., PC 2/56, fol. 267; see Roberts, *Schemes and undertakings*, p. 63.

[79] Clarendon MSS 80, fol. 247, ? to Coronel, 10 Oct. 1663; cf. P.R.O., SP 84/167/210, De Bacquoy to Williamson, 21 Sept. [1663]; Carte MSS 33, fol. 120, O'Neill to Ormonde, 9 Sept. 1663; Pepys, *Diary*, IV, 366.

[80] Greaves, *Deliver us from evil*, pp. 174–92.

[81] *Ibid.*, p. 172, cf. p. 199 for Wharton's and Stockdale's alleged involvement; Add. MSS 38015, fol. 79v, Southwell to Sir George Lane, n.d., but cf. Carte MSS 46, fol. 162, Brodrick to Ormonde, 27 Feb. 1664.

[82] *Hist. MSS Comm.*, Ormonde MSS 81, fol. 140–1, Anglesey to Ormonde, 23 Jan. 1664; Clarendon MSS 81, fol. 59, Brodrick to Cornbury, 29 Jan. 1664, fol. 70, S. Bowman to Cornbury, 1 Feb. 1664, fol. 106, Coronel to Clarendon, 15 Feb. 1664, fol. 108, Coronel to the king, 19 Jan. 1664.

indicate how severely he would deal with his supporters.[83] At the end of February he declared in council that 'if any of his privy council abet my Lord Bristol he will remove him from the council, if any of his servants he will dismiss them his service, if any other person he will forbid them his presence', and at about the same time he spoke to all assembled in the privy chamber to warn that he expected full support from all his friends against Bristol and his associates: 'and those that do I will requite them, and those who do otherwise I shall cry guilty with them justice I see must be done, and let them not delude themselves into a belief to find me tame'.[84]

In the interval before the new session opened, Bristol wrote to several ministers and the king himself in an attempt to force himself back into favour by threatening a troublesome parliament. His letter to Charles hinted at his possession of dangerously explosive material, suitable only for his own eyes. But Bristol no longer had much support to help him. When Anglesey received a letter from him, he was so worried by the king's earlier threats that he hurried round to deliver it to his master. The opening of the session was delayed by an abortive attempt to arrest the earl as he came to parliament, but when it did open, three days late on 21 March, he did not appear in person.[85] Instead, his wife and daughter stood at the entrance to the lords chamber and asked all who entered to present a petition on his behalf. Caernarvon, Chandos, Bolingbroke, and others all nervously refused it, but Northampton, who had also received a letter from Bristol, accepted, and delivered the petition to the Speaker. In the ensuing debate, Lucas supported Northampton's motion that it should be read, arguing that it concerned the privilege of the house, but York's motion, that it be put off till the next day, was finally accepted.[86] On the 22nd York arrived early, and spoke to several lords, including Lucas: but in the debate, Northampton and Lucas continued to demand that Bristol's letter be opened and read. Northampton told the house that Bristol was a peer despite all that was alleged against him, and was still entitled to the privileges of his peerage and to the sympathy of those who had suffered with him, for the king, at least until any of the charges against him had been proved: but in the end, the house voted to send the unopened

[83] See e.g., *Hist. MSS. Comm.*, 12th report, appendix, part VII (1890), MSS of S. H. Le Fleming, Sir G. Fletcher to Fleming, 21 Jan. 1664.

[84] Carte MSS 46, fol. 162; B.L., Add. MSS 38015, fol. 79.

[85] Clarendon MSS 81, fol. 151, Bristol to the king, 20 March 1664, cf. fol. 155, Bristol to Albemarle, 20 March 1664, fol. 153, Bristol to the Speaker of the house of lords, 19 March 1664; *Hist. MSS. Comm.*, Ormonde MSS, III, 150–1, Anglesey to Ormonde, 9–12 March 1664; see also West Sussex Record Office, Orrery papers, MS 13223(4), Massarene to Orrery, n.d. [Feb. 1664], for Bristol's attempts to canvass M.P.s.

[86] Carte MSS 44, fol. 513, Brodrick to Ormonde, 26 March 1664; Carte MSS 76, fol. 7, Salisbury to Huntingdon, [22 March, 1664]; B.L., Add. MSS 38015, fol. 77, Southwell to ?, [22 March 1664]; Bodl., Rawlinson MSS A 130, fol. 2.

letter to the king, for which Charles returned fulsome thanks on the 23rd.[87] Northampton and Lucas appear to have been Bristol's only real defenders. The catholic Lord Stafford, and even Ashley, were said to have supported the court's demands that the letter be passed to the king, and Salisbury remarked on the 22nd that 'Lauderdale & Ashley Cooper are now quite silent, and as I suppose taken into the chancellor's friendship.'[88] Bristol's defeat in 1664 was the end of the affair: in late April Pepys wrote that the business was 'hushed up, and nothing made of it – he gone and the discourse quite ended'.[89]

From the session of early 1664 the court had in any case something else with which to occupy itself: the increasing likelihood of war with the United Provinces. Ormonde's presence in England for much of the year, which meant that the flow of letters to him on court affairs was stopped, and O'Neill's death in October, which removed the most informative of his correspondents, mean that court politics for a year or two are rather obscure: yet there are some important indications of the changes which the prospect of war, and the war itself, provoked. There remained, indeed, much suspicion that the rivalry between Bennet and Clarendon continued,[90] and disagreements over the war and its conduct may have brought it back out into the open. Clarendon and Southampton were deeply opposed to the war; and Clarendon, in his account of its origins, alleged that Bennet and the servants of the duke of York enthusiastically encouraged the duke's appetite for war and the merchants' animus against the Dutch. In fact the war owed its origins as much to miscalculated brinkmanship on either side as to deliberate bellicosity, although it is clear that York was avid for the opportunity of military glory, and Bennet may have been less reluctant for war than many of his colleagues.[91] More important than the war's origins to the future shape of court politics was its effect in the emergence of two new men as powerful figures in their own right. The preparations for, and waging of the war placed the duke of York, as lord admiral, in a central position in the government and to some extent diminished the importance of those – such as Clarendon – who had little to do with the forces. York, although hard-working and an administrator of competence, relied heavily on a set of able, even brilliant, subordinates. Principal among them was his secretary, William Coventry, who possessed an instinctively professional bureaucratic mind, matched with enormous energy and an unbounded confidence in his own opinion. Less able, perhaps, but a charmer who could easily straddle both the court of the court wits and the court of the privy council, was Sir Charles Berkeley, one of

[87] *L.J.*, 584, 585; Carte MSS 76, fol. 7; Rawlinson MSS A 130, fols. 2, 5.
[88] Carte MSS 76, fol. 7.   [89] Pepys, *Diary*, V, 137.   [90] Pepys, *Diary*, V, 208.
[91] Clarendon, *Life*, II, 1–10; see also Seaward, 'The house of commons committee of trade and the origins of the second Anglo-Dutch war'.

York's large military coterie. During the autumn and winter of 1664–5 Bennet seems to have courted both men, building on earlier acquaintance in an attempt, perhaps, to create an indefatigable ministerial triumvirate. In the new creations of honours of 1665 Berkeley added the earldom of Falmouth to the Irish peerage of Fitzharding he had acquired in 1663, and Bennet became earl of Arlington. A few months later, in June, Coventry was knighted and made a privy councillor – although, by that time, Falmouth was dead.[92] Nevertheless, the relationship was not one of complete unanimity: a hiatus in Coventry's letters to Bennet from December to April and some hints in his letters to Falmouth indicate that Bennet and Coventry were far from in complete agreement. They seem to have fallen out over the reward to be given to Sir Robert Paston for his services in moving the supply in the commons in November 1664, and their disagreement was public enough for a visit Coventry made to Clarendon to have raised many eyebrows. Falmouth attempted to mediate between Coventry and Arlington; but Falmouth himself went to see Clarendon, probably at the end of May, during a brief absence from the fleet where he was accompanying the duke. Clarendon's account of the interview suggests that Falmouth, perhaps convinced by the arguments of Coventry in his many papers of advice to him, was anxious that the war should be ended: both men – possibly in opposition to Arlington's opinion – hoped to stop the war before any serious fighting took place.[93] Falmouth's promise – and a possible new alliance – was never realised; he was killed at the Battle of Lowestoft in June, and Coventry, whose elevation to the council had been strongly resisted by Clarendon, settled into a firm alliance with Arlington.[94]

The full-scale war into which England had entered, almost by accident, made a harmonious relationship between court and parliament essential. Only by proper responses to government requests for supply could fleets be kept in repair, in victuals, and in men. But the 1663 session had shown up, once more, the dangers inherent in the relationship between court and parliament. Harmony and co-operation between them was inevitably wrecked once ministers gave themselves up to factional conflict. There had, in 1663,

[92] See Coventry's letters to Arlington, P.R.O., SP 29/104/104, 149, 105/50, 75, 76, 82, 92, 93, 118/12, 36, 119/68, 121/53, 54; see above, p. 86, n. 80, for their earlier relationship.

[93] B.L., Add. MSS 32094, fols. 46, 48–9, Coventry to Falmouth, 1 April 1665; B.L., Althorp MSS C1, Arlington to Coventry, 17 April 1665; P.R.O., PRO 31/3/114, French ambassadors to Louis XIV, 17/27 April 1665; Clarendon, *Life*, II, 128–9; for the date of Falmouth's visit to Clarendon, compare Clarendon's account with *The journal of Edward Montagu first earl of Sandwich 1659–65*, ed. R. C. Anderson, Publications of the Navy Records Society, LXIV (1929), 212, 220.

[94] See Coventry's resumed letters to Arlington, P.R.O., SP 29/123/87, 124/29, 126/11, 128/1, 35, 53, 62, 75, 129/11, 19, 26, 29, 40, 131/30, 46, 72, 73, 132/11, 37, 49, 65; Clarendon, *Life*, II, 186–7.

been genuine causes for parliamentary anger, real grievances which provoked protests against court policy. But properly managed, these could be contained. In 1663, however, the conflict of Bristol and Bennet with Clarendon had made the government's direction of the commons almost impossible. Bennet's creation of an independent faction made it possible for him to challenge the dominance of Clarendon's own management committee: and with government representatives in the house thus divided, they could provide no effective leadership; the debates of the commons were left to be guided by no more than the interests and whims of individual private members and the feebly-contested polemic of the government's critics. As Henry Coventry, one of Clarendon's management committee, wrote in May, 'either all things are in the dark or better eyes than mine have lost their sight. I am for my own part as assiduous both at court and in the house as I can be, and as inquisitive as my temper will give me leave, and yet I can neither tell you what the house intends nor what we at Whitehall wish they should.'[95] When the king finally realised that the direction of parliamentary business was impossible without the mutual co-operation of the court managers, he took steps to reconcile Clarendon and Bennet and their factions in the commons. With their coalition ensured, Bristol could be safely discarded; despite his popularity and his alliance with 'country' M.P.s, his personal influence in the commons was negligible. Clarendon and Bennet's parliamentary factions, on the other hand, made them indispensable.

One of the lessons of 1663 and 1664 was that much of this sort of difficulty could be avoided if the king took better command of his court. His intervention in 1663 had been decisive, and in 1664 his very public announcement of the displeasure to which anyone aiding Bristol was liable had the desired effect in dissuading almost all the earl's old supporters from involving themselves in his quarrel a second time: when the countess of Bristol offered Chandos her husband's petition, he 'leapt back swore he would [not] touch the paper for forty pound; believed it not the part of a kinswoman to offer such a thing to him'.[96] But 1663 had shown that sometimes Charles seemed so sunk in lethargy or pleasure that his capacity to take a firm hold over his warring ministers was small. With the plague, first noticed in the summer of 1665, establishing its grip on the country, and the prospect of a second year's war forcing England's economy into depression and her people into gloom, it was evident that in the next session of parliament firm leadership would be essential if popular discontent was not once more to become the instrument of factious courtiers.

[95] *Hist. MSS. Comm.*, Ormonde MSS, III, 52, Coventry to Ormonde, 12 May 1663; cf. Carte MSS 46, fol. 37, Bennet to Ormonde, 11 April 1663, Carte MSS 32, fol. 405, O'Neill to Ormonde, 15 May 1663, fol. 477, O'Neill to Ormonde, 26 May 1663.
[96] Carte MSS 44, fol. 513, Brodrick to Ormonde, 26 March 1664.

10

War: October 1665–November 1666

At the end of 1665, the government could look back with some satisfaction on the first year of the war: the duke of York's striking victory over the Dutch fleet off Lowestoft in June had won the English navy a redoubtable reputation; politically, the parliamentary sessions of 1664–5 and 1665 reproduced the harmony and co-operation of that of 1664; fears that the war might produce a resurgence of radical conspiracy against the monarchy seemed unfounded. Even the court seemed more tranquil than it had been for some time: with Bristol's challenge to Clarendon's hegemony definitely defeated, no new focus of power looked likely to take its place, even if there remained some very real personal conflicts about the conduct of the war, about patronage, and about command. But during the course of 1666 a conjunction of events produced a decline into a sharp economic, political, and military crisis, more serious than anything that had happened since the winter and spring of 1659–60; a crisis which was to put the survival – and certainly the power – of the restored monarchy in doubt.

Although England had had the better of the naval encounters of 1665, her diplomacy was less fortunate. During 1665 and 1666 she became increasingly isolated. Louis XIV, his attempts to mediate having failed, reluctantly accepted his obligations to the Dutch under a defensive alliance of 1662: on 16 January 1666 he, too, declared war.[1] Although the entry of France into the conflict was greeted with enthusiasm by many Englishmen for whom she increasingly represented the antithesis of all the English virtues and values,[2] and although it was obvious that Louis had no intention of wholeheartedly throwing in his forces to ensure a crushing English defeat, French participation was a severe blow, decisively tipping the diplomatic balance in favour

---

[1] For the negotiations, see K. H. D. Haley, *An English diplomat in the low countries: Sir William Temple and John De Witt, 1665–72* (Oxford, 1986), and Hartmann, *Charles II and Madame*, pp. 154–76; *The Oxford Gazette*, 1666, no. 6.

[2] See above, p. 125, and P.R.O., SP 29/144/37, Sir Edward Nicholas to Williamson, 4 Jan. 1666, and B.L., Althorp MSS B6, Lady Ranelagh to the earl of Burlington, 31 Jan. 1666.

of the Dutch. England's one firm ally, the bishop of Münster, was forced out of the war by French military pressure in the winter of 1665–6. Other potential allies – Brandenburg and Sweden – were persuaded into neutrality; and one, Denmark, slipped into alliance with the United Provinces in February, and eventually into war with England in September.[3] Negotiations with the Emperor Leopold and even with a Spain concerned about Louis XIV's designs on the Spanish Netherlands produced no more than frustration.[4] English efforts to incite unrest in the United Provinces were disastrously mishandled, and an abject failure.[5] England's diplomatic isolation was perhaps not quite as serious as it seemed – there remained a general reluctance among the allies the Dutch had collected to become actively involved; yet with the backing of France and the smashing of the Orangist conspiracy, as well as the denial of allies to England, it seemed less and less likely that the United Provinces would succumb ultimately either to English power or to internal convulsion.

The fighting of 1666 underlined England's inability, now, to inflict a decisive defeat on the Dutch. The English fleet itself narrowly avoided disaster at the beginning of June when part of it sustained the full attack of the Dutch in the Four Days' Battle. Despite a severe battering, the fleet was repaired in time to fight again, at the end of July, and this time to claim a (modest) victory, followed up by Sir Robert Holmes's raid on the Dutch coastal town of Ter Schelling. But English naval successes had the unfortunate result of convincing Louis XIV that there was a real threat of the defeat of the Dutch, and from the late summer he allowed his navy to take a more active part in the war.[6] Dividing the energies of the English fleet, the Franco-Dutch alliance sapped English strength and reinforced Dutch resilience. After February 1666 it was difficult to see how England could win the war.

An even more obvious lesson of the campaign of 1666 was the limited ability of naval finances to cope with the navy's needs. Naval finance had been a source of disquiet from well before the war.[7] As the principal officers of the navy attempted to prepare the fleet for sea in early 1666, they complained incessantly to the lord treasurer of the inadequacy of their provision with money; their needs still far exceeded – by over £1 million – all the money voted by parliament in October 1665.[8] With immense effort, the navy board

---

[3] Haley, *An English diplomat*, pp. 53–87; Sir Keith Feiling, *British foreign policy, 1660–72* (London, 1930), pp. 157–62, 184–95.
[4] Feiling, *British foreign policy*, pp. 163–83.
[5] P. Geyl, *Orange and Stuart, 1641–72* (London, 1969), pp. 197, 208–12, 220–56.
[6] See Hutton, pp. 241–5, for a fuller account of the 1666 campaign.
[7] See above, pp. 113, 115.
[8] See the reports of the officers of the navy, in Coventry MSS 96, fol. 108v, and *The further correspondence of Samuel Pepys, 1662–79*, ed. J. R. Tanner (London, 1929), pp. 120–3, 132–40; and Pepys, *Diary*, VII, 35, 36–7, 37 n. 1, 43, 48 n. 2, 122–3, 125, 205–6.

managed to set out a fleet in 1666 despite the unwillingness of its suppliers to allow further credit, and the consequently inflated prices it was forced to pay.[9] But by the end of the season the problems of setting out another fleet for the next were coming to seem utterly intractable: the navy's debt, the board told parliament in October, now stood at £930,000; and in a report to the duke of York in November, it complained that its lack of money was completely choking its ability to do the king any service at all.[10]

Further pressures were placed on government finance by the problems of coastal defence. There was a short-lived fear of invasion in January, occasioned by the preparations of the French fleet;[11] more serious was the scare in later June, when the Dutch put to sea three weeks before the English fleet could be refitted after the Four Days' Battle. Three new regiments for which commissions had previously been issued were now raised, and new commissions issued for additional companies and troops in existing regiments.[12] To pay for them on top of the heavy demands of the navy in June and July, the government had to search for any unused supplies of money: it decided to use whatever remained in the hands of the local militia officers of the three £70,000 monthly assessments which the Militia Act had permitted to be raised.[13] There were some protests from the counties at the removal to London of all the resources for their defence, although they proved no obstacle;[14] and the disbandment of the troops in September, just before the beginning of the parliamentary session, prevented their becoming a popular grievance.[15]

The problems of navy finance, and the obstacles to the rapid mobilisation of a national army, were but reflections of deeper difficulties in the treasury itself. Throughout the war the government was at best on the brink of

[9] See below, pp. 241, 249.
[10] *Further correspondence of Samuel Pepys*, pp. 145–54.
[11] P.R.O., SP 29/146/24, the king to the lord lieutenant and deputies of Essex, 25 Jan. 1666; *Oxford Gazette*, nos. 27, 28, 31; Carte MSS 222, fol. 89, newsletter, 6 Feb. 1666.
[12] P.R.O., PC 2/59, fols. 37r–v, 48.
[13] *Ibid.*, fol. 37v.
[14] B.L., Add. MSS 37820, fol. 153v; *Hist. MSS. Comm.*, MSS in Various Collections, II (1903), Sir George Wombwell's MSS, p. 123 (Arlington's reply to Lord Fauconberg's objection); P.R.O., SP 29/162/140, Lord Newport to Williamson, 14 July 1666. Cf. SP 29/161/30, Albemarle to Arlington, 7 July 1666. R. M. Dunn (ed.), *Norfolk lieutenancy Journal, 1660–76*, Norfolk Record Society, XLV (1977), pp. 12–13, claims that the expedient was 'strictly illegal'. But although it was assumed in the Militia Act (14 Car. II, c.3, para. XXII, S.R., 362) that the money would be spent on the militia, there was no clear statement against bringing it out of the counties and disbursing it nationally.
[15] A. Browning (ed.), *The memoirs of Sir John Reresby* (Glasgow, 1936), p. 61; Leeds Archives Department, Archives of the earl of Mexborough, Correspondence of Sir John Reresby, MEX/R/3/26, Sir George Savile to Reresby, 29 Sept. 1666.

financial collapse. This was not simply the result of inadequate funding: at the end of the war accounts of expenditure on and money voted for the war balanced remarkably well. The problem lay not so much with the revenue itself, but with the government's debt and credit difficulties. Already in 1663, the extent to which future revenue was anticipated to pay for current needs was crippling;[16] at the beginning of the war the government was burdened with debts of £1.25 millions, the revenue was already anticipated by £665,491, and issues were exceeding annual income by £652,193. In order to free some of the branches of the revenue which had been anticipated so far ahead, Southampton recommended in his report of March 1665 that some of the most recent windfall – the £2.5 million of the Royal Aid granted in the 1664–5 session – be used to pay off a proportion of the old debts and anticipations.[17] This may have happened: it is probable that some of the Royal Aid went towards clearing 'old bills' of the armed forces; the amount available for the war itself correspondingly declined.[18] As a result, the government was always paying for last year's navy; it was constantly behind in its payments and building up new debts at interest. Raising credit to pay for them provided the other half of the government's difficulties. Shortage of liquid capital – and hence loans – in the economy was a recurrent problem of seventeenth-century finance,[19] but the problem was made considerably worse by the government's heavy demands for cash on the outbreak of war. These rapidly overtook the City's capacity to oblige;[20] when the taxes on which such loans were secured came in more slowly than was expected, lenders either lacked sufficient cash, or were too concerned about the prospects of repayment to provide fresh credit.[21] Already in April 1665, Southampton was almost in

---

[16]   B.L., Harleian MSS 1223, fol. 235.
[17]   *Ibid.*, fol. 235; Chandaman, p. 209.
[18]   Chandaman, p. 211; this may explain the discrepancy of £780,000 reported by the parliamentary commission in December 1667 between the commission's and the government's accounts of what had been spent on the war (*ibid.*, pp. 210–11), and may also explain the very many anticipation tallies struck on the Royal Aid in the very early months of its operation (*ibid.*, pp. 178–9, and appendix III, pp. 341, 349 and 364, n. 5). See also Pepys, *Diary*, VI, 75.
[19]   See D. C. Coleman, 'Sir John Banks, financier: an essay in government borrowing under the late Stuarts', in *Essays in the economic and social history of Tudor and Stuart England in honour of R. H. Tawney*, ed. F. J. Fisher (Cambridge, 1961), pp. 204–11; Thirsk and Cooper (eds.), *Seventeenth century economic documents*, pp. 25–7, 65–6, 82–5, 86–7, 88–90; and see the difficulties of raising loans 1660–4, in G. V. Chivers, 'The City of London and the state', pp. 219–73, especially 252. See also below, pp. 306–7.
[20]   See Roseveare, 'The advancement of the king's credit', pp. 34–5, for the extent to which the issue of privy seals to the navy in November and December absorbed the market's resources.
[21]   See C. A. F. Meekings, 'The City loans on the hearth tax, 1664–8', *Studies in London history*, ed. A. E. J. Hollaender and W. Kellaway (London, 1969), pp. 335–8, 341–2, 345–6; Pepys, *Diary*, VI, 267.

despair: 'why will not people lend their money?' he cried at a meeting with the officers of the navy; 'why will they not trust the king as well as Oliver?'[22]

Sir George Downing's provisos to the Additional Aid of October 1665 had been designed to alleviate some of these difficulties: they would, he hoped, encourage loans by guaranteeing more prompt and certain repayment. Despite the hostility of the banking community, his and his allies' efforts to publicise the scheme did bring in substantial sums.[23] But the government's use of treasury imprest orders to pay for goods tended to throw onto the navy's creditors the burden of obtaining money from them in advance of the yield of the tax on which they were secured; and they could only raise money to continue trading by selling the orders – often at a large discount.[24] In any case, the sums raised still did not match the insatiable demands of the navy, and the government was forced once more to turn to the City for a £100,000 loan in June 1666;[25] and as the sum registered on the Act began to approach the amount it was to raise, lenders became nervous that the yield of the tax might be insufficient to guarantee their repayment. By the middle of 1666 the government was again in acute need of fresh and immediate cash.[26]

There were also problems with the yield of the revenue, which bore some of the responsibility for the inelasticity of the money market. The slow payment of taxes into the treasury inhibited its repayment of loans: and for this the almost irresistible opportunities for profit that seventeenth-century tax collection methods afforded the collectors were partly to blame.[27] The heavy burden of taxation from 1665 to 1667 added to the difficulties: from Christmas 1665, with the Royal and Additional Aids running concurrently, the country was paying £120,902 a month in assessments, more than in the heaviest assessments of the Interregnum.[28] Not surprisingly, there were many complaints about the weight of the taxes and about the slowness of payment, although their yield held up remarkably well.[29] The effects of the war were more acutely felt elsewhere, in the decline of the revenue from the customs, excise and hearth tax, which cut the Crown's ordinary revenue in 1665–7 to

[22] Pepys, *Diary*, VI, 78; see Meekings, 'The City loans on the hearth tax', p. 345, and Roseveare, 'The advancement of the king's credit', p. 38, for attempts to encourage loans with interim interest payments in June and September 1665.
[23] Roseveare, 'The advancement of the king's credit', pp. 59–68, 79; see above, pp. 126–7.
[24] *Ibid.*, pp. 76–7; D. C. Coleman, *Sir John Banks, baronet and businessman* (Oxford, 1963), pp. 34–6.
[25] Roseveare, 'The advancement of the king's credit', pp. 80–1.
[26] Pepys, *Diary*, VII, 131, 184.
[27] For complaints against receivers, see Pepys, *Diary*, VI, 211; and see Chandaman, pp. 182–3, and *Calendar of treasury books*, II, 44, for the reforms instituted in 1667 as a result.
[28] I.e., 16/17 Car. II, c. 1, 17 Car. II, cc. 1, 9; cf. G. E. Aylmer, *The state's servants: the civil service of the English republic, 1649–1660* (London, 1973), pp. 320–1, and table 44.
[29] E.g., P.R.O., SP 29/160/104; *Hist. MSS. Comm.*, 5th report, appendix (1876), MSS of R. Cholmondley Esq., p. 348; Chandaman, pp. 179–80.

only £650,000, just over half of its normal value.[30] As there is no evidence of a decline in ordinary expenditure to meet the shortfall, the government must have dug into the funds available for the war – in particular into the proceeds from the sale of prizes, for which money the king appointed a treasurer, Lord Ashley, independent of the controls of the treasury and exchequer.[31]

To some extent, the government's problems were simply those of the economy as a whole, forced into recession by the war, and depressed further by the effects of the virulent plague that broke out in London in the summer of 1665, and the fire which devastated the City in September 1666. International trade was naturally the hardest hit by the war, as the activities of enemy fleets and privateers disrupted shipping. The war seriously set back the expansion of English overseas trade: the East India Company's exports dropped away dramatically, and the Baltic trade shrank almost to nothing.[32] The domestic economy, particularly the staple industry, woollen manufacturing, was further depressed as a result, provoking efforts to revive the cloth trade by removing the restrictions on the export of woollens.[33] In trades associated with the war, of course, the navy's demands and its shortage of credit produced a boom in prices: yet opportunities for profit were limited by the government's inability to pay for the goods it ordered.[34]

The plague was past its worst in London by early 1666, and the court was able to return to Whitehall in February; but many other towns in the South and East were still badly infected throughout the year. The disaster's effects on the economy were considerable (although incalculable), as seriously affected towns ceased to fulfil their role as market centres, and trade with them ceased: the price of labour rose, while industrial output fell.[35] In London, the fire destroyed much of the commercial and financial area, and dealt a further blow to merchants already hit by the decline in international trade, destroying goods and assets valued at between £7 million and £10 million.[36]

---

[30] Chandaman, pp. 212–13. [31] *Ibid.*, pp. 132, 135–6.

[32] C. G. A. Clay, *Economic expansion and social change: England 1500–1700*, 2 vols. (Cambridge, 1984), II, 181; K. N. Chaudhuri, 'Treasure and trade balances: the East India Company's export trade, 1660–1720', *Econ. Hist. Rev.*, 2nd series, XXI (1968), 482, 492, 497, table 1; R. W. K. Hinton, *The Eastland trade and the common weal in the seventeenth century* (Cambridge, 1959), p. 103, and appendix D, pp. 226–30; cf. C. A. J. Skeel, 'The Canary company', *Eng. Hist. Rev.*, XXXI (1916), 537.

[33] Pepys, *Diary*, VI, 11–12; Steele, nos. 3458 and 3489.

[34] E. B. Schumpeter, 'English prices and public finance, 1660–1822', *The Review of Economic Statistics*, XX (1938), 22 and 34 (table 4).

[35] Hutton, pp. 246–7; for a list of royal proclamations announcing the closure of markets, see W. G. Bell, *The Great Plague in London in 1665*, revised edn (London, 1951), pp. 343–4; P. Slack, *The impact of plague in Tudor and Stuart England* (London, 1986), pp. 188–92.

[36] W. G. Bell, *The Great Fire of London in 1666* (London, 1920), pp. 223–4; Hutton, pp. 247–9.

The most vocal sufferers from the depression, however, were perhaps those in the agricultural sector, beset by other difficulties; agricultural problems affected the most powerful interest group in the country, the landed gentry. From 1664, agricultural production quickly recovered from the low levels of the last two decades. The prices of grain and cattle of all kinds slumped.[37] Rents correspondingly fell, squeezing gentry incomes. The early 1660s marked the beginning of a period of low prices and agricultural depression which lasted until the mid-eighteenth century: gradually farmers adjusted to the changed conditions by improving their land and its profitability; in the 1660s, most landlords were only painfully beginning to come to terms with their new difficulties. They came at a time, too, when borrowing money, either for tenants to pay rent, or for landlords to improve land, was more than ordinarily difficult, with London sources fully stretched by government demands, and others reluctant to lend in times of political uncertainty.[38]

By the summer of 1666 the depression had produced distress in many areas.[39] On their own account, the gentry were deeply worried by their falling rents, which threatened both their incomes, and their position at the apogee of the social and political hierarchy; the declining profitability of agriculture implied the dissolution of the old, stable life of the English countryside. For rural communities, it implied the abandonment of farming by many families, the creation of a more fragmented, rootless society. The acceleration of the decline of the cloth trade bred unemployment and poverty where there had once been wealth and plenty.[40] Few can have been more aware of these problems than M.P.s, who, even if they failed to appreciate or to be affected by them themselves, were subject to fierce pressure from their friends and neighbours among the gentry and yeomen of their communities to seek some sort of solution for the plight of the countryside: inevitably, the solutions they seized on were of the simplest kind.

For many, the difficulties of farming were easily explained by the unfair competition of imported products, principally the large and growing trade in exporting Irish cattle and sheep to England, on which the Irish economy was

[37] Thirsk (ed.), *Agricultural history of England and Wales*, V, ii, 56–7, 76–8, appendix III, tables i, ii, iii and xii.
[38] *Ibid.*, p. 75; Davies, 'Country gentry and falling rents', pp. 86–9; see above, pp. 41–2. For the difficulties of extracting rent from tenants in the mid-1660s, see also the 1665 Act for a more speedy and effectual proceeding upon distresses and avowries for rents, 17 Car II, c. 7, *S.R.*, 579.
[39] See P.R.O., SP 29/159/118; Milward, *Diary*, pp. 5, 10; D. Gardiner (ed.), *The Oxinden and Peyton letters, 1642–70* (London, 1937), p. 307; Pepys, *Diary*, VII, 188, 196, 230, 242, 342.
[40] E.g., P.R.O., SP 29/159/118, Daniel Fleming to Williamson, 25 June 1666; Bodl., MSS Add. C. 305, fol. 183, Bishop Ward to Sheldon, 18 June 1666; Nottingham University Library, Portland Collection, Cavendish MSS PW1/269, marquis of Dorchester to the earl of Ogle, 11 June 1666; Clark (ed.), *The life and times of Anthony Wood*, II, 86.

heavily dependent throughout the seventeenth century.[41] English cattle breeders blamed the fall in their prices on the influx of much cheaper animals than their own; and although some English graziers benefited from Irish cattle imports by fattening the normally poor beasts for the market, others found their old, unimproved grassland unable to compete: consequently they could not produce beef as cheaply as the arable farmers, with their new improved grasses, could. When the price of beef fell, their profits might be cut to levels at which it was uneconomic to continue farming. Irish imports produced lower prices and profits, forcing landowners to cut rents to keep their tenants in business. Irish cattle could also, in part, be blamed for the scarcity of money, as imports were paid for with exports of bullion: Ireland became the beguilingly simple explanation for both of what seemed to be the fundamental problems of the English economy.[42] Concern about the volume of Irish imports had already produced a clause in the 1663 Act for the Encouragement of Trade, limiting imports (by restricting them to the early part of the year) to lean cattle alone, preserving the graziers' trade in fattening them.[43]

The 1663 Act, although it made the trade more difficult, did little actually to reduce the volume of imports: further complaints were inevitable, therefore, when the great slump in prices, particularly of beef cattle, came in 1665 and 1666.[44] In the Oxford session of 1665, Sir Richard Temple, himself badly affected by falling rents, introduced a bill for the complete prohibition of Irish cattle imports. Under pressure from the Irish government, the Bill was blocked in the lords: but despite a considerable body of opinion against it, even in the commons, observers reckoned that the pressure for it was ultimately irresistible.[45] M.P.s, wrote Lord Burlington to Ormonde after the end of the session, were 'so much pressed by the gentry and commons of every county to pursue that design, that they conceive they cannot do their country a more acceptable service than perfecting that work'.[46] There was no sign of a decline in the feeling against Irish cattle during 1666, as prices and rents

---

[41] D. Woodward, 'The Anglo-Irish livestock trade in the seventeenth century', *Irish Historical Studies*, XVIII (1972–3), 494, 497.

[42] Thirsk (ed.), *Agricultural history of England and Wales*, V, ii, 348; C. A. Edie, 'The Irish Cattle Bills: a study in Restoration politics', *Transactions of the American Philosophical Society*, new series, LX, part 2 (1970), 7–10.

[43] 15 Car. II, c. 7, paras. X–XII, *S.R.*, 451; Edie, 'The Irish Cattle Bills', pp. 11–13; Woodward, 'The Anglo-Irish livestock trade', pp. 499–500.

[44] Thirsk (ed.), *Agricultural history of England and Wales*, V, ii, appendix III, table 3.

[45] *C.J.*, 617, 619, 620; *L.J.*, 694, 695; Edie, 'The Irish Cattle Bills', pp. 17–21; Davies, 'Country gentry and falling rents', p. 88.

[46] Carte MSS 34, fol. 537, 15 Jan. 1666; cf. *ibid.*, fol. 463, Sir Winston Churchill to Ormonde, 29 Oct. 1665, fol. 464, Lord Conway to Ormonde, 29 Oct. 1665.

continued to fall: Ormonde began to lobby furiously against the revived bill that was to be expected in the forthcoming session of parliament.

The clamour of breeders and some graziers against Irish cattle was so loud that other solutions to the depression were difficult to be heard above it: there was, though, wide support for restrictions on other imports, as an answer to the flight of currency from the country and its consequent scarcity, as well as (in some cases) to the uncompetitiveness of English goods.[47] Imports of French and Dutch goods – still entering the country, despite the war – were an obvious target for discrimination. The government, however, was reluctant to go so far as banning foreign imports, for fear of inviting reprisals against English commodities, and of reducing the revenue from the customs; only token measures – such as a rule that English manufactures alone should be worn at court – seemed likely to be put into effect.[48]

The worries expressed in 1666 were not, however, exclusively economic ones. The war, the plague, the fire, and economic decline, all contributed a new impetus to the sense of uncertainty and instability that pervaded English politics. The troubles of the country led easily to a jealousy of the extravagance of the court; the corruption of government officials, less noticed or more tolerated in times of lower taxation and a more buoyant economy, were now more objectionable and more visible as the war brought wealth to a few. For sure, the volume of protests against the court's immorality, luxury, and corruption during most of 1666 seems to have been little greater than it was during the rest of the 1660s, or even than the standard seventeenth-century complaints of the artificiality and dishonesty of a courtier's life. Yet the explosion of such protest at the beginning of the 1666–7 session of parliament, in satire, in conversation and in elections, seems to suggest a considerable subterranean revulsion of opinion away from the court. As the country gentleman felt (in his blackest moments) threatened with ruin and humiliation by his declining rental income, it was easy to compare his plight with the obvious wealth of the court, and of some ministers; with the profits that bankers were assumed to be amassing in various ways from war debt; and with the enormous wealth which Irish landowners – worse still, catholic Irish landowners – were thought to enjoy from their cattle export trade. The wealth of court and courtiers seemed not merely to contrast with the poverty of the country, but to be its cause. Instead of that firm conjunction of country gentry, cavalier, and government against the threats of religious dissent and

---

[47] For concern about the export of bullion, see the 1663 speech of 'Sir J' (presumably Sir Thomas is meant) Littleton mentioned in Carte MSS 77, fol. 645, earl of Salisbury to the earl of Huntingdon, 29 June 1663.
[48] Carte MSS 34, fol. 440, Southwell to Ormonde, 19 Oct. 1665; cf. Evelyn, *Diary*, III, 306, 465, and *Cal. Cl. S.P.*, V, 470–1, Downing to Clarendon, 3/13 March 1665.

social and political upheaval for which so many had hoped in 1660, the government, having wavered in its commitment to crushing religious dissent, now seemed also to be withdrawing from its alliance with the country.

More easily expressed – because it less obviously implied criticism of the government and the king – was a more metaphysical instability: the heavy burdens which God had chosen to impose upon the nation clearly indicated His displeasure. Some laymen could interpret them in a complacently political way – a judgement of the sins of the murderers of Charles I[49] – but many more possessed a wider sense of the meaning of God's heavy hand: to them, it was His just retribution against a nation more generally consumed by sin; as Evelyn confided to his diary in October 1666, the sufferings of the country were no more than it deserved, 'for our prodigious ingratitude, burning lusts, dissolute court, profane and abominable lives, under such dispensations of God's continued favour, in restoring Church, prince and people from our late intestine calamities, of which we were altogether unmindful even to astonishment'.[50] Such a sense of the weight of sin was in part the product of the Church's own appeal for national repentance, in which the successive disasters visited on England were valuable ammunition.[51] John Dolben, the dean of Westminster, drew the terrible moral in a sermon preached to the house of commons on the fast day for the fire in October 1666; England, like God's chosen nation, had provoked His wrath with the sins and rebellions of her people; the Israelites He had tried to amend, and to bring forth the fruits of the moral virtues he had originally infused into them with his judgements and his corrections; but that failing, 'then came the axe to cut them down as a fruitless fig-tree'. England risked a similar fate.[52]

The chilling possibility of national annihilation was more than just preacher's rhetoric. Throughout 1666 the prospect of a total collapse of the government was never very far from the minds of ministers and officials: particularly, perhaps, those involved with the navy who conversed regularly with Pepys – who were probably more aware than anybody of the impending dangers; but no one could have been ignorant of the poverty of country and City, or of the inadequacies in the administration of the war – of which the

[49] E.g., Gardiner (ed.), *The Oxinden and Peyton letters*, p. 391, Thomas Oxinden to Henry Oxinden, 14 Sept. 1666.
[50] Evelyn, *Diary*, III, 464; cf. Sir John Lowther's (for whose royalism and religious sobriety, see H.P., II, 769) forebodings: C. B. Philips (ed.), *Lowther family estate books*, Surtees Society, CXCI (1976–7), 179; A. Macfarlane (ed.), *The diary of Ralph Josselin*, British Academy Records of Social and Economic History, new series, III (London, 1976), p. 530; E. B. Sainsbury (ed.), *A calendar of the court minutes of the East India Company, 1664–7* (Oxford, 1925), p. 249, the Company to Thomas Dethick & Co., 14 Sept. 1666.
[51] Spurr, 'Anglican apologetic and the Restoration Church', pp. 153–7.
[52] Milward, *Diary*, p. 13.

state of the royal dockyards was the clearest possible evidence.[53] Some, though, sought the causes of the nation's difficulties more deeply, in themselves, their sins and corruption, and in their society. The feelings of instability and insecurity of 1666 provoked one of the seventeenth century's classic responses, visceral anti-catholicism, a searching into the political and religious cancer at the heart of English life. The plague and the war could scarcely be blamed on the catholics, although they might be taken as a sign of God's displeasure at their effective toleration. Yet fears of the catholic threat tended to arise along with alarms of invasion, particularly by the French;[54] and when the fire broke out in London, a number of coincidences, as well as the popular association of fire with catholic repression and conspiracy, immediately suggested popish involvement.[55] There followed an anti-catholic reaction of unusual virulence: even the normally phlegmatic Clarendon told Ormonde that 'since I was born, I never knew so great a sharpness and animosity against the Roman Catholics, as appears at this present. I mean amongst persons of quality and condition.'[56] Fear of popery, like providentialism, was an attitude most firmly rooted in puritan responses; yet unease about catholic strength was widespread even among those who discounted the patently circumstantial evidence that the fire had been started deliberately.[57] Old campaigners against popery like William Prynne sensed the unease, and revelled '*stylo veteri*' in the 'fears and jealousies, of plots and designs of jesuits, and Romanists against our Church and religion'.[58]

If the pressures of war produced tensions in the country and its alienation from the court, they also revived tensions within the court itself. Although observers still liked to define court politics in terms of a struggle between Bristol's and Clarendon's factions, this no longer really reflected reality.[59] No one, now, saw any advantage in supporting Bristol, still excluded from court; Arlington himself, though he retained connections with others of Bristol's old associates, grew away from them: his marriage in April 1666 to Freule van Beverweert, Lord Ossory's sister-in-law, brought him much closer to Ossory and his father, Ormonde, and distanced him from Ormonde's long-standing

---

[53] Pepys, *Diary*, VII, 55 (for Sandwich), 180, 184, 186, 188, 315 (for Sir William Coventry), 24, 62, 131, 160, 196, 281 (for Carteret), 61, 130–1, 233 (for Sir Philip Warwick); Carte MSS 34, fol. 516, bishop of Limerick to Ormonde, 29 Nov. 1665.

[54] *Hist. MSS. Comm.*, 12th report, appendix, part VII, MSS of S. H. Le Fleming Esq. (1890), p. 41, Fleming to Williamson, 3 Aug. 1666, and Alan Bellingham to Fleming, 25 Aug. 1666.

[55] Miller, *Popery and politics*, pp. 103–4.

[56] Carte MSS 47, fol. 127, 22 Sept. [1666]; see also Clarendon, *Life*, II, 288.

[57] See, e.g., P.R.O., SP 29/171/128, 129; Hutton, pp. 249–50.

[58] SP 29/180/68, Dr Isaac Basire to Williamson, 4 Dec. 1666.

[59] B.L., Egerton MSS 627, fols. 77–9, 82, 90v ('Relation d'Angleterre', 1665); Pepys, *Diary*, VII, 260–1.

enemy, Buckingham.[60] Buckingham himself, though sometimes mentioned as Bristol's successor as leader of an anti-Clarendon faction, was showing few signs of seizing a political role. But his immense capacity for giving – and taking – offence was at least partly attributable to a belief that his rank and abilities were undervalued, and that men whose standing was far below his own engrossed power and preferment. Having failed to become president of a revived council of the North, he sought a role in the direction of the war, regularly attending meetings of the admiralty committee of the privy council, and attempting, unsuccessfully, to demand a place in the council of war in the fleet in April 1665.[61] Buckingham possessed a dangerous talent for popularity: his generosity to the seamen in the fleet was remarked on, and his sympathy with nonconformity and antipathy to bishops and to Common Prayer were likely to recommend him more widely.[62] But his popularity among the gentry – particularly among the gentry of the West Riding of Yorkshire, where his main estates lay – rested mostly on his easy sociability and lavish entertainment, which he showed to wide admiration in the summers of 1665 and 1666, while commanding the militia and a newly raised regiment in Yorkshire.[63] Yet in his assiduous courting of the Yorkshire gentry (as well as of Lady Shrewsbury) and his wide acquaintance in London society, there was little to suggest in the summer of 1666 that Buckingham was planning to lead a fresh assault on the current administration.

In fact, the most apparent danger to court unity came from quite another quarter. From William Coventry's elevation to the council and knighthood in June 1665, he soon became in indispensable councillor, a central figure in the government's policy discussions, Arlington's ally, and a rival to Clarendon's pre-eminence in the private committee. Clarendon was offended by his readiness to overturn past decisions, and by his political attitudes – especially a smaller regard for the formalities of law and procedure than he thought suitable in a councillor. As with the arrival of Bennet into the administration, three years before, a new mind with a different approach to the conduct of business and to policy could plunge it into confusion, as personal and professional rivalries and animosities were kindled. Coventry's position in the

---

[60] For the marriage, see Carte MSS 222, fol. 99, newsletter, under 14 April 1666; for its implications in Ormonde and Arlington's relationship, see Carte MSS 46, fol. 286 *et seqq.*; see Carte MSS 46, fol. 235, Arlington to Ormonde, 9 Jan 1666, and P.R.O., SP 29/140/24, Arlington to Williamson, 29 Dec. 1665 for his relationship with Buckingham and Sunderland (now firmly married to Bristol's daughter).

[61] B.L., Add. MSS 37820, notes of the admiralty committee's meetings; B.L., Althorp MSS C6, Lord Ogle to Sir George Savile, 22 April 1665.

[62] *Hist. MSS Comm.*, MSS of R. R. Hastings Esq., II, 149, earl of Salisbury to the earl of Huntingdon, 5 April 1665; P.R.O., SP 29/191/91, William Leving's statement against Buckingham.

[63] Browning (ed.), *The memoirs of Sir John Reresby*, pp. 56–61.

navy board and the navy's heavy demands on the treasury placed him in almost inevitable conflict with treasury officials; the navy's insistence on constant supplies of ready cash had brought its relations with them very low by the end of 1665. In late September a quarrel in the countil between Coventry's employer and admirer, York, and Lord Treasurer Southampton seems to have led to a proposal, backed by York, to replace Southampton with a commission.[64] Although Clarendon saw off this suggestion, Southampton remained for some time sensitive to York's hostility, a suspicion that showed itself in the very public struggle over the succession to Edward Montagu as master of the queen's horse.[65] Rumours of Southampton's replacement, perhaps by Arlington, continued to circulate, however, and Southampton and Clarendon also regarded the insertion of Downing's clauses into the Additional Aid Act of October as another attempt to undermine the treasurer.[66] Even if, for the moment, the inter-departmental quarrel was smoothed over, there were throughout 1666 plenty of fresh causes for friction.[67] From 1665, Coventry's growing influence with York and the king challenged Clarendon's hold on government policy; but it was not yet sufficient to replace it. Without decisive leadership at the centre, the existence of two such different, conflicting conceptions of policy in the court might lead at best to confusion, at worst to faction. In 1666 the king showed as little sign as he had in 1663 of providing that leadership. The lack of clarity in government decision-making held particular dangers for the next meeting of parliament.

That meeting the government attempted to hold off as long as possible. A further imposition of taxation would be barely supportable so soon after the last, and the next session was certain to produce a new bill for the prohibition of Irish cattle imports, and probably irresistible demands for an inquiry into the way the money voted for the war had been spent.[68] On 31 October 1665, parliament had been prorogued to February, in case the predicted entry of France into the war made an early meeting necessary; but one was not expected, and the further prorogation to 23 April came as no surprise.[69]

---

[64] *Hist. MSS. Comm.*, 4th report (1874), part 1, appendix, MSS of the earl De La Warr, p. 203, Lady Charnock to the earl of Dorset, 27 Sept. 1665; Clarendon, *Life*, II, 234–8, cf. 213–17.

[65] *Ibid.*, II, 176–85; Carte MSS 34, fol. 431, Southwell to Ormonde, 12 Oct. 1665; P.R.O., SP 29/131/52, T. Rosse to Williamson, 29 Aug. 1665.

[66] Carte MSS 34, fol. 486, Southwell to Ormonde, 15 Nov. 1665, fol. 537, same to same, 30 Dec. 1665; Clarendon, *Life*, II, 215–32.

[67] For problems over the implementing of Downing's loans scheme, see H. Roseveare, *The treasury 1660–1870: the foundations of control* (London, 1973), p. 25.

[68] Cf. above, p. 128, for the commons' resolution of 1665.

[69] E.g., B.L., Althorp MSS B6, Lady Ranelagh to Burlington, 19 Jan. 1666; *Parliamentary history*, IV, 332.

Whether or not a session would be held then depended largely on the government's estimate of its financial health at the beginning of the new campaigning season: in mid-March it was still assumed at high levels in the government that there would be a meeting,[70] but at the end of that month, or the beginning of April, a decision was taken to put off parliament until the end of the Summer – perhaps on the basis of encouraging reports of the success of Downing's efforts to solicit further loans.[71]

But within a month or two of the decision, and particularly after the damage done to the fleet in the Four Days' Battle, the government's financial problems reasserted themselves. In late May officials were again concerned about the government's declining credit; by early June they were worried that the City might refuse a request for a loan of £100,000.[72] The latter worry was unfounded; but a fresh attempt to obtain further loans on the Additional Aid met with more laments of country poverty than success.[73] By the end of June, with the Dutch fleet cruising off the unprotected English coast, many were predicting disaster. Clarendon was even asking some of his friends to put their minds to how money could best be raised – without parliamentary approval – in an emergency.[74]

The victory secured over the Dutch at the end of July removed the immediate danger, but not the underlying need: only another parliamentary grant could meet it.[75] The navy board turned its attention to preparing for the forthcoming session by attempting to put its confused accounts in some order.[76] In August Ormonde and the Irish privy council began lobbying furiously against the anticipated move to bar Irish cattle imports. Despite Clarendon's assurance, other ministers and officials hinted that the government, if forced to choose between saving the Irish cattle trade and

70 Coventry MSS 44, fol. 321, Sir William Morrice to William Coventry, 23 March 1666; Pepys, *Diary*, VII, 64, 77–8.
71 P.R.O., PC 2/58 fol. 199v; Steele, no. 3457; P.R.O., SP 29/151/42, report of payments made on the Act up to 3 March, received in Arlington's office in mid March; see also SP 29/152/40, Sir John Duncombe to Arlington, on Lord Townshend's success in raising loans. For further requests for loans, see Bodl., MS Add. C. 308, fol. 59v, Sheldon to the bishops, 30 March 1666; Carte MSS 222, fol. 99; Roseveare, 'The advancement of the king's credit', p. 75.
72 Pepys, *Diary*, VII, 130–1, 159–60, 171.
73 P.R.O., SP 29/158/93, the king to the earl of Exeter, 12 June 1666, 95, [Arlington] to Sir Francis Cobb, 12 June 1666, SP 29/159/119, Fleming to Williamson, 25 June 1666, and SP 29/160/139–45; Nottingham University Library, Portland Collection, Cavendish MSS Pw1/269, Dorchester to Ogle, 11 Juane 1666; and cf. Althorp MSS C6, Ogle to Sir George Savile, 21 June 1666.
74 Essex County Record Office, Bramston MSS D/DEb 25/7, Clarendon to Sir John Bramston, 5 July [1666]. For the date, see Macfarlane (ed.), *The diary of Ralph Josselin*, pp. 528–9; Pepys, *Diary*, VII, 184, 186, 196.
75 See Sir Philip Warwick, in Pepys, *Diary*, VII, 233.
76 Ibid., pp. 235, 239–40, 262, 288, 291; see also Coventry MSS 97, fol. 269.

bankruptcy, would have little option but to abandon its resistance.[77] For the court was well aware that the forthcoming session was likely to be a rough one: there were rumours of an inquiry into the administration of the war, attacks on Coventry, Arlington, Sandwich, Carteret, and Ashley, even the impeachment of Clarendon;[78] there was much resentment of the abuses of naval administration, and of the threat to gentry incomes represented by Irish cattle; and it was highly probable that the government's critics might use all this to win concessions from the government. But while it is obvious that what Milward soon came to refer to as 'Mr Garraway and that party' must have laid some sort of preparations for the session in view of the effectiveness of the challenge they quickly presented to the court, it seems that the pattern of politics that was to emerge in the session of 1666–7 was largely spontaneous: and the crisis that quickly ensued was due as much to government confusion as to an 'opposition's' sophistication.

When parliament met on 21 September the commons responded encouragingly to the king's plea for a new grant with a vote of thanks for his 'great care' in the management of the war, and a resolution for supply. But the resolution was obtained so easily in part because the house was not yet full, still dominated by the London-based court members: Arlington would warily say only that the houses seemed 'reasonably well inclined' to grant further taxes.[79] For there were less encouraging signs to accompany the vote: it was followed by a decision to request accounts of the monies granted for the war in accordance with (and probably promoted by the same men as) the resolution of October 1665; without a true estimate of the cost of the war in past years, its movers argued, it would be difficult to arrive at a satisfactory sum to be raised in this.[80]

Government departments were fairly ready to oblige: after a weekend spent juggling with figures, Sir Philip Warwick, as Southampton's secretary, Carteret, as treasurer of the navy, and Sir John Duncombe, as treasurer of the ordnance, delivered in their accounts to the commons.[81] In the long ensuing

---

[77] Carte MSS 51: letters of Ormonde to Arlington, 7 Aug. (fol. 208), and 12 Sept. 1666 (fol. 219), to Sir W. Coventry, 29 Aug. 1666 (fol. 464); Carte MSS 48, fols. 415 and 420, Ormonde to Clarendon, 11, 26 Aug. 1666; Carte MSS 34, fol. 32, Irish privy council to the king; Carte MSS 47, fol. 125v, Clarendon to Ormonde, 18 Aug. [1666]; Carte MSS 46, fol. 365; Arlington to Ormonde, 11 Sept. 1666; Edie, 'The Irish Cattle Bills', p. 23.

[78] Pepys, *Diary*, VII, 248, 260–1, 262, 285–6, 287, 325; Clarendon, *Life*, II, 319–20.

[79] *Parliamentary history*, IV, 331–3; C.J., 625; L.J., X, 4; Carte MSS 46, fol. 377, Arlington to Ormonde, 22 Sept. 1666; cf. Holland's speech of 4 Oct., Bodl., Tanner MSS 239, fol. 71v.

[80] C.J., 625: the vote of thanks to the king was taken to the lords by William Garraway; Carte MSS 46, fol. 377; Carte MSS 72, fol. 97, Sir Edward Massey to Ormonde, 22 Sept. 1666.

[81] Pepys, *Diary*, VII, 294, 295, 296, cf. 301–2; C.J., 628; Milward, *Diary*, p. 8; there exists a copy of the accounts delivered in by Warwick at B.L., Add. MSS 18764, fols. 50–2; those delivered in by Carteret presumably formed the book he showed to Pepys on 24 September.

debate the accounts underwent sharp censure; the committee which was appointed to examine them included many of the most prominent critics – Garraway, Littleton, Tompkins, and Temple. Nevertheless, the committee's choice of a chairman – Sir William Lowther – may not have been unsatisfactory to the court, as Lowther, although a 'country cavalier' of much the same stamp as Garraway, was apparently a friend of Warwick.[82] Some committee members like John Milward were soon bored by the intricacies of government accounting, and fell away from its meetings: but others, more determined, defeated government hopes that this would lead to the disintegration of the committee. They created sub-committees to deal with the accounts of each department; the navy's accounts, in particular, were subjected to a fierce scrutiny by a sub-committee of Birch, Garraway, Sir William Thompson, and Edmund Boscawen.[83]

The government's effort to secure a new grant had soon been lost amid the inspection, which every day strengthened M.P.s' concern about taxation and corruption. But every day the need for finance grew: on 1 and 2 October the fleet returned to the Nore, its ships requiring repair, and its seamen payment.[84] It was perhaps these pressing needs that provoked an attempt to move forward the discussion of supply on 4 October. Sir John Holland's speech on this occasion is probably representative of a general mood: the war, the plague, the fire, 'scarcity of money', and the weight of taxation was crippling the country; 'commodities of our own growth bear no price, our markets dead, tenants broke, or discouraged, we have our lands thrown into our hands (condition of some of us) and yet our payments heavier than ever'. But the war, he acknowledged, had to be carried on, at whatever cost. Although the house would have to wait for the accounts committee's report before it could decide on how much to give, it could at least now discuss the ways and means of supply. The house concluded a lengthy debate by requiring the committee to speed its report of the last two years' cost of the war: evidently many concurred with Holland in being anxious to keep the furnaces of war well stoked; but they were also eager to avoid, in so far as it was possible, overburdening their countrymen further than was essential.[85] The government

[82] *C.J.*, 628; Milward, *Diary*, p. 8; Pepys, *Diary*, VII, 298; P.R.O., SP 29/126/1, Lowther to Warwick, 1 July 1665.
[83] Milward, *Diary*, pp. 9–11; Pepys, *Diary*, VII, 300, 301–2, 303, 304 and n. 2, 305–7; *C.J.*, 629.
[84] Pepys, *Diary*, VII, 279, 286, 304, 312–13, 315; Tanner (ed.), *Further correspondence of Samuel Pepys*, pp. 142–3, Pepys to Sir William Penn, 6 Oct. 1666.
[85] *C.J.*, 630; Milward, *Diary*, p. 14, gives a confused account of this debate and its conclusions; Bodl., Tanner MSS 239, fols. 71v–74v. The speech is undated, but 4 Oct. is the most likely occasion for which it was prepared.

was apparently encouraged by the general tenor of the debate, which seems to have given it more credit in the City.[86]

Over the next few days, the committee finalised its accounts, ready to present to the house its war estimates. Despite some departmental worries, when Lowther presented its report in the commons on 11 October it was far from unacceptable to the government; the estimates seem to have been fairly close to figures which Sir William Coventry had himself prepared – he and Pepys were fairly happy with the report. It judged that over the past two years the total cost of the navy, its stores and its ordnance, had been £3,223,110: the cost of a further year's war at sea would therefore be £1,611,555.[87] There followed some lengthy wrangling: £30,000 was without much objection added to the estimate for the cost of caring for the sick and wounded, but an attempt by the ordnance officers to add £54,000 was rejected on a division; the tellers against it were two prominent 'country' leaders, Whorwood, and Temple's near neighbour, Sir Thomas Lee. To officials' relief, however, the report was finally approved: the government had passed a major hurdle on the way to supply.[88]

But its overwhelming concern to obtain fresh supply as quickly as possible was matched by M.P.s' anxious desire to obtain some sort of relief from falling prices and falling rents as soon as they could. So while the investigation of accounts proceeded in committee, the house of commons itself was occupied with what many members regarded as the most crucial measure for the country's relief, the prohibition of cattle imports. The widely expected bill was introduced the day after the king's speech. Although its preamble was based on the failed 1665 Bill, the new Bill contained important differences. The earlier version had laid prohibitive import duties on imports from Ireland of cattle, sheep, swine, and beef, pork, and bacon, and banned any bulk imports; the new one simply banned all imports, and declared illegal imports to be a 'nuisance'.[89] The penalties and limitations of the 1665 Bill

---

[86] Carte MSS 217, fol. 338, Lord Anglesey to Ormonde, 6 Oct. 1666; see also Pepys, *Diary*, VII, 312–13.

[87] Carte MSS 222, fol. 125v, newsletter of 9 Oct.; *C.J.*, 632, 633, 634; for Coventry's and Pepys's worries about discrepancies, see Coventry MSS 101, fol. 50v, and Pepys, *Diary*, VII, 317; cf. Coventry's own calculations, Coventry MSS 98, fol. 240; part of the report itself, with some critical remarks on it made in 1678, is at B.L., Harleian MSS 6277, fols. 1–2v; the full report, taken from Lowther's own copy, is in the Pepys Library, Magdalene College, Cambridge, MS 2266, no. 152; some of the figures are copied out by Milward under 17 October, *Diary*, pp. 26–7; for Coventry's and Pepys's reactions to the report, see Pepys, *Diary*, VII, 318–19.

[88] For Lee's 'country' affiliations, see the other occasions in this session in which he was a teller: *C.J.*, 647, 654, 658, 666, 669, 683, 686.

[89] The 1665 Bill is in H.L.R.O., Parchment Collection, Box 13; see also Edie, 'The Irish Cattle Bills', pp. 19–20; there exists no copy of the 1666 Bill as introduced: this account is deduced from Sir Heneage Finch's speech at the second reading, Leicestershire Record Office, Finch

were no longer felt sufficient; but this attempt to prevent any cattle coming in at all was likely to divide country opinion, and threaten the Bill's success. A total ban attacked the interests of the many graziers who were still able to profit from fattening Irish livestock. The addition of the word 'nuisance' complicated the issue further: the declaration that imports were a 'nuisance' implied that they were self-evidently wrong, and against natural law; laws against such *mala in se* could not, it was accepted, be dispensed with by the king's prerogative. The addition hinted at a concern that the king might allow some individuals licences to import cattle contrary to the Act when it was passed: and it is possible that it was attributable to the anti-Irish, and anti-Ormonde feeling (Ormonde was himself heavily involved in the Irish cattle trade, and was probably the most likely beneficiary of a licence to import) which was frequently manifested in the ensuing debates.[90]

Unusually, the Bill was opposed even at its first reading, by three Norfolk landowners, Sir Charles Harbord, Sir William Doyley, and Sir John Holland.[91] At the second reading the solicitor general made a passionate and lengthy speech against its rationale, its justice, and its prudence, with some bitter reflections on the distrust of the king and the government implied by the addition of the word 'nuisance'; recognising the pressure for the Bill he suggested more moderate measures, including the imposition of quotas on imports. Yet his requests for delay were ignored (despite some admiration for his speech) and the Bill committed. Government ministers accepted that notwithstanding the fierce opposition of some graziers, it was virtually unstoppable in the lower house.[92] The discussions in the committee largely concerned the Bill's seizure provisions for illegally imported cattle rather than the Bill itself: the committee seems to have restricted the power of confiscation to parish officers. When the Bill was reported by Edward Seymour on 5 October, Finch again spoke at length and with passion against it and particularly against the 'nuisance' clause: although forced by Sir Richard Temple to admit that its insertion was far from unprecedented, he continued to argue that whether something was, or was not, a 'nuisance', was not a

MSS, Box 4965, P.P. 16, pp. 18–20; Edie (pp. 24–5) argues from the addition at the end of this speech that the word 'nuisance' was added at the second reading, and was not in the Bill from the beginning. Yet Finch is clearly referring to something already in the Bill, not a proposed amendment, and it is unlikely that such an amendment would have been inserted before the committee stage.

90 For the significance of the word, see Finch's speech (see above, n. 88); for Ormonde's involvement in the Irish cattle trade, see Carte MSS 51, fol. 219v, Ormonde to Arlington, 12 Sept. 1666.

91 C.J., 626; Milward, *Diary*, pp. 3–4.

92 C.J., 627–8; Milward, *Diary*, pp. 7–8; Finch MSS, Box 4965, P.P. 16, pp. 15–20; Carte MSS 35, fol. 86, Sir Heneage Finch to Ormonde, 29 Sept. 1666; Carte MSS 217, fol. 336, Anglesey to Ormonde, 29 Sept. 1665.

matter for a decision of parliament but ought to be self-evident. Its addition
was motivated not by a concern for English rents, he argued, but by a desire
to restrict the royal prerogative which would delight republican radicals.
These arguments seem to have found little support, and some even found
them offensive; more, though, approved of his continued objections to the
clause concerning confiscation of suspected illegal imports, and despite
worries that recommitment might allow Irish interests time to delay the Bill
– or even to talk it out – a division sent it back to committee, and the required
clause, allowing appeals against seizure, was added to remove the
objection.[93]

On 13 October the Bill received its third reading. In a long and heated
debate those groups opposed to it attempted at least to moderate its
provisions. In his final speech on the Bill, Finch pleaded for the prohibition to
be stayed for a year; others proposed, as he had earlier, a quota system, or a
delay until the war was over. But in the final vote on the Bill, Sir Edward
Massey and Sir Allen Brodrick, the tellers against it, were defeated by 165 to
104, and Edward Seymour was entrusted with carrying it up to the house of
lords.[94]

Supply, and Irish cattle, were the two greatest burdens on the minds of the
government and of country gentry respectively: but the other proposals made
and initiatives taken in the first three weeks of the new session indicate the
extent of the malaise which many M.P.s felt was threatening the country. On
22 September, in a long and apparently rather formless debate, the commons
discussed many aspects of the current economic crisis, but in particular the
scarcity of coin (which produced some criticism of the bankers, as well as
proposals for coining plate and for a land registry), and the scale of foreign
imports. A committee was appointed, with Prynne as its first member, to
look into all these problems.[95] Its first fruit was the bill introduced on
28 September by Sir George Downing for 'increasing the stock of money in
the kingdom', which took up the suggestion made on the 22nd to encourage
owners of plate to exchange it at the mint for cash to its full value; to pay for
the compensation, a small extra duty was to be laid on imported wines.[96] In
response to a further motion, a committee considered lifting the laws which

[93] C.J., 631, 632; Milward, *Diary*, pp. 9, 15, 17; Carte MSS 35, fol. 86; Finch MSS, Box 4965,
P.P. 16, pp. 21–3; P.R.O., SP 29/174/85, Sir Thomas Clifford to Arlington, 6 Oct. 1666.
[94] C.J., 635; Finch MSS, Box 4965, P.P. 16, pp. 24–6; Milward, *Diary*, p. 22; Carte MSS 35,
fol. 101, Brodrick to Ormonde, 13 Oct. 1666.
[95] C.J., 626; Milward, *Diary*, pp. 4–5; for Prynne's involvement in economic legislation, see the
committees on Irish cattle and exports, C.J., 627, 628, and Seaward, 'The house of commons
committee of trade and the origins of the Second Anglo-Dutch War', pp. 444–5, 447.
[96] Milward, *Diary*, p. 10; cf. the Act as passed, 18/19 Car. II, c. 5, S.R., 598–600; C.J., 629,
631.

restrained the free export of certain goods and livestock, and thus helped to hold down their prices; although when Downing reported the committee's recommendations on 8 October it suggested only a bill against the importation of all French goods, and, until it could be completed, a request to the king for an immediate ban by proclamation.[97]

This request was to occasion a little embarrassment in government circles, but this was nothing compared with the trouble caused it by the commons' investigation into the Canary company. The company's charter, passed under the Great Seal on 17 March 1665, had granted it a monopoly of the trade in Canary wine, with the object of overcoming the Canary authorities' obstruction of English traders and the producers' demands for what the merchants believed were artificially high prices. The company had experienced enormous difficulties in enforcing its charter, even among its own members: indeed, the complaints against it were more in connection with the orders and byelaws it made than against the monopoly itself. Dissident members of the company had already petitioned the privy council; and on 1 October, perhaps encouraged by the commons' current interest in economic issues, they petitioned the house as well. But 'country' leaders in the house were rather more outraged by the monopoly (or recognised in it a useful issue to arouse the indignation of the commons) than interested in specific grievances: after a fairly long debate, the house appointed a committee, headed by Edward Seymour, and including Temple, Tompkins, Littleton, and Birch, which was instructed not just to look into the particular faults of the company, but also to consider 'the former laws against monopolies; and examine, how they are observed; and wherein it is fit to reinforce them'. Further petitions against various other monopolies were referred to the same committee on 9 and 12 October: the burgeoning attack on monopolies suggested the beginnings of a campaign against court corruption; and, since Clarendon was well known to have been the company's patron, it may have been quickened by the belief that an investigation might turn up material for an impeachment.[98]

The commons spent time, too, in considering less tangible aspects of the current malaise: the concern about the strength of popery and its responsibility for the fire, and the need for a national repentance and moral reformation. On 25 September, the planned debate on the accounts of the navy was pushed aside by a debate on the fire, 'whether it was by the hand of God, or by design, and whether a committee should be named for examination of it'. Although many took the government's view that the fire was an accident, there were enough, including Sir John Maynard and Sir Charles Harbord, the

[97] *C.J.*, 627, 631, 632, cf. 633; Milward, *Diary*, pp. 6, 17.
[98] *C.J.*, 629, 632–3, 635; Milward, *Diary*, p. 10; Skeel, 'The Canary company'; Carte MSS 47, fol. 124v, Clarendon to Ormonde, 18 Aug. [1666], cf. fols. 104v, 110, 112.

surveyor general, to carry the question for a committee: for some time this committee fuelled the popular interest for the rumours and anecdotes of a conspiracy for the firing of London.[99] If popery pressed from one side, atheism and blasphemy threatened from the other: on the day after the dean of Westminster and the vicar of St Margaret's had both preached to the commons on repentance (at services on the day of fasting for the fire), a committee was appointed to consider the strengthening of the laws against atheism and irreligious behaviour. Moralists from all places on the religious spectrum were included – ex-presbyterians like Grimston (its first member), Prynne, Massey, and Irby; men of (probably) dissenting sympathies like Roger Pepys, and men closely connected to the hierarchy of the Church, like Charlton and Berkenhead. A few days later a bill against atheism and profaneness was produced and read: such irreligion, it declared, was to the 'high dishonour of God, provoking of his fierce wrath and drawing down of his most severe and exemplary judgements', and it laid down heavy punishments – including transportation and forfeiture – for a denial of the fundamentals of the Christian faith, and lesser penalties for blasphemy and profanity.[100] On the day after it was committed, on 16 October, fears were also expressed about the publication of 'such books as tend to atheism, blasphemy or profaneness, or against the essence or attributes of God', in particular those of Hobbes and Thomas White: the suppression of these works was also referred to the committee.[101] There had been several such bills introduced since 1661; but only that of 1663 had been anywhere near as successful as this one. Often instigated by men of a puritan stamp, they usually attracted the support of devout Churchmen; but this time the Bill seems to have survived for longer than usual as it caught the national mood of repentance.[102]

Over these first three weeks of the session, and in the weeks to come, there were signs that that mood of religious foreboding might turn into one of more open political anger. The very existence of parliament, with the opportunities for caballing and gossip that it afforded, may have been partly responsible for the increasingly focussed nature of political criticism. Stories of the conduct of the court were widespread in mid-October, when the court was at its most ebulliently offensive to respectable opinion. Lord Herbert resolved not to

[99] C.J., 627, 629, 633, 636; Milward, Diary, p. 7; P.R.O., SP 29/174/139, newsletter, 11 Oct. 1666.
[100] C.J., 630, 632, 636; Milward, Diary, pp. 12–13, 18, 24–5; H.L.R.O., Parchment Collection, Box 14 (31 Jan. 1667), contains the Bill as engrossed and sent to the lords.
[101] C.J., 636; Milward, Diary, p. 25; Hobbes and White were already linked in Roger Coke's A survey of the politicks of Mr Thomas White, Mr Thomas Hobbs, and Mr Hugo Grotius (London, 1662); see also Aubrey's story, Aubrey, Brief lives, I, 339.
[102] For previous bills against profanity, see C.J., 437, 440, 454, 456, 467, 470, 472, 473, 492, 496, 515, 525, 535, 539, 545, 580, 581, 616; L.J., 530, 535, 546; for the subsequent progress of the 1666 Bill, see C.J., 682, 687; L.J., X, 96, 98.

attend a lavish ball in honour of the queen's birthday on 19 November because (apart from the expense), it was 'a thing so unsuitable to the times'.[103] Libels began to circulate attacking the court's corruption and immorality.[104] Resentment of the court and courtiers was plainly expressed at several by-elections: at Morpeth on 27 September, where Joseph Williamson was defeated, and most notably in the rejection of Baptist May at Winchilsea on 4 October.[105] The government, anxious to stem a rising tide of anti-court comment, considered suppressing the coffee houses, or at least limiting the liberties taken with its reputation inside them.[106]

Yet the government's capacity for firm action was in decline, as ministers divided over policy and some courtiers seized the opportunity to wield power. Buckingham finally emerged from the political backwoods to set himself up as a leader and co-ordinator of the attack on the administration. His intentions were no doubt largely to force himself into office: his loud protestations of his 'wonderful affections and reverence' for his country, and his dismay at the court's 'declared malignity against the liberty of the subject' may indeed have been, as Clarendon alleged, mere window-dressing.[107] Yet his motives were perhaps more various than this suggests: Buckingham possessed a lively contempt of almost everybody, and particularly of the king's current ministers, a feeling which was easily convertible – even in a man as closely identified with so many of the vices of the court as was Buckingham – into a hatred of the court and of courtiers which well suited the prevailing mood.[108] He also had personal reasons to espouse 'country' values: Clarendon claimed that he had had a violent quarrel with Castlemaine, and had consequently offended the king;[109] and in April 1667 Pepys heard that his rental income, like that of many M.P.s and country gentry, had been drastically cut by the depression. If nothing else, his hatred of Ormonde and his falling rents would

---

103 *Hist. MSS. Comm.*, 12th report, appendix, part IX (1891), MSS of the duke of Beaufort, pp. 54–5, Lord Herbert to Lady Herbert, 17 Nov. 1666; see also Pepys, *Diary*, VII, 323, 325–6, 371–2; Evelyn, *Diary*, III, 465–6; Carte MSS 34, fol. 459, Lord Conway to Ormonde, 27 Oct. 1666.
104 Pepys, *Diary*, VII, 341–2; Bodl., MS Eng. Hist. e. 87 appears to date to late 1666.
105 *H.P.*, I, 346–7, 503, and cf. the Plympton Erle election, 206; Pepys, *Diary*, VII, 337.
106 Clarendon, *Life*, II, 298–9: the story cannot be accurately dated, but according to Clarendon's version, the discussion seems to have taken place either shortly before, or after the opening of the session.
107 Clarendon, *Life*, II, 322.
108 See Buckingham's poetry and commonplace book, printed in Villiers, George, duke of Buckingham, *Buckingham: public and private man*, ed. C. Phipps, The Renaissance Imagination, vol. XIII (New York, 1985), and the play he wrote with Sir Robert Howard in 1669, *The country gentleman*, ed. A. H. Scouten and R. D. Hume (London, 1976).
109 Clarendon, *Life*, II, 322; Henry Killigrew had also offended her at about this time (Pepys, *Diary*, VII, 336–7, 337 n. 1): for Killigrew's association with Buckingham, see Sir Walter Scott (ed.), *Memoirs of Count Grammont by Anthony Hamilton* (London, 1905), p. 358.

have combined to make him one of the fiercest proponents of the Irish Cattle Bill.[110]

In Clarendon's account, Buckingham's association with 'country' peers and M.P.s began fairly early, perhaps before the session had started: he sought the company and opinions of men like Temple, Seymour, Garraway and Sir Robert Howard and shared with them his distaste for the corruptions of the court; he was said to have taken to listening in to the debates of the commons; and on 5 October he initiated a long debate in the lords of revenue abuses.[111] Buckingham's sudden reforming zeal was greeted with some mirth, more scepticism and much scorn; but he was given leave to draw up a bill which by 22 November had received two readings and was committed: by that stage, ministers were all too aware of the seriousness of his challenge.[112]

But the greatest threat to the government's business in parliament lay as much in its own response to such challenges. As in 1663, the difficulties it met with in parliament, the worries about possible attempts to impeach individual ministers, and possibly unacknowledged, but nevertheless profound, rivalries at court, produced a potent mixture which could paralyse the government's capacity for coherent, effective action. Clarendon hinted at the beginning of this process: those, he claimed, who directed the government's business in the commons (meaning, principally, Clifford and Sir William Coventry) were more nervous than before of opposition; and rather than attempt to convince the most obstructive M.P.s of the government's case with reason and argument, they resorted to cruder methods, 'promises of reward and preferment'. As a result, some of the government's other parliamentary managers (presumably those associated with himself) largely abdicated from running its business.[113] In fact Coventry, at least, was alive to some of the dangers of rewarding the troublesome:[114] but the main point at issue in the developing debate between the factions was rather how far to give in to the evidently genuine concern of M.P.s on some issues in order more easily to secure supply. Joined to this professional dilemma was the personal dilemma of some ministers – Clarendon cited Lord Ashley – who felt threatened by parliamentary inquiry and hence were anxious not to be seen to oppose the commons' wishes.[115] By the beginning of November, the effectiveness of government leadership was noticeably in decline: in a letter reminiscent of that Henry Coventry had written during the session of 1663, Brodrick told

[110] Pepys, *Diary*, VIII, 158.
[111] Clarendon, *Life*, II, 321–2; Milward, *Diary*, p. 22; cf. *C.J.*, 635.
[112] P.R.O., SP 29/174/85, Sir Thomas Clifford to Arlington, 6 Oct. 1666; Pepys, *Diary*, VII, 309, cf. 325; *L.J.*, X, 33, 76: the first reading is not apparently recorded in the Journal. See also H.L.R.O., Committee Minutes, B.L., 23 Nov. 1666, 17 Jan. 1667.
[113] Clarendon, *Life*, II, 327–30.
[114] Pepys, *Diary*, VII, 311.   [115] Clarendon, *Life*, II, 319–20.

Ormonde that the court M.P.s 'are in truth able to carry any vote (we firmly resolve) within these walls, but to deal frankly with your grace we are not directed as formerly and being left to the accident of wind and tide, in a popular assembly, drive at random, the consequence will be fatal if not timely prevented'.[116] The man most able to prevent it was also the man who seemed least inclined to do so: as in 1663, Charles seemed to all observers to have escaped from the difficult world of politics into his life of ease and pleasure. As the danger of chaos seemed ever more present, the king, so Carteret told Pepys, 'minds it not, nor will be brought to it', while 'his servants of the house do, instead of making the parliament better, rather play the rogue one with another, and will put all in fire'.[117]

From mid-October to the end of November these problems, and their consequences, all became more glaring. In its efforts to obtain supply, the court's performance was at its most lamentable. On 11 October, following the presentation of the committee's estimates of expenditure on the war, the commons proceeded to debate supply. 'Country' leaders attempted to limit the sum: Temple proposed that £1.6 million be voted, roughly the sum the committee had claimed to be the cost of the fleet for a year. As court M.P.s pointed out, the committee's estimate showed only part of the costs of the war; it included, for example, no provision for land forces in case of invasion. As important as the debate over the sum to be raised, however, was the debate over how it was to be raised. The insistence of 'country' leaders that the money must be raised by a land tax – not all that welcome to country gentlemen already overburdened with assessment taxation – can only have been due to the unacceptability of the alternative proposal offered by the court, of a general excise.[118]

The excise, and the 1666 debates about it, so soon became part of 'country party' mythology (thanks to Andrew Marvell), that it is important to examine the government's reasons for wanting it.[119] Doubtless part of its attraction was, as the 'country' tradition alleged, that in expanding the permanent revenue it might help to reduce the government's reliance on parliament. But in the conditions of 1666 the tax was particularly appropriate. The Royal and Additional Aids had placed a heavy fiscal burden on land: a new assessment to run concurrently with them would be an almost intolerable burden; but if

---

[116] Carte MSS 35, fol. 118, 3 Nov. 1666.
[117] Pepys, *Diary*, VII, 370, cf. 320.
[118] *C.J.*, 634, 635; Milward, *Diary*, pp. 20, 21–2. Milward's account of the debate on 12 October is unreliable, its version of the 'country' leaders' actions ambiguous and confused. Perhaps the most likely interpretation would be that they wished to close the issue of how the money was to be raised as soon as possible, before the court could surprise them with a motion for the excise.
[119] 'The last instructions to a painter', in Margoliouth, I, 141–65, ll. 105–306.

the tax was not to run with them, then payment of it could begin only when they and the one month's assessment for the duke of York were finished, in January 1668. In the present state of uncertainty, few would be willing to lend money with no prospect of repayment for more than a year ahead. But collection of an additional excise could begin immediately, and attract credit at once; in the circumstances, the excise seemed the most practical answer to the government's needs.[120]

In spite of its undeniable attractions, however, some later thought that insisting on it had been a serious mistake: it would have been far better to have accepted the firm proposal for a land tax than to spend precious weeks haggling over the excise's merits. And indeed, the existence of two rival proposals confused many who found it difficult to decide between the virtues and the inconveniences of the two schemes – despite the ritual disapproval of the excise.[121] Holland expressed what was apparently a common wish, for all proposals to be examined closely on their merits; and although there was apparently no formal vote to do so, it seems to have been the practice that the house and the committee of the whole followed – spending more time and energy than the government would have liked in considering numerous complex suggestions.[122]

At least the government did succeed on 12 October in ending the day with a resolution to supply a specific sum, and a sum – £1.8 million – £200,000 higher than that Temple had mentioned.[123] But the only cautious welcome which it gave the vote was amply justified the following week, a week of debates on how the money should be raised which seemed to get nowhere. Brodrick called them 'wild debates', and they seem to have provoked country gentry into cataloguing their miseries: 'the bankers are called caterpillars, the usurers threatened to have their monies forced from them by our wise country gentlemen who say they cannot sell their corn or cattle to supply even the present land rate'.[124] The commons' animosity towards the bankers had been aroused principally by the suggestion – made on 15 October by Humphrey Orme, M.P. for Peterborough – that £1.6 million could be raised if the government agreed to surrender the hearth tax in return for an immediate grant of eight times its annual value. The proposal caught the imagination of country M.P.s, delighted at the opportunity to remove a tax so widely

---

[120] Chandaman, pp. 54–7; cf. Pepys, *Diary*, V, 68–9, and VII, 286; see also George Cocke's paper in support of an excise at P.R.O., SP 29/170/130, and Carte MSS 35, fol. 105, Brodrick to Ormonde, 20 Oct. 1666.
[121] E.g., Carte MSS 47, fol. 142, Anglesey to Ormonde, 26 March 1667.
[122] Bodl., Tanner MSS 239, fols. 67–8; Milward, *Diary*, p. 21.
[123] *C.J.*, 635; Milward, *Diary*, pp. 21–2.
[124] Carte MSS 35, fols. 101, 105r–v, Brodrick to Ormonde, 13, 20 Oct. 1666; cf. Carte MSS 46, fol. 385, Arlington to Ormonde, 13 Oct. 1666, and Pepys, *Diary*, VII, 321.

resented, and they received with satisfaction the arguments that were put forward on its behalf: the popularity of such a measure; that it would be a much better fund for credit than a land tax would be (so much so, apparently, that the £200,000 which had been added to the war estimate of £1.6 million as it was said to cover interest charges, could now be dropped); and that it could also be the way to remove the excise, 'and so reduce all payments to the old way of subsidies'. But only the first of these arguments had very much weight. Even if some were anxious to prevent any expansion of the royal permanent revenue, there was no pressure for its actual reduction; indeed, the point that the hearth tax should be replaced by some other permanent source of revenue – an excise on tobacco, sugar, and pepper was mentioned – seems to have been established early on. The claim that the sale of the hearth tax would provide excellent credit was answered by the argument that at the current state of the money market, a sum amounting to eight times its normal yield simply could not be found; Orme's estimate of £200,000 for the tax's annual yield was greatly exaggerated; and such a project involved immense and complicated problems – particularly that of apportioning payments between landlords and tenants.[125]

One other difficulty in the way of abandoning the hearth tax was apparently not mentioned, perhaps deliberately. In March 1666, the government had let out the hearth tax to farm to three City merchants, who represented a large syndicate: the new farmers paid the generous advance of £250,000, and agreed to a rent of £145,000 rising to £170,000 in the seventh year. Abandoning the tax would mean reneging on the agreement – for which the advance had already been paid – and would cause untold damage to the London financial community.[126] Some in government, believing that the Crown was already too much in the City's hands, seem to have believed this was none too bad a thing: Sir William Coventry disliked the farming of the hearth tax, and appears to have supported this scheme;[127] but the lord treasurer, who had arranged the farm, and those in the treasury and naval administration who had close links with the City, could scarcely countenance it.

On 16 October, perhaps because the government had managed for the moment to suppress the hearth tax scheme, discussion returned to the alternatives of a land tax and the excise; the court, according to Milward,

[125] *C.J.*, 636; Milward, *Diary*, pp. 23–4; for hearth tax yields, see Chandaman, pp. 92–1, and above, p. 116.
[126] Chandaman, pp. 92–3; Meekings, 'The City loans on the hearth tax', p. 347.
[127] P.R.O., SP 29/140/71, Sir William Coventry to Arlington, 31 Dec. 1665; Pepys, *Diary*, VIII, 143–4; cf. Clarendon, *Life*, II, 361, for an obscure hint that someone in the government was pressing the king to accept the hearth tax scheme, and p. 342 for Coventry's animosity towards the bankers.

strongly urging the latter, the 'presbyterian party' the former. But it remained clear that neither proposal was very welcome to M.P.s reluctant to burden their communities. In two speeches, Holland enumerated the country's objections to either scheme.[128] The land tax, though it produced a definite sum and was cheaper to collect than the excise, would be an intolerable weight on land already groaning under taxation; it was no very good foundation for credit; and there were great inequalities in the way it was distributed over the country – Holland himself had for some time been demanding a reduction in Norfolk's contribution.[129] The excise raised different worries: the bureaucracy it would call into existence would consume much of the revenue it collected, and 'will soon become as so many vermin and caterpillars to devour us'; once the excise was set up, it was unlikely to be removed again; and practically, setting up such a new tax would take much time, in fixing the commodities and rates to be charged.[130]

Such difficulties meant that M.P.s could not be easily diverted from the attractive prospect of offering something to their friends and countrymen to make further taxation more bearable: on 18 October, an old cavalier, Samuel Sandys, seconded by Henry Williams, suggested that money should be raised by a sort of forced loan, authorised by parliament, from 'all rich and moneyed men' and great officials; the motive behind the suggestion may have been, as some suspected, an attack on the presbyterians.[131] Yet the proposal did not seriously impede the hearth tax scheme, and on the 18th there seemed to be a real possibility that it might be implemented: it may even have been that some in government were prepared to contemplate it seriously. According to Milward 'it was affirmed' that the scheme would be the quickest way to raise the money, as long as the estimate of the tax's annual yield was correct, as long as a replacement for it was worked out which would not become as great a cause of grievance as the hearth tax itself, and as long as landlords, not tenants, should pay. Other impositions suggested on the 18th – an excise on luxury goods, a stamp duty, a tax on corn – appear to have been for replacements for the hearth tax. A committee was appointed to discover the real

---

[128] *C.J.*, 636; Milward, *Diary*, p. 25; Bodl., Tanner MSS 239, fols. 63v–68. Robbins (Milward, *Diary*, pp. 307–12) obeys Holland's instruction in the MS that the third of the three speeches on supply in 1666 should be 'placed before the former two speeches' (i.e., these two). But it is uncertain that this means that it was delivered before them, and it seems more likely that the arrangement is not chronological. Indeed, the two speeches may not have been given on any particular occasion, but may simply summarise the arguments against these methods of supply.

[129] Bodl., Tanner MSS 239, fols. 65–6v, cf. fols. 38r–v, 44v–45 and above, p. 129, for his efforts to reduce Norfolk's share.

[130] Bodl., Tanner MSS 239, fols. 63–4v; cf. Carte MSS 35, fol. 105, 20 Oct. 1666, Brodrick to Ormonde.

[131] Milward, *Diary*, p. 27; Carte MSS 35, fol. 105.

annual value of the hearth tax, and to consider the best means of compensation.[132] On the 25th it endorsed the original, and excessive, estimate of £200,000; although the government's desire to get the estimate correct, to avoid false optimism about how much eight years' value of it would come to, was probably tempered by the fact that a high estimate would at least increase the value of the compensation on offer. But at the end of the week some doubt still appeared to be hanging over the scheme, for the most obvious objection held good: few people would be able to afford the lump payment of eight times the hearth tax rate in the present circumstances. The sale was bound to fail.[133]

At the end of the second week of these debates, the government's frustration was mounting. Although the hearth tax proposal had been strongly pressed, there was as yet no firm decision about what should replace it, while enthusiasm for the scheme itself was declining: yet neither the excise, nor the land tax had obtained strong support. As Brodrick complained, the result was too many new proposals, 'new projects being daily offered ere the old be duly weighed'. Some of these, as Downing later said, came from the court itself, unable to decide firmly on a proposal both satisfactory to itself and acceptable to parliament.[134]

At the beginning of the next week, the government gently attempted to speed up a decision with a royal message drawing attention to the urgency of the matter, and denying that there were any negotiations for peace. The latter denial was perhaps a mistake. Although some of the government's fiercest critics may have believed that its intention was to withdraw from the war once it had secured a supply, and divert the money for other purposes, it was not an allegation which seems to have been widely discussed up to now; the government's denial may have given it wider publicity. The message did at first appear to have some effect. But although it was Garraway who proposed that a bill for the hearth tax scheme should be discussed and either firmly rejected or accepted, others demanded that its chances of acceptance should be increased by comparing, first, the merits of excise and land tax, and then the best of these with the hearth tax scheme. After two weeks the whole issue seemed to be back where it had begun: most of the day on the 30th was used up in deciding whether to debate the excise or the land tax first. The house did, however, order a bill for the hearth tax scheme to be drawn up, and the completion of the petition to the king for the prohibition of French imports

[132] *C.J.*, 637–8; Milward, *Diary*, pp. 26, 27–8; Carte MSS 35, fol. 105.
[133] *C.J.*, 638, 640, 641, 643; Milward, *Diary*, pp. 30–2; Carte MS 34, fols. 459v–60, Conway to Ormonde, 27 Oct. 1666.
[134] Carte MSS 35, fol. 109, Brodrick to Ormonde, 27 Oct. 1666; Pepys, *Diary*, VII, 380–1; cf. Carte MSS 46, fol. 392, Arlington to Ormonde, 27 Oct. 1666; Margoliouth, II, 42, Marvell to Mayor Franke, 27 Oct. 1666.

seems to have inspired a new proposal, for an excise on foreign goods. Yet this initiative was perhaps a fresh indication of government confusion; proposed by Colonel Birth (who had made a similar suggestion the previous week) it was taken up by the solicitor general as a means of reducing the sum to be raised by a land tax. But other court members – Clifford and Sir Charles Harbord – continued to press for the full inland excise. The foreign excise proposal was greeted with considerable enthusiasm: a committee was appointed to consider it in greater detail. From this, Birch reported on 2 November. His report was torn to shreds and the proposal shelved: but although debate turned back to the land tax on the following day and continued well into the afternoon, still no decision could be reached.[135]

Three weeks had now passed since the resolution of 12 October: the debates of the last week had clearly shown how the government was in complete disarray over which proposal to support. Brodrick hinted on 3 November at the disintegration of the court's parliamentary management; a meeting the following evening (Sunday, 5 November) would, he hoped, bring some clarity to the government's actions.[136] This meeting – perhaps of the private committee of the council – seems to have resolved, probably on Carteret's advice and against Coventry's opposition, firmly to disavow the hearth tax scheme, to drop the excise, and concentrate instead on a combination of the land tax with other expedients.[137] In a message to the commons on the next day they sat for business, 8 November, the king effectively put an end to the hearth tax scheme by announcing that he would not allow it, and an assurance was also given (presumably by court M.P.s) that there would be no further effort to obtain a general excise. The court received its reward: Garraway (who had perhaps been consulted by the government, as one of the most constructive of its critics) proposed that of the £1.8 million, £1,320,000 should be raised by an eleven months' assessment of £120,000 a month, to follow the current assessments; the remainder should be raised by a mixture of poll tax, stamp duty, and foreign excise. That some of the money should be raised by an assessment was accepted in a division by other moderate 'country' M.P.s, Gower and Lee, although they did not endorse the sum Garraway had mentioned to be raised by it (which would mean continuing the current level of the land tax to the end of 1668); an indication, perhaps, that still they hankered after less burdensome solutions for the main part of

135 C.J., 643, 644, 645, 646; Milward, Diary, pp. 33–4, 35, 36.
136 Carte MSS 35, fol. 118, Brodrick to Ormonde, 3 Nov. 1666.
137 For Coventry's opposition see Pepys, Diary, VIII, 143–4; cf. Clarendon, Life, II, 361. Duncombe's opposition to the land tax in the debate on 8 November is perhaps an indication that he, like his mentor Coventry, continued to resent the abandonment of the hearth tax scheme: C.J., 647.

the taxation. The new poll tax proposal attracted M.P.s, designed as it was to reduce the weight of taxation on land and place some of it instead on money and salaries. It, and the stamp duty, were accepted with little difficulty, although presbyterians were said to have opposed it, clinging still to their favourite solution of the land tax, and attempting to avoid a tax on the moneyed.[138] The foreign excise was more firmly contested. The 'presbyterian party' leader, Swinfen, attempted to halt the debate, and 'country' leaders tried at least to limit the excise's collection to the point of entry of the goods, presumably to prevent the extension of the army of excise officials and to place obstacles in the way of a later expansion of the excise to domestically produced goods as well. On this they were narrowly defeated, and on the final division on the proposal, M.P.s' approval of a tax which in theory hurt only foreign producers overcame their distrust of the excise; it was passed by an overwhelming majority.[139]

Government concessions and a firm plan of action had at last produced results, although the length and heat of the debate showed that plenty of dangers still lay in the path of supply; on the following day the government's critics diverted the house into a discussion of the by now desperate clamours of the seamen for pay; they alleged mismanagement and demanded a bill for the establishment of a statutory committee to examine, on oath, the accounts of the departments responsible. Similar proposals had been made before by the group of M.P.s led by Vaughan and Littleton: before, they had been easily suppressed, but now M.P.s were more jealous of the government's financial management; the motion was again rejected, but by only eleven votes.[140] Despite its failure, M.P.s clearly felt that the accounts which had so far been brought into the house were inadequate, for they accepted an alternative proposal, that the accounts should be examined by a joint committee of lords and commons, which would enable officials to be questioned on oath: a request was sent to the lords for such a committee to be appointed, and on the following day the commons revived their old committee of accounts, to the alarm of Sir William Coventry and the navy board.[141]

But at least the progress in supply was not reversed: on 10 November a

---

[138] For an early mention of the Poll Bill, see Margoliouth, II, 43, Marvell to Mayor Franke, 6 Nov. 1666; for the tax, see Chandaman, pp. 163–4; see Pepys, *Diary*, VII, 387–8, for Lord Crew's reaction to the poll.

[139] *C.J.*, 647: note particularly Seymour's support for the foreign excise; Milward, *Diary*, pp. 38–9.

[140] See above, p. 120; the 'Mr Vaughan' who told against the motion is unlikely to be John Vaughan, as *H.P.* (III, 629) claims: this would be almost inconceivable, and Vaughan was absent this session (see above, p. 48 and n. 63). The teller is more likely to have been Roger Vaughan, whom Coventry looked upon as a possible court spokesman: P.R.O., SP 29/171/104, Coventry to Arlington, 27 Sept. 1666.

[141] *C.J.*, 647–8; Milward, *Diary*, p. 39; Pepys, *Diary*, VII, 364.

committee was appointed to bring in an estimate of the sum to be raised by the stamp duty, and in the following week the house worked hard in committee of the whole settling the details of the poll. These the chairman of the committee, Robert Milward, reported to the house on the 17th. In contrast to previous polls, which rated people according to rank, the centre of this tax was a flat rate of a shilling on all liable to pay. Its role in tapping wealth untouched by the assessments was made explicit; all personal estate (save that already taxed in the assessments) was subject to a further tax at 1 per cent; the profits of public office, perquisites, pensions, and the incomes of lawyers, physicians, and servants were also to be taxed at varying rates. Aliens and nonconformists were to be charged double. On the same day, the house ordered that a bill be brought in along these lines.[142] A few further changes were made subsequently, possibly at the instance of the committee of lawyers entrusted with drawing up the Bill: the house reversed the earlier decision not to tax people by their titles, and added a scale of charges set at half those of the 1660 poll; they resolved, too, that the house also had a right to tax the clergy on their titles. On the 26th the Bill had its first reading.[143] At the end of six weeks since the resolution to grant £1.8 million, there was at last one bill – out of a proposed four – on the table. 'Country' leaders were starting to show a little anger that supply was beginning to come without major concessions from the court: Whotwood narrowly escaped a reprimand when he complained, bitterly, on the 12th that 'when we have raised the king's supply we may go home like fools, as we came'.[144]

Divided, confused, and battered in the commons, the government might have seen the lords as a place of refuge where it would be permitted to win some of its contests out of a respect forgotten in the lower house. Certainly, those connected with the court hoped that the Irish Cattle Bill could be quietly laid to rest amongst the peers: but the duke of Buckingham (for whom they may have been coming to feel a new respect), Lord Ashley, and a resentment of Irish cattle imports in the upper house no less than in the lower, was largely to defeat them.[145] But even if it did pass, Irish lobbyists comforted themselves with the king's declared determination to refuse the Bill when it was presented to him, although in their soberer moments they realised that with the

[142] *C.J.*, 648, 649, 650, 650–1; Milward, *Diary*, pp. 40–3; Margoliouth, II, 44, Marvell to Mayor Franke, 13 Nov. 1666; Carte MSS 35, fol. 130, Brodrick to Ormonde, 17 Nov. 1666; P.R.O., SP 29/178/69, newsletter, 15 Nov. 1666; Chandaman, pp. 147, 163–4; cf. *Hist. MSS. Comm.*, MSS of R. R. Hastings Esq., II, 372, Conway to [Sir George Rawdon], 10 Nov. 1666, which is much at variance with the other accounts.

[143] *C.J.*, 653, 654; Milward, *Diary*, pp. 45–6 (in which some of the business of 26 November has been misattributed to the 24th); Carte MSS 46, fol. 402r–v, Arlington to Ormonde, 20 Nov. 1666.

[144] Carte MSS 46, fol. 396, Arlington to Ormonde, 10 Nov. 1666; Milward, *Diary*, pp. 40–1.

[145] Carte MSS 46, fol. 385, Arlington to Ormonde, 13 Oct. 1666.

weight of popular pressure for the Bill, it would be better if it were never presented.[146] The Bill was read for the first time on 16 October; despite a vigorous attack by the Irish lobby, its supporters won its commitment to the whole house the following Monday.[147] A heated, and very evenly divided debate continued for the rest of the week. By the end of the second day, despite the desperate opposition and pleas for delay from English protestant settlers and Irish catholics, the preamble of the Bill was accepted. But while the lords would not forgo the Bill, they had sufficient respect for the royal prerogative to accept the replacement of the word 'nuisance' with the anodyne 'detriment and mischief'.[148]

During these debates Buckingham had emerged as the leader of the Bill's supporters, and of the government's critics in the lords, if only by virtue of being the loudest, most uncompromising, and least temperate. When Buckingham was absent from the house for two days – by reason of a violent quarrel with Ossory, which ended with both of them committed into temporary custody – there was no further progress on the Bill.[149] In fact it was not until 8 November, after the house had taken a few days off for the All Saints' day and 5 November holidays, that it took up discussion of it again. In a lengthy and exhausting debate in committee of the whole house, Clarendon and the other supporters of Ireland tried hard to mitigate the Bill's seizure and penalty provisions, although the changes that were suggested by a subcommittee were ultimately rejected by the committee of the whole on the 10th. The objections of the Church to the ban on fish imports which the Bill also included were also overruled, and the Bill, now completely passed in committee with only one significant amendment – the replacement of the word 'nuisance' – was ready to be reported to the house.[150]

Members of the Irish lobby, having failed to suppress the Bill in committee, were more confident of their ability to dispose of it in the house itself; and increasingly they recognised the need to do so. Despite the king's frequently

---

[146] Carte MSS 217, fols. 342 and 344, Anglesey to Ormonde, 16, 20 Oct. 1666; Carte MSS 46, fol. 387, Arlington to Ormonde, 16 Oct. 1666.
[147] *L.J.*, X, 13; Carte MSS 217, fol. 344; Clarendon, *Life*, II, 333.
[148] *L.J.*, X, 15–18; Bodl., MS Rawlinson A 130, fol. 62v–63 (which attributes the decision on the 26th to the 27th); H.L.R.O., MS Minutes, H.L., vol. 13, 22–26 Oct. 1666, Committee Minutes, H.L., 22, 23 and 26 Oct. 1666, Main Papers, H.L., 22 Oct. 1666; Carte MSS 217, fol. 346, Anglesey to Ormonde, 23 Oct. 1666; Carte MSS 34, fol. 459, Conway to Ormonde, 27 Oct. 1666.
[149] Carte MSS 34, fol. 459, Conway to Ormonde, 27 Oct. 1666; Carte MSS 35, fol. 111, Brodrick to Ormonde, 27 Oct. 1666; Carte MSS 46, fol. 394, Arlington to Ormonde, 3 Nov. 1666; Carte MSS 217, fol. 348, Anglesey to Ormonde, 27 Oct. 1666; Bodl., Rawlinson MSS A 130, fol. 64; Clarendon, *Life*, II, 333–8; *L.J.*, X, 18–19, 19–20, 22.
[150] *L.J.*, X, 24, 25; H.L.R.O., Committee Minutes, H.L., 8, 9, 10 Nov. 1666, MS Minutes, vol. 13, 8–10 Nov. 1666; Bodl., MS Rawlinson A 130, fols. 64v–65; Carte MSS 217, fol. 353; Carte MSS 35, fol. 120, Conway to Ormonde, 10 Nov. 1666.

iterated insistence that he would never assent to it, it was obvious that he would be hard put to refuse a Bill which so many of the gentry and nobility considered vital for their economic survival.[151] On 12 November Lord Robartes reported the Bill: debate was renewed then and on the 16th, over the replacement of 'nuisance'; finally the committee's decision to substitute 'detriment and mischief' was accepted. The proviso for exempting Scottish cattle was rejected, despite the efforts of Ashley, Lauderdale, and Arlington; but the attempts of the Irish lobby to exempt 20,000 cattle that Ormonde had offered to send in order to help feed the inhabitants of devastated London were more successful. Even so, and notwithstanding an appeal from the City, there remained fierce opposition to what was seen as a ruse to benefit private interests under the cloak of charity. If the Bill's supporters could hardly be seen directly to reject so apparently beneficial a scheme, they did their best to make it as little to the taste of the Irish as they could. Buckingham, Ashley, and Lucas tried to limit the exemption to dead meat, to be sent over before the next Michaelmas – well before it would be ready. Anglesey claimed to have got the house to reject these conditions when their draft proviso was offered to the house on 19 November, though he was not helped by Ossory's bitter comment on one of its promoters, Ashley, that he spoke 'like one of Oliver Cromwell's councillors': some, though not all, of the proviso's restrictions on the gift were removed. With the addition of a proviso explicitly excepting the importation of horses, the Bill was ready for its third reading, on the 23rd.[152]

As widely predicted, it was passed, with its three main amendments – the removal of the word 'nuisance' and of the exemption of Scotland, and the addition of the proviso for the cattle for London. The 115 opponents were consoled by the fact that it had passed by a slimmer majority than had been expected, and some thought there was still scope to wreck it in the commons; but now that the insult to the prerogative had been removed, few believed that the king would veto it.[153] The government's hopes that the Bill could be suppressed in the upper house had been ruined, and, as Clarendon and Anglesey observed, it had been so largely through the efforts of courtiers. The Irish lobby felt betrayed. Anglesey enumerated for Ormonde the members of

---

[151] *Ibid.*, fol. 120, 124 (Burlington to Ormonde, 10 Nov. 1666); Carte MSS 46, fol. 396, Arlington to Ormonde, 10 Nov. 1666.

[152] *L.J.*, X, 26, 30, 31, 32; H.L.R.O., MS Minutes, H.L., vol. 13, 12, 16 Nov. 1666, Committee Minutes, H.L., 17 Nov. 1666, Main Papers, H.L., 22 Oct. 1666, annex a, 1; Bodl., MS Rawlinson A 130, fols. 65v, 66v, 67; Carte MSS 47, fol. 136v, Anglesey to Ormonde, 13 Nov. 1666; Carte MSS 217, fol. 354, Anglesey to Ormonde, 20 Nov. 1666; Edie, 'Irish Cattle Bills', p. 30; Clarendon, *Life*, II, 344–6.

[153] *L.J.*, X, 34; H.L.R.O., MS Minutes, H.L., vol. 13, 23 Nov. 1666; Bodl., MS Rawlinson A 130, fol. 67v; Carte MSS 35, fol. 144, Brodrick to Ormonde, 27 Nov. 1666, fol. 148, Conway to Ormonde, 27 Nov. 1666; Carte MSS 217, fol. 357, Anglesey to Ormonde, 24 Nov. 1666.

the privy council and the king's servants among the principal advocates of the Bill: Southampton, Robartes, Manchester, Ashley, Buckingham, Dorchester, Oxford, Carlisle, Berkshire, and Gerrard.[154] Lord Conway was so struck by this that he thought (improbably) that the king had given at least tacit consent to a project of Ashley, Lauderdale, and Arlington to expand the Scottish cattle trade and settle the profits on the duke of Monmouth.[155] Many Irish lords, as well as Clarendon, considered that the ferocity of some courtiers against Irish cattle was attributable to their intense jealousy and hatred of Ormonde, the architect of an Irish land settlement which many considered to discriminate against English settlers in favour of Irish catholics. Buckingham's long-standing animosity towards the Irish viceroy was well known, and when, in early January, Conway inquired of Ashley why he was so insistent on Ireland's ruin, Ashley admitted that the Bill was an 'unnatural act', but claimed that 'the fault was in our present governors who by the settlement of Ireland, the book of rates, and other principles of government did endeavour to divide the interest of the two kingdoms', and that the poverty of Ireland was 'upon these lords, that have driven the English out of the sea ports and corporate towns, and filled them up with Irish'.[156] Ashley clearly cherished a profound suspicion of the wealthy Irish élite and a distrust of the Irish catholic influences among them: his actions implied a fear that an old English nobility would be edged out of its power and lands by the upstart Irish; if Irish cattle imports continued, he claimed, rents in Ireland would rise as much as they fell in England, and in a few years Ormonde's estate would exceed the vast lands of the earl of Northumberland. He sponsored, too, an attack in the committee of privileges on the efforts of Irish peers to usurp the precedence of the English, and was said to be preparing a bill to alter the Irish book of rates.[157] A champion of the privileges of the house of lords, Ashley saw in Ireland an obscure nobility sucking away the wealth and the honour of England, with a government so open to catholic subversion that it threatened the health of protestantism in England.[158]

Why some other courtiers supported the Bill is less clear: they may simply have shared the general perception that the decline in English rents was to be

[154] Carte MSS 217, fol. 353; cf. Carte MSS 47, fol. 128, Clarendon to Ormonde, 10 Nov. 1666, and Carte MSS 35, fol. 120, Conway to Ormonde, 10 Nov. 1666.

[155] Carte MSS 35, fol. 126, Conway to Ormonde, 13 Nov. 1666.

[156] *Ibid.*, fols. 240, 259, Conway to Ormonde, 5, 19 Jan. 1667; cf. Carte MSS 47, fol. 130, Clarendon to Ormonde, 24 Nov. 1666, Carte MSS 217, fol. 354v, Anglesey to Ormonde, 20 Nov. 1666; Clarendon, *Life*, II, 323, 332.

[157] Clarendon, *Life*, II, 332; for the Irish peerage case, see *L.J.*, X, 28–9; Bodl., Rawlinson MSS A 130, fol. 65v; Carte MSS 35, fols. 125–6, Conway to Ormonde, 13 Nov. 1666.

[158] For his interest in the privileges of the lords, and his opposition to the 1665 Plague Bill, see Carte MSS 34, fol. 468, Brodrick to Ormonde, 2 Nov. 1665. Cf. Clarendon's more cynical explanation of his conduct, *Life*, II, 319–20, and Haley, *Shaftesbury*, pp. 187–93.

laid to Ireland – most of them were as concerned for their rents and profits as any 'country' peer. Manchester and Robartes, ex-presbyterian lords, may have agreed with Ashley's fear of catholic influence in Ireland; Robartes may also have resented his replacement by Ormonde as lord lieutenant in 1661.[159] Southampton's support for the Bill was perhaps an indication of the split in the government between those willing to compromise in order to gain supply, and others convinced that concessions had to be resisted, at almost any cost. Arlington, at any rate, was beginning to hint that the Bill would have to be accepted.[160] As with the government's efforts to obtain supply, divisions on court strategy might eventually damage its attempts to keep control of parliament.

As 'country' leaders in both houses recognised the government's diffi-culties, they pressed it harder. On 29 October Edward Seymour reported from the commons' committee appointed to consider the Canary patent: the committee's resolution that it was illegal, a monopoly, and a grievance was accepted by the house, although the more radical demands for an impeach-ment of the patentees were for the moment rejected in favour of a joint appeal with the lords to the king for the patent's withdrawal.[161] Action in the lords – probably because of Clarendon's attempt to suppress the matter – was dilatory; only on 12 November did the house discuss it, and then the hearing was continually put off: to the 24th, the 29th, and then to 3 December.[162] In fact the government had already taken action which may have been designed to calm the feeling against the patentees: on 12 November it issued a proclamation on the petition of some Spanish merchants, stopping the Canary wine trade altogether on the grounds of the Canary authorities' inter-ference.[163] But the commons were now considering monopolies more widely: publishing privileges came under scrutiny by a committee appointed to consider whether the Licensing Act needed to be reinforced – a committee which included many of the 'country' leaders.[164]

The commons' attempt to draw from the government a proclamation against French imports also caused some embarrassment, even though in

[159] Clarendon, *Life*, I, 395–8, 461–5; see especially 462 for Robartes's contempt for the Irish catholic nobility.
[160] Carte MSS 46, fol. 396, Arlington to Ormonde, 10 Nov. 1666.
[161] *C.J.*, 643; Milward, *Diary*, p. 33; Carte MSS 35, fol. 118, Brodrick to Ormonde, 3 Nov. 1666.
[162] *L.J.*, X, 25, 26, 30, 35, 38.
[163] P.R.O., SP 29/177/115, newsletter, 8 Nov. 1666; Steele, no. 3482. Cf. SP 29/178/5, a draft of the proclamation, dated October.
[164] *C.J.*, 636, 641, 642, 657, 665, 666, 672, 675, 679, 682; *Hist. MSS. Comm.*, MSS of the duke of Beaufort, p. 54, Lord Herbert to Lady Herbert, 14 Nov. 1666; P.R.O., SP 29/178/69, newsletter, 15 Nov. 1666. See also Thomas, *Sir John Berkenhead*, pp. 210–11.

principle the government appears to have accepted the case for one. For a while it resisted the pressure for it in the lords, combating it with obviously trivial arguments, easily disposed of by the commons' spokesmen at a conference with the upper house. The lords gave in, and agreed to petition with the commons for a ban: the government now accepted, and a proclamation was published accordingly on 10 November.[165] In fact, the government's efforts to suppress or delay the vote may have had a wider significance than its stated objections suggested; in early October the earl of St Albans arrived in England from Paris, ostensibly on the queen mother's business, but actually bearing hints of Louis XIV's inclination to peace. On 18 October Charles wrote to his sister, the duchess of Orleans, in response. The government was possibly anxious not to threaten these encouraging gestures with a belligerent proclamation on trade: on the other hand, it was equally anxious not to give the commons the impression that there was any chance of a peace which would free them from the obligation of providing supply for the coming year's war. By the end of October, however, the king may have felt less certain of the genuineness of the French overtures, and accepted the pressure for the proclamation.[166]

But the greatest excitement, for the commons at least, and for the government the most irritating diversion from the business of supply, was the investigation into the causes of the Fire of London. Many found the inquiry gripping and frightening; Sir Edward Harley credulously reported to his wife the hints, rumours, and suppositions which the committee heard as evidence.[167] On 20 October the house appointed a committee headed by Prynne to investigate further the reports of a catholic conspiracy. Six days later its findings were described by Giles Hungerford, a Whitchurch M.P. of dissenting and parliamentarian connections: most dramatically, he exhibited two daggers, examples of hundreds found by Sir Richard Browne in the cellars of a City house, and linked, by intercepted letters and other information, to catholic plotters. Ex-presbyterians, such as Harley, Marvell, and Sir Thomas Crew, found all this evidence of a planned massacre – like St Bartholomew's day – highly disturbing; the committee's recommendations, to ask the king to banish catholic priests, disarm catholic laymen, and to weed them out from all government offices, were quickly accepted; and the government did not try, as it had in 1663, to moderate their suggestions. On 10 November a

[165] *L.J.*, X, 10, 11, 12, 14, 15, 16, 19, 20, 22; *C.J.*, 639, 644, 645; H.L.R.O., MS Minutes, H.L., vol. 13, 12 and 15 Oct. 1666; Bodl., MS Rawlinson A 130, fol. 61v; Steele, no. 3481.
[166] Hartmann, *Charles II and Madame*, pp. 184–5; Haley, *An English diplomat*, pp. 103–5.
[167] *Hist. MSS. Comm.*, 14th report, appendix, part II, MSS of the duke of Portland, III (1894), 301–2, 20 Oct. 1666.

proclamation was issued in precisely the terms the commons had requested.[168]

The concern shown in the house at the popish threat reflected the wider worries in the country at large. Both Pepys and Conway commented on the similarity of the atmosphere to that of 1641, and there were certainly rumours flying around reminiscent of those current twenty-five years before.[169] There were reports that Albemarle and Sir John Robinson had been dismissed, the latter replaced as lieutenant of the Tower by a papist; that large numbers of strangers had been noticed passing to and from Ireland; that armed horsemen were daily seen riding in the country; that enormous quantities of arms had been found in the house of Sir Kenelm Digby's son; and that the papists were planning a massacre of protestants.[170] When fire destroyed part of the stables at Whitehall on the night of 9–10 November, the immediate assumption was that it was the signal for some catholic uprising to begin. As Brodrick told Ormonde the following day, 'many dismal apprehensions possess the minds of the credulous'.[171]

Vague rumours of catholic conspiracies were not all the government had to worry about: there were more tangible threats to public order. Unpaid seamen were becoming violent in their demands: on 19 October they rioted, and two months later another riot had to be quelled by the army.[172] Protests against taxation in the country were no less violent. The discussions of the scheme for the replacement of the hearth tax in the commons made it difficult for the tax's collectors to extract money due from taxpayers who were eagerly awaiting news of their relief; when their hopes were dashed by the king's refusal to part with the tax, the collectors received the brunt of their disappointment – they were met with resistance all over the country. On 19 December a proclamation was issued demanding an end to the obstruction of the collectors, and ordering local officers of the peace to co-operate with

[168] C.J., 638–9, 641–2, 649, 650, 651; L.J., X, 21, 22, 29, 32; Milward, *Diary*, p. 32; *Hist. MSS. Comm.*, MSS of the duke of Portland, III, 302, Sir Edward to Lady Harley, 27 Oct. 1666; P.R.O., SP 29/176/62, newsletter, 27 Oct. 1666; Pepys, *Diary*, VII, 343, 356–7; Margoliouth, II, 42, Marvell to Mayor Franke, 27 Oct. 1666; Carte MSS 34, fols. 459–60, Conway to Ormonde, 27 Oct. 1666; Carte MSS 217, fol. 348v, Anglesey to Ormonde, 27 Oct. 1666. For Hungerford, see *H.P.*, II, 616–17, cf. 617–18; for the committee's further proceedings, see C.J., 653, 655, 682; Milward, *Diary*, pp. 45–6. There seems no reason for *H.P.*'s (II, 593) attribution of the report of 24 Nov. to Sir Edward, rather than Giles, Hungerford.
[169] Carte MSS 34, fols. 459–60, Conway to Ormonde, 27 Oct. 1666; Pepys, *Diary*, VII, 343; Carte MSS 47, fol. 128, Clarendon to Ormonde, 10 Nov. 1666.
[170] P.R.O., SP 29/175/26, 176/108, 127, 177/56, 80, 178/134; Pepys, *Diary*, VII, 360, 364–5.
[171] Carte MSS 35, fol. 122; Pepys, *Diary*, VII, 362–4; *Hist. MSS. Comm.*, MSS of R. R. Hastings Esq., II, 372–3, Conway to Sir G. Rawdon, 10 Nov. 1666.
[172] Pepys, *Diary*, VII, 330, 332, 355, 415–16; *Hist. MSS. Comm.*, MSS of the duke of Portland, III, 303, D. de Repas to Sir Robert Harley, 22 Dec. 1666; P.R.O., PC 2/59, fol. 121.

them: but the hearth tax disturbances were only the first of several outbreaks of tax-related unrest throughout 1667.[173]

Most alarmingly, for the last two weeks in November events in Scotland seemed to make the parallels with 1641 frighteningly exact. A small nonconformist rising near Dumfries grew, by 27 November, to a rebellion of about 1000; already, on 24 November, the government was sufficiently disturbed to inform Ormonde and think of sending up English troops. In fact, on the 28th the rebels were forced to retreat and then beaten in the Pentland Hills outside Edinburgh by Scottish troops, but the news remained ambiguous until authoritative accounts arrived on the evening of 2 December.[174] The alarm was short, but while it lasted it was very sharp: a full scale rebellion combined with the government's financial difficulties, the discontent of the seamen and the country, and the sympathy of English dissenters for the Scottish, might easily have been more successful than even its leaders hoped. Pepys heard from the earl of Peterborough's servant that the nobility were lukewarm about voluntary measures for the defence of the kingdom, when many of them had received no repayment for the soldiers they had raised in the summer against a possible invasion.[175] Although now the immediate danger was over for some time the government was convinced that a wider conspiracy was involved; the possibility of a further uprising remained to haunt it.[176]

Domestic politics, too, seemed less and less stable. An impeachment of Clarendon was rumoured; and Bristol was said to be again active in preparing one.[177] There do appear to have been some, albeit cautious, moves towards preparing charges against the chancellor: the petitions against a chancery decree presented to the lords on 17 November were probably politically backed, as those presented in January seem to have been.[178] But the obscure efforts of semi-court factions to remove ministers caused the government far fewer problems than their own inability to agree on workable strategies: as Brodrick, Carteret, Downing, Lord Crew, and George Cocke complained, the court's difficulties in the supply debates were largely of its

[173] C. A. F. Meekings (ed.), *Dorset hearth tax assessments, 1662–4* (1954), p. xxxiv; P.R.O., PC 2/59, fols. 113v–117; SP 29/180/88, 181/15; Carte MSS 35, fol. 148v, Conway to Ormonde, 27 Nov. 1666; Steele, no. 3483.
[174] Pepys, *Diary*, VII, 377, 381, 382, 384, 390–1, 395, 396–7; Carte MSS 35, fols. 148v and 162, Conway to Ormonde, 27 Nov. and 4 Dec. 1666; Carte MSS 46, fol. 404, Arlington to Ormonde, 24 Nov. 1666; Carte MSS 47, fol. 130, Clarendon to Ormonde, 24 Nov. 1666.
[175] Pepys, *Diary*, VII, 395.
[176] O. Airy (ed.), *The Lauderdale papers*, vol. I, Camden Society, new series, XXXIV (1884), 248–68.
[177] Carte MSS 35, fols. 148v, 197, 240v, Conway to Ormonde, 27 Nov., 2 Dec. 1666, and 5 Jan. 1667, cf. fol. 144v, Brodrick to Ormonde, 24 Nov. 1666, and Pepys, *Diary*, VII, 404–5; see also Lister, *Life of Clarendon*, III, 441–2, for Bristol's petition of 14 October.
[178] L.J., X, 31; Clarendon MSS 84, fols. 359–60, 361 and 362; cf. below, pp. 295–6.

own making; because of its failure to decide on the method of supply it preferred, court M.P.s were unable to provide clear leadership, and so, as Cocke said, gave 'leisure and occasion to the other part to run away with what the court would not have'.[179]

Clearly, there was something wrong with the co-ordination of the government's business in the house of commons, but precisely what it was remains obscure. Clarendon blamed many of the troubles of the session on Arlington's and Coventry's willingness to reward parliamentary dissent, to concede defeat too easily by giving in to the demands of the discontented. Coventry does, indeed, appear to have been more ready than some to compromise with the government's critics, strongly supporting the hearth tax scheme.[180] But concessions in themselves would not have produced the near-paralysis in government business in parliament since October. The main problem was rather the division at court between alternative strategies. Judging by the bitterness it still aroused in April 1667, the debate at court over whether or not to accept the hearth tax scheme was a particularly nasty one.[181] Clarendon partly glossed this division as one between Coventry and Arlington on the one hand, cravenly giving in to the commons' demands in order to secure supply, and himself on the other, firmly standing by the law and the legitimate royal prerogative. Some of this may have been true: but it also seems that by this stage the struggle for control of parliament between Coventry and Arlington and Clarendon had become almost an end in itself, perhaps given added urgency by a feeling that impeachments of some government ministers were not far away; in such a situation, each would be anxious to make his own hold over the court party in parliament as strong as possible. When, on 27 November, Clarendon's principal manager of the commons, Sir Hugh Pollard, suddenly died, he was succeeded almost immediately in his old office of comptroller of the household by Arlington's confidant and parliamentary agent, Sir Thomas Clifford. A few days later Clifford was made a privy councillor. Arlington appears to have been anxious to establish his protégé as Pollard's successor before anyone else could assume his mantle.[182]

These signs of a disintegrating government added more fuel to the fears of many that some sort of political collapse was imminent, even if few could say what form it was likely to take. Conway, worried about invasion or rebellion, suggested that 10,000 Irish troops be sent over; Clarendon, writing to Ormonde on 24 November, apostrophised: 'Oh God send us peace or you

[179] Carte MSS 35, fol. 118, Brodrick to Ormonde, 3 Nov. 1666; Pepys, *Diary*, VII, 370, 380–1, 388, 402.
[180] Clarendon, *Life*, II, 327–8.
[181] Pepys, *Diary*, VIII, 143–4.
[182] Carte MSS 46, fol. 406, Arlington to Ormonde, 27 Nov. 1666; P.R.O., PC 2/59, fol. 117v.

and I shall see ill days again'.[183] In fact the prospects for peace did provide the one glimmer of good news. Although approaches to the Dutch in September had fallen on stony ground, the French overtures of October seemed more encouraging. Hopes that they might produce an agreement fluctuated wildly, but in mid-December Arlington was confident enough to describe the negotiations to Ormonde.[184] Peace, accompanied by a large parliamentary grant for war which could then be diverted to pay off the government's debts, would, Arlington suggested, be the best – perhaps the only – way to put the administration back on its financial and political feet. Others easily guessed that such a policy was at least at the back of ministers' minds, but the suspicion that it might be outraged those who believed that much of the money given for the war had already found its way into ministers' and courtiers' pockets. As rumours of peace increased, the belief that a similar fate might befall the present grant made M.P.s even less willing to untie the purses of their countrymen; ministers attempted to quell any optimism about the possibility as they urged that even to negotiate, the government needed to be able to demonstrate a capacity to carry on the war.[185] As the country entered a bitterly cold winter, most people, without the benefit of the ministers' hopes, could look forward only to another year of military stalemate and commercial paralysis.

[183] Carte MSS 35, fol. 120, Conway to Ormonde, 10 Nov. 1666; Carte MSS 47, fol. 130, cf. Pepys, *Diary*, VII, 350, 351, 354–5, 358, 360, 362, 367, 369–70, 371, 382, 383, 387, 393, 395.
[184] Carte MSS 46, fol. 425v, 18 Dec. 1666; Feiling, *British foreign policy*, pp. 195–201, 209–10; Haley, *An English diplomat*, pp. 100–5; Clarendon, *Life*, II, 378–82.
[185] Pepys, *Diary*, VII, 361, 369–70, 375, 404, 411; Carte MSS 46, fol. 426v, Arlington to Ormonde, 18 Dec. 1666.

⫷ 11 ⫸

Defeat: December 1666–September 1667

By the end of November, the government had at last succeeded in tabling the Poll Bill; after the frustration of six weeks with scarcely any progress on the revenue, now there did seem to be some prospect of moving forward. Yet the next six weeks were to be the most frustrating of all for the court, and the most disturbing for the country: and as the new campaigning season approached, the need for finance grew every day more pressing, the possibility of disaster nearer. There was one new obstacle to supply, the pressure generated in the commons for a joint parliamentary committee to inspect departmental accounts. In a debate on 22 November the lords, on the basis of a report on the precedents of 1641 and 1661 from the committee of privileges, rejected the commons' request for a joint committee. But the government was anxious not to antagonise parliamentary opinion by refusing to allow any further inspection: so at a conference on the 28th, Buckingham (because the original spokesman for the lords, Clarendon, was ill) told M.P.s that the house was willing that there should be an examination of the accounts on oath, but claimed that investigations such as they proposed were unprecedented. Although the commons resolved to consider the matter on 1 December, debate then was squeezed out by consideration of the Poll Bill; soon, it was to be rendered irrelevant by government critics who a few days later took the court completely by surprise.[1]

On 26 November the Poll Bill itself had been referred to the committee of the whole house, which was occupied with it for most of the next week. Some of the debates picked up both the anti-nonconformist and anti-clerical themes which (for once) had been little heard in this session, with some lengthy debates on the double taxation of nonconformists, of the rates at which doctors of divinity were to be charged, and of special extra rates to be charged to those who kept nonconformist ministers (the latter a proposal whose main

---

[1] *L.J.*, X, 26–7, 29, 33, 34, 37; *C.J.*, 655; Bodl., MS Rawlinson A 130, fols. 65v, 67v; H.L.R.O., Committee Minutes, 22 Nov. 1666; see above, pp. 144–6 for the precedents of 1641 and 1661; Milward, *Diary*, p. 49.

276

motive was apparently to have a joke at Colonel Birch's expense: it was ended, rather impatiently, by the Speaker). Some time was saved when it was resolved that the commissioners to administer the tax were to be the same as those appointed in the 1665 Royal Aid; clauses for encouraging credit on the money it raised, such as those in the Royal and Additional Aids, were added; and a sub-committee was appointed to work out some details of the tax's assessment and collection. 'Country' attempts to delay the Bill's progress by adjournment or diversion met with little success, perhaps in part because the news from Scotland had persuaded M.P.s of the urgency of supply.[2] On 4 December the committee, sitting morning and afternoon, completed the Bill; on the 6th it was reported, and ordered to be engrossed. But on the following day, as debate on the details continued, the 'country' leaders succeeded in turning M.P.s' minds away from the need for taxation (now that the threat from Scotland had receded) and back to government corruption. What may have helped them – and were possibly publicised deliberately – were the stories circulating of Lady Castlemaine's freedom with the royal purse, and of the royal purse's own immense consumption of public money.[3]

Two provisos were presented on the 7th: the first, presented by Edward Rigby, an old presbyterian, was apparently aimed at Carteret, whose fees it proposed to remove. This was perhaps the attack on Carteret that navy officials had expected for some time; but it was rejected, as being 'unreasonable'. Although Carteret's fees, and those of the exchequer officials which the proviso was also to reduce, were ultimately lowered by statute in this session, Rigby's proposal had apparently gone too far.[4] But the other proviso, offered by William Garraway and possibly seconded by Sir Robert Howard, received much more support. After the failure of the lords to agree to a joint accounts committee, he revived the proposal made in early November for a statutory committee to examine the accounts of the money which had been given for the war. Over the protests of government M.P.s that annexation of such a proviso to the Poll Bill was 'not proper', the proviso was put to a division, and committed by a majority of thirty-six.[5]

The government was surprised and horrified: Arlington complained that it 'expresseth a manifest distrust' of the court's management of the war. The king was said to be furious at so great a blow to his prerogative, as well as

[2] *C.J.*, 653, 655, 656, 657; Milward, *Diary*, pp. 49–53.
[3] *C.J.*, 657–8; Milward, *Diary*, p. 56; Pepys, *Diary*, VII, 404.
[4] For the navy officials' fears, see Pepys, *Diary*, VII, 319, 321–3, 334, 342, 356; Rigby may have been harbouring some resentment of the court because of the dismissal by the council of his complaint against Lord Derby in May, P.R.O., PC 2/59, fol. 27; see also *H.P.*, III, 333.
[5] *C.J.*, 659; Milward, *Diary*, p. 56; Margoliouth, II, 46–7, Marvell to Mayor Franke, [10] Dec. 1666; Carte MSS 46, fol. 412, Arlington to Ormonde, 8 Dec. 1666; for Howard's involvement, see Pepys, *Diary*, VII, 399–400, and *C.J.*, 662.

reluctant to have disbursements made on his personal order too closely examined.[6] Although the government was desperate for money, it would rather not have the Poll Bill at all than have it with this proviso. Ministers agreed to make every effort to prevent it from being accepted; to that end, M.P.s were, according to Clarendon, to 'be prepared' by being left in no doubt of the king's objections.[7]

When debate on the proviso was resumed in committee of the whole on the afternoon of 10 December, the court did at least succeed in having Coventry and Clifford included among the twenty-four M.P.s – most of them the chief 'country' leaders – who were to make up the commons' share of the accounts commission. But the court's main object was to keep the proviso out of the Bill altogether: on 12 December, Sir Hugh Cholmley, possibly repeating something that had been said in the debate on the day before, told Pepys that parliament had been told plainly that the king 'would dissolve them rather than pass the Bill with the proviso'. Such a threat and its implications were perhaps too much for many of the proviso's weaker supporters, and on the 11th it was resolved not to add it to the Poll Bill but to make it instead into a separate bill. Even so, the proviso's sponsors were evidently anxious that it should still be considered to be closely linked with the poll. Assuming that the two readings it had received as a proviso would serve for it as a bill, the new Accounts Bill was committed the same day, reported the next, and engrossed. The same day the Poll Bill, with a watered-down version of Rigby's proviso limiting the fees taken on sums issued out of the poll money by the treasurers of the navy and ordnance, was also ordered to be engrossed. On 13 December, both Bills received their third readings and were passed on up to the lords.[8]

The Poll Bill was now, it seemed, out of the worst danger of further delay: yet the court did not greet its passage with any great enthusiasm. The whole Bill expressed the country's suspicion of the government and the court: officials, the holders of royal pensions, and members of the royal household were subjected to unusually severe taxation; the fees of the navy and ordnance treasurers were sharply limited; and most irritating, although it aroused little comment, was a proviso restricting any expenditure out of the poll money on the army to £30,000 – a legacy of some of the fears which had been earlier, if cautiously, expressed, of the expansion of the army. It was uncertain, in any case, how effective a solution to the government's problems the tax could be: a committee which reported to the house on 13 December

[6] Carte MSS 46, fol. 412; Pepys, *Diary*, VII, 399–400, 401, 402; Clarendon, *Life*, II, 319–21, 364.
[7] *Ibid.*, II, 320–1.
[8] *C.J.*, 660–2; P.R.O., SP 29/173/26; Pepys, *Diary*, VII, 404.

estimated its value at £540,035; but apart from the sum of £82,035 to come from the rate on honours, based on the yield of the 1660 poll, this was no better than a guess.[9] As Conway told Ormonde, the Bill was 'such an extravagant thing, that nothing but extremities could move the king to accept it'.[10]

There remained to be completed the other projects for raising the full £1.8 million, the assessment, and the stamp duty. A bill for the assessment was brought in by the solicitor general on 4 December, and by the 10th it had received its second reading; but debates on it were hampered by ignorance about the yield of the poll tax and uncertainty about how much should also be raised by the stamp. The first difficulty was solved by the estimate presented on 13 December; although as Marvell remarked, it was a committee's estimate, unconfirmed by the house and subject to revision. The second was solved by an estimate of the stamp duty's yield from a committee appointed over a month before; 'country' leaders, strongly resisting the stamp project, attempted unsuccessfully to suppress the report. The estimate – of £100,325 a year – was delivered, and a bill for the duty received a first reading.[11] At the second reading, two days later, 'country' leaders, as Pepys heard from William Ashburnham and Sir Steven Fox, tried hard to stop the Bill; the court's majority for commitment, however, of eighty-nine to fifty-two, was a fairly encouraging one.[12]

Despite these signs of progress, that evening the government's parliamentary managers appear to have made two decisions to speed matters: first, to drop the sealed paper and foreign excise projects, and secondly, to abandon the usual few weeks' recess over Christmas and the new year in the hope that the country gentry would disperse anyway, leaving ample court majorities to complete the essential business. Both decisions, it would seem, Clarendon opposed; on both he was overruled. Sir John Nicholas was waspish about the decision to abandon the Bill; Matthew Wren, Clarendon's secretary, was furious. As he pointed out, had the government wanted to rely mainly on the land tax, it might have been secured weeks before; it seemed pointless to abandon the stamp duty now, merely out of what Nicholas called 'compliance to Sir Rich[ard Temple] and his friends'. The dropping of the Bill failed to produce the desired effect either, because the reason for the court's decision to sit over Christmas was transparently obvious. When Sir

---

[9] *C.J.*, 662; P.R.O., SP 29/181/44, the committee's estimate; the Act is 18/19 Car. II, c. 1, the clause on expenditure on the army is para. 31, *S.R.*, 394. As there is no indication of it being added to the Bill after the engrossment, it must have been in the Bill by the time it was sent to the lords.

[10] Carte MSS 35, fol. 197v, 29 Dec. 1666.

[11] *C.J.*, 658, 659, 661–2; P.R.O., SP 29/181/97, newsletter, 13 Dec.

[12] *C.J.*, 662; Pepys, *Diary*, VII, 407.

William Morrice announced on the morning of 15 December that parliament would adjourn only for the main festival days, alarmed 'country' leaders immediately took steps to prevent the predictable drop in the attendance of M.P.s: they moved that all those who had been given licence to leave be summoned back, all those who had failed to attend at all be sent for in custody, and that the house should be called over on 2 January; and they demanded, and obtained, a committee to draw up a bill against absentee-ism.[13] But the most significant thing about the government's decision was possibly its indication that Clarendon was no longer powerful enough to impose his own will in matters of parliamentary management: Arlington, Clifford, and Coventry – who, as he complained, were far more inclined to appeasement than he was – were now the decisive voices.

When the house returned to discussing finance, on the 17th, 'country' leaders continued to try to delay the land tax, to reduce the amount it would raise, and to secure an adjournment: they opposed the court's efforts to revise the poll tax estimate in order to increase the sum to be obtained by the land tax, and they attempted to change the present fixed rate assessment into a proportional one. Further time was spent over how to make up the sum which was to be cut from London's contribution, because of the fire. But by 22 December, as the house voted to adjourn for a week over Christmas, most of the details of the Bill were complete.[14] 'Country' efforts to delay it were renewed after the house met again on the 29th. As rumours of peace increased in strength, so speculation grew that the court hoped to obtain both a peace and the money. Once more, progress on the Bill declined: 'country' leaders managed to postpone discussion and then to adjourn the house again until after the new year: then, pushed aside by M.P.s' excitement over matters which seemed to many both more interesting and more important, the Bill languished, and it was a further two weeks before the government could again secure a debate on it.[15]

The court suffered further (if less intractable) frustrations in the lords: the Poll Bill, read first on 14 December and again the following day, had been brought up with the sums with which peers were to be charged for their titles already written in. The lords took this for an invasion of their privileges; members of the court seem to have protested against the taxation of the officers and servants in the royal household, and of pensioners; and there were also objections against the double taxation of aliens and of non-

[13] Carte MSS 35, fols. 171 and 238v, Brodrick to Ormonde, 15 Dec. 1666, 5 Jan. 1667; B.L., Egerton MSS 2539, fol. 77, Sir John to Sir Edward Nicholas, 19 Dec. 1666; Pepys, *Diary*, VII, 408; *C.J.*, 663.

[14] *C.J.*, 664, 665, 666, 668; Carte MSS 46, fols. 426, 428, Arlington to Ormonde, 18, 22 Dec. 1666; Margoliouth, II, 48, Marvell to Mayor Franke, 22 Dec. 1666.

[15] *C.J.*, 669; for the currency of rumours of peace, see Pepys, *Diary*, VII, 412, 420.

conformists. In the ensuing debates in committee of the whole house, from 18 to 22 December, the peers produced new clauses to protect their privileges. On the 29th the Bill was read a third time and accepted: but courtiers were now gloomily forecasting that the commons would reject their amendments and so completely block the Bill's passage.[16]

For the Accounts Bill, which was brought up to the lords along with the Poll Bill, the court had other plans. Although it received two readings, Clarendon was adamant that a bill so destructive to the royal prerogative should not pass. After the debate on the second reading on 19 December he succeeded in persuading the house to petition the king for the appointment of a royal commission instead.[17] Clarendon devoted great attention to the reply: the commons were to be offered a royal commission which included almost all of those they had themselves named, while it conceded no precedent for a statutory inspection of royal accounts. He carefully scrutinised the list of commissioners in the Bill, leaving out of the royal commission both obviously government members (all – Clifford, Coventry, Carr, and Harbord – men of the Arlington–Coventry group) and those whose criticism of the government was thought purely factional. The peers he added included his protégé, Bridgewater; Lord Conway; the ex-presbyterian Lord Crew; and the 'country cavalier' lords, Aylesbury and Lucas.[18] When the royal commission was announced in the king's answer to the lords' petition, the court's critics were said to be incensed at the omission of the 'duke of Buckingham, my Lord Ashley, my Lord Northampton, and other confederates with the commoners', enraged with the chancellor, and planning 'such a remonstrance, as shall obstruct the payment of all the money they have given'.[19] Nevertheless, the lords accepted the commission, and on 3 January communicated the king's message to the commons at a conference.

The commons reacted angrily to this, one of a crop of conferences in which the lords had delivered unpalatable messages; when Sir Robert Howard reported to the house, it quickly voted the lords' abandonment of the Bill and decision to petition the king without reference to themselves to be 'unparliamentary and of dangerous consequence'. A group of the most prominent 'country' members drew up arguments to be used at a further conference: it was against the 'right and settled course of parliament', they claimed, for any

[16] *L.J.*, X, 47–8, 51, 53, 54, 55–6; H.L.R.O., MS Minutes, H.L., vol. 13, 19, 20 Dec. 1666, Committee Minutes, H.L., 21 Dec. 1666, Main Papers, H.L., 19 Dec. 1666, papers h and i (the new clauses for rating the peers); Carte MSS 35, fol. 197v, Conway to Ormonde, 29 Dec. 1666.

[17] *L.J.*, X, 47, 52, 54

[18] P.R.O., SP 29/173/26, a list of the commissioners in the Bill with emendations by Clarendon; SP 29/182/94 is a later list, and 182/95 is Clarendon's draft of the king's answer to the lords' petition.

[19] *L.J.*, X, 57; Carte MSS 35, fol. 197v.

bill to be communicated to the king by one house until the whole was agreed by both. On 9 January their reasons were presented to the lords.[20] The peers' tampering with the Poll Bill had also infuriated the lower house: the commons accepted (after dividing) their abandonment of double taxation of nonconformists, the change in date from which the act was to be effective, and other minor alterations; but they rejected the clauses for the rating of peers and members of the royal household – it was unprecedented, they claimed, for the lords to grant separately, in another place in the Act, a tax which was the same as that granted by the commons.[21] The lords were conciliatory, and drew up a compromise clause. But with, by this time, complete deadlock on the Irish Cattle Bill, it remained to be seen whether or not the commons would accept the new clause, or attempt to use it as a lever with which to extract concessions from the court.[22]

The Irish Cattle Bill itself had been returned to the commons by the lords on 24 November, with the replacement of 'nuisance' by 'detriment and mischief', the new proviso permitting the import of 20,000 cattle for the relief of the City of London and the removal of Scotland's exemption. When the amendments were debated on the 27th the alteration of the word 'nuisance' was rejected, although by a slim margin in a division. The exclusion of the Scottish exemption was accepted with little demur. Courtiers attempted at least to improve the London proviso, with the loud support of the London M.P.s, and Arlington felt that the commons were more inclined to charity than the lords had been: the house voted that instead of being shipped over as slaughtered beef, the cattle should be brought over live, despite objections 'that it is only a blind to bring over greater quantities to other purposes without any real intention in the kingdom of Ireland to avail these poor people'.[23] But when the amended proviso was reported to the house by Edward Seymour, the decision was not merely reversed, but the whole proviso rejected: London members may have felt that dead cattle were not worth arguing for. On 14 December Sir Robert Howard, Temple, Sir Robert Atkins, and Sir Richard Ford delivered to the lords the house's reasons for their refusal of these alterations. Howard and Temple rejected all the arguments against the word 'nuisance'; there was nothing novel, they pointed out, about laws limiting the royal prerogative to dispense.[24]

The rejection of the compromise over 'nuisance' represented complete defeat for the court: its endeavours to avoid an unwelcome limitation of the

[20]   *C.J.*, 670, 672–3; Carte MSS 217, fol. 366, Anglesey to Ormonde, 5 Jan. 1667.
[21]   *C.J.*, 671, 672, 673, 675; Margoliouth, II, 49, Marvell to Mayor Franke, 5 Jan. 1667.
[22]   *L.J.*, X, 72–3, 74–5; H.L.R.O., MS Minutes, H.L., vol. 13, 12 Jan. 1667.
[23]   *C.J.*, 653, 654; Milward, *Diary*, p. 47; Carte MSS 46, fol. 406, Arlington to Ormonde, 27 Nov. 1666; Carte MSS 35, fol. 160v, Brodrick to Ormonde, 1 Dec. 1666.
[24]   *C.J.*, 658, 660, 661; *L.J.*, X, 47, 48–50; Milward, *Diary*, pp. 54–5.

royal prerogative had clearly failed. Yet the Irish lobby saw in it a gleam of hope. Many of them were now convinced that the Bill was pressed on by malice against the prerogative rather than by the genuine worries of land-owners; so Anglesey and Burlington now reasoned that if the lords were to insist on removing the word, the commons would rather lose the whole Bill than compromise; by refusing to give in to the commons, they thought, the lords could strangle the Bill in a dispute between the two houses.[25] The strategy followed by the government over the next few weeks was, indeed, to reject entirely the word 'nuisance'; in the debate on 17 December on the report of the conference with the commons, Clarendon urged that it was 'against the king's prerogative, an affront, and diminution to him, an unreasonable, improper, unusual and nonsense word', while Buckingham, Lucas, and Ashley contradicted him. Clarendon finally won; the house appointed a committee to draw up reasons for its removal, to be presented at a conference – although it also offered, as a compromise, that if the Bill passed, the king might be petitioned not to grant any dispensations from it. The reasons, when they emerged from some evidently stormy committee meetings, stressed the restraint on the prerogative that 'nuisance' implied, the unlikelihood that the king would in any case grant dispensations, and the fact that the planned petition would sufficiently ensure that he did not: but the Bill's supporters had managed to avoid the inclusion of any suggestion that the word was unprecedented, or was an illegitimate limitation of the prerogative; and another attempt to insert such a claim was rejected when the reasons were reported to the house on 29 October.[26]

The government had accurately guessed that there was enough reluctance in the lords to infringe the royal prerogative to remove the word 'nuisance', but too much feeling against Irish cattle to hope for the Bill's outright rejec-tion. In fact some of the Bill's promoters do seem to have been ready to compromise: it was probably in the debate on 29 December that Ashley suggested that such a word as 'felony' or 'praemunire' could be used instead. It was rather the court that was anxious not to blur the distinction between the Bill with 'nuisance' in it and the Bill without: Clarendon mocked Ashley's motion, saying it might as well be called an 'adultery'.[27] As predicted, the commons, on learning of the lords' action at a conference on 2 January, voted overwhelmingly to adhere to the word 'nuisance': the majority for adhering

[25] Carte MSS 215, fol. 310, Burlington to Ormonde, 5 Jan. 1667; Carte MSS 217, fols. 358, 360, Anglesey to Ormonde, 27 Nov., 11 Dec. 1666; cf.Carte MSS 35, fol. 197, Conway to Ormonde, 29 Dec. 1666, and B.L., Egerton MSS 2539, fol. 77v, Sir John to Sir Edward Nicholas.
[26] *L.J.*, X, 48–50, 54, 57–8; H.L.R.O., MS Minutes, H.L., vol. 13, 17 Dec. 1666, Committee Minutes, H.L., 18 and 21 Dec. 1666; Bodl., MS Rawlinson A 130, fol. 71.
[27] Carte MSS 35, fol. 197, Conway to Ormonde, 29 Dec. 1666.

was more than trebled; and Lord Conway reported that there were even suggestions that the Bill should be annexed to the Assessment Bill in the same way as the accounts proviso had been to the Poll Bill. At a conference on 9 January the commons made clear their absolute refusal to accept the removal of the word. When the lords turned on Saturday 12 January to debating the report of this conference they, too, adhered.[28] The impasse which the government seems to have wanted had arrived; but now that it had, few believed that the situation could long remain like this. 'It cannot hold long at this pass', wrote Anglesey; Burlington stressed the lords' continued resolve not to give way; and Brodrick described how the Bill's supporters, temporarily nonplussed, made vague threats of 'I know not what dangers likely to ensue' if, among other things, the Bill failed.[29]

The Irish Cattle Bill was only one of several matters over which the lords and commons were in dispute by the middle of January. Pressure from the lower house and from 'country' politicians in the lords did little to speed up the peers' consideration of the patent of the Canary Company: arguing that this was a judicial matter, to be heard by counsel at the bar of the house, the government cheerfully avoided any proceedings on it at all. Its opponents contested the point – the proper procedure, as Buckingham and Lucas argued on 29 November when no counsel against the company appeared for yet another hearing, was not a judicial hearing at all, but for the house itself to decide whether the patent was illegal or not. Clarendon and York, having failed to have the house drop the whole business, succeeded in obtaining a further postponement, to 3 December. When counsel against the patent once more failed to appear, the government tried again to suppress the matter: Anglesey claimed that the vote of the commons, and hence the procedure promoted by Buckingham and Lucas, was irregular and a usurpation of the lords' jurisdiction. The committee of privileges, to whom the issue was referred, reported two precedents of the commons informing the lords of grievances which were to be redressed; but when the report was discussed, on 7 December, the court continued to override opposition, claiming that the precedents referred to occasions on which the commons' complaint had been made at a conference rather than by message, as in this case. The houses voted obediently to inform the commons that they had infringed the lords' right of judicature: after a long debate on 10 December, in which the patent's

[28] *C.J.*, 670, 671, 673; *L.J.*, X, 71–2; Pepys, *Diary*, VIII, 9–10; Carte MSS 35, fol. 240v, Conway to Ormonde, 5 Jan. 1667.

[29] Carte MSS 215, fol. 318, Burlington to Ormonde, 12 Jan. 1667; Carte MSS 217, fol. 368v, Anglesey to Ormonde, 12 Jan. 1667; Carte MSS 35, fol. 246, Brodrick to Ormonde, 12 Jan. 1667.

opponents attempted again to turn the debate on to the legality of the company's charter, a terse message was agreed and delivered the same day.[30]

The commons clearly felt a little resentment about the lords' defence of their judicature, since, as they pointed out, the peers had accepted their votes against French commodities and papists without objection; nevertheless, eager to secure action against the patent, they agreed to proceed as the precedent dictated, preparing in detail arguments against the patent which were presented to the upper house on 19 December.[31] At a conference marred by an unseemly scuffle between two of the lords' managers, Buckingham and Dorchester,[32] Sir Robert Howard, Edward Seymour, Temple, and Downing described the commons' complaints against the company. The limitation of the trade in the Canaries to members of the company, and the rules limiting membership made it a monopoly, they claimed, in contravention of the Common Law and of a statute of 1606 which prohibited the creation of any monopoly of trade with Spain and Portugal; the king might dispense with neither, as they guaranteed the subjects' fundamental rights. The charter contained particular illegalities as well; and the company rather obstructed than protected English trade. Seymour closed by with a broad hint: 'it was no wonder if patents of this nature were sometimes procured, because importunity of ministers might prevail for grants that are uneasy'.[33]

The lords accepted that they should proceed by examining the commons' complaints. On 7 January they heard the king's and patentees' counsel in the charter's defence. They denied that it was a monopoly, illegal, or damaging to trade; and its *non obstante* clause, they claimed, was perfectly valid against the 1606 Act – and even if it was not, that Act was limited only to the 'dominions of Spain' which did not include the Canaries.[34] A speech that replied to these arguments, and reiterated some of the commons, may have been delivered on the same occasion. The *non obstante*, its author alleged, was a clear indication that its drafters recognised its illegality; but if such a dispensation could be granted from an Act which enshrined the subjects' rights, where might it end? 'If the king can in one particular destroy by a patent this highest and most sacred security, that a subject of England can have for what he possesseth, by the same rule he may certainly take away the

[30] *L.J.*, X, 38–9, 42–3; *C.J.*, 661; H.L.R.O., MS Minutes, H.L., vol. 13, 29 Nov., 3 Dec. 1666; Bodl., MS Rawlinson A 130, fols. 69–70.
[31] *C.J.*, 661, 664, 665; *L.J.*, X, 63.
[32] For which, see *L.J.*, X, 52–3, 55, 56; Bodl., MS Rawlinson A 130, fols. 71v, 72v; Pepys, *Diary*, VII, 414–15; and Clarendon, *Life*, II, 338–9.
[33] *L.J.*, X, 62–5.
[34] *Ibid.*, 67; Bodl., MS Rawlinson A 130, fol. 73v; Clarendon MSS 92, fols. 266–71. This speech is endorsed by Clarendon as 'Mr Jones's argument upon the Canary charter'. Jones was one of the counsel for the patentees (the others were Sir William Scroggs and Mr Simson) who spoke on 7 January.

lands, privilege or right of the subjects whatsoever.' He reminded the house
of the 1663 Indulgence Bill, and of the argument then used against it: like ship
money, it would destroy any security the people had in all they possessed,
freeing the king from the bonds of law. Royal dispensation from statute in the
present case, he claimed, held the same dangers. The whole speech, it might
be suggested, was directed against Clarendon, echoing his own voice on law
and archly quoting the very argument he had himself used in the 1663 debate
on the Ecclesiastical Powers Bill. Its author may have been Ashley,
Clarendon's antagonist in that debate.[35]

If this is true, it shows how the Canary company issue was pushed not
entirely innocently: at the conference Seymour had remarked on government
corruption, and this speech was perhaps directed against the allegedly
corrupt chancellor. Yet there was much genuine feeling, particularly from the
outports, against such London-based monopolies; and there were some
passionate campaigners for free trade, such as Downing.[36] Such pressure,
however, came largely from commercial interests in the commons: most of
the lords had less expertise in and less concern for such matters, which no
doubt explains the government's ease in avoiding the subject for so long. The
same reason, added to the intervention of other matters of more pressing
urgency or of greater interest, explains why after its airing on the 7th, further
consideration of the patent was continually postponed.

One of those other matters was the charges presented by the commons
against Viscount Mordaunt. The impeachment of Mordaunt may have been
a cynical effort by unscrupulous politicians to pursue wider objectives
through the ruin of a hapless and not very important official: but to the
members of the commons who heard the allegations against him, Mordaunt's
misdemeanours were more than isolated crimes, and profoundly representative of the sort of corruption and abuse of power with which they believed
the government to be riddled. Mordaunt had for long been a controversial
figure, arousing much enmity through his activities as an independent and
uncontrollable royalist conspirator in the 1650s. Since the Restoration, he
had been rewarded with the governorship and captaincy of Windsor Castle.
The proceedings against him related to the saga of his conflict with William
Tayleur, an employee at the castle, that began when Mordaunt interfered
with Tayleur's attempt to be elected M.P. for Windsor in 1661, and continued with his alleged attempted rape of Tayleur's daughter, his use of

---

[35] B.L., Stowe MSS 303, fols. 109–26.
[36] Carte MSS 35, fol. 197v, Conway to Ormonde, 29 Dec. 1666; even Brodrick thought the
patent a grievance, *ibid.*, fol. 191, Brodrick to Ormonde, 29 Dec. 1666; cf. *C.J.*, 577, the
debate on the merchant adventurers, and see, for the issue in the reign of James I, P. Croft,
'Free trade and the house of commons, 1605–6', *Econ. Hist. Rev.*, 2nd series, XXVIII
(1975), 17–27.

soldiers to remove him from a debtors' prison to jail in the castle, and his imprisonment of him there for twenty weeks. Mordaunt claimed that Tayleur's charges were no more than a malicious attempt to avoid a prosecution currently depending for peculation and corruption, which, according to the surveyor general, Sir John Denham, was such that 'it goes beyond all that any accountant ever made'.[37] But whether or not Tayleur was guilty of some sordid petty corruption, the charges against Mordaunt smacked of something grander, the military's disregard for the rules of law, of the constitution, even of common decency. Even John Evelyn, a friend of both Mordaunt and his wife, was shocked by the nature of the 'foul and dishonourable' charges, of '*tyranny* . . . incontinence and suborning'.[38] For some it was simply the most graphic illustration of a creeping corruption of the worst kind that was gradually engulfing the government.

Tayleur presented his petition against Mordaunt on 2 November. It was referred to the committee of grievances, where, at the end of the month, it produced several days of acrimonious and confused debate.[39] The committee's report was not heard until 18 December, when after long debate, the house voted to impeach Mordaunt. A committee, headed by Sir Thomas Gower, was set up to draw up charges. On 21 December Prynne presented them to the house: stressing Tayleur's royalist service in the Interregnum, Mordaunt's arbitrary and oppressive action and his carelessness of the laws of England in his words and his deeds, they were accepted and delivered to the lords at a conference on 29 December (after some careful consultation of precedent).[40] The business alarmed the government: Brodrick thought it more dangerous, 'I mean for the example', than the attack on the Canary patent. Ministers apparently believed it to be a sort of trial impeachment, to test both the procedure and parliament's response to it. They were correspondingly eager to suppress it. Although Anglesey reported the effect of the conference with the commons to the house on 3 January, and the committee of privileges was asked to consider the precedents of such cases, there was little haste in their proceedings. On 10 January, when the earl of Dorset reported from the committee, Mordaunt was given a further week to prepare his defence. The government hoped, if it could, to play the matter out until the tax bills were finished and it could end the session.[41]

The complaints against Mordaunt were not the only allegations of corrup-

---

[37] The detailed charges are in *C.J.*, 666–7, and Mordaunt's answer is in *L.J.*, X, 77–9; cf. P.R.O., SP 29/176/43, Sir John Denham to Williamson, 26 Oct. 1666; see *H.P.*, I, 131; Witcombe, *The cavalier house of commons*, p. 49 and n. 5.
[38] Evelyn, *Diary*, III, 468–9.
[39] *Ibid.*; *C.J.*, 645, 646; Margoliouth, II, 46, Marvell to Mayor Franke, 1 Dec. 1666.
[40] *C.J.*, 660, 666–7, 669.
[41] Carte MSS 35, fol. 191v, Brodrick to Ormonde, 29 Dec. 1666; *L.J.*, X, 60–2, 70.

tion and misconduct. Charges were made in the committee of grievances against the actions of Lord Willoughby as governor of Barbados, which were only stopped by Willoughby's death by drowning during a campaign against the French off Guadeloupe.[42] In the session of October 1667 these allegations were to inspire one of the charges against Clarendon.[43] There were other vexations as well: 'country' leaders fought back against the court's attempts to diminish their influence with audacity and success. Acutely conscious of the government's ability to carry important divisions with a large block of votes on which it might depend, they had made frequent moves to have the house called over and defaulters brought back to Westminster.[44] The court's attempt on 15 December to keep the house sitting right through the normal Christmas break outraged them, and caused them to move for a bill to punish defaulters: those whom the house appointed to draft one were probably its movers – Littleton, Garraway, Howard, Meres, and Temple, and the lawyers, Prynne, Maynard, Atkins, and Charlton. Their draft received a first reading on 17 January, and was committed on the 19th.[45]

Other laws on elections were inspired by the heated debate in early January over the court's attempt to overturn the Winchilsea election result, where its candidate, Baptist May, had been resoundingly defeated. The Winchilsea election had been notorious for the cheating on both sides, and the influence that the Crown, through the warden, exerted over all Cinque Ports elections was well known. The court's principal contention, that the election was void because the mayor, a dissenter, held office in contravention of the Corporation Act, was accepted by the committee of elections, but on 10 January was decisively rejected by the house on the arguments of Littleton, Atkins, and Colman.[46] Two days after this debate, two bills were presented relating to elections: the first was an attempt to prevent any undue interference at the poll by outsiders, especially soldiers, and to abolish such practices as the distribution of drink and provision of entertainment, and the corrupt manipulation of residence requirements. The Bill, Brodrick wrote, would 'never pass,

---

[42] Margoliouth, II, 46, Marvell to Mayor Franke, 1 Dec. 1666; for the dispute between Willoughby and the assembly of Barbados, see *Hist. MSS. Comm.*, MSS of the duke of Portland, III, 292–6, 300; see Haley, *Shaftesbury*, pp. 185, 237–8, for Ashley's interest in the issue, which he may have had something to do with raising. See also *Cal. Cl. S.P.*, V, 540–1, 550, 562.

[43] Clarendon, *Life*, II, 546–61.

[44] *C.J.*, 646, 649, 651, 656, 663, 670, 676, 678–9.

[45] *C.J.*, 663, 678, 683, 683–4; Milward, *Diary*, p. 70; Carte MSS 35, fol. 271v, Brodrick to Ormonde, 19 Jan. 1667.

[46] *C.J.*, 636, 649, 660, 663, 671, 673, 674; Milward, *Diary*, p. 60: the debate is there misattributed to 11 January – the heading '11 January' should come at the top of p. 61. *H.P.*, I, 503.

but shows their animosity'.[47] Such bills had been presented before during the 1660s, and were not simply a product of the government's current difficulties;[48] yet the interest that this aroused, and its provisions against the involvement of the military, seem to indicate a rather heightened mistrust of the government's intentions. The other bill read on the 12th, one to ensure the religious conformity of both electors and the elected, was probably also suggested by the details of the Winchilsea case, and may have been either an attempt by the defenders of the Church to capitalise on it, or a court riposte to the 'country' bill.[49]

By mid-January, with proceedings on the Assessment Bill halted in the commons, with the Poll Bill, the Accounts Bill and the Irish Cattle Bill stuck fast in disputes between the two houses, and with the lords provoking the commons by their foot-dragging on the Canary patent and Mordaunt's impeachment, it was evident that the crisis of the session had arrived. The normal operation of parliament, of redress of grievances and granting of money, had seized up, and without the money on which continuing the war depended, the rest of the administration looked likely to seize up as well. There were few who underestimated the dangers of the situation: 'either the kingdom will be reduced to a commonwealth', wrote Conway on 5 January, 'or the king must dissolve this present and govern by some other medium if the parliament will not supply him with money to maintain that war which they do engage him in'.[50]

The government's leadership in the commons had improved, certainly, perhaps because Arlington and Coventry were now indisputably in control of it: whatever the merits of the decision of 14 December to abandon the foreign excise and stamp duty and concentrate on the assessment, it was at least a decision. But the problem was for the moment beyond remedy merely by the tightening of court discipline. 'Country' leaders had mastered the commons with great skill. In late December and early January ministers and court M.P.s complained bitterly of the tactics by which they sought to manipulate milder members.[51] Their skill, however, was not the fundamental reason for their effectiveness. Moderate M.P.s were reluctant to engage in anything that might seem disloyal or factious; but the anger and desperation of the country

[47] *C.J.*, 675, 676; Milward, *Diary*, p. 65; Carte MSS 35, fol. 271v, Brodrick to Ormonde, 22 Jan. 1667.
[48] *C.J.*, 438, 546.
[49] *C.J.*, 678; Milward, *Diary*, p. 65.
[50] Carte MSS 35, fol. 240, Conway to Ormonde, 5 Jan. 1667.
[51] *Ibid.*, fols. 197v, Conway to Ormonde, 29 Dec. 1666, 240v, same to same, 5 Jan. 1667, 246, Brodrick to Ormonde, 5 Jan. 1667; Carte MSS 217, fols. 366 and 368, Anglesey to Ormonde, 5 and 12 Jan. 1667; B.L., Egerton MSS 2539, fol. 77, Sir John Nicholas to Sir Edward Nicholas, 19 Dec. 1666; Bodl., MS North c. 10, fol. 124, Francis North to [Lord North], 16 Jan. 1667.

had made them as anxious as the more advanced of the government's critics to alleviate the burden of taxation, and to lighten the extra load caused by court corruption and Irish competition. 'Country' politicians – whether factious and disruptive, or genuinely concerned for the public interest – could gain their support with ease for as long as the causes of 'country' irritation were not seriously attended to.

Clearly, the impasse that had been reached by the middle of January could scarcely be allowed to continue. While it did, neither preparations for peace, nor for war, could proceed: and without preparations for war, the next campaign might soon be lost by default.[52] Up to now the government's strategy appears to have been as Lord Brouncker explained it to Pepys on 8 January: to prevent any real progress on the impeachment, the Canary patent, the Irish Cattle Bill and the Accounts Bill until the money bills were passed; then the house could be prorogued, suppressing them all. But as was increasingly obvious, the commons could easily be persuaded to progress slowly, or not at all, on the money bills in order to force the government to accede to their most cherished projects.

The debate over how to get out of this stalemate seems to have come to a head in the weekend of 12 and 13 January with the maturing of the conflict, visible even early on in the session, between those who demanded firmness against the commons and those who urged the need for concessions. As Arlington had wistfully written to Ormonde on the 5th, if only the government had gracefully made some easy concessions earlier on in the session, the present trouble might have been avoided; and it was Arlington and Coventry, Clarendon indicated, who were the strongest advocates of breaking the deadlock by offering an olive-branch or two.[53] The arguments for doing so were self-evident: the Crown needed money now, there seemed no very safe means of obtaining it than from this parliament, and the leaders of the present discontents seemed to possess influence largely from the anger of ordinary M.P.s over matters such as Irish cattle. Once a few well-chosen concessions were made, moderate M.P.s, if still suspicious of the court, would at least be able to see with more clarity the necessity of supply, and the power of Buckingham, Temple, Littleton, and the rest would be broken. Yet there were also powerful and compelling arguments against surrender: to accept any of the 'country's' current preoccupations would involve the creation of precedents limiting royal powers and prerogatives;[54] and although concessions might appease moderates and break the influence of the 'country' leaders, it was as possible that they might rather add to their prestige, and

---

[52] See Carte MSS 49, fol. 376, Ormonde to Conway, 19 Jan. 1667.
[53] Carte MSS 46, fol. 435; Clarendon, *Life*, II, 328–9, 346.
[54] Carte MSS 35, fol. 191, Brodrick to Ormonde, 29 Dec. 1666.

encourage them to make further demands – something that was particularly worrying for those, like Clarendon, who were aware that the next demand might be their own removal, or even impeachment. The very prospect of surrendering bits of royal power under parliamentary pressure appalled Clarendon who pointed out how easily the commons' encroachments could lead to the decay of monarchy, and Sheldon, aware how fragile the ascendancy of the Church might be if not backed wholly by the authority of the Crown.[55] Such arguments were perhaps not very helpful when the king seemed almost to be, as Ormonde told Sir William Temple, under a 'necessity of consenting to unreasonable things';[56] yet the opponents of concessions do seem, more constructively, to have argued that the better course was to break the power of the 'country' leaders by dissolving this parliament and obtaining a new one, disrupting all the connections and cabals they had built up in this.[57] But this would involve a delay of at least a month, as well as the abandonment of the two financial bills – which at least existed – for the uncertain prospect of supply in a new parliament.

On the evening of Sunday, 13 January, at a meeting at the lord chancellor's, the private committee were persuaded by Arlington and perhaps also by the treasurer of the navy, Sir George Carteret, to drop the government's objection to the inclusion in the Irish Cattle Bill of the word 'nuisance'.[58] Only Clarendon dissented. On the morning of the following day, as the house was again due to debate the Bill, the duke of York conveyed the decision to the court lords and the bishops, many of whom, with York himself, withdrew as a vote to agree with the lower house was taken and passed. The Irish lobby and many others were furious. Sheldon told Brodrick that 'the king was resolved to ruin himself, and it would not be in their powers to preserve him'; Anglesey and Burlington complained that victory on the Bill had been snatched from their grasp. Many entered formal protests against the vote.[59]

Undoubtedly, the decision, when communicated to the commons on the same day, did remove the final obstacle to the passage of the Poll Bill: the lords' compromise proviso on the rating of the peers, presented to the lower house along with their capitulation on the Irish Bill, was accepted with alacrity, and returned to the lords with the comment that they had agreed to

[55] See Clarendon, *Life*, II, 347–52, 450–1; Carte MSS 45, fols. 212, 214, Sheldon to Ormonde, 25 Feb., 16 March 1667; cf. Carte MSS 51, fol. 283, Ormonde to Arlington, 23 Jan. 1667.

[56] Carte MSS 47, fol. 304, Ormonde to Sir William Temple, 14 Oct. 1666.

[57] Clarendon, *Life*, II, 330–1; cf. Conway's proposal, Carte MSS 35, fol. 240.

[58] *Ibid.*, fol. 30, Brodrick to Ormonde, 14 Jan. 1667, fol. 259, Conway to Ormonde, 19 Jan. 1667; Carte MSS 47, fol. 138, Anglesey to Ormonde, 15 Jan. 1667; Pepys, *Diary*, VIII, 18; cf. Arlington's justification of the decision to Ormonde, Carte MSS 46, fols. 438, 440, 15 and 19 Jan. 1667; Clarendon, *Life*, II, 346.

[59] *Ibid.*; *L.J.*, X, 74–5; Carte MSS 35, fol. 30; Carte MSS 47, fol. 138; Carte MSS 215, fol. 318, Burlington to Ormonde, 15 Jan. 1667.

the proviso 'by way of gratitude, and to shew their desires of maintaining a good correspondence between the two houses'.[60] Yet progress on the assessment seemed unaffected: the government had failed to have it debated on 15 January, and although on the next day it was discussed for the first time in over two weeks, it was only after strong resistance. On the 17th it was again neglected.[61] On the evening of the 15th Arlington had gloomily written to Ormonde that the concession on the Irish Cattle Bill was evidently not enough: 'I am afraid less than the Bill of Accounts and Canary Company will not content them, nay suspect their frowardness so far as to believe when all is done the same stomach will make them cut off a part of the assessment in case the peace be made.'[62] When, on 18 January, the king came to pass the Poll Bill and the Irish Cattle Bill, he sharply told the assembled houses that there were no preparations for peace which might make them wary of completing the Assessment Bill, and rebuked them for their distrust of him.[63] The speech had some effect: despite the 'country' leaders' resistance, it produced an agreement to proceed with the assessment;[64] and at last, on the 19th, there was some real progress in the details of the Bill. But the government's critics, anxious still to retain their influence in the house and to keep up their pressure against the court, worked hard to revive all the old anger against the management of the war and the corruption of officials, in particular, the officers of the navy board. Carteret and Coventry attempted to defend themselves and their departments, but failed to prevent the presentation and commitment of a proviso to guarantee that part of the money would be spent on the seamen (whose distress was by now all too evident by their violence and unruliness). The committee to which it was referred, headed by Downing, Littleton, Garraway, Gower, and Edward Boscawen, met that night to complete the proviso's details 'with a universal consent of all the disagreeing members', as Arlington grumbled. But the vehemence of the 'country' leaders was a sign that their power was diminishing: with the Irish Cattle Bill passed, the majority of M.P.s had less sympathy with their other aims; they had to create much greater interest in the issue of corruption if they were to continue to obstruct the government. And vehement though they may have been, they were more chary than before of making very radical proposals: although Arlington expressed concern that they intended to present another proviso to cut half of the grant if peace was settled, none appeared.[65]

---

[60] *L.J.*, X, 74–5; *C.J.*, 675–6; Carte MSS 35, fol. 30.
[61] *C.J.*, 677; Milward, *Diary*, p. 64.
[62] Carte MSS 46, fol. 438; cf. Carte MSS 35, fol. 259, Conway to Ormonde, 19 Jan. 1667.
[63] *L.J.*, X, 80–1.
[64] *C.J.*, 678–9; Clarendon, *Life*, II, 360–1; Pepys, *Diary*, VIII, 19–20.
[65] *C.J.*, 679; Carte MSS 46, fol. 440v–1, Arlington to Ormonde, 19 Jan. 1667; Carte MSS 35, fol. 259, Conway to Ormonde, 19 Jan. 1667; Milward, *Diary*, p. 67; Pepys, *Diary*, VIII, 20–

Aware that the Assessment Bill was almost their last hostage, the 'country' leaders attempted to delay its passage; but now its completion before the Accounts Bill, or the impeachment of Mordaunt, seemed almost inevitable.[66] The proviso for the payment of seamen was completed and accepted by the house on the 21st; with the government now considerably more confident that the power of its critics in the commons was broken, St Albans was despatched to France to begin peace negotiations in earnest.[67] Two days later, the Bill received its final reading and was passed; in the lords, to the immense relief of the government, it was rushed through in three days.[68]

The passage of the Assessment Bill further limited the power of the government's critics to embarrass it. Yet there remained to them one last opportunity to squeeze concessions from it. After long discussions, a bill to establish regulations which would govern the rebuilding of the City after the Fire had received a first reading in the commons at the end of December, and by mid-January was being discussed in committee.[69] The government was anxious that the Bill should pass: without it, it was difficult to see how the reconstruction of the City could begin. But there was strong opposition to it from an 'obstinate party' in London's common council. As several feared, this was now patronised by members wanting to delay the end of the session and perhaps to force a surrender on the impeachment, the Canary Company, or the Accounts Bill.[70]

The Accounts Bill lay neglected, but not forgotten, between the two houses: the commons had angrily rejected the lords' substitution of an appeal to the king for their Bill at the conference on 9 January. For some time the peers avoided discussing the matter: when they did, on 15 January, their first reaction appears to have been to contest the lower house's arguments on precedent.[71] But after the debate on the 18th, the government appears to have changed its mind: while progress in the commons on the Assessment Bill was still depressingly slow, further concessions were perhaps still required. On the following day the lords decided to accept the Bill, but to avert the worst consequences of the precedent by making it clear that the function of the accounts committee it established was merely to examine the departmental

---

1; Carteret seems soon before the debate on the 19th to have become aware of charges against him and took steps to suppress them: see *ibid.*, p. 18, and P.R.O., SP 29/188/136, Carteret to the commissioners of the navy, 17 Jan. 1667.
[66] Margoliouth, II, 52, Marvell to Mayor Franke, 22 Jan. 1667.
[67] *C.J.*, 680, 683; Milward, *Diary*, p. 71; Carte MSS 35, fol. 275, St Albans to Ormonde, 23 Jan. 1667.
[68] *L.J.*, X, 90, 91, 92; Carte MSS 46, fol. 442v, Arlington to Ormonde, 26 Jan. 1667.
[69] *C.J.*, 669, 670.
[70] Carte MSS 46, fols. 440v and 442v, Arlington to Ormonde, 19, 26 Jan. 1667; Carte MSS 35, fol. 381, Brodrick to Ormonde, 26 Jan. 1667.
[71] *L.J.*, X, 75, 81–2; Bodl., Rawlinson MSS A 130, fol. 75v.

accounts and to report on them to parliament, not to allow or to disallow them; in short, its role was to be purely informal. Furthermore, the examination was apparently to be strictly limited to the money given specifically for the purposes of the war.[72] When the Bill was further debated on the 24th, the house drew up a new list of twenty-four lords commissioners, with privy councillors excluded at their own request. The Bill was read a third time and passed: at a conference on the same day, the lords returned it to the commons.[73]

The commons seemed oddly reluctant to take up the Bill again: 'country' leaders may have felt that there was a risk that it would be accepted by more moderate M.P.s. It was finally discussed on 7 February, two weeks after the conference with the lords. The government's critics mounted a fierce attack on the lords' amendments, repudiating the limitation of the committee's role, and arguing (against Henry Coventry's defence) that it should be allowed to investigate all moneys used for the war, not simply those the grant of which stipulated that they should be spent on it alone. There were signs that the commons would reject the lords' version of the Bill and adhere to their own.[74]

The lords were also frustrating the discontented in the lower house by stalling over Mordaunt's impeachment. After Mordaunt's answers to the charges against him were delivered to the commons on 21 January, the peers seemed fairly ready to continue with the trial, assigning counsel to the accused and ordering witnesses to appear. The commons listed their own managers for the impeachment: the 'country' leaders, Temple, Seymour, and Gower; the 'presbyterian' leader Swinfen; and the lawyers, Maynard, Atkins, Seys, Prynne, William Montagu, Richard Colman, and Francis Goodrick. It was a list far from dominated by the court's opponents, and as Brodrick hinted, several of its members were far from enthusiastic, or even interested, in the proceedings.[75] As soon as the trial began, on 26 January, it was halted by arguments over procedure which the government was quick to exploit: the business degenerated into wrangles between the houses, which ended with the lords refusing to discuss the point, resenting the commons' interference with their right to order their own judicial business. The lower house protested in a conference about the lords' refusal to hold a conference on the subject; but the lords claimed that their action was neither unprecedented,

---

[72] L.J., X, 82; H.L.R.O., MS Minutes, H.L., vol. 13, 19 Jan. 1667; cf. Milward, *Diary*, p. 81.
[73] L.J., X, 88–9.
[74] C.J., 691, 692; Milward, *Diary*, pp. 81–2; for the government's attitude to the Bill, see Macray (ed.), *Notes which passed at meetings of the privy council*, p. 55.
[75] C.J., 677, 680, 681; Milward, *Diary*, p. 64; L.J., X, 77–9, 81, 83, 85; Carte MSS 35, fol. 281, Brodrick to Ormonde, 26 Jan. 1667; cf. Carte MSS 46, fol. 440v, Arlington to Ormonde, 19 Jan. 1667.

nor destructive to the freedom of the proceedings of parliament. The whole issue had declined into farce.[76] By now it was the day before the adjournment, and it was fairly clear that proceedings on the impeachment had been effectively prevented and that the government's critics were neither numerous nor influential enough in the lords to bring it to a satisfactory conclusion. In trying to avoid any serious action on the Canary patent, the government at first simply used delay. When the lords finally considered the matter on 24 January, it turned to obfuscation instead. The house referred to the judges the decision on the question of whether the statute of 1606 made the patent illegal, or whether the statute's limitation to the 'dominions of Spain' excluded the Canaries. The judges' equivocal answer shed little light on the difficulty, and there, despite an attempt by the commons to urge the lords into some action on the last day of the session, the whole matter rested.[77]

Similarly anti-climactic was the event of the investigations into the causes of the Fire. The report of the committee was delivered by Sir Robert Broke to the commons on 22 January: but the evidence he presented was scarcely comprehensible, consisting of the vaguest of rumours and suppositions. Some of the most strongly anti-catholic members were impressed: Marvell reported it to be 'full of manifest testimonies' that the fire had been caused by 'a wicked design'. Milward, though, conveyed a more general sentiment: 'I cannot conceive that the house can make anything of the report.'[78]

The end of the session meant the end, too, of the tentative efforts of the 'country' leaders, begun at the height of the political crisis in mid-January, to push their attack further. On 14 and 16 January two petitions were presented to the lords complaining (like those of November) of chancery decrees of the lord chancellor. Both of those, and another presented on the 29th (which more promisingly implied Clarendon's corruption and favouritism), were delivered to Clarendon for his answers to them; the chancellor's reply, given by the earl of Bridgewater in his absence, was read on 4 February. The latter decree became in October 1667 one of the pieces of evidence on which impeachment proceedings against Clarendon were based, and it seems clear that the motive in presenting the petitions now was to prepare evidence (and

[76] *L.J.*, X, 92, 93–4, 96–7, 98, 99–101, 103, 104, 106–7; Bodl., Rawlinson MSS A 130, fol. 80; *C.J.*, 684, 685–6, 688–9, 690, 691; Milward, *Diary*, pp. 72–3, 74–5, 76; for the precedents involved in both issues, see Foster, *The house of lords*, pp. 159–60, 177.

[77] *L.J.*, X, 70, 74, 75, 76, 83, 89, 91, 108.

[78] *C.J.*, 681; Margoliouth, II, 52, Marvell to Mayor Franke, 22 Jan. 1667; Milward, *Diary*, p. 69; for Sir Thomas Littleton's scepticism, see Burnet, *History*, I, 414–15; for details of the report, see *Hist. MSS. Comm.*, 10th report, appendix, part IV (1885), MSS of Capt. Stewart, pp. 114–16, which includes the testimony of Sir John Maynard, and 9th report, appendix, part II (1884), MSS of Henry Chandos Pole-Gell Esq., p. 397. See also Miller, *Popery and politics*, p. 104, n. 53, for the subsequent printing of the committee's report.

the house) against him.[79] But by the end of the month, the endeavours of the government's critics to retain the flagging interest of M.P.s – particularly after many had been forced to stay at Westminster over Christmas – were doomed to failure: in any event, now that the supply bills had been passed, further concessions from the court or substantial proceedings on the other grievances were unlikely. The government still needed to secure the London Bill, but this, despite an attempt to delay it at the last moment by supporters of the common council's objections, passed the commons on 4 February, and was quickly assented to by the lords.[80] A bill to amend the Act for the Poll Tax, drawn up after the Act's publication revealed 'several horrible oversights to the prejudice of the king', was passed rapidly through both houses with little apparent difficulty.[81] On 8 February the king's arrival in the house of lords cut short proceedings in both houses on the Accounts Bill and on Mordaunt's impeachment: he prorogued parliament, with some sharp remarks on the provisos in the Assessment Bill, and requested members of both houses to 'use your utmost endeavours to remove all those false imaginations in the hearts of the people, which the malice of ill men have industriously infused into them, of I know not what jealousies and grievances'.[82]

After almost five months, the destruction of the Irish cattle export trade, and of much of the powerful international reputation that England had built up in the first two years of the war, the government had at last secured from parliament what was theoretically a sufficient sum to sustain another year's fighting. There had been plenty of indications in advance that the session of 1666–7 would be a troublesome one, but ministers were nevertheless shocked by the sudden turbulence of a parliament which had more usually (except in 1663) shown itself to be malleable and deferential.

That turbulence was primarily attributable to a complex of attitudes and feelings irritated by the combined effects of war and economic crisis. A sudden decline in the profits and rents of farming brought home to gentry the

---

[79] L.J., X, 74, 95; H.L.R.O., MS Minutes, H.L., vol. 13, 16 and 31 Jan. 1667, Main Papers, H.L., 16 and 29 Jan. 1667; see also *Hist. MSS. Comm.*, 8th report, appendix, MSS of the house of lords, 1666–70, pp. 108, 110–11; Carte MSS 35, fol. 280v, Conway to Ormonde, 2 Feb. 1667.

[80] C.J., 689, 691; L.J., X, 103, 104, 105.

[81] C.J., 684, 686, 687; L.J., X, 98, 100; for the inadequacies of the poll tax – and this Bill's failure to remove all of them – see Pepys, *Diary*, VIII, 30, 33, 38, 66–7; P.R.O., SP 29/193/59; B.L., Add. MSS 29551, fol. 251, Jeffreys to Hatton, 25 Feb. 1667; 18/19 Car. II, c. 6, *S.R.*, 601.

[82] *Parliamentary history*, IV, 359–60. Coventry interpreted the reference to the provisos as a malicious reference to Downing's loans scheme (and the speech was probably written by Clarendon, as it is fully quoted in the *Life*, II, 362–3), although it seems as likely that it was intended to refer to the limitations imposed on the disbursement of the money, in para. X, or in the Poll Bill: Pepys, *Diary*, VIII, 140.

unsettling reality of the impermanence of their prosperity and social power. They directed their anger at what they saw as the causes of that decline. Much of it they channelled into the protectionist struggle against Irish cattle, seen by many of those involved as more than just a clash of economic interest: the Bill, Lord Delamere told the earl of Ailesbury, concerned no less than the 'good of England'.[83] With an Irish catholic, upstart nobility profiting at the expense of English rents, they would soon replace the English gentry and nobility in wealth and power: and such an outcome, it was hinted, was one positively favoured by the Irish viceroyalty.

Irish cattle and Irish landowners were not the only enemies, however: the gentry were little less bitter about the perceived growth of other forms of wealth not rooted in land, and, indeed, competing with it. At any time of difficulty, the parasitic nature of the financial sector, feeding off the gentry's wealth as it destroyed it, aroused the jealousy and resentment of the landed. But during the war it seemed even more corrupt, as heavy taxation appeared simply to add to the enormous profits of the banking and merchant community. Anglican royalists, with their stereotype of the rich, hypocritical presbyterian financier, and their worries about the continued predominance of the royalist, land-owning, conservative gentry, were perhaps the most prone to suspicions of war finance, but for ex-presbyterians and the puritanically-minded, corruption could equally indicate the profligacy, irreverence and lack of concern for the public good which they could see spreading through government and society. Those of more puritan convictions were more likely than others to accept the evidence of a popish conspiracy and infiltration, and it seems clear that parliament as a whole, despite a strong reaction against catholics, remained confused or unconvinced about the evidence that they were, indeed, involved in plotting. More general was a rather vaguer, but still disturbing, sense that God's hand had again turned against His chosen people: only repentance and reformation could save the country from the worse consequences of its – and the court's – sins.

Resentment against the court had many roots: a whole series of fears of the subversion of the *status quo* by the poverty of the land, the corruptions of the City and the court, and the impending judgement of God. Yet all might have subsided rather more quickly and the 'country' leaders might never have gained the influence among members that they did, had it not been for two things. Arlington, in early January, regretted that the government had failed to make concessions early on in the session, perhaps to acknowledge the

---

[83] Wiltshire Record Office, Ailesbury Papers, 1300/558, endorsed [16]66; *Hist. MSS. Comm.*, 15th report, appendix, part VII (1898), MSS of the marquis of Ailesbury, p. 175, Delamere to Ailesbury, 17 Dec. 1666.

feeling against Irish cattle imports.[84] When the court finally bowed to the inevitable and accepted the Irish Cattle Bill as it stood, the up until then firm opposition to it on other measures collapsed, as moderates, satisfied with the concession and tired of their long stay at Westminster, began to throw off the leadership of men such as Temple, Littleton, Garraway, and Howard – although the evidence of government corruption and the long and desperate struggle over the Irish Cattle Bill left memories which would embitter politics in the future. Secondly, court politics had given a rather inchoate opposition some form and direction: 'all the disorders', complained Sheldon after the session had ended, 'have arisen from the king's family and servants'.[85] Buckingham and Ashley helped to build up an opposition leadership which could present a real challenge to the government's efforts to manage the business of both houses: but perhaps more important than this was the court's inability, for much of the session, to provide any coherent leadership of its own. Divided by disagreements over its strategy and by conflicts of power, for some time the government seemed unable to come to any firm decisions about how to control parliament.

The paralysis of court policy when the government was riven by faction, and the tendency of discontented courtiers in the lords to combine with dissatisfied M.P.s were both natural and common phenomena of seventeenth-century parliaments, and both make nonsense of any easy identification of 'court' and 'country' parties.[86] Yet the session of 1666–7 is remarkable for the extent to which that identification was made; Arlington's efforts to encourage M.P.s to support government business with the judicious distribution of favours, which (if Clarendon is to be believed) became more visible during this session, were perhaps largely responsible. The government's willingness to requite services with gifts and bribes received unwelcome satirical attention – in a libel found in the house of commons at the end of October, listing 'divers great sums to be given away by the king' (principally to M.P.s),[87] and most famously in Andrew Marvell's 'Last instructions to a painter', written, probably, on the eve of the parliamentary session which opened in October 1667. Marvell's account of the supply debate in the session of 1666–7 was built around the notion of a virtuous, independent 'country', set against a corrupt, diseased, bribed court.

---

[84] Carte MSS 46, fol. 435, Arlington to Ormonde, 5 Jan. 1667.
[85] Carte MSS 45, fol. 212, Sheldon to Ormonde, 25 Feb. 1667.
[86] See Russell, *Parliaments and English politics*, pp. 5–29.
[87] Pepys, *Diary*, VII, 342. The libel is described as being 'directed to Sir John Maynard'. For Maynard's interest in the issue, see Milward, *Diary*, p. 201.

> the *Court* and *Country*, both set right,
> On opposite points, the black against the white.
> Those having lost the Nation at *Trick track*,
> Those now advent'ring to win it back.[88]

Marvell's analysis of the members of each 'party' made them a good deal less coherent than this suggests, recognising that each was made up of groups and individuals which were far from constantly in agreement or co-operation. Yet the notion, at least, of a 'court party' was already a commonplace of political comment and seems to have become more regularly used during the session, despite the general reluctance to acknowledge the existence of any divergence of interests within parliament. Courtiers themselves preferred to refer to 'all that depend on the court', a number that Brodrick reckoned at about 140; but they told Ormonde that 'country' leaders talked, in private, of a 'court party'.[89] Although Arlington's efforts to build up a group of government supporters in the commons had been proceeding for a long time before 1666, the session of 1666–7, showing far more clearly than before a split in the interests of the 'court' and the 'country', had brought in its wake a much greater awareness of the court's manipulation of parliament.[90]

Another reason for the increasing identification of a 'court party' was perhaps the greater sophistication of its rivals. For sure, no 'country party' existed, and members and sympathisers of the government who wished to describe the opposition to it were usually forced into complicated and often ill-humoured circumlocutions: 'the peevish people', as Charles called them.[91] Yet while in previous sessions of this parliament opposition to government intentions had frequently and sometimes successfully been mounted by some individuals and groups – by John Vaughan and his allies, and by a widely recognised 'presbyterian' faction – only in this session (and to some extent in 1663) did they coalesce sufficiently to baffle the government for any long period, perhaps because this session was one dominated by issues which united, rather than divided them: the poverty of the country, the wealth, profligacy and corruption of the court. Yet such an 'opposition' was inevitably fissile, its life brief. The division between 'presbyterians' and the others was plain in the supply debates where the former championed a land tax while others sought more attractive solutions to the problem of taxation.

---

[88] Margoliouth, I, 143, ll. 107–10; for Marvell's later satire and comment on the issue of parliamentary corruption – and for comment by others – see Browning, 'Parties and party organization in the reign of Charles II', p. 25.

[89] Carte MSS 35, fols. 105, 118, 171, 246, 271v.

[90] Cf. the greater number of references to 'courtiers' and 'court party' in Milward and Pepys in this session than in those before or after it: Milward, *Diary*, pp. 20, 21, 25, 29, 47, 230; Pepys, *Diary*, IV, 58, V, 331, VII, 356, 370, 380–1, 388, 399, 401, 402, 407, 408, 416.

[91] Macray (ed.), *Notes which passed at meetings of the privy council*, p. 55; see also Brodrick, in Carte MSS 35, fols. 30v, 238, 271v, and Pepys, *Diary*, VIII, 18; Milward, *Diary*, p. 33.

But more important, the ability of the 'country' leaders to maintain pressure on the government depended on their success in retaining their influence over more moderate M.P.s, 'their calmer neighbours' as Brodrick called them.[92] The leaders themselves were diverse, and it is not clear how far they co-operated: at their centre, of course, were those who had gathered around John Vaughan in the early 1660s, including Littleton, Temple, and Garraway; there were others, like Sir William Lowther, Sir Thomas Gower, Brome Whorwood, Sir Thomas Tompkins, Edward Seymour, and Colonel Strangwayes, whom the government had found troublesome – particularly in financial matters – before. Some association between them there must have been, but it remains hard to demonstrate beyond the frequency with which these men were appointed together to the same committees and as managers of conferences.

The government was rather more surprised and annoyed by the co-operation between the discontented in the commons and some members of the lords than by the cabals in the house of commons itself. Bristol, Buckingham, Ashley, and Northampton were all accused of fostering contacts in the commons, besides unnamed others: but of these Buckingham was undoubtedly the principal.[93] Buckingham possessed sounder foundations for his political challenge than had Bristol in 1663, in his careful nurturing of his own little group in the commons. His influence there has been said to rest on a Yorkshire clientele,[94] and it is clear that he was popular in the county, that his marriage to Lord Fairfax's daughter brought him wide connections among its presbyterian families, and that his appointment as lord lieutenant of the West Riding gave him some opportunity to enlarge his circle of Yorkshire friends and clients.[95] A small group of them were closely involved with Buckingham and with opposition politics in parliament. Sir Henry Belasyse (elected at Grimsby in November 1666) and Sir Thomas Osborne were among the duke's firmest friends in the tribulations he was to face in the coming year, although neither was a major figure in the 'country' leadership.[96] Sir Thomas Gower, close to Lord Fairfax, a little sympathetic towards nonconfirmists, and one of the principal investigators of the 1663 Yorkshire plot, was probably associated with Buckingham for all these reasons; and he and the other Yorkshire M.P., Sir William Lowther, were rather more

[92] Carte MSS 35, fol. 238; cf. Carte MSS 46, fol. 434.
[93] Carte MSS 35, fols. 197, 240; Carte MSS 217, fol. 368; Clarendon, *Life*, II, 321–3.
[94] Browning, 'Parties and party organization in the reign of Charles II', p. 31; though cf. his *Danby*, I, 59–60.
[95] See also his apparent leadership of Yorkshire politics, in the 1661 Yorkshire militia scheme, Clarendon MSS 206, fol. 24, Dutch ambassadors to the states general, 13/23 Dec. 1661.
[96] *H.P.*, I, 617; Browning, *Danby*, II, 8–34.

prominent among the government's critics.[97] But Buckingham's main associates in the commons – Temple, Seymour, Garraway, and Howard – had no strong Yorkshire connections.[98] With some, he may have shared common concerns: his interest in toleration had perhaps already helped to bring him alliances with Bristol and Lord Ashley; and Ashley, Buckingham, and Sir Robert Howard were all apparently friends of the Cromwellian and tolerationist Sir Charles Wolseley.[99] Osborne, later the standard bearer of anglican royalist reaction, was something of an anomaly among Buckingham's political allies. Indeed, it is clear that Buckingham's faction was a rather loose, feeble one: despite its existence, his power ultimately rested (as had Bristol's) not on his personal following, but on the immense energy and passion he devoted to the co-ordinating of an incoherent opposition movement, and becoming himself the champion of the dissatisfactions of a nation; when those dissatisfactions seemed to decline, so, too, did his power.

For the moment, indeed, some of the violence had gone out of that dissatisfaction. Yet the session of 1666–7 had revealed a new trend in politics: increasingly, the greatest threats to stability seemed to come not from radical subversion, but from the court and its corruption. Many were surprised and shocked by the sort of things that were now openly being said, and the frequently-expressed fears of a return to the convulsions of the 1640s seemed now to ring more true to more people than they had since 1660.[100] Yet what many felt was not a wish to rebel, but a great anguished yearning for the king to discard his mistresses and give up his pleasures, sweep from his Augean court the corrupt ministers, the pampered women and the sycophants, and himself take command. Until he did so, Pepys and Colonel Reymes agreed in February 1667, nothing could be done to haul the government out of crisis: but the possibility seemed horribly remote, for 'nobody would or had authority enough with the king to tell him how all things go to wrack and will be lost'.[101]

---

[97] For Gower, see *H.P.*, II, 425; for his sympathy for nonconformists, see Sheffield Central Library, Wilson of Bromhead MSS, Wil.D.274/9 [Osborne] to Bennet, 4 April 1664, cf. 7; see also Browning, *Danby*, III, 38–9.

[98] Clarendon, *Life*, II, 321.

[99] For Buckingham and Wolseley, see *ibid.*, II, 436; for Howard, see *H.P.*, II, 595; for Wolseley, see Worden, 'Toleration and the Cromwellian protectorate', pp. 229–33.

[100] Carte MSS 34, fol. 459, Carte MSS 35, fols. 126, 240v, Conway to Ormonde, 27 Oct., 13 Nov. 1666, 5 Jan. 1667; Carte MSS 217, fol. 366, Anglesey to Ormonde, 5 Jan. 1667; Carte MSS 47, fol. 138, same to same, 15 Jan. 1667; Pepys, *Diary*, VIII, 24; Clarendon, *Life*, II, 347–9.

[101] Pepys, *Diary*, VIII, 68, cf. 37, 38, and VII, 349, 350, 370, 404–5, and Bodl., MS Eng. Hist. e. 87, fol. 10, no. 25.

Ministers were left to pick up the pieces of what had been, for them, an awful session. Some attempts were made to meet parliamentary criticism – although the creation of a royal commission on public accounts, based on the Bill drafted by the commons, was the only one of a number of rumoured reforms that saw the light of day.[102] And the commission was itself a failure. All those named to it had been included in Clarendon's proposed royal commission of December; but the 'country' politicians among them – particularly Sir Thomas Littleton and William Garraway – were suspicious of the commission, and reluctant to participate. They disputed its terms endlessly: only after a personal interview with the king, on 4 June, did they finally agree to sit. Little further good could be expected from it. On 1 May Lord Lucas, one of its members, pointed out the uselessness of the whole affair: its members regarded it only as a 'forced, packed business of the king', allowed only to query the accounts, not to pass them. Within a week or two of its meeting with the king, the commission appears to have ceased meeting entirely.[103]

The government's attempts at repression were no more successful than its attempts at conciliation. Buckingham had apparently said or done enough during the session to anticipate some legal action against him after it – he made himself scarce soon after the prorogation – but the origins of the accusations against him are obscure.[104] It seems most likely that they lay with Arlington, who obtained from Sir Roger Langley, a Yorkshire gentleman with a grudge against the duke, access to two informers with wide connections in dissenting and radical circles.[105] The part of their evidence on which the government seems most to have relied concerned Buckingham's association with John Heydon, a slightly deranged Rosicrucian scholar who had been involved before in radical anti-government conspiracy.[106] Heydon had been arrested on 24 January and questioned by Arlington, Morrice, William Coventry, and Clifford concerning his discussions with Buckingham about plans for a rebellion by the seamen, and the astrological casting of the king's nativity.[107] A month later, the king dismissed the duke from his place on the

[102] Pepys, *Diary*, VIII, 50, 70; Carte MSS 35, fol. 305, Brodrick to Ormonde, 9 Feb. 1667.
[103] P.R.O., PC 2/59, fols. 180v, 192v, 208; SP 29/179/173 (Thomas Lee to Williamson, n.d., but late May), 192/57 (draft of the commission), 194/91 (newsletter, 21 March 1667), 201/120 (the commission to the king, 24 May 1667), 203/149 (newsletter, 8 June), Clarendon, *Life*, II, 364–5; *Cal. S.P. Dom.* 1666–7, p. 526
[104] B.L., Add. MSS 27872, fol. 8v; Clarendon, *Life*, II, 436.
[105] For Langley, see Browning, *Danby*, I, 29; *H.P.*, I, 489; B.L., Add. MSS 27872, fols. 12 and 15; cf. Carte MSS 35, fol. 302, 'Mr Leaveing' to Sir George Lane, 7 Feb. 1667, and fol. 304; Yorkshire Archaeological Society, Leeds, Slingsby MSS, DD 149/98, information of Jeremy Bower.
[106] Greaves, *Deliver us from evil*, p. 220.
[107] *Hist. MSS Comm.*, 12th report, appendix, part VII, MSS of S. H. Le Fleming (1896), p. 44, newsletter, 29 Jan. 1667, cf. MSS of A. G. Finch, III, 413–17; Carte MSS 35, fols. 304 and

council and all his offices, and ordered his arrest.[108] But Buckingham went to ground, defying all the government's efforts to find him;[109] although its fears of the consequences of his removal from the lieutenancy of the West Riding – of mass resignations among his deputies, and refusals to co-operate with his successor, the earl of Burlington – proved unfounded: in the event only two, Sir George Savile and Sir Thomas Osborne, along with a number of minor militia officers, gave up their commissions.[110]

These attempts to deal with the government's political problems could in any case not mask the economic foundations of its and the country's present plight: distress and resistance to taxation grew. The new poll tax was stiffly opposed by the unusually heavily taxed poor; collectors were hampered by the Act's ambiguous and sometimes unworkable provisions, and by local tax commissioners who sometimes condoned and even abetted evasion.[111] Some resistance and protests were accompanied by expressions of sympathy for Buckingham, and of sinister rumours of the progress of papists in government: Buckingham's only crime, it was said, had been too enthusiastic a persecution of popery.[112] Most basic of all to the government's difficulties was its shortage of credit. Most of the £1.8 million voted by parliament was contained in a tax which would not begin to be collected for another twelve months: few were willing to lend with no better security than the assessment. The bankers, Carteret complained, simply would not, or could not, lend him money for the navy. The poll tax was no better as a fund of credit, since its problems were widely known.[113] Even if loans could be procured, the navy's immense and growing debt, which would have to be paid in part at least before the board could even begin to prepare a fleet,

329, Brodrick to Ormonde, 2 March 1667; cf. P.R.O., SP 29/191/91, 192/112, 137, 164 and SP 29/187/160.

[108] *Hist. MSS. Comm.*, Le Fleming MSS, p. 45, newsletter, 26 Feb. 1667; Carte MSS 35, fol. 323, Lord Carlingford to Ormonde, 26 Feb. 1667; Carte MSS 46, fol. 457, Arlington to Ormonde, 26 Feb. 1667; Clarendon, *Life*, II, 435–6.

[109] *Ibid.*, II, 437; Clarendon MSS 85, fols. 96–7, report of Sergeant Barcroft; Steele, no. 3486; for his refuges, see Browning (ed.), *The memoirs of Sir John Reresby*, p. 66; P.R.O., SP 29/193/86, R.H. to Williamson, 11 March 1667; Yorkshire Archaeological Society, Leeds, Slingsby of Scriven MSS DD 56, M5/21, Henry Slingsby to Sir Thomas Slingsby, 16 April [1667]; B.L., Add. MSS 27872, fols. 8, 10.

[110] Browning (ed.), *The memoirs of Sir John Reresby*, p. 65; B.L., Althorp papers A 30, Burlington to Arlington, n.d., and Robert Boyle to Burlington, 4 May 1667; and see Reresby's correspondence in West Yorkshire Archive Department, Leeds, MEX/R/2 and 3, and Sir Thomas Slingsby's in Yorkshire Arch. Soc., Leeds, DD 149 and DD 56, M5.

[111] P.R.O., SP 29/193/59, 113, 194/84, 137, 196/20, 39; B.L., Add. MSS 29551, fol. 253; Pepys, *Diary*, VIII, 66, 84; *Hist. MSS. Comm.*, 3rd report, appendix, MSS of Sir Philip de Malpas Grey-Egerton, p. 245; see also SP 29/195/89 and 196/20 for the continuing problems of hearth tax collection.

[112] P.R.O., SP 29/193/45, 86, 194/44, 196/67, 197/161; B.L., Add. MSS 29551, fol. 253.

[113] Pepys, *Diary*, VIII, 140, 143–4, cf. 290.

meant that an ultimate collapse of naval finance would only be postponed until the following year. And without ready money, as Pepys spelled out to the king, York, Southampton, and Carteret in mid-March, he and his colleagues at the navy board could do nothing.[114]

The only hope was that nothing would need to be done, that peace could be settled before the next campaigning session. Indeed, negotiations had been encouraging, pushed on by the French, anxious to clear the way for their projected invasion of the Spanish Netherlands.[115] There were spasms of optimism followed by troughs of pessimism; but there were just enough of the former for the private committee of the council, faced with a depressing report from the navy board and the impossibility of raising immediate money, to agree at the end of February that no major fleet should be fitted out. Only squadrons of third-rates and below would put to sea, to protect trade and attack Dutch merchant shipping. Coastal defences would be strengthened, and England would be safe behind its sea wall: the Dutch, troubled by the French attack on Flanders, would be unlikely to invade.[116] All the ministers seem to have been unhappy about the decision, but, as Carteret told Pepys, 'it was not choice, but only force'. Although the government kept it as quiet as it could, by mid-March it was obvious, and as hopes of peace plummeted with news from over the channel it provoked misgivings.[117] It made peace more necessary than ever: and in the last two weeks of April ministers closed to an agreement with the French. England's non-intervention against the French attack on Flanders was assured, in return for an engagement to secure peace from the Dutch on acceptable terms.[118]

It was perfectly plain that the English government relied heavily on this French promise: even more so as, when negotiations finally began at Breda in mid-May, the Dutch remained adamant about most of their war demands and the French seemed to make little effort to persuade them to be otherwise: as French troops pushed quickly into Flanders, Louis preferred to assure the Dutch of his good intentions towards them. Nevertheless, they were distinctly nervous of Louis's actions on their western borders, and were eager to end their naval war so they might turn to this threat: but to them, the English seemed ludicrously obdurate, particularly over the long-disputed island of

---

[114] *Further correspondence of Samuel Pepys*, pp. 162–7; cf. Pepys, *Diary*, VIII, 111–12.

[115] Feiling, *British foreign policy*, pp. 213–18; Clarendon, *Life*, II, 374–5.

[116] *Further correspondence of Samuel Pepys*, pp. 158–61; Clarendon, *Life*, II, 365–71; Pepys, *Diary*, VIII, 62, 88, 98.

[117] Pepys, *Diary*, VIII, 110, 117; cf. Carte MSS 35, fol. 356v, Brodrick to Ormonde, 16 March 1667, and Carte MSS 47, fol. 476, Sir William Coventry to Ormonde, 12 March 1667. See also B.L., Althorp MSS B6, Lady Ranelagh to Burlington, 20 April 1667.

[118] *Cal. Cl. S.P.*, V, 393, 591, 595, 598, Clarendon to St Albans, 18, 22 and 23 March, St Albans to Clarendon, 3/13 April 1667; see also Lister, *Life of Clarendon*, III, 455–9; Clarendon, *Life*, II, 393–4.

Pulorun. In their negotiations with the French, the English had agreed not to let Pulorun stand in the way of a treaty; but they continued, in their discussions with the Dutch, to insist on its return in accordance with the 1654 Treaty of Westminster. The Dutch remained unaware of the Anglo-French agreement, and convinced that the English would not come to terms without securing their way on the issue. In the hope of bringing a quick end to the war, De Witt, in late April and early May, drew up plans to take advantage of England's naval weakness with an attack on the English fleet moored uselessly in the Medway. At the end of May, the Dutch fleet put to sea.[119]

As the prospect of a naval disaster loomed, tension in the court grew. Sir William Coventry and Sir George Carteret angrily disputed responsibility for the collapse of naval finance.[120] Rumours of the removal of Southampton and his replacement by Sandwich, Arlington or Coventry were prevalent in mid-March, while peace negotiations were thought to be failing.[121] Thereafter, they died away for a time, until late April, when the treasurer, who had been unwell for several months, became very ill.[122] His death was confidently predicted, and there followed in the three weeks until it occurred, and for almost a week afterwards, a fierce struggle over the succession. Clarendon lost: his endeavours to have Southampton replaced by his own protégé, Bridgewater, and at all events not by a commission composed of his *bête noire*, William Coventry, and his and Arlington's cronies – Clifford and Sir John Duncombe – were finally rejected by the king and by York. Clarendon succeeded only in adding to the commission two peers, the chancellor of the exchequer, Lord Ashley, and the duke of Albemarle, to add a little to its dignity. The commission's existence and membership were interpreted, even by Clarendon himself, as a demonstration of the chancellor's declining power and Coventry's increasing influence: it was, he wrote, 'an accident that made a fatal breach into the chancellor's fortune, with a gap wide enough to let in all that ruin which soon after was poured upon him'.[123]

In the early days of June the Dutch fleet arrived off the South-East coast. At first, the government's fear was that its commanders planned an invasion: for a few days it made frantic efforts to assemble all available soldiers, and to raise new regular regiments.[124] But on 10–13 June, the Dutch, scorning the

[119] Feiling, *British foreign policy*, pp. 219–22; Haley, *An English diplomat*, pp. 115–16.
[120] Pepys, *Diary*, VIII, 143–4, 149, 164–5, 179–80.
[121] *Ibid.*, VIII, 96, 118–19.
[122] *Ibid.*, VIII, 80; Clarendon, *Life*, II, 400.
[123] Clarendon, *Life*, II, 399–400, 409–14; Carte MSS 35, fols. 400 and 465v, Brodrick to Ormonde, 30 April and 8 June 1667; Carte MSS 46, fols. 476 and 478, Arlington to Ormonde, 18, 22 May 1667; Carte MSS 47, fol. 152, Anglesey to Ormonde, 21 May 1667; Pepys, *Diary*, VIII, 190, 195, 223–4; P.R.O., SP 29/201/194.
[124] Pepys, *Diary*, VIII, 248, 255; P.R.O., PC 2/59, fols. 223v, 225v, 227, 228; SP 29/204/23; P. G. Rogers, *The Dutch in the Medway* (London, 1970), p. 69.

new defences designed to bar the approaches to the naval dockyards at Chatham, sailed up the Medway almost to the town, took the *Royal Charles*, the flagship of the last two years' campaigns, and burnt three more of the navy's finest first rates and several smaller ships, before they fell back down the river on the ebb tide on 14 June, and retired into the Thames estuary. There they remained, blockading the South-East coast and providing a constant threat of a second attack.[125]

In London, there was an outburst of anguish, anger, and fear as the disaster which had been expected for so long finally broke; mobs turned their rage against Clarendon, whom they openly abused, crying out that he had betrayed his country for money. All over the country there were appalled denunciations of treachery and popish conspiracy about the king, which could only explain so appalling a calamity.[126] At court, the news was greeted with despondency or despair: 'they who remember that conjuncture', Clarendon wrote a few years later, 'and were then present in the galleries and privy lodgings at Whitehall, whither all the world flocked with equal liberty, can easily call to mind instances of such wild despair and even ridiculous apprehensions, that I am willing to forget, and would not that the least mention of them should remain'.[127]

Worse than the scale of the naval defeat or even than the humiliation inflicted on the government, was the blow it dealt to its solvency. As the scale of the danger became apparent, money vanished into the country: Pepys sent much of his own gold away with his wife and father on 13 June, but was unable to obtain the rest from his banker. Some bankers were reduced to stalling their customers' demands for cash. If the banks did not break, Brodrick told Ormonde on the 15th, it would be a miracle.[128] Depositors were well aware of how much they had lent to the government, and were worried that the government might cancel its debts: a proclamation issued on 18 June, guaranteeing the punctual payment of the exchequer's debts, and the solvency of the goldsmiths had some effect in reassuring them, and perhaps in preventing the total collapse of the bankers.[129] Yet it did nothing to increase the sums available to the government; and as its sources of credit dried up, and customs receipts were stifled by the Dutch blockade of the Thames, there was scarcely any money available to prepare defence measures. The government ordered its new levies of soldiers – whose addition

[125] Rogers, *The Dutch in the Medway*, pp. 83–117.
[126] Pepys, *Diary*, VIII, 264–5, 269, 270; P.R.O., SP 29/205/2, 77, 84, 117, 128, 206/1, 43, 47, 64; Carte MSS 35, fol. 478; Carte MSS 215, fol. 351; Evelyn, *Diary*, III, 485.
[127] Clarendon, *Life*, II, 418–19.
[128] Pepys, *Diary*, VIII, 263, 274, 275–6. Cf. 528–9; Carte MSS 35, fol. 478.
[129] P.R.O., PC 2/59, fol. 235v; Steele, no. 3493; see the two drafts prepared by Clarendon, Clarendon MSS 85, fols. 439–40 and 445–6, and *Cal. Cl. S.P.*, V, 617, n. 1.

to the permanent establishment would cost, it estimated, over £260,000 a year – without any money to pay for them.[130] It appealed for money: to the City, to lawyers and clergy, to the East India Company, to the country at large through the lords lieutenant. The new levies were cut back as far as was possible; and in Chester, an ancient feudal due was revived to raise 3000 marks.[131]

Some seem to have suggested radical solutions to these difficulties. It was perhaps Conway who was the Irish earl mentioned by Brodrick as suggesting that an Irish – and inevitably catholic – army might be brought over for England's defence, and probably to impose military rule. Certainly by mid-July some such plan to raise an army and 'so to make the government like that of France' was rumoured in London.[132] There was another rumour, that the government intended a deal with the dissenters; and there were, certainly, some at court – perhaps Anglesey in particular – who urged granting liberty of conscience as part of a solution to the crisis.[133] Yet these schemes were peripheral to what many saw as the central question: whether or not to summon parliament sooner than the date – 10 October – to which it had been prorogued. In the two weeks which followed the Dutch raid, debate raged in council. The king's first reaction was angrily to recall his ambassadors from Breda: but after a discussion in council on 14 June, he succumbed to reality and decided to leave them. The government expected in any case that the negotiations would now fall apart: although it quickly conceded to the Dutch the two major points still at issue, it was deeply concerned that their victory might make the Dutch demand new, and unacceptable terms.[134] If war was to continue, money had to be found from somewhere – and parliament seemed the only practicable source.[135] Ministers were also under immense popular pressure to allow parliament to sit. On 18 June it was said that the king had forestalled a petition for it from the City; there were demonstrations for a parliament in Westminster on 14 June; and many of those Pepys talked with

130 Carte MSS 35, fol. 478; Pepys, *Diary*, VIII, 290; Carte MSS 46, fols. 490, 492, Arlington to Ormonde, 15, 18 June 1667; Carte MSS 75, fol. 530v, Arlington to Sandwich, 20 June 1667.
131 Pepys, *Diary*, VIII, 283–4; *Cal. S.P. Dom.*, 1667, p. 221; Bodl., MS Add. C. 308, fol. 94v, Sheldon to bishop of London, 24 June 1667; Clarendon MSS 85, fol. 332–3, king to Clarendon, 21 June 1667; P.R.O., SP 29/208/90; *Hist. MSS. Comm.*, 12th report, appendix, part V, MSS of the duke of Rutland, II (1889), 10, king to the earl of Rutland, 29 June 1667.
132 Carte MSS 35, fol. 489, Brodrick to Ormonde, 22 June 1667; cf. fol. 120, Conway to Ormonde, 10 Nov. 1667; Pepys, *Diary*, VIII, 332.
133 Carte MSS 35, fol. 489; cf. Bodl., Tanner MSS 45, fol. 202, Roger Pepys to John Hobart, 2 July 1667; P.R.O., SP 29/205/78, 206/1.I, 47, 116.I, 207/107, 208/47; Clarendon MSS 85, fols. 336–7; Pepys, *Diary*, VIII, 265.
134 Coventry MSS 44, fol. 43, Morrice to Henry Coventry, 14 June 1667; *Cal. Cl. S.P.*, V, 616–17, Clarendon to St Albans, 15 June 1667.
135 Carte MSS 46, fol. 492v, Arlington to Ormonde, 18 June 1667; Carte MSS 47, fol. 158, Anglesey to Ormonde, 15 June 1667.

– and Pepys himself – regarded it as the only credible solution to the nation's trials.[136]

Nevertheless, there were compelling arguments against holding a meeting of parliament. Clarendon pointed out that the legality of recalling parliament to a date before that to which it had been prorogued was questionable; and although the government received advice from Prynne which got over the scruple, the chancellor's point was as much that it might give the government's critics one further cause to hold up proceedings.[137] In any case, it was unclear how parliament could help: it would require at least twelve days' notice of its assembly; and when assembled, even if its members had no objection to the legality of its assembly, and even if they were willing to grant more taxation, getting a bill through both houses would require more time than was available in the circumstances. Besides, it was doubtful whether more taxation (or at least more assessment taxation) was needed: it was said that there remained £700,000 uncharged on the last assessment. The real need was for ready cash. As Carteret told Pepys on 18 June, 'the parliament itself cannot be thought able at present to raise money, and therefore it will be to no purpose to call one'. Anglesey was equally dubious, as were even some M.P.s.[138] If the prospects that parliament might solve the government's problems were small, the likelihood that it would add to them was immense. There were many indications of the continued strength and vitality of the government's critics within the commons: the activity of some of them on the accounts commission gave them a reason to remain in London and to communicate frequently with each other when they might have been merely inactive in the country; and the production of the play *The change of crowns* by Edward Howard, Sir Robert Howard's brother, in April, including scripted and unscripted satire on government corruption, showed an undiminished boldness in challenging the court.[139] There were many rumours that if parliament sat it would tear into the court.[140] Already, before a decision was taken on whether or not to hold parliament, the government made approaches to some of its more moderate opponents. On 8 June Osborne had a sometimes angry interview with the king, but received hints of favour and preferment; a week or so later, after the disaster, the government was even more anxious to mollify its critics. Lord St John, apparently a friend

---

[136] W. Durrant Cooper (ed.), *The Savile correspondence*, Camden Society, LXXI (1858), 15–16, Henry to Sir George Savile, 18 June 1667; Pepys, *Diary*, VIII, 268, 282, 285, 292.
[137] Clarendon, *Life*, II, 419–23; Carte MSS 35, fol. 478v, Brodrick to Ormonde, 15 June 1667.
[138] Clarendon, *Life*, II, 424; Pepys, *Diary*, VIII, 277; Carte MSS 47, fol. 160, Anglesey to Ormonde, 22 June 1667; Bodl., Tanner MSS 45, fol. 202.
[139] See Edward Howard, *The change of crownes*, ed. F. R. Boas (London, 1949); Pepys, *Diary*, VIII, 167–8, 173.
[140] *Ibid.*, VIII, 271, 273, 282, 304; Carte MSS 35, fols. 474, 484.

of Buckingham's, whose scuffle with Andrew Henley in Westminster Hall during the last session had rendered him liable to severe penalties, was allowed to compound for his fine and was received back into the king's favour; Sir Robert Howard and Samuel Sandys were said to have agreed not to oppose the government in parliament, and Colonel Strangewayes to have been bought off with promises of preferment for his second son.[141] Ministers anxiously sought to fix the blame for the disaster elsewhere than on themselves: Sir Peter Pett, the navy commissioner at Chatham, was arrested on 17 June and questioned before a committee of the council. Arlington candidly admitted that if Pett was not guilty, 'the world would think them all guilty'. Coventry, too, urged that somebody – anybody but Albemarle, who was too popular – should be found responsible. Pepys concluded them 'all upon their own purgation'.[142]

In this atmosphere of *sauve qui peut*, it was natural that those who felt themselves most threatened by public opinion should be the most vigorous opponents of the revocation of parliament. Carteret, the treasurer of the navy, and answerable for the failure of navy finance, and his patron Clarendon were well known to be strongly against it.[143] Clarendon urged again for a dissolution instead: again, it was ruled out. But there were more alternatives than this to a session: the immediate need, Clarendon pointed out – to provide the troops that were required for the defence of the coast with pay, food and shelter – could best be met by imposing free quarter on the local inhabitants, and levying some sort of forced loan to be repaid out of the next parliamentary supplies.[144] As he argued later, in *A brief view and survey*, for the government to take such liberties at times of extreme emergency was perfectly within its powers under the law; such strictly temporary measures for public defence were no violation of the right of property.[145] Clarendon was not advocating military rule, or the abolition of parliament; yet others may have been, and the chancellor's suggestion for free quarter and a forced loan appears to have become confused with yet more drastic proposals. A third opponent of a meeting of parliament was said to be the duke of York; and York was associated now, as he had been before, with plans to impose the

---

[141] Browning, *Danby*, II, 31–4; Carte MSS 35, fols. 484, 488, Brodrick to Ormonde, 17 and 22 June 1667; for St John and Henley, see P.R.O., SP 29/179/136, newsletter, 29 Nov. 1666.

[142] Pepys, *Diary*, VIII, 278–9; Carte MSS 35, fol. 484.

[143] *The Savile correspondence*, p. 17, Henry to Sir George Savile, 20 June 1667; Pepys, *Diary*, VIII, 277, 292–3; Carte MSS 46, fol. 492, Arlington to Ormonde, 18 June 1667; P.R.O., SP 29/205/76.

[144] Clarendon, *Life*, II, 425; for his earlier wishes to dissolve parliament, see *ibid.*, II, 330–1, above, p. 291, and Carte MSS 35, fol. 290, Conway to Ormonde, 2 Feb. 1667; see also Carte MSS 45, fol. 212.

[145] Clarendon, *A brief view and survey*, pp. 176–8.

royal will with an army.[146] The coincidence of such reports with the actual recruitment of considerable reinforcements for Charles's small permanent army gave them greater credence.

Clarendon attributed the pressure in the council for a meeting of parliament to several of its most recent members – presumably Duncombe, Clifford, and Coventry; these, the effective members of the treasury commission, were no doubt anxious for as rapid a solution as possible to the government's financial problems, and as in the 1666–7 session, probably ready to make large concessions in order to obtain one. Yet most of the council, including the king himself, were said to accept the arguments for recalling parliament, if the war was to continue.[147] It was principally waiting for news from Breda that held up the final decision until 25 June, when it seems to have been precipitated by rising fears that the Dutch, jubilant at their success, would raise their demands. The following day a proclamation was published recalling parliament to Westminster on 25 July.[148]

The arguments of the past two weeks had been aggressive and recriminatory: popular anger, and what must have seemed the imminent collapse of the government, put a severe strain on its members. In one of the first council meetings after the disaster, Clarendon was said to have announced that he had been opposed to the war from the beginning, and therefore washed his hands of the whole business; Anglesey, who reproached him for indulging in self-vindication, was himself not above it; and neither was the king who angrily complained to London aldermen on 13 June that the laying up of the fleet had been contrary to his own opinion, and that he had been betrayed.[149] The debate over calling parliament was unusually acrimonious. That it had finally gone against Clarendon testified to his declining influence and Coventry's rising power. Even Brodrick, one of Clarendon's closest allies, acknowledged it: 'how happy a progress my noble friend Sir William Coventry makes in his Majesty's and his Royal Highness's favour', he wrote to Ormonde four days after the decision was taken, 'and how happily he supplies the chancellor's part when absent from council table I suppose your grace hears at large, without doubt no man at the board is abler to sustain it'.[150] Despite Brodrick's unconcern (and the many who valued both

---

[146] *The Savile correspondence*, p. 17; Pepys, *Diary*, VIII, 292–3, 332.

[147] Clarendon, *Life*, II, 421; cf. *The Savile correspondence*, p. 17; P.R.O., SP 29/205/76, John Rushworth to Lady ?, 15 June 1667; Carte MSS 46, fol. 492, Arlington to Ormonde, 18 June 1667.

[148] *Ibid.*, fol. 496v, Arlington to Ormonde, 25 June 1667; Carte MSS 35, fol. 494v, Brodrick to Ormonde, 25 June 1667; cf. B.L., M 636/21, Nathaniel Hobart to Sir Ralph Verney, 26 June 1667; Pepys, *Diary*, VIII, 285. Steele, no. 3495.

[149] Pepys, *Diary*, VIII, 287–8; Carte MSS 47, fol. 158, Anglesey to Ormonde, 15 June 1667; P.R.O., SP 29/205/78, ? to Lord Conway, 15 June 1667; cf. PC 2/59, fol. 229v.

[150] Clarendon, *Life*, II, 421–6; Carte MSS 35, fol. 502v, Brodrick to Ormonde, 29 June 1667.

Clarendon's patronage and Coventry's friendship were placed in an awkward position, so his sang-froid was perhaps rather studied) Coventry's progress presented Clarendon with a dangerous threat at a time when he who was both unpopular and had lost influence might easily be left out in the cold of parliamentary fury.

The proclamation was greeted with much relief in the country at large. 'I hope', Nathaniel Hobart wrote to Sir Ralph Verney on the day after it appeared 'his Majesty will now . . . be advised by those that really love him, and his interest which is indeed the interest of the nation'; Pepys greeted it as the 'best news I have heard a great while'.[151] Others, particularly those at court, were considerably less enthusiastic. Brodrick contemplated gloomily the prospect of 'an English house of commons, warmed with the dog days, and their own ill humours'.[152] As soon as the announcement was made the government looked for means of pacifying its critics: on the same day it published new procedures for redressing the seamen's complaints about their pay, and Sir William Coventry urged the navy board to prepare detailed accounts. To widespread astonishment, Sir George Carteret was allowed to leave his office of treasurer of the navy, and disproving the rumours that he had been dismissed and disgraced, exchanged it with Anglesey's, of vice-treasurer of Ireland. Rumours flew – that Mordaunt had been replaced as governor of Windsor Castle with Prince Rupert, and that the Canary company's patent had been called in.[153] But these were quickly disappointed, although on 28 June a council committee was appointed to discuss the Canary trade, and it heard some suggestions of the company for amendments to its charter which, they hoped, would mollify its opponents.[154]

The government did, however, step up its discussions with 'country' leaders. Martin Clifford, Buckingham's secretary, and Sir Robert Howard appealed to Clarendon and the king for the charges against the duke to be lifted. Sir William Scroggs (who had been Buckingham's counsel in the Roos peerage case in January) may also have lobbied the king. It was clear in the approaches to Clarendon that Buckingham suspected Arlington to be responsible for the allegations against him, and hoped to obtain his revenge – perhaps in collaboration with the chancellor. It was equally clear that the

[151] B.L., M 636/21, 26 June 1667; Pepys, *Diary*, VIII, 292.
[152] Carte MSS 35, fol. 502, Brodrick to Ormonde, 29 June 1667; cf. fol. 496; Pepys, *Diary*, VIII, 303.
[153] Steele, no. 3494; P.R.O., SP 29/207/26, Coventry to navy board, 26 June 1667; Pepys, *Diary*, VIII, 295, 297, 301; Carte MSS 35, fol. 502; *Hist. MSS. Comm.*, 14th report, appendix, part IX (1895), MSS of the earl of Lindsey, p. 367, Charles Bertie to Osborne, 29 June 1667; P.R.O., SP 29/207/113, James Thurston to Conway, 29 June 1667; Bodl., MS North c. 10, fol. 187, Francis North to Lord North [27 June 1667]; B.L., Althorp MSS B6, Lady Ranelagh to Burlington, 29 June 1667; Bodl., Tanner MSS 45, fol. 202.
[154] P.R.O., PC 2/59, fol. 242v; Clarendon MSS 85, fol. 263.

king, although exhibiting much coldness towards the duke, was no longer really prepared to go on with the charges.[155] The danger which might attend such an action was shown when Buckingham, by now presumably satisfied that his prosecution would be feeble, gave himself up on 28 June. He extracted the maximum publicity from the event: his surrender seemed more like a triumph. On the way, he dined in Bishopsgate, in company with Lord Rivers and the M.P.s Lord Buckhurst and Lord Vaughan; there were some claims that the duke of Monmouth was also present. 'Really he is at this day a very popular man,' wrote Pepys, 'the world reckoning him to suffer upon no other account than that he did propound in parliament to have all men questioned that had to do with the receipt of the taxes and prizes.'[156]

Hopes of peace waxed and waned by the day: but despite further (though ineffective) action by the Dutch navy,[157] Dutch politicians and diplomats were less demanding than had at first been feared; and although the English were forced to a few further concessions, agreement on a draft treaty was reached at Breda on 30 June. At first the government balked at some of the demands: but after long and very secret discussions in council on 10 and 11 July, the English ambassador at the talks, Henry Coventry, was sent back to accept them.[158] As expectations of peace grew, the belief that parliament would meet after all declined. As early as 11 July it was assumed that the session would be a very short one, if it took place at all.[159] Yet ministers were unwilling to dispense with a meeting until absolutely certain that the Dutch and other major signatories had ratified the treaty; and news of this was desperately slow in coming. Even on 23 July, twelve days after Coventry's departure and only two before the assembly of parliament, there was no assurance that the peace had been concluded. Ministers resolved that as soon as parliament met on the 25th it would be adjourned to the following

[155] Clarendon, *Life*, II, 439–42; Carte MSS 35, fols. 502 and 520 (Lord Carlingford to Ormonde, 2 July 1667). For Scroggs, see Pepys, *Diary*, VIII, 22.
[156] Pepys, *Diary*, VIII, 302; Carte MSS 35, fol. 502; B.L., Althorp MSS B4, Lord Clifford to Burlington, 29 June 1667, B5, Lord Graham to Burlington, 29 June, 9 July 1667; *Hist. MSS. Comm.*, Le Fleming MSS, p. 51, newsletter, 2 July 1667; Pepys, *Diary*, VIII, 302.
[157] Rogers, *The Dutch in the Medway*, pp. 120–3.
[158] Carte MSS 47, fol. 164, Anglesey to Ormonde, 6 July 1667; Carte MSS 222, fol. 160, newsletter, 2 July 1667; Carte MSS 35, fol. 534, Edward Cooke to Ormonde, 9 July 1667; Carte MSS 46, fol. 166, Arlington to Ormonde, 13 July 1667; B.L., Althorp MSS B6, Lady Ranelagh to Burlington, 6 July 1667, B7, Lawrence Hyde to Burlington, 13 July 1667; Bodl., MS North c. 10, fol. 185, Francis North to Lord North, 11 July 1667; Pepys, *Diary*, VIII, 328, 329–30.
[159] Bodl., MS North c. 10, fol. 185, cf. fol. 188; B.L., Althorp MSS B6, Lady Ranelagh to Burlington, 18 July 1667; Carte MSS 35, fol. 559, Brodrick to Ormonde, 20 July 1667.

Monday, the 29th, in the hope that by then confirmation would have arrived.[160]

Political activity, though, was little diminished by the imminence of peace. Buckingham's fate excited great interest. On 1 July he was examined in the Tower by Arlington, Morrice, Sir William Coventry, and Clifford, and on the 8th he appeared before the council. On both occasions he denied the charges against him. Although opinion varied on the extent to which Buckingham was guilty, it was fairly clear that he was no longer in any real danger: one of the chief witnesses against him was now dead, and the king was obviously unlikely to press a prosecution.[161] Clarendon was scandalised, though, by how lightly the charges were dismissed: a letter, which he hinted was undeniably in Buckingham's hand and gave evidence of some sort of treasonous activity, the duke claimed to have been written by his sister. The king and Arlington accepted the explanation. The chancellor plainly suspected some sort of collusion, and common gossip suggested that Castlemaine had badgered the king into leniency: she may have felt that co-operation with Buckingham now might protect her from criticism in the forthcoming parliament.[162] But Clarendon's suspicions were evidently wider. Buckingham's behaviour during his examination before the council made it obvious that he considered Arlington to be the author of his misfortunes, and it was clear that he would do as much as he could to take his revenge. The presence of the parliamentary leaders, Howard and Sir Thomas Meres, at the council chamber during the hearing, underlined his ability to do so.[163] It was perhaps natural for ministers involved in his persecution and now aware that the king was likely to let him go, to seek to ingratiate themselves with him as much as they could.

Buckingham was released on the evening of Sunday 14 July. Now the government began to fall apart in earnest. The duke appears to have made two approaches to Clarendon, once in a personal visit, and again through Martin Clifford and Matthew Wren. Both times Clarendon rebuffed, against Wren's advice, Buckingham's tentative offers of a combination against Arlington. The rejection seems to have forced Buckingham to accept instead, much against his will, an alliance with Arlington himself: Clarendon claimed

[160] Carte MSS 35, fols. 559, 568 (Brodrick to Ormonde, 23 July 1667); Carte MSS 46, fol. 510, Arlington to Ormonde, 23 July 166[7]; B.L., Althorp MSS B7, Lawrence Hyde to Burlington, 23 July 1667.

[161] B.L., Add. MSS 27872, fols. 13–14, notes of the examination on 1 July; B.L., Althorp MSS C2, Sir W. Coventry to Sir G. Savile, 2 July 1667, B6, Lady Ranelagh to Burlington, 9 July, B5, Lord Graham to Burlington, 9 July; Carte MSS 35, fol. 534.

[162] Clarendon, *Life*, II, 441–3; Pepys, *Diary*, VIII, 331, 334.

[163] *Ibid.*, VIII, 330, 342.

that the king made immense efforts to reconcile the two.[164] Sir William Coventry seems also to have taken some steps to assure himself of Buckingham's goodwill, through his nephew and the duke's ally Sir George Savile.[165] As Carteret told Pepys on 26 July, the court was in turmoil, split in rivalry between Clarendon and another – perhaps Coventry or Arlington – whom he did not name. The king, as on earlier, similar occasions, retreated from the need for firm action into vacillation and pleasure: even his coldness towards Buckingham seemed unlikely to last.[166]

With or without Buckingham's leadership and the contention of the court, the wider political discontent was daunting enough. During late June and July new causes of unrest were added to the fury over the corruption, incompetence, and (as some suspected) conspiracy which had brought defeat in the Medway. The fairly firm prospects of peace, which might have been expected to assuage popular anger, evoked more ambiguous reactions. With trade almost dead, peace and the lifting of the Dutch blockade were desperately needed;[167] but the blow to national pride was ferociously resented, and some said that the loss of naval supremacy to the Dutch would do as much damage to England's trade as continuing the war would have done. The truth was, as Pepys summarised it, 'no wise man that I meet with, when he comes to think of it, but wishes with all his heart a war; but that the king is not a man to be trusted with it'; unflattering comparisons with Cromwell and Louis XIV were common.[168]

The events of the summer had brought a complete collapse in any confidence in the administration's capacity to govern the country with any degree of competence. But an incompetent government was not necessarily a harmless one, and the rumours that were circulating indicated a fairly general belief that it was capricious as well. In 1666 the gentry had suspected corrupt court interests of striking at their economic power by promoting imports of Irish cattle, and of overbearing their declining landed wealth with the huge profits to be made from the war. By 1667 they felt they faced something even more sinister: a deliberate conspiracy to cut away both their social and their political predominance. Baptist May was quoted as urging the king 'to crush

---

[164] Clarendon, *Life*, II, 455–6; Carte MSS 35, fol. 549, Brodrick to Ormonde, 16 July 1667; Pepys, *Diary*, IX, 361.

[165] Coventry MSS 2, fol. 24, Buckingham to Coventry, 20 July 1667.

[166] Pepys, *Diary*, VIII, 355–6; Carte MSS 220, fol. 259, Ossory to Ormonde, 16 July 1667; Carte MSS 35, fol. 561, Brodrick to Ormonde, 20 July 1667, cf. fol. 522v, same to same, 2 July, and fol. 534v; Carte MSS 48, fol. 465, Ormonde to Clarendon, 20 July 1667.

[167] P.R.O., SP 29/209/67; Carte MSS 47, fol. 166.

[168] Pepys, *Diary*, VIII, 335, cf. 332, 335–6, 354–5; P.R.O., SP 29/210/121; *Hist. MSS. Comm.*, 14th report, appendix, part IX (1895), MSS of the earl of Lindsey, p. 369, Charles Bertie to Sir Thomas Osborne, 9 July 1667. B.L., Althorp MSS C5, Mr Hervey to Sir G. Savile, 18 July 1667.

the English gentlemen, saying that 300 *l.* a year was enough for any man';
Clarendon, it was claimed, had denied 'that three or four hundred country
gentlemen could either be prudent men or statesmen', and told Charles to rule
by an army. The rumours of a plan to impose military rule with the army that
was still being recruited gained wide publicity and wide acceptance. Even
some courtiers and officials, such as Thomas Povey and Sir Hugh Cholmley,
believed them.[169] The replacement of parliament by a standing army would
blow away the last remnant of that 'special relationship' by which, the gentry
believed, England should be ruled.

Political discontent took more concrete forms as well. Pepys heard that
there were many petitions being prepared to be presented to parliament, and
his cousin, Roger Pepys, told him of the pressure on M.P.s from their
countrymen to attend the coming meeting. Many arrived early in London:
Brodrick reported on 23 July that John Vaughan had already come up, having
broken his resolution never to attend parliament again.[170] The most visible
sign of unrest was perhaps the fresh outbreak of satirical libels, all of them
containing a strong anti-Clarendon sentiment; one was directed against the
Irish government, and Ormonde in particular, and was said to be backed, in
some way, by Lord Robartes and Lord Ashley; another was found by Lord
Anglesey in Whitehall; others were discovered even at the door of the king's
bedchamber.[171] There is some evidence of the energetic caballing and canvassing of the government's critics in preparation for the session: on the 28th,
Buckingham's associates, the M.P. Sir Henry Belasyse and Tom Porter, dined
at the London home of Sir Robert Carr, another 'country' leader of the
1666–7 session; and the French warned St Albans that they had intelligence
that Spanish diplomats in London were seeing English politicians 'by which
they hoped to stir humours in the parliament contrary to the king's service',
and, he told Clarendon, 'your quiet'.[172] But although the king talked of how
government members might try to withstand parliamentary fury, the court,

[169] Pepys, *Diary*, VIII, 324, cf. 332, 361, 366–7; Clarendon, *Life*, II, 469; cf. Bodl., Tanner MSS
45, fol. 202; P.R.O., SP 29/208/47, 210/102, 121.
[170] Pepys, *Diary*, VIII, 361; Carte MSS 35, fol. 568, Brodrick to Ormonde, 23 July 1667; Carte
MSS 215, fol. 359v, same to same, 30 July 1667; cf. Bodl., Tanner MSS 45, fol. 205, J.H. to
John Hobart, 1 Aug. 1667.
[171] *Hist. MSS. Comm.*, MSS of the marquess of Ormonde, new series, III (1904), 272, Edward
Vernon to Ormonde, 16 July 1667; MSS of the earl of Egmont, II (1909), 17, Robert
Bowyers to Robert Southwell, 9 July 1667; Carte MSS 35, fol. 568; Hutton, pp. 271–3 and
n. 16, p. 368; for other libels, of dates perhaps from July to December, see P.R.O., SP
29/211/132, 215/79; Bodl., MS Top Cheshire c. 6, fol. 196v, and Tanner MSS 306b,
fol. 372.
[172] Clarendon MSS 85, fol. 357, St Albans to Clarendon, 20 July 1667; Pepys, *Diary*, VIII, 363.
See also Witcombe, *Charles II and the cavalier house of commons*, p. 64, and C. Roberts,
'The impeachment of the earl of Clarendon', *Cambridge Historical Journal*, XIII (1957),
13–14, for the Imperial ambassadors' involvement in later conspiracies against Clarendon.

relying on news of peace, and hoping that the expectation of it would prevent many M.P.s from coming up to London, made few preparations for the meeting.[173]

As the houses assembled on 25 July, the government still intended to adjourn them over the weekend. To the surprise of some, there was a great attendance in the commons of 200 or 300 M.P.s, including 'all the discontented party, and indeed, the whole house seems to be no other almost'.[174] When the Speaker announced the king's pleasure for an adjournment to the following Monday, the commons' reaction caught the government completely off its guard. As Turnor asked the house to vote its adjournment, Sir Thomas Tompkins, backed by a general clamour, demanded to be heard first. Though he referred to the poverty of the country, the weight of taxes, and the diversion of revenues into the pockets of 'private persons', he spoke mainly against another grievance: since the last session, he said, the king had 'raised an army, and the people are afraid and talk aloud, that he intends to govern by a standing army'; he proposed a petition to the king for their disbandment.[175] William Garraway and Littleton supported him: only Sir William Coventry attempted to answer them. With perhaps other speeches in its favour, the petition was carried; the councillors in the house were commissioned to take it to the king. Only then did the members allow the Speaker to adjourn.[176]

The motion was soon famous, and deeply embarrassed the government. Ministers explained how the king had intended all along to disband the troops, and Carteret complained that now, when he did it, it would seem only as if it was done in compliance with the commons' wishes.[177] But this evidence of parliamentary turbulence made the definitive news of peace brought with the treaty itself by Sir John Coventry on the night of Friday, 26 July, all the more welcome.[178] The decision to dismiss parliament was confirmed: and on Monday the 29th the court took no chances of a repetition of Thursday's scene. Both houses were eager for one: they were packed, and those present

---

[173] Carte MSS 35, fol. 559, Brodrick to Ormonde, 20 July 1667; B.L., Althorp MSS B7, Lawrence Hyde to Burlington, 23 July 1667.

[174] Pepys, *Diary*, VIII, 352; B.L., Egerton MSS 2539, fol. 105, Sir John to Sir Edward Nicholas, 25 July 1667; Bodl., Tanner MSS 45, fol. 204, Roger Pepys to John Hobart, 25 July 1667.

[175] The fullest account of Tompkins's speech is in Carte MSS 35, fol. 649, ? to Ormonde, 10 Aug. 1667, although this anonymous letter's details of the ensuing debate are contradicted in places by the other accounts.

[176] *Ibid.*; Pepys, *Diary*, VIII, 352–3 (derived from the M.P.s Batten, Ford and Penn); B.L., Harleian MSS 4712, fol. 142, Brodrick to [Henry Coventry]; Bodl., Tanner MSS 45, fol. 204; Milward, *Diary*, pp. 82–3.

[177] Carte MSS 46, fol. 513v, Arlington to Ormonde, 27 July 1667; Carte MSS 47, fol. 170, Anglesey to Ormonde, 27 July 1667; Pepys, *Diary*, VIII, 355.

[178] B.L., Althorp MSS B4, Lord Clifford to Burlington, 27 July 1667; Carte MSS 35, fol. 576, Brodrick to Ormonde, 27 July 1667.

in the lords included even Bristol – he and Clarendon were said to have warily 'saluted each other'. But the Speaker timed his entry into the commons so that he had scarcely taken his place by the time that black rod was at the door to summon the house to the lords for the king's speech. As all were aware, the speech was not to open the parliament, but to close it: it was short and cold, announcing merely the peace, and denying any intention of retaining the new troops beyond its completion. With that, parliament was prorogued to the date it had originally been supposed to meet, 10 October.[179]

Whatever short-term relief the prorogation may have afforded the government, it did nothing to lift the political crisis. Public reaction to it was almost uniformly unfavourable: Pepys wrote emotionally of the frustration of the honest 'country' members who had come up all to no purpose, 'neither to serve their country, content themselves, nor receive any thanks from the king'. It was commonly believed that parliament would not be allowed to sit in October either, 'so as, if it be possible, never to have parliament more'.[180] Lord Chief Justice Bridgman told Brodrick that calling parliament in the first place had been a mistake, and proroguing it was an even greater one: now a meeting in October was unavoidable, as members, their expectations of calling the government to account disappointed, 'will be yet more exasperate, if denied to vent their petulant humours in a full assembly, and spread the infection through their respective counties'.[181]

The government in any case had little choice but to allow parliament to sit, as expected, in ten weeks' time. The energetic work of the new treasury commission exposed the full extent of the disorder of the Crown's finances: on 3 August Arlington confidentially disclosed to Ormonde that the government's debts had grown to £2 million, and expenditure was still exceeding revenue at a rate of £600,000 a year. There was scarcely any prospect of raising substantial loans. Effectively, the Crown was bankrupt.[182] The political prospects seemed little better. On 30 July Arlington wrote that, despite the peace, there 'is a war and discontent in the generality of men's minds that looks as terrible to us and I cannot see what the king can do to extinguish or pacify it'. Unless parliament could eventually clear the Crown's debt, the government would 'moulder to nothing in a short time under the weight of its

---

[179] Carte MSS 35, fol. 649; Carte MSS 215, fol. 319, Brodrick to Ormonde, 30 July 1667; Bodl., Tanner MSS 45, fol. 205, J.H. to John Hobart, 1 Aug. 1667; *Hist. MSS. Comm.*, MSS of R. R. Hastings Esq., II, 154, Ferdinando Davys to the earl of Huntingdon; Pepys, *Diary*, VIII, 360–1; Milward, *Diary*, p. 84.
[180] Pepys, *Diary*, VIII, 362; Milward, *Diary*, p. 84; *Hist. MSS. Comm.*, MSS of R. R. Hastings Esq., II, 154; Carte MSS 35, fol. 649v; cf. P.R.O., SP 29/212/4, 88, 213/95, 118, 214/80.
[181] Carte MSS 35, fol. 595, Brodrick to Ormonde, 10 Aug. 1667.
[182] Carte MSS 46, fols. 520 and 530, Arlington to Ormonde, 3 and 10 Aug. 1667; Carte MSS 47, fol. 499; Sir W. Coventry to Ormonde, 27 July 1667; B.L., Althorp MSS B6, Sir John Reresby to Burlington, 31 July 1667.

necessities though it should be attacked no other way'.[183] Somehow, the court would have to find means to make the ensuing session more amenable, or at least amenable enough.

Attempts to suppress the criticism, such as had been tried in February with the arrest of Buckingham, were no longer feasible. Buckingham was too popular to be touched. The liberty taken to criticise the government by almost everybody could scarcely be checked with the resources at its command – although there were signs that its irritation with the gossip of coffee-houses was on the verge of provoking it into action.[184] The best hope of quieting parliamentary anger lay rather in reform. On the same day that parliament was dismissed, the council appointed a committee of the treasury commissioners, the two secretaries, the lord chamberlain, Bridgewater and Anglesey, to recommend deep cuts in expenditure. As Arlington accepted, the most likely effect would be (in the short term, at least) to infuriate courtiers, themselves not incapable of doing some damage in the following session: and sure enough, the committee's investigations and suggestions were soon causing offence and annoyance to the holders of fees and perquisites.[185]

More determined approaches were made to the dissenters, as well. On 10 August Ormonde's anonymous correspondent told him a 'dam'd story' that the courtiers were prepared, in order to pacify the commons, to sacrifice the clergy; and he knew that Clarendon had been making much of the nonconformist ministers and had had several meetings with John Owen, with whom he had before discussed the future of the Church.[186] An agreement with dissenters was unlikely to pacify the present parliament. But Clarendon may have been interested in one rather as a prelude to a dissolution: by placing religion at the centre stage of a new parliament – in which he expected presbyterians to predominate – he may have been hoping to divert the anticipated turmoil. James believed in later life that although the presbyterians had approached Clarendon at some stage, the chancellor rebuffed them, thinking that their aim was to divide the duke and the king; but their discussions may have been more productive than he thought.[187] When parliament did meet, Sir Robert Atkins and Colonel Birch were the sponsors of a bill for com-

---

[183] Carte MSS 46, fols. 516–17, Arlington to Ormonde, 30 July 1667.
[184] See the comment in the newsletter of 30 July, *Hist. MSS. Comm.*, Le Fleming MSS, p. 52; cf. P.R.O., SP 29/211/28; Carte MSS 35, fol. 634, Lord Carlingford to Ormonde, 13 Aug. 1667, and fol. 649; Pepys, *Diary*, VIII, 362.
[185] P.R.O., PC 2/59, fol. 262; Carte MSS 46, fol. 516v, Arlington to Ormonde, 30 July 1667; Pepys, *Diary*, VIII, 394–5; Carte MSS 35, fol. 595v. For the committee's proceedings, see Pepys, *Diary*, VIII, 378, 391–2, and 391, n. 4; Carte MSS 35, fols. 595v, 624, 632 (Brodrick to Ormonde, 3, 10 and 13 Aug. 1667) and 628 (Clifford to Ormonde, 13 Aug. 1667); Carte MSS 220, fols. 263, 280, Ossory to Ormonde, 10 Aug., 3 Sept. 1667; Clarendon, *Life*, II, 533. The committee's report is at B.L., Egerton MSS 2543, fols. 129–34.
[186] Carte MSS 35, fols. 649–50.   [187] Clarke, *Life of James the Second*, I, 431–2.

prehension – and both men were among Clarendon's strongest defenders in the proceedings against him in October and November, as Baxter commented.[188] At the beginning of August, Sheldon was deeply concerned for the Church in the forthcoming session; and by the end of September he was greatly disenchanted with the chancellor.[189]

Somehow, too, the disputes of the court had to be rendered harmless: with ministers eager to avoid becoming the victims of parliamentary attack and royal pusillanimity, there seemed little prospect that they would present a tranquil, united front against the forthcoming onslaught. One conflict, between Clarendon and Coventry, had the potential to be peculiarly damaging. Coventry complained of Clarendon that he was 'so great at the council-board and in the administration of matters, there was no room for anybody to propose any remedy to what was amiss or to compass anything, though never so good for the kingdom, unless approved of by the chancellor'. Yet Coventry was rather similar himself: to Pepys's admiration, and Clarendon's annoyance, he was as dominant, and domineering, as the chancellor.[190] It was unlikely that two such personalities could co-exist without at least a very close personal alliance. Instead, they had become rivals in policy and power: most of the clashes of policy which had occurred over the past year or so were associated with disagreements between them. As with the rivalry of Bennet and Clarendon in 1662–3, the government was in danger of being crippled by the power-struggles of its ministers.

Ministerial relations were even more embittered by a recognition that any resolution of the crisis would involve some sacrifices to popular opinion. Mordaunt covered himself shortly after the parliament was dismissed by taking out a pardon under the Great Seal.[191] In any case, it seemed that now the sacrifices required would have to be altogether more distinguished. According to Clarendon, at the prorogation Coventry was freely saying that the chancellor would have to go.[192] There were rumours of impeachments on all sides: it was said that had parliament sat longer, charges would have been prepared against Clarendon, Arlington, Carteret, and Coventry.[193] A judicious dismissal or two, anticipating the action that parliament would inevitably take in October, might take some of the heat out of both popular and parliamentary unrest.

[188] Thomas, 'Comprehension and indulgence', pp. 196–8; Sylvester (ed.), *Reliquianae Baxterianae*, part III, pp. 20–1.
[189] Carte MSS 45, fols. 222, 228, 232, Sheldon to Ormonde, 27 Aug., 28 Sept., 29 Oct. 1667; Bodl., MSS Add. C. 308, fol. 97v, Sheldon to the bishop of St David's, 3 Aug. 1667.
[190] Pepys, *Diary*, VIII, 415, cf. 347–8; Clarendon, *Life*, II, 190–1; cf. Carte MSS 35, fol. 502v, Brodrick to Ormonde, 29 June 1667.
[191] Carte MSS 35, fol. 595.
[192] Clarendon, *Life*, II, 430.   [193] Carte MSS 35, fols. 649–50.

But despite the pressure from Clarendon's court rivals for his removal, the first moves which led to his dismissal were, ironically, made by his friends. The year 1667 had been one of immense personal loss for the chancellor. The death of his friend, Southampton, for him a personification of all the old aristocratic virtues, had been followed by those of his two royal grandchildren, the two sons of the duke and duchess of York, and of his wife. Her death afflicted him deeply: it was, he admitted, 'so sudden, unexpected and irreparable a loss that he had not courage to support'.[194] Visitors found him depressed and dejected.[195] One of his first reactions to his bereavement was to complain freely of the burden of his office, and express a desire to retire from political life: his son-in-law, York, took him at his word, and Coventry, seeing an ideal opportunity to dispense of the chancellor with the least possible fuss, encouraged him and the king to persuade Clarendon to resign.[196] The king was, for the moment, easily convinced that Clarendon's resignation would remove much of the odium attached to the government. Probably in the week between the countess of Clarendon's funeral on 17 August and the 24th, Charles sent York to Clarendon to suggest that his resignation before the beginning of the next session would both pull the teeth of the attack, and save Clarendon himself. The chancellor had clearly not intended his effusions of grief to be taken too literally: he was taken aback and told York he was perfectly confident of his ability to defend himself from whatever charges were levelled against him. In any case, he could not afford to retire: in November he claimed that his debts, chiefly occasioned by the building of Clarendon house in Piccadilly, amounted to £23,000 or £24,000, and his estate after these had been paid would not yield £2,000 a year. It was also obvious that he would be better able to resist any charges in the forthcoming session as a minister than as an ex-minister to whom nobody was beholden. Besides, resignation would seem like an admission of responsibility for the disaster – an admission which Clarendon, 'too proud of a good conscience', absolutely refused to make. He requested an interview with the king.[197] As he pressed the king to keep him on, his enemies lobbied furiously for his dismissal. Castlemaine and Baptist May were said to be hectoring the king to remove him; the duke of York dismissed Henry Brouncker from his own service for demanding the same thing; Arlington was cautiously arguing

---

[194] Clarendon, *Life*, II, 443–4; Lister, *Life of Clarendon*, II, 485, n.; see the letters of Lawrence Hyde and Lady Ranelagh in B.L., Althorp MSS B6 and B7.

[195] Carte MSS 35, fol. 657, Carlingford to Ormonde, 24 Aug, 1667; Carte MSS 217, fol. 402, Anglesey to Ormonde, 24 Aug. 1667.

[196] This is roughly what Pepys and others made of the affair, and it seems confirmed by Coventry's central role in it: Pepys, *Diary*, VIII, 410, 416, 506, IX, 476; cf. B.L., Althorp MSS C1, Charles Bates to Sir G. Savile, 27 Aug. 1667.

[197] Clarendon, *Life*, II, 445–6, 490; cf. the schedule of debts in Lister, *Life of Clarendon*, III, 535–40.

that it would be best both for the chancellor himself and for the government's business if he were now to go.[198] They were matched by Clarendon's friends. York tried to make up for the damage he had already done by urging Charles to retain him; his wife, the duchess, joined in pleading for her father; Sheldon, the duke of Albemarle, and even, according to Sir Richard Ford, Buckingham (who had still made no reconciliation with Arlington) joined in his defence.[199]

Charles was further swayed by Clarendon himself in an interview he had with the king and James on the morning of the 26th. The king, the chancellor argued, should never show himself to be daunted by the fear of parliament. That evening the rumour was that the king had now decided against his removal: Arlington was dismayed; Anglesey complained that Charles's irresolution was no use to anybody. By the 29th Carteret, one of Clarendon's greatest allies, was hoping the whole affair would blow over. Then suddenly, the king made up his mind: on the evening of 30 August he sent Secretary Morrice to Clarendon to demand the Seals.[200]

However widely expected, Clarendon's fall was still a shock: the chancellor had been the most prominent feature of the English political landscape for so long that it was difficult to imagine the government without him. The ostensible reason for his removal, that it might ease the king's difficulties in parliament, was not a bad one, even if it later became obvious that it merely created new problems. But the real reasons lay deeper. The king mentioned Coventry's argument, that Clarendon's dominance in the council prevented him from receiving other advice;[201] but more deeply still, Clarendon went finally because the king had been roused into a jealousy for the preservation of his own power and authority. Charles was said to have complained rather feebly that his chancellor 'would not let him speak himself in council'.[202] Some said that Charles was furious with Clarendon for his part in preserving the virtue of Frances Stuart, the object of his most recent desire, by marrying her off to the duke of Richmond. Lauderdale wrote at the time that he had never seen Charles 'more offended than he is at the duke and all concerned'.[203] But the marriage had taken place some months before; and if it had anything to do with the dismissal, it was probably merely that it was another instance of the way Clarendon thwarted the king's will and crossed his wishes. For a while, Clarendon, by pointing out that by making so

[198] Pepys, *Diary*, VIII, 404, 406, 434, 525; Clarendon, *Life*, II, 451; Carte MSS 46, fol. 540, Arlington to Ormonde, 27 Aug. 1667.
[199] Clarendon, *Life*, II, 446; Carte MSS 46, fol. 540; Pepys, *Diary*, VIII, 402.
[200] Clarendon, *Life*, II, 446–55; Pepys, *Diary*, VIII, 401–2, 406, 409–10; Carte MSS 35, fol. 657, 690 (Brodrick to Ormonde, 31 Aug. 1667); Carte MSS 217, fol. 402; Carte MSS 46, fol. 540v.
[201] B.L., Althorp MSS C2, Sir William Coventry to Savile, 3 Sept. 1667.
[202] Pepys, *Diary*, VIII, 427.
[203] National Library of Scotland, MSS 7023, fol. 30, Lauderdale to Tweeddale, 2 April 1667.

momentous a concession to parliament he was risking the loss of his entire authority, had given him cause to reconsider. Ultimately, however, it was Clarendon's visible obstruction of his will that was more irritating than parliament's – at present – theoretical obstruction. As Morrice brought the purse containing the Seals back to Whitehall, 'under his arm like a bagpipe', it seemed that a new age had arrived: 'oh it would do your heart good to see what a new world we have here and how bravely all the king's business goes on', enthused Lauderdale to Tweeddale, two weeks later; 'now we have no green room, all is fairly treated in council, and now the king is the king himself'.[204]

---

[204] *Ibid.*, fol. 85, same to same, 31 Aug. 1667, and MS 3136, fol. 23, same to same, 14 Sept. 1667.

12

Conclusion

Clarendon's dismissal was not, of course, the end of the crisis: his impeachment by parliament when it met in October and the struggle for power which followed his downfall for a long time frustrated the government's efforts to resolve it. But it was the end of an administration and of a policy. In his years in power, Clarendon had sought the Crown's military, constitutional, and financial security within a respect for the law, liberty, and property which, he believed, were the foundations of stability. His and their purpose, he told the Cavalier Parliament in 1661, was to complete the work of the Convention which had invited the king home:

It will be your glory so to establish him in his power and greatness, so as to annex monarchy to the nation, that he and his posterity shall be never again forced to be abroad, that they be invited home, nor in danger to be restored; so to rivet monarchy to the hearts, and to the understandings of all men, that no man may ever presume to conspire against it.[1]

Clarendon's object was neither the construction of a constitutional compromise, nor the rigid recreation of the pre-War system of government. Rather it was the restoration of stability and unity to the country by the reconstruction of a strong monarchy beside a powerful law.

These preoccupations are visible in the legislative programme of 1661–5. The government attempted to reduce the privileges and autonomy of corporations and the power and importance of parliament where it felt these had been inflated above their ancient extent. It sought security through a small army, the suppression of dissidence through control over the press, curbs on political demonstrations, and a new definition of treason. But Clarendon constantly defended the sanctity of the law – particularly against those royalists anxiously trying to recover their lands and their fortunes; no attempt was made to repeal the acts which had outlawed methods of taxation that, under Charles I, had been seen as an arbitrary threat to the peaceful possession of private property; and the restoration of Star Chamber and the

[1] *Parliamentary history*, IV, 199.

prerogative courts, whose procedures and behaviour had seemed to call into question the rights and liberties of the individual, were considered only with the utmost caution and hesitancy. Even the way in which Clarendon set about managing parliament indicated his sensitivity to the need to avoid offending its members' sensibilities. Unobtrusively and quietly, he tried to guide them to his favoured conclusion, attempting to prevent any imputation of interfering with parliamentary privileges and liberties – while at the same time, seeking to curb parliament's potency.

The war – which Clarendon tried hard to avert – did much to ruin his plans. For its heavy and urgent financial demands once more extended the importance of parliament, the only body which might supply them, and put paid to any further progress on the repair of the Crown's ordinary revenue or the reconstruction of its authority. And the economic crisis to which it contributed did much to produce the bitter political crisis of 1667.

The expulsion of Clarendon and his assumptions from the centre of affairs left a vacuum both of power – which the king's other ministers spent years struggling to fill – and of policy. It was the beginning of a period dominated by different concerns: by Charles's and James's more determined efforts to obtain toleration for catholics; by Charles's obscure and bizarre negotiations with France; and by his declining resolve to abide by the laws and the customs of the constitution. Following English politics from his exile in France, Clarendon was dismayed by the course of events. The Declaration of Indulgence, published in March 1672, showed Charles now openly flouting the interpretation of the law that had triumphed in 1663: the renewal of war against the Dutch at the same time threatened all the peace and security that Clarendon had worked to achieve: the Stop of the exchequer demonstrated how little the government was prepared to keep to its own rules when it no longer suited it: and Charles's liaison with a new, French mistress indicated that the court itself had mended none of its ways. In May 1673 Clarendon completed his *Brief view and survey* of *Leviathan*. In it, he pointedly appealed to princes in general – and perhaps to its dedicatee, Charles II, in particular – that it was high time that the sovereign power should

declare, that it doth not approve those doctrines, which may lessen the affections and tenderness of princes towards their subjects, and even their reverence to God himself, if they thought that they could change religion, and suppress the Scripture it self; and that their power over their subjects is so absolute that they give them all that they do not take from them; and property is but a word of no signification, and lessens the duty and obedience of subjects, and makes them less love the constitution of the government they live under; which may prove so destructive to them, if they have a temptation from their passions or their appetite to exercise the authority they justly have.[2]

---

[2] Clarendon, *A brief view and survey*, p. 63; cf. Clarendon MSS 87, fols. 185–6, Clarendon to Cornbury, 7/17 March 1674, for Cornbury's doubts about the book's publication.

If the crisis of 1667 had made Charles II and his ministers more anxious to free themselves of irritating parliamentary oversight – and less fastidious about how they tried to achieve it – it may have made others rather more anxious to strengthen it. That kings were never more powerful than when in harmony with their subjects, and that the king was never more absolute than when he sat with his lords and his commons in parliament, were commonplaces of English, if not European, political rhetoric. But when such rhetoric was used (as Sir William Temple used it in September 1667, attributing the thought to some people at Brussels) to imply that the king ought 'to pursue what he finds the parliament judge to be the common interest of his kingdom', the commonplace was being taken a good deal further.[3] Vaughan, Littleton, Temple, and others had spent much of the 1660s in an (admittedly futile) attempt to retain limitations placed on the Crown in the early 1640s; to establish greater parliamentary oversight of the government and (more successfully) to limit what they believed to be royal encroachments on the subjects' liberties. From very early in the 1660s, there had been murmurings that the court was seeking to raise a large standing army and the king wanted to rule by his arbitrary power alone. Such sentiments were expressed as yet by only a few; and Vaughan and his associates formed only a minority in the commons – albeit an influential one. But by 1667 their influence had expanded, and those sentiments were much more readily entertained. Remarks such as Temple's might have suggested an ultimate hope that the king, in his own phrase, would become a mere doge of Venice; an object of dignity and ceremony, but no power. Whatever other lessons may have been drawn from the crisis of 1667, one of the most obvious was that which had been drawn in 1663 by Lord Peterborough: there was no longer any room for limitations or 'mixed monarchy'. The choice was between a sovereign parliament, or a truly sovereign king.

That was not to say, of course, that those conclusions were necessarily correct: the experience of the Civil War so occupied the minds of politicians that the slightest signs of parliamentary disagreement tended to invite morbid parallels with 1641 from all but the most phlegmatic. Given those expectations, it was indeed difficult for a properly co-operative relationship to be re-established: but that one could be re-established seemed clear from the relatively tranquil sessions of 1661–2, the early years of the war, and from the remarkable harmony of that of 1670. Even in the session of 1666–7, dissatisfaction with the government among most M.P.s was far from fundamental. After the court's surrender on the cherished project of a very vocal majority of either house – the Irish Cattle Bill – opposition on other matters collapsed: the government secured its supply and suppressed all those other matters with

[3] Quoted in Haley, *An English diplomat*, p. 139.

which 'country' leaders had been constantly vexing it. And the part of courtiers themselves in causing the troubles of 1666–7, as those of 1663, was widely acknowledged. Half of the government's problems stemmed from Charles's inability to put his own house in order. Opinions such as Vaughan's could arouse interest, and occasionally persuade some into supporting him and his allies. During the 1670s they were to become considerably more influential. For the moment, however, they achieved real prominence only when M.P.s had already been irritated by actions of the government which hurt them more immediately.

Among the issues which most effectively irritated them was religion: time and again, M.P.s rejected the government's efforts to moderate the harsh ecclesiastical settlement they seemed to prefer. Yet their hostility towards nonconformity was not uncomplicatedly the product either of the gentry's devotion to the anglican liturgy and hierarchy, or of their recognition of the Church of England's role in supporting their own hegemony. A persuasive and influential minority did, indeed, have the determination to protect the Church from presbyterian dilution and from any more radical infringement of its monopoly of the country's religious life. For a larger proportion of M.P.s, that aim was far from paramount. Yet the Church lobby possessed the political standing to lead parliament into the persecution of dissent, and the arguments to convince its members of its necessity, playing on their fears of renewed civil strife and social insubordination. However uncomfortable many M.P.s may have felt about countenancing religious persecution, such arguments were enough to carry a majority in favour of the strongest measures. Yet none was exclusively religious in tone.

For it was neither constitutional politics nor religion that chiefly occupied the minds of most members of this cavalier and anglican parliament. What concerned them most deeply was rather their sense of decline. Whichever way they looked, M.P.s and the gentry from whose ranks they came felt they saw cause to fear a decline of their power, their influence and their wealth – even to fear for their lives. Falling prices, and (for royalists) the havoc wreaked in their estates by punitive measures after the war, threatened their incomes. As these decayed, so too did their influence. Rich wartime profiteers – probably presbyterians – and corrupt courtiers elbowed them away from royal favour and preferment, the means to restore their fortunes; they fed off the country gentry, draining them of strength as they increased their own. As the gentry's wealth decayed, and their influence in Whitehall declined, so too did their power in their communities: the common people, they felt, paid them less respect and demanded more wages. Most disturbing of all was the radicalism of the sectaries, from whom some feared for their lives. All these discontentments and resentments were, to some extent, related to religion: the sectary and the presbyterian manifested, in flesh and blood, the less tangible subversion of the gentry's position – on the one hand by direct violence, on the other by a more insidious corruption.

What the gentry felt they needed, above all, was a stability in which they could restore their estates and rebuild their influence. If they sought to establish their power, it was only to preserve, not to extend, their position. They had looked forward, happily, to the restoration of the monarchy and all that had gone with it: the harmonious co-operation of Crown and gentry for their mutual benefit. It was not long before they found that their idea of stability did not necessarily agree with the court's. They fended off attempts to replace the militia with a standing army; they were unimpressed by plans to reduce local autonomy; and they were appalled by measures to reduce the ecclesiastical laws to the prerogative of the king. In 1667, all their worries rose rapidly to the surface. The war and an agricultural crisis had accelerated their decline and shown up the corruptions of the City and the court, a court so viciously perverted that it had rather rule by an army than face justice in parliament. Those who had fought for the king, no less than those who had fought for parliament, were incensed. Far from restoring the old relationship of the Crown and the gentry, and far from conforming the alliance of the Crown and the royalists, the court seemed intend on ignoring and insulting them. The year 1667 appeared to mark not just the end of an administration, or of a policy, but also the limits to the reconstruction of the old regime.

APPENDIX

COMMITTEE MEMBERS ON ECCLESIASTICAL BILLS,
1661–1665

The committees included for this list of M.P.s most frequently appointed for committees on ecclesiastical legislation, with the dates of their appointment are: Uniformity Bill (3 July 1661), Corporation Bill (20 June 1661), Commissioners for Ecclesiastical Causes (Church Courts) Bill (9 July 1661), Ecclesiastical Jurisdiction (7 June 1661), Conventicles (29 April 1663), relief from the Act of Uniformity (30 June 1663), committee to consider the Act of Uniformity and the Declaration of Indulgence (19 Feb. 1663), Conventicles (2 April 1664), Five Mile Bill (17 Oct. 1665). Also included are members involved in the management of conferences etc., on the bill for confirming the Convention's Ministers Act (4, 18 Feb., etc., 1662).

M.P.S APPOINTED TO

9 committees: Milward, R.
8 committees: Berkenhead; Crouch; Lord Fanshaw.
7 committees: Atkins; Clifford; Rinch, H.; Goodrick, J.; Holte; Knight, J.; Talbot, J.
6 committees: [Ashburnham, John];[1] Burwell; [Churchill, W.]; Duncombe; Goodrick, F.; Harbord, C.; Heath, J.; Kelyng; Lake; [Montagu, W.]; [Vaughan, J.]; Warwick.
5 committees: Allen; Bramston; Bruce; Charlton; [Coventry, H.]; Gawdy; Gower; Holland; Kirkby; Legge; Littleton; Lowther, W.; Musgrave, P.; Strangwayes, G.; Temple; [Throckmorton, B.]; Thurland, Walpole; [Wyndham, Hugh]; Yorke, W.

---

[1] Names in square brackets indicate that there is a possibility of confusion with other M.P.s of the same surname. In these cases, the initial or Christian name is that of the man to whom the majority of the references seem most likely to refer.

SELECT BIBLIOGRAPHY

This bibliography is intended primarily as a guide to the literature on politics in the 1660s and as an index to short titles used in the text. All manuscript and primary sources are listed: but secondary works cited for comparative purposes are not, unless frequently referred to.

MANUSCRIPT SOURCES

Bodleian Library, Oxford
MSS Add. C. 302, 303, 305, 308 (Sheldon correspondence)
Carte MSS 31–6, 44–9, 217, 221, 222, 232 (Ormonde's papers)
   73, 75 (Sandwich papers)
   76, 77 (Huntingdon papers)
   81 (Wharton's papers)
   130 (Somerset papers)
Clarendon MSS 74–85, 87, 92, 106, 107, 109
MS Eng. Hist. b. 205 (Warner MSS), b. 212 (Clarendon's lieutenancy correspondence), e. 87 (Prose satire)
MS Eng. Lett. c. 210 (Yelverton–Parker correspondence)
MS North c. 10 (North family correspondence)
MS Top Cheshire c. 6 (Miscellaneous papers)
Rawlinson MSS A 130 (Henchman diary), D 922 (Parliamentary papers)
Rawlinson MSS Letters 107 (Miscellaneous letters), 109 (Letters to John Thornton)
Smith MSS 29 (Peirce's correspondence)
Tanner MSS 45, 47, 48, 49 (Miscellaneous Sancroft, etc., papers), 306b (Miscellaneous papers)
   239 (Holland's speeches)

Bristol University Library
Bull of Shapwick MSS

British Library, London
Althorp MSS A30, B4, B6, B7, C1, C2, C6

Additional MSS
10116–17 (Rugge's Diurnal)
11043 (Scudamore papers)
11053 (Papers concerning Herefordshire)

11324 (West country families' papers)
12510 (Miscellaneous papers)
15857 (Evelyn papers)
18674 (Exchequer accounts)
18979 (Fairfax correspondence)
21922 (Letter book of Sir R. Norton)
22919–20 (Correspondence of Sir G. Downing)
23119–20 (Lauderdale papers)
23215 (Correspondence of Lord Conway)
27382 (Miscellaneous papers)
27447 (Paston correspondence)
27531 (Diary of the countess of Warwick)
27872 (Papers concerning the duke of Buckingham)
28053 (Osborne correspondence)
32094 (Malet papers)
32500 (North correspondence)
34217 (Miscellaneous papers)
35865 (Miscellaneous papers)
36988 (Paston correspondence)
37425 (Miscellaneous papers)
37820 (Council minutes of Sir E. Nicholas)
38015 (Correspondence of Sir R. Southwell)
41654 (Townshend papers)
45538 (Papers of Philip Henry)
61483 (Digby papers)

Egerton MSS
627 (Relation d'Angleterre)
2043 (Reymes's diary)
2537, 2539 and 2543 (Papers of Sir E. Nicholas)
2717 (Gawdy correspondence)
2979 (Heath papers)

Harleian MSS
1223 (Miscellaneous financial papers)
1509 (Proceedings of the commissioners for prizes)
1579 (Miscellaneous papers)
2043 (R. Holmes's historical collections)
4712 (Miscellaneous correspondence)
6277 (Parliamentary, etc., accounts)
7001 (Miscellaneous correspondence)

Lansdowne MSS
525 (Prynne's parliamentary collections)
805 (Miscellaneous collection)
841 (Miscellaneous papers)
1236 (Letters of Charles II)

Loan MSS
29 (Portland MSS)
57 (Bathurst MSS)

Microfilm, etc.
M455 (Stationers' Company MSS)
M636 (Verney MSS)
RP 409 (Carlingford papers)

Sloane MSS
3828 (Miscellaneous papers)
4107 (Miscellaneous papers)

Stowe MSS
744 (Dering papers)
180 (Papers of Sir R. Temple)
302–3 (Miscellaneous political papers)
304 (Papers of Sir R. Temple)

Essex Record Office, Chelmsford
Bramston MSS

Glasgow University Library
MSS T.3.11 (Hyde papers)

Gloucestershire Record Office, Gloucester
Ducie MSS
Badminton MSS

Hereford and Worcester Record Office, Worcester
Pakington MSS (microfilm)

Hertfordshire Record Office, Hertford
Ashridge Collection
Verulam MSS

House of Lords Record Office, London
Braye MSS
House of Lords Committee Minute Books
House of Lords Main Papers
House of Lords Manuscript Minutes
House of Lords Parchment Collection

Kent Archives Office, Maidstone
U269 (Sackville MSS)

Lambeth Palace Library, London
MS 1394 (Twysden letter book)

Leeds Archive Department
Archives of the earl of Mexborough

Leicestershire Record Office, Leicester
Finch MSS

Longleat House, Warminster, Wiltshire
Coventry MSS
Thynne MSS

National Library of Scotland, Edinburgh
MSS 3136, 7023

Northamptonshire Record Office, Northampton
Isham MSS

Nottinghamshire Record Office, Nottingham
Savile of Rufford MSS

Nottingham University Library
Portland Collection, Cavendish MSS
Galway MSS

Pepys Library, Magdalene College, Cambridge
MS 2266

Public Record Office, London
30/24 (Shaftesbury MSS)
PC 2/55–9 (Privy Council Registers)
PRO 31/3 (Transcripts of French diplomatic correspondence relating to England)
SP 29 (State Papers, Charles II)
SP 44 (State Papers, letter books)

Sheffield Central Library
Wilson of Bromhead MSS

West Sussex Record Office, Chichester
Wiston MSS
Orrery papers

Yorkshire Archaeological Society, Leeds
Slingsby MSS, DD 56, 149

PRINTED PRIMARY SOURCES

A—, F. *A letter from a gentleman in Grayes Inn, to a justice of the peace in the country, explaining the Act of Uniformity in that part which doth concern unlicensed preachers*, no place or date of publication [1662]

Arber, E. (ed.) *A transcript of the registers of the company of stationers of London, 1554–1640*, 5 vols., London, 1875–94

Aubrey, John, *'Brief lives', chiefly of contemporaries, set down by John Aubrey between the years 1669 and 1696*, ed. A. Clark, 2 vols., Oxford, 1898

Bagot, William Lord. *Memorials of the Bagot family*, Blithfield, 1824

The correspondence of Isaac Basire, ed. W. N. Darnell, London, 1831

Reliquiae Baxterianae: or Mr Richard Baxter's narrative of the most memorable passages of his life and times, ed. M. Sylvester, London, 1696

Beddard, R. A. (ed.) 'An unpublished memoir of Archbishop Sheldon', *Bodleian Library Record*, X (1976–82)

B[ellamy], T[homas]. *Philanax Anglicus: or a Christian caveat for all kings, princes and prelates, how they entrust a sort of pretended protestants of integrity, or suffer them to commix with their respective Governments*, London, 1662

Berkenhead, Sir John. *Cabala, or an impartial account of the nonconformists' private designes*, London, 1663

The autobiography of Sir John Bramston, ed. Lord Braybrooke, Camden Society, old series, XXXII (1845)

Brown, T. (ed.) *Miscellanea aulica: or, a collection of state Treaties, never before publish'd*, London, 1702

Browning, A. (ed.) *English historical documents, 1660–1714*, London, 1953

Bruce, Thomas, earl of Ailesbury. *Memoirs, written by himself*, Publications of the Roxburghe Club, 2 vols., London, 1890

Burnet, Gilbert. *Burnet's history of my own time*, ed. O.Airy, 2 vols., Oxford, 1897–1900

A supplement to Burnet's history of my own time, ed. H. C. Foxcroft, Oxford, 1902

The genuine remains in verse and prose of Mr Samuel Butler, author of Hudibras, ed. R. Thyer, 2 vols., London, 1759

Calamy, Edmund. *A (farewell) sermon preached at Aldermanbury Church Dec. 28 1662*, London, 1662

Calendar of the Clarendon state papers preserved in the Bodleian Library, ed. O. Ogle, W. H. Bliss, W. D. Macray, and F. J. Routledge, 5 vols., Oxford, 1869–1970

Calendar of the proceedings of the committee for compounding, ed. M. A. E. Green, London, 1889–92

Calendar of state papers, domestic series, of the reign of Charles II, ed. M. A. E. Green, F. H. Blackburne Daniel, and F. Bickley, 28 vols., London, 1860–1939

Calendar of state papers and manuscripts relating to English affairs, existing in the archives and collections of Venice, ed. R. Brown, London, 1864–

Calendar of treasury books, 1660– , preserved in the Public Record Office, ed. W. A. Shaw, London, 1904–

Cardwell, E. *A history of conferences and other proceedings connected with the revision of the Book of Common Prayer*, 3rd edn, Oxford, 1849

Cavendish, Margaret, duchess of Newcastle. *The life of William Cavendish, duke of Newcastle to which is added the true relation of my birth, breeding, and life*, ed. C. H. Firth, London, 1886

Chamberlain, Edward. *The late war parallel'd, or a brief relation of the five years civil wars of Henry the third*, London, 1660

Clarke, J. S. *The life of James the Second, king of England, etc., collected out of memoirs writ of his own hand*, 2 vols., London, 1816

Cobbett, W. and Wright, J. *The parliamentary history of England, from the earliest period to 1803*, 36 vols., London, 1806–20

Coke, Roger. *Justice vindicated from the false fucus put upon it, by Thomas White, gent, Mr Thomas Hobbes, and Hugo Grotius*, London, 1660

Collection des lettres et mémoires trouvés dans les porte-feuilles du Maréchal du Turenne, ed. P. H. de Grimoard, 2 vols., Paris, 1782

A Collection of scarce and valuable tracts ... selected from ... public as well as private libraries, particularly that of the late Lord Somers, ed. W. Scott, 2nd edn, 13 vols., London, 1809–15

Collins, Arthur (ed.) *Letters and memorials of state*, 2 vols., London, 1746

[Constantine, William]. *The reader's speech of the Middle Temple at the entrance into his reading, Febr. 29, 1663/4*, London, 1664

Corker, J. *Stafford's memoires*, London, 1681

The correspondence of John Cosin: with other papers, part II, ed. G. Ornsby, Surtees Society, LV (1872)

The poems and fables of John Dryden, ed. J. Kinsley, Oxford, 1970

Dunn, R. M. (ed.) *Norfolk Lieutenancy Journal 1660–76*, Norfolk Record Society, XLV (1977)

The correspondence of Bishop Brian Duppa and Sir Justinian Isham, ed. Sir Gyles Isham, Northamptonshire Record Society, XVII (1955)

The Diary of John Evelyn, ed. E. S. de Beer, 5 vols., Oxford, 1955

Firth, C. H. and Rait, S. R. (eds.) *Acts and ordinances of the Interregnum*, 3 vols., London, 1911

G—, A. *Some few questions concerning the Oath of Allegiance propos'd by a catholic gentleman in a letter to a person of learning and honour*, London, 1661

Gauden, John. *A discourse concerning publick oaths*, London, 1662

Grey, Anchitell. *Debates of the house of commons from the year 1667 to the year 1694*, 12 vols., London, 1763

H—, J. *A letter from a person of quality to a principal peer of the realm, now sitting in parliament occasioned by the present debate upon penal laws*, London, 1661

Hakewill, W. *The manner how statutes are enacted in parliament by passing of bills*, London, 1670

Memoirs of Count Grammont by Anthony Hamilton, ed. Sir Walter Scott, London, 1905

The political works of James Harrington, ed. J. G. A. Pocock, Cambridge, 1977

Heath, James. *The glories and magnificent triumphs of the blessed restitution of his sacred majesty K. Charles II*, London, 1662

A new book of loyal English martyrs and confessors, London, [1663]

H[eylyn], P[eter]. *The stumbling block of disobedience and rebellion cunningly laid by Calvin in the subject's way, discovered, censured and removed*, London, 1658

Historical Manuscripts Commission. 4th report part I, appendix, De La Warr MSS

5th report (1876) part I, appendix, MSS of the duke of Sutherland

6th report (1877) part I, appendix, MSS of Sir H. Ingilby and Sir R. Graham

8th report (1881) part I, appendix, MSS of the Corporation of Trinity House

10th report appendix, part IV (1885), MSS of Stanley Leighton, M.P.

11th report appendix, part V (1887), MSS of the earl of Dartmouth

12th report appendix, part V (1889), MSS of the duke of Rutland, vol. II

12th report appendix, part VII (1890), MSS of S. H. Le Fleming

12th report appendix, part IX (1891), MSS of the duke of Beaufort

14th report appendix, part IX (1895), MSS of the earl of Lindsey

15th report appendix, part VII (1898), MSS of the marquess of Ailesbury and the duke of Somerset

MSS of A. G. Finch Esq., 4 vols. (1913–65)

MSS of R. R. Hastings Esq., 4 vols (1928–47)

MSS of J. M. Heathcote Esq (1899)

MSS of the earl of Verulam (1906)

MSS of the marquess of Ormonde, K.P., new series, 8 vols. (1902–20)

MSS in various collections, 8 vols. (1901–13)

MSS of the viscount de L'Isle at Penshurst, 6 vols. (1925–66)

The history and proceedings of the house of commons, from the Restoration to the present time, 13 vols., London, 1742–3

The history and proceedings of the house of lords, from the Restoration to the present time, 8 vols., London, 1742–3

Hobbes, Thomas. *Leviathan*, ed. C. B. Macpherson, Harmondsworth, 1968

Howard, Edward. *The change of crowns*, ed. F. R. Boas, London, 1949

Howard, Sir Robert. *Five new plays*, London, 1700

  The great favourite, or, the duke of Lerma, London, 1668

An humble representation of the sad condition of many of the king's party, [London], 1661

Hyde, Edward, first earl of Clarendon, *A brief view and survey of the dangerous and pernicious errors to church and state in Mr. Hobbes's book, entitled Leviathan*, Oxford, 1676

  The history of the Rebellion and Civil Wars in England, ed. W. D. Macray, 6 vols., Oxford, 1888

  The life of Edward earl of Clarendon, 2 vols., Oxford, 1857

  Religion and policy, and the countenance and assistance each should give the other, 2 vols., Oxford, 1811

Hutchinson, Lucy. *Memoirs of the life of Colonel Hutchinson*, ed. J. Sutherland, London, 1973

Ichabod: or five groans of the Church: prudently foreseeing, and passionately bewailing, her second fall, London, 1663

The Intelligencer, London, 1663–6

Jones, J. R. (ed.) 'Court dependents in 1664', *Bulletin of the Institute of Historical Research*, XXXIV (1961), 81–91

The diary of Ralph Josselin, ed. A. Macfarlane, British Academy Records of Social and Economic History, new series, III, London, 1976

Journals of the house of commons, London, 1742–

Journals of the house of lords, London, 1767–

Kidson, R. M. (ed.) 'The gentry of Staffordshire', and 'Active parliamentarians during the Civil War', in *Collections for a history of Staffordshire*, Staffordshire Record Society, 4th series, II (1958)

Lake, Sir Edward. *Memoranda: touching the oath ex officio, pretended self-accusation and canonical purgation*, London, 1662

The Lauderdale papers, ed. O. Airy, vol. I, Camden Society, new series, XXXIV (1884)

L'Estrange, Roger. *A caveat to the cavaliers: or an antidote against mistaken cordials: dedicated to the author of a cordial for the cavaliers*, London, 1661

  Considerations and proposals in order to the regulation of the press: together with diverse instances of treasonous, and seditious pamphlets, proving the necessity thereof, London, 1663

  A memento: directed to all those that truly reverence the memory of King Charles the Martyr . . . the first part, London, 1662

  A modest plea both for the caveat, and the author of it, London, 1661

A lively pourtraict of our new-cavaliers, commonly called presbyterians, clearly shewing that his Majesty came in not upon their account. In a compendious narrative of our late Revolutions, London, 1661

Lloyd, David. *Memoirs of the lives, actions, sufferings and deaths of those noble, reverend, and excellent personages, that suffered*, London, 1668

John Locke: Two tracts on government, ed. P. Abrams, Cambridge, 1967
The London Gazette, London, 1666–
Lowther family estate books, ed. C. Philips, Surtees Society, CXCI (1976–7)
Mackay, C. (ed.) *The cavalier songs and ballads of England*, London, 1863
Macpherson, J. *Original papers; containing the secret history of Great Britain, from the Restoration, to the accession of the house of Hanover*, 2 vols., Dublin, 1775
The poems and letters of Andrew Marvell, ed. H. M. Margoliouth, 2 vols., Oxford, 1927
The Mather papers, Collections of the Massachusetts Historical Society, 4th series, VIII (1868)
Mercurius publicus, London, 1660–3
The diary of John Milward, ed. C. Robbins, Cambridge, 1938
The journal of Edward Montagu, first earl of Sandwich, 1659–65, ed. R. C. Anderson, Publications of the Navy Records Society, LXIV (1929)
Newton, S. C. (ed.) 'The gentry of Derbyshire in the seventeenth century', *Derbyshire Archaeological Journal*, LXXVI (1966), 1–30
The notebook of Sir John Northcote, ed. A. H. A. Hamilton, London, 1877
Notes which passed at meetings of the privy council between Charles II and the earl of Clarendon, 1660–67, ed. W. D. Macray, Publications of the Roxburghe Club, London, 1896
Owen, David. *Herod and Pilate reconciled*, London, 1663
A complete collection of the sermons of the reverend and learned John Owen, D.D., London, 1721
The Oxford Gazette, Oxford, 1665–6
The Oxinden and Peyton letters, 1642–70, ed. D. Gardiner, London, 1937
Parker, Samuel. *Bishop Parker's history of his own time*, tr. Thomas Newlin, London, 1727
The diary of Samuel Pepys, ed. R. Latham and W. Matthews, 11 vols., London, 1970–1983
The further correspondence of Samuel Pepys 1662–79, ed. J. R. Tanner, London, 1929
Phillips, Fabian. *Tenenda non tollenda; or, the necessity of preserving tenures in capite and by knight service*, London, 1660
The plea, case, and humble proposals of the truly-loyal and suffering officers, London, 1663
[Pocock, N.] (ed.) 'Illustrations of the state of the Church during the Great Rebellion', *The Theologian and Ecclesiastic*, VI–XV (1848–54)
Pointz, Sir Robert. *A vindication of monarchy and the government long established in the Church and kingdom of England*, London, 1661
Pollock, F. and Holdsworth, W. S. 'Sir Matthew Hale on Hobbes: an unpublished MS', *Law Quarterly Review*, XXXVII (1921)
[Prynne, W.] *Summary reasons, humbly tendered to the most honourable house of peers by some citizens and members of London and other cities, borough corporations, and ports, against the new intended Bill for Governing and Reforming Corporations*, no place or date of publication [1661]
The Rawdon papers, consisting of letters . . . to and from Dr. John Bramhall, London, 1819
Le reading del Monsieur Denshall sur L'Estatute de Finibus. fait anno 4. H. 7., no place of publication, 1662
The memoirs of Sir John Reresby, ed. A. Browning, Glasgow, 1936

Robbins, C. (ed.) 'The election correspondence of Sir John Holland of Quidenham, 1661', *Norfolk Archaeology*, XXX (1947–52), 130–9

'Five speeches, 1661–3, by Sir John Holland, M.P.', *Bulletin of the Institute of Historical Research*, XXVIII (1955), 189–202

Roberts, C. (ed.) 'Sir Richard Temple's discourse on the parliament of 1667–1668', *Huntington Library Quarterly*, XX (1956–7), 137–44

The diurnal of Thomas Rugg, ed. W. Sachse, Camden Society, 3rd series, XCI (1961)

S—, P—. *A letter from an anti-hierarchical divine in the country, to a member of the house of commons, concerning the bishops being restored to their votes in parliament*, London, 1661

Sainsbury, E. B. (ed.) *Calendar of the court minutes of the East India Company, 1664–7*, Oxford, 1925

The Savile correspondence, ed. W. Durrant Cooper, Camden Society, old series, LXXI (1858)

The complete works of George Savile, first marquess of Halifax, ed. W. Raleigh, Oxford, 1912

Sitwell, Sir George (ed.) *Letters of the Sitwells and Sacheverells*, 2 vols., Scarborough, 1900–1

Something that lately passed in discourse between the king and R. Hubberthorne, London, 1660

Sorbières, Samuel. *Relation d'une voyage en angleterre où sont touchées les plusieurs choses, qui regardent l'estat des sciences, de la religion, & autres matières curieuses*, Paris, 1664

State papers, collected by Edward, earl of Clarendon, ed. R. Scrope and T. Monkhouse, 3 vols., Oxford, 1767–86

State tracts: being a collection of several treatises relating to the government, London, 1693

Statutes of the realm, 11 vols., London, 1810–28

Thirsk, J. and Cooper, J. P. (eds.) *Seventeenth-century economic documents*, Oxford, 1972

Twysden, Sir Roger, *Certain considerations upon the government of England*, ed. J. M. Kemble, Camden Society, old series, XLV (1849)

Villiers, George, duke of Buckingham. *Buckingham: public and private man*, ed. C. Phipps, The Renaissance Imagination, vol. XIII, New York, 1985

The works of his grace George Villiers, duke of Buckingham, 2 vols., London, 1775

Villiers, George, duke of Buckingham and Howard, Sir Robert. *The country gentleman*, ed. A. H. Scouten and R. D. Hume, London, 1976

Violet, Thomas. *To the king's most excellent majesty and to the lords spiritual and temporal; with the commons assembled in parliament*, no place or date of publication [1662]

Warwick, Sir Philip. *Memoirs of the reign of King Charles I*, 2nd edn, London, 1702

Waterhouse, Edward. *The gentleman's monitor; or, a sober inspection into the vertues, vices and ordinary means, of the rise and decay of men and families*, London, 1665

Whalley, Peniston. *The civil rights, and conveniences of episcopacy, with the inconveniences of presbytery asserted*, London, 1661

Whitehead, G. *The christian progress of that ancient servant and minister of Jesus Christ, George Whitehead*, London, 1725

Wilkins, D. (ed.) *Concilia Magnae Britanniae et Hiberniae*, 4 vols., London, 1737

Winstanley, W. *The loyal martyrology, or brief catalogues and characters of the most eminent persons who suffered for their conscience during the late times of rebellion*, London, 1665

Wood, Anthony. *The life and times of Anthony Wood, antiquary, of Oxford, 1632–95, described by himself*, ed. Andrew Clark, 6 vols., Oxford Historical Society, 1891–1900

  Athenae Oxonienses, ed. F. Bliss, 5 vols., London, 1813–20

SECONDARY SOURCES

Abernathy, G. R. 'Clarendon and the Declaration of Indulgence', *Journal of Ecclesiastical History*, XI (1960), 55–73

  'The English presbyterians and the Stuart Restoration, 1648–1663', *Transactions of the American Philosophical Society*, new series, LV, part 2 (1955)

Ashcraft, R. *Revolutionary politics and Locke's 'Two treatises of government'*, Princeton, New Jersey, 1986

Aylmer, G. E. *The state's servants: the civil service of the English Republic, 1649–1660*, London, 1973

Barbour, V. *Henry Bennet, earl of Arlington*, Washington, 1914

Beddard, R. A. 'Of the duty of subjects: a proposed fortieth article of religion', *Bodleian Library Record*, X (1978–82)

  'The Restoration Church', in *The restored monarchy, 1660–1688*, ed. J. R. Jones, London, 1979, pp. 155–75

  'The retreat on toryism: Lionel Ducket, member for Calne, and the politics of conservatism', *Wiltshire Archaeological Magazine*, LXXII–LXXIII (1980), 75–106

  'Wren's mausoleum for Charles I and the cult of the royal martyr', *Architectural History*, XXVII (1984), 36–49

Bell, W. G. *The Great Plague in London in 1665*, revised edn, London, 1951

  The Great Fire of London in 1666, London, 1920

Blackwood, B. G. *The Lancashire gentry and the Great Rebellion 1640–1660*, Chetham Society, 3rd series, XXV (1978)

Bond, M. *The records of parliament*, London, 1971

Bosher, R. S. *The making of the Restoration settlement: the influence of the Laudians, 1649–1662*, Westminster, 1951

Broad, J. 'Gentry finance and the Civil War: the case of the Buckinghamshire Verneys', *Econ. Hist. Rev.*, 2nd series, XXXII (1979), 183–200

Browning, A. 'Parties and party organization in the reign of Charles II', *Trans. Roy. Hist. Soc.*, 4th series, XXX (1948), 21–36

  Thomas Osborne, earl of Danby and duke of Leeds, 3 vols., Glasgow, 1951

Carlyle, E. I. 'Clarendon and the privy council, 1660–1667', *Eng. Hist. Rev.*, XXVII (1912), 251–73

Carter, D. P. 'The Lancashire lieutenancy', unpublished M.Litt. dissertation, Oxford University, 1981

Chandaman, C. D. *The English public revenue 1660–1688*, Oxford, 1975

Chaudhuri, K. N. 'Treasure and trade balances: the East India Company's export trade, 1660–1720', *Econ. Hist. Rev.*, 2nd series, XXI (1968), 480–502

Childs, J. *The army of Charles II*, London, 1976

Chivers, G. V. 'The City of London and the state, 1658–1664, a study in political and financial relations', unpublished Ph.D thesis, Univeirsity of Manchester, 1961

Christie, W. D. *A life of Anthony Ashley Cooper, first earl of Shaftesbury*, 2 vols., London, 1871

Clay, C. G. A. *Economic expansion and social change: England 1500–1700*, 2 vols., Cambridge, 1984

'The price of freehold land in the later seventeenth and eighteenth centuries', *Econ. Hist. Rev.*, 2nd series, XXVII (1974), 173–89

Coleby, A. M. *Central government and the localities: Hampshire 1649–1689*, Cambridge, 1987

Coleman, D. C. 'Sir John Banks, financier: an essay in government borrowing under the late Stuarts', in *Essays in the economic and social history of Tudor and Stuart England in honour of R. H. Tawney*, ed. F. J. Fisher, Cambridge, 1961, pp. 204–30

Sir John Banks, baronet and businessman, Oxford, 1963

The complete peerage, ed. G. E. C[okayne] and V. Gibbs, new edn, 13 vols., London, 1910–40

Coward, B. *The Stanleys, Lords Stanley and earls of Derby, 1385–1672: the origins, wealth and power of a landowning family*, Chetham Society, 3rd series, XXX (1983)

Daly, J. W. 'The implications of royalist politics, 1642–6', *Historical Journal*, XXVII (1984), 745–55

'John Bramhall and the theoretical problems of royalist moderation', *Journal of British Studies*, XI (1971), 26–44

'The origins and shaping of English royalist thought', *The Canadian Historical Association Historical Papers* (1974), 15–35

Sir Robert Filmer and English political thought, Toronto, 1979

Davies, G. 'The political career of Sir Richard Temple, 1634–97', *Huntington Library Quarterly*, IV (1940), 47–83

The Restoration of Charles II, London, 1955

Davies, M. G. 'Country gentry and falling rents in the 1660s and 1670s', *Midland History*, IV (1977–8), 86–96

Davis, R. W. 'Committee and other procedures in the house of lords, 1660–1685', *Huntington Library Quarterly*, XLV (1982–3), 20–35

'The presbyterian opposition and the emergence of party in the house of lords in the reign of Charles II', in *Party and party management in parliament, 1660–1784*, ed. Clyve Jones, Leicester, 1984, pp. 1–35

The dictionary of national biography, ed. L. Stephen and S. Lee, 63 vols., London, 1885–1900

Douglas, D. C. *English scholars*, London, 1939

Drake, F. *Eboracum, or the history and antiquities of the city of York*, London, 1736

Edie, C. A. 'The Irish Cattle Bills: a study in Restoration politics', *Transactions of the American Philosophical Society*, new series, LX, part 2 (1970)

'The popular idea of monarchy on the eve of the Stuart Restoration', *Huntington Library Quarterly*, XXXIV (1976), 343–73

Feiling, Sir Keith. *British foreign policy, 1660–72*, London, 1930

A history of the Tory party, 1640–1714, Oxford, 1924

Fletcher, A. 'The enforcement of the Conventicle Acts, 1664–1679', in *Persecution and toleration*, Studies in Church History, XXI, Oxford, 1984, pp. 233–46

The outbreak of the English Civil War, London, 1981

Reform in the provinces: the government of Stuart England, London, 1986

Foster, E. R. *The house of lords, 1603–1649: structure, procedure and the nature of its business*, Chapel Hill, 1983
Foster, Frances Arnold. *Studies in Church dedications*, 3 vols., London, 1899
Foxcroft, H. C. *The life and letters of Sir George Savile, bart., first marquis of Halifax*, 2 vols., London, 1898
Gardiner, S. R. *The constitutional documents of the Puritan Revolution, 1628–1660*, Oxford, 1889
    History of England from the accession of James I to the outbreak of the Civil War, 10 vols., London, 1883–4
Gay, E. F. 'Sir Richard Temple, the debt settlement, and estate litigation, 1653–75', *Huntington Library Quarterly*, VI (1942–3), 255–91
Geyl, P. *Orange and Stuart, 1641–72*, London, 1969
Goldie, M. A. 'John Locke and Restoration anglicanism', *Political Studies*, XXXI (1983), 61–95
    'Sir Peter Pett, sceptical toryism and the science of toleration in the 1680s', in *Persecution and toleration*, Studies in Church History, XXI (1984), 247–73
Grant, W. D. *Margaret the first: a biography of Margaret Cavendish, duchess of Newcastle*, London, 1957
Greaves, R. L. *Deliver us from evil: the radical underground in Britain, 1660–3*, New York, 1986
Green, I. M. 'The persecution of "scandalous" and "malignant" parish clergy during the English Civil War', *Eng. Hist. Rev.*, XCIV (1979), 507–31
    The re-establishment of the Church of England 1660–1663, Oxford, 1978
Habakkuk, H. J. 'Landowners and the Civil War', *Econ. Hist. Rev.*, 2nd series, XVIII (1965), 130–51
    'The land settlement and the Restoration of Charles II', *Trans. Roy. Hist. Soc.*, 5th series, XXVIII (1978), 201–22
Haley, K. H. D. *The first earl of Shaftesbury*, Oxford, 1968
    An English diplomat in the low countries: Sir William Temple and John De Witt, 1665–72, Oxford, 1986
Hardacre, P. H. *The royalists during the Puritan Revolution*, The Hague, 1956
Harris, F. R. *The life of Edward Montagu, K.G., first earl of Sandwich*, 2 vols., London, 1912
Harris, T. 'The bawdy-house riots of 1668', *Historical Journal*, XXIX (1986), 537–56
    London crowds in the reign of Charles II, Cambridge, 1987
Hartmann, C. H. *Charles II and Madame*, London, 1934
Hatsell, J. *Precedents and proceedings in the house of commons*, new edn, 4 vols., London, 1818
Henning, B. D. (ed.) *The history of parliament: the house of commons, 1660–1690*, 3 vols., London, 1983
Hinton, R. W. K. *The eastland trade and the common weal in the seventeenth century*, Cambridge, 1959
Hirst, D. M. *The representative of the people? Voters and voting in England under the early Stuarts*, Cambridge, 1975
Holiday, P. G. 'Land sales and repurchases in Yorkshire after the Civil Wars, 1650–1670', *Northern History*, V (1970), 67–92
Holmes, C. *Seventeenth-century Lincolnshire*, Lincoln, 1980
Hurwich, J. J. 'A "fanatick town": the political influence of dissenters in Coventry, 1660–1720', *Midland History*, IV (1977), 15–48

Hutton, R. *The Restoration, a political and religious history of England and Wales, 1658–67*, Oxford, 1985

Ive, J. G. 'The local dimension of defence: the standing army and militia in Norfolk, Suffolk and Essex, 1649–1660', unpublished Ph.D thesis, University of Cambridge, 1986

Jenkins, P. *The making of a ruling class: the Glamorgan gentry, 1640–1790*, Cambridge, 1983

Jones, G. F. T. 'The Bristol affair, 1663', *Journal of Religious History*, V (1968–9), 16–30

Jones, J. R. *Charles II royal politician*, London, 1986
Country and court, England, 1658–1714, London, 1978
'Parties and parliament', in *The restored monarchy, 1660–88*, ed. J. R. Jones, London, 1979, pp. 48–70

Jose, N. *Ideas of the Restoration in English literature*, London, 1984

Kemp, B. *King and commons, 1660–1832*, London, 1965

Kenyon, J. P. *The popish plot*, Harmondsworth, 1974
Robert Spencer, earl of Sunderland, London, 1958
The Stuart constitution, Cambridge, 1966

Kishlansky, M. A. *Parliamentary selection: social and political choice in early modern England*, Cambridge, 1986

Kitchin, G. *Sir Roger L'Estrange: a contribution to the history of the press in the seventeenth century*, London, 1913

Lacey, D. R. *Dissent and parliamentary politics in England 1661–1689*, New Brunswick, 1969

Le Neve, J. and Hardy,a T. D. *Fasti ecclesiae Anglicanae*, 3 vols., Oxford, 1854

Letwin, W. *The origins of scientific economics. English economic thought, 1660–1776*, London, 1963

Lister, T. H. *The life and administration of Edward, first earl of Clarendon*, 3 vols., London, 1837–8

Macgillivray, R. *Restoration historians and the English Civil War*, The Hague, 1974

Mason, W. G. 'The annual output of Wing-listed titles, 1649–84', *The Library*, 5th series, XXIX (1974)

Matthews, A. G. *Walker revised*, Oxford, 1948

May, T. E. and Vardon, T. *A general index to the Journals of the house of commons*, London, 1852

Meekings, C. A. F. 'Introduction', in *Surrey hearth tax, 1664*, Surrey Record Society, XVII (1940)
'The City loans on the hearth tax, 1664–8', in *Studies in London history*, ed. A. E. J. Hollaender and W. Kellaway, London, 1969, pp. 335–70

Miller, J. 'Charles II and his parliaments', *Trans. Roy. Hist. Soc.*, 5th series, XXXII (1982), 1–23
'The Crown and the borough charters in the reign of Charles II', *Eng. Hist. Rev.*, C (1985), 53–84
James II: a study in kingship, Hove, 1978
Popery and politics in England, 1660–1688, Cambridge, 1973
'The potential for "Absolutism" in later Stuart England', *History*, LXIX (1984), 187–207
'The Restoration monarchy', in *The restored monarchy, 1660–88*, ed. J. R. Jones, London, 1979, pp. 30–47

Mintz, S. I. *The hunting of Leviathan*, Cambridge, 1962

Morrill, J. S. 'The Church in England, 1642–1649', in *Reactions to the English Civil War, 1642–9*, ed. J. S. Morrill, London, 1982, pp. 89–114

Mullett, M. A. 'Conflict, politics, and elections in Lancaster, 1660–88', *Northern History*, XIX (1983), 61–86

Ogg, D. *England in the reign of Charles II*, 2nd edn, 2 vols., Oxford, 1954

Packer, J. W. *The transformation of anglicanism, 1643–1660 with special reference to Henry Hammond*, London, 1969

Pocock, J. G. A. *The ancient constitution and the feudal law*, reissue, Cambridge, 1987

Procter, F. and Frere, W. H. *A new history of the Book of Common Prayer*, 3rd impression, London, 1929

Pruett, J. H. *The parish clergy under the later Stuarts: the Leicestershire experience*, Urbana, Illinois, 1978

Ralph, J. *The history of England during the reigns of K. William, Q. Anne and K. George I*, 2 vols., London, 1744–6

Ranke, L. von. *A history of England, principally in the seventeenth century*, 6 vols., Oxford, 1875

Ratcliff, E. C. 'The Savoy Conference and the revision of the Book of Common Prayer', in *From uniformity to unity, 1662–1962*, ed. O. Chadwick, and G. F. Nuttall, London, 1962, pp. 91–148

Reay, B. 'The authorities and early Restoration quakerism', *Journal of Ecclesiastical History*, XXXIV (1983), 69–84
'The quakers, 1659, and the Restoration of the monarchy', *History*, LXIII (1978), 193–213

Robbins, C. 'The repeal of the Triennial Act in 1664', *Huntington Library Quarterly*, XII (1948–9), 121–40
'The Oxford session of the Long Parliament of Charles II, 9–31 October 1665', *Bull. Inst. Hist. Res.*, XXI (1946–8), 214–24

Roberts, C. *The growth of responsible government in Stuart England*, Cambridge, 1966
'The impeachment of the earl of Clarendon', *Cambridge Historical Journal*, XII (1957), 1–18
Schemes and undertakings: a study of English politics in the seventeenth century, Columbus, Ohio, 1985

Roberts, S. K. *Recovery and Restoration in an English county: Devon local administration, 1646–70*, Exeter, 1985

Roebuck, P. *Yorkshire baronets 1640–1760, families, estates and fortunes*, Oxford, 1980

Rogers, P. G. *The Dutch in the Medway*, London, 1970

Roseveare, H. 'The advancement of the king's credit, 1660–1672', Ph.D thesis, University of Cambridge, 1962
'Prejudice and policy: Sir George Downing as parliamentary entrepreneur', in *Enterprise and history: essays in honour of Charles Wilson*, ed. D. C. Coleman and P. Mathias, Cambridge, 1984, pp. 135–50
The treasury 1660–1870: the foundations of control, London, 1973

Routledge, F. J. *England and the Treaty of the Pyrenees*, Liverpool, 1953

Russell, C. S. *Parliaments and English politics, 1621–29*, Oxford, 1979

Sacret, J. H. 'The Restoration government and municipal corporations', *Eng. Hist. Rev.*, XLV (1930), 232–59

Schoenfeld, M. P. *The restored house of lords*, The Hague, 1967

Schumpeter, E. B. 'English prices and public finance 1660–1822', *The Review of Economic Statistics*, XX (1938), 28–37

Schwoerer, L. G. *'No standing armies!' The antiarmy ideology in seventeenth-century England*, Baltimore, 1974

Seaward, P. C. 'The house of commons committee of trade and the origins of the Second Anglo-Dutch War, 1664', *Historical Journal*, XXX (1987), 437–52

'A Restoration publicist: James Howell and the earl of Clarendon, 1661–6', *Historical Research*, LXI (1988), 123–31

Shirley, E. P. *Stemmata Shirleiana*, London, 1873

Siebert, F. S. *The freedom of the press in England, 1476–1776*, Urbana, 1952

Skeel, C. A. J. *The council in the marches of Wales*, London, 1904

'The Canary company', *Eng. Hist. Rev.*, XXXI (1916), 529–44

Skinner, Q. 'The context of Hobbes's theory of political obligation', in *Hobbes and Rousseau: a collection of critical studies*, ed. M. Cranston and R. S. Peters, New York, 1972, pp. 109–42

Slack, P. *The impact of plague in Tudor and Stuart England*, London, 1986

Smith, A. Hassell. 'Militia rates and militia statutes, 1558–1663', in *The English commonwealth, 1547–1640: essays in politics and society presented to Joel Hurstfield*, ed. P. Clark, A. G. R. Smith, and N. Tyacke, Leicester, 1979, pp. 93–110

Sommerville, J. P. *Politics and ideology in England, 1603–40*, London, 1986

Spalding, R. *The improbable puritan: a life of Bulstrode Whitelocke, 1605–75*, London, 1975

Spurr, J. 'Anglican apologetic and the Restoration Church', unpublished D.Phil. thesis, University of Oxford, 1985

Stradling, R. A. 'Anglo-Spanish relations 1660–68', unpublished PhD thesis, University of Wales, 1968

Swainson, C. A. *The parliamentary history of the Act of Uniformity*, London, 1875

Swatland, A. 'The house of lords in the reign of Charles II, 1660–81', unpublished Ph.D thesis, University of Birmingham, 1985

Thirsk, J. *The agricultural history of England and Wales*, vol. V, two parts, Cambridge, 1984–5

'The sales of royalist land during the Interregnum', *Econ. Hist. Rev.*, 2nd series, V (1952–3), 188–207

Thomas, P. W. *Sir John Berkenhead, 1617–1679*, Oxford, 1969

Thomas, R. 'Comprehension and indulgence', in *From uniformity to unity 1662–1962*, ed. O. Chadwick and G. F. Nuttall, London, 1962, pp. 189–253

Trevor-Roper, H. R. *Archbishop Laud 1573–1645*, London, 1940

Edward Hyde, earl of Clarendon, Oxford, 1975

Tuck, R. ' "The ancient law of freedom": John Selden and the Civil War', in *Reactions to the English Civil War, 1642–1649*, ed. J. S. Morrill, London, 1982, pp. 37–61

Natural rights theories their origins and development, Cambridge, 1979

Underdown, D. *Royalist conspiracy in England 1649–1660*, New Haven, 1960

Walker, J. 'The censorship of the press during the reign of Charles II', *History*, new series, XXXV (1950), 219–38

Webb, S. S. ' "Brave men and servants to his Royal Highness": the household of James Stuart in the evolution of English imperialism', *Perspectives in American History*, VIII (1974), 55–80

Webster, C. *The great instauration: science, medicine and reform 1621–60*, London, 1975

Western, J. R. *The English militia in the eighteenth century*, London, 1965
  Monarchy and revolution: the English state in the 1680s, London, 1972
Weston, C. C. and Greenberg, J. R. *Subjects and sovereigns: the grand controversy over legal sovereignty in Stuart England*, Cambridge, 1981
Whiteman, E. A. O. 'The episcopate of Dr. Seth Ward, bishop of Exeter and Salisbury', unpublished D.Phil. thesis, University of Oxford, 1951
  'The re-establishment of the Church of England, 1660–3', *Trans. Roy. Hist. Soc.*, 5th series, V (1955), 111–31
  'The restoration of the Church of England', in *From uniformity to unity, 1662–1962*, ed. O. Chadwick and G. F. Nuttall, London, 1962, pp. 60–72
Williams, J. B. 'Newsbooks and letters of news of the Restoration', *Eng. Hist. Rev.*, XXIII (1908), 252–76
Witcombe, D. T. 'The cavalier house of commons: the session of 1663', *Bulletin of the Institute of Historical Research*, XXXII (1959), 181–91
  Charles II and the cavalier house of commons 1663–74, Manchester, 1966
  'The parliamentary career of Sir William and Henry Coventry', unpublished B.Litt. thesis, University of Oxford, 1954
Woodward, D. 'The Anglo-Irish livestock trade in the seventeenth century', *Irish Historical Studies*, XVIII (1972–3)
Worden, B. *The Rump Parliament*, Cambridge, 1974
  'Toleration and the Cromwellian protectorate', in *Persecution and toleration*, Studies in Church History, XXI (1984), pp. 199–233
Wormald, B. H. G. *Clarendon: politics, history and religion 1640–1660*, Cambridge, 1951
Wynne, William. *The life of Sir Leoline Jenkins*, 2 vols., London, 1724
Yale, D. E. C. 'Hobbes and Hale on law, legislation, and the sovereign', *Cambridge Law Journal*, XXXI (1) (1972), 121–56

INDEX

Abernathy, G. R., on religious settlement, 27, 179

'absolutism', 3–4, 23–4, 42–4

acts, *see* statutes

Africa, Anglo-Dutch competition in, 120

agriculture, dearths of 1658–62, 104; depression of late 1660s, 41–2, 104, 129, 242–4, 251, 260, 327

Ailesbury, earls of, *see* Bruce

Albemarle, *see* Monck

Aldeburgh, 81

Aldworth, Richard, 64

Alexander VII, Pope, 227

Allen, Sir Thomas, 328

anabaptists, 171

Anderson, Sir Francis, 90

Anglesey, *see* Annesley, Arthur, earl of

anglicans, 28–9, 31, 50; in parliament, 56–7, 62–70, 80, 96–8, 162–3, 168, 184, 193–5

Annesley, Arthur, earl of Anglesey, 14, 54, 94, 133, 177, 189, 202, 231, 232, 268, 283, 284, 287, 291, 307, 308, 311, 315, 318, 321; religious opinions of, 31, 189, 190

anti-catholicism, 246, 255–6, 272, 297, 303, 306; addresses against priests, 186, 223, 271, 285; Bill against growth of popery, 185–6, 188; committee on catholic plots, 271–2; *see also* Roman Catholics

Apsley, Sir Allen, 81, 84, 90, 117, 145, 225

Arlington, *see* Bennet, Henry, lord

army, 141, 272; cost of, 141, 278; expansion of, 21, 22, 24, 43–4, 96, 144–7, 149, 180, 238, 273, 305, 306–7, 310, 315, 325; of Interregnum, 11, 71, 103, 197, 209; protests against, 43–4, 146, 147, 316, 325, 327; *see also* militia

Arundell of Trerice, Richard, Lord, 37 n. 9

Arundell of Wardour, Henry, Lord, 169

Ashburnham, John, 89 n. 114, 90, 106, 109, 328

Ashburnham, William, 279

Ashley, *see* Ashley-Cooper, Anthony, Lord

Ashley-Cooper, Anthony, Lord Ashley, 14, 37, 55, 89, 94, 126–7, 133, 144, 151, 154, 183, 186, 189, 191, 206, 212, 213, 228, 230, 233, 241, 250, 258, 281, 286, 298, 305, 315; and Irish Cattle Act, 266, 268, 269, 283; religious opinions of, 31–2, 181, 219, 301

Ashton, Sir Ralph, 153, 171

assessment, 108–9, 122–3, 259; *see also* supply, debates on

atheism, bills against, 256

Atkins, Col., 158, 159

Atkins, Sir Robert, 81, 83, 105, 107, 185, 282, 288, 294, 319; religious views of, 98, 328

Aubrey, John, 40 n. 19

Aylesbury, 203

Bacon, Francis, Viscount St Alban, 79

bankers, in crisis of 1666, 306; criticism of, 254, 260, 297; and government credit, 112, 124–5, 126–7, 303; and treasury order scheme, 240

baptists, 171

Basing House, Hampshire, 205

Bastide de la Croix, agent of Fouquet, 105

Barbados, misdeeds of Lord Willoughby in, 288

Bartet, Isaac, agent of Mazarin, 16, 24, 141

Barwick, Dr John, 65

Bath, *see* Grenville, John, earl of

Baxter, Richard, 179 n. 85

Beave, Serjeant, 19 n. 38

Bedford, *see* Russell, William, earl of

Bedfordshire, 63

Belasyse, Sir Henry, and Buckingham, 300, 315

Belasyse, John, Lord, 35 n. 38, 144

Belasyse, Thomas, Viscount Fauconberg, 37

345

Cominges, Gaston-Jean-Baptiste de, 223,
224, 225
Comprehension, 1668 Bill for, 68–9, 95, 195,
318–19
Compton, James, earl of Northampton, 97,
132, 189, 193, 198, 300; and Buckingham, 281; and Bristol's impeachment of
Clarendon, 213, 229, 230, 232–3
conspiracies, 11, 12, 43–4, 141; alleged, in
1661, 143–5, 172, in 1662, 149; Bristol
and, 231; Yorkshire rising of 1663, 136,
138, 189–90, 194–5; *see also* Venner's
rebellion
convocation, of 1640, 168; of 1661, 164
Conway, Edward, Viscount, 42 n. 30, 269,
274, 281, 284, 289, 307
Cope, Sir Anthony, 56
Cornwall, 80, 87; duchy of, 81
Coronel, Sir Augustine, 226, 231
corporations, Bills concerning, 156; in
Interregnum, 152; opinions on, 151–2;
regulation of, 151–7; *see also* statutes
corruption, 51–2, 53–6, 108, 113, 128–9,
130, 211, 213–14, 217, 221, 230, 308,
314–15; attacked, in parliament of
1666–7, 244–5, 255, 256–7, 258, 277,
278, 285–6, 297; of 1667, 316; in navy,
alleged, 265; of parliament, 91–2,
298–9; *see also* court
Coryton, Sir John, 80, 85, 89 n. 114, 91, 156
Cosin, John, bishop of Durham, 59, 64, 174,
176
council of the marches of Wales, 83;
re-establishment of, 134–5, 137
council of the North, 74, 96; proposed
re-establishment of, 134–7
court, criticism of, in 1666–7, 244–5, 256–7,
276, 278; *see also* corruption
Courtenay, Sir William, 209
court of augmentations, 120
court of exchequer, 109
court of wards and liveries, 23, 43, 103, 104,
140
Covenant, Solemn League and, 30, 164;
declaration against, 155, 157, 173, 175,
177, 187, 188–9, 189 n. 134
Coventry, Anne, 65
Coventry, Henry, 40 n. 19, 139, 143, 184,
206, 222, 223, 224, 225, 226, 235, 294;
ambassador at Breda, 312; and parliamentary management, 80, 83, 84,
258; religious views of, 65, 98 n. 176, 328
Coventry, Sir John, 316
Coventry, Mary, 65
Coventry, Thomas, Lord, 65

Coventry, Sir William, 15, 40 n. 19, 65, 77,
115, 121, 123, 126, 146, 224, 233–4,
250, 309; and Bennet, 85–6, 233–4; and
Buckingham, 302–3, 313, 314; and the
City, 261; and Clarendon, 23, 234,
247–8, 296 n. 82, 310–11, 319, 321; as
informant of Pepys, 7; and naval
administration, 234, 247–8, 252, 265,
292, 305, 311, 319–20; and parliamentary management, 84, 85–6, 87, 90, 258,
264, 265 n. 140, 274, 280, 281, 289,
290–1, 316; and prize commission, 89;
and treasury commission, 305, 310
Craven, William, Lord, 206
Crew, John, Lord, 55, 76, 212, 273; and
public accounts commission, 281
Crew, Sir Thomas, 271
Croft, Herbert, bishop of Hereford, 177
Crofts, William, Lord, 231
Cromwell, Oliver, 314
Crosland, Sir Jordan, 87, 88, 89, 90, 185
Crouch, Thomas, 97, 188, 328
Crown lands, 11, 156, 208; Bill to void grants
of, 116; revenue of, 106–7, 114, 115
Culpepper, Thomas, 59; *see also* Colepepper
Cumberland, duke of, see Rupert, Prince
customs, 106–7, 114, 115, 119, 120; Bill
against abuses in, 109; Bill for appro-
priating to navy, 115–16; decline in,
240–1

Danvers, Sir John, 7
D'Aubigny, Ludovic Stuart, seigneur de,
227, 228
Declaration of Breda, 18, 26, 56, 162, 168,
184
Declaration of Indulgence, of 1662, 88,
113–14, 150 n. 95, 181–2, 184, 221; and
Bill concerning ecclesiastical affairs,
181–4, 185, 186, 189, 222, 286
Declaration of Indulgence, of 1673, 324
Delamere, *see* George Booth, Lord
Denbigh, 201
Denham, Sir John, 68, 287
Denmark, 237
Derby, *see* Stanley, Charles, earl of
De Vere, Aubrey, earl of Oxford, 269
Devonshire, 80, 87
Devonshire, *see* Cavendish, Christiana,
countess of
Digby, Anne, countess of Bristol, 232, 235
Digby, George, earl of Bristol, 95, 169, 173,
175–6, 177, 204, 218–22, 224, 225,
247, 317; attempted impeachment of
Clarendon, 39, 88, 90, 188, 189, 213–14,

Fire of London, 241, 246, 251, 293; par-
    liamentary inquiry into, 255–6, 271–2,
    295
Firth, C. H., 5
Fletcher, Sir George, 136
Flintshire, 201, 202
Ford, Sir Richard, 109, 282, 321
forest laws, 160
Forest of Dean, 114, 116
Foster, Lord Chief Justice Sir Robert,
    19 n. 38, 203, 207–8
Four Days' Battle, 237, 238, 249
Fowke, John, 111, 157 n. 129
Fox, Sir Steven, 279
Frampton, Thomas, 63
France, 246, 315, 324; ambassadors of, 7;
    animosity towards, 111, 125, 236–7,
    248; campaign against, 288; and
    England, 23–5, 219, 221; and Dutch
    war, 125, 236–7, 248; imports from,
    address against, 244, 255, 263, 270–1,
    285; invasion of Spanish Netherlands,
    304; queen mother in, 32
Freschville, John, Lord, 37 n. 9, 207, 211
Fuller, William, 170

Gardiner, S. R., 5
Garraway, William, 95, 121, 227, 250, 251,
    258, 263, 264, 277, 288, 298, 300, 301,
    302, 316
Gauden, John, bishop of Exeter and (1662)
    Worcester, 144, 172 n. 50, 173, 174,
    176, 177, 219
Gawdy, Sir William, 110, 328
gentry, and interest rates, 112, political
    attitudes of, 43–52, power of, 2, 49–50,
    242, 296–7, 314–15, 326–7; relation-
    ship with Crown, 50–2, 327; religious
    attitudes of, 56–70
Gerard, John, 75
Gerrard of Brandon, Charles Lord, 97, 230,
    269
Giavarina, Venetian resident in England, 143,
    221
Gilby, Col. Anthony, 90
Glynne, Sir John, 55, 202, 203
Goodrick, Francis, 202, 294, 328
Goodrick, Sir John, 122, 127–8, 145, 328
Goodwin, Thomas, 175
Gower, Edward, 95
Gower, Sir Thomas, 264, 292, 300, 328; and
    impeachment of Mordaunt, 287, 294
Gray, Angel, 205, 206
Great Tew, Lord Falkland's house at, 28–9
Green, I. M., on religious settlement, 27, 57,
    58, 60, 62

Grenville, John, earl of Bath, 80 n. 46, 229
Grey, Anchitell, his *Debates*, 6
Grey of Warke, William Lord, 202
Grimsby, 300
Grimston, Sir Harbottle, 45 n. 46, 55, 70
Guadeloupe, actions against French near, 288

Habakkuk, Sir John, 208
Hale, Sir Matthew, 44, 55
Hales, John, 28
Halifax, *see* Savile, George, marquis of
Hallam, Henry, on the Restoration, 1–2
Hammond, Charles, 54, 66, 210
Hammond, Dr Henry, 64–5
Harbord, Sir Charles, 80 n. 47, 106, 108, 253,
    255, 264, 281; and inspection of revenue,
    1663, 114–15, 116, 117, 118; religious
    views of, 66, 98
Harley, Sir Edward, 271
Harrington, James, 39–40, 40 n. 19, 43, 49,
    144
Hatton, Christopher, Lord, 230
Hawarden, 201, 202
Hay, John, earl of Tweeddale, 322
hearth tax, 85, 117–18, 119, 120, 129;
    farmers of, 260; proposed abolition of,
    1666, 260–1, 262, 263–4, protests
    against, 272; yield of, 111–12, 113, 114,
    116, 130, 260; *see also* statutes, taxation
Heath, John, 43, 97, 156, 187, 328
Heath, Robert, 43
Henchman, Humphrey, bishop of London, as
    diarist?, 6 n. 15
Henley, Andrew, 309
Henrietta, duchesse d'Orleans, and peace
    negotiations, 271
Henrietta Maria, queen mother, 220, 227;
    and catholics, 32, 219; household of,
    186; jointure of, 103, 106
Herbert, Sir Henry, 36
Herbert, Philip, earl of Pembroke, 55, 171
Herbert, William, Lord, 146, 256–7
Herefordshire, 223
Hertfordshire, and the Conventicle Bill, 186
Heydon, John, 302
Heylin, Peter, 66, 165 n. 11
Hickes, James, 73
Higgons, Sir Thomas, 90
high commission, 23, 158; abolition of
    confirmed, 168; *see also* statutes
Hobart, Nathaniel, 311
Hobbes, Thomas, 17, 39, 40 n. 19, 69, 151;
    books of, censured, 256; Clarendon on,
    20–1
Holmes, Sir Robert, 237
Holland, Sir John, 158, 253, 328; speeches of,